Thomas Edie Hill

Hill's Souvenir Guide to Chicago And the World's Fair

Thomas Edie Hill

Hill's Souvenir Guide to Chicago And the World's Fair

ISBN/EAN: 9783744724876

Printed in Europe, USA, Canada, Australia, Japan

Cover: Foto ©Andreas Hilbeck / pixelio.de

More available books at **www.hansebooks.com**

HILL'S

SOUVENIR GUIDE

TO

CHICAGO

AND

THE WORLD'S FAIR

BY

THOMAS E. HILL

Author of "*Hill's Manual of Social and Business Forms*," etc.

"Westward the course of Empire takes its way."—*Berkeley*

Copyright, 1892, by LAIRD & LEE

CHICAGO

LAIRD & LEE, Publishers

1892

TO

AMERICANS

AND

PEOPLE IN ALL PARTS OF THE WORLD ABOUT TO VISIT

THE

Great Columbian Exposition:

TO

THOSE INHABITANTS OF CHICAGO NOT YET FULLY ACQUAINTED

WITH

Their Own City:

TO

ALL PERSONS DIRECTLY OR INDIRECTLY INTERESTED

IN

The Metropolis of the West,

THIS BOOK

IS

DEDICATED.

PREFACE.

THIS seems to be a small book, but count the words upon a page, and, by comparison with other and larger books, the great amount of reading which it contains will be readily estimated.

A special effort has been made to have this Guide small in bulk, so that it might be conveniently carried in the pocket, and be always at hand to answer the questions it may be called upon to solve.

Examination will show that it is not an advertising medium but, in miniature, a general cyclopædia of the world, describing the great thoroughfares of travel, and affording information of much service to those who journey to and from any part of the earth.

Being designed to be conveniently opened and consulted, whether in the library, on the railway train, or in the crowded street car, all broad-spreading folding maps had to be done away with. The advantage of the new plan here adopted may be fully realized by examining page 114, which shows the City of Chicago divided into 13 divisions. Each division, on the succeeding 13 pages, occupies a full page, and presents to the eye all the old or new streets in that division.

By a little study of the directions on page 80, the reader becomes acquainted with the Street Index, and is enabled, without the inconvenience of a large folding map, to discover in fifteen seconds the location of any street in the city.

While mistakes, which subsequent editions will correct, will doubtless be found in this work, several thousand dollars have been expended in its preparation, and over one year of time, with a large force of assistants, has been required by the author to put the matter, herein contained, into proper form, and to bring the volume down to the compact shape in which it is here presented to the public.

If it has the general sale which a concise, useful handbook for travelers should have, and be found a serviceable Guide to Chicago and the Columbian Exposition, the purpose of this conscientiously prepared work will be fulfilled by

THE PUBLISHERS.

Alphabetical and Classified Index of Contents.

Alphabetical and Classified Index of Contents.

ALPHABETICAL INDEX---WORLD'S COLUMBIAN EXPOSITION

INFORMATION CONCERNING THE SURFACE OF THE GLOBE.

Geographical Knowledge Which All Persons Should Have Who Journey To and From Foreign Countries.

JOURNEY is in contemplation, which may take the traveler a long distance, possibly half-way or entirely around the world. Before starting, it is desirable to know where the tourist is going, what will be seen, and the features of interest on the way to the destination.

This involves a knowledge of geography in general, and leads to an examination of the surface of the world, known in the group of planets as the earth; which, held in position in space through the law of gravitation, has been proven by human observation and experience to be spherical in form.

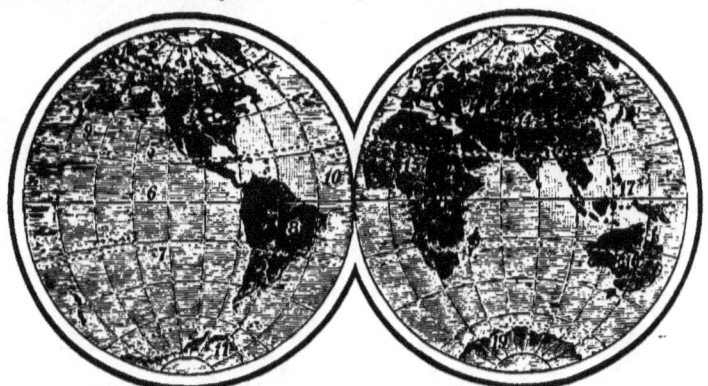

Names of the General Divisions of the World.

Explanation of Figures.—1. Siberia. 2. Arctic Ocean. 3. Alaska. 4. North America. 5. Tropic of Cancer. 6. Equator. 7. Tropic of Capricorn. 8. South America. 9. Pacific Ocean. 10. Atlantic Ocean. 11. Unexplored South Polar Continent. 12. Great Britain. 13. Europe. 14. Asia. 15. Africa. 16. Australia. 17. Equator. 18. Japan. 19. Unexplored South Polar Continent.

Geographical Outlines of the Earth.

The above illustration shows the general contour of the land surface on the earth, there being two great divisions of the globe, consisting of what is known as the eastern and western hemispheres.

In the eastern hemisphere are the countries of Europe, Asia, Africa and the great islands which are included in Oceanica. In the western hemisphere, North America and South America.

The lines extending from side to side on the map are denominated lines of latitude, and number 90 degrees each way from the equator. The lines extending from top to bottom are known as lines of longitude, and are numbered in different countries from different points, as longitude from Washington, from Greenwich, from Paris, etc.

These lines are used in designating location, whether on land or sea, and are of especial service to navigators, who, aided by compass and chart, find it necessary to be continually informed as to their position, which is indicated by longitude and latitude.

Map of Europe, Including Portions of Asia and Africa.

Bounded on the south by the Mediterranean Sea, Black Sea and Caucasus Mountains; on the east by the Caspian Sea, Ural River and Ural Mountains; on ne north by the Arctic Ocean, and on the west by the Atlantic Ocean.

See Description on Following Pages.

Principal localities and objects, worthy of general attention, in Europe, portions of Asia and Africa. See letters and figures on opposite map.

A 1. North Pole.	**D** 7. Edinburgh.	**E** 11. Italy.	**F** 8. Tripoli.
B 1. Greenland.	**D** 8. England.	**E** 12. Corsica.	**F** 9. Greece.
B 2. Arctic Ocean.	**D** 9. London.	**E** 13. Sardinia.	**F** 10. Candia.
B 3. Spitzbergen.	**D** 10. Str'its of Dover.	**E** 14. Rome.	**F** 11. Alexandria.
B 4. Hammerfest.	**D** 11. Belgium.	**E** 15. Adriatic Sea.	**F** 12. Isthmus of Suez.
B 5. North Cape.	**D** 12. Holland.	**E** 16. A'stria-H'ng'ry.	**F** 13. Cyprus.
B 6. Nova Zembla.	**D** 13. Germany.	**E** 17. Vienna.	**F** 14. Turkey in Asia.
C 1. Iceland.	**D** 14. Berlin.	**E** 18. Servia.	**F** 15. Syria.
C 2. Arctic Circle.	**D** 15. Denmark.	**E** 19. Turkey.	**F** 16. Jerusalem.
C 3. Faroe Islands.	**D** 16. Baltic Sea.	**E** 20. Bulgaria.	**F** 17. Persia.
C 4. Shetland Isl'ds.	**D** 17. Stockholm.	**E** 21. Roumania.	**G** 1. Trop. of Cancer.
C 5. Norway.	**D** 18. Poland.	**E** 22. Black Sea.	**G** 2. Sahara Desert.
C 6. Sweden.	**D** 19. Russia.	**E** 23. Constantinople.	**G** 3. Egypt.
C 7. Lapland.	**D** 20. St. Petersburg.	**E** 24. Crimea.	**G** 4. River Nile.
C 8. Finland.	**D** 21. Moscow.	**E** 25. Caucasus Mts.	**G** 5. Cairo.
C 9. Gulf of Bothnia.	**E** 1. Portugal.	**E** 26. Don River.	**G** 6. Red Sea.
C 10. White Sea.	**E** 2. Spain.	**E** 27. Volga River.	**G** 7. Mecca.
C 11. Ural Mountains.	**E** 3. Pyrenees Mts.	**E** 28. Caspian Sea.	**G** 8. Arabia.
C 12. Siberia.	**E** 4. France.	**F** 1. Lisbon.	**G** 9. Persian Gulf.
D 1. Atlantic Ocean.	**E** 5. English Chan'l.	**F** 2. Sts.of Gibraltar.	**H** 1. Soudan.
D 2. Ireland.	**E** 6. Paris.	**F** 3. Morocco.	**H** 2. Africa.
D 3. Queenstown.	**E** 7. Strasburg.	**F** 4. Algeria.	**H** 3. Abyssinia.
D 4. St. Geo'g's Ch'l.	**E** 8. Bavaria.	**F** 5. Mediter'n'n Sea.	**I - 1.** Equator.
D 5. Liverpool.	**E** 9. Switzerland.	**F** 6. Sicily.	
D 6. Scotland.	**E** 10. Alps.	**F** 7. Malta.	

Description of Notable Objects, Cities, Localities and Regions in Europe.

A 1. North Pole. An imaginary point at the extreme northern end of the globe, any direction from which would be south.

B 1. Greenland. An immense continental island, a large portion of which lies within the arctic circle; the northern part, in consequence of extreme cold, has never been explored.

B 2. Arctic Ocean. An extensive, unexplored sea, surrounding the North Pole, and extending southward to the continents of Europe, Asia and America.

B 3. Spitzbergen. A group of islands, the whole covering an area of 30,000 square miles; too cold to be inhabited, the only tree which grows there being the miniature polar willow, which attains the height of two inches, with leaves not larger than a man's finger-nail. Numerous grasses and flowering plants abound, however, in the warmer seasons, which continue through July, August and September.

B 4. Hammerfest. The most northern town in Europe. During two summer months the sun is continually above the horizon and the heat is very great. The winter is sufficiently mild to allow the fishing industry to go forward. Population about 2,100.

B 5. North Cape. The extreme northern point of land in Europe, from which tourists and others who journey there, look northward upon the silent, unknown Arctic Sea.

B 6. Nova Zembla. Large island surrounded by several smaller ones. Belongs to Russia. Is 600 miles long, about 50 miles wide. No permanent inhabitants there. Extremely cold and desolate.

C 1. Iceland. Celebrated for the advanced civilization of its people in spite of its severely cold climate. It is notable, also, for its Hecla Volcano and its numerous hot springs and geysers, in the warm waters of which the inhabitants frequently wash clothing. Earthquakes here have been frequent.

C 2. Arctic Circle. The imaginary circle used by geographers to designate the southern limit of the arctic regions. Within this circle there is a long period of the year during which the sun does not set; and also a period during which it is not seen.

C 3. Faroe Islands. A group of 22 islands, 17 of which are inhabited. Belongs to Denmark. Area, 500 square miles; about half the size of Rhode Island. Population about 11,000.

C 4. Shetland Islands. Include about 100 islands, the largest of which is 60 miles long, and from 3 to 10 wide. Population highly intelligent, and well educated. Numbers about 30,000. These islands are celebrated as the original home of the Shetland horse, the diminutive size and docile disposition of which have made it a great favor-

SHETLAND PONY.

ite among the children of the civilized portion of the earth. Owing to extensive exportation the little animal is becoming scarce in Shetland.

C 5. Norway. The extreme northwestern portion of Europe, the people of which are almost universally well educated and intelligent.

C 6. Sweden. Area, 173,974 square miles. Population, in 1890, 4,784,675. Education, which is compulsory, is universally diffused among all the people, in the country districts as well as in the cities. Occupation largely agricultural.

C 7. Lapland. A region of the country to the far northward of Sweden and Norway. The Laplanders, in consequence of a continually cold climate, are

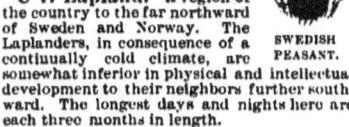

SWEDISH PEASANT.

somewhat inferior in physical and intellectual development to their neighbors further southward. The longest days and nights here are each three months in length.

C 8. Finland. A province in Russia, with an area of 144,254 square miles, three times as large as the State of New York, one-third of the province being covered with marshes and lakes. Has eight months of winter, and no sunlight during portions of December and January. Lutheran in religion. Population, in 1890, nearly 2,400,000.

C 9. Gulf of Bothnia. About 400 miles long; breadth, 100 miles.

C 10. White Sea. An inlet of the Arctic Ocean. Covers an area of 47,000 square miles; a little larger than Ohio.

C 11. Ural Mountains. The boundary line, for 1,333 miles, between Europe and Asia.

C 12. Siberia. A vast extent of territory in northeastern Russia, bounded on the north by the Arctic Ocean, east by the Pacific Ocean south by the Chinese Empire, and west by the Ural Mountains, Ural River and the Caspian Sea. In the southern portion of the region here designated, is the penal colony of Russia, to which point prison-

SIBERIAN DOG TEAM.

ers have been sent for the past 240 years. In the extreme northward are the arctic regions, where the inhabitants make much use of dogs for transportation. Area, 4,824,563 square miles. Population, in 1885, 4,313,680.

D 1. Atlantic Ocean. That great body of water, to the eastward of Europe and Africa, over which all Europeans must pass in order to reach the American continent. Is the great water highway of the civilized world.

D 2. Ireland. An island 306 miles long and 182 miles wide, being, with an area of about 31,759 square miles, a little smaller than Indiana. Is subject to the British government. Population, in 1841, was 8,190,597; in 1881 it was 5,159,839, and in 1891, 4,706,-162. Population continues to decrease, owing to emigration.

D 3. Queenstown. The first port of entry that gladdens the eyes of the tourist who is on the way from American ports to Liverpool. Named in honor of Queen Victoria, who visited here in 1849. Population, in 1881, was 9,755.

D 4. St. George's Channel. Is 100 miles long and 65 miles wide.

D 5. Liverpool. Second largest city in England. Principal port of embarkation for United States of America. Population, 517,-116. Is 3,210 miles from New York City.

D 6. Scotland. Forms the northern part of Great Britain; divided from England by the rivers Sark and Liddell, the Cheviot Hills and the River Tweed. Area, nearly 30,000 square miles; considerably smaller than Indiana. Population, in 1891, 4,033,103.

D 7. Edinburgh. Capital of Scotland. Celebrated as a great publishing center, for its university, for its castle, for its literary achievements, and for the monuments of Walter Scott, Robert Burns, David Hume and others. Population, 261,970.

SCOTTISH HIGH-LANDER.

D 8. England. Area, including Wales, 58,362 square miles; about the size of Michigan. Population, in 1891, 29,001,018. The most widely known, the wealthiest, and one of the most powerful of the countries of Europe. Its people have penetrated into all lands; its commerce brightens all the seas; its language is diffused throughout all the world, its influence has permeated and advanced the civilization of all the earth. The rapid spread of the English language shows that this will ultimately become the language of the entire civilized world, a fact which is made manifest by the study of English in nearly all the educational institutions of the different countries on the globe. There is much need, however, of an improved method of spelling, as the present English system is exceedingly defective, the foreigner having much difficulty in acquiring the language for this reason.

D 9. London. The largest city on the globe. Capital of the British Empire. Is 60 miles inland from the sea. London proper covers 122 square miles. Population, 4,221,452. Area of Chicago, in 1891, was 181 square miles, with a population, in 1890, of 1,098,576. London began its corporate exist-

ence and elected its first mayor in 1189,but was a city of very considerable importance in the time of Christ; its origin dating back to a time unknown. Its growth, at the present time, is enormously great, 9,000 houses being constructed each year, 28 miles of new streets and 100,000 new population being added yearly. The London police force, necessary for the preservation of order, includes an immense number of the best specimens of physical manhood in the kingdom.

D 10. Straits of Dover. The channel dividing England from France; is 18 miles wide at its narrowest place. It is believed that at one time England and the continent were connected at this point by a narrow neck of land.

D 11. Belgium. Area, 11,373 square miles; about the size of Maryland. Its government is a limited monarchy. Mostly a low, flat country. Its capital is Brussels, having a population of 482,158. Population of Belgium, in 1890, 6,030,043. Is the most densely populated country in Europe, having 530 persons to the square mile.

LONDON POLICEMAN.

D 12. Holland. The country of the Dutch, called by the people themselves the "Country of the Netherlands." Monarchial government. Protestant in religion. Area, 12,680 square miles; a little larger than New Hampshire. Population, in 1887, 4,450.870, being 350 persons to the square mile. A low, marshy country, much of the land being below the level of the sea, from the encroachments of which it is protected by dikes.

D 13. Germany. Area, 211,168 square miles; about the size of Texas. Population, 49,421,064. Population to square mile, 234 persons. Protestant in religion. Monarchial government. Celebrated for its general diffusion of education among the masses, its philosophy and its schools of advanced thought.

D 14. Berlin. Capital of Germany. Population, 1,609,536. One of the most beautiful cities of Europe, the population of which has trebled in the last 34 years, owing to a large influx of rural population. The liability to disturbance, in so large a city, makes a large police force necessary; the long coat and general costume of a Berlin policeman is herewith shown.

BERLIN POLICE-MAN.

D 15. Denmark. Area, 14,-789 square miles; about twice the size of New Jersey. Population, in 1890. 2,172,205, being 146 to the square mile. Capital, Copenhagen. Population, 320,000. Condition of the laboring classes is happy. Small amount of labor-saving machinery in the country; most articles of clothing and furniture are made in the homes of the people. All have opportunity for employment. Education compulsory, and the educational institutions of the country have reached a high degree of perfection.

D 16. Baltic Sea. Is 900 miles long and from 100 to 200 miles wide. The region southward of this sea was formerly a part of Poland.

D 17. Stockholm. Is the capital of Sweden. Population, 245,317. On one side of the city are the famous zoological gardens, located in one of the finest public parks in Europe. From Sweden comes to the United States an intelligent, industrious, order-loving class of immigrants, who readily adopt the customs of the country and become excellent citizens.

POLANDER.

D 18. Poland. Area about the size of Texas. Population, in 1859, was 24,000,000. Towards the latter part of the last century its territory was divided among the countries of Russia, Prussia and Austria. Warsaw, the former capital of Poland, is a beautiful city of 450,000 population. Has a highly cultured and well-governed people.

POLISH OFFICER.

D 19. Russia. Extends over a large share of the northern regions of the globe; has an area of 8,457,289 square miles. Population, 108,787,215.

D 20. St. Petersburg. Capital of Russia. Population, 936,226. Climate severe in winter, pleasant in summer. The Winter Palace, in this city, is the largest and most magnificent palace in the world. During the residence of the Emperor herein, there are 6,000 people within its walls. Owing to the severity of the climate, in the winter season, the people dress themselves in the warmest of fur clothing. For the purpose of greater protection from cold, the male sex allows the hair and beard to grow to a considerable length.

D 21. Moscow. Ancient capital of Russia. Population, 753,469. Celebrated as being the city which Napoleon, with his army, entered in 1812; at which time the town was set on fire by the Russians, in 500 places at once, burning 11,840 houses to the ground, compelling the evacuation and disastrous retreat of the French army from Russia, in the dead of winter.

RUSSIAN.

E 1. Portugal. The most western part of Europe, lies west of Spain. Is 368 miles long and 100 miles broad. Population, in 1881. 4,708,178. Capital, Lisbon; population, 246,343.

E 2. Spain. Situated in southwestern Europe. Area, 196,173 square miles; about the size of California. Population, in 1887, 17,550,216. Monarchial in government; Catholic in religion. Bull fighting was abolished by Charles IV., but was re-established as a national amusement by Joseph Bonaparte, a brother of Napoleon, the mass of the people being passionately fond of the sport. The bull-fighting season, in Madrid, begins in April, and lasts until November, occupying one afternoon in each week, the proceeds going to the fund of the general hospital. Great numbers attend these exhibitions, it being a general dress occasion, very high prices being charged for admission

SPANISH BULL FIGHTER.

E 3. Pyrenees Mountains. A range of mountains, on the boundary line between France and Spain, extending a distance of 240 miles. The rapid climbing of these mountains by the guides, and those that frequent them, requires a special costume and that skill which comes from practice.

E 4. France. One of the most highly cultivated regions of Europe; possessing a favorable climate and very fertile soil, adapted to the growth of cereals, fruits, and especially the vine. Area, about 204,090 square miles, being about 620 miles long and 550 miles wide. Population, in 1886, 38,218,903. Republican in government.

PYRENEES MOUNTAINEER.

E 5. English Channel. An arm of the Atlantic Ocean leading toward the Straits of Dover.

E 6. Paris. Capital of the French Republic. Is a wondrously beautiful and cleanly kept city; the asphalt pavement used in many streets being so smooth as to permit of its being washed at regular times by a large force of workmen. Is the second largest city in the world. Population, 2,344,550. Is a very ancient city, which began to be known as Paris in the fourth century. Has been a center of beauty, art and literature for the last 200 years. Is continually being visited by an immense number of tourists from all parts of the earth. Very efficient in its police system, this being the home of Bertillon, the inventor of the Bertillon system of criminal identification, by which, through a series of measurements of the various parts of the body, identification is absolute when a subsequent measurement of the same individual is made.

PARIS POLICEMAN.

E 7. Strasburg. Principal town of Alsace. Famous for its cathedral and for its astronomical clock, which represents the planetary system. Population, 111,987.

E 8. Bavaria. Area, 29,032 square miles; about half the size of Illinois. Population, in 1890, 5,589,382. Monarchial government. Religion, Catholic. Before males can marry, they must perform certain military service, and prove capacity for supporting a family. Capital, Munich; population, 349,000.

E 9. Switzerland. Area, 15,981 square miles; a little larger than Maryland. Population, in 1888, 2,933,334. Capital, Berne; population, 47,150. Most mountainous country in Europe. Education compulsory and generally diffused among the masses. Celebrated for its Alps Mountains, its superior watches, its charming lakes and the clear, beautiful complexion and ruddy faces of its peasant girls.

SWISS GIRL.

E 10. Alps. Most extensive system of lofty mountains in Europe, the highest peak being Mount Blanc, 15,810 feet.

E 11. Italy. Is 600 miles long and 300 miles wide, including Sicily, Sardinia and other islands. Its area is 110,655 square miles; about twice the size of Iowa. Population, in 1890, 30,158,408. Celebrated for its delightful climate, its fruits, its art attractions and its Vesuvius and Etna volcanoes. The beautiful Italian city of Venice is a place of great resort for tourists, being built on 117 islands, separated by 150 canals, and united by 380 bridges; all the main traffic passing along the canals.

BRIDGE IN VENICE.

E 12. Corsica. An island in the Mediterranean. Area, 3,340 square miles; about half the size of New Jersey. Population, 258,507. Famous as the birthplace of Napoleon Bonaparte.

E 13. Sardinia. Large island in the Mediterranean, 166 miles long, 90 miles wide. Area, 9,361 square miles; about the size of New Hampshire. People dark-complexioned. Education not very generally diffused. Population about 400,000.

E 14. Rome. On the Tiber River, 16 miles from the sea. Founded, it is supposed, 753 years before Christ. Celebrated for its St. Peter's Church, its Coliseum, its works of art, its ancient history, its former power among nations, its great antiquity, and as being the seat of Papal authority. Population, 427,684. The city is supposed to have had a population of 2,000,000 at the time of Christ. Rome at that time had 400 temples. The Pantheon, built by Agrippa, 27 B. C., is still standing.

ITALIAN PEASANT GIRL.

The city had covered walks, supported by columns and open at one side. These were used for recreation and the transaction of business, in some cases being adorned with paintings and works of art. The covered walk, or double sidewalk, will doubtless come into use in several of the great cities of the United States, as a means of allowing pedestrians to move more freely through the streets.

E 15. Adriatic Sea. Is 450 miles long and 90 miles wide.

E 16. Austria-Hungary. In Central Europe. Area, 261,649 square miles; about the size of Texas. Population, 42,749,329. Monarchial government.

E 17. Vienna. Capital of the Austrian Empire. Population, 1,- 378,530. Celebrated for its university, its department of medicine being renowned throughout the world. The Imperial Royal Palace is an ancient building consisting of various parts, erected at different times. The imperial library, in one portion of the palace, contains 410,000 volumes, 12,000 of which were printed before the year 1500. Among the public places of popular resort is the Prater, said to be the largest park in Europe.

E 18. Servia. Formerly belonged to Turkey. Area, about 18,757 square miles; twice the size of Massachusetts. Population, in 1890, was 2,096,043. Mountainous and heavily timbered country; inhabited by an intelligent people.

E 19. Turkey. The present extent of the Ottoman Empire is 1,710,000 square miles. Population, 32,500,- 000. Grouped mainly around the eastern waters of the Mediterranean Sea: composed of various provinces and states, some under direct control of the Sultan, some practically independent. Mohammedan in religion. Reading, writing and the study of the Koran form the curriculum of study with the Mohammedans. Limited in

TURK.

means of transportation from one part of the country to another. The products of Turkey are wax, raisins, dried figs, saddlery, olive oil, silks, red cloth, dressed goat skins, swords of superior quality, shawls, carpets, dye-stuffs, embroidery, attar of roses, plum brandy, etc. While formerly it was a capital offense to follow any other than the Mohammedan religion, the government has now become much more tolerant, the Musselman being free to change his religion as he may choose. A reform has been introduced, in late years, in the establishment of primary schools throughout the country.

E 20. Bulgaria. One of the Turkish dependencies. Area, 32,932 square miles; about the size of Maine. Wheat and Indian corn among the common productions of the soil. Though nominally the people belong to the Greek Church, very many do not adopt that religion. Population, about 2,000,000.

E 21. Roumania. A kingdom in the southeast of Europe. Area, 46,- 314 square miles; about the size of New York. Population, 5,376,- 000, including about 400,000 Jews and 200,000 Gypsies. The country became independent of Turkey at the close of the Russo-Turkish war, in 1878.

ROUMANIAN.

E 22. Black Sea. Large inland body of water entered from the Mediterranean through the Straits of Dardanelles. Is 720 miles long, 380 miles wide. Named "Black" on account of its liability to sudden and violent storms and dense fogs.

E 23. Constantinople. Capital of Turkey. Population, in 1885, 871,561. The Palace of the Sultan, in this city, is a most imposing building, inclosed by a wall 7½ miles in circuit, within which are a variety of mosques, gardens and large edifices; is capable of containing 20 000 persons.

E 24. Crimea. A peninsula jutting into the Black Sea, in the south of Russia, being 190 miles long and 110 miles wide. Population of Crimea, 705,000. Sebastopol, on the south of Crimea, was the principal point of the Crimean War, undertaken, in 1854, by Turkey, England, France and Sardinia, in behalf of Turkey, to prevent the aggressions of Russia on the Black Sea. The siege of Sebastopol continued from October 9, 1854, to September 8, 1855, at which time an important fortress was stormed by the French and English, and the Russians evacuated the city. The loss of life, within the year, was: English, 24,000; French, 63,500; Russian, estimated at 500,000.

E 25. Caucasus Mountains. An important range of mountains between the Black and Caspian Seas, nearly 700 miles long; were long the rendezvous of certain Caucasian tribes, who were the terror of surrounding civilization. These were subjugated by the Russians in 1871. Mt. Elburz, in this range, is 18,526 feet high, being the highest mountain in Europe. Many mountains in this range are above the line of perpetual snow. The former inhabitants of this region were classed by ethnologists as types of the highest mental and most perfect physical development, and included the white race in general throughout Europe. The inhabitants of the Caucasus, at the present time, are excluded from the above classification, and are considered

CLEAR FEATURES OF THE CAUCASIAN RACE.

to belong more closely to the sallow, flat-faced Mongols, whom they more nearly resemble than they do the higher order of Europeans.

E 26. Don River. Is 1,325 miles long. Empties into the sea of Azov. In the spring the river is navigable for a distance of 600 miles.

E 27. Volga River. The most important river in Russia and the longest in Europe; length, 2,400 miles. Rises in the Valdai Mountains; empties into the Caspian Sea.

E 28. Caspian Sea. The largest inland salt sea in the world; 700 miles long, 200 miles wide.

F 1. Lisbon. Capital of Portugal. Population, in 1878, 253,496. A picturesque and beautiful city; very old and contains many important educational institutions. An earthquake here, in 1755, destroyed a large portion of the city and 60,000 people.

F 2. Straits of Gibraltar. Connecting the Atlantic with the Mediterranean Sea. Are 15 miles wide at the narrowest point. On the north is the rock of Gibraltar, 1,439 feet high, upon which are stationed the most powerful of guns, making it a fortress that is considered almost impregnable. Has been controlled and held by the British since 1783.

F 3. Morocco. An old and decaying city in the northwest of Africa. Population, 50,000.

F 4. Algeria. A country in the northwest of Africa, under French control since 1830. Area, about 122,910 square miles. Population, in 1886, 3,817,465.'

F 5. Mediterranean Sea. Length, 2,320 miles; greatest breadth, 1,080 miles. Receives a constant and strong current from the Atlantic through the Strait of Gibraltar. Was the "Great Sea" of the ancients.

F 6. Sicily. The most fertile and most populous island in the Mediterranean. Area, 10,000 square miles; a little larger than New Hampshire. Population, 2,584,099.

F 7. Malta. An island owned by the British, 17 miles long and 9 miles wide. Has very strong fortifications. Population, in 1880, was 154,892, including 24,000 English-born and foreigners.

F 8. Tripoli. One of the Barbary states in north Africa. Area, 399,000. Population, about 1,010,000. The seaport town called Tripoli has an estimated population of 30,-000.

F 9. Greece. Area, 24,977 square miles; half the size of Ohio. An old country and long celebrated for literature, oratory, art, philosophy and the high condition of its civilization. Population, 2,187,208. Athens, the capital, was founded 1,550 years before Christ.

GREEK.

F 10. Candia. Large island in the Mediterranean. Is 160 miles long, and from 6 to 35 miles wide. Under control of Turkey. Population, 200,-000. Greek mythology claims this island to have been settled by a highly civilized people 1,300 years before Christ.

F 11. Alexandria. Founded by Alexander the Great in 332 B. C. For centuries after the time of its foundation was the capital of Egypt. Population, 227,064.

F 12. Isthmus of Suez. A neck of land, 72 miles wide at the narrowest part, connecting the continents of Asia and Africa. Celebrated in later years for the Suez Canal, connecting the Mediterranean and the Red Sea, and opened to navigation in 1870, by a procession of English steamers and vessels of other countries, in the presence of several rulers of the old world.

F 13. Cyprus. Controlled by England. Is 150 miles long and 55 miles wide. The population, in 1891, was 209,291.

F 14. Turkey in Asia. A large area of the Ottoman Empire, comprising 680,000 square miles. The prevailing religion of the people being the Mohammedan, tall minarets of the mosques, a specimen of which is shown, are a striking, characteristic feature of the country. Estimated population, 16,333,000.

F 15. Syria. In Asiatic Turkey. Area, 146,000 square miles; about the size of California. The

MOSQUE.

region of the Holy Land mentioned in the Bible. Reached a high civilization during the reigns of David and Solomon, at which time political union was secured among a people that hitherto had been scattered into small tribes, continually fighting one another. Later under control of the Romans, it was

subsequently held by the Arabs, from whom it passed into the possession of Turkey in the sixteenth century. The people are mostly Mohammedan. Population, about 2,000,000.

F 16. Jerusalem. The Jewish capital of Palestine. Its origin and early history very obscure. Its late history begins with David, who made this his place of residence, the city being known as the "City of David." Reached its greatest power and magnificence under Solomon, who built the Temple. Was captured and the Temple destroyed by incoming armies. The city rebuilt, and again destroyed by the Romans in the year 70. Afterwards rebuilt, it came under the dominion of the Turks in 1077. Population, 18,000, of whom 5 000 follow Mohammed, 8,000 are Jews who reject Christ, the remainder being mostly Christians. The city has few advantages and attractions aside from its religious associations.

F 17. Persia. Large Kingdom in Asia; 900 miles long from east to west, and 700 miles from north to south. Estimated population, 7,653,600; mostly Mohammedan in religion. The government pure despotism. Capital, Teheran; population, 200,000.

G 1. Tropic of Cancer. Explained in the description of North America.

G 2. Sahara Desert. In North Africa. An immense expanse of sandy waste, stretching from the Atlantic Ocean eastward to the River Nile. Is about 3,000 miles long and 1,000 miles wide, in Africa; extends even across into Arabia. The climate is one of great extremes and of intense dryness. The level basins are vast regions of sand, driven by the winds into a resemblance of ocean waves. In various valleys are springs and ac cumulations of rainfall, making oases, these places being marshy fields having frequently considerable population. Those habitable places support in all a population of about 2,500,000, consisting of Arabs, Negroes and others.

PERSIAN.

G 3. Egypt. One of the oldest countries, in history, on the globe, having a civilization dating back thousands of years before Christ; the records of which are very indistinct. It contains many remarkable ruins, the evidences still existing of a once singularly imposing and colossal architecture, as seen in the pyramids, the obelisks, the sphinxes, and other mammoth objects in sculpture. The Pyramid of Cheops is said to have required the labor of 100,000 men for twenty years. It covers 14 acres and is 460 feet in height.

"SHIP OF THE DESERT."

G 4. River Nile. Originates in the Victoria Nyanza Lake, Central Africa. Flows 3,370 miles, emptying into the Mediterranean. Has had an annual overflow, at the same time, within a few hours, and within a few inches of the same height, year after year, for unknown ages. Along its borders are the wonderful ruins of ancient Egypt, and evidences of the highest civilization of pre-historic times.

G 5. Cairo. The capital of modern Egypt. Situated on a sandy plain, 150 miles by rail from Alexandria. Is located near where the Nile divides into several great rivers on its way to the sea. Founded in 969. Population, in 1882, 374,838.

G 6. Red Sea. An inlet of the Indian Ocean, separating Arabia, on the east from Egypt, Nubia and Abyssinia, on the west. Length, over 4,100 miles; from 20 to 230 miles wide. Called "Red" Sea from

NUBIAN WOMAN.

the red and purple rocks that line its borders, from the red color given its waters, sometimes by seaweed, and in some places by red sandstone and reddish coral reefs. Has been an important water thoroughfare for thousands of years, recorded mention being found of its navigation 1,400 years before Christ. Has attained its great importance, as a means of communication between the east and Europe, since the opening of the Suez Canal, in 1870.

G 7. Mecca. One of the oldest towns of Arabia. Situated about 45 ml.es eastward from the Red Sea. Celebrated as the birthplace of Mohammed. The town has a fixed population of about 50,000, who obtain a living mainly from the patronage of pilgrims, who come

ARAB.

from Mohammedan countries, annually, to the number of many thousands. No paving existing in the streets, they are excessively dusty in summer and muddy in the rainy season. The chief mosque, known as the "House of God," holds 35,000 persons. Mohammed was born in Mecca, November 10, 570. His father, a merchant in humble circumstances, died ten months after his birth, and his mother six years later. The child then lived with his grandfather, who died two years later. He afterwards lived with two uncles, and with them traveled extensively through Arabia. Was at one time a shepherd, later a linen-trader, and subsequently was in the employ of a wealthy widow named Kadijah whom he married, and by whom he had six children—four daughters and two sons. About this time there were troublesome periods in the religious world. A reform was needed in Arabia. Mohammed, when about forty years old, retired to a cave, gave himself up to meditation, and after a time received the messages, which, it was claimed, came from God; being recorded by attendants, they became the Bible of the Mohammedans, called the Koran. He was several times expelled from Mecca, fleeing at last, for his life

to Medina, where he died at the age of sixty-three. Wrought many good works, and was sufficiently persecuted to call the attention and sympathies of millions of people to the reforms which he inaugurated.

G 8. Arabia. The great peninsula in the southwest of Asia. Is 1,500 miles long and

ARABIAN HORSE.

800 miles wide; having a population of about 5,000,000. This was, for a time, since the advent of Mohammed, a region of advanced ideas in philosophy, science and poetry. This also is the region of the camel, which has been styled "the ship of the desert." Here, likewise, the Arabian horse has been raised for several thousand years.

G 9. Persian Gulf. An arm of the Indian Ocean which extends between Arabia and Persia a distance of 650 miles, being from 55 to 250 miles wide.

H 1. Soudan. A vast tract of country in Northern Africa, which is the habitable region, in Africa, of the negro race; has a population estimated at 10,000,000.

H 2. Africa. More fully described in the chapter devoted to Africa.

H 3. Abyssinia. An extensive tract of country in the highlands of East Africa, the inhabitants of which resemble the Arabs in physical characteristics and the structure of their language. Area, 129,000 square miles. Population, about 3,000,000.

ABYSSINIAN.

I-1. Equator. The figures at the lower left-hand corner of the map, which resemble the figure eleven, designate the location of the equator, which is more fully defined in the descriptions of other maps, this line crossing those portions of the earth which are most directly under the vertical rays of the sun, and are consequently the warmest.

Temperature and Rainfall in Various Cities of the World.

CITIES.	Mean Annual Temperature.	Annual Average Rainfall, Inches.	CITIES.	Mean Annual Temperature.	Annual Average Rainfall, Inches.	CITIES.	Mean Annual Temperature.	Annual Average Rainfall, Inches.
Alexandria	69.0	10	Florence	59.2	41	Munich	48.4	
Algiers	64.3	27	Frankfort	50.0		Naples	60.3	30
Amsterdam	49.9		Geneva	52.7	32	Nice	58.0	29
Archangel	33.0		Genoa	61.1	47	Odessa	48.0	
Astrakhan	50.1	6	Glasgow	49.8	44	Para	81.0	71
Athens	63.0		Hague	52.0		Paris	51.3	22
Bagdad	74.0		Hamburg	47.0		Pekin	53.0	27
Barcelona	63.0		Havana	79.1	91	Port Said		2
Berlin	48.2	24	Hong Kong	73.0	101	Prague	50.2	14
Bermuda	72.0	55	Honolulu	75.0		Quebec	40.3	
Berne	46.0	46	Iceland	39.0	30	Quito	60.9	
Birmingham	48.2		Jerusalem	62.6	16	Rio Janeiro	77.2	29
Bombay	81.3	75	Lima	73.3		Rome	60.5	31
Bordeaux	57.0	30	Lisbon	61.4	27	Rotterdam	51.0	23
Brussels	50.7	29	London	50.8	25	San Domingo	81.3	108
Buda-Pesth	51.0	17	Lyons	53.0	28	Shanghai	59.0	
Buenos Ayres	62.8		Madeira	66.0	25	Smyrna	60.0	24
Cairo	72.2		Madrid	58.2	9	St. Petersburg	39.6	17
Calcutta	82.4	76	Malta	66.0	26	Stockholm	42.3	20
Canton	71.0	39	Manchester	48.8	36	Sydney	65.8	49
Cape Town	62.0	23	Manilla	78.4		Tobolsk	32.0	
Cayenne		116	Maranham		277	Trieste	55.0	43
Cherrapongee *		610	Marseilles	58.3	23	Valdivia	52.0	106
Christiania	41.5		Melbourne	57.0	29	Valparaiso	64.0	
Constantinople	56.5		Mexico	60.9		Venice	55.4	
Copenhagen	46.6	19	Milan	55.1	38	Vera Cruz	77.0	180
Delhi	77.0	24	Montevideo	62.0	44	Vienna	51.0	19
Dublin	50.1	29	Montreal	44.6		Warsaw	50.2	
Edinburgh	47.1	38	Moscow	40.0				

* In Southwestern Assam. It is the wettest place in the world. In 1861 the rainfall there reached 905 inches.

NOTE.—Mean annual temperature of the globe is 50° Fahr. The average rainfall is 36 inches.

(Proclaimed by the Secretary of the Treasury, January 1, 1892.)

COUNTRY.	The Standard Metal Money of the Country.	The Coin Known as the Monetary Unit.	Value in United States Money.	COINS OF VARIOUS COUNTRIES, AND THEIR VALUE IN UNITED STATES MONEYS.
Arg'tine Rp..	G'ld and Silver	Peso.....	$0.96,5..	Gold: Argentine ($4.82,4) and ½ Argentine. Silver: peso and divisions.
Aust.-Hung'y	Silver†	Florin ...	...34,1..	Gold: 4 florins ($1.92,9), 8 florins ($3 85 8), ducat ($2.28,7) and 4 ducats ($9.15,8). Silver: 1 and 2 florins.
Belgium ...	Gold and Silve	Franc.....	...19,3..	Gold: 10 and 20 francs. Silver: 5 francs.
Bolivia......	Silver..........	Boliviano	...69,1..	Silver: Boliviano and divisions. [2 milreis.
Brazil......	Gold.........	Milreis.....	...54,6..	Gold: 5, 10 and 20 milreis. Silver: ½, 1 and
Brit. N. Amer.	Gold.	Dollar ...	..1.00 ..	....
Cen. America	Silver..........	Peso......	...69,1..	Silver: peso and divisions.
Chili........	Gold and Silver	Peso......	...91,2..	Gold: escudo ($1.82,4), doubloon ($4.56.1), condor ($9.12,3). Silver: peso and divisions.
China.......	Silver..........	Ta- (Shanghai.	..1.02.1..	....
		el. (Haikwan.	..1.13.7..	...................................[Silver: peso.
Colombia.....	Silver..........	Peso......	...69,1..	Gold: condor ($9.64,7) and double-condor.
Cuba.......	G'ld and Silver	Peso......	...92,6..	Gold: doubloon ($5.01,7). Silver: peso.
Denmark....	Gold	Crown......	...26,8..	Gold: 10 and 20 crowns.
Ecuador.....	Silver..........	Sucre	...69,1..	Gold. condor ($9·64.7) and double - condor. Silver: sucre and divisions.
Egypt..... ..	Gold	Pound ...	..4 94,3..	Gold: pound (100 piastres), 5, 10, 20 and 50 piastres. Silver: 1, 2, 5, 10 and 20 piastres.
Finland	Gold	Mark......	...19,3..	Gold 20 marks ($3.85,9), 10 marks ($1 93).
France......	Gold and Silver	Franc....	...19,3..	Gold: 5, 10, 20, 50 and 100 francs. Silver: 5 francs.
Germ'n Emp.	Gold	Mark.....	...23,8..	Gold: 5, 10 and 20 marks. [ereign.
Great Britain	Gold...........	Pound	..4.86,6½	Gold: sovereign (pound sterling) and ½ sov-
Greece......	Gold and Silver	Drachma..	...19,3..	Gold: 5, 10, 20, 50 and 100 drachmas. Silver: 5 drachmas.
Hayti	G'ld and Silver†	Gourde ..	...96,5..	Silver: Gourde. [divisions.
India.......	Silver..........	Rupee....	...32,8..	Gold: mohur ($7.10,5). Silver: rupee and
Italy.	G'ld and Silver†	Lira......	...19,3..	Gold: 5, 10, 20, 50 and 100 liras. Silver: 5 liras.
Japan......	G'ld and Silver*	Yen {Gold	{..99.7..	Gold: 1, 2, 5, 10 and 20 yen.
		{Silvr.	{..74,5..	Silver: yen.
Liberia	Gold	Dollar	..1.00 ..	....
Mexico.....	Silver..........	Dollar....	...75....	Gold: dollar ($0 98.3), 2½, 5, 10 and 20 dollars. Silver: dollar (or peso) and divisions.
Netherlands.	Gold and Silver	Florin ...	...40,2..	Gold: 10 florins. Silver: ½, 1 and 2½ florins.
Newfo'ndland	Gold	Dollar ...	..1.01.4..	Gold: 2 dollars ($2.02,7).
Norway ...·.	Gold	Crown....	...26,8..	Gold · 10 and 20 crowns.
Peru...	Silver..........	Sol......	...69,1..	Silver: sol and divisions.
Portugal....	Gold	Milreis...	..1.08...	Gold: 1, 2, 5 and 10 milreis. [($3.86).
Russia	Silver†	Rouble ...	{..77,2..	Gold: imperial ($7.71,8) and ½ imperial
		{	{..55.3..	Silver: ¼, ½ and 1 rouble.
Spain	Gold and Silver	Peseta....	...19,3..	Gold: 25 pesetas. Silver: 5 pesetas.
Sweden ...	Gold	Crown....	...26,8..	Gold: 10 and 20 crowns. [5 francs.
Switzerland..	Gold and Silver	Franc....	...19,3..	Gold: 5, 10, 20, 50 and 100 francs. Silver:
Tripoli	Silver..........	Mahbub..	..62,3..	....
Turkey.....	Gold	Piastre.....	...4.4..	Gold. 25, 50, 100. 250 and piastres. [bolivars.
Venezuela...	Silver..........	Bolivar....	...13.8..	Gold: 5, 10,20, 50 and 100 bolivars. Silver: 5

* Gold the nominal standard; silver practically the standard. † Silver the nominal standard; paper the actual standard, the depreciation of which is measured by the silver standard.

NOTE.—Foreigners will find that the above values fluctuate with the rates of exchange.

Amount of Money in Circulation for Each Person in Different Countries.**

Estimated amount of gold, silver and paper money in circulation, from a communication, by the Director of the U. S. Mint, to the "North American Review."

COUNTRIES.	Gold.	Silver.	Paper.	Money Per Each Person.	COUNTRIES.	Gold.	Silver.	Paper.	Money Per Each Person.
Austria.......	$1.00	$2.25	$6.50	$9.75	Italy.........	$4.51	$1.94	$6.81	$13.26
Australia ...	25.00	...	1.75	26.75	Japan........	2.25	1.25	1.40	4 90
Belgium......	10.66	9.02	8.85	28.53	Mexico.......	.43	4.31	.17	4.91
British India..	...	3.53	11	3.64	Netherlands..	5.55	14.44	8.89	28.88
Canada......	3.56	1.11	8.89	13.56	Norw'y Sw'd'n	3.72	1.16	3.14	8 02
Central Amer.	...	.17	.67	.84	Portugal....	8.00	2 00	1.20	11.20
Cuba.......	10.00	1.00	20.00	31.00	Russia	1.68	.53	4.42	6.63
Egypt.......	14.20	2.14	...	16.43	Spain........	5.56	6.91	5.22	17.69
France.......	23 53	18.30	2.72	44.55	South America	1.29	.71	8.57	10 56
Germany.....	10.42	4.48	3.12	18.02	Switzerland ..	5 00	5 00	4.67	14.67
Gr't Britain..	14.41	2.02	1.57	18.60	Turkey.......	1.52	1.36	...	2.88
Greece.......	.91	1.82	6.36	9.09	United States.	11.06	7.33	6.78	25.17

** The "Hill Banking System," which favors government ownership of banks, denies that the above amounts are in actual circulation. The losses to depositors, through the present system of individual banking for profit, have so weakened confidence in banks, as to induce great numbers of people to hide their money, causing scarcity, high rates of interest, suppression of business, large accumulations in the hands of the few and poverty for the many. These conditions, it is claimed, would be changed, were the goverment to suppress all banks, and do the banking for the people, thus creating absolutely safe places for deposit, resulting in money becoming so abundant that it could be loaned at very low interest, causing revival of business, giving employment to the idle and prosperity to all, through universal circulation of money.

Map of Asia, Including a Portion of Australia.

This map represents those parts of the earth where the human race had already advanced to a high degree of civilization thousands of years ago, at a period no authentic record of which remains.

See Description on Following Pages.

To find the localities here mentioned on the opposite map, observe the corresponding figures on each page, the numbers growing larger from the top of the map downward.

A 1. North Pole.	E 4. Caspian Sea.	G 2. Suez Canal.	I - 1. Africa.
B 1. Nova Zembla.	E 5. Sea of Aral.	G 3. Red Sea.	I - 2. Indian Ocean.
B 2. Arctic Ocean.	E 6. Turkestan.	G 4. Arabia.	I - 3. Ceylon.
B 3. New Siberia.	E 7. Lake Balkash.	G 5. Mecca.	I - 4. Sumatra.
C 1. Arctic Circle.	E 8. Altai Mountains	G 6. Persian Gulf.	I - 5. Malay Penins'la.
C 2. Norway and Sweden.	E 9. Chinese Empire.	G 7. Beloochistan.	I - 6. Sts. of Malacca.
	E 10. Chinese Wall.	G 8. India.	I - 7. Singapore.
C 3. Russia in Eur'pe	E 11. Pekin.	G 9. Calcutta.	I - 8. Borneo.
C 4. Ural Mountains.	E 12. Corea.	G 10. Ganges River.	J 1. Java.
C 5. Siberia.	F 1. Turkey in Asia.	G 11. Burmah.	K 1. Madagascar.
C 6. Behring Strait.	F 2. Persia.	G 12. Tonquin.	K 2. North Australia.
D 1. St. Petersburg.	F 3. Afghanistan.	G 13. Canton.	L 1. Western Australia.
D 2. Irtish River.	F 4. Himalaya Mts.	G 14. Hongkong.	
D 3. Omsk.	F 5. Thibet.	G 15. Formosa.	L 2. Queensland.
D 4. Tomsk.	F 6. China.	G 16. Pacific Ocean.	L 3. Brisbane.
D 5. Lake Baikal.	F 7. Grand Canal.	H 1. Arabian Sea.	M 1. South Australia.
D 6. Sea of Okhotsk.	F 8. Nanking.	H 2. Bombay.	M 2. New South Wales.
D 7. Kamtchatka.	F 9. Shanghai.	H 3. Madras.	
D 8. Behring Sea.	F 10. Yellow Sea.	H 4. Bay of Bengal.	M 3. Victoria.
D 9. Aleutian Islands.	F 11. Sea of Japan.	H 5. Siam.	M 4. Melbourne.
E 1 Black Sea.	F 12. Japan.	H 6. Cochin China.	M 5. Sydney.
E 2. Constantinople.	F 13. Yokohama.	H 7. China Sea.	N 1. Tasmania.
E 3. Caucasus Mts	G 1. Trop. of Cancer.	H 8. Philippine Isles.	N 2. Hobart.

Localities, Cities and Regions in Asia and Australia Described.

Points Already Described: A 1, B 1, B 2, B 3, C 1, C 2, C 3, C 4, C 5 and D 1, described in description of Europe; C 6, described in description of North America.

D 2. Irtish River. An important river in Russia, which rises in the Altai Mountains, flows 2,200 miles northwest and empties into the Obi River.

D 3. Omsk The capital of western Siberia, 1,795 miles east of Moscow. Has a population of about 31,000. Is the headquarters of about 5,000 Russian soldiers.

D 4. Tomsk. Capital of the territory of Tomsk. Between this town and Omsk, and to the northward, for hundreds of miles, is the region into which are sent the Russian exiles. Population of the city of Tomsk, in 1884, was 31,380.

D 5. Lake Baikal. Extensive lake in the interior of Russia; 370 miles long and from 20 to 70 miles wide.

D 6. Sea of Okhotsk. Large inlet of the North Pacific Ocean, 1,000 miles long and 500 miles wide.

D 7. Kamtchatka. A peninsula in the southeast of Siberia; 725 miles long and 190 miles wide. Contains twelve active volcanoes. In its valleys is a luxuriant growth of vegetation. At its latest census had a population of 5,846; a hardy race of people, who live in caves in winter and in slightly built sheds in summer.

D 8. Behring Sea. A part of the North Pacific Ocean, commonly known as the Sea of Kamtchatka. Sometimes spelled "Bering."

D 9. Aleutian Islands. A group of 150 islands, which belong to Alaska, now a part of the United States. Population, 8,000. These islands, forming a kind of bridge between America and Asia, render probable the opinion, largely entertained, that the inhabitants of the American continent originally came across these islands from Asia.

E 1, E 2, E 3 and E 4. Described in the description of Europe.

E 5. Sea of Aral. Is 265 miles long and 145 miles wide.

E 6. Turkestan. Extensive region in Central Asia, occupied by various races.

E 7. Lake Balkash. Is 300 miles long and 75 miles wide.

E 8. Altai Mountains. An extensive range of mountains extending from east to west and forming the northern boundary of Chinese Tartary.

CHINAMAN.

E 9. Chinese Empire. A vast territory in Eastern Asia, supposed to have an area of 4,468,750 square miles, and a population of 400,000,000. Later estimates place the population at 300,000,000. The people are wholly absorbed in their own affairs and, excepting the few who have been abroad, know nothing of other countries. The religion of Confucius teaches that the highest virtues are imitation of, and obedience to, superiors, to parents and persons in authority. While this teaching is wholesome, in many respects, it has made the Chinese a race of imitators, who are averse to any change in costume, manners or methods of doing business.

E 10. Chinese Wall. An immense wall, 1,250 miles long, built about 220 years before Christ, as a protection against the Tartar tribes.

E 11. Pekin. Capital of the Chinese Empire since 1406. Surrounded by a great wall, 30 miles in circumference, inclosing an area of about 25 square miles. Is 100 miles from the sea and 60 miles from the great Chinese wall. Population, about 1,648,800.

E 12. Corea. A peninsula of Eastern Asia. Area, 79,414 square miles. Population, 10,518,937. An isolated people, of whom not much is known.

F 1. Turkey in Asia. Described in the description of Europe.

F 2. Persia. Described in the description of Europe.

F 3. Afghanistan. Located on the northwest of India. About 600 miles long from east to west, and 450 miles from north to south. Population, about 4,000,000. Mohammedan in religion.

F 4. Himalaya Mountains. A Sanscrit name meaning "the abode of snow." The most elevated and stupendous mountain system on the globe; the highest peak being Mount Everest, 29,000 feet, or 5½ miles, high.

F 5. Thibet. In Central Asia. Area, 700,000 square miles. Much of the territory abandoned to wild animals. Population estimated at 6,000,000. Is a dependency of China, and not much is known, by the outside world, of this country or its people.

F 6. China. The area of China proper, including eighteen provinces, is 1,534,953 square miles. Length, from north to south, 1,860 miles; width, 1,520 miles. Is about one-third of the area of the Chinese Empire.

F 7. Grand Canal. In the eastern part of China. Is 650 miles long, and connects Tien-tsin with Hang-chow. Is of great service in facilitating the interior commerce of the country.

F 8. Nanking. Formerly the capital of China. Has an estimated population of 349,-000. Is surrounded by an immense wall, 30 feet in thickness, and, in some places, 70 feet high.

F 9. Shanghai. The most important maritime city of China. Contains a greater number of foreigners than any other Chinese city, having 145,500 people of foreign birth, against a native population of 156,000.

F 10. Yellow Sea. Is a shallow inlet between China and the Peninsula of Corea.

F 11. Sea of Japan. The name of a large body of water lying between Japan and Corea, being about 1,200 miles long and 600 miles wide.

F 12. Japan. An ancient empire, consisting of four large and many small islands. Comprises an area estimated at 147,697 square miles; having a population, in 1890, of 40,072,084. Is said to have a written history extending back 2,500 years. Its authentic history begins about the year 400. Is rapidly advancing in higher civilization.

JAPANESE GIRL.

F 13. Yokohama and Tokio. Most important of the cities opened to commerce in Japan. Yokohama is the city first reached by the trader going westward on the journey around the world after leaving San Francisco. Population, 115,012. Tokio, capital of Japan, 17 miles from Yokohama, is divided into eight districts by several canals; has upward of sixty temples, and a population, in 1889, of 1,378,132.

G 1. Tropic of Cancer. Described in the description of Europe.

G 2. Suez Canal. An important waterway connecting the Red Sea with the Mediterranean Sea. Its opening was one of the most important maritime events of modern times, reducing the distance between western Europe and India nearly 4,000 miles. It is said that water communication for small vessels was made here 600 years before Christ, and existed for 1,400 years. Napoleon I. conceived the idea of a great ship canal, and De Lesseps carried the plan to successful conclusion, no locks being necessary, the waters of the Mediterranean and the Red Sea being nearly on a level.

G 3, Red Sea; G 4, Arabia; G 5, Mecca, and G 6, Persian Gulf, described in the description of Europe.

G 7. Beloochistan. Area, about 106,-000 square miles. Population, about 500,000.

G 8. India. Very ancient in civilization, and a very interesting portion of the world, principally under the dominion of Great Britain. Area, 1,533,726 square miles. Population, in 1891, was 284,614,-210. This is the land of the elephant, the serpent and the tiger. It contains, in some portions of the country, a highly civilized and very wealthy people.

ELEPHANT.

G 9. Calcutta. The capital and metropolis of British India. Will ever be celebrated for an event which occurred in 1756. The city, at that time, was captured by an invading force, the commander of whom confined for one night, the 146 men who surrendered, in a cell 120 feet square, having one small aperture for the admission of air. Only 23 survived the horrors of the place and were found alive in the morning, the place being fitly known afterwards as the "Black Hole of Calcutta." Has rapidly grown in wealth and importance in later years. Population, 466,459.

G 10. Ganges River. Rises in the Himalaya Mountains, and flows eastward 1,557 miles to the Bay of Bengal. Celebrated as the sacred river of the Hindoos. On the banks of the river, in the vicinity of Benares, where the Ganges is joined by the Jumna River, is an especially alleged holy place, to which hundreds of thousands of Hindoos repair to wash away their sins. Is a very muddy river, owing to the overflow of its banks. Its navigation is difficult for steamers, owing to the fact that its waters, corrode rapidly the cocks and valves of the engines. A priestly costume is shown herewith.

HINDOO.

G 11. Burmah. Area, 198,792 square miles. Population, about 9,053,900. Rice is the main product of the country.

G 12. Tonquin. A French possession obtained from Annam. In Eastern Asia, in 1884. Contains 35,000 square miles. Population, 9,000,000 principally Chinese.

G 13. Canton. An old city occupied by two races, namely, the Tartars and Chinese; separated by a wall having four gates. Was, for a long time, the only Chinese city open to foreigners; its principal export is being tea and silks. Population, 1,600,000.

G 14. Hongkong. An island about 11 miles long and from 2 to 5 miles wide, distant 100 miles southeast of Canton. Belongs to England, and has a population of 221,441, of whom over 200,000 are Chinese. Is a military station for the protection of British commerce.

G 15. Formosa. An island on the east coast of China, 237 miles long and 70 miles wide, containing three distinct populations: the Chinese, the subjugated aborigines and the uncivilized aborigines, the latter living on the eastern portion of the island. Here tattooing is a universal custom. Population, 500,-000, broken up into many tribes and clans, among whom petty wars are common.

TIGER. THE MOST DANGEROUS WILD ANIMAL IN ASIA.

G 16. Pacific Ocean. Described at G 1, in the description of North America.

H 1. Arabian Sea. Large body of water between Arabia and India.

H 2. Bombay. Is located on an island of the same name, and has a population of 804,470, consisting principally of Hindoos, and of a small number of Mohammedans and others. The city is rapidly rising in importance as the principal commercial port of India.

H 3. Madras. An important chief city in the province of Madras. Has a population of 449,950. The province has an area of 143,345 square miles, and a population of 35,588,850.

H 4. Bay of Bengal. A large portion of the Indian Ocean, stretching from Madras to Malacca, about 1,200 miles.

H 5. Siam. An extensive country, under a monarchy, in southeastern Asia, containing forty-one provinces. Area, 280,550 square miles. Population, from 4,000,000 to 6,000,000. The capital, Bangkok, has a population of 600,000.

H 6. Cochin China. An old province of southern Asia, the southern part of which was ceded by Annam to France, in 1862 and 1867. French Cochin China includes an area of 22,958 square miles, with a population of 1,642,182. Has a rich soil, but an unfavorable climate for Europeans.

H 7. China Sea. The extensive body of water lying between Cochin China and the Philippine Islands.

H 8. Philippine Islands. Numbering more than 1,400; having a supposed area of 114,356 square miles and a population of about 5,636,000, three-fourths of whom are governed by Spain, the remainder being under the control of native princes. Were discovered in 1521, by Magellan. This is the most important cigar-tobacco region in the east.

TOBACCO
PLANT.

I-1. Africa. More fully described in the succeeding chapters relating to Africa.

I-2. Indian Ocean. One of the five great divisions of the universal ocean, lying to the eastward of Africa and to the southward of Asia.

I-3. Ceylon. An island southeast of the southern extremity of India, being 266 miles long and 140 miles wide. Population, 3,008,239, being descendants of colonists from the valley of the Ganges, having retained, for many centuries, the habits, costumes and general appearance of their ancestors. In the northern part of the island have been discovered, in the depths of the forests, the ruins of ancient cities, which, in grandeur and magnificence, fully equal the famous antiquities of Egypt, and indicate the former high order of civilization once existing here, of which no authentic record is known.

I-4. Sumatra. An island 1,040 miles long and 266 miles wide. Population, about 5,000,000; mostly Malays, who profess Mohammedanism. All the fruits of the tropics abound here, and the elephant, tiger, leopard, bear, wild swine, antelope, deer, monkey and ant-eater, roam the forests at will.

I-5. Malay Peninsula. The southernmost region in Asia; about 600 miles in length and from 45 to 210 miles wide. Population, 850,000. Is but little known in the interior, the tiger and other wild animals having here undisputed sway.

I-6. Strait of Malacca. Is 520 miles long and from 25 to 200 miles wide. In this strait are the British settlements of Singapore, Malacca and Penang.

MALAY.

I-7. Singapore. The name of an island situated about three-quarters of a mile from the Malay Peninsula. Is 27 miles long and 14 miles wide; the seat of government being the town of Singapore, having a population, in 1881, of 139,208. Immense numbers of vessels annually enter the harbor at this point, the number of foreign ships, in 1890, being 3,646. The climate is delightful for a country within one degree of the equator. The temperature ranges from 70 to 90; the nights are cool; the atmosphere is almost uniformly serene. The rainy days of the year number about 167. Owing to there being no restric-

tions, the population is rapidly becoming Chinese. The favorable climate permits such rapid growth of vegetation as to cause the island to be covered, outside of the town, with a dense forest, which it is difficult to keep cleared away. The greatest danger to the inhabitants is the tiger, which swims over the strait from the mainland, and kills, on the average, it is claimed, about one person a day on the island of Singapore.

I-8. Borneo. One of the largest islands in the world. Is about 800 miles long and 700 miles wide. Population, 1,183,974, including a considerable variety of races, mostly yellow or dark skinned, enjoying various degrees of civilization. Has a delightful climate, notwithstanding its equatorial position. Luxuriant vegetation, including all the fruits, spices and vegetables which thrive in the hot climates. The forests abound in monkeys, orang-outangs, tigers, bears, wild oxen and deer; the trees being illuminated with birds of brilliant plumage; parrots, pheasants, peacocks and pigeons. The greatest part of the island is ruled by the Dutch.

J I. Java. On the journey from Singapore to Australia, the island of Java is conspicuously in view. Is 666 miles long and from 56 to 136 miles wide. Belongs to Holland. Has an estimated number of 20,898,523 inhabitants, being one of the most densely populated regions of the world. The race is Malay in complexion and feature. Is celebrated for its rice, coffee, and the fruits and flowers peculiar to the equatorial regions.

JAVANESE
LADY.

K 1. Madagascar. The third largest island in the world, being 975 miles long and 350 miles at its greatest width; and having a population of about 3,500,000. The inhabitants are divided into numerous tribes, of which the governing tribe is the Hova, whose language was reduced to writing about the year 1820, by missionaries of the London Missionary Society, who introduced here the art of printing six years afterwards. Climate temperate and healthy in the highlands of the interior. Three races: whites, negroes and Malays. Under French protectorate.

NATIVE OF
MADAGASCAR.

K 2. North Australia. The most northern portion of the Australian continent, discovered in 1605, about the same time, by expeditions under the command of the Dutch and the Spaniards respectively; although it was probably known to the Chinese much earlier. Owing to the warm climate of this portion of Australia, it has never been occupied by a people as highly civilized as that inhabiting the south of the island. The greatest breadth of Australia from north to south is upward of 2,000 miles, and the length from east to west is nearly 2,600 miles.

L 1. Western Australia. First settled in 1829. The climate here is one of the healthiest and most enjoyable in the world—the southern portion resembling the climate of England. There are two seasons, wet and dry; the wet lasting from April to September. Climate and soil admirably adapted to silk-worm-raising and vine-growing. Population, in 1891, 49,782.

L 2. Queensland. The most recently organized of the Australian colonies. Became a colony, distinct from New South Wales, in 1859. The summer is the rainy season, and is naturally hot. Both the productions of tropical and temperate countries can be cultivated with success in Queensland. Population, in 1891, 393,863. In 1890 there were 2,142 miles of railroad in operation. Schools and educational advantages are of a high grade.

L. 3. Brisbane. Is the capital of Queensland. In 1890 had a population of 93,000. Is an important seaport with a great future, as the country, to the westward, is developing.

M 1. South Australia. Since July, the entire territory in the central part of Australia, both north and south, has been included under the one name of South Australia, the whole having, in 1891, an estimated population of 315,048, exclusive of aborigines. First colonized in 1836. Capital: Adelaide, which had, in 1890, a population of 133,220. Had 5,623 miles of telegraph lines in 1890. Government administered by a governor and a parliament of two houses.

M 2. New South Wales. In southeastern Australia. Named by its first explorer, Captain James Cook, in 1770. Was first settled at Port Jackson, near Botany Bay, in 1788, by a penal colony of 750 persons, brought over from England in six transports and three store-ships. The bad reputation of Botany Bay has long since passed, and to-day the people, in all the essentials of civilization, are far advanced. The gold fields, discovered in 1851, up to the close of 1890 yielded $190,375,860. One of the animals, native here, is the kangaroo.

KANGAROO.

M 3. Victoria. Is the extreme southeastern colony of Australia, and, although the smallest of the Australian colonies, is, in size, 490 miles long and 300 miles wide. This has been the principal gold-producing region of Australia, the yield from 1851 to the close of 1890, being $1,137,411,500. About 3,000 miles of railways are in operation in the colony, all owned by the government. These railways, after transporting the people very cheaply, pay a handsome revenue to the government. The climate of the country is delightful, and pleasant to contemplate, when we realize that while we are worried by snow and ice in Europe and the United States, the people of Australia, in January, are in the midst of their golden harvest time.

M 4. Melbourne. The capital of Victoria, having, in 1891, a population of 491,378. Is noted for its university, museum, mint, public gardens, observatory, public

library, hospitals, grand churches and other monuments of advanced civilization.

M 5. Sydney. Capital of New South Wales. Had a population, at last census, of 386,400. It stands amid scenery of great beauty; extends four miles north and south and three miles east and west. Has 115 miles of streets and 3,800 acres of parks and open spaces. Is widely celebrated for the beauty and grandeur of its public buildings—the wonder of all travelers being that such taste should have been developed, such perfection attained and such magnificence realized, in the brief space of the country's history.

N 1. Tasmania. A large island lying to the southward of Australia. Is 240 miles long and 200 miles wide. Discovered by Tasman, December 1, 1642, and named by him Van Diemen's Land, which name was afterwards changed in honor of the discoverer. Was first settled, in 1803, by soldiers and convicts, from Sydney. Has had a steady growth since 1817, the population, in 1889, being 146,149. Has a very healthy climate, and is a summer resort for the people of Australia during their warmest seasons. Population composed of well-educated and highly intelligent people. The beautiful lyre-bird is native here.

LYRE-BIRD.

N 2. Hobart. The capital of Tasmania. Has a population, including its suburbs, of 38,000.

New Zealand. Is situated about 1,200 miles eastward from Australia, and includes three islands explored by Tasman, under direction of the East India Company, in 1642. Was settled by Europeans in 1814. The entire area of the islands is a little smaller than Great Britain and Ireland. Had, in 1891, a European population of 626,658, and a native population of 41,523, the latter of whom inhabit chiefly the north island. The government, in 1890, owned 1,842 miles of railway, and 132 miles were under construction. The climate and soil are similar to those of England. The capital is Wellington, having a population of 33,224. Auckland, the chief city, contains, with its suburbs, 51,287 inhabitants; and Dunedin has 45,865 inhabitants.

Names of People and Languages of Different Nations.

COUNTRY.	Name of People.	Language They Speak.
Austria	Austrians	German, Hungarian and Slavonic.
Arabia	Arabs, Arabians	Arabic.
Afghanistan	Afghans	Persian and Hindostanee.
Algeria	Algerines	Chiefly Arabic.
Abyssinia	Abyssinians	Abyssinian.
Australasia	Australasians	Dutch, English and native.
Brazil	Brazilians	Portuguese.
Bolivia	Bolivians	Spanish.
Belgium	Belgians	Flemish and French.
Beloochistan	Beloochees	Beloochee and Hindostanee.
Canada	Canadians	English and French.
Chili	Chilians	Spanish.
China	Chinese	Chinese.
Denmark	Danes	Danish.
Egypt	Egyptians	Arabic and Italian.
England	English	English.
East Indies	East Indians	Hindoostanee, Bengalee, Siamese, Malay, etc.
France	French	French.
Greenland	Greenlanders	Danish and Esquimaux.
Germany	Germans	German.
Greece	Greeks	Greek.

COUNTRY.	Name of People.	Language They Speak.
Holland	Dutch	Dutch.
Hindoostan	Hindoos	Hindoostanee and others.
Iceland	Icelanders	Icelandic.
Ireland	Irish	English and Irish.
Italy	Italians	Italian.
Japan	Japanese	Japanese.
Mexico	Mexicans	Spanish.
Norway	Norwegians	Danish.
Poland	Poles	Polish.
Peru	Peruvians	Spanish.
Paraguay	Paraguayans	Spanish.
Prussia	Prussians	German
Portugal	Portuguese	Portuguese.
Persia	Persians	Persian.
Russia	Russians	Russian.
Sweden	Swedes	Swedish.
Switzerland	Swiss	German, French and Italian.
Spain	Spaniards	Spanish.
Siberia	Siberians	Russian (mostly).
Siam	Siamese	Siamese.
Scotland	Scotch	English and Gaelic.
Turkey	Turks	Turkish.
United St'tes	Americans	English.
Venezuela	Venezuelans	Spanish.
West Indies	West Indians	Spanish.
Wales	Welsh	English and Welsh.

NAME OF CITY	Population.	NAME OF CITY.	Population.	NAME OF CITY.	Population.
Africa—Estimated Population.		**Asia—Ind. Archipelago.**		**Europe—Great Britain.**	
Abomey	50,000	Batavia	99,109	Aston	53,844
Antananarivo	75,000	Samarang	50,000	Bath	51,790
Bida	80,000	Surabaja	90,000	Burnley	58,882
Chartum	50,000	Surakarta	50,000	Bury	51,582
El-Obeid	50,000			Cardiff	85,378
Ibadan	50,000	**Asia—Japan.**		Cork	78,361
Illorin	70,000	Hiroshima	75,760	Croyden	78,947
Jakoba	50,000	Sendai	52,074	Derby	80,410
Kabebo	50,000	Tokushima	57,003	Gateshead	65,873
Kuka	60,000	Wakayama	62,197	Greenock	67,427
Kunasi	70,000	Yokohama	64,313	Halifax	73,633
Lagos	60,000			Huddersfield	81,825
Marokko	50,000	**Asia—Persia.**		Ipswich	50,762
Ogbomoscho	50,000	Ispahan	60,000	Leith	60,033
Ojo	70,000	Meschhed	60,000	Northampton	51,880
Port Louis	64,300	Rescht	60,000	Norwich	87,843
Salaga	50,000			Paisley	55,587
Zanzibar	80,000	**Asia—Russia.**		Plymouth	75,096
America, Brit. N.		Khokand	50,000	Preston	96,532
Quebec	62,446	Taschkent	86,233	Rochdale	68,860
Toronto	86,415	**Asia—Turkey.**		St. Helens	57,234
Amer.,N.-Mex'co Est. Pop.		Aleppo	75,000	Southampton	60,235
Guadalajara	93,875	Bagdad	67,000	South Shields	56,922
Guanajuato	63,000	Beirut	80,000	Stockport	59,544
Merida	56,000	Brusa	70,000	Swansea	63,739
Puebla	75,000	Diarbekir	60,000	Wakall	58,568
Queretaro	48,000	Erzerum	55,000	Wolverhampton	64,303
Zacatecas	50,000	Kintahia	60,000	York	54,198
America, South.		Manissa	60,000	Ystradyfodwg	55,617
Caracas	73,509	Mossul	75,000	**Europe—Italy.**	
La Paz	76,372	**Asia—Turkestan.**		Alessandria	62,464
Quito	80,000	Buchara	70,000	Bari	60,575
Santa Fe de Bogota	84,000	Jarkand	80,000	Brescia	60,636
Valparaiso	97,737	Kaschgar	70,000	Ferrara	75,513
Asia—Afg'nistan--Est. Pop.				Livorno	97,615
Cabul	60,000	**Europe—Austria-Hung.**		Lucca	68,063
Chulum	60,000	Brunn	82,660	Modena	58,058
Herat	50,000	Cracovia	66,095	Padua	72,174
Maimene	60,000	Debreczin	51,122	Perugia	51,354
Asia—Arabia.		Graz	97,791	Pisa	53,924
Sana	50,000	Maria-Theresiopolis	61,367	Ravenna	60,573
Asia—India.		Szegeden	73,675	Reggio	50,651
Allyghur	58,539	**Europe—France.**		Verona	68,741
Arcot	53,474	Amiens	74,170	**Europe—Netherlands.**	
Aurungabad	60,000	Angers	68,049	Utrecht	77,431
Beekaneer	60,000	Besancon	57,067	**Europe—Roumania.**	
Bellary	51,766	Brest	69,110	Galacz	80,000
Bhangulpur	69,678	Dijon	55,453	Jassy	90,000
Bhurtpoor	60,000	Grenoble	51,371	**Europe—Russia.**	
Chicacole	50,000	Le Mans	55,347	Astrakhan	69,319
Cuttack	50,878	Limoges	65,765	Berdischew	56,980
Dacca	69,212	Montpellier	56,005	Cherson	60,921
Dhrangdra	90,737	Nancy	73,225	Dunaberg	64,513
Furruckabad	79,204	Nice	66,279	Jelissuwetgrad	51,774
Goruckpur	51,117	Nimes	63,552	Nikolajew	66,335
Gya	66,843	Orleans	57,264	Orel	76,601
Hourah	97,784	Reims	93,823	Reval	50,488
Hubli	50,000	Rennes	60,974	Samara	63,400
Hue	55,188	Roubaix	91,757	Taganrog	63,025
Jubbulpur	48,831	Toulon	70,103	Tula	63,510
Kainte	48,831	Tourcoing	51,895	Wilna	93,763
Kathmandu	50,000	Tours	52,209	**Europe—Spain.**	
Kurrachi	53,526	Versailles	48,324	Cadiz	65,028
Madura	51,987	**Europe—Germany.**		Carthagena	75,908
Maisur	57,815	Aachen	95,669	Cordova	49,855
Mirut	81,386	Augsburg	75,476	Granada	76,108
Mirzapur	67,274	Braunschweig (Bruns-		Jerez de la Frontera	64,533
Moradabad	62,417	wick)	85,174	Lorca	52,934
Multan	50,878	Dortmund	78,435	Murcia	91,805
Muttra	59,281	Erfurt	58,385	Palma	58,224
Nagpur	84,441	Essen	65,074	Saragossa	84,575
Oothna	59,292	Frankfort on Oder	54,084	Valladolid	52,206
Pallee	50,000	Gorlitz	55,705	**Europe—Sweden.**	
Peshawur	58,430	Halle	81,949	Gothenburg	91,033
Saigon	60,000	Kassel	64,088	**Europe—Switzerland.**	
Salem	50,012	Krefeld	90,241	Basel (Bale)	61,399
Shahjehanpur	72,136	Lubeck	55,399	Geneva	68,310
Sholapur	53,403	Mainz (Mayence)	65,701	Zurich	75,956
Singapore	97,111	Mannheim	61,210	**Europe—Turkey.**	
Tanjore	52,175	Metz	54,072	Adrianople	62,000
Trichinopoly	76,530	Mulhausen	69,760	Saloniki	80,000
Vellare	51,500	Posen	68,318	Serajewo	50,000
		Stettin	99,550		
		Wiesbaden	55,437		

Map of Africa, Showing Parts of Europe and Asia.

Africa is bounded on the south by the Atlantic and Indian Oceans; on the east by the Indian Ocean and the Red Sea; north by the Mediterranean Sea, and on the west by the Atlantic Ocean.

See Description on Following Pages.

The points of interest numbered from E 2 to I-1, inclusive, are described in the Description of Europe, but are again enumerated here.

E 2. Spain	F 15. Syria.	I - 1. Equator.	K 2. St. Helena.
E 11. Italy.	F 16. Jerusalem.	I - 2. Liberia.	K 3. Benguela.
F 2. St. of Gibraltar.	F 17. Persia.	I - 3. River Niger.	K 4. Lake Nyassa.
F 3. Morocco.	G 1. Tr'pic of Cancer.	I - 4. Yambuya.	K 5. Mozambique.
F 4. Algeria.	G 2. Sahara Desert.	I - 5. Emin Pasha.	K 6. Moz'bique Chnl.
F 5. Mediterr'an Sea.	G 3. Egypt.	I - 6. Albert Nyanza,	K 7. Madagascar.
F 6. Sicily.	G 4. Nile River.	I - 7. Indian Ocean.	L 1. Tropic of Capri-
F 7. Malta.	G 5. Cairo.	J 1. Ascension Isl'nd.	corn.
F 8. Tripoli.	G 6. Red Sea.	J 2. Mouth of Congo.	L 2. Kimberley.
F 9. Greece.	G 7. Mecca.	J 3. Congo State.	L 3. Zululand.
F 10. Crete.	G 8. Arabia.	J 4. Vict'ria Nyanza.	L 4. Port Natal.
F 11. Alexandria.	G 9. Persian Gulf.	J 5. Lk. Tanganyika.	M 1. Cape Colony.
F 12. Isthmus of Suez.	H 1. Soudan.	J 6. Ujiji.	M 2. Cape Town.
F 13. Cyprus.	H 2. Africa.	J 7. Zanzibar.	M 3. C'p. of G'd Hope.
F 14. Turkey in Asia.	H 3. Abyssinia.	K 1. S. Atlantic Oc'n.	M 4. S. Indian Ocean.

Notable Regions, Cities and Objects in Africa.

I-2. Liberia. An independent negro republic in the southwestern part of upper Africa. Area, 14,000 square miles. Population, 1,050,000; mostly blacks, 18,000 of whom are immigrants from America. Founded by the American Colonization Society, in 1821, as a home for emancipated negroes. Climate rather warm and unhealthy for Europeans. Soil is fertile. Drainage is improving the healthfulness of the region, and its future is encouraging.

I-3. River Niger. Rises to the northward of Liberia, flows about 2,600 miles, east and south, emptying into the Gulf of Guinea.

I-4. Yambuya. Celebrated in connection with Stanley's latest exploration of Africa, up the Congo River: this being the point,1,300 miles from the ocean, where Major Bartellot was left in command of a number of natives, as a base of supplies.

STANLEY AND NEGRO DWARF.

I-5. Location of Emin Pasha. This is the region of the Province where Emin was found by Stanley.

I-6. Albert Nyanza. A large lake—one of the headwaters of the Nile—in east central Africa. Is 300 miles long and 92 miles wide.

I-7. Indian Ocean. Described in description of Asia.

J 1. Ascension Island. Is 800 miles from St. Helena. Discovered in 1501, on Ascension Day; hence its name. Occupied by the British since 1815. Is 7½ miles long and 6 miles wide. Population, 500, comprising naval officers and seamen.

J 2. Congo River. Flows 1,700 miles from the interior of Africa. Is navigable 460 miles from its mouth up to the rapids, near Stanley Pool. Above the rapids it is again navigable for a distance of 900 miles up to Stanley Falls. It is proposed to connect the two navigable portions of the river by means of a railway line around the rapids.

J 3. Congo Free State. Lies south of the River Congo, and covers an area of 802,000 square miles, and includes an estimated population of 8,000,000, principally uncivilized tribes.

J 4. Victoria Nyanza. Discovered by Captain Speke in 1858. Is 220 miles long and 180 miles wide.

AFRICAN LION.

J 5. Lake Tanganyika. Discovered by Speke in 1858. Is 350 miles long and from 15 to 60 miles wide.

J 6. Ujiji. An African village of considerable importance, about 750 miles from Zanzibar. Formerly a slave-market, it is now a center for the exchange of goods for ivory. The dwellings comprise those made of sun-dried bricks, and native huts. The population consist of Arabs and representatives of various African tribes. It was here that Stanley found Livingstone, October 28, 1871.

NATIVE OF ZANZIBAR.

J 7. Zanzibar. Located on an island of the same name. Has a population of about 100,000. Governed by native Sultan.

K 1. South Atlantic Ocean. Described elsewhere, under the head of "Atlantic Ocean."

K 2. St. Helena. British island in the South Atlantic. Discovered by the Portuguese in 1501; afterwards owned by the Dutch, and subsequently taken by the English in 1673. Is 10½ miles long and 6½ miles wide. Had a population, in 1891, of 4,116. Is 1,140 miles from the nearest point of the African continent. Has a delightful climate. Population consists of government officials, old-time European residents, and negroes, the fertility of the soil easily supporting the inhabitants. Has been celebrated for seventy years as the place to which Napoleon I. was banished by the English government, and where he lived from October 15, 1815, till May 5, 1821, when he died at a place now known as "Longwood," a farm-house three-quarters of a mile inland from Jamestown, on the seaboard. Twenty years after his death, during the reign of Louis Philippe, by permission of the English government, his remains were removed from the island of St. Helena to Paris, where they now rest, beneath an imposing monument, in the Hotel des Invalides.

K 3. Benguela. A mountainous region in western Africa, the boundaries of which are undefined; having an estimated population of about 140,000. Is well watered and has a very luxuriant vegetation.

K 4. Lake Nyassa. Was discovered by Dr. Livingstone in 1861. Is 300 miles long and 26 miles wide.

K 5. Mozambique. Is the capital of the province of the same name, and contains about 9,000 inhabitants. Population of the province, 300,000.

K 6. Mozambique Channel. Is about 1,000 miles long and 450 miles wide.

K 7. Madagascar. Lies in the Indian Ocean, 450 miles to the eastward of the African continent. See Madagascar, in Asia.

NATIVE OF MADAGASCAR.

L 1. Tropic of Capricorn. Described in description of South America.

L. 2. Kimberley. Widely known as the region of the Kimberley diamond mines. The value of the diamonds taken out, in these mines, in 1890, was $20,810,050. Population of Kimberley City, 28,643.

L. 3. Zululand. A rough, mountainous region, inhabited by a race of warlike Kaffirs, who were formed into a powerful kingdom about the beginning of this century. Became a British colony in 1887. During a war between the British and the natives, in 1878, the young Prince Imperial of France was killed, while out on a skirmishing expedition.

ZULU WARRIOR.   **L. 4. Port Natal.** Port of eutry to the Province of Natal, and is becoming a flourishing city, having the principal harbor on the coast of southeastern Africa.

M 1. Cape Colony. Includes the diamond mines of Kimberley, the Cape of Good Hope and the southern extremity of Africa. This also includes the region of ostrich farming and great sheep pastures. Has an agreeable climate favorable for consumptives. The elephant,

buffalo, lion, rhinoceros, giraffe, hippopotamus, leopard, hyena, jackal, zebra and antelope, formerly here, have retreated before advancing civilization to the jungles and forests of the more northern regions of Africa.

OSTRICH.

M 2. Cape Town. Capital of Cape Colony. Had, in 1891, a population of 51,083. Is a growing and prosperous city, the character of its inhabitants being known by its churches, which include the Catholic, Episcopal, Presbyterian, Lutheran, Wesleyan and Congregational. Is lighted by electricity; is handsomely paved, and surrounded, in its suburbs, with beautiful villas.

M 3. Cape of Good Hope. Discovered by Bartholomew Diaz, a Portuguese navigator. In 1486, and given its present name by the King of Portugal, as its discovery afforded a hope of a new and easier way of reaching India.

M 4. South Indian Ocean. Has no definite limit, but is supposed to terminate at the parallel which runs between the southern extremity of Africa and Australia; south of which is the Antarctic Ocean.

Principal Countries of the World; Population, Religion and Government.

COUNTRY.	Population.	Inhabitants to Square Mile.	Capital.	Prevailing Religion.	Form of Government.
China (Estimated)*	303,241,969	93.7	Pekin	Buddhic	Empire.
India	274,000,000	184.3	Calcutta	Hindoo	Empire.
Russia (Est.)	108,787,214	13	St. Petersburg	Greek Church	Empire.
United States †	62,622,250	18	Washington	Protestant	Republic.
German Empire	49,421,065	227.1	Berlin	Protestant	Monarchy.
Austria-Hungary	42,749,329	168.5	Vienna	Catholic	Monarchy.
France	38,218,903	187.2	Paris	Catholic	Republic.
Japan	40,072,684	265	Tokio	Buddhic	Empire.
Great Britain ‡	38,000,000	290	London	Protestant	Monarchy.
Italy (Est.)	30,158,408	267.5	Rome	Catholic	Monarchy.
Turkish Empire	32,500,000	20.2	Constantinople	Mohammedan	Monarchy
Spain	17,550,216	88	Madrid	Catholic	Monarchy.
British America	5,000,000	1.2	Ottawa	Protestant	Monarchy.
Brazil	14,000,000	4.3	Rio Janeiro	Catholic	Republic.
Mexico (Est.)	10,000,000	15.3	Mexico City	Catholic	Republic.
Belgium	6,030,043	530	Brussels	Catholic	Monarchy.
Bavaria	5,589,382	182.7	Munich	Catholic	Monarchy.
Sweden	4,478,675	27	Stockholm	Protestant	Monarchy.
Persia (Est.)	7,653,600	13.2	Teheran	Mohammedan	Monarchy.
Portugal	4,708,178	135.2	Lisbon	Catholic	Monarchy.
Holland **	4,450,870	356	The Hague	Protestant	Monarchy.
Colombia	3,500,000	9.9	Bogota	Catholic	Republic.
Switzerland	2,933,334	184	Berne	Protestant	Confederation.
Peru	3,000,000	6	Lima	Catholic	Republic.
Australasia	3,935,494	1.2	Melbourne *†	Protestant	Monarchy.
Chili (Est.)	2,665,000	9	Santiago	Catholic	Republic.
Bolivia (Est.)	1,380,000	2.9	Sucre	Catholic	Republic.
Denmark (Est.)	2,172,205	156.3	Copenhagen	Protestant	Monarchy.
Wurtemberg	2,036,556	261.8	Stuttgart	Protestant	Monarchy.
Norway	2,000,000	14	Christiania	Protestant	Monarchy.
Venezuela	2,121,988	3.5	Caracas	Catholic	Republic.
Argentine	3,000,000	3.6	Buenos Ayres	Catholic	Republic.
Greece	2,187,208	87	Athens	Greek Church	Monarchy.
Baden	1,656,817	272.1	Karlsruhe	Catholic	Grand Duchy.
Guatemala	1,427,116	30.5	New Guatemala	Catholic	Republic.
Ecuador	1,004,651	8.5	Quito	Catholic	Republic.
Hesse	994,614	318.8	Darmstadt	Protestant	Grand Duchy.
Liberia (Est.)	1,050,000	74.6	Monrovia	Protestant	Republic.
Hayti (Est.)	500,000	94.1	Port au Prince	Catholic	Republic.
Uruguay	687,194	9.5	Montevideo	Catholic	Republic.
San Salvador	651,130	91.5	San Salvador	Catholic	Republic.
Nicaragua (Est.)	310,000	7	Managua	Catholic	Republic.
Honduras (Est.)	431,917	9	Tegucigalpa	Catholic	Republic.
San Domingo	350,000	34	San Domingo	Catholic	Republic.
Paraguay	440,000	5	Asuncion	Catholic	Republic.
Costa Rica (Est.)	213,785	10.3	San Jose	Catholic	Republic.
Hawaii (Est.)	86,647	12	Honolulu	Protestant	Monarchy.

* Includes Corea.   † Includes the Territories.   ‡ Includes Ireland.   ** Includes Netherlands.
*† Australasia has seven organized colonies—New South Wales, Victoria, Queensland, South Australia, Western Australia, New Zealand and Tasmania.   The capital of Victoria is Melbourne.

NAME OF RIVER.	Length in Miles.	Country in Which Located.	Where It Rises.	Where It Empties.
Amazon	3,944	Peru, Ecuador and Brazil	Andes Mountains	Atlantic Ocean
Amoor	2,200	Eastern Asia	Irkutsk—Mongolia	Sea of Okhotsk
Araguay	1,300	Brazil	Latitude, 19° S	River Amazon
Arkansas	2,170	Utah, Ind. Ter., Colorado	Rocky Mountains	Mississippi River
Brahmaputra	1,500	Asia	Upper Assam	Bay of Bengal
Chingua	1,150	Brazil	Diamantí Mountains	River Amazon
Colorado	2,000	Utah, Wyoming Territory and California	Southeast Utah	Gulf of California
Columbia	1,400	Oregon, Washington, British North America	Rocky Mountains	Pacific Ocean
Congo	1,700	Congo and Loango, Africa	Interior Africa	Atlantic Ocean
Danube	1,750	Central Europe	Black Forest, Baden	Black Sea
Dnieper	1,200	Russia	Government of Smolensk	Black Sea
Euphrates	1,600	Western Asia	Armenia	Persian Gulf
Ganges	1,557	Hindustan	Himalaya Mountains	Bay of Bengal
Hoang-Ho	2,500	China	Thibet	Yellow Sea
Indus	1,960	Asia	Mt. Kailas, Thibet	Arabian Sea
Irrawaddy	1,200	Farther India	British Burmah	Bay of Bengal
Irtish	2,200	North Asia	Altai Mountains	River Obi
Japura	1,000	Brazil and Colombia	Unit'd St'tes of Colombia	Amazon River
Kama	1,200	Russia	Government of Viatka	Volga River
Kiou-long kiang	1,200	Thibet, China, etc	Thibet	China Sea
Kuskoquim	1,500	Alaska	Alaska	Pacific Ocean
Kwickpak	1,800	Alaska	Rocky Mountains	Behring Strait
Lena	2,500	Siberia	Near Irkutsk	Arctic Ocean
Mackenzie	1,700	British North America	Great Slave Lake	Arctic Ocean
Madeira	2,000	South America	Bolivia	River Amazon
Mississippi	2,616	North America	Itaska Lake, Minn	Gulf of Mexico
Missouri *	3,096	United States	Rocky Mountains	Mississippi River
Murray	1,000	Victoria, Australia	Warragong Mountains	Lake Victoria
May Kuang	1,300	China	Thibet	China Sea
Niger	2,300	Central Africa	Western Coast	Gulf of Berien
Nile	3,500	Northeast Africa	Blue Rvr. & White Rvr. Lat. 15° 34′ N., Long. 32° 30′ 58″ E.	Mediterranean Sea
Obi	2,700	Asiatic Russia	Little Altai Mountains	Gulf of Obi
Orange	1,000	South Africa	Nr. lat. 29° S. long. 30° E.	Atlantic Ocean
Orinoco	1,500	Venezuela	Sierra de Parima	Atlantic Ocean
Paraguay	1,800	Paraguay and Brazil	Matto Grosso, Brazil	Parana River
Parana	1,800	Uruguay	Brazilian Mountains	La Plata River
Pilcomayo or Araguai	1,000	Bolivia and Paraguay	Bolivia	Paraguay River
Platte (or Nebraska)	1,200	Wyoming and Colorado	Wind Mts., Wyoming Ter., Park Mts., Colo.	Missouri River
Red River and Branches	2,100	Texas, Indian Territory, Arkansas, Louisiana	Northwestern Texas	Mississippi River
Rio Grande	1,800	United States and Mexico	Rocky Mountains	Gulf of Mexico
Rio Negro	1,200	Colombia and Venezuela	Colombia Hills	Amazon River
Sayhalien	1,000	Manchuria	Mongolia	Sea of Okhotsk
San Francisco	1,400	Brazil	Sierra Veretntes	Atlantic Ocean
Saskatchewan	1,000	British North America	Rocky Mountains	Lake Winnipeg
Senegal	1,000	Senegambia	Mount Cooro	Atlantic Ocean
Shat-el-Arab	1,800	Persia	Euphrates and Tigris	Persian Gulf
Tigris	1,150	Turkey and Persia	Armenian Mountains	Persian Gulf
Tocatines	1,300	Brazil	Cordilleras Mountains	River Para
Ucayali	1,200	Peru	Near Cuzco	Amazon River
Ural	1,800	Russia	Government of Mensk	Caspian Sea
Uruguay	1,020	Brazil and Uruguay	Santa Catherine, Brazil	Parana River
Volga	2,400	Russia	Valdai Mountains	Caspian Sea
Yang-tse-Kiang	2,500	China	East Thibet	Yellow Sea
Yellowstone	1,000	Dakota, Wy. Ter. and Mont	Yellowst'ne L'ke,Wy.Ter	Missouri River
Yenisei	2,300	Siberia	Mongolia	Arctic Ocean
Yukon	1,850	Alaska	British Columbia	Pacific Ocean
Zambesi	1,800	Eastern Africa	Abt.lat. 11° S.,long.23° E.	Indian Ocean

* Total length of continuous stream, from its headwaters to the Gulf of Mexico, 4,194 miles.

Height of Waterfalls in Different Parts of the World.

NAME OF FALL.	WHERE LOCATED.	Height in Feet	NAME OF FALL.	WHERE LOCATED.	Height in Feet
Bridal Veil Fall	Yosemite	900	Niagara Falls *	North America	164
Cerosola Cascade	Alps, Switzerland	2,400	Passaic Falls	New Jersey	71
Falls of Arve	Savoy	1,100	Tivoli Cascade	Near Rome	40
Falls of St. Anthony	Upper Mississippi	60	Virgin Tears Creek	Yosemite	1,000
Falls of Terni	Near Rome	300	Waterfall Mountain Cascade	South Africa	85
Fryer's	Nr. Loch Ness, Scotl'd	200	Yosemite Falls	California	1,500
Genesee Falls	Rochester, N. Y	96			
Lauterbrunnen	Lake Thun, Switzerland	900			
Lidford Cascade	Devonshire, Eng	100			
Missouri Falls	North America	90			
Montgomery Falls	Quebec, Canada	250			
Natchkikin Falls	Kamtchatka	300			
Nile Cataracts	Upper Egypt	40			

* These falls are steadily receding up Niagara River, the wearing away of them, in some portions of them, having been at least 100 feet since 1841, pieces of rock falling from time to time. The other portions of the falls have not visibly receded during the same period.

Map of the Continent of South America.

Portions of this continent were occupied by civilized human beings, for unknown ages, prior to its occupancy by the Spaniards. Its modern discovery was made by Americus Vespucci, who landed on the coast of Brazil in 1499.

See Description on Opposite Page.

To find the points designated, begin at the upper part of the map and follow to the right and downward, across the map. The points marked from G 16 to I-6, on the opposite map, are described on the map of North America.

I-5. Equator. The imaginary circle, on the earth's surface, which is midway between the North and South Poles, and, being almost continually beneath the vertical rays of the sun, represents the warmest portion of the earth.

I-6. Orinoco. A great river of northern South America, 1,960 miles long.

I-7, I-8, I-9. The Guianas. Three territories belonging respectively to the English, Dutch and French, each a little larger than the State of New York.

J 1. Quito. The capital of the Republic of Ecuador, located near the Equator, between two ranges of the Andes. By the earthquake of March, 1859, property to the extent of $3,000,000 was destroyed. From that calamity, however, the city has recovered. Population about 80,000.

J 2. Ecuador. The Spanish name for Equator; a republic covering an area 500 miles from north to south, and, from east to west, nearly 800 miles, having an area of 250,000 square miles. Population, 1,004,651, besides 600,000 wild Indians.

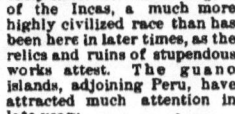

PERU INDIAN.

J 3. Peru. Area, 508,718 square miles. Population, 3,000,000. In early times this was the region of the Incas, a much more highly civilized race than has been here in later times, as the relics and ruins of stupendous works attest. The guano islands, adjoining Peru, have attracted much attention in late years.

J 4. Amazon River. The largest river in the world, the main mouth of which is about 50 miles wide; and the whole delta, where it empties, is nearly 200 miles from shore to shore. Rises in Peru and flows about 4,000 miles; allows of navigation, on the main river and its tributaries, for about 50,000 miles. On its bosom float the giant Victoria Regia and other great aquatic plants, native to the equatorial regions.

J 5. Brazil. The largest territory of the South American continent; is about 2.600 miles long and 2,500 miles wide. Population about 11,000,000, including nearly 1,000,000 aboriginal Indians.

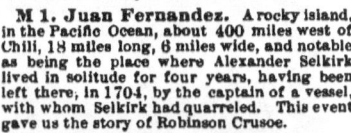

BRAZILIAN.

K 1. Lima. The capital of Peru; a beautiful city of about 200,000 population. Founded by Pizarro, in 1535. The summer, in this region, begins in December, and the winter in June. The university here, built in 1576, is the oldest in America.

K 2. Andes Mountains. A great mountain chain, extending, nearly parallel with the Pacific Ocean, almost the whole length of the continent, a distance of about 4,500 miles; claimed by some writers to be the southern continuation of the Rocky Mountains of North America. The highest peak is the Nevada de Sorata, close to Lake Titicaca, and is estimated to be 21,286 feet in height.

K 3. Lake Titicaca. A great lake in the valley between the mountain ranges of southern Peru.

K 4. Bolivia. A Republic so named after Bolivar, a distinguished warrior who fought in this region in behalf of freedom. Has an area of 850,000 square miles, and had a population, at the last census, of 1,380,000.

L 1. Chili. The southwestern Republic of South America; extends 1,240 miles along the coast, with an average breadth of 120 miles. Population, 2,665,000.

L 2. Argentine Republic. Population nearly 3,000,000, about one-half being of pure European descent. The negro element is small. In climate and government, similar to the United States.

L 3. Paraguay. Area, 90,000 square miles. Population about 440,000, including 130,000 Indians, a female of whom is here shown.

L 4. Rio de Janeiro. The largest and most important commercial city of South America. Capital of Brazil. Population, in 1889, was about 350,000.

PARAGUAY INDIAN.

L 5. Tropic of Capricorn. An imaginary line indicating the southern boundary of the torrid zone.

M 1. Juan Fernandez. A rocky island, in the Pacific Ocean, about 400 miles west of Chili, 18 miles long, 6 miles wide, and notable as being the place where Alexander Selkirk lived in solitude for four years, having been left there, in 1704, by the captain of a vessel, with whom Selkirk had quarreled. This event gave us the story of Robinson Crusoe.

M 2. Valparaiso. The most important trading port of Chili. Population, in 1885, was 95,000.

M 3. Santiago. Stands at the west boundary of the Andes. Subject to earthquakes; houses consequently are but one story in height. Population, in 1890, was 225,000. Contains a university and school of arts.

M 4. Rio de la Plata. The principal river of southern South America; 200 miles long.

M 5. Buenos Ayres. Capital of the Argentine Republic; a beautiful city, the public buildings of which would honor any city in Europe. Traversed by street cars. Four lines of railway connect it with the interior. Population about 250,000.

M 6. Montevideo. Capital of Uruguay; built on a rocky peninsula, one mile square. An important city. Population, 120,000.

N 1. Patagonia. Most southern region of South America. Length, 1,000 miles; greatest breadth, 480 miles. Inhabited by two tribes of Indians, who are rather above the average size.

O 1. Straits of Magellen. Are 300 miles long and from 5 to 30 miles wide. So named from Magellan, the first navigator who sailed through them, in 1519, with five ships and 236 men. Navigation through these straits is difficult.

PATAGONIAN.

O 2. Terra del Fuego. "Land of Fire;" so called from the numerous volcanoes which have prevailed in this region. Is a collection of islands located at the southern extremity of South America. Climate raw and cold. The only quadrupeds on the island are dogs. Inhabited by a low order of negroes, who are brutal and coarse in their instincts.

O 3. Cape Horn. The most southern point of an island of that name at the southern extremity of Terra del Fuego; named after Hoorn, in Holland, by a native of that town who discovered the Cape about 1610.

O 4. Falkland Islands. A group of about 200 islands, 300 miles northeast of the Strait of Magellan, belonging to England. Have a population of about 1,200.

P 1. Graham's Land. An island in the Southern Pacific, discovered by Biscoe in 1832.

Map of the North American Continent.

Occupied, two thousand or more years ago, by the Mound Builders; more recently by the red men, called Indians; opened to civilization by Christopher Columbus, who discovered the Bahama Islands, October 12, 1492.

See Description on Following Pages.

When examining the map of North America figures will be found extending from left to right, beginning with A 1 and A 2, in the arctic regions; succeeding which are B 1, etc., in the regions south of latitude 80; while, south of latitude 70 are C 1, and so on, down to Central America. Letters and figures on the map indicate important localities. By examining the map the letters and figures will be readily found indicating points that are thus described:

Localities and Objects Designated on the Map by Letters and Figures.

A 1. North Pole.	D 9. St't of Belle Isle.	E 30. Gf.St.Lawrence.	G 6. Mexico.
A 2. Highest Point of Arctic Exploration.	E 1. Vancouver Is'd	E 31. Newfoundland.	G 7. Sierra Madre.
B 1. Point Barrow.	E 2. Victoria, B. C.	F 1. San Francisco.	G 8. Rio Grande.
B 2. Cape Sabin.	E 3. Mt. St. Helens.	F 2. Sierra Nev. Mts.	G 9. Monterey, Mex.
B 3. Baffin's Bay.	E 4. Portland, Ore.	F 3. San Diego.	G 10. Gulf of Mexico.
B 4. Greenland.	E 5. Columbia Riv'r.	F 4. Salton Lake.	G 11. Galveston, Tex.
B 5. Spitzbergen.	E 6. Boundary Line.	F 5. Colorado River.	G 12. New Orleans.
C 1. Siberia, Russia.	E 7. Salt Lake, Utah.	F 6. Mexic'n B'nd'ry.	G 13. Florida.
C 2. Behring's Str'it.	E 8. Yellowstone Pk.	F 7. Rocky Mo'nt'ns.	G 14. St. Augustine.
C 3. Alaska.	E 9. Missouri River.	F 8. Denver, Colo.	G 15. Havana.
C 4. Yukon River.	E 10. Dakota.	F 9. Santa Fe.	G 16. Cuba, W. Indies
C 5. Can. Dominion.	E 11. St. Paul, Minn.	F 10. Indian Ter.	G 17. Watling Island.
C 6. McKenzie River.	E 12. Duluth, Minn.	F 11. Arkansas River.	H 1. Mexico City.
C 7. Great Bear L'ke.	E 13. Lake Superior.	F 12. Red River.	H 2. Popocatepetl.
C 8. Great Slave Lke.	E 14. Mackinac.	F 13. Mississippi Rivr.	H 3. Vera Cruz, Mex.
C 9. Hudson Bay.	E 15. Lake Michigan.	F 14. St. Louis, Mo.	H 4. Yucatan, S. A.
C 10. Hudson Strait.	E 16. Chicago.	F 15. Ohio River.	H 5. Guatemala.
C 11. Davis Strait.	E 17. Lake Huron.	F 16. Cincinnati, O.	H 6. Honduras.
C 12. Iceland.	E 18. Detroit, Mich.	F 17. Alleghany Mts.	H 7. Nicaragua.
C 13. Norway.	E 19. Lake Erie.	F 18. Charleston, S. C.	H 8. Nicaragua Lke.
C 14. Arctic Circle.	E 20. Cleveland.	F 19. Cape Hatteras.	H 9. Caribbean Sea.
D 1. Mt. St. Elias.	E 21. Buffalo, N. Y.	F 20. Wash'gton, D.C.	H 10. Jamaica.
D 2. Mt.Fairweath'r.	E 22. Lake Ontario.	F 21. Phil'delphia,Pa.	H 11. Hayti, W. Inds.
D 3. Sitka, Alaska.	E 23. Montreal, Can.	F 22. Bermuda Isl'ds.	I 1. Ish. of Panama.
D 4. Mt. Brown.	E 24. New York, N. Y.	F 23. Atlantic Ocean.	I 2. Aspinwall.
D 5. Lake Winnipeg.	E 25. Boston, Mass.	G 1. Pacific Ocean.	I 3. U.S.of Cl'mbia.
D 6. Winnipeg.	E 26. Mt.Washington.	G 2. Guadaloupe Is.	I 4. Venezuela, S. C.
D 7. Lake Nipigon.	E 27. St.Lawrence Rr.	G 3. Tropic of Cancer	I 5. Equator.
D 8. Labrador.	E 28. Quebec, Can.	G 4. Low. Calif'rnia.	
	E 29. Nova Scotia.	G 5. Glf. of Calif'rnia.	

Description of Notable Objects on the North American Continent.

A 1. The North Pole. An imaginary point where the lines of longitude are supposed to converge.

A 2. The Point Nearest the North Pole, reached by arctic navigators, being Lockwood Island, discovered by the Greeley expedition in May, 1883, and supposed to be about 450 miles from the North Pole. Failing to get supplies, the expedition started southward, and camped at Cape Sabin (see B 2), about 420 miles southwest of Lockwood Island, where they were rescued in a dying condition by the relief expedition under guidance of Commander W. S. Schley, 7 being rescued alive, 17 having died before relief arrived.

B 1. Point Barrows. The northernmost point of Alaska, and the most northern point of the United States' possessions.

B 2. Cape Sabin. A locality that will always be notable as the place where the Greeley explorers went into camp and waited for relief, which did not come until the majority of the party had died.

B. 3. Baffin's Bay. So named after William Baffin, who first explored the region in 1816. It is a large inland sea, 1,000 miles long and 500 miles wide.

B 4. Greenland. A region of unknown extent northward, said to have been discovered in the ninth century by an Icelander. Dr. Kane extended his explorations northward, across Greenland, to within 520 miles of the North Pole. The whole face of the northern portion is covered with a sheet of ice and snow. The face here shown is that of  a Greenland woman, a representative of a race that are widely scattered throughout the colder regions of the north. Their dress consists principally of skins, and is much alike for both sexes.

GREENLANDER.

B 5. Spitzbergen. A group of islands covering about 30,000 English square miles. Covered with nearly perpetual snow and glaciers.

C 1. Siberia. A vast territory in North Asia, belonging to Russia, 4,000 miles long and 2,600 wide.

C 2. Behring's Strait. Explored by Vitus Behring in 1728; is nearly 50 miles wide from Alaska to Siberia, with three uninhabited islands nearly midway between. Towards the middle the water is about 120 feet in depth. With a railroad spanning the distance between Alaska and Siberia, either above water or in a tunnel under the water, nearly all portions of the world could be traversed by continuous railways.

C 3. Alaska. Belongs to the United States; comprises 565,862 square miles; population about 35,000; small proportion are whites Purchased of Russia, in 1867, for $7,200,000. Alaskan waters are the home of the fur seal, the largest weighing about 700 pounds.

FUR SEAL.

C 4. Yukon River. The principal river of Alaska; rises in the Rocky Mountains, in the Canadian Dominion, flows 2,000 miles, and empties into the Pacific Ocean some 400 miles southwest of Behring Strait.

C 5. Canadian Dominion. A vast area of country in the northern part of North America, usually designated as British America, contains 3,500,000 square miles, extending from the Atlantic to the Pacific Ocean, and from the United States to the Arctic Ocean. Population about 5,000,000.

C 6. Mackenzie River. An important river of British America, 1,773 miles long. Runs through Athabasca and Great Slave Lakes, and empties into the Arctic Ocean.

C 7. Great Bear Lake. By observing a perfect map of North America it will be seen that a chain of lakes extends from the Arctic Ocean, near Alaska, eastward to the Gulf of St. Lawrence. The most northerly of these is Great Bear Lake, the area of surface of which is estimated to be 14,000 square miles.

C 8. Great Slave Lake. Next, south of Great Bear, is Great Slave Lake, 300 miles in length by 50 in width, and, like other lakes in this region, wholly frozen over for six months in the year.

C 9. Hudson Bay. A great inland sea, on the borders of which the Hudson Bay Company, which was established in 1670, held control until 1869; at which time their possessions were transferred to the Dominion of Canada for the sum of $1,500,-000, they only reserving their trading posts and a small amount of land around each post. During the year 1856 their employes numbered 3,000 persons and upward, principally engaged in the capture of fur-bearing animals.

TRAPPER.

C 10. Hudson Strait is a body of water joining Hudson Bay with the Atlantic Ocean; is 450 miles in length, by 60 miles in width; is bridged with solid ice for ten months in the year, and, during the time it is not frozen, is beset by icebergs and detached floes of ice.

C 11. Davis Strait. So called from the name of the navigator who first discovered it. Connects Baffin's Bay with the Atlantic Ocean, being at its narrowest point 160 miles in width.

C 12. Iceland. An island 300 miles in length by 200 miles in width; in the northernmost part of the Atlantic in the conflues of the Arctic Ocean; belongs to the kingdom of Denmark. Is about 800 miles from Norway and 300 from Greenland. Settled by Norwegians in the latter part of the ninth century; has thus been open to civilization over 1,000 years. Possessed once a climate much more warm than now. Had at one time, it is supposed, a population of 100,000, but latterly, owing to intense cold, its population has been steadily decreasing, its inhabitants emigrating into the Canadian Dominion and northern parts of the United States. In spite of cold and poverty its people have been noted for literary attainments and scientific acquirements.

C 13. Norway. Forms, with Sweden, one joint kingdom; is 1,100 miles long and 250 miles wide; has, however, its own government, legislative machinery, army and navy, after the manner of each separate State in the United States. Its population, almost wholly rural, in religion is strongly Lutheran, and all persons holding public offices of trust must belong to that church. To the extreme northward of Norway and Sweden is the home of the Laplander, and the native haunt of the reindeer, which is the principal source of wealth of the Laplander.

REINDEER.

C 14. Arctic Circle. A circle drawn around the North Pole which is supposed to divide the arctic regions from the temperate zone.

D 1. Mt. St. Elias. A volcanic mountain between Alaska and British America; is 19,000 feet in height and is the highest peak in North America.

D 2. Mt. Fairweather. In northeast Alaska; is 14,900 feet, or 2¾ miles, in height.

D 3. Sitka. The capital of Alaska, on the coast, in the southernmost part of that territory.

D 4. Mt. Brown. Is 15,900 feet high, in the Rocky Mountains, near Mt. Hooker, in the same range of mountains; the latter being 15,675 feet in height.

D 5. Lake Winnipeg. Is 90 miles north of Minnesota; is 264 miles long, 85 miles wide.

D 6. Winnipeg. Capital of Manitoba; celebrated for its schools and advanced civilization. Population, 30,000.

D 7. Lake Nipigon. An important lake at the head of Nipigon River, renowned as a resort for fishermen.

D 8. Labrador. A portion of the North American continent supposed to have been visited by the Northmen in the ninth century; is a cold, frigid region a large portion of the year, and is settled largely by the Esquimaux. Is under British rule.

D 9. Strait of Belle Isle. A narrow neck of water separating Labrador from Newfoundland.

ESQUIMAUX.

E 1. Vancouver Island. Is 270 miles long, 50 miles wide, and has, with its chief town, Victoria, a large and growing population. Under British rule.

E 2. Victoria. Capital of the province of British Columbia; stands at the southeast extremity of Vancouver Island.

E 3. Mt. St. Helens. In the southeast of Washington State; 13,400 feet high. Mt. Hood, in northern Oregon, is 11,225 feet high.

E 4. Portland, Ore. See "Principal Cities of the United States." This is a region, owing to mild, moist and favorable climate, of remarkable fruit and vegetable production.

E 5. Columbia River. Largest stream on the western coast of the United States, being 1,000 miles long.

E 6. Boundary Line, between the United States and the British Dominion.

E 7. Salt Lake. An extensive sheet of salt water, 70 miles long and 30 miles wide, having an average depth of 7 or 8 feet, and nowhere over 30 feet in depth. Its surface is over 4,200 feet above the sea. Nine islands are found in this lake, some of which are 3,250 feet above the level of its surface. No living creature is found in its waters, which constitute one of the purest and most concentrated brines in the world. Receives fresh water from two sources, but has no outlet.

E 8. Yellowstone Park. Is 65 miles long and 55 miles wide; contains from 5,000 to 10,000 springs, and 50 geysers that throw water to a height of from 50 to 200 feet. Was set apart by Congress as a public park in 1872.

E 9. Missouri River. The longest continuous river in the world; springs out in the Rocky Mountains, in Montana, runs north 200 miles, thence east 1,200 miles, thence southeast to the mouth of the Kansas River, thence east to the Mississippi, thence south, in union with the Mississippi, to the Gulf of Mexico; its entire length being 4,500 miles; 2,540 miles being navigable, in high water, up from the Mississippi.

E 10. Dakota. So called from the Dakota Indians; was set apart as a territory in 1861, and admitted into the Union as two States in 1889. A bountiful wheat-growing region.

WHEAT.

E. 11. St. Paul. See "Principal Cities of the United States."

E 12. Duluth. See "Principal Cities of the United States."

E 13. Lake Superior. Is the largest body of fresh water in the world, being 355 miles long and 160 wide; is 600 feet above the level of the sea; its average depth is 1,000 feet, its bottom thus being 400 feet below the level of the sea.

E 14. Mackinac. An island located at the northern extremity of Michigan, in the straits of Mackinac; is a national park 3 miles long by 2 miles wide; is much frequented as a summer resort.

E 15. Lake Michigan. The second in size of the great fresh-water lakes; lies wholly in the United States, 240 miles long and 88 miles wide in some places.

E 16. Chicago. See description in other parts of this work. In the vicinity of Chicago, and to the westward, throughout the Mississippi valley, are the great prairies where the rank growth of vegetation has blossomed and gone to decay, every year for centuries, creating a wondrously fertile soil, adapted to the growth of that important cereal known as corn.

CORN.

E 17. Lake Huron. One of the five great lakes. Separates the Canadian Dominion from the State of Michigan. Area, 20,000 square miles. Depth, 1,000 feet. Its surface is 584 feet above the level of the ocean. Contains 3,000 islands.

E 18. Detroit. See "Principal Cities in the United States."

E 19. Lake Erie. Length, 240 miles; breadth, from 30 to 60 miles. Average depth about 120 feet.

E 20. Cleveland. See "Principal Cities in the United States."

E 21. Buffalo. See "Principal Cities in the United States."

E 22. Lake Ontario. Easternmost of the five great lakes, is 196 miles long and 55 miles wide, being, in some places, 600 feet deep.

E 23. Montreal. The largest city of Canada, 400 miles from New York, 180 miles from Quebec and 2,750 miles from Liverpool, England. Population, 140,747.

E 24. New York City. See "Principal Cities in the United States"

E 25. Boston. See "Principal Cities in the United States."

E 26. Mt. Washington. One of the highest of the White mountains, in the State of New Hampshire, is 6,285 feet high; has a carriage road and railway to its summit, on the top of which is a signal-service station and a hotel.

E 27. St. Lawrence River. Rises at the lower end of Lake Ontario and empties into the Gulf of St. Lawrence, being 750 miles long. Including the chain of lakes it is 2,200 miles long up to Duluth.

E 28. Quebec. The location where this city is situated was discovered by Jacques Cartier in 1553, and founded by Champlain in 1608. Throughout the Canadian Dominion one of the principal sports of the country is that of tobogganing on the frozen snow, in the long winter season. Capital of the Province of Quebec. Population, 62,446.

TOBOGGANING.

E 29. Nova Scotia. A small province belonging to the Canadian Dominion, 280 miles long and from 50 to 100 miles in width. Contains about 400 lakes and a population of 440,572. Capital city, Halifax.

E 30. Gulf of St. Lawrence. Lies westward of Newfoundland, and is the entrance to the St. Lawrence river.

E 31. Newfoundland. An island and province of the Canadian Dominion, at the eastward extreme of the North American continent; is 370 miles in length, 200 in breadth.

F 1. San Francisco. See "Principal Cities in the United States."

F 2. Sierra Nevada Mountains. Extending 450 miles in length along the eastern boundary of California. These mountains, nearly always covered with melting snow, are the head waters of many streams and rivers which furnish moisture to the valleys below. They are also the reservoirs of immense quantities of gold quartz, which have given the Pacific coast its great reputation for gold production. In these, and the Rocky Mountains, are found the mountain lion, the grizzly bear and the antelope, the latter being one of the varieties of deer common in this region.

ANTELOPE.

F 3. San Diego. Seaport city and port of entry, having a superior harbor, in lower California. Modern discovery by Cabrillo in 1542. First settled in 1769. A new town commenced in 1867. Has many attractions both as a summer and winter resort. Will become a large city. Population in 1890, 16,159.

F 4. Salton Lake. A newly formed lake in southern California, supposed, at first, to come from the Colorado River. Extends over an area 30 miles long, 10 miles wide, having a depth of from 3 to 4 feet. With the stoppage of the mysterious source that feeds it, this lake may disappear, its bottom being turned again into a bed of hot sand.

F 5. Colorado River. Rises in southeastern Utah, flows first west and then south 2,000 miles, emptying into the Gulf of California.

F 6. Boundary Line of Mexico. Extending from the Pacific Ocean to the Gulf of Mexico, a distance of about 1,400 miles. To the eastward are the Texas cattle-ranges, and the cowboys in long hair and broad-brimmed hats.

COWBOY.

F 7. Rocky Mountains. Extending from Mexico to the Arctic Ocean, a distance of 2,500 miles, being over 1,000 miles wide in the U. S.

F 8. Denver. See "Principal Cities in the United States."

F 9. Santa Fe. Capital of New Mexico. An old Spanish-Mexican town, founded in 1605, and for over 200 years occupied by Spaniards. Emigration of American traders began here in 1803. Population, 8,000.

F 10. Indian Territory. A region having about 10,000 square miles, originally set apart by the government in 1843 for the use of the Indians. In 1890 contained a population, exclusive of Oklahoma, of 119,000.

F 11. Arkansas River. Excepting the Missouri, the largest branch of the Mississippi. Rises in the Rocky mountains and flows 2,170 miles, southeast ward, to the Mississippi, being navigable, for eight months of the year, for a distance of 800 miles from its mouth.

INDIAN GIRL.

F 12. Red River. Rises on the east border of New Mexico, flows southeast 2,100 miles; empties into the Mississippi 341 miles from the Gulf of Mexico.

F 13. Mississippi River. The principal river of North America and, including its chief branch, the Missouri, the longest in the world. Rises in the highlands of Minnesota and flows southward 2,616 miles. The picture of the Indian here shown represents the original red man of the Mississippi Valley, when fully dressed in Indian costume.

INDIAN CHIEF. **F 14. St. Louis.** See "Principal Cities in the U. S."

F 15. Ohio River. Formed by the union of the Alleghany and Monongahela at Pittsburg, Pa.; thence flows southwest to the Mississippi, 950 miles. Navigable through its entire length.

F 16. Cincinnati. See "Principal Cities in the United States."

F 17. Alleghany Mountains. Extending from Cape Gaspe, on the Gulf of St. Lawrence, southwest to Alabama, 1,300 miles. Are the dividing ridge between the Atlantic and the Mississippi valley.

F 18. Charleston. See "Principal Cities in the United States." Since the early settlement of the States this has been a region celebrated for the growth of cotton. Although cotton is a native of the tropical parts of Asia, Africa and America, its cultivation has extended far into the temperate zones. How far back in the history of the world dates the manufacture of cloth from this plant is not certain. It was known in Arabia in the fifth COTTON PLANT. century, was manufactured in Spain in the tenth century, and Columbus, on his arrival here, found cotton to be the principal fabric in the attire of the natives.

F 19. Cape Hatteras. A dangerous point for ships on the sea, at the extreme eastern point of North Carolina.

F 20. Washington. See "Principal Cities in the United States."

F 21. Philadelphia. "See Principal Cities in the United States."

F 22. Bermuda Islands. So named because first discovered by Bermudez, a Spaniard, in 1527. Were colonized in 1609. There are 500 islets, which, in all, contain about 12,000 acres, the whole occupying about 20 miles in length by 6 miles in breadth.

F 23. Atlantic Ocean. That ocean, at the eastward of America, which divides the old world from the new, extending from the arctic circle on the north to the ant-arctic circle on the south; is 5,000 WHALE. miles wide at the widest and 1,600 miles in width at the narrowest point. A familiar object to sailors and ocean travelers is the whale, found in the waters of all the seas and oceans.

G 1. Pacific Ocean. That great body of water at the westward of America, being about 9,000 miles long by 10,300 miles broad, at its greatest breadth. Its area covering about two-fifths of the entire globe.

G 2. Guadeloupe Island. Three hundred miles to the westward of lower California.

G. 3. Tropic of Cancer. That line which is supposed to be the northern boundary of the equatorial region.

G 4. Lower California. That portion of California which is principally in Mexican territory; a very dry, rocky and forbidding region, having a population numbering about 12,000 persons, the most of whom live near the southern extremity of the peninsula.

G. 5. Gulf of California. Divides lower California from the rest of Mexico. Is 700 miles long and from 40 to 100 miles wide.

G 6. Mexico. Occupies the southern part of the North American continent; occupied by a race of beings, about the seventh century, called the Toltecs; subsequently, in the twelfth century, by the Aztecs, who remained here until the conquest of the country, by Cortez, in 1519. Present population is little less than 10,000,000. A type of the higher order of Mexicans is MEXICAN. shown herewith; many of them a refined and cultured people.

G 7. Sierra Madre. The name of the southern portion of the Rocky Mountains which are in Mexico.

G 8. Rio Grande River. Has a total length of about 1,800 miles, and for 1,100 miles forms the boundary between Mexico and the United States. Navigable for 450 miles from the sea.

G 9. Monterey, Mexico. The most thriving city of Northern Mexico, having, in 1880, a population of about 37,000. Founded in 1596.

G 10. Gulf of Mexico. Basin of the Atlantic Ocean, covering an area of 800,000 square miles.

G 11. Galveston. See "Principal Cities of the United States."

G 12. New Orleans. See "Principal Cities of the United States."

G 13. Florida. The most southern portion of the United States, 400 miles long; average width, 120 miles. A very general and favorite resort, in the winter season, because of its mild climate.

G 14. St. Augustine. The oldest city in the United States. The region hereabouts first made known to Europeans by Ponce de Leon, who landed near the city in 1512. The city, itself, founded in 1565. A favorite resort for people from the north in the winter season. Widely known because of its magnificent Ponce de Leon hotel.

G 15. Havana. The capital of Cuba and the most important city in the West Indies. Founded by Velasquez, in 1511. Population of Havana and its suburbs, 300,000.

G 16. Cuba. Largest of West India Islands. Length, 750 miles; average width, 50 miles. Population about 1,500,000 The white people of Cuba are of Spanish descent, and among the ladies are types of a very high order of beauty.

G 17. Watling Island. One of the Bahamas, being the island on which, it is supposed, Columbus first landed, October 12, CUBAN LADY. 1492, upon his arrival in the New World, 70 days after leaving Spain.

H 1. Mexico City. Capital of the Mexican Republic. Situated on an elevated plateau; is laid out with great regularity, being about three miles square. Supposed to have been founded by the Aztecs in 1325. Population, 350,000.

H 2. Volcano Popocatepetl. Largest volcano in Mexico, a mountain about 10 miles southwest of Mexico City. Is 17,720 feet above sea level. Though it emits smoke, no eruption has taken place since 1540.

H 3. Vera Cruz. Leading harbor on the eastern coast of Mexico.200 miles from the Mexican capital; built in semicircle and surrounded by a strong wall. Population about 17,000.

H 4. Yucatan. A Mexican peninsula jutting into the Gulf of Mexico. Discovered by the Spaniards in 1517.

H 5. Guatemala. In Central America. Area, 46,774 square miles; nearly as large as Ohio. Has a population of 1,427,116. Many Northerners have recently come here and engaged in the cultivation of coffee and bananas.

CENTRAL AMERICAN INDIAN.

H 6. Honduras. A Republic in Central America about the size of Indiana, having a population of nearly 432,000. Was discovered by Columbus on his fourth voyage, in 1502. Is being rapidly opened to settlers from the United States. The peculiar headgear of some of the Central American Indians is well shown in our illustration. Area, 42,658 square miles.

H 7. Nicaragua. A Republic of Central America, near the size of the State of New York. Population about 310,000. Has several smoking volcanoes, and a soil that produces, in abundance, all the fruits and vegetables of the tropics. Area, 51,660 square miles.

H 8. Lake Nicaragua. A sheet of water 110 miles long and from 30 to 50 miles wide. The Nicaragua Canal, now being constructed, will extend from the Pacific Ocean to this lake, and from this lake to the Atlantic Ocean. Length of waterway, 170 miles, being 40 miles of canal, and 130 miles of navigation through the lake, the Francisco and the San Juan Rivers. The plan requires eight locks and a canal from 80 to 120 feet wide at the bottom, from 80 to 340 feet wide at the top, and of a depth sufficient for the largest vessels. Estimated cost, $65,-000,000. Atlantic 8 feet higher than Pacific.

H 9. Caribbean Sea. That part of the Atlantic Ocean, between the coasts of Central and South America and the large islands of the West Indies. Is the turning point of the Gulf Stream, which sends a flow of water into the Gulf of Mexico, and flows out at the southern extremity of Florida, in an estimated volume of 3,000 Mississippi Rivers.

H 10. Jamaica. One of the West India Islands belonging to England, a little less in size than New Jersey. Length, 135 miles; 21 to 49 miles wide. Population, 581,000.

H 11. Hayti. Largest of the West India Islands, Cuba excepted; 400 miles long, 150 miles wide at the widest point. Is near the size of New Hampshire. Population about 500,000, nearly all negroes. Climate tropical and unhealthy. Soil fertile. Discovered by Columbus in 1493. The warm, moist climate of the West India Islands is admirably adapted to the growth of the sugar cane, whence come the West India molasses and the well-known brown sugar.

SUGAR CANE.

I-1. Isthmus of Panama. Narrow neck of land, connecting North and South America, a high range of mountains forming the barrier between the Atlantic and Pacific Oceans, which, at this point, are about 31 miles apart. The proposed Panama Canal, by De Lesseps, which has been abandoned from lack of funds, was to have been 45½ miles in length, from sea to sea, and was to have run beside the railway, now constructed from Aspinwall to Panama.

I-2. Aspinwall. Sometimes called Colon, is built on the coral island of Manzanilla. Was founded by the Panama Railway Company, in 1850, and derives its name from W. H. Aspinwall, one of the principal railway shareholders. Has a population of about 9,000, mostly negroes. The locality is much healthier than formerly, and is becoming a city of considerable importance, particularly as a point for the shipment of bananas.

I-3. United States of Colombia. The name for several confederated States, in this portion of South America, the area of which is 502,000 square miles; about seven times as large as the six New England States.

I-4. Venezuela. A portion of Northern South America. Includes nineteen separate States and Territories, and contains a population of 2,198,825. Republican government.

I-5. Equator. The imaginary partition line midway between the North and South Poles; divides the northern from the southern hemisphere, and crosses those regions which, being directly under the sun's vertical rays, are the warmest parts of the earth.

Harvest Time in Different Parts of the World.

To many people the spring and summer, which precede the harvest, are the most delightful in which to travel To others, the most charming season is that in which the grains and fruits of the country have attained their maturity.

Should this latter season be that which shall be selected by the tourist, the following will be interesting as giving the period of wheat-gathering in different countries:

In **January** the wheat is harvested in Australia, New Zealand, Chile and the Argentine Republic.

In **February and March** the harvest has extended into upper Egypt and India.

In **April** it is in lower Egypt, India, Persia, Syria, Asia Minor, Cyprus, Mexico and Cuba.

In **May** it reaches perfection in Algeria, Central Asia, China, Japan, Morocco and Texas.

In **June** it has reached into Oregon, California, Alabama, Mississippi, Georgia, North Carolina, South Carolina, Virginia, Kentucky, Tennessee, Kansas, Arkansas, Colorado, Utah, Missouri, Turkey, Greece, Italy, Spain, Portugal and the south of France.

In **July** it has extended into New England, New York, Pennsylvania, Ohio, Indiana, Michigan, Illinois, Iowa, Wisconsin, southern Minnesota, Nebraska, upper Canada, Roumania, Germany, Switzerland and the south of England.

In **August** the harvest is actively going forward in central and northern Minnesota, Dakota, Manitoba, Lower Canada, Columbia, Belgium, Holland, Great Britain, Denmark, Poland and central Russia.

In **September and October** it has reached up into Scotland, Norway, Sweden and the north of Russia.

In **November** it is proceeding in Peru and South Africa, and in **December** it is in Burmah.

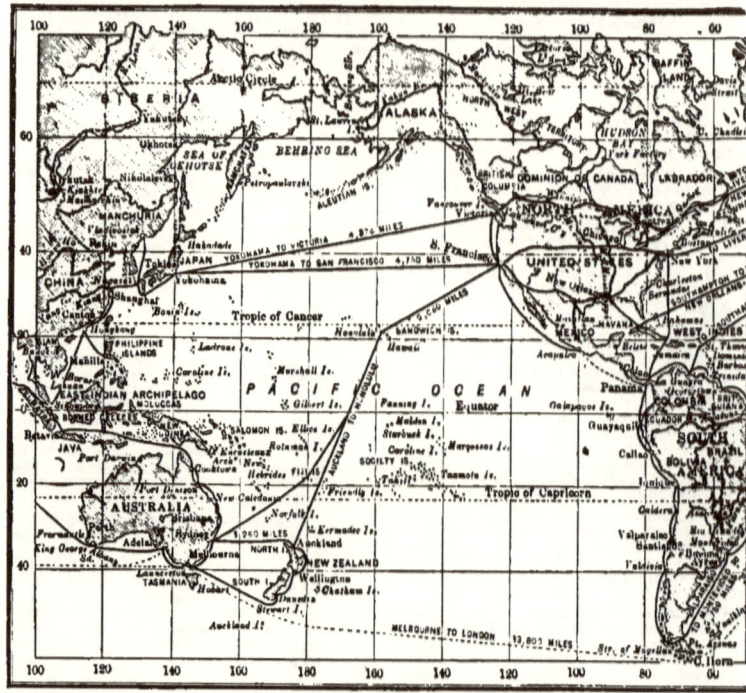

ACROSS NORTH AMERICA AND THE PACIFIC OCEAN, GOING WESTWARD.

Around the World in 67 Days, 13 Hours and 3 Minutes, by George Francis Train.

The map, which is seen at the head of this and the opposite page, represents the principal divisions of the earth, the different countries, and the great avenues of commerce and travel on land and water, in traversing long distances, from one portion of the earth to another, or in going around the world; the above diagram of routes of travel being almost a copy of the Bartholomew map containing the Commercial Track Chart of the World.

The distance covered and the time required in traveling between countries and important central cities on the globe, are well illustrated by George Francis Train, who went around the world, under the auspices of R. F. Radebaugh, of the Tacoma Ledger, leaving Tacoma, Wash., on March 18, 1890, and making the following record:

	MILES.	DAYS.
Tacoma to Yokohama	4,300	16
Yokohama to Hong Kong	1,630	8
Hong Kong to Singapore	1,430	5
Singapore to Colombo	1,570	6
Colombo to Aden	2,093	7
Aden to Suez	1,308	4
Suez to Port Said	87	1
Port Said to Brindisi	1,100	3
Brindisi to Southampton	1,200	2
Southampton to New York	3,000	6
New York to Tacoma	3,300	3
	21,018	61

Owing to occasional fogs and unavoidable delays, six days more time than that outlined above were consumed.

It will be seen that the distance traversed was 21,081 miles; nearly 4,000 less than had been supposed was the distance around the globe. This shorter distance is the result of traveling, most of the time, in a northern altitude, the distance being much less than

when the journey around the world is made on the line of the equator.

The articles of baggage carried by Mr. Train consisted of an ordinary satchel, and small leather trunk. His wardrobe comprised two suits—the one for cold being of warm woolen, a red Turkish fez cap, and sealskin overcoat. In the tropics and throughout the warmer portions of his journey he wore a white linen sack coat and pure white linen throughout, helmet hat, and white baseball shoes. Our illustration shows the latter costume.

After going around the world and carefully reviewing the incidents and delays liable to occur on another such journey, Mr. Train announced his belief that, aided by the rapid-sailing steamers, the building of which is in contemplation, he could go around the world in 50 days, the distances and time between points being indicated in the following table:

GEORGE F. TRAIN ON HIS JOURNEY AROUND THE WORLD.

	MILES.	DAYS.
Tacoma to Yokohama	4,300	10
Yokohama to Hong Kong	1,630	3½
Hong Kong to Singapore	1,430	3½
Singapore to Aden via Colombo	3,663	8
Aden to Port Said via Suez	1,395	3½
Port Said to Brindisi	1,100	2
Brindisi to Southampton	1,200	1½
Southampton to New York	3,000	6
New York to Tacoma	3,300	3½
Coaling, contingencies and accidents		8
Total time required by this estimate		50

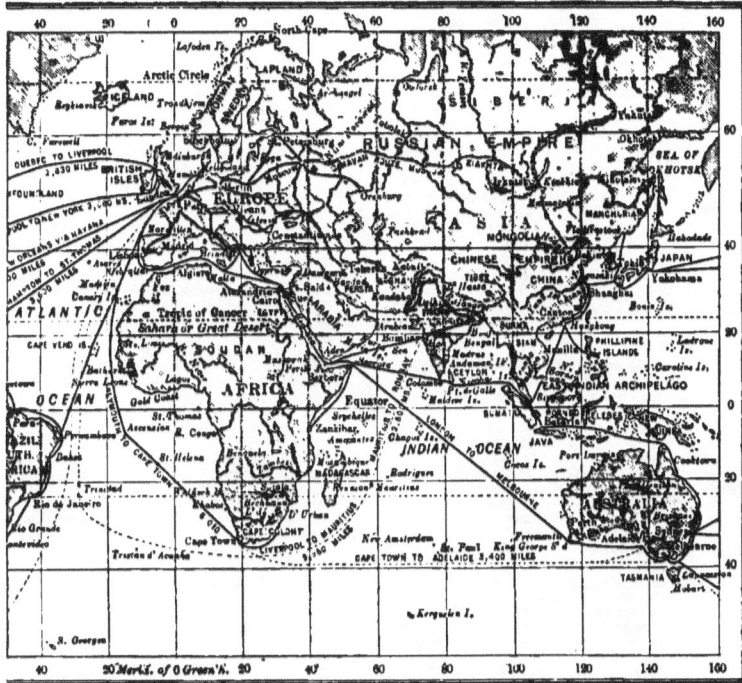

ACROSS THE ATLANTIC, EUROPE AND ASIA, GOING EASTWARD.

Around the World in 72 Days, 6 Hours and 11 Minutes, by Nellie Bly.

Miss Nellie Bly's journey around the globe, under the management of the New York World, may be summarized as follows:

Left New York at 9:40 A. M., Nov. 14, 1889. Had rough seas across the Atlantic. Anchored off Southampton, Eng., at 2.30 A. M., Nov. 23. Up to London, forward into France, and had a pleasant visit with Jules Verne, the author of "The Tour of the World in Eighty Days," at his home at Amiens. Received his wish for Good Luck, a kiss from Madame Verne, and sped on to Calais, there taking sleeping car for Brindisi, in the southern part of Italy. There embarked on a steamer of the Peninsular & Oriental Line for the Isthmus of Suez, arriving at Port Said, November 27. Thence across the Red Sea to the beautiful city of Aden, and from there across the Arabian Sea to Colombo, on the island of Ceylon, where five days' time was passed in waiting for a connecting boat going eastward, arriving at Singapore on the 18th of December. After visiting the points of interest during the few hours' stop, passage was continued, reaching Hong Kong December 23. Was compelled to wait five days in China, spending Christmas in Canton. Left Hong Kong December 28, and reached Yokohama, where she was warmly welcomed, news of her journey having come from New York via San Francisco. Left Yokohama January 7; had bad weather across the Pacific Ocean. Arrived at San Francisco. January 21, and in a special train, sped across the

United States, arriving at New York, January 25, 1890.

Great credit is due to the projectors of this, the first enterprise of its kind, by which Miss Bly encircled the earth in the time she did. It was a trial never before undertaken, as a test to determine the period of time absolutely required to go this journey.

Expense of Going Around the World.

Route 1. From Chicago to San Francisco; Pacific Mail Steamer to Yokohama and Hong Kong; Peninsular & Oriental Steamer to Singapore, Colombo, through Red Sea, Suez Canal, Malta, Gibraltar, London; rail to Liverpool; steamer to New York; rail to Chicago. First Class, $753.

Route 2. Chicago to San Francisco; Pacific Mail Steamer to Yokohama; Japanese Mail Steamer to Shanghai; Peninsular & Oriental Steamer to Hong Kong, Singapore, Ceylon, Madras, Calcutta; railroad, across India to Bombay, Peninsular & Oriental Steamer to Suez; rail to Cairo; steamer to Malta, Gibraltar, Liverpool, New York; rail to Chicago. First Class, $850.

Route 3. Route No. 2 to Cairo. Thence by steamer to Brindisi; by rail to Naples, Rome, Florence, Turin, Paris, London, Liverpool; steamer to New York; rail to Chicago. First Class, $883.

Route 4. Route No. 2 to Cairo. Rail to Alexandria; mail steamer to Athens; Austrian Lloyds steamer to Constantinople; Orient Express to Buda Pesth, Vienna, Strasburg, Paris, London, Liverpool; steamer to New York; rail to Chicago. First Class, $912.

NELLIE BLY ON HER JOURNEY AROUND THE WORLD.

A Journey by Carter H. Harrison. Distance Traveled, 45,000 Miles.

CARTER H. HARRISON.

As Mr Harrison himself relates, he left his home in Chicago, repaired to Winnipeg, Manitoba, and there, on the 29th of July, 1887, started on his "race with the sun," around the world. The following are the principal cities which he visited during his journey:

BANFF, and its hot springs, on the CanadianPacific Railroad; arrived July 31.

VICTORIA, Vancouver's Island. While waiting here a week for steamship, made various excursions into the surrounding country Left Vancouver, August 29.

YOKOHAMA; arrived September 15. From that to Kobe. Left Kobe, October 26, and sailed south on the Sea of Japan.

NAGASAKI, China; stopping here for coal.

SHANGHAI; excursions from this place. Then south on Eastern Sea of China.

HONG KONG. Left Hong Kong, November 20, sailing south on China Sea.

SINGAPORE, via Bangkok, arriving December 8. Sailed south from Singapore to the Equator, stopping at Rhio and an unknown island. Then returned to Singapore.

RANGOON; arrived December 20, after stopping for several hours at Penang. Excursion from Rangoon, December 22, to Mandalay and Prome.

CALCUTTA; arrived January 3, 1888. Excursion to Darjeeling.

BENARES, India, 556 miles, by rail, northwest of Calcutta.

DELHI, via Cawnpore and Agra. From Delhi to Lahore and Peshawur; then back to Delhi.

BOMBAY, 890 miles southwest, via Ulwah, Jeypore, Ajmere, Ahmedabad, Baroda, Surat.

MADRAS, India, via Hyderabad.

TUTICORIN, India, via Pondicherry, Tanjore, Trichinopoly and Madura. Had now spent about two months in India, and traveled nearly 5,000 miles in that time.

COLOMBO, Ceylon. Excursion to Kandy. Left Colombo for Suez, March 15.

ADEN, Arabia, 2,093 miles northwest; arrived March 22.

SUEZ, Egypt, 1,308 miles northwest; arrived March 26. Excursions up the Nile to Cairo, Thebes and Assouam. Sailed from Alexandria April 18.

ATHENS, Greece; CONSTANTINOPLE, via Smyrna. Left Constantinople, May 12, and sailed up the Bosphorus into the Black Sea.

VIENNA, Austria, via Varna, Bucharest, Belgrade, Buda-Pesth and Presburg.

MOSCOW, about 1,250 miles northeast of Vienna. Then southeast to Tiflis, via Veronij, Rostof, Novocherkash and Vladikavkas. Then to the Caspian Sea, via Baku and Balakhaner. North on the Caspian Sea to the Volga River; up the Volga River.

ST. PETERSBURG, via Kazan, Saratof, Samara, Nijni-Novgorod, Yaroslav, Kastroma and Rybinsk. Excursion to Peterhof, about 20 miles from St. Petersburg.

ULEABORG Finland via Wiborg, Nyslott, Kuopio and Idensalmi. An excursion from Uleaborg to the Arctic Circle.

HELSINGFORS, Finland, by rail, via Tammersfors and Tavastehuus.

ABO, Finland, by steamboat; then west on Baltic Sea to Stockholm, and from that to Christiania. Excursions from Christiania to Konsberg and other places.

COPENHAGEN; thence south through Zealand to Gjedserodde; steamer for Warnemunde, in Mecklenburg.

BRUSSELS, via Berlin, Hamburg, Hanover, Frankfort-on-the-Main and Cologne.

PARIS, DIEPPE, LONDON.

LIVERPOOL, NEW YORK, CHICAGO.

Total distance traveled, about 45,000 miles. Time, 15¾ months.

EASTWARD, AROUND the WORLD in EIGHTY DAYS, from LONDON to LONDON.

BY PHILEAS FOGG, THE HERO OF JULES VERNE'S NOVEL, "THE TOUR OF THE WORLD IN EIGHTY DAYS."

Phileas Fogg left London, England, at 8:45 P. M., Wednesday, October 2, 1872, and arrived at—

PARIS, 7:20 A. M., Thursday, October 3.

TURIN, Italy, via Mont Cenis, 6:35 A. M., Friday, October 4.

BRINDISI, Italy, 4 P M., Saturday, October 5.

SUEZ, Egypt, 11 A. M., Wednesday, October 9.

ADEN, Arabia, 1,310 miles from Suez, evening of October 14.

BOMBAY, 4:30 P. M., Sunday, October 20. From Bombay east across India, by rail. From Kholby to Allahabad, a distance of 50 miles, on the back of an elephant, the railroad not being finished between these two points. During this 50-mile journey, Phileas Fogg and his fellow-travelers heroically rescue a lady from the hands of the natives, who are about to burn her as a sacrifice. The lady accompanies Mr. Fogg to the end of his tour.

CALCUTTA, by rail, via Benares, 7 A. M., October 25.

SINGAPORE, 4 A. M., October 31. About 1,300 miles from Hong Kong.

HONG KONG, 7 A. M., November 6. Being too late for the steamer going to Yokohama, Mr. Fogg finds a pilot-boat, offers au immense sum of money for its use, and sails on it 800 miles to Shanghai, so as to take passage on the American mail steamer at that place.

YOKOHAMA, Japan, November 14.

SAN FRANCISCO, 7 A. M., December 3.

OGDEN, Utah, 2 P. M., December 6. Excursion to Salt Lake City. At Fort Kearney, Nebraska, Mr. Fogg again acts the hero; but in consequence of this he and his company are delayed, and the train goes on without them. As there is snow on the ground, they travel to Omaha, a distance of about 200 miles, on an ice-boat, or "sloop-rigged sledge."

CHICAGO, by rail, 4 P. M., December 10.

NEW YORK, 9:35 P. M., December 11.

QUEENSTOWN, 1 A. M., Saturday, December 21.

LIVERPOOL, 11:40 A. M., Saturday, December 21.

LONDON, 8:50 P. M., Saturday, December 21, five minutes later than the time appointed. At least, that was the date of arrival as Mr. Fogg at first believed; but he afterwards discovered that "he had, without suspecting it, gained a day on his journey, because he had made the tour of the world going to the east. . . . While he, traveling towards the east, saw the sun pass the meridian 80 times, his colleagues, remaining in London, saw it pass only 79 times." The actual date of arrival in London was, therefore, Friday, December 20, and Mr. Fogg had accomplished the tour in less than eighty days.

A Journey for Pleasure and Sight-seeing, Consuming 2½ Years of Time.

General Grant left Philadelphia, May 17, 1877, and sailed down the Delaware River, in a small steamer, to Newcastle, where he embarked on an ocean steamship. Below is a list of the countries through which he traveled, with the places of interest, in each country, in the order in which he visited them:

IRELAND.—Queenstown, May 27.

ENGLAND.—Liverpool, Manchester, Leicester, Bedford and London. Excursion from London to Southampton, where General Grant's daughter was residing; also to Windsor, at the invitation of the Queen. From London to Folkestone, July 5; thence to the Continent.

BELGIUM.—Ostend, Brussels.

GERMANY. — Cologne, Coblentz, Wiesbaden, Frankfort-on-the-Main, Homburg, Salburg, Heidelberg, Baden and the Black Forest.

SWITZERLAND. — Lucerne, Interlaken, Berne, Geneva. Then back to Britain, via northern Italy, Alsace and Lorraine.

SCOTLAND. — Edinburgh, Dunrobin, Dornoch, Inverness, Glasgow, Ayr, Loch Lomond.

ENGLAND. — Newcastle - upon - Tyne, Yarrow, Tynemouth, Sunderland, Sheffield (September 26), Stratford-on-Avon, Leamington, Southampton, Birmingham, London, Brighton. Then back to London, and from that, October 24, to Folkestone; thence to the Continent, for second tour there.

FRANCE.—Boulogne, Paris, Villefranche.

ITALY.—Naples, Mt. Vesuvius and Pompeii.

SICILY.—Palermo, December 23.

MALTA.—Valetta, December 28. Embarked for Egypt, December 31.

EGYPT. — Alexandria, Cairo, Siout, Gizeh, Keneh, Thebes. Then back to Memphis and Port Said.

PALESTINE.—Jaffa, Ramleh, Jerusalem, Bethlehem, Nazareth, Damascus, Beyrout.

TURKEY.—Constantinople, March 3, 1878.

GREECE.—Athens, and the plains of Marathon.

ITALY.—Rome, Florence, Venice, Milan.

FRANCE.—Paris, May 7, during the Paris Exposition.

HOLLAND.—The Hague, Rotterdam, Amsterdam, Haarlem.

GERMANY.—Berlin, June 26. Thence to Hamburg.

DENMARK.—Copenhagen, July 7.

SWEDEN and NORWAY. —Gottenburg, Christiania, Stockholm. Then east across the Baltic Sea and the Gulf of Finland.

RUSSIA. — St. Petersburg, Peterhof, Cronstadt, Moscow, Warsaw.

AUSTRIA.— Vienna, August 18.

GERMANY.—Munich, Augsburg, Ulm, Schaffhausen.

FRANCE.—Besançon, St. Etienne, Vichy, Limoges, Perigueux, Bordeaux, Biarritz.

SPAIN.—Irun, San Sebastian, Tolosa, Vergara, Vittoria, Madrid (October 28).

PORTUGAL.—Lisbon. Excursion to Cintra, 15 miles distant.

SPAIN.—Cordova, Seville, Cadiz.

IRELAND. — Dublin (January 3, 1879). Dundalk, Omagha, Strabane, Londonderry, Coleraine, Ballymena, Belfast. Thence back to Dublin, and from that to Kingston, embarking there for England.

INDIA.—Bombay, via Paris, Marseilles, Alexandria and Suez. Excursion to the island of Elephanta. From Bombay to Allahabad, Agra, Jeypore, Amber, Bhurtpoor, Benares, Delhi, Calcutta.

CHINA.—Hong Kong (April 30), via Singapore, Bangkok and Saigon. From Hong Kong to Canton, Macao, Swatow, Amoy, Shanghai, Tientsin.

JAPAN.—Nagasaki (June 21), Yokohama, Tokio, Nikko. Then back to Yokohama, embarking there for the United States, September 3.

UNITED STATES.—San Francisco, September 20. Excursion to the Yosemite Valley. Trip by steamer to points in Oregon and Washington. From San Francisco to Chicago, arriving November 12, 1879.

GEN. U. S. GRANT.

DUE WEST, AROUND the WORLD, by M. M. BALLOU, from BOSTON to BOSTON.

WITH A PARTY OF COOK TOURISTS.—TIME, TEN MONTHS; EXPENSE TO EACH, WITH GUIDE, $2,000

Mr. Ballou left Boston, Mass., on the morning of September 16, 1882, for his journey westward around the world. The following are the principal places of interest on the route which he traveled, with the time occupied in reaching them:

NIAGARA FALLS, 500 miles, in a day and a night.

CHICAGO, 513 miles west, in a day and a night.

SALT LAKE CITY, 1,600 miles west, in 4 days and nights.

SAN FRANCISCO, 800 miles west. in 2 days and 1 night. Excursion from San Francisco to the Yosemite Valley.

YOKOHAMA, Japan, 4,700 miles west, in 3 weeks. Excursion from Yokohama to Kamakura, Tokio and Nikko.

KOBE, at northern entrance to Sea of Japan, in 2 days, by steamship. Excursion to Kioto, Lake Biwa and Osaka.

NAGASAKI, Japan, in 2 days and 2 nights. Left Nagasaki November 29.

HONG KONG, China, 1,100 miles south, arriving December 5. By steamship up the Pearl River to Canton. Left Hong Kong, for Singapore, December 12.

SINGAPORE, East Indies, arriving Dec. 17.

PENANG, East Indies, by steamship in 2 days.

COLOMBO, Ceylon, west about 1,300 miles, arriving December 25.

KANDY, Ceylon, about 75 miles, by rail.

TUTICORIN, the extreme point of southern India, about 100 miles west.

MADRAS, India, via Madura, Trichinopoly and Tanjore, about 400 miles. Embarked for Calcutta January 11.

CALCUTTA, India, a 5 days' voyage northeast, on the Bay of Bengal, arriving January 15. From Calcutta north about 400 miles, by rail, to Darjeeling. Back to Calcutta.

BOMBAY, India, via Benares, Cawnpore, Delhi, Lahore, Umritsar, Agra and Jeypore, about 2,710 miles. Embarked, February 9, for Suez.

SUEZ, Egypt, about 3,000 miles from Bombay. Then to Zagazig, Cairo and Port Said.

VALETTA, on the island of Malta, about 1,000 miles, in 4 days.

GIBRALTAR, Spain, about 1,000 miles, arriving March 11. Excursion to Tangier.

MALAGA, Spain, nearly 100 miles eastward, by sea, arriving March 15.

MADRID, Spain, via Granada and Cordova, about 194 miles. Excursion to Toledo.

BORDEAUX, France, via Burgos, San Sebastian and Bayonne, about 390 miles.

PARIS, France, about 400 miles northeast. Thence northeast to Antwerp. Embarked at Antwerp for New York, July 14.

NEW YORK, about 3,000 miles west, in 12 days, arriving July 24.

BOSTON, 207 miles northeast, the same evening. Entire distance traveled, about 40,000 miles. Time consumed, a little more than 10 months.

1492.

TIME
CROSSING
THE
ATLANTIC:
70 DAYS,
BY
COLUMBUS.

1892.

TIME
CROSSING
THE
ATLANTIC:
5 DAYS,
16 HOURS,
31 MIN.

STEAMSHIP MAJESTIC, WHITE STAR LINE, LIVERPOOL TO NEW YORK.

SUGGESTIONS TO PEOPLE WHO INTEND TO TRAVEL BY STEAMSHIP,
Particularly to Those Who Contemplate Coming to the United States.

Trunks. For convenience a small, leather trunk, well strapped, with a good lock, will be best. Have full name plainly painted on the end. The regulation size to go under steamer beds is about 32 inches long by 15 to 18 inches wide, and from 12 to 15 inches deep.

Passports. No passports are required in visiting the United States. Revenue officers inspect baggage upon arrival at American ports, to see whether passenger brings articles of commerce to sell. Baggage and most articles for personal use are admitted duty free.

Time of Departure. Be early at the boat on the day of departure, that you may get all your baggage securely in your room an hour before the boat leaves. You have time thus to compose yourself and to give full and careful directions, if any such are to be given, to friends and others before you leave.

Baggage. One hundred and fifty pounds of baggage are allowed to each passenger on the railways of the United States. On the steamers the allowance to each first-class ticket is 20 cubic feet; to second-class tickets, 15 cubic feet; steerage tickets, 10 cubic feet. Ten cubic feet is equal to a good-sized trunk.

Money. A quantity of gold and silver coins, carefully secured, will be convenient in traveling. Foreigners are advised to investigate concerning exchanging their money into United States money (see money table elsewhere), before embarking for the United States. The letter of credit, obtained at the bank or of steamship lines, will enable the traveler to draw money as required, in various cities, and thus avoid the necessity of carrying much money on the person.

Steerage Table Fare. Steerage passengers are, on the average, furnished with the following bill of fare: Oatmeal porridge, coffee, fresh-baked rolls and butter, being varied on certain days with hash or Irish stew; soup at dinner, boiled beef, pork, or fish, with potatoes and bread. Roast beef and dessert for Sunday dinner. Food is placed on the middle of the table, and passengers help themselves. Steerage passengers furnish their own cups, plates and other utensils, as well as their own bedding.

Tourists' Garments. On the steamship, ladies should be provided, when on deck, with a sufficiency of dress, warm woolen wrapper, warm knit slippers, a nubia or close hood and a carriage robe. For general travel in the States, a dark-colored dress, suitable for the cars and sight-seeing, an evening dress, winter underwear for all seasons, linen for two or three weeks, a warm shawl, strong, easy boots, a gossamer waterproof and necessary toilet articles. Gentlemen should have a strong, warm, business suit, an extra suit, winter underclothing, linen for two or three weeks, light woolen overcoat and a gossamer overcoat. Each sex should, for convenience sake, carry as little baggage as possible.

State Rooms. The most desirable rooms are near the center of the ship. In the lately built steamers the state rooms are about equally desirable, whether outside or inside rooms.

Clothing. Travelers should be provided with an abundance of woolen clothing when on the ocean. Warm garments are required in Chicago and all the Northern States, from the 1st of November to the 1st of April.

Surplus Baggage. All baggage, being conveyed by immigrants and others, not absolutely necessary, on the ship, should be marked "Not Wanted," that it may go immediately into the general baggage room of the ship. It should also be so marked that it can be readily identified when wanted.

Passenger Accommodation. First-class cabin passengers have ample promenade room on the decks, usually amidships. Second-class have somewhat more restricted quarters, depending on location of state room. Steerage passengers generally occupy the forward portions of the steamer. On recently built steamers, their opportunities for exercise are ample, and all their accommodations are comfortable.

Steamer Chairs. Passengers are expected to furnish their own seating accommodation on the steamer deck. For this purpose steamer chairs are for sale at a cheap rate near the point of embarkation. These should be plainly marked with owner's name. They can be stored at steamboat offices until tourist returns; or, if owner does not return, can be shipped as baggage to point of destination anywhere in the States.

In American Ports. On arrival of each immigrant vessel at her dock, she is boarded by certain officers, who examine baggage, with reference to importation of articles which should pay duty. Baggage being passed, it is then checked, placed on transfer boats, and conveyed with passengers to the Barge Office, where immigrants are examined by a medical staff, and then passed on to the registration department, where they give name, age, occupation, nationality and destination. If the indications are that they may become a public charge, such persons are returned by the same vessel on which they arrived, to the place from which they came. But an opportunity is given to the friends, should they call, to guarantee that they shall not become a public charge, and they are then allowed to leave the department, in the care of their friends. Parties expecting friends by steamer call at the information bureau, and obtain permission to see them, and, when desired, if identity is proven, are allowed to take their friends away, baggage being kept at the Barge Office, free of charge, until called for. A railroad ticket office, in the Barge Office, furnishes tickets at cheapest rates to all parts of the country, and checks baggage to destination; 150 pounds of baggage to each immigrant being allowed to go free.

Also List of Abbreviations Used in Describing Lines.

(Al.)..Allan State Line.-New York to Glasgow.
(Am.)..American Line.—Phila. to Liverpool.
(An.)..Anchor Line.—New York to Glasgow.
(At.)..Atlas Line.—N.Y.to W.Inds. & Cent Am.
(B.)..Baltic Line.—New York to Copenhagen.
(Ca.)..Castle Line.—London to South Africa.
(Cl.)..Clan Line.—Liverpool to India
(C. G. T.)...Compagnie Generale Transatlantique.—New York to Havre
(C. R. & H.)..Costa Rica & Honduras S S Line.
(Cu.)..Cunard Line.—New York to Liverpool
(F.)..Fabre Line.—New York to Naples.
(F. R. I.)..Florio Rubattino Italian Line.
(G.)..Guion Line.—New York to Liverpool
(H.)..Hall Line.—Liverpool to Bombay, India.
(H. A. P.)..Hamburg American Packet Co.
(H. & C. A.)..Honduras & Cent. Amer S S. Co
(I.)..Inman Line.—New York to Liverpool.
(I N.)..Insular Nav. Co.—New York to Lisbon.
(M. M.)..Messageries Maritimes Lines.
(M S.)..Morgan S. S. Lines.—N O. to Havana.
(N.)..National Line.—New York to Liverpool.

(N. A. S. N.)..Netherlands Am. S. Nav. Co.
(N. L.)..Norddentscher Lloyd S. S. Co.
(N. Y. & C.)..New York & Cuba Mail S S. Co.
(N. Y. & P. R.)..New York & Porto Rico S S. Co.
(N. Z. S.)..New Zealand Shipping Company
(Oc.)..Oceanic S. S. Co.—San F. to Sandwich Is.
(Or.)..Orient Line.—London to Gibraltar
(P. H.)..Patrick Henderson's Line.—To India.
(P. & O.)..Peninsular & Oriental Line.—London to India and Australia.
(P. M.)..Pacific Mail S. S. Co.—San F. to Japan.
(Q. R. M.)..Queensland Royal Mail Line.
(Q. S.)..Quebec S. S. Co.—N. Y. to West Indies.
(R. "D")..Red "D" Line.—N. Y. to W. Indies.
(R. S.)..Red Star Line.—New York to Antwerp.
(S., S. & A.)..Shaw, Savill & Albion Co.
(T.)..Thingvalla Line.—New York to Sweden.
(U.)..Union Line.—Southampton to S. Africa.
(U. D. H.)..Union Direct Hamburg Line.
(U. S. & B.)..U. S. and Brazil Mail S. S. Co.
(W.)..Wilson Line.—New York to London.
(W. S.)..White Star Line.—N. Y. to London.

OTHER ABBREVIATIONS.—d., Time in days. m., Distance in miles. 1st, First class or "cabin passage." 2nd, Second class, second cabin or "intermediate." 3rd, Third class or "steerage."

RATES OF FARE FROM EUROPEAN CITIES TO CHICAGO VIA NEW YORK.

Change in Rates of Fare.—The traveler should understand that rates of fare are liable to great fluctuations, depending upon combinations, competition, seasons of the year and occasional pressing demand for passenger transportation; the rates being slightly lower in winter than in summer. The rates here given are the average winter rates. For exact information consult the nearest steamship offices.

Explanation.—To understand abbreviations relating to distance, time and rates of fare from various cities to Chicago, see Berlin, for example, the description of which is as follows: From Berlin to Chicago the distance is 5,297 miles, requiring 11 days to make the journey. By the Anchor Line the fare, 1st class, is $99, $104, $114, according to location of state room; 2nd class, $72; 3rd class (which is usually steerage accommodations), $51; and by the American Line, 3rd class, the fare is $36. On certain large fine boats the 2nd class accomodations are superior to 1st class on others; hence the difference in prices on different boats. From New York, or any American port, to Chicago, passengers furnish their own board

AALESUND, NORWAY.—(W. S.) 2nd, $83, $88; $133. (G.) 2nd, $73, $78; 3rd, $59.
AARHUS, DENMARK.—(T.) 3rd, $39.
ABO, FINLAND.—(W. S.) (Cu.) (I.) (T.) 3rd, $45. (Al.) (N.) 3rd, $40. (Am.) 3rd, $43.
AMSTERDAM, HOLLAND.—4,897m., 11d. (N. A. S. N.) 1st, $65, $70, $75, $80; 2nd, $49; 3rd, $33. (An) 1st, $87, $92, $102; 2nd, $63; 3rd, $35. (W. S.) (Cu.) (I.) (Am.) 3rd, $35. (Al.) (N.) 3rd, $33.
ANCONA, ITALY.—(F. R. I.) 1st, $116.
ANTWERP, BELGIUM.—4.912m., 11d. (W. S.) 2nd, $66, $71, $116; 3rd, $35. (G.) 2nd, $56, $61; 3rd, $42. (R. S.) 1st, $70, $80, $90. $95, $100, $110, $120; 2nd, $52; 3rd, $34. (An.) 1st, $77, $82, $92; 2nd, $61; 3rd, $35. (Cu.) (I.) (Am.) 3rd, $35. (Al.) (N.) 3rd, $33.
ATHENS, GREECE.—6.567m.. 14d. (F. R. I.) 1st, $138. (F.) 3rd, $56.
BELFAST, IRELAND.—(Am.) 2nd, $47: 3rd, $32. (Al.) 2nd, $47; 3rd, $33. (W. S.) (Cu.) (I) 3rd, $33. (N.) 3rd, $31. (An.) 3rd, $32.
BERGEN, NORWAY.—(Al) 1st, $72, $77, $82, $87, $97; 3rd, $37. (An.) 1st, $95, $100, $110; 2nd, $64; 3rd, $37. (W. S.) 2nd, $78, $83, $128; 3rd, $39. (G.) 2nd, $68, $73; 3rd, $54. (Am.) 2nd, $68; 3rd, $37. (Cu.) (I.) (T.) 3rd, $39. (N.) 3rd, $34.
BERLIN, GERMANY.—5,297m., 11d. (An.) 1st, $99, $104. $114; 2nd, $72; 3rd, $51. Am.)3rd, $36.
BJORNEBORG, FINLAND.—(W. S.) (Cu.) (I.) (T.) 3rd, $45. (Al.) (N.) 3rd, $40. (Am.) 3rd, $43.
BOULOGNE, FRANCE.—(N. A. S. N.) 1st, $65, $70, $75, $80; 3rd, $33.
BREMEN, GERMANY.—5,147m., 11d. (An.) 1st, $80, $85, $95; 3rd, $35. (Al.) 1st, $70, $75, $80, $85, $95; 3rd, $33. (N. L.) 1st, $95 to $145; 2nd, $61; 3rd, $39. (W. S.) 2nd, $71, $76, $121; 3rd, $35. (Am.) 2nd, $61; 3rd, $35. (N.) 3rd, $33. (I.) 3rd, $35.

BRINDISI, ITALY.—6,117m., 12d. (F. R. I.) 1st $100.
BRISTOL, ENGLAND.—(W. S.) 2nd, $60, $65; $110; 3rd, $35. (G.) 2nd, $50, $55; 3rd, $36. (Cu.) (I.) 3rd, $35. (Al.) (Am.) (An.) 3rd, $34. (N.) 3rd, $33.
BRODY, AUSTRIAN GALICIA.—(Am.) 3rd, $42.
BRUSSELS, BELGIUM.—4,887m., 11d. (An.) 1st, $86, $91, $101; 2nd, $62; 3rd, $41.
BUCHAREST, ROUMANIA.—(Am.) 3rd, $50.
CARDIFF, ENGLAND.—(W. S.) 2nd, $60, $65; $110; 3rd, $35. (G.) 2nd, $50, $55; 3rd, $36. (Cu.) (I.) 3rd, $35. (Al.) (Am.) (An.) 3rd, $34. (N.) 3rd, $33.
CATANIA, SICILY.—(F. R. I.) 1st, $115.
CHRISTIANIA, NORWAY.—5,562m., 13d. (Au.) 1st, $90, $95, $105; 2nd, $62; 3rd, $37. (Al.) 1st, $81, $86, $91, $96, $106; 2nd, $65; 3rd, $37. (T.) 1st, $68; 2nd, $53; 3rd, $39. (Am.) 2nd, $68; 3rd, $37. (G.) 2nd, $68, $73; $54. (W. S.) 2nd, $78, $83, $128; 3rd, $39. (Cu.) (I.) 3rd, $39. (N.) 3rd, $34.
CHRISTIANSAND, NORWAY.—(An.) 1st, $81, $86, $96; 2nd, $62; 3rd, $37. (Al.) 1st, $71, $76, $81, $86, $96; 3rd, $37. (T.) 1st, $68; 2nd, $53; 3rd, $39. (W. S.) 2nd, $78, $83, $128; 3rd, $39. (Am.) 2nd, $68; 3rd, $37. (Cu.) (I.) 3rd, $39. (N.) 3rd, $34.
CONSTANTINOPLE, TURKEY.—6,722m., 15d. (F. R. I.) 1st, $152. (F.) 3d, $59.
COPENHAGEN, DENMARK.—5,487m., 12d. (An.) 1st, $81, $86, $96; 2nd, $62; 3rd, $37; (Al.) 1st, $71, $76, $81, $86, $96; 3rd, $37. (T.) 1st, $68; 2nd, $53; 3rd, $39. (W. S.) 2nd, $76, $81, $126; 3rd, $39. (G.) 2nd, $68, $73; $54. (Am.) 2nd, $66; 3rd, $37. (Cu.) (I.) 3rd, $39. (B.) 3rd, $38. (N.) 3rd, $34.
CORFU, IONIAN ISLANDS.—(F. R. I.) 1st, $100.
DARDANELLES, TURKEY.—(F. R. I.) 1st, $126.
DRESDEN, GERMANY. — 5,467m., 11d. (An.) 1st, $102, $107, $117; 2nd, $74; 3rd, $53

DRONTHEIM, NORWAY.—(W. S.) 2nd, $83, $88, $133; 3rd, $39. (Am.) 2nd, $73. (Al.) (An.) 3rd, $37. (I.) 3rd, $39. (N.) 3rd, $34.
DUBLIN, IRELAND.—(W. S.) (Cu.) (I.) 3rd, $34. (Al.) (An.) (Am.) 3rd, $33. (N.) 3rd, $32.
ESBJERG, DENMARK.—(W. S.) (Cu.) (I.) (T.) 3rd, $39. (Al.) (Am.) 3rd, $37. (N.) 3rd, $34.
EYDTKUHNEN, GERMANY.—(Am.) 3rd, $39.
FAYAL, AZORES.—(I. N.) 1st, $80; 3rd, $37.
FLORENCE, ITALY.—5,712m., 12d. (An.) 1st, $118, $123, $133; 2nd, $86; 3rd, $65.
FLORES, AZORES.—(I. N.) 1st, $80; 3rd, $37.
FREDERIKSHAVN, DENMARK.—(T.) 3rd, $39.
GALATZ, ROUMANIA.—(Am.) 3rd, $50.
GAMLA KARLEBY, FINLAND.—(W. S.) (Cu.) (I.) (T.) 3rd, $45. (Al.) (N.) 3rd, $40. (Am.) 3rd, $43.
GENOA, ITALY.—5,527m., 11d. (An.) 1st, $120, $140; 3rd, $43.— (F.) 1st, $95, $105; 3rd, $43. (N. L.) 1st, $100 to $270; 3rd, $43. (F. R. I.) 1st, $98; 3rd, $43. (R. S.) 3rd, $43.
GIBRALTAR, SPAIN.—6,067m., 14d. (An.) 1st, $80, $100; 3rd, $41. (N. L.) 1st, $100 to $270; 3rd, $43. (F. R. I.) 1st, $80; 3rd, $41.
GLASGOW, SCOTLAND. — 4,287m., 11d. (An.) 1st, $65, $70, $80; 2nd, $47; 3rd, $32. (Al.) 1st, $55, $60, $65, $70, $80; 2nd, $47; 3rd, $32. (W. S.) 2nd, $60, $65, $110; 3rd, $33. (G.) 2nd, $50, $55; 3rd, $36. (Am.) 2nd, $47; 3rd, $32. (Cu.) (I.) 3rd, $33. (N.) 3rd, $31.
GOTHENBURG, SWEDEN.—5,667m., 13d. (T.) 1st, $68; 2nd, $53; 3rd, $39. (An.) 1st, $90, $95, $105; 2nd, $62; 3rd, $37. (Al.) 1st, $77, $82, $87, $92, $102; 2nd, $63; 3rd, $37. (W. S.) 2nd, $76, $81, $126; 3rd, $39. (G.) 2nd, $66, $71; 3rd, $52. (Am.) 2nd, $66; 3rd, $37. (N.) 3rd, $34. (I.) 3rd, $39.
HAMBURG, GERMANY.—5,252m., 11d. (G.) 1st, $85, $95, $115, $135, $155, $179, $215; 2nd, $58, $63; 3rd, $44. (H. A. P.) 1st, $70, $80, $95, and up; 2nd, $67, $77; 3rd, $36, $39. (An.) 1st, $81, $86, $96; 2nd, $69; 3rd, $35. (Al.) 1st, $70, $75, $80, $85, $95; 3rd, $33. (Am.) 2nd, $58; 3rd, $35. (W. S.) 2nd, $68, $73, $118; 3rd, $35. (Cu.) (I.) 3rd, $33. (N.) 3rd, $33.
HANGO, FINLAND.—(W. S.) (Cu.) (I.) (T.) 3rd, $45. (Al.) (N.) 3rd, $40. (Am.) 3rd, $43.
HAVRE, FRANCE.—4,852m., 9d. (C. G. T.) 1st, $100, $120, $180, up to $820; 2nd, $77; 3rd, $37. (G.) 1st, $85, $95, 115, $135, $155, $179, $215; 2nd, $59, $64; 3rd, $45. (N. L.) 1st, $160 to $410; 2nd, $67. (Am.) 2nd, $58; 3rd, $35. (W. S.) (Cu.) (I.) (An.) 3rd, $35. (N.) 3rd, $33.
HELSINGFORS, FINLAND.—(W. S.) (Cu.) (I.) (T.) 3rd, $46. (Al.) (N.) 3rd, $41. (Am.) 3rd, $44.
HULL, ENGLAND.—(W.) 1st, $60, $65.
JACOBSTAD, FINLAND.—(W.S.) (Cu.) (I.) (T.) 3rd, $45. (Al.) (N.) 3rd, $40. (Am.) 3rd, $43.
JASSY, ROUMANIA.—(Am.) 3rd, $46.
KALMAR, SWEDEN.—(T.) 3rd, $39.
KINGSTON, IRELAND.—(H. & C. A.) 1st, $70.
KRISTINESTAD, FINLAND.—(W. S.) (Cu.) (I.) (T.) 3rd, $45. (Al.) (N.) 3rd, $40. (Am.) 3rd, $43.
LEGHORN, ITALY.—(An.) 1st, $120, $140; 3rd, $43. (N. L.) 1st, $100 to $270; 3rd, $45. (F.R.I.) 1st, $100; 3rd, $43. (F.) 3rd, $43.
LEIPZIG, GERMANY. — (An.) 1st, $99, $104, $114; 2nd, $72.
LISBON, PORTUGAL.—6,247m., 13d. (I. N.) 1st, $110; 3rd, $49.
LIVERPOOL, ENGLAND.—4,452m..9d. (W.S.) 1st, $70, $80, $100, $120, $140, up to $520; 2nd, $57, $62 $107; 3rd, $33. (G.) 1st, $70, $80, $100, $120, $140, $164, $200; 2nd, $47, $52; 3rd, $33. (Cu.) 1st, $80, $100, $120, $145; 2nd, $52; 3rd, $33. (I.) 1st, $70, $80, $100, $120, up to $520; 2nd, $47, $52; 3rd, $33. (Al.) 1st, $65, $68, $73 $78, $88; 2nd, $52; 3rd, $34. (Am.) 2nd, $47; 3rd, $32. (An.) 3rd, $32. (N.) 3rd, $31.

LIVORNO, ITALY.—(R. S.) 3rd, $43.
LONDON, ENGLAND.—4,652m., 10d. (N.A.S.N.) 1st, $68, $73, $78, $83; 2nd, $51; 3rd, $45. (G.) 1st, $77, $87, $107, $127, $147, $171, $207; 2nd, $50, $55; 3rd, $36. (R.S.) 1st, $70, $80, $96, $106, $116, $126; 2nd, $58; 3rd, $33. (An.) 1st, $79, $84, $94; 2nd, $58; 3rd, $33. (Al.) 1st, $69, $74, $79, $84, $94; 2nd, $57; 3rd, $33. (W.) 1st, $60, $65. (N. L.) 1st, $160 to $410. (W. S.) 2nd, $61, $66, $111; 3rd, $33. (Am.) 2nd, $51; 3rd, $32. (Cu.) (I.) 3rd, $33. (N.) 3rd, $31.
LONDONDERRY, IRELAND.—(An.) 1st, $65, $70. $80; 2nd, $47; 3rd, $32. (Al.) 1st, $55 to $65; 3rd, $33. (Am.) 2nd, $47; 3rd, $32. (W. S.) (Cu.) (I.) 3rd, $33. (N) 3rd, $31.
MALMO, SWEDEN.—(T.) 1st, $68; 2nd, $53; 3rd, $39. (G.) 2nd, $68, $73; 3rd, $54. (W. S.) (Cu.) (I.) 3rd, $39. (An.) (Al.) (Am.) 3rd, $37. (N.) 3rd, $34.
MALTA, south of SICILY.—6,192m, 14d. (F. R. I.) 1st, $120.
MARSEILLES, FRANCE.—5,472m., 11d. (F.) 1st, $85 to $95; 3rd, $41. (F. R. I.) 1st, $100; 3rd, $41. (R. S.) 3rd, $41.
MESSINA, SICILY.—(An.) 1st, $120, $140; 3rd, $47. (F. R. I.) 1st, $115; 3rd, $47. (F.) (R. S.) 3rd, $47. (N. L.) 3rd, $49.
MILAN, ITALY.—5,527m., 11d. (N. L.) 1st, $100 to $270; 3rd, $45. (F.) (R. S.) 3rd, $43.
MUNICH, BAVARIA.—5,522m., 11d. (An.) 1st, $106, $111, $121; 2nd, $77; 3rd, $56.
NAPLES, ITALY.—6,107m., 13d. (An.) 1st, $129, $134, $144; 2nd, $94; 3rd, $43. (F.) 1st, $95 to $105; 3nd, $43. (N. L.) 1st, $100 to $270; 3rd, $45. (F. R. I.) 1st, $108; 3rd, $43. (R. S.) 3rd, $43.
ODERBURG, MORAVIA.—(W. S.) (Cu.) (I.) 3rd, $39. (Am.) 3rd, $38.
ODESSA, RUSSIA.—6,367m., 14d. (F. R. I.) 1st, $156. (Am.) 3rd, $52. (F.) 3rd, $65.
OSWIECINE, AUSTRIA.—(W. S.) (Cu.) (I.) 3rd, $39.
PALERMO, SICILY.—(F.) 1st, $100 to $110; 3rd, $47. (N. L.) 1st, $100 to $270; 3rd, $49. (F. R. I.) 1st, $115; 3rd, $47. (An.) 1st, $120, $140; 3rd, $47. (R. S.) 3rd, $47.
PARIS, FRANCE.—4,932m., 9d. (N. A. S. N.) 1st, $71, $76, $81, $86; 2nd, $53; 3rd, $37. (G.) 1st, $85, $95, $115, $135, $155, $179, $215; 2nd, $59, $64; 3rd, $45. (R. S.) 1st, $78, $88, $98, $103, $108, $118, $128; 2nd, $58. (An.) 1st, $87, $92, $102; 2nd, $64; 3rd, $43. (C. G. T.) 1st, $106, $126, $186; 2nd, $81; 3rd, $40. (Am.) 2nd, $61; 3rd, $38. (W. S.) (Cu.) (I.) 3rd, $38. (N.) 3rd, $36.
QUEENSTOWN, IRELAND.—4,162m., 9d. (W. S.) 1st, $70, $80, $100, $120, $140, up to $520; 2nd, $57, $62, $107; 3rd, $33. (G.) 1st, $70, $80, $100, $120, $164, $200; 2nd, $47, $52; 3rd, $33. (Cu.) 1st, $80, $100, $120, $145; 2nd, $52; 3rd, $33. (I.) 1st, $70, $80, $100, $120, up to $520; 2nd, $47, $52; 3rd, $33. (Am.) 2nd, $47; 3rd, $32. (N.) 3rd, $31.
REYKJAVIK, ICELAND.—(Am.) 3rd, $48.
ROME, ITALY.—5,942m, 12d. (An.) 1st, $123, $128, $138; 2nd, $90; 3rd, $69.
ROTTERDAM, HOLLAND.—4,847m., 11d. (N. A. S. N.) 1st, $65, $70, $75, $80; 2nd, $49; 3rd, $33. (An.) 1st, $77, $82, $92; 2nd, $61; 3rd, $35. (W. S.) (Cu.) (I.) (Am.) 3rd, $35. (N.) 3rd, $33.
ST. MICHAELS, AZORES.—(I. N.) 1st, $80; 3rd, $37.
SALONICA, TURKEY.—(F. R. I.) 1st, $150.
SOUTHAMPTON, ENGLAND.—4,592m., 9d. (H. A. P.) 1st, $120 to $170; 2nd, $77; 3rd, $39. (N. L.) 1st, $146 to $396; 2nd, $67; 3rd, $39.

STAVANGER, NORWAY.—(Al.) 1st, $81, $86, $91,
$96, $106; 2nd, $65; 3rd, $37. (An.) 1st,
$95, $100, $110; 3rd, $37. (Am.) 2nd,
$68; 3rd, $37. (W. S.) 2nd, $78, $83,
$128; 3rd, $39. (G.) 2nd, $68, $73; 3rd,
$54. (Cu.) (I.) (T.) 3rd, $39. (N.) 3rd,
$34.
STETTIN, GERMANY.—(B.) 3rd, $34. (Cu.) 3rd,
$42.
STOCKHOLM, SWEDEN.—5,887m., 13d. (Am.)
2nd, $73; 3rd, $40. (W. S.) 2nd, $83,
$88, $133, 3rd, $42. (Cu.) (I.) (T.) 3rd,
$42. (An.) 3rd, $40. (N.) 3rd, $37.
THRONDJEM, NORWAY.—(An.) 1st, $111, $116,
$126. (G.) 2nd, $73, $78; 3rd, $59. (Cu.)
(T.) 3rd, $39. (Am.) 3rd, $37.

TRIESTE, AUSTRIA.—5,822m., 13d. (F. R. I.)
1st, $116. (An.) (F.) 3rd, $48.
TURIN, ITALY.—5,432m., 12d. (N. L.) 1st, $100
to $270; 3rd, $45. (R. S.) (F.) 3rd, $43.
ULEABORG, FINLAND.—(W. S.) (Cu.) (I.) 3rd,
$46. (Al.) (N.) 3rd, $41. (T.) 3rd, $47.
(Am.) 3rd, $44.
VENICE, ITALY.—5,692m., 13d. (An.) 1st,
$113, $118, $128; 2nd, $83; 3rd, $62.
(F. R. I.) 1st, $116.
VIENNA, AUSTRIA.—5,652m., 13d. (An.) 1st,
$115, $120, $130; 2nd, $83; 3rd, $63.
(Am.) 3rd, $40.
WASA, FINLAND.—(Cu.) (I.) (T.) (W. S.) 3rd,
$45. (Al.) (N.) 3rd, $40. (Am.) 3rd,
$43.

Rates of Fare from Points in Asia, Africa, Australia, New Zealand and Tasmania, to Chicago, via New York

ADELAIDE, AUSTRALIA.—16,227m., 60d. (N.
Z. S.) 1st, $416, $467; 2nd, $236, $261;
3rd, $115, $125, $135. (N. L.) 1st, $386;
2nd, $215; 3rd, $105. (Or.) 1st, $361,
$415, $450; 2nd, $203, $236, $261; 3rd,
$120, $131, $140. (S. S. & A.) 1st, $415,
$467; 2nd, $236, $261; 3rd, $111, $121,
$131. (P. & O.) 1st, $401, $425, $450;
2nd, $203 to $237. (Am.) 2nd, $195; 3rd,
$113, $123, $133. (I.) (W. S.) 3rd, $114,
$124, $134.
ALBANY, AUSTRALIA.—(Or.) 1st, $361, $415,
$450; 2nd, $203, $236, $261; 3rd, $120,
$131, $140.
ALEXANDRIA, EGYPT.—7,062m., 16d. (F. R. I.)
2nd, $119. (F.) 3rd, $59.
ALGIERS, AFRICA.—(C. G. T.) 1st, $145; 2nd,
$106; 3rd, $56.
ALGOA BAY, SOUTH AFRICA.—(Ca.) 1st, $287,
$302; 2nd, $174, $184; 3rd, $99 to $115.
ASCENSION ISLAND, west of AFRICA.—(Ca.) 1st,
$307; 2nd, $189; 3rd, $116.
AUCKLAND, NEW ZEALAND.—(N Z. S.) 1st, $416,
$467; 2nd, $236, $261; 3rd, $125, $135.
(S. S. & A.) 1st, $415, $467; 2nd, $236,
$261; 3rd, $111, $121, $131. (N. L.) 1st,
$372; 2nd, $339; 3rd, $115. (Am.) 2nd,
$227; 3rd, $133. (W. S.) (I.) 3rd, $114,
$124, $134.
BATAVIA, JAVA.—13,712m., 42d. (Q. R. M.)
1st, $364; 2nd, $203; 3rd, $116.
BLUFF, NEW ZEALAND.—(N. L.) 1st, $372; 2nd,
$339; 3rd, $115. (W. S.) 3rd, $114, $124,
$134.
BOMBAY, INDIA. — 10,677m., 28d. (Cl.) 1st,
$340; 2nd, $203. (H.) 1st, $339; 2nd,
$203. (P. O.) 1st, $440. 2nd, $227.
BOWEN, AUSTRALIA.—(Q R. M.) 1st, $380; 2nd,
$203; 3rd, $116
BRISBANE, AUSTRALIA.—(Or.) 1st, $376, $413,
$440; 2nd, $210, $236, $261, 3rd, $120,
$131, $140. (Q. R. M.) 1st, $380; 2nd.
$203; 3rd, $116. (P. & O.) 1st $450; 2nd,
$237. (Am.) 2nd, $220; 3rd, $114, $124.
$133. (W. S.) 3rd, $115. (N. L.) 3rd, $110.
BUNDABERG, AUSTRALIA.—(Q. R. M.) 1st, $380;
2nd, $203; 3rd, $116.
CAIRNS, AUSTRALIA.—(Q. R. M.) 1st, $380; 2nd,
$203; 3rd, $116.
CALCUTTA, INDIA.—12,032m., 31d. (Cl.) 1st,
$352; 2nd, $203. (P. & O.) 1st, $440;
2nd, $267.
CAMPBELLTOWN, AUSTRALIA.—(Am.) 2nd, $227;
3rd, $113, $123, $133.
CANTERBURY, NEW ZEALAND.—(N. Z. S.) 1st,
$416, $467, 2nd, $236, $261; 3rd, $115,
$125, $135. (S. S. & A.) 1st, $415, $467;
2nd, $236, $261; 3rd, $111, $121, $131.
(Am.) 2nd, $227; 3rd, $113, $123, $133.
CAPE TOWN, SOUTH AFRICA.—12,157m., 31d.
(Ca.) 1st, $271, $287; 2nd, $164, $174;
3rd, $99, $105, $115. (U.) 1st, $271,
$287; 2nd, $164, $174, 3rd, $99, $110.
(N. Z. S.) (S. S. & A.) 1st, $287; 2nd, $174;
3rd, $94, $105. (I.) 3rd, $93, $98.
CEYLON, south of INDIA.—(P & O.) 1st, $440;
2nd, $267.

COLOMBO, CEYLON.—(Or.) 1st, $361, $415,
$450; 2nd, $203, $236, $261; 3rd, $120,
$131, $140. (Cl.) 1st, $340; 2nd, $203.
(N. L.) 1st, $376; 2nd, $203.
COOKTOWN, AUSTRALIA.—(Q. R. M.) 1st, $380;
2nd, $203; 3rd, $116.
DARDANELLES, TURKEY.—(F. R. I.) 1st, $120.
DELAGOA BAY, SOUTH AFRICA.—12,432m., 46d.
(Ca.) (U.) 1st, $323, $338. 2nd, $199,
$210; 3rd, $120, $125, $136.
DUNEDIN, NEW ZEALAND.—(N. L.) 1st, $372;
2nd, $339; 3rd, $115.
EAST LONDON, SOUTH AFRICA.—(Ca.) (U.) 1st,
$297, $312; 2nd, $179, $189; 3rd, $105,
$110, $120.
FREEMANTLE, WEST AUSTRALIA. — (Or.) 3rd,
$120, $131, $140.
GISBORNE, NEW ZEALAND.—(Am.) 2nd, $227;
3rd, $113, $123, $133. (W. S.) 3rd, $114,
$124, $134.
HOBART, TASMANIA.— (N. Z. S.) 1st, $416,
$467; 2nd, $236, $261; 3rd, $115, $125,
$135 (Or.) 1st, $376, $415, $450; 2nd,
$203, $236, $261; 3rd, $120, $131, $140.
(S. S. & A.) 1st, $415, $467; 2nd, $236.
$261; 3rd, $111, $121, $131. (P. & O.)
1st, $450; 2nd, $237. (Am.) 2nd, $195;
3rd, $113, $123, $133. (W. S.) 3rd, $114,
$124, $134. (N. L.) 3rd, $103.
KING GEORGE'S SOUND, AUSTRALIA.—(P. & O.)
1st, $401, $425, $450; 2nd, $203 to $227.
KNYSNA, SOUTH AFRICA.—(U.) 1st, $287, $302;
2nd, $174, $184; 3rd, $99, $105, $115.
(Ca.) 1st, $302; 2nd, $184; 3rd, $105,
$115.
KURRACHEE, INDIA.—11,242m., 31d. (Cl.) 1st,
$340; 2nd, $203. (H.) 1st, $339; 2nd,
$203. (P. & O.) 1st, $440; 2nd, $227.
LAS PALMAS, CANARY ISLANDS.—(Ca.) 1st, $179;
2nd, $103; 3rd, $63.
LAUNCESTON, TASMANIA.—(N. Z. S.) 1st, $416,
$467; 2nd, $236, $261; 3rd, $115, $125,
$135. (Or.) 1st, $376, $415, $450; 2nd,
$203, $236, $261; 3rd, $120, $131, $140.
(S. S. & A.) 1st, $415, $467; 2nd, $236.
$261; 3rd, $111, $121, $131. (P. & O.)
1st, $450; 2nd, $237. (N. L.) 3rd,
$103.
MACKAY, AUSTRALIA.—(Or.) 1st, $391, $430,
$440; 2nd, $227, $252, $281; 3rd, $126,
$135, $145. (Q. R. M.) 1st, $380; 2nd,
$203; 3rd, $116.
MADAGASCAR, east of SOUTH AFRICA. — (Ca.)
1st, $364; 2nd, $231. 3rd, $151. $170.
MADEIRA, northwest of AFRICA.—6,257m., 15d.
(U.) 1st, $174, $184; 2nd, $95, $107;
3rd, $93. (Ca.) 1st, $184; 2nd, $103;
3rd, $63. (I. N.) 1st, $95.
MADRAS, INDIA.—11,437m., 30d. (Cl.) 1st,
$352; 2nd, $203. (P. & O.) 1st, $440;
2nd, $267.
MARYBOROUGH, AUSTRALIA.—(Or.) 1st, $381,
$420, $440; 2nd, $242, $205, $271; 3rd,
$120, $131, $140. (Q. R. M.) 1st, $380;
2nd, $203; 3rd, $116. (Am.) 2nd, $234;
3rd, $114. $124, $133. (W. S.) 3rd,
$115, $125, $134.

MAURITIUS, east of MADAGASCAR.—13,262m., 39d. (Ca.) 1st, $264; 2nd, $231; 3rd, $151, $170.

MELBOURNE, AUSTRALIA.—(N. Z. S.) 1st, $416, $467; 2nd, $236, $261; 3rd, $115, $125, $135, (Or.) 1st, $361, $415, $450; 2nd, $203, $236, $261; 3rd, $120, $131, $140. (S. S. & A.) 1st, $415, $467; 2nd, $236, $261; 3rd, $111, $121, $131. (N. L.) 1st, $406; 2nd, $227; 3rd, $105. (P. & O.) 1st, $401, $425, $450; 2nd, $203 to $237. (Am.) 2nd, $195; 3rd, $113, $123, $133. (W. S.) (I.) 3rd, $114, $124, $134.

MOSSEL BAY, SOUTH AFRICA.—(Ca.) 1st, $287, $302; 2nd, $174, $184; 3rd, $99, $105, $115.

NAPIER, NEW ZEALAND.—(Am.) 2nd, $227; 3rd, $113, $123, $133. (W. S.) 3rd, $114, $124, $134.

NATAL, SOUTH AFRICA.—(Ca.) (U.) 1st, $307, $323; 2nd, $189, $200; 3rd, $110, $115, $125.

NELSON, NEW ZEALAND.—(Am.) 2nd, $227; 3rd, $113, $123, $133. (W. S.) 3rd, $114, $124, $134.

NORMANTON, AUSTRALIA.—(Q. R. M.) 1st, $380; 2nd, $203; 3rd, $116.

OTAGO, NEW ZEALAND.—(N. Z. S.) 1st, $416, $467; 2nd, $236, $261; 3rd, $115, $125, $135. (S. S. & A.) 1st, $415, $467; 2nd, $236, $261; 3rd, $111, $121, $131.

PENANG, STRAITS SETTLEMENTS. — 12,647m., 36d. (P. & O.) 1st, $441; 2nd, $236.

PICTON, NEW ZEALAND.—(Am.) 2nd, $227; 3rd, $113, $123, $133. (W. S.) 3rd, $114, $124, $134.

PORT ALFRED, SOUTH AFRICA.—(Ca.) (U.) 1st, $297, $312; 2nd, $179, $189; 3rd, $105, $110, $120.

PORT CHALMERS, NEW ZEALAND.—(W. S.) 3rd, $114, $124, $134.

PORT ELIZABETH, SOUTH AFRICA.—(Ca.) (U.) 1st, $287, $302; 2nd, $174, $184; 3rd, $99, $105, $115.

PORT LYTTLETON, NEW ZEALAND.—(W. S.) 3rd, $114, $124, $134.

RANGOON, INDIA. — 12,822m., 35d. (P. H.) 1st, $390; 2nd, $284.

ROCKHAMPTON, AUSTRALIA.— (Or.) 1st, $386, $430, $440; 2nd, $222, $247, $276; 3rd, $120, $131, $140. (Q. R. M.) 1st, $380; 2nd, $203; 3rd, $116. (Am.) 2nd, $240; 3rd, $114, $124, $133. (W. S.) 3rd, $115, $125, $134.

RUSSELL, NEW ZEALAND.— (N. L.) 1st, $372; 2nd, $339; 3rd, $115.

ST. HELENA, west of AFRICA.—10,192m., 28d. (U.) 1st, $271, $287; 2nd, $164, $174; 3rd, $99, $110. (Ca.) 1st, $271; 2nd, $164; 3rd, $94, $99.

SINGAPORE, STRAITS SETTLEMENTS.—13 087m., 38d. (N. L.) 1st, $424; 2nd, $242. (P. & O.) 1st $441; 2nd, $236.

SMYRNA, TURKEY IN ASIA.—(F. R. I.) 1st, $126. (F.) 3rd, $57.

SYDNEY, AUSTRALIA.— (N. Z.S.) 1st, $416, $467; 2nd, $236, $261; 3rd, $115, $125, $135. (Or.) 1st, $361, $415, $450; 2nd, $203, $236, $261; 3rd, $120, $131, $140. (S. S. & A.) 1st, $415, $467; 2nd, $236, $261; 3rd, $111, $121, $131. (N. L.) 1st, $372; 2nd, $339; 3rd, $105. (P. & O.) 1st, $401, $425, $450; 2nd, $203 to $237. (Am.) 2nd, $195; 3rd, $113, $123, $133. (I.) (W. S.) 3rd, $114, $124, $134.

TARANAKI, NEW ZEALAND.—(W. S.) 3rd, $114, $124, $134.

TAURANGA, NEW ZEALAND.—(Am.) 2nd, $227; 3rd, $113, $123, $133. (W. S.) 3rd, $114, $124, $134.

TENERIFFE, CANARY ISLANDS.—6,557m., 19d. (U.) 1st, $179; 2nd, $102; 3rd, $63. (N. Z. S.) 1st, $176; 2nd, $112. (S., S. & A.) 1st, $175; 2nd, $151.

TOWNSVILLE, AUSTRALIA. — (Or.) 1st, $391, $430, $440; 2nd, $227, $252, $281; 3rd, $126, $135, $145. (Q. R. M.) 1st, $380; 2nd, $203; 3rd, $116. (Am.) 2nd, $245; 3rd, $119, $128, $138. (W. S.) 3rd, $120, $129, $139.

WELLINGTON, NEW ZEALAND.—(N. Z. S.) 1st, $416, $467; 2nd, $236, $261; 3rd, $115, $125, $135. (S., S. & A.) 1st, $415, $467; 2nd, $236, $261; 3rd, $111, $121, $131. (N. L.) 1st, $372; 2nd, $339; 3rd, $115. (Am.) 2nd, $227; 3rd, $113, $123, $133. (I.) (W. S.) 3rd, $114, $124, $134.

Rates of Fare from Points in Central America, South America, Mexico and the West Indies, to Chicago, via New York.

ANTIGUA, LEEWARD ISLANDS.— 2,702m., 10d. (Q. S.) 1st, $80; 2nd, $67; 3rd, $38. (At.) 1st, $95.

ARECIBO, PORTO RICO.—(N.Y.& P.R.) 1st, $90. ASPINWALL, U. S. OF COLOMBIA.—3,217m., 9d. (At.) 1st, $90.

AUX CAYES, HAYTI.—(At.) 1st, $90.

BAHIA, BRAZIL.—6,782m., 22d. (U. S. & B.) 1st, $160; 2nd, $83.

BARBADOES, WINDWARD ISLANDS.—3,057m., 9d. (Q. S.) 1st, $80; 2nd, $67; 3rd, $38. (U. S. & B.) 1st, $80; 3rd, $43. (H. & C. A.) 1st, $80.

BELIZE, HONDURAS.—3,272m., 10d. (At.) (H. & C. A.) 1st, $80.

BERMUDA, east of UNITED STATES.—1,692m., 3d. (Q. S.) 1st, $50; 2nd, $37; 3rd, $28.

BLUEFIELDS, NICARAGUA.—(At.) 1st, $110.

BUENOS AYRES, SOUTH AMERICA.— 8,957m., 30d. (U. S. & B.) 1st, $205; 3rd, $103.

CAMPEACHY, MEXICO.—(N. Y. & C.) 1st, $90; 2nd, $57.

CARTHAGENA, U. S. OF COLOMBIA.—3,357m., 13d. (At.) 1st, $95.

CIENFUEGOS, CUBA.—(N. Y. & C.) 1st, $80; 2nd, $47.

COLON, U. S. OF COLOMBIA. — 3.217m., 9d. (At.) 1st, $90.

CURACAO, WEST INDIES.—2,942m., 8d. (R."D") 1st, $95; 2nd, $57.

DOMINICA, LEEWARD ISLANDS.—2,832m., 10d. (Q. S.) 1st, $80; 2nd, $67; 3rd, $38.

FONTERA, MEXICO.— (N. Y. & C.) 1st, $90, 2nd, $57.

GONAIVES, HAYTI.—(At.) 1st, $90.

GREYTOWN, NICARAGUA.— 3,722m., 8d. (At.) 1st, $110. (H. & C. A.) 1st, $80.

HAVANA, CUBA.—2,312m., 4d. (N. Y. & C.) 1st, $50, $60; 2nd, $32, $37.

JACMEL, HAYTI. — 2,822m., 8d. (At.) 1st, $90.

JEREMIE, HAYTI.—(At.) 1st, $100.

KINGSTON, JAMAICA—2,732m., 8d. (At.) (H. & C. A.) 1st, $70

LA GUAYRA, VENEZUELA.—3,157m., 11d. (R. "D") 1st, $100; 2nd, $67.

LIVINGSTON, GUATEMALA.—3,407m., 11d. (H. & C. A.) 1st, $90.

MARANHAM, BRAZIL.—4,717m., 16d. (U. S. & B.) 1st, $140; 3rd, $73.

MARTINIQUE, WINDWARD ISLANDS. — 2,892m 10d. (Q. S.) 1st, $80; 2nd, $67; 3rd, $38. (U. S. & B.) 1st, $80; 2nd, $43.

MONTEVIDEO, SOUTH AMERICA.—8,827m., 29d. (U. S. & B.) 1st, $205; 3rd, $103.

MOSQUITO COAST PORTS, CENTRAL AMERICA.— (At.) 1st, $110, $120.

NASSAU, BAHAMA ISLANDS.—2,017m., 5d. (N. Y. & C.) 1st, $60; 2nd, $37.

PARA, BRAZIL.— 4,372m., 13d. (U. S. & B.) 1st, $120; 2nd, $63.

PERNAMBUCO, BRAZIL.—6,337m., 17d. (U. S. & B.) 1st, $150; 2nd, $78.

PETIT GOAVE, HAYTI.—(At.) 1st, $100.

PONCE, PORTO RICO. — (N. Y. & P. R.) 1st, $90.

PORT-AU-PRINCE, HAYTI.—2,512m., 8d. (At.) 1st, $90.

PORT LIMON, COSTA RICA.—3,777m., 10d. (At.) 1st, $100.
PORTO CORTEZ, HONDURAS.—(H. & C. A.) 1st, $90.
PROGRESO, MEXICO.—(N. Y. & C.) 1st, $80; 2nd, $57.
PUERTO CABELLO, VENEZUELA.—3,072m., 13d. (R. "D") 1st, $100; 2nd, $67.
RIO DE JANEIRO, BRAZIL.—7,642m., 26d. (U. S. & B.) 1st, $165; 3rd, $88.
ST. CROIX, WINDWARD ISLANDS.—(Q. S.) 1st, $80; 2nd, $67; 3rd, $38.
ST. JOHN, PORTO RICO.—(N. Y. & P. R.) 1st, $80.
ST. KITTS, LEEWARD ISLANDS.—2,712m., 9d. (Q. S.) 1st, $80; 2nd, $67; 3rd, $38.
ST. LUCIA, WINDWARD ISLANDS.—2,937m., 9d. (Q. S.) 1st, $80; 2nd, $67; 3rd, $38.
ST. MARC, HAYTI.—(At.) 1st, $90.

ST. THOMAS, WEST INDIES.—2,562m., 7d. (U. S. & B.) 1st, $80; 3rd, $43.
SANTA MARTHA, U. S. OF COLOMBIA.—3,227m., 14d. (At.) 1st, $95.
SANTIAGO DE CUBA.—(N. Y. & C.) 1st, $80; 2nd. $47.
SANTOS, BRAZIL.—7,892m., 26d. (U. S. & B.) 1st, $170; 2nd, $93
SAVANILLA, U. S. OF COLOMBIA.—3,292m., 14d. (At.) 1st, $85.
TAMPICO, MEXICO.—3,162m., 8d. (N. Y. & C.) 1st; $90; 2nd, $57.
TRINIDAD, WINDWARD ISLANDS.—3,282m., 7d. (Q. S.) 1st, $80; 2nd, $67; 3rd, $38.
TRUXILLO, CENTRAL AMERICA.—(H. & C. A.) 1st, $90.
TUXPAN, MEXICO.-(N.Y.&C.) 1st, $90; 2nd, $57.
VERA CRUZ, MEXICO.—3,412m., 14d. (N. Y. & C.) 1st, $80; 2nd, $57.

Rates of Fare from Mexico, Central America and Havana, to Chicago, via New Orleans.

BLUEFIELDS, NICARAGUA.—(M. S.) Cabin, $63; Deck, $36.
HAVANA, CUBA.—(M. S.) Cabin, $58; Deck, $36.
MEXICO CITY, MEX. (via Galveston).—(M. S.) Cabin, $86; Deck, $54.
MEXICO CITY, MEX. (via Morgan City),—(M. S.) Cabin, $74; Deck, $45.

PORT LIMON, COSTA RICA—(C. R. & H.) Cabin, $63, $73; Deck, $31, $41.
VERA CRUZ, MEX. (via Galveston).—(M. S.) Cabin, $75; Deck, $45.
VERA CRUZ, MEX. (via Morgan City).—(M. S.) Cabin, $63; Deck, $36.

Rates of Fare from Points in India, China, Japan, Australia, New Zealand, Mexico and the West Coast of America, to Chicago, via San Francisco.

ACAJUTLA, SAN SALVADOR.—(P. M.) 1st, $170; 3rd, $95.
ACAPULCO, MEXICO.—(P.M.) 1st, $155; 3rd, $87.
ADELAIDE, AUSTRALIA.—11,933m., 33d. (Oc.) 1st, $292; 3rd, $156. (P. M.) 1st, $448; 3rd, $181, $235.
AMAPALA, HONDURAS.-(P.M.) 1st, $170; 3rd, $95.
ANTOFOGASTA, CHILI.—(P. M.) 1st, $347; 3rd, $152.
ARICA, PERU.—(P. M.) 1st, $435; 3rd, $145.
AUCKLAND, NEW ZEALAND.—9,208m., 25d. (Oc.) 1st, $270; 3rd, $145.
BALLENITA, ECUADOR.—(P. M.) 1st, $243; 3rd, $121.
BUENAVENTURA, COLOMBIA.—(P. M.) 1st, $214; 3rd, $112.
BOMBAY, IND.-(P.M.) 1st, $398; 3rd, $151, $200.
BRISBANE, AUSTRALIA.—11,278m., 33d. (Oc.) 1st, $285; 3rd, $152. (P. M.) 1st, $413; 3rd, $146, $220.
CALCUTTA, INDIA.—(P. M.) 1st, $313; 3rd, $111, $180.
CALDERA, CHILI.—(P.M.) 1st, $352; 3rd, $152.
CALLAO, PERU.—(P. M.) 1st, $301; 3rd, $135.
CHAMPERICO, GUATEMALA.—(P. M.) 1st, $170; 3rd, $95.
CHRISTCHURCH, NEW ZEALAND. — (Oc.) 1st, $296; 3rd, $161.
COBIJA, BOLIVIA.—(P. M.) 1st, $344; 3rd, $150.
COLOMBO, CEYLON.—(P. M.) 1st, $373; 3rd, $137, $186.
COQUIMBO, CHILI.—(P.M.) 1st, $360; 3rd, $154.
CORINTO, NICARAGUA.-(P.M.) 1st, $175; 3rd, $97.
DUNEDIN, NEW ZEALAND. — (Oc.) 1st, $300; 3rd, $163.
ESMERALDAS, ECUADOR.—(P. M.) 1st, $236; 3rd, $119.
ETEN, PERU.—(P. M.) 1st, $292; 3rd, $131.
GUAYAQUIL, ECUADOR.—(P. M.) 1st, $265; 3rd, $124.
HOBART, TASMANIA.—(Oc.) 1st, $295; 3rd, $160.
HONGKONG, CHINA.—9,078m., 26d. (P. M.) 1st, $238; 3rd, $96, $145.
HONOLULU, SANDWICH ISLANDS.—4,733m., 12d. (Oc.) 1st, $145; 3rd, $70.
HUASCO, CHILI.—(P. M.) 1st, $356; 3rd, $154.
IQUIQUE, PERU.—(P.M.) 1st, $339; 3rd, $147.
LA LIBERTAD, SAN SALVADOR. — (P. M.) 1st, $170; 3rd, $95.
LA UNION, SAN SALVADOR.—(P. M.) 1st, $170; 3rd, $95.
LEVUKA, FIJI ISLANDS.—(Oc.) 1st, $309; 3rd, $161.

MANILA, PHILIPPINE ISLANDS. — (P. M.) 1st, $288; 3rd, $104, $160.
MANTA, ECUADOR.— (P. M.) 1st, $243; 3rd, $121.
MANZANILLO, MEX.—(P.M.) 1st, $145; 3rd, $82.
MAZATLAN, MEX.—(P. M.) 1st, $135; 3rd, $75.
MELBOURNE, AUSTRALIA.—11,353m., 31d. (Oc.) 1st, $282; 3rd, $151. (P. M.) 1st, $438; 3rd, $176, $225
MOLLENDO, PERU.—(P.M.) 1st, $331; 3rd, $145.
OCOS, GUATEMALA.—(P.M.) 1st, $170; 3rd, $95.
PACASMAYO, PERU.—(P.M.) 1st, $292; 3rd, $131.
PANAMA, COLOMBIA.—(P. M.) 1st, $185; 3rd, $102.
PAYTA, PERU.—(P. M.) 1st, $287; 3rd, $129.
PENANG, STRAITS SETTLEMENTS.—(P. M.) 1st, $293; 3rd, $116, $170.
PIMENTEL, PERU.—(P.M.) 1st, $292; 3rd, $131.
PISAGUA, CHILI.—(P. M.) 1st, $339; 3rd, $147.
PISCO, PERU.—(P. M.) 1st, $309; 3rd, $137.
PORT ANGEL, MEX.—(P.M.) 1st, $160; 3rd, $90.
PORT CHALMERS, NEW ZEALAND. — (Oc.) 1st, $300; 3rd, $163.
PORT LYTTLETON, NEW ZEALAND.— (Oc.) 1st, $296; 3rd, $161.
PUNTA ARENAS, COSTA RICA.—(P. M.) 1st, $175; 3rd, $97.
ROCKHAMPTON, AUSTRALIA.—(Oc.) 1st, $296; 3rd, $158.
SALAVERRY, PERU.--(P.M.) 1st, $294; 3rd, $132.
SALINA CRUZ, MEXICO.—(P.M.) 1st, $160; 3rd, $90.
SAN BENITO, MEX.—(P.M.) 1st, $160; 3rd, $90.
SAN BLAS, MEXICO.—(P.M.) 1st, $140; 3rd, $80.
SAN JOSE DE GUATEMALA.—(P.M.) 1st, $170; 3rd, $95.
SAN JUAN DEL SUR, NICARAGUA.—(P. M.) 1st, $175; 3rd, $97.
SINGAPORE, STRAITS SETTLEMENTS.—11,328m., 41d. (P. M.) 1st, $268; 3rd, $110, $160.
SYDNEY, AUSTRALIA.—10,658m., 30d. (Oc.) 1st, $270; 3rd, $145. (P. M.) 1st, $428; 3rd, $176, $225.
TONALA, MEXICO.—(P. M.) 1st, $160; 3rd, $90.
TUMACO, COLOMBIA.—(P. M.) 1st, $221; 3rd, $114.
TUTUILA, SAMOA.—(Oc.) 1st, $270; 3rd, $145.
VALPARAISO, CHILI.—(P. M.) 1st, $367; 3rd, $155.
WELLINGTON, NEW ZEALAND.—9,578m., 26d. (Oc.) 1st, $290; 3rd, $158.
YOKOHAMA, JAPAN.—7,813m., 22d. (P. M.) 1st, $220; 3rd, $96, $130.

Allan-State Line.
GLASGOW AND NEW YORK. ESTABLISHED 1891.

STEAMSHIPS	Year When Built	Gross Tonnage	Registered Horse Power	Length in Feet	Br'dth in Feet
St. of California	1892	6,000		400	46
St. of Nebraska*	1880	3,985	650	385	43
St. of Indiana	1874	2,528	400	329	36
St. of Georgia	1873	2,490	400	330	36
St. of Nevada	1874	2,488	400	332	36
St. of Penns'via	1873	2,472	400	331	36
Arcadian †	1872	931	100	205	
Assyrian	1880	3,970	500	360	
Austrian	1867	2,458	300	319	
Buenos Ayrean	1879	4,005	500	385	
Canadian	1872	2,906	280	349	
Carthaginian	1884	4,214	520	386	
Caspian	1870	2,728	300	349	
Circassian	1872	3,724	500	415	
Corean	1881	3,488	400	360	
Grecian	1879	3,613	400	360	
Hibernian	1881	2,997	380	351	
Lucerne	1878	1,925	220	291	
Manitoban	1865	2,975	300	338	
Monte Videan	1887	3,500		330	
Nestorian	1866	2,689	275	317	
Newfoundland	1872	919	130	212	
Norwegian	1865	3,523	350	375	
Nova Scotian	1858	3,305	400	366	
Parisian	1881	5,359	800	440	
Peruvian	1863	3,038	500	373	
Phoenician	1864	2,425	250	334	
Polynesian	1872	3,983	675	400	
Pomeranian	1882	4,364	550	381	
Prussian	1869	3,030	400	340	
Rosarian	1887	3,500		330	
Sardinian	1875	4,376	600	400	
Sarmatian	1871	3,647	600	370	
Scandinavian	1870	3,068	400	338	
Siberian	1884	3,904	500	372	
Waldensian	1861	2,256	250	322	

Anchor Line.
GLASGOW AND NEW YORK. ESTAB. 1852.

STEAMSHIPS	Year When Built	Gross Tonnage	Registered Horse Power	Length in Feet	Br'dth in Feet
City of Rome*	1881	8,144	1,500	561	53
Anchoria	1874	4,168	617	408	40
Bolivia	1873	4,050	1,120	400	40
Circassia	1878	4,272	600	400	42
Devonia	1877	4,270	600	400	42
Ethiopia	1873	4,005	720	402	42
Furnessia	1880	5,495	600	445	45

Bordeaux Line.
BORDEAUX AND NEW YORK. ESTAB. 1880.

STEAMSHIPS	Year When Built	Gross Tonnage	Registered Horse Power	Length in Feet	Br'dth in Feet
Chateau Lafite	1881	3,462	450	366	41
Panama	1881	1,357	180	281	36
Tancarville	1881	1,463	200	285	36

French Line.
HAVRE AND NEW YORK. ESTAB. 1860.

STEAMSHIPS	Year When Built	Gross Tonnage	Registered Horse Power	Length in Feet	Br'dth in Feet
La Touraine	1890	8,000		536	55
La Gascogne	1886	7,283		508	52
La Bourgogne*	1886	7,303		508	52
La Champagne	1886	6,922		508	51
La Bretagne	1886	6,920		508	51
La Normandie	1882	6,217		459	50

Guion Line.
LIVERPOOL AND NEW YORK. ESTAB. 1842.

STEAMSHIPS	Year When Built	Gross Tonnage	Registered Horse Power	Length in Feet	Br'dth in Feet
Alaska	1881	6,250	1,800	500	50
Arizona	1879	5,147	1,200	464	46
Nevada	1868	3,617	400	345	43
Wisconsin	1870	3,700	600	378	43
Wyoming	1870	3,723	600	366	43

Inman Line.
LIVERPOOL AND NEW YORK. ESTAB. 1850.

STEAMSHIPS	Year When Built	Gross Tonnage	Registered Horse Power	Length in Feet	Br'dth in Feet
City of Paris	1889	10,499	2,000	580	63
City of N. York	1888	10,499	2,000	580	63
City of Berlin	1874	5,526	1,000	510	44
City of Chicago	1883	5,202	900	430	45
City of Chester	1873	4,770	850	444	44
C. of Richmond	1873	4,780	700	440	43

Amsterdam-Netherlands Line.
ROTTERDAM AND NEW YORK. ESTAB. 1874.

STEAMSHIPS	Year When Built	Gross Tonnage	Registered Horse Power	Length in Feet	Br'dth in Feet
Spaarndam*	1881	4,539	600	430	42
Maasdam	1872	3,984	600	420	41
Veendam	1872	3,707	600	420	41
Werkendam	1881	3,657	400	410	39
Amsterdam	1879	3,627	400	411	39
Obdam	1880	3,558	400	411	39
Rotterdam	1878	3,329	350	390	38
Didam	1891	2,750	600	340	40
Dubbeldam	1891	2,750	600	340	40

Cunard Line.
LIVERPOOL AND NEW YORK. ESTAB. 1840.

STEAMSHIPS	Year When Built	Gross Tonnage	Registered Horse Power	Length in Feet	Br'dth in Feet
Etruria*	1885	7,718	2,500	501	57
Umbria	1884	7,718	2,500	501	57
Aurania	1883	7,268	1,500	470	57
Servia	1881	7,391	1,000	515	52
Gallia	1879	4,808	700	430	44
Bothnia	1874	4,535	600	422	42
Scythia	1875	4,550	600	420	42
Pavonia	1882	5,587	700	430	46
Cephalonia	1882	5,517	700	430	46
Catalonia	1881	4,841	600	429	43

Hamburg-American Line.
HAMBURG AND NEW YORK. ESTAB. 1847.

STEAMSHIPS	Year When Built	Gross Tonnage	Registered Horse Power	Length in Feet	Br'dth in Feet
Fuerst Bismarck	1891	12,000		520	58
Normannia*	1890	12,000		520	57
Augusta Victoria	1889	10,000		460	56
Columbia	1889	10,000		460	56
Scandia	1889	4,372	700	374	44
Wieland	1874	3,504	600	384	40
Gellert	1874	3,533	600	374	40
Suevia	1874	3,609	500	364	41
Rugia	1882	3,467	400	357	43
Rhaetia	1883	3,553	425	351	43
Bohemia	1881	3,410	360	351	40
Moravia	1883	3,739	310	360	40
Slavonia	1883	2,274	250	300	37
Polaria	1882	2,724	300	300	38
Polynesia	1881	2,196	270	298	36
Russia	1889	4,017	700	374	44
Italia	1889	3,498	400	344	44

North German Lloyd.
BREMEN AND NEW YORK. ESTAB. 1857.

STEAMSHIPS	Year When Built	Gross Tonnage	Registered Horse Power	Length in Feet	Br'dth in Feet
Kaiser Wm. II	1888	6,990		450	49
Spree	1890	6,963		462	49
Havel	1890	6,963		462	49
Lahn*	1887	5,581		448	49
Saale	1886	5,381		439	48
Trave	1886	5,381		438	48
Aller	1885	5,381		438	48
Ems	1884	5,192		429	47
Elder	1883	4,719		429	47
Elbe	1881	4,510		418	44

Red Star Line.
ANTWERP AND NEW YORK. ESTAB. 1873.

STEAMSHIPS	Year When Built	Gross Tonnage	Registered Horse Power	Length in Feet	Br'dth in Feet
Friesland*	1889	7,116	800	470	51
Westernland	1883	5,736	700	440	47
Noordland	1883	5,212	500	400	47
Waesland	1867	4,752	500	435	42
Belgenland	1878	3,692	600	402	40
Rhynland	1879	3,689	600	402	40
Pennland	1870	3,760	500	361	41
Switzerland	1874	2,816	290	329	38
Nederland	1873	2,839	290	329	38

White Star Line.
LIVERPOOL AND NEW YORK. ESTAB. 1870.

STEAMSHIPS	Year When Built	Gross Tonnage	Registered Horse Power	Length in Feet	Br'dth in Feet
Teutonic	1889	9,685	2,400	582	58
Majestic*	1889	9,861	2,400	582	58
Britannic	1874	5,004	760	455	45
Germanic	1874	5,008	760	455	45
Adriatic	1871	3,888	600	437	40
Celtic	1872	3,867	600	437	40
Runic	1889	4,649	520	430	45
Cufic	1888	4,639	520	430	45
Nomadic	1891	5,749	600	460	49
Tauric	1891	5,749	600	460	49

* Commodore steamers. In the Allan-State Line, after † steamers sail from Quebec; Portland, Boston, Philadelphia and Baltimore, to Liverpool, Glasgow and London.

NOTE.—For the above figures we are largely indebted to the New York World Almanac.

Number of Steamers. There are about 10,000 steamers at present afloat on the various great rivers, seas and oceans.

Mail Steamships. The Cunard Line has carried the ocean mails since 1840. The earlier steamers of this line, for several years, were all side-wheelers.

First Ocean Propeller. The method of moving vessels by screw propulsion, was invented by Ericsson, in 1836, and was practically applied on the Great Britain, which made the trip from Liverpool to New York in 14 days, 21 hours, in 1845.

First Steamer Crossing Ocean. The Savannah, 380 tons, launched at Corlear's Hook, New York, in 1818, was the first vessel using steam to cross the ocean, the journey from Savannah to Liverpool being made in 1819, in 25 days, using steam 18 days.

Fog. The passenger should not grumble at fog. It should be understood that this dense mist is the method pursued by Nature in taking up moisture from the ocean into the atmosphere, to be wafted in clouds thousands of miles inland, to fall upon the earth in refreshing rain.

Crossing Ocean—Time in 1838. The Great Western, 750 tons, the largest steamer at that time, made the journey from Bristol, England, to New York in 15 days, April, 1838; brought over 7 passengers; carried back 66 passengers, and made return trip in 14 days. Coal consumed on westward trip, 655 tons; consumed on return trip, 392 tons.

The Great Eastern. Designed by Brunel, was begun at Millwall, London, in 1854, and was launched in 1858. Was 680 feet long, 83 feet broad; draught of 25 feet. Had screw engines of 4,000 horse-power, and paddle engines of 2,600 horse-power. Served in the laying of the Atlantic Cable, but was unfitted for ocean use in competition with the more rapid-sailing vessels, which made their journeys at less expense. Was sold in 1887, for $40,000, and broken up.

Stores for One Trip.—On one of the recent departures of a great liner from New York her larder was stocked with the following, says an authority on steamship travel: 20,000 pounds of fresh beef (a portion of this, although all was available, was intended for the return trip, beef being cheaper here than in Liverpool) ; fresh pork,500 pounds; mutton, 3,500 pounds; lamb, 450 pounds; veal, 500 pounds; sausage, 200 pounds; liver, 230 pounds; corned beef, 2,900 pounds; salt pork, 2,200 pounds; bacon, 479 pounds; hams, 500 pounds; tongues, 8 dozen; sweetbreads, 200; fish, assorted, 2,100 pounds; oysters, 5,000; clams, 5,000; soft-shell crabs, 500; green turtle, 200 pounds; turkeys, 50; geese, 50; fowls, 248; chickens, 150; squabs, 300; snipe, 500; quail, 500; ducklings, 216; wild game, 108 pair. Butter, 1,500 pounds; eggs, 1,200; condensed milk, 400 quarts; fresh milk, 1,000 quarts; ice cream, 400 quarts. Apples, 12 barrels; pears, 10 boxes; musk-melons, 160; water-melons, 60; oranges, 16 boxes; peaches, 10 crates; bananas, 10 bunches; huckleberries, 100 quarts; gooseberries, 100 quarts; cherries, 250 quarts; currants, 100 quarts; grapes, 75 pounds; lemons, 14 cases; pineapples, 100; plums, 150 quarts; strawberries, 250 quarts; raspberries, 250 quarts. Flour, 125 barrels; potatoes, 140 barrels; lettuce, 72 dozen; asparagus, 30 dozen; green peas, beans, tomatoes, 15 crates each, Brussels sprouts, 10 baskets. Crackers, cakes in large variety, and a quantity of pickles, sauces, spices, extracts, pates de foie gras, truffles, caviare, canned and dried and fresh vegetables, and general groceries in the most generous quantity. About 500 other items appeared on her list of stores, besides wines, spirits, beer, mineral waters, cigars, etc.

A Knot.—In sailor phrase a knot is a nautical mile, and includes 6,080 feet. By United States surveyors' measure a mile includes 5,280 feet.

Passenger Steamer Capacity. The greatest number of immigrants ever brought by a single ship, was 1,767, by the steamer Egypt, belonging to the National Line, in 1873. In the warm climates thousands of passengers, on ships, go from one portion of the world to another, living and sleeping, during their travels, only on the steamer decks.

Icebergs. Icebergs appear in February, March and April, and often linger until October and November. Most of the bergs have their origin in West Greenland. Thousands are there set adrift every 12 months, and have been a year, and some of them several years, in reaching the track of the transatlantic steamers, having possibly been locked in several winters and freed in the summer, during their passage far enough south to be seen by steamer passengers.

Speed and Danger. Experience has proved that the greater the speed the greater the safety, rapid-sailing vessels being able to escape the area of fog and storm more quickly than the slow ship. The rapid sailer can be more easily manoeuvred than the slower vessel, and if collision becomes unavoidable, the great impetus of the rapid-sailing ship will cause it to cut the opposing vessel in two, with but little damage to itself.

Growing Safety. With the many improved devices introduced into ship-building, in the past few years, accidents at sea have been less and less frequent. Among the numerous improvements is that of constructing the steamer in such a manner that there are several water-tight compartments, so that should there be collision, and one part of the vessel be broken in, the other compartments being uninjured, the ship proceeds with little hindrance to the end of the journey. Latterly, vessels have been so constructed that a fire in one compartment cannot be communicated to another portion of the ship. Arrangements are now made for the scattering of oil in case of a storm, and the use of the double screw permits the vessel to proceed though one of the screws be broken. In the year 1890 nearly 2,000 trips were made from New York to various European ports, and about 200,000 cabin passengers were carried, besides nearly 372,000 immigrants landed at Castle Garden, and all this without accident.

Facts and Figures. There are 29 regular lines of steamships running between New York and European ports, of which 23 carry passengers. Other lines run to other parts of the world. The Teutonic and Majestic, of the White Star Line, and the La Touraine, of the French Line, each cost $2,000,000. Other well-known steamers cost $1,500,000 each. The great White Star steamers can carry 1,500 passengers and 2,500 tons of freight. The large Inman ships may carry each 1,200 passengers and 2,700 tons of freight, while the great Cunarders have each accommodations for 1,600 passengers and 800 tons of freight. Freight steamers now go from New York to Liverpool in 10 days. The largest load of freight ever carried was by the Nomadic, of the White Star Line, in August, 1891, being 9,591 tons, besides the necessary coal for the voyage. The largest number of cattle, at one time, was carried by the England, of the National Line, in September, 1889, being 1,022 head. Over 2,000 vessels, loaded with grain, sailed from New York in 1891. Over 90 vessels are in the fruit trade between the United States, West Indies and Central America. Over 70 tank steamships go out from the American ports carrying oil, and latterly numerous molasses ships, carrying molasses in bulk, have come into use.

STEAMSHIP LAHN, NORTH GERMAN LLOYD LINE, BREMEN TO NEW YORK.

AN ANSWER TO THE MANY QUESTIONS THAT ARE ASKED ABOUT SHIPS.

Flags on Steamships. The forward flag on the topmast is the flag of the country to which the steamer is going; the second is the company flag, the third gives the name of the boat; the fourth, the rank of the captain; fifth indicates a mail steamer, and sixth, the flag of the country from which the steamer comes. Sometimes the flag indicating the name of the ship, captain's flag and mail flag are not displayed.

Speed and Distance. The rapidity with which a rapid-sailing propelling steamer travels is ascertained by the number of revolutions or movements made per minute in certain portions of the machinery. It is also learned by the dropping of an object attached to a line into the water, at the side of the stern of the vessel, which, remaining nearly stationary, allows the operator to know the speed by the number of knots which the line runs out in a certain number of seconds. The drop line, called the log-line, contains a small string tied into a knot at about every 47 feet and 3 inches; hence the name "knot." The number of miles traveled per day is known by latitude and longitude, which is understood by study of the fixed stars at night and observation of the sun at noonday.

Funnel Colors and Flags. Some of the well-known lines of transatlantic steamers are known by the color of their funnels and the peculiarity of their house-flags; thus: Allen Line—funnel, red, with white ring under black top; flag, red, white and blue, with red pennant above. Anchor Line—funnel, black; flag, white swallowtail, with red anchor. Bordeaux Line—funnel, white, with black top; flag, white, red border, three red crescents in center, blue letters C. B. N. V. in corners. Cunard Line—funnel, red, with black top; flag, red, with yellow lion in center. French Line—funnel, red, with black top; flag, white, red ball in corner, and the name of company. Gulon Line—funnel, black, with red band, black top; flag, blue, with diamond in center containing a black star. Hamburg-American Line—funnel, white and blue, with an anchor and yellow shield bearing the letters H. A. P. A. G. Inman Line—funnel, black, white band, black top; flag, red, white square in upper corner with black diamond. National Line—funnel, white, with black top; flag, union-jack in square red field, blue and white cross in center. North German Lloyd Line—funnel, cream; flag, key and anchor crossed in center of an oak leaf wreath, black. Red Star Line—funnel, cream color, black top, with red star; flag, white swallowtail, with red star. Rotterdam Line—funnel, black, with green band; flag, one white and two green stripes, N. A. S. M. in center. State Line—funnel, blue, with red ring under black top; flag, blue swallowtail, with red and white stripes at top and bottom, and letter S. in star and center. White Star Line—funnel, cream, with black top; flag, swallowtail, containing white star.

Fastest Steamer-Sailing. The following is the best record made by fast-sailing steamers between New York and various European ports, up to the spring of 1892:

5 days 16 hours 31 min., by the Teutonic, of the White Star Line, going 2,778 miles, from Queenstown to New York, August 14-19, 1891.

5 days 20 hours 22 min., by the Majestic, going 2,866 miles, from Queenstown to New York, February 18-24, 1892, making 20¾ miles per hour, being the fastest speed on record.

6 days 14 hours 15 minutes, by the Fuerst Bismarck, of the Hamburg Line, from Southampton to New York, May 9-15, 1891. Distance, 3,075 miles.

6 days 12 hours 54 minutes, by the Fuerst Bismarck, from New York to Southampton, June 18-25, 1891.

6 days 16 hours 34 min., by the La Touraine, of the French Line, from Havre to New York, June 20-27, 1891. Distance, 3,170 miles.

Steamship Names. The bow is the extreme forward part of the ship. The stern is the after part. Forward is the fore part of the vessel. Aft, is the rear part. Amidships is the central part of the vessel. Starboard is the right side of the ship, looking forward. Port, the left side. The Index Guide gives the following description of sails; namely, that the masts are the fore-mast, main-mast and mizzen-mast. The parts of the masts are the fore-mast, fore-top-mast, fore-top gallant-mast, fore-royal-mast, and similarly for the other masts; thus, main-mast, main-top-mast, mizzen-top-mast, etc. Booms are round, heavy, wooden spars to which the sails are attached—the jib-boom extending from the bowsprit, the flying-jib-boom being attached to, but extending beyond, the jib-boom. The main and mizzen booms are attached to the main and mizzen-masts, the spanker boom extends aft from the mizzen-mast. Yards are strong, horizontal, wooden spars, extending crosswise the ship, to which the sails are attached along, up the masts. The principal sails are the jib and flying-jib, long triangular sails extending from the fore-mast to the jib-booms, and along the masts upward from the deck to the try-sail, the fore-course or fore-sail, fore-top-sail, fore-top-gallant-sail, fore-royal-sail, fore-sky-sail, and similarly for each of the other masts; thus, main-try-sail, main-sail, main-top-sail, mizzen-top-sail, etc., and spanker, the stern-most sail, extending from the spanker boom to the gaff. The ensign or ship's colors are attached to the gaff. Shrouds are the ropes used to sustain the masts, and extend from the fore-top to the sides of the ship (the rope ladders). The other ropes, used as supports to the masts, are designated stays, and are named from that part of the mast to which they are attached, as fore-stay, mizzen-stay, fore-royal-stay, mizzen-top-gallant-stay, etc. The jib-boom, flying-jib-boom and several of the sails here mentioned, are not required and are not used on the large modern steamers.

1792.

FROM

SAN · · · ·

· FRANCISCO

—TO—

NEW YORK:

167 DAYS.

1892.

FROM

SAN · · · ·

· FRANCISCO

—TO—

NEW YORK:

4 DAYS · · ·

12½ HOURS.

ADVICE CONCERNING BAGGAGE, HEALTH AND GENERAL CONDUCT.

Climate. To the foreign tourist the most pleasant season to visit in the United States is from May 15 to October 15.

Fear Not. Do not worry from fear of accident when traveling. Remember that a vastly greater number of accidents happen at home, from falling off ladders, falling down stairs, being kicked, run-away with, struck by lightning or cut by sharp instruments, than occur from railway traveling.

Accident Insurance. If you are so certain that you will be injured while traveling that you are willing to wager a small sum of money, on that belief, the accident-insurance agent at the station, where you usually get your railroad ticket, will bet with you six hundred to one that you will not. This is shown in his willingness to guarantee you $3,000 in case you are injured, if you will invest 25 cents in the purchase of an accident insurance ticket, good for three days.

Distance in One Hour. The following is the best record to date: Vulture flies 150 miles; railroad passenger train goes 64 miles; pigeon flies 60 miles; river steamboats, 26 miles; bicycling, 23 miles; ocean steamers, 20 miles; man running, 11½ miles; man walking, 8 miles. In estimating time required to reach a given place, it is safest to allow 20 miles per hour by rail, and 12 miles per hour by water. In the table of distances and fares from various parts of the world to Chicago, the time given is that which is allowed for the transmission of the mails.

In the Satchel. The following articles are essential to the complete traveling outfit for gentlemen—ladies probably adding a few more: Brush-broom, hair-brush, looking-glass, nail-brush, tooth-powder, tooth-brush, traveling-cap, fruit-knife, night-shirt, sponge, soap, studs, ties, gloves, pomade, comb, lozenges, collars, cuffs, corkscrew, matches, spectacles, shirts, envelopes, perfumery, cards, maps, pencils, scissors, needles, pins, thread, string, buttons, slippers, handkerchiefs, writing-paper, note-book, guide-book, washing-book, sling-strap, pocket-compass, address-cards, court-plaster, field-glass.

Precautions. Carefully secure tickets, checks keys and money when traveling. Be provided with a sufficiency of small silver change for convenience in making petty purchases. Keep hand-baggage carefully under the eye, and have all baggage so clearly marked that you will readily know it your self and no one be liable to take it away through mistake in exchange for his own. Keep your watch with local time, and be in readiness in your place for traveling always before time. It is the careless, unsuccessful person that gets "left," and it is a most ludicrous sight to see a person running after a train.

Pull Down the Blinds. Many injuries have been received by passengers on railway trains, because of stones thrown through the windows by scoundrels after nightfall. The traveler should guard against the danger by always lowering the blinds after dark.

On Time. Be early at the depot. Get tickets, attend to the checking of baggage, and select seats with reference to the sunny or shady side, as you prefer. Telegraph ahead to your friends at what time you will arrive, and the road over which you will come, that they may know at what hour and at what depot to go to receive you.

Sociability. Many travelers lose a large share of the benefit arising from traveling, by drawing themselves into a shell, and neglecting to converse with their fellow travelers. The fellow passenger is, perhaps, fully conversant with all the region through which the train passes, and by affording the opportunity, through conversation, may give a large amount of information.

Guide Books and Maps. Before starting on a journey to a region where the traveler has not been before, it is wise to get time-tables from the ticket agent, all maps necessary and a supply of guide books, if any are published, fully describing the locality to be visited; all of which should be consulted as the traveler visits the regions mentioned. A journey is thus made much more interesting and profitable.

Rewards for Services. On the sleeping car the porter usually blacks boots, brushes clothing, furnishes pillows, guards baggage, etc., for which service each male passenger, when near the journey's end, pays 25 cents. Ladies, when traveling alone, do the same. On steamers, passengers allow "boots" 50 cents for the journey across the ocean; the chairman the same amount for the care of the chair; the room steward, $2.50 for attendance in the state-room, and $2.50 to the table-waiter. In order to secure good attention, pay these attendants just before leaving the ship and not until then.

Regular Habits when Traveling. Beware of eating at all hours on railway trains. Eat as nearly as possible at the regular meal time, and always deliberately, even though time be short, at the eating room. Make special effort to get your usual amount of sleep, and if you rise unrefreshed from lack of sleep, after washing face and hands, return to your state-room or closet with towels, one wet, the other dry, and after putting aside your clothing, wet all parts of the body; follow by wiping with the dry towel, and conclude with a brisk and vigorous rubbing over the whole person. This exercise puts the blood into even circulation and the physical system into the best possible condition for health and enjoyment.

Map of the States and Territories. When States Were Settled, Areas, Capitals, Etc.

Year Settled.	STATES AND TERRITORIES.	Area in Sq. Miles.	Population in 1890.	No. to Sq. Mile.	Admitted to the Union.	CAPITAL OF THE STATE.	Population of the Capital.	In Congress. Sena-tors.	Repre-'tive.
1711	Alabama	52,250	1,508,073	29.5	1814	Montgomery	21,790	2	8
1799	Alaska ‡	557,390	30,329			Sitka	1,188		
1540	Arizona ‡	113,020	59,691	5		Prescott	1,759		
1685	Arkansas	53,850	1,125,385	21.2	1836	Little Rock	22,496	2	5
1769	California	158,360	1,204,002	7.8	1850	Sacramento	26,272	2	6
1858	Colorado	103,925	410,974	3.9	1876	Denver	106,670	2	1
1633	Connecticut*	4,990	745,861	149.4	1788 †	Hartford	53,182	2	4
1627	Delaware*	2,050	167,871	81.9	1787 †	Dover	3,061	2	1
1634	Dist. of Col'mbia	70	229,796	3,282.8		Washington	229,796		
1565	Florida	58,680	390,435	6.6	1845	Tallahassee	2,934	2	2
1733	Georgia *	59,475	1,834,366	30.8	1788 †	Atlanta	65,515	2	10
1811	Idaho	84,800	84,229	1.0	1890	Boise City	2,311	2	1
1720	Illinois	56,650	3,818,536	67.4	1818	Springfield	24,852	2	10
1690	Indiana	36,350	2,189,030	60.2	1816	Indianapolis	107,445	2	13
	Indian Terr'ry ‡	64,690	119,000	1.8		Tahlequah			
1833	Iowa	56,025	1,906,729	34.0	1846	Des Moines	50,067	2	11
1850	Kansas	82,080	1,423,485	17.3	1861	Topeka	31,809	2	7
1775	Kentucky	40,400	1,855,436	45.9	1792	Frankfort	8,500	2	11
1699	Louisiana	48,720	1,116,828	22.9	1812	Baton Rouge	10,397	2	6
1625	Maine	33,040	660,261	19.9	1820	Augusta	10,521	2	4
1634	Maryland*	12,210	1,040,431	85.2	1788 †	Annapolis	7,625	2	6
1620	Massachusetts*	8,315	2,233,407	268.6	1788 †	Boston	446,507	2	12
1670	Michigan	58,915	2,089,792	35.4	1837	Lansing	12,630	2	11
1846	Minnesota	83,365	1,300,017	15.6	1857	St. Paul	133,156	2	5
1716	Mississippi	46,810	1,284,887	27.4	1817	Jackson	6,041	2	7
1764	Missouri	69,415	2,677,880	38.5	1821	Jefferson City	6,732	2	14
1861	Montana	146,080	131,769	1.0	1889	Helena	13,834	2	1
1854	Nebraska	76,855	1,056,793	13.7	1867	Lincoln	55,491	2	3
1861	Nevada	110,700	44,327		1864	Carson City	3,950	2	1
1623	New Hampshire*	9,305	375,827	40.3	1788 †	Concord	16,948	2	2
1624	New Jersey*	7,815	1,441,017	184.2	1787 †	Trenton	58,488	2	7
1540	New Mexico ‡	122,580	144,863	1.1		Santa Fe	6,185		
1614	New York*	49,170	5,981,934	121.6	1788 †	Albany	94,640	2	34
1663	North Carolina*	52,250	1,617,340	30.9	1789 †	Raleigh	12,798	2	9
1846	North Dakota	70,195	182,425	2.5	1889	Bismarck	2,186	2	1
1788	Ohio	41,060	3,666,719	89.3	1803	Columbus	90,398	2	21
1889	Oklahoma ‡	3,183	61,071	19.1		Guthrie	5,511		
1811	Oregon	96,039	312,490	3.2	1859	Salem	7,000	2	1
1682	Pennsylvania*	45,215	5,248,574	116.1	1747 †	Harrisburg	40,221	2	28
1636	Rhode Island*	1,250	345,343	276.2	1790 †	Prov. & N'port		2	2
1670	South Carolina*	30,570	1,147,161	37.5	1788 †	Columbia	14,508	2	7
1846	South Dakota	76,850	327,848	4.2	1889	Pierre	3,235	2	2
1757	Tennessee	42,050	1,763,723	41.9	1796	Nashville	76,309	2	10
1690	Texas	265,780	2,232,220	8.3	1845	Austin	15,324	2	11
1847	Utah ‡	84,990	206,495	2.4		Salt Lake City	45,025		
1725	Vermont	9,565	332,205	34.0	1791	Montpelier	3,617	2	2
1607	Virginia*	42,450	1,648,911	38.8	1788 †	Richmond	80,838	2	10
1811	Washington	69,180	349,516	5.0	1889	Olympia	4,698	2	1
1862	West Virginia*	24,780	760,448	30.6	1862	Charleston	6,734	2	4
1669	Wisconsin	56,040	1,683,697	30.0	1848	Madison	13,392	2	9
1858	Wyoming	97,890	60,589	6	1890	Cheyenne	11,693	2	1

NOTE.—Large star in each State, on Map, indicates location of State capital. * The original 13 States. † Date of adoption o.' State constitution. ‡ Territory; not yet organized as a State.

Forty-four States and five Territories are shown on the opposite map.

The star in the upper northwest corner of Wyoming indicates the location of Yellowstone Park.

The area of the United States, including Territories, is 3,607,604 sq. miles.

UNITED STATES CAPITOL, WASHINGTON, D. C.

The two stars in the inclosure immediately above the State of Texas, on the map, indicate the location of the Public Land Strip to Oklahoma.

The three stars directly above Oklahoma, indicate the location of the Cherokee Outlet to the Indian Territory.

Alaska, a territory containing 557,990 square miles, and described in description of North America, is not shown on the opposite map.

The territory of Columbia, termed a district, lies midway on the line between Maryland and Virginia, and is not shown on the map. Capital, Washington, seat of United States Government.

Delaware lies eastward of Maryland, and is too small to be easily distinguished on the map. Chicago is in N. E. corner of Ill. See dagger.

Connecticut and Rhode Island lie directly south of Massachusetts. The location of Connecticut is indicated by the letters C. T., and Rhode Island lies eastward of Connecticut; too small to be easily designated on the map.

Description of the Area Occupied by, and Early Settlement of, the United States.

The greatest length of the territory from the Atlantic to the Pacific Ocean, occupied by the United States, on the parallel of 42°, is 2,768 miles; and its greatest breadth, from Point Isabel, Tex., to the northern boundary of North Dakota, is 1,650 miles. The Mexican boundary line is 1,500 miles in length. The boundary line separating the United States from the British possessions is about 3,400 miles long.

The first attempt at civilized settlement, in the United States, was made on the Island of Roanoke, off the coast of North Carolina, where a colony from England was placed under the command of Sir Richard Grenville, in 1585. Having trouble with the Indians, several of the settlers were killed, and the remainder returned to England. In 1587 John White landed a party of 108 persons, and returned to England after founding the city of Raleigh, named after Sir Walter Raleigh. Here Virginia Dare, the first white child, native of the United States, was born. In 1590, John White returned with a fleet, but all traces of the colonists, left three years before, had vanished. Their fate has never been ascertained.

In 1540, French fur-traders founded a settlement on Manhattan Island, where the city of New York now stands, but the next year they abandoned the country. A party of Huguenots, driven from France, sought refuge in South Carolina, where they built Port Royal, in 1562; but subsequent famine compelled them to abandon the colony. In 1565, the Spaniards, on the east coast of Florida, founded St. Augustine, the oldest existing town in the United States. The first permanent English settlement was made at Jamestown, Virginia, in 1607, the colony consisting of 105 emigrants, more than one-half of whom died within six months, from privation or at the hands of the Indians. Newly arrived immigrants from England, however, swelled the number of colonists to 200, in the year 1610.

Hendrick Christænson, a Hollander, in 1612, made a small redoubt enclosing four log huts, as a place in which to live and receive furs, on Manhattan Island, on the site where is now located No. 29 Broadway, New York City. A Dutch settlement, in 1614, was founded at Albany, N. Y. In 1620, the Puritans, a company of British refugees, numbering 102 persons, driven out of England through religious persecution, landed at Plymouth, Mass., at a point known as Plymouth Rock. In 1623 the Virginia colonists, then numbering 2,500, feeling themselves strong enough to assume the offensive, attacked the Indians; this resulted in a desultory warfare which continued for twenty-four years.

From the feeble efforts thus begun, the settlement of the country has continued until its population now numbers 63,000,000; there being within the confines of the United States over 550 cities, each having, at the present time, more than 6,000 inhabitants, one hundred of the leading cities being here mentioned.

Principal Cities of the United States Containing 25,000 Inhabitants and Over.

Akron, O. About 35 miles south of Cleveland. First settled in 1824. Important manufacturing center, and the seat of Buchtel College. Pop. 27,702.

Albany, N. Y. On the Hudson River, 145 miles north of New York City. Next to Jamestown, Va., and St. Augustine, Fla., the oldest town in the U. S. Founded by the Dutch in 1614. Named in honor of the English Duke of Albany. The State Capitol, located here, when completed, will have cost $22,000,000. Pop. 94,640.

Allegheny, Pa. Opposite Pittsburg, Pa. Contains Western Penitentiary of Pennsylvania, three theological seminaries, and Western University of Pennsylvania. Pop. 104,967.

Allentown, Pa. Is 59 miles north of Philadelphia. Favorably situated in a region within easy reach of slate, coal and iron. Seat of Muhlenberg College. Pop. 25,183.

Altoona, Pa.—Picturesque in situation. Contains the extensive car works of the Pennsylvania Railroad, in which over 5,000 men are employed. Pop. 30,269.

Atlanta, Ga. One of the leading educational and manufacturing cities in the Southern States, having 590 factories already established here. Capital of the State. Situated in a healthy region, rich in gold, iron and other minerals, and with a very productive soil. Pop. 65,515.

Auburn, N. Y. Abounds in seminaries of learning, but is more widely known for its State Prison, which usually contains over 1,000 inmates. Pop. 25,887.

Augusta, Ga. Third city of the State. Contains iron foundries, cotton and flour mills, tobacco factories and numerous public institutions. Pop. 33,150.

Baltimore, Md. Known as the "Monumental City," from its many monuments. Located 200 miles from the Atlantic Ocean. Founded in 1727. Pop. 433,547.

Bay City, Mich. An important city in Michigan for the shipment of salt, and sawed lumber. Directly connected by water and rail with all points of the Northwest. Pop. 27,826.

Binghampton, N. Y. Well known for its public institutions, among which are the State Inebriate Asylum, State Home for Indigent Children, Dean Female College, etc. Pop. 35,093.

Birmingham, Ala. A new and rapidly growing southern city, already famous for its manufactories of iron and steel. Pop. 26,241.

Boston, Mass. Capital of the State. Founded in 1630. Its original owner, John Blackstone, sold his right and title five years after for £30. First church built in 1632; first wharf, 1673. First postmaster, 1677; first newspaper, "Boston News-Letter," 1704. Great fire, loss $70,000,-000, in 1872. Stands in the very front rank, socially, intellectually and politically. Pop. 446,507.

Bridgeport, Conn Distinguished for its manufactories of carriages, harness, firearms, sewing machines, and as having been the home of P. T. Barnum, who expended much of his wealth in beautifying the city. Pop. 48,856.

Brocton, Mass. A very prosperous and well-known manufacturing city. Pop. 27,278.

Brooklyn, N. Y. Founded by the Dutch in 1625. Is widely known for its navy-yard, its many churches, its beautiful Prospect Park, its Greenwood Cemetery and its stupendous bridge, half a mile long and 135 feet above water, connecting it with New York. Pop. 804,377.

Buffalo, N. Y. Terminus of upper lake navigation; at the head of Erie Canal, which is 364 miles long. Contains extensive woolen factories, saw-mills, iron-works, and has facilities for shipbuilding. Pop. 254,457.

Cambridge, Mass. Settled in 1630. Seat of Harvard University, founded in 1638, by the Rev. John Harvard. Famous also for its Mount Auburn Cemetery, the beauty of its homes, and the intellectual culture of its people. Delightfully situated on Charles River, opposite Boston. Pop. 69,837.

Camden, N. J. On the Delaware River, opposite Philadelphia. Possesses numerous manufactories; has several ship-yards and dry docks. A flourishing city. Pop. 58,274.

Canton, O. Is the seat of St. Vincent Roman Catholic College; is in the midst of a rich grain-growing region, and is an important manufacturing and coal-mining city. Pop. 26,327.

Charleston, S. C. Founded in 1672. Was prominent in its zeal for independence during the revolutionary war with England, and was the first to inaugurate a war for secession from the United States, by firing on Fort Sumter in behalf of the Confederacy in 1860. Has many churches, a large orphan asylum and the State Medical College. Pop. 54,592.

Chattanooga, Tenn. Located in a very picturesque and beautiful region of the State. Came into prominence during the rebellion through a hard-fought battle between the Confederates and Gen. Sherman's army. Pop. 29,109.

Chelsea, Mass. Contains important manufactories, a United States Marine Hospital, a fine Public Library, an Academy of Music, and all the accessories of a highly cultured people. Pop. 27,850.

Cincinnati, O. Commercial metropolis of the State. Is the center of a network of railways, and has superior facilities for water transportation, by canal to Lake Erie, and by the Ohio River to the ocean. Picturesque in location, its suburbs containing many charming, palatial homes. Pop. 296,300.

Cleveland, O. Known as the "Forest City." Is a charming city in which to live, its famous Euclid Ave., lined on either side with elegant homes, having no front fences, being conceded to be one of the most beautiful streets in the world. Is favorably located for manufacturing and commercial purposes, and is a very rapidly growing city. Pop. 261,546.

NEW YORK STATE CAPITOL, ALBANY, N. Y.

Columbus, O. Capital of the State. Is the seat of the Lutheran University, Ohio Agricultural and Mechanical College, two Catholic seminaries and the Starling Medical College. Has a large inland trade. Pop. 90,398.

Covington, Ky. Is connected by bridge with Cincinnati. Is in fact one of the great suburbs of the latter city, being a beautiful place in which to reside. Pop. 37,375.

Dallas, Tex. In the past few years, has been one of the most rapidly growing cities of the State of Texas; its numerous manufactories and superior educational institutions attracting much wide-spread attention. Pop. 38,140.

Davenport, Ia. Is located on the banks of the Mississippi River. Is the seat of Griswold College and other important institutions. Pop. 25,161.

Dayton, O. One of the wealthiest cities in this region. Is the terminus of numerous railways which center here. The Soldier's Home, with its ample grounds, is one of the prominent attractions of this part of the State. Pop. 58,868.

Denver, Colo. Capital of the State. Settled in 1858. Its wide and well-shaded streets, its imposing public buildings, its wealth and enterprise— all these are a surprise to the traveler who first looks upon the city. Pop. 106,670.

Des Moines, Ia. Capital of the State. Has a large inland trade. Is a rapidly growing city. The State Capitol, costing $3,000,-000, is one of the most imposing public edifices in the country. Pop. 50,067.

Detroit, Mich. One of the oldest cities in the country, having been founded, in 1670, as an outpost for the prosecution of the fur trade. Has long been an important manufacturing point, and the center of lumber and copper industries. Pop. 205,669.

Dubuque, Ia. Situated on a bluff 200 feet above the Mississippi River, 450 miles north of St. Louis. Settled by Julian Dubuque, a French trader, in 1788. Abundantly supplied with educational institutions and general public buildings. Pop. 30,147.

Duluth, Minn. A city which in 1869 was a forest. To-day it bids fair to become one of the great metropolitan cities of the Northwest. Is favorably located at the head of the great lakes. Pop. 32,725.

East Saginaw, Mich. Contains large manufactories, lumber mills and machine shops. Pop. 46,137.

Elizabeth, N. J. Is one of the important suburbs of New York. Although at one time heavily oppressed with a debt, the result of rapid extension of street-paving, the recent rapid growth of the city, from a population of 28,229, in 1880, to its present size, has dispelled all doubt as to the future of this beautiful residence town. Pop. 37,670.

Elmira, N. Y. Widely known for its State reformatory of the criminal classes. It is also the center of extensive manufactories. Pop. 28,070.

Erie, Pa. Has long been one of the prominent shipping ports on Lake Erie. Is a large manufacturing center and the terminus of the Erie & Pittsburg railroad. Pop. 39,699.

Evansville, Ind. One of the prosperous cities on the Ohio River is the city of Evansville, which grew from 29,280, in 1880, to a population of 50,674, according to the 1890 census.

Fall River, Mass. Terminus of one of the leading lines of steamers carrying passengers between New York and Boston. Has superior water-power, numerous cotton-mills and other manufactories. Has a large and safe harbor. Pop. 74,351.

Fort Wayne, Ind. Is an important railroad center, having extensive car shops. It is also the seat of numerous educational institutions, among which are the Lutheran College, Methodist Episcopal College, and Catholic Convent and Academies. Pop. 35,349.

Galveston, Tex. The largest sea-coast city in Texas. Is located on the island of Galveston, which is 28 miles long and from 1¼ to 3¼ miles wide; which island was, for four years, prior to 1821, the rendezvous of a pirate named Lafitte. Pop. 29,118.

Grand Rapids, Mich. A rapidly growing city, especially noted for its large furniture manufacturing industry, superior specimens of this class of goods having gone into the homes of people in all parts of the world. First settled in 1833. Has doubled in population during the past ten years, being the largest city, at this writing, in the western part of Michigan. Pop. 64,147.

Harrisburg, Pa. Is 107 miles northwest of Philadelphia. First settled by John Harris, in 1793, and, for a time, known as Harris Ferry. Became the capital of the State in 1812. Pop. 40,221.

Hartford, Conn. A prominent book-publishing and insurance center; also noted for its manufactory of firearms and for the beautiful architecture of several of its public buildings. Some of the most noted literary people reside here, and some of the most beautiful homes in the United States are within the confines of the city. Pop. 53,182.

Haverhill, Mass. One of the cities of New England particularly noted for the manufacture of boots and shoes of the finest grades. First settlement here made in 1640. Incorporated in 1645. Received a city charter in 1870. A fine granite and bronze monument has lately been erected to commemorate the heroism of the early settlers, who suffered much from the attacks of savages. Pop. 27,322.

Hoboken, N. J. One of the leading suburbs of New York, with which it is connected by frequent ferry boats. Connected with Jersey City, and other neighboring cities, by street cars. It is noted for its large coal trade. Pop. 43,561.

Holyoke, Mass. Situated on the Connecticut River, 105 miles west of Boston. Claimed to be the largest manufacturing center of paper in the world. At the same time contains large factories for the making of silk, woolen and cotton goods. Pop. 35,528.

Houston, Texas. Has steamboat connection with Galveston, being situated on Buffalo Bayou, 49 miles northwest of Galveston. Named after Gen. Samuel Houston, president of Texas when it was an independent Republic,

STATE CAPITOL, BOSTON, MASS.

subsequently governor of Texas and a United States Senator. Pop. 27,411.

Indianapolis, Ind. Capital of the State, situated 100 miles northwest of Cincinnati. First railway entered the city in 1847. To-day 15 lines converge here. The State Asylums for the deaf and dumb, the blind, and the insane, and the State Reformatory for women, are located here. Pop. 107,445.

Jersey City, N. J. Is the terminus of numerous lines of railway, steamers and of the Morris Canal, all pointing towards New York. Is naturally a large supply point for the metropolis, iron, zinc, steel goods, watches, glass and sugar being largely obtained here. Pop. 163,987.

Joliet, Ill. Celebrated for its well-conducted penitentiary, for its iron and steel works, and as a large distributing point for coal and stone. Is an important railroad center. Pop. 27,407.

Kansas City, Mo. Widely known as a leading city of Missouri, having large packing and agricultural interests. Situated in the midst of the broad plains over which formerly roamed great herds of buffaloes, elk and deer. Pop. 132,416. Lies opposite Kansas City in Kansas; the two cities being separated by the Missouri River. The population of the latter city, in Kansas, is 38,271.

La Crosse, Wis. Is the seat of large manufacturing interests, including lumber and ship-building. Is 196 miles northwest of Milwaukee. Incorporated as a city in 1856. Has rapidly increased in population of late. Pop. 25,053.

Lancaster, Pa. Is the seat of Marshall College, which belongs to the German Reformed Church. Is 68 miles west of Philadelphia. Was founded in 1730, and was the State capital from 1799 to 1812. Is the center of a rich agricultural region, and contains a large watch manufactory. Pop. 39,090.

Lawrence, Mass. Situated on the Merrimac River, 26 miles by rail from Boston. Is emphatically a manufacturing city; its waterpower, which is very efficient, is supplied by a dam across the river, and distributed by a canal 1 mile long and 14 feet deep. The cotton and woolen mills here employ thousands of workmen, the average output being 28,800,-000 yards per week, varying from broadcloths to ginghams. Pop. 44,559.

Lincoln, Neb. Beautifully situated in a prairie region. Is the capital of the State, and contains penitentiary, insane asylum, home for the friendless, and University of Nebraska. In its vicinity are limestone quarries and salt springs. Pop. 55,491.

Long Island City, N. Y. Separated from New York City by the East River. Is the terminal point of several railroad lines, and has numerous industrial establishments, including granite works, chemical works, pianos, carriages and carpets. Pop. 30,396.

Los Angeles, Cal. The metropolis of Southern California, situated 17 miles from the ocean. Was founded in 1781, by the Spaniards, and received the name "Town of the Queen of the Angels," as a tribute to the beauty and general charm of the place. Is the center of a fine orange and grape growing country, and as a resort for invalids is a place of importance. Increased in population from 11,180, in 1880, to 50,294, in 1890.

STATE CAPITOL, HARTFORD, CONN.

Louisville, Ky. Founded in 1780, and named in honor of Louis XVI. of France, then aiding in the struggle for independence. Claimed to be the largest market in the world for leaf tobacco. Is also a great center for pork packing, tanning of leather, production of whisky, and the manufacture of mechanical and agricultural implements. Pop. 161,005.

Lowell, Mass. Known because of its superior manufacturing power, on the Merrimac River, as the "Manchester of America," its extensive cotton mills giving it also the name of the "Spindle City." Named after Francis Cabot Lowell, from whose plans the town was mainly developed. Pop. 77,605.

Lynn, Mass. Widely known as a center for the manufacture of boots and shoes, this industry being established here in 1750 by a Welshman, John Adam Dagyr. The output of this manufacture, in 1880, was 16,276,380 pairs, at which time about 12,000 workmen were employed. The tanning and dressing of sheep and goat skins, and the making of morocco leather, are industries extensively conducted at this point. Pop. 55,684.

Manchester, N. H. An important manufacturing town, situated on the Merrimac River, its principal industries being cotton goods, paper, locomotives and starch. About $8,000,-000 are invested in manufactures at this point, and in the single article of cloth the output, in yards, numbers 143 miles per day. Pop. 43,983.

Memphis, Tenn. The largest city on the Mississippi River between St. Louis and New Orleans. Is the most extensive interior cotton market in the United States. Laid out as a village in 1820; incorporated as a city in 1831. The largest sea-going vessels are able to ascend the Mississippi River to this point. Pop. 64,586.

Milwaukee, Wis. Largest city in Wisconsin, developed largely through its manufacturing interests, which include clothing, cigars, cooperage, leather, bricks, sash, doors and blinds, machinery, flour and beer. The lake tonnage is about as large at this port as at Baltimore or Philadelphia. A very beautiful city, many miles of its streets being lined with charming residences. Pop. 204,150.

Minneapolis, Minn. Is the nineteenth in population, though one of the youngest cities, in the United States. Is widely known as the great center in the Northwest for the manufacture of wheat flour, the capacity of the 24 flouring mills, situated on the picturesque St. Anthony River at this point, being 37,850 barrels per day. Next in importance is the lumber output of the city, closely followed by the manufacture of furniture and agricultural implements. Will, in connection with its sister city, St. Paul, be the great metropolis of the upper Northwest. Pop. 164,738.

Mobile, Ala. The only seaport in Alabama, and the largest city in the State. Mobile Bay, on which the city is situated, is the outlet for several navigable rivers, and is the terminus of several important railways. Mobile was founded in 1702, under the administration of the French, who, at that time, were in possession of a large portion of the territory now comprising the Southern States. Pop. 31,822.

Nashville, Tenn. Capital city of Tennessee. Contains hospitals, penitentiary, four universities, custom-house, lunatic asylum, Protestant and Catholic orphan asylums, and other public institutions. Was settled in 1780. Became the capital of the State in 1843. The "Hermitage," formerly the residence of General Jackson, near the city, is a place of much interest. Contains large cotton factories and numerous manufacturing enterprises. Pop. 76,309.

Newark, N. J. Is the largest city in the State, and is celebrated as a manufacturing center, being called the "Birmingham of America"; its industries including jewelry, tanning, celluloid, hats, boots and shoes, trunks, carriages, hardware, edge-tools, silk, thread, sewing machines, etc. Settled by Puritans from Connecticut in 1666. Pop. 181,515.

New Bedford, Mass. Situated on the ocean side, 55 miles south of Boston. Long known as a center of whale-fishing in New England, over 400 vessels hailing from this port in 1854. With the decline of this industry the number of boats has lessened; but even to-day the fleet numbers over 100. The decline in whaling has been followed by the general introduction of manufacturing. Was settled by the Quakers in 1664. One of the wealthiest cities in the State. Pop. 40,705.

New Haven, Conn. Widely celebrated for its Yale College, and for its many beautiful streets, which are embowered in majestic elm trees. Is also a great industrial center, this city having over 800 manufacturing institutions, which employ many millions of capital. Settled, in 1638, by nearly 300 English immigrants of more than average wealth and business ability. Pop. 81,298.

New Orleans, La. Settled by the French in 1718. Located 100 miles from the mouth of the Mississippi River. Extends for six miles along the river bend, which gives it its name, "Crescent City." Is the natural entering port to the United States for all the vast productive countries bordering upon the Gulf of Mexico. Covers an area of 155 square miles, including within its limits many homes of great beauty. Pop. 242,039.

New York, N. Y. Situated on Manhattan Island, which is 13¼ miles long, its average width being 1¾ miles, this being but a small portion of the city. Is closely connected by bridge and ferries with Brooklyn, and by ferry with Jersey City and other adjoining cities, which are in reality a part of this great metropolis. Through railway connections and the Erie Canal, has been for 60 years the metropolitan American city; its public buildings, its mammoth private enterprises and its great wealth attracting world-wide attention. Pop. 1,515,501.

Norfolk, Va. Situated on the Elizabeth River, 106 miles southeast of Richmond. Is the seat of the United States navy yard, and is one of the most important cotton markets in the United States. Founded in 1705. Connects by steamer with all Atlantic ports. Pop. 34,871.

Oakland, Cal. Is the delightful and principal residence suburb of San Francisco. Derives its name from the groves of oaks in the midst of which it has been built, which trees are ever-green and bear their foliage throughout the entire year. The California Military Academy and other schools make it an educational center, while the outskirts of the city contain numerous manufacturing institutions. Pop. 48,682.

Omaha, Neb. Lately has had a phenomenal growth, being fitly called the "Magic City." Connected with Council Bluffs by a bridge across the Missouri River, costing $1,500,000. Is the third city in the world in the meat-packing industry, and is in the midst of a very rich agricultural country, which is yet in the beginning of its development. Pop. 140,452.

Paterson, N. J. Well known for the manufacture of railway locomotives, and equally celebrated as a silk-manufacturing center, 25 corporations being engaged in that industry alone. Its abundant manufacturing facilities results from its great water-power, the Passaic River here affording a fall of 50 feet. Sewing machines, iron bridges, brass wares, etc., are among its other manufactures. Pop. 78,347.

Pawtucket, R. I. Lies on both sides of the Pawtucket River, which falls about 50 feet at this point, affording such strength of water-power as to induce Samuel Slater, in 1790, to construct here a cotton-mill, which was the first of its kind in America. Is now the center of nearly 100 different manufacturing industries, among them being large factories for the making of cotton and woolen cloths, steam-engines, fire-engines, etc. Pop. 27,633.

Peoria, Ill. A city of recent rapid growth, situated on the Illinois River at the south of Peoria Lake, 159 miles south of Chicago. Is the third city in the State in population. Has important railway connections, 12 railroads centering at this point. Is the terminus of a line of steamers plying between this city and St. Louis. Has five daily newspapers and many manufacturing industries, among them being the extensive distillation of whiskies and the making of agricultural implements. Pop. 41,024.

Philadelphia, Pa. Settled originally by the Swedes, and so occupied when William Penn found it, and commenced his labors here in 1682. Is the great manufacturing center of the United States, steamers from this point carrying its products to all parts of the world. It is an extremely quiet, order-obeying, cleanly city, a large percentage of its people owning their homes. Its beautiful Fairmount Park, the largest owned by any city in the country, contains 2,791¼ acres. Pop. 1,046,964.

Pittsburg, Pa. On account of the natural deposits of bituminous coal and natural gas in the vicinity, has become one of the leading manufacturing cities west of the Allegheny Mountains, its principal industries being glass and glass ware, iron, steel and copper. Seventy-five different establishments being engaged exclusively in glass ware manufacture, employing 6,442 workmen. The city's 1,380 manufacturing institutions employ $105,401,481 of capital, and give work to 85,936 employes. Pop. 238,617.

STATE CAPITOL, RICHMOND, VA.

Portland, Ore. Is situated 100 miles from the Pacific Ocean, on the Willamette River, and 640 miles north of San Francisco by water. Is an important railroad center, and the most populous city on the Pacific Coast north of San Francisco. Pop. 46,385.

Portland, Me. Is 105 miles northeast of Boston. Is the largest city in Maine. First settled in 1632, and named Casco Neck, which was finally changed to the present name in 1786. Has a superior harbor, usually free from ice in the coldest winters, which has long been used as the winter port for steamers between Great Britain and Canada. Pop. 36,425.

Providence, R. I. One of the capitals of the smallest State in the Union. Was settled in 1636 by a colony of refugees from Massachusetts, under Roger Williams. Is a city of numerous manufactories and a fine array of beautiful homes. Is the seat of several educational institutions, among them being Brown University. Pop. 132,146.

Pueblo, Colo. One of the rapidly growing Colorado cities, located on the Arkansas River, 100 miles south of Denver; its importance being largely due to numerous railway connections. Is destined to be a great manufacturing center, especially for those industries into which iron largely enters. Pop. 24,558.

Quincy, Ill. Is the third largest city in the State, being handsomely situated on a limestone bluff on the eastern bank of the Mississippi River, 160 miles by river above St. Louis and 263 miles by rail southwest of Chicago. Quincy Bay, an arm of the Mississippi River, at this point, makes the best natural harbor for steamboats on the upper Mississippi. Pop. 31,494.

Reading, Pa. Is 58 miles northwest of Philadelphia, at the intersection of 16 railway lines; those transportation facilities afford superior opportunities for manufacturing, the iron industries largely predominating. Is picturesquely located on the Schuylkill River. Pop. 58,661.

Richmond, Va. Was founded in 1742. Is situated on seven hills, and most favorably located to secure perfect drainage and cleanly streets, every rainfall carrying all refuse material on the thoroughfares immediately to the sewers, whence it goes to the ocean through the rapid current of the James River. Was an important central Confederate point during the early part of the War of the Rebellion. Its famous "Libby Prison" is now one of the sights of Chicago. Is the capital of the State; its State-house, seen on another page, presents a very imposing appearance. Pop. 81,388.

Rochester, N. Y. Celebrated as a great center of floriculture and fruit-growing, the Rochester nurseries having a world-wide reputation. As a result of special attention being directed to landscape ornamentation, the place itself is a city of great beauty, its streets being lined with the most perfectly grown trees in great variety. Was distinguished early as an agricultural center, its well-known flour-mills giving it long the name of the "Flour" City, which name is yet retained, the preponderance of blossoms in the city, however, causing a change of spelling to that of "Flower" City. Its art gallery, its university, and its astronomical observatory have all contributed to give it further renown. Pop. 133,896.

Rockford, Ill. On the Rock River, 92 miles northwest of Chicago. Has superior water-power, the result of a dam 800 feet in length, built in 1844, which power has greatly aided in the establishment of the many manufacturing industries of the city, among them being those for the making of furniture, agricultural implements, watches, silver-ware, cutlery, nails, bolts, woolen and cotton goods, paper, flour, etc. Is a city of many charming homes. Pop. 23,584.

Sacramento, Cal. Capital of California 135 miles by rail northeast of San Francisco, on the east bank of the Sacramento River. The State Capitol, a view of which we present, cost $2,500,000, and stands in the center of the city, in the midst of a park of 50 acres. Was settled in 1841, by John Augustus Sutter, a Swiss military officer. The discovery of gold on his property, in 1848, changed the whole history of California The place was known at first as Sutter's Fort, and subsequently as Sacramento. Pop. 26,386.

Saginaw, Mich. An important lumber center, and lately distinguished for its salt works. Lies on an elevated plateau, 100 miles northwest of Detroit, and 18 miles from Lake Huron, by the Saginaw River, which is navigable for the largest vessels that sail the lakes. Pop. 46,322.

St. Joseph, Mo. Is an important railway center, in the midst of a rich agricultural region, about 260 miles from St. Louis. Ranks as the third city in the State in its wholesale business, and among its manufactories are flour-mills, starch works, boot and shoe factories, pork-packing establishments, wagon factories, etc. Pop. 53,324.

St. Louis, Mo. The principal city of the central Mississippi Valley, founded in 1764, by Pierre Laclede Liguest. In 1771, and for 30 years after, the Spanish governor made his residence here. This region came into the possession of France in 1800, and into the possession of the United States by purchase in 1803. St. Louis is the great metropolis of the Southwest, possessing many unrivaled advantages, resulting principally from superior geographical position. The Mississippi River, at this point, is spanned by two immense bridges, one of which cost over $6,000,000. For its public parks, beautiful suburbs, manufactories and educational institutions this city has long been celebrated. Pop. 451,770.

St. Paul, Minn. The capital of Minnesota, and at the head of navigation for the great steamers on the Mississippi River. Is in the center of a very fertile agricultural region, and, when united with the city of Minneapolis, must be the metropolis of the great Northwest. Twenty-eight lines of railway radiate from this city, and during the summer season about 300 passenger trains arrive and depart daily. First white settler arrived here in 1832. Pop. 133,156.

Salem, Mass. Is 16 miles from Boston, in which city a large share of its population finds employment. Attained early notoriety by its effort for the extermination of witchcraft in this country. Was settled in 1626, and, excepting Plymouth, is the oldest town in New England. Though quite an extensive manufacturing point, the city is principally noted for its historical and literary associations. Pop. 30,801.

Salt Lake City, Utah. Capital of Utah Territory, and long noted as the capital seat of

STATE CAPITOL, SPRINGFIELD, ILL.

Mormonism. The city contains several unique and interesting physical features. Is laid out chess-board fashion, each street being 137 feet wide, and all the blocks 40 rods square. Shade and fruit trees have been freely planted, and on each side of every north and south street flows a rapid-running stream of pure water in an open channel. Founded July, 1847. The great Mormon Temple, a long time in building, and erected at great expense, has recently been completed. The influence of Mormonism in this city, however, is not so strong as formerly. Pop. 44,843.

San Antonio, Tex. Is an old Spanish town, settled early in the history of the country. Is 547 miles west of New Orleans, and is handsomely situated on the San Antonio River, on a branch of the Southern Pacific railroad, 256 miles from the ocean at Galveston. Has had a rapid growth since the Civil War, being an important railroad and commercial center, especially in the distribution of cotton, wool and hides. Pop. 37,673.

San Francisco, Cal. The great metropolis of the Pacific Coast, situated on the borders of the Bay of San Francisco, one of the best harbors in the world, being 40 miles long and 10 miles wide, the entrance to it being known as the Golden Gate. A Catholic mission founded here in 1776. First house of modern construction built in 1835. First survey of streets in 1839. Had a population of 1,000 in 1848. Is a place of great attraction to tourists, its Golden Gate Park, its Seal Rocks, its Chinatown, its rugged hills, its beautiful architecture, its grand hotels and charming suburbs, affording never-failing interest to the traveler. Pop. 298,997.

Savannah, Ga. Capital of Georgia, and the largest city in the State. Located on the Savannah River, 18 miles from its mouth. Like many other prosperous Southern cities, has a steadily increasing traffic and an excellent prospect for future rapid growth. Has a superior harbor, and as a cotton market is, next to New Orleans, the largest in the United States. Of its thirty churches thirteen are used by the colored people. Pop. 43,189.

Scranton, Pa. Is a great coal-mining center, and the seat of numerous iron manufactories, including locomotives, rails, mining machinery, steam boilers, stoves, carriages, edge-tools, etc. Pop. 75,215.

Seattle, Wash. A leading city of the newly organized State of Washington. Settled in 1852, by New Yorkers. Named in honor of Seattle, the most powerful Indian chief of that region. Is the location of the Washington State University, and the base of supplies for a large region inland, in which are mines, lumber camps and extensive agricultural interests. Pop. 42,837.

Sioux City, Ia. Situated in the midst of a rich agricultural region. Is an important railroad center, five great trunk lines meeting here, and reaching out from this point to all parts of the country. Is the headquarters for steamboat lines on the upper Missouri River. Has extensive stockyards in the suburbs, and in the business center numerous large jobbing houses. Pop. 37,806.

Somerville, Mass An important suburb of Boston, two miles northwest of Boston State-house. Has recently been annexed, and is now a part of the city of Boston. At the last census the following was its pop., 40,152.

Springfield, Mass. The largest city in Western Massachusetts, situated on the Connecticut River. Was settled in 1636. One of the leading railway centers of the State. Is very handsomely located, and in architectural adornment is a very beautiful city. Is very evenly balanced in educational advantages, in commercial facilities and manufacturing industries; among the leading establishments are the government armory, arsenal, and machine shops, situated on 20 acres, nearly half a mile from the city. Pop. 44,179.

Springfield, O. Is the seat of Millenburg Lutheran College. Is 80 miles north of Cincinnati, and 130 miles south of Lake Erie. Being the center of a rich agricultural region, has become a center of trade and manufacturing for the population of that portion of the State. Pop. 31,895.

Syracuse, N. Y. One of the central cities of the State of New York, so favorably situated for the gathering of State delegates to all great meetings as to make this a desirable assembling place; hence it has been called the "Convention City." The salt springs in the vicinity yield from 7,000,000 to 8,000,000 bushels of salt per annum. Is also a large manufacturing center. Pop. 88,143.

Tacoma, Wash. Situated on the Northern Pacific Railroad, at the south of Puget Sound. Has been termed the "City of Destiny," because of its rapid growth and promise for the future. Is the terminus of several great trunk lines of railway, and of several steamship lines. Its situation at the base of the Cascade and Olympic Mountains is very picturesque. Climate mild and equable. Pop. 36,006.

Taunton, Mass. Is situated on Taunton River, 35 miles south of Boston. Like the most of Massachusetts towns, is largely devoted to manufacturing, prominent among these industries being the Mason Locomotive Works, which give employment to more than 1,000 men. The Taunton Copper Company occupy an area of nearly 15 acres. Great planing and paint mills, store and hardware specialties are also among the works here. Settled in 1639. Pop. 25,448.

Terre Haute, Ind. Lies in the midst of a rich agricultural country, on the Wabash River, 73 miles west of Indianapolis. Is important as a manufacturing and railroad center. The State Normal School, the Polytechnic Institute and Providence Hospital are located here. Extensive coal mines exist in the near vicinity, aiding in the furnishing of power for the many manufactories at this point. The spacious groves and beautiful lawns around the homes, are among the conspicuous features of this city. Pop. 30,217.

Toledo, O. Is situated near the western extremity of Lake Erie. Has a fine harbor, is the northern terminus of the Miami & Erie Canal, and is the focus of 17 railroad lines, which converge at this point. Is the center of manufacturing industries, which employ over $5,000,000 capital, the annual disbursements to employes being nearly $3,000,000. Settled about 1812. Pop. 81,434.

Topeka, Kas. Capital of Kansas, is located on both banks of the Kansas River, 67 miles west of Kansas City. Prominent as a railroad center, several great trunk lines passing through the city. Is handsomely laid out, with broad streets. Contains the State asylum for the insane. Coal mines and

STATE CAPITOL, SACRAMENTO, CAL.

stone quarries in the vicinity are profitably worked. The repair shops of the Atchison, Topeka & Santa Fe Railroad Line, located here, give employment to a large force of operatives. Pop. 31,007.

Trenton, N. J. Is the capital of New Jersey, being 33 miles northeast of Philadelphia and 57 miles from New York. Has been celebrated since the days of the Revolution, for Washington's attack on the British troops, whom he surprised by crossing the Delaware River, when it was supposed, at that time, that the ice was impassable. Its near proximity to the coal fields of Pennsylvania, and its great water-power, make this a superior manufacturing center. Pop. 57,458.

Troy, N. Y. On the east bank of the Hudson River, 147 miles north of New York City. Its industrial institutions give employment to over 23,000 people in the various manufactories, which include iron, steel, stoves, linen goods, railway cars, coaches, omnibuses, etc. Is the seat of Rensselaer Polytechnic Institute, which was, for many years, the leading engineering school in the United States, and still maintains a high reputation. Settled by the Dutch, in 1752. Pop. 60,956.

Utica, N. Y. A leading central city of New York State, 180 miles northwest of New York City. Is the chief market for cheese in the United States. Clothing, boots and shoes are also among its extensive industries. One of the State lunatic asylums is located here. The Erie Canal and five great trunk lines of railroads open the commerce of the city to all portions of the country. Pop. 44,007.

Washington, D. C. Is the capital city of the United States. Situated on the east bank of the Potomac River, 185 miles from the Atlantic Ocean. Is under the immediate control of the United States government, its affairs being administered by three commissioners appointed by the President. The climate of this city is characterized by great humidity, long-continued but not excessive heat in summer, and mild winters. Snow seldom falls here, and never lies long on the ground. Contains wider streets than any other city on the globe, the avenues ranging in width from 120 to 160 feet. The entire cost of the Capitol, to date, has been $13,000,000. Pop. 230,392.

Waterbury, Conn. Situated in one of the beautiful valleys of the State. Is a city of charming residences, and is the greatest center on earth for the manufacture of brass goods. Among its other industries are the manufacture of clocks, watches, carriages, photographic supplies, stove and harness trimmings, varnish, silver-plated ware, etc. Particularly is it celebrated for its watches, furnished at so low a price as to enable nearly every youth in the country to own one. Pop. 28,646.

Wheeling, W. Va. The largest city in the State; stands on the eastern bank of the Ohio River, and on an island in the river; this island is connected with the mainland by a suspension bridge 1,010 feet in length. Is popularly known as the "Nail City," from the large number of cut nails made in its workshops. Has extensive iron and steel works, also manufactories of glass and queensware, wine from home-grown grapes, cigars, tobacco, lanterns and leather. Settled in 1769. Pop. 34,522.

Wilkesbarre, Pa. Named after John Wilkes and Colonel Barre, in 1770. Is intersected by four great railways. Rich coal mines, in the near vicinity, add much to the wealth and prosperity of the city; aiding, as they do, in the making of large incomes through receipts from anthracite coal, and in furnishing power for the manufacture, at this point, of locomotives, rope, castings, etc. Pop. 37,718.

Williamsport, Pa. Is one of the most extensive lumber marts in the country. The exceptionally picturesque location of the place, bordered by a river and surrounded by hills, together with the healthfulness of its climate, has tended to make this, in recent years, a popular summer resort. Pop. 27,132.

Wilmington, Del. The largest city in the State of Delaware. Is a railroad center of considerable importance. Its manufactories give employment to over 8,000 people, its industries including the manufacture of paper, iron and steel, ship-building, wagons, carriages, steam-engines, brick, glass, cotton, gunpowder, matches, etc. Settled by the Swedes in 1638. Pop. 61,431.

Worcester, Mass. Includes, besides its closely built section, fourteen villages of various sizes. Contains large manufacturing industries, prominent among them being iron and steel factories, foundry and machine-shop products and tools; second to the metal industries is the manufacture of boots and shoes. Pop. 84,665.

Yonkers, N. Y. A suburb of New York City, largely occupied by residents of that metropolis. Its site is very hilly, consisting of ridges forming terraces parallel to the river. Though having extensive manufactories, its importance largely consists in its being a desirable residence suburb, within an hour of the business center of New York. Pop. 32,033.

Youngstown, O. A manufacturing city, dealing largely in coal and iron. Situated on the Mahoning River, about 65 miles from Cleveland. The output from its manufactories has easy access to all parts of the country, through five great trunk lines of railroads. Pop. 33,220.

Zanesville, O. Occupies the site of one of the earliest settlements in the Northwest Territory. Became the capital of that portion of the States in 1804, and the State legislature convened here from 1810 to 1812. Is situated on the Muskingum River, which is navigable for steamers from the Ohio and Mississippi River. Pop. 21,009.

STATE CAPITOL, AUSTIN, TEXAS.

ATTRACTIVE PLEASURE RESORTS IN THE VICINITY OF CHICAGO.

Prominent among the quiet, delightful resting places are the following:

Geneva Lake, Wis. Is 86 miles from Chicago, on the Wisconsin Division of the Northwestern Railroad. Is reached in three hours by rail. Fare, $2.40. Is one of the most popular of the western resorts. The lake is eight miles long and two miles wide. Fish abound in its waters, while its shores are lined with the charming residences and the tents of those who tarry there in summer time.

Glen Ellyn, Ill. Is 22 miles west of Chicago, on the Galena Division of the Northwestern Railroad. Reached in 40 minutes. Fare, $1.15, round trip from Chicago; by monthly ticket is 13 cents each way. Location very picturesque; contains steep hills, secluded vales, fine lake for boating, several rapid-flowing springs, hundreds of acres of grove and forest, boarding houses and a large hotel surrounded by an extensive park, devoted to pleasure purposes. Delightful town for a brief sojourn; charming place for permanent home.

Oconomowoc, Wis. Is 116 miles from Chicago, on the Chicago, Milwaukee & St. Paul Railroad. Reached in 3 hours and 40 minutes. Fare, $3.40. Is situated in the beautiful Wisconsin Lake region, the town being located on an isthmus between Fowler's Lake and Lac la Belle. Is the summer home of many wealthy Chicago people, the numerous lakes in the vicinity being favorable for fishing and yachting.

St. Joseph, Mich. Is 60 miles eastward from Chicago, on the opposite side of Lake Michigan. Reached by steamer in 3½ hours. Fare on excursion boats, $1 for round trip from Chicago. Is a noted fruit region, and contains numerous hotels. Is visited by thousands of people, throughout the season, for bathing purposes; its long stretch of safe, sandy beach being admirably adapted to that use. Is rapidly growing in popularity as a pleasure resort.

A MAP PARTIALLY SHOWING THE CHICAGO RAILROAD SYSTEM.

Explanation.—The very small dimensions of the above map forbid the proper showing of many railroads which center in Chicago. Several lines between Sioux City and Fargo are not shown in the above. No space is allowed for several other lines running eastward and southward; but enough is shown to demonstrate that Chicago is already a great railroad center, having very superior transportation facilities, by rail, to all parts of the United States.

Distances, Rates of Railroad Fare, Cost of Telegraphing from Various Cities in the United States to Chicago, and Advice Concerning Railroad Tickets.

Fluctuations.—While a majority of the railroad companies, whose lines center in Chicago, have agreed to maintain the following rates of fare, it should be understood that prices are liable to change. We give the rates to Chicago from the following cities at the time of going to press.

Unlimited Tickets. With these the traveler can stop an indefinite length of time at any regular stations throughout the journey, tickets being good until used

Limited Tickets. These are sold at reduced rates in consideration of the traveler agreeing to go to his or her destination within a certain specified number of days.

Round-Trip Tickets. Travelers are advised, before purchasing a regular single-trip ticket, to inquire concerning round-trip and excursion tickets, which are often sold at a great reduction in price from regular rates.

Meals and Sleeping Berths. On most long journeys by rail, parlor and sleeping cars are attached to through trains, on which the passenger pays, over and above the regular fare, one dollar per day, and two dollars per night for use of sleeping berth. Many railroad trains also have dining-cars attached, on which meals are furnished at 75 cents each. Meals can be had at nearly all railway eating-houses, at from 50 cents to 75 cents each.

NAME OF CITY.	Population of City in 1890	Miles Distant from Chicago.	RATES OF FARE.				Limit of Days in which Ticket Must be Used.	TELEGRAPH RATES.			
			Cost of 1st Class Unlimited Ticket.	Limited to Certain Time.				Day Rates.		Night Rates.	
				Cost of 1st Class Ticket.	Cost of 2nd Class Ticket.			First 10 Words.	Each Add'al Word.	First 10 Words.	Each Add'al Word.
								Cents.	Cents.	Cents.	Cents.
Akron, O.	27,601	346	$10.30	$.9.20	$7.50	1	25	2	25	1
Albany, N. Y.	94,923	837	19.15	19.00	16.00	2	50	3	30	2
Albuquerque, N. M.	5,518	1,377	43.00	40.50	32.60	3	75	5	75	5
Alexandria, Va.	a	14,339	840	25.35	17.65	15.15	2	50	3	30	2
Allegheny, Pa.	b	105,287	478	14.00			2	25	2	25	1
Allentown, Pa.	25,228	913	22.25	18.00	15.50	2	50	3	30	2
Altoona, Pa.	30,337	585	17.50	15.50	13.50	2	50	3	30	2
Amsterdam, N. Y.	17,336	795	18.42		16.00	2	50	3	30	2
Annapolis, Md.	c	7,604	833	23.50	18.10	15.60	2	50	3	30	2
Atchison, Kan.	13,963	556	10.00				35	2	25	1
Atlanta, Ga.	d	65,533	795	22.95	21.20	19.10	2	40	2	30	2
Atlantic City, N. J.	13,055	877	24.00	19.25	16.50	2	50	3	30	2
Auburn, N. Y.	25,858	682	16.01		13.00	2	40	3	30	2
Augusta, Ga.	33,300	966	27.40	25.00	22.35	4	50	3	30	2
Aurora, Ill.	19,688	38	1.12				25	2	25	1

a Via Penn. Lines, through Washington.
b Baltimore & Ohio Railroad.

c Baltimore & Ohio, or Chicago & Erie.
d Via cities of Cincinnati and Chattanooga.

NAME OF CITY.	Population of City in 1890	Miles Distant from Chicago.	RATES OF FARE.			Limit of Days in which Ticket Must be Used.	TELEGRAPH RATES.			
			Cost of 1st Class Unlimited Ticket.	Limited to Certain Time.			Day Rates.		Night Rates.	
				Cost of 1st Class Ticket.	Cost of 2nd Class Ticket.		First 10 Words. Cents.	Each Add'al Word. Cents.	First 10 Words. Cents.	Each Add'al Word. Cents.
Austin, Tex............	14,575	987	$32.15	$31.35	$23.00	3	.60	4	40	3
Baltimore, Md.........	434,439	853	22.50	17.50	15.00	2	40	3	30	2
Bangor, Me............	19,163	1,263	30.90	28.50	25.00	4	60	4	40	3
Battle Creek, Mich....	13,197	165	4.15				25	2	25	1
Bay City, Mich........	27,839	287	8.75	7.20		1	25	2	25	1
Bayonne, N. J.........	19,033	911	22.25				50	3	30	2
Beatrice, Neb.	13,836	628	15.60	14.35		1	40	3	30	2
Belleville, Ill........	15,361	282	7.55				25	2	25	1
Biddeford, Me.........	14,443	1,128	26.83	24.50	21.50	4	60	4	40	3
Binghampton, N. Y....	35,005	739	18.15	17.00	14.75	2	40	3	30	2
Birmingham, Ala......	26,178	651	19.85	19.50	15.00	2	50	3	30	3
Bloomington, Ill......	20,484	126	3.75				25	2	25	1
Boston, Mass..........	448,477	1,020	23.65	22.00	19.00	2	50	3	30	2
Bridgeport, Conn......	48,866	968	22.93	21.15	18.15	3	50	3	30	2
Brighton, Mass........	13,000	1,019	23.65	22.00	19.00	2	50	3	30	2
Brooklyn, N. Y........	806,343	912	22.25	20.00	17.00	2	50	3	30	2
Buffalo, N. Y........ a	255,664	542	13.50	12.50	10.50	1	25	2	25	1
Burlington, Ia........	22,565	206	6.17				25	2	25	1
Burlington, Vt........	14,590	1,182	23.00		19.00	3	50	3	30	2
Cairo, Ill............	10,324	365	10.94		9.50	1	25	2	25	1
Canton, O.............	26,189	367	11.00	9.75	8.00	1	25	2	25	1
Cedar Rapids, Ia......	18,020	258	6.75				25	2	25	1
Charleston, S. C......	54,955	1,108		25.00		4	50	3	30	2
Chattanooga, Tenn.....	29,100	687	18.15	17.10	15.00	2	40	3	30	2
Chester, Pa........ b	20,226	828	24.40	18.25	15.50	2	50	3	30	2
Cheyenne, Wyo.....c	11,690	1,017	28.65	28.15		2	60	4	40	3
Cincinnati, O.........	296,908	293	8.80	8.00			25	2	25	1
Cleveland, O..........	261,353	357	10.00		8.00	1	25	2	25	1
Clinton, Ia...........	13,619	146	4.27				25	2	25	1
Columbia, S. C.....d	15,353	837	31.20	25.00	22.35	4	50	3	30	2
Columbus, Ga.........	17,303	738	24.50	23.30	17.80	3	50	3	30	2
Columbus, O..........	88,150	314	9.20	8.35	7.00	1	25	2	25	1
Concord, N. H........	17,004	1,083	24.57	22.25	19.25	3	60	4	40	3
Council Bluffs, Ia.....	21,474	488		12.50		1	35	2	25	1
Covington, Ky........	37,371	293	8.80	8.00			25	2	25	1
Cumberland, Md......	12,729	669	20.00	16.35	14.50	2	50	3	30	2
Dallas, Tex...........	38,067	991	26.95	26.65	20.25	3	60	4	40	3
Danbury, Conn.......	16,552	915	22.33	20.55	17.55	3	50	3	30	2
Davenport, Ia.........	26,872	183	5.02				25	2	25	1
Dayton, O.........e	61,220	265	8.70	7.50			25	2	25	1
Decatur, Ill..........	16,841	179	4.45				25	2	25	1
Denver, Colo..........	106,713	1,113	30.65	28.15		2	60	4	40	3
Des Moines, Ia........	50,093	357	10.15	10.00			35	2	25	1
Detroit, Mich.........	205,876	280	7.75				25	2	25	1
Dover, N. H..........	12,790	1,117	26.00	24.35	21.35	4	50	3	30	2
Dubuque, Ia..........	30,311	188	5.45				25	2	25	1
Duluth, Minn.........	33,115	477	13.55				25	2	25	1
Easton, Pa............	14,481	928	22.25	18.00	15.50	2	50	3	30	2
East St. Louis, Ill.....	15,169	282	5.75			1	25	2	25	1
Eau Claire, Wis.......	17,415	312	9.35				40	3	30	2
Elgin, Ill.............	17,823	36	1.10				25	2	25	1
Elizabeth City, N. J. f..	37,764	898	22.25	18.00	16.00	2	50	3	30	2
Elmira, N. Y.........	30,893	682	16.45	15.75	13.30	1	40	3	30	2
Erie, Pa..............	40,634	452	12.75		9.50	1	25	2	25	1
Evansville, Ind,.......	50,756	338	8.65				25	2	25	1
Fairfield, Ia..........	3,391	257	7.60				50	3	30	2
Fall River, Mass......	74,398	1,069	24.41	22.00	19.00	3	50	3	30	2
Fargo, N. D...........	5,664	745	18.48			4	50	3	30	2
Fernandina, Fla.......	2,803	1,275		25.00			60	4	40	3
Findlay, O............	18,553	234	7.15				25	2	25	3
Fitchburg, Mass.......	22,037	969	22.97	21.00	18.00	2	60	4	40	1
Fond du Lac, Wis......	12,024	148	4.45				25	2	25	1
Fort Wayne, Ind.......	35,393	148	4.45				25	2	25	1
Fort Worth, Tex.......	23,076	1,023	27.85	26.65	20.10	3	60	4	40	3
Galesburg, Ill.........	15,264	163	4.88				25	2	25	1
Galva, Ill.............	2,409	140	4.18				25	2	25	1
Galveston, Tex........	29,084	1,150	33.45	31.95	23.90	3	60	4	40	3
Geneva Lake, Wis......	2,297	85	2.40				25	2	25	4
Gettysburg, Pa..... g..	3,221	771	23.00	17.50	15.00	3	50	3	30	2
Grand Rapids, Mich...	60,278	181	5.40				25	2	25	1
Green Bay, Wis........	9,069	242	5.94				40	3	30	2
Hamilton, O..........	17,565	269	8.05	7.50		1	25	2	25	1
Hannibal, Mo.........	12,857	329	7.70	7.25		1	25	2	25	1
Harrisburg, Pa........	39,385	716	21.50	17.25	14.75	2	50	3	30	2
Hartford, Conn.......	53,230	1,011	21.99	20.50	17.50	3	50	3	30	2
Hastings, Neb.........	13,584	638	17.15	16.70		2	50	3	30	2
Haverhill, Mass.......	27,412	1,049	25.00	23.35	20.35	3	50	3	30	2

a Via Port Huron.　　b Penn. Lines.
c Via Council Bluffs.
d Via Louisville, Nashville and Atlanta.
e Cleveland, Cincinnati, Chicago & St. Louis Railroad (Big Four).

f Chicago & Grand Trunk Railroad, Niagara Falls Short Line, or Baltimore & Ohio Railroad.
g Penn. Lines, or Lake Shore & Michigan Southern Railroad.

NAME OF CITY.	Population of City in 1890.	Miles Distant from Chicago.	RATES OF FARE. Cost of 1st Class Unlimited Ticket.	Limited to Certain Time. Cost of 1st Class Ticket.	Cost of 2nd Class Ticket.	Limit of Days in which Ticket Must be Used.	TELEGRAPH RATES. Day Rates. First 10 Words.	Day Rates. Each Add'l Word.	Night Rates. First 10 Words.	Night Rates. Each Add'l Word.
Helena, Mont.	13,834	2,007	$51.50	$50.00	$36.50	4	.75	5	.60	4
Hoboken, N. J.	43,648	911	22.25	20.00	17.00	2	.50	3	.30	2
Holyoke, Mass.	35,637	945	21.69	20.00	17.00	2	.50	3	.30	2
Hot Springs, Ark.	8,086	693	20.25	18.75		2	.50	3	.30	2
Houston, Tex.	27,557	1,099	31.95	30.45	22.40	3	.50	3	.30	2
Hudson, N. Y.	9,970	846	19.81	19.66	16.66	2	.50	3	.30	2
Indianapolis, Ind.	105,436	193	5.50	5.00		1	.25	2	.25	1
Iowa City, Ia	7,016	237	6.64				.35	2	.25	1
Jackson, Mich	20,798	197	5.50				.25	2	.25	1
Jackson, Miss.	5,920	708	22.04	22.00	15.50	2	.50	3	.30	2
Jacksonville, Fla.	17,201	1,248	32.75	25.00		4	.60	4	.40	3
Jamestown, N. Y.	17,038	540	14.00	12.00	10.00	1	.35	2	.25	1
Janesville, Wis	10,836	91	2.73				.25	2	.25	1
Jefferson City, Mo.	6,742	408	11.05	9.75		1	.35	2	.25	1
Jersey City, N. J.	163,003	911	22.25	20.00	17.00	2	.50	3	.30	2
Johnstown, Pa. a	21,805	546	16.35	14.35	12.35	1	.50	3	.30	2
Joliet, Ill.	23,264	37	1.66				.25	2	.25	1
Kalamazoo, Mich.	17,853	142	4.00				.25	2	.25	1
Kansas City, Kas.	38,316	458		10.00			.30	2	.25	1
Kansas City, Mo.	132,716	458		10.00			.30	2	.25	1
Keokuk, Ia.	14,101	250	7.15				.25	2	.25	1
Kingston, N. Y.	21,261	866	20.83	20.00	17.00	2	.50	3	.30	2
Knoxville, Tenn.	22,535	503	17.00	16.00		2	.50	3	.30	2
La Crosse, Wis	25,090	280	7.86				.25	2	.25	1
Lafayette, Ind.	16,243	131	3.60				.25	2	.25	1
Lancaster, Pa. a	32,011	753	22.53	18.25	15.50	1	.50	3	.30	2
Lansing, Mich.	13,102	245	5.05				.25	2	.25	1
Leadville, Colo.	10,384	1,284		36.15		3	.60	4	.40	3
Leavenworth, Kas.	19,768	484		10.00			.35	2	.25	1
Lebanon, Pa. a	14,664	741	22.22	18.00	15.50	2	.50	3	.30	2
Lewiston, Me.	21,701	1,167	27.83	25.50	22.50	3	.60	4	.40	3
Lexington, Ky.	21,567	373		10.40		1	.30	2	.25	1
Lima, O.	15,981	208	6.25				.25	2	.25	1
Lincoln, Neb.	55,154	552	14.40	14.35		1	.40	3	.30	2
Little Rock, Ark.	25,874	627	17.85	16.35		2	.50	3	.30	2
Lockport, N. Y.	16,038	534	14.38	13.38	11.38	1	.40	3	.30	2
Logansport, Ind.	13,328	117	3.50				.25	2	.25	1
Long Branch, N. J. b	7,231	901	26.25	20.00	17.00	2	.50	3	.30	2
Los Angeles, Cal.	50,395	2,243	72.50	70.00	45.00	6	.75	5	.75	5
Louisville, Ky.	161,129	297	9.00	8.60		1	.25	2	.25	1
Lowell, Mass.	77,696	1,039	23.82	21.50	18.50	2	.50	3	.30	2
Lynn, Mass.	55,727	1,029	24.35	22.70	19.70	2	.50	3	.30	2
McKeesport, Pa.	20,741	559	14.45	12.45	10.45	1	.40	3	.30	2
Macon, Ga.	22,746	898	24.90	23.83	19.20	3	.50	3	.30	2
Madison, Wis.	13,426	138	3.92				.25	2	.25	1
Manchester, N. H.	41,126	1,068	24.21	21.89	18.89	3	.60	4	.40	3
Mansfield, O.	13,743	293	8.70	8.00	7.00	1	.25	2	.25	1
Marquette, Mich.	9,093	390	10.87				.40	3	.30	2
Memphis, Tenn. c	64,495	517	15.85	15.40	12.00	2	.40	3	.30	2
Meriden, Conn.	21,652	1,004	22.39	20.90	17.90	3	.50	3	.30	2
Milwaukee, Wis.	204,468	85	2.55				.25	2	.25	1
Mobile, Ala.	31,076	845	25.95	22.00	16.00	2	.50	3	.30	2
Montgomery, Ala.	21,833	870	22.80	20.50	15.00	2	.50	3	.30	2
Montreal, Can.	240,000	844	22.25	18.00	15.00	2	.50	3	.30	2
Muskegon, Mich.	22,702	190	5.75				.25	2	.25	1
Nashville, Tenn.	76,168	482	13.65	13.50	12.20	2	.35	2	.25	1
New Albany, Ind.	21,059	317	8.75	7.75		1	.25	2	.25	1
Newark, O. d	14,270	347	10.20	8.35	7.00	1	.25	2	.25	1
New Bedford, Mass.	40,733	1,084	24.56	22.85	19.85	3	.60	4	.40	3
New Britain, Conn. e	16,519	972	22.23	19.00	17.00	2	.50	3	.30	2
New Brunswick, N.J. a	18,603	885	25.57	19.85	17.00	1	.50	3	.30	2
New Haven, Conn.	81,298	915	22.74	21.25	18.25	2	.50	3	.30	2
New London, Conn.	13,757	1,036	23.78	22.00	19.00	2	.50	3	.30	2
New Orleans, La.	242,039	915	27.55	23.00	16.50	2	.50	3	.30	2
Newport, Ky.	24,918	293	8.80	8.00			.25	2	.25	1
Newport, R. I.	19,457	1,060	24.81	22.00	19.00	3	.50	3	.33	2
New York, N. Y.	1,515,301	912	22.25	20.00	17.00	2	.40	3	.30	2
Niagara Falls, N. Y. f	5,502	513	13.05	12.50	10.50	1	.50	3	.30	2
Norfolk, Va. a	34,871	957	32.95	23.00	20.50	3	.50	3	.30	2
Norristown, Pa. g	19,791	838	24.50	18.25	15.50	2	.50	3	.30	2
North Adams, Mass.	16,074	876	20.47	20.00	17.00	2	.50	3	.30	2
Northampton, Mass.	14,990	954	21.99	20.00	17.00	2	.60	4	.40	3
Norwich, Conn.	16,156	1,051	23.38	22.00	19.00	3	.50	3	.30	2
Omaha, Neb.	140,452	497		12.75		1	.35	2	.25	1
Oshkosh, Wis.	22,836	165	4.97				.40	3	.30	2
Oswego, N. Y.	21,842	687	16.66		14.66	1	.50	3	.30	2
Ottumwa, Ia.	14,001	281	8.43				.40	3	.30	2

a Pennsylvania Lines, or Lake Shore & Michigan Southern Railroad.
b Pennsylvania Lines and Baltimore & Ohio Railroad.
c Via Cairo and Fulton.
d Via Columbus.
e Chicago & Grand Trunk, Niagara Falls Short Line, or Chicago & Erie Railroad.
f Chicago & Grand Trunk Railroad.
g Pennsylvania Lines.

NAME OF CITY.	Population of City in 1890.	Miles Distant from Chicago.	Cost of 1st Class Unlimited Ticket.	Limited to Certain Time. Cost of 1st Class Ticket.	Cost of 2nd Class Ticket.	Limit of Days in which Ticket Must be Used.	Day Rates. First 10 Words.	Each Add'al Word.	Night Rates. First 10 Words.	Each Add'al Word.
Paducah, Ky.	12,797	400	$11.67	$11.23	$10.00	2	30	2	25	1
Passaic, N. J.	13,028	885	22.25	18.00	16.00	2	50	3	30	2
Paterson, N. J.	78,347	883	22.20	20.00	17.00	2	50	3	30	2
Pensacola, Fla....a	11,750	972	28.53	22.00	16.00	2	60	4	40	3
Peoria, Ill.	41,024	146	4.25				25	2	25	1
Petersburg, Va.	22,680?	911	27.25				50	3	30	2
Philadelphia, Pa.	1,046,964	823	24.00	18.25	15.50	2	40	3	30	2
Pittsburg, Pa.	238,617	468	14.00	12.00	10.00	1	25	2	25	1
Pittsfield, Mass.	17,281	883	20.32	20.00	17.00	2	50	3	30	2
Port Huron, Mich.	13,543	335	7.34				25	2	25	1
Portland, Me.	36,425	1,128	26.83	24.50	21.00	3	50	3	30	3
Portland, Or.	46,385	2,465	79.50	69.50	44.50	6	75	5	75	5
Poughkeepsie, N. Y.	22,206	863	20.63	20.00	17.00	2	50	3	30	2
Providence, R. I.	132,146	1,035	23.81	22.00	19.00	3	50	3	30	2
Pueblo, Colo.	24,558	1,107	30.65	28.15		2	60	4	40	3
Quebec, Can.	75,447	1,116	25.35	21.00	16.50	3	50	3	30	2
Quincy, Ill.	31,494	263	7.25				25	2	25	1
Racine, Wis.	21,014	62	1.85				25	2	25	1
Reading, Pa.	58,661	770	22.25	18.00	15.50	3	50	3	30	2
Richmond, Ind.	16,608	223	6.70	6.25		1	25	2	25	1
Richmond, Va....b	81,388	933	28.70	21.00	18.50	3	50	3	30	2
Rochester, N. Y.	133,896	599	14.52	12.38		1	40	3	30	2
Rockford, Ill.	23,584	93	2.50				25	2	25	1
Rock Island, Ill.	13,634	181	4.97				25	2	25	1
Sacramento, Cal.	26,386	2,260	72.50	70.00	45.00	6	75	5	75	5
Saginaw, Mich.	46,322	291	8.45	6.90		1	25	2	25	1
St. Joseph, Mo.	53,324	469		10.00			35	2	25	1
St. Louis, Mo.	451,770	282		6.00			25	2	25	1
St. Paul, Minn.	133,156	410	11.50				25	2	25	1
Salem, Mass....c	30,801	1,039	24.50	22.85	19.85	2	50	3	30	2
Salt Lake City, Utah.	44,843	1,566	52.50	50.00	40.00	4	75	5	60	4
San Antonio, Tex.	37,673	1,315	34.55	33.75	24.60	3	75	5	60	4
Sandusky, O....d	18,471	291	8.25		7.45	1	25	2	25	1
San Francisco, Cal.	298,997	2,411	72.50	70.00	45.00	6	75	5	75	5
Santa Fe, N. M.	6,185	1,342	41.05	38.55	31.35	3	75	5	75	5
Saratoga Springs, N. Y.	11,975	855	19.54		16.80	2	75	5	75	5
Savannah, Ga.	43,189	1,088	36.60	25.00	23.25	4	50	3	30	2
Schenectady, N. Y.	19,902	813	18.74		16.00	2	50	3	30	2
Scranton, Pa.	75,215	801	20.20	18.00	15.50	2	40	3	30	2
Seattle, Wash.	42,837	2,361	79.50	69.00	44.50	6	75	5	75	5
Sheboygan, Wis.	16,359	137	4.11				30	2	25	1
Shenandoah, Pa....e	15,944	805	22.85	18.00	15.50	2	50	3	30	2
Sioux City, Ia.	37,806	515	12.75			1	35	2	25	1
Somerville, Mass.	40,152	1,019	23.65	22.00	19.00	2	60	4	40	3
South Bend, Ind.	21,819	86	2.55				25	2	25	1
Spokane Falls, Wash...f	19,922	2,014	68.00	66.50	43.00	6	75	5	75	5
Springfield, Ill.	24,963	185	4.75				25	2	25	1
Springfield, Mass.	44,179	937	21.49	20.00	17.00	3	50	3	30	2
Springfield, Mo.	21,850	492	14.60	13.10		1	50	3	30	2
Springfield, O.	31,895	311	8.65	7.50		1	25	2	25	1
Steubenville, O.	13,394	426	13.70	11.00	9.50	1	25	2	25	1
Syracuse, N. Y.	88,143	680	16.12		13.98	1	40	3	30	2
Tacoma, Wash.	36,006	2,320	79.50	69.50	44.50	6	75	5	75	5
Tallahassee, Fla.	2,934	1,339		25.00	22.40	4	60	4	40	3
Taunton, Mass.	25,448	1,059	24.06	22.00	19.00	3	50	3	30	2
Terre Haute, Ind.	30,217	229	5.36				25	2	25	1
Toledo, O.	81,434	235	7.00		6.00	1	25	2	25	1
Topeka, Kas.	31,007	522	14.01	11.50		1	40	3	30	2
Toronto, Can.	172,800	515	12.45		11.00	1	50	3	30	2
Trenton, N. J.	57,458	855	24.80	19.05	16.30	1	50	3	30	2
Troy, N. Y.	60,956	834	19.15	19.00	16.00	2	50	3	30	2
Utica, N. Y.	44,007	745	17.18		15.04	2	50	3	30	2
Vicksburg, Miss.	13,373	753	23.35	22.00	16.50	3	50	3	30	2
Waltham, Mass.	18,707	1,009	23.65	22.00	19.00	2	60	4	40	3
Washington, D. C....g	230,392	813	22.50	17.50	15.00	2	40	3	30	2
Waterbury, Conn.	28,646	920	22.96	20.50	17.50	3	50	3	30	2
Wheeling, W. Va....g	34,522	451	14.15	11.00	9.50	1	25	2	25	1
Wichita, Kas.	23,853	744	18.65	16.15		2	50	3	30	2
Wilkesbarre, Pa.	37,718	824	19.95	18.00	15.50	2	40	3	30	2
Wilmington, Del.	61,431	849	24.75	18.00	15.50	2	50	3	30	2
Winnipeg, Man.	25,000	845	25.70		22.85	3	50	3	30	2
Winona, Minn.	18,208	297	8.62				25	2	25	1
Worcester, Mass.	84,665	985	22.71	21.00	18.00	3	50	3	30	2
Yankton, S. D.	3,670	603	15.15				60	4	40	3
York, Pa....h	20,793	744	22.28	17.50	15.00	1	50	3	30	2
Youngstown, O.	33,220	406	11.90	10.50	8.90	1	25	2	25	1
Zanesville, O....g	21,009	385	11.50	8.75	7.75	1	25	2	25	1

a Via Louisville.
b Pennsylvania Lines and Lake Shore & Michigan Southern Railroad.
c Via Boston.
d Lake Shore & Michigan Southern R. R.
e Pennsylvania Lines, or Lake Shore & Michigan Southern Railroad.
f Northern Pacific Railroad.
g Baltimore & Ohio Railroad.
h Via Pittsburg and Harrisburg.

THE FOLLOWING RULES ARE ADOPTED BY THE CHICAGO RAILROAD ASSOCIATION FOR EXCESS OF BAGGAGE, LOWER RATES BEING CHARGED ON EXCESS TO CERTAIN POINTS ON PACIFIC COAST.

Allow Free 150 pounds for each passenger holding full ticket, 75 pounds each half ticket. To find the excess baggage rate to any point, first ascertain the *lowest* first-class unlimited ticket rate to that point. Then find that rate in the table below, under the head of "Fares," and opposite such rate you will find the rate per 100 pounds. In computing charges for less than 100 pounds, multiply the number of pounds by the rate so given, divide by 100, and you have the amount to be collected. Thus, suppose the excess of baggage is 45

SAMPLES OF GENERAL BAGGAGE.

ANY PIECE OF BAGGAGE THAT WEIGHS MORE THAN 250 POUNDS WILL NOT BE ACCEPTED FOR TRANSPORTATION AS BAGGAGE ON PASSENGER TRAINS. THESE RULES ADOPTED IN 1892.

pounds and suppose the cost of ticket is $50.01, in which case the rate per 100 pounds would be $6.05. (See table.) To ascertain the cost of transporting the 45 pounds of excess, we multiply the $6.05 by 45 and the result is 27225; dividing by 100, cutting off two right-hand figures, we have 272 cents, or $2.72.

In computing charges, all weights and rates must end in 0 or 5, and in no case must a less amount than 25 cents be charged for any shipment. In the above the baggage-master would probably make the sum $2.70.

FARES.	Charge for 100 Pounds.	FARES.	Charge for 100 Pounds.	FARES.	Charge for 100 Pounds.	FARES.	Charge for 100 Pounds.
$0.05 to $1.25.$	.15	$25.86 to $26.25.$	3.15	$50.46 to $50.85.$	6.10	$75.01 to $75.45.$	9.05
1.26 " 2.10	.25	26.26 " 26.70	3.20	50.86 " 51.25	6.15	75.46 " 75.85	9.10
2.11 " 2.50	.30	26.71 " 27.10	3.25	51.26 " 51.70	6.20	75.86 " 76.25	9.15
2.51 " 2.95	.35	27.11 " 27.50	3.30	51.71 " 52.10	6.25	76.26 " 76.70	9.20
2.96 " 3.35	.40	27.51 " 27.95	3.35	52.11 " 52.50	6.30	76.71 " 77.10	9.25
3.36 " 3.75	.45	27.96 " 28.35	3.40	52.51 " 52.95	6.35	77.11 " 77.50	9.30
3.76 " 4.20	.50	28.36 " 28.75	3.45	52.96 " 53.35	6.40	77.51 " 77.95	9.35
4.21 " 4.60	.55	28.76 " 29.20	3.50	53.36 " 53.75	6.45	77.96 " 78.35	9.40
4.61 " 5.00	.60	29.21 " 29.60	3.55	53.76 " 54.20	6.50	78.36 " 78.75	9.45
5.01 " 5.45	.65	29.61 " 30.00	3.60	54.21 " 54.60	6.55	78.76 " 79.20	9.50
5.46 " 5.85	.70	30.01 " 30.45	3.65	54.61 " 55.00	6.60	79.21 " 79.60	9.55
5.86 " 6.25	.75	30.46 " 30.85	3.70	55.01 " 55.45	6.65	79.61 " 80.00	9.60
6.26 " 6.70	.80	30.86 " 31.25	3.75	55.46 " 55.85	6.70	80.01 " 80.45	9.65
6.71 " 7.10	.85	31.26 " 31.70	3.80	55.86 " 56.25	6.75	80.46 " 80.85	9.70
7.11 " 7.50	.90	31.71 " 32.10	3.85	56.26 " 56.70	6.80	80.86 " 81.25	9.75
7.51 " 7.95	.95	32.11 " 32.50	3.90	56.71 " 57.10	6.85	81.26 " 81.70	9.80
7.96 " 8.35	1.00	32.51 " 32.95	3.95	57.11 " 57.50	6.90	81.71 " 82.10	9.85
8.36 " 8.75	1.05	32.96 " 33.35	4.00	57.51 " 57.95	6.95	82.11 " 82.50	9.90
8.76 " 9.20	1.10	33.36 " 33.75	4.05	57.96 " 58.35	7.00	82.51 " 82.95	9.95
9.21 " 9.60	1.15	33.76 " 34.20	4.10	58.36 " 58.75	7.05	82.96 " 83.35	10.00
9.61 " 10.00	1.20	34.21 " 34.60	4.15	58.76 " 59.20	7.10	83.36 " 83.75	10.05
10.01 " 10.45	1.25	34.61 " 35.00	4.20	59.21 " 59.60	7.15	83.76 " 84.20	10.10
10.46 " 10.85	1.30	35.01 " 35.45	4.25	59.61 " 60.00	7.20	84.21 " 84.60	10.15
10.86 " 11.25	1.35	35.46 " 35.85	4.30	60.01 " 60.45	7.25	84.61 " 85.00	10.20
11.26 " 11.70	1.40	35.86 " 36.25	4.35	60.46 " 60.85	7.30	85.01 " 85.45	10.25
11.71 " 12.10	1.45	36.26 " 36.70	4.40	60.86 " 61.25	7.35	85.46 " 85.85	10.30
12.11 " 12.50	1.50	36.71 " 37.10	4.45	61.26 " 61.70	7.40	85.86 " 86.25	10.35
12.51 " 12.95	1.55	37.11 " 37.50	4.50	61.71 " 62.10	7.45	86.26 " 86.70	10.40
12.96 " 13.35	1.60	37.51 " 37.95	4.55	62.11 " 62.50	7.50	86.71 " 87.10	10.45
13.36 " 13.75	1.65	37.96 " 38.35	4.60	62.51 " 62.95	7.55	87.11 " 87.50	10.50
13.76 " 14.20	1.70	38.36 " 38.75	4.65	62.96 " 63.35	7.60	87.51 " 87.95	10.55
14.21 " 14.60	1.75	38.76 " 39.20	4.70	63.36 " 63.75	7.65	87.96 " 88.35	10.60
14.61 " 15.00	1.80	39.21 " 39.60	4.75	63.76 " 64.20	7.70	88.36 " 88.75	10.65
15.01 " 15.45	1.85	39.61 " 40.00	4.80	64.21 " 64.60	7.75	88.76 " 89.20	10.70
15.46 " 15.85	1.90	40.01 " 40.45	4.85	64.61 " 65.00	7.80	89.21 " 89.60	10.75
15.86 " 16.25	1.95	40.46 " 40.85	4.90	65.01 " 65.45	7.85	89.61 " 90.00	10.80
16.26 " 16.70	2.00	40.86 " 41.25	4.95	65.46 " 65.85	7.90	90.01 " 90.45	10.85
16.71 " 17.10	2.05	41.26 " 41.70	5.00	65.86 " 66.25	7.95	90.46 " 90.85	10.90
17.11 " 17.50	2.10	41.71 " 42.10	5.05	66.26 " 66.70	8.00	90.86 " 91.25	10.95
17.51 " 17.95	2.15	42.11 " 42.55	5.10	66.71 " 67.10	8.05	91.26 " 91.70	11.00
17.96 " 18.35	2.20	42.51 " 42.95	5.15	67.11 " 67.50	8.10	91.71 " 92.10	11.05
18.36 " 18.75	2.25	42.96 " 43.35	5.20	67.51 " 67.95	8.15	92.11 " 92.50	11.10
18.76 " 19.20	2.30	43.36 " 43.75	5.25	67.96 " 68.35	8.20	92.51 " 92.95	11.15
19.21 " 19.60	2.35	43.76 " 44.20	5.30	68.36 " 68.75	8.25	92.96 " 93.35	11.20
19.61 " 20.00	2.40	44.21 " 44.60	5.35	68.76 " 69.20	8.30	93.36 " 93.75	11.25
20.01 " 20.45	2.45	45.00 " 45.45	5.40	69.21 " 69.60	8.35	93.76 " 94.20	11.30
20.46 " 20.85	2.50	45.01 " 45.45	5.45	69.61 " 70.00	8.40	94.21 " 94.60	11.35
20.86 " 21.25	2.55	45.46 " 45.85	5.50	70.01 " 70.45	8.45	94.61 " 95.00	11.40
21.26 " 21.70	2.60	45.86 " 46.25	5.55	70.46 " 70.85	8.50	95.01 " 95.45	11.45
21.71 " 22.10	2.65	46.26 " 46.70	5.60	70.86 " 71.25	8.55	95.46 " 95.85	11.50
22.11 " 22.50	2.70	46.71 " 47.10	5.65	71.26 " 71.70	8.60	95.86 " 96.25	11.55
22.51 " 22.95	2.75	47.11 " 47.50	5.70	71.71 " 72.10	8.65	96.26 " 96.70	11.60
22.96 " 23.35	2.80	47.51 " 47.95	5.75	72.11 " 72.50	8.70	96.71 " 97.10	11.65
23.36 " 23.75	2.85	47.96 " 48.35	5.80	72.51 " 72.95	8.75	97.11 " 97.50	11.70
23.76 " 24.20	2.90	48.36 " 48.75	5.85	72.96 " 73.35	8.80	97.51 " 97.95	11.75
24.21 " 24.60	2.95	48.76 " 49.20	5.90	73.36 " 73.75	8.85	97.96 " 98.35	11.80
24.61 " 25.00	3.00	49.21 " 49.60	5.95	73.76 " 74.20	8.90	98.36 " 98.75	11.85
25.01 " 25.45	3.05	49.61 " 50.00	6.00	74.21 " 74.60	8.95	98.76 " 99.20	11.90
25.46 " 25.85	3.10	50.01 " 50.45	6.05	74.61 " 75.00	9.00	99.21 " 100.00	12.00

There are six centrally located railroad passenger depots in the city, designated by name and number as follows: Thus—

Depot No. 1 is known as the "Michigan Central" or "Illinois Central depot," at the eastern end of Lake street, East Side of the city.

No. 2 is known as the "Northwestern depot," corner of Wells and Kinzie streets, North Side.

No. 3 is known as the "Canal Street depot," or "Union depot," corner of Canal and Adams streets, West Side.

No. 4 is known as the "Van Buren St. depot," or "Rock Island depot," corner of Van Buren and Sherman streets, South Side.

No. 5 is known as the "Harrison street depot," or "Grand Central depot," at the corner of Harrison street and Fifth avenue, South Side.

No. 6 is known as the "Polk street depot," or "Dearborn station," corner of Polk street and Fourth avenue, South Side.

Names of Different Railroads Centering in Chicago.

Different roads are designated by single small letters, express lines by italic letters, and the direction, in which roads extend, by single capital letters; thus—

a —**Chicago & West Michigan R. R.** Runs south and east. *a*

b —**Cleveland, Cincinnati, Chicago & St. Louis R. R., Kankakee Line, "Big Four."** Runs south. *a* } Use Depot No. 1, foot of Lake St.

c —**Illinois Central Railroad.** Runs south. *a*

d —**Michigan Central R. R.** Runs south and east. *a*

e —**Galena Division, Northwestern R. R.** Runs west. *a*

f —**Milwaukee Division, Northwestern R. R.** Runs north. *a-c* } Use Depot No. 2, corner Kinzie & Wells streets.

g—**Milwaukee, Lake Shore & Western R. R.** Runs northwest.

h—**Wisconsin Division, Northwestern R. R.** Runs northwest. *a*

i —**Chicago, Alton & St. Louis R. R.** Runs southwest. *c*

j —**Chicago, Burlington & Quincy R. R.** Runs southwest. *a*

k—**Chicago & Council Bluffs Division, Chicago, Milwaukee & St. Paul R. R.** Runs northwest. *b* } Use Depot No. 3, corner Canal and Adams streets.

l —**Chicago & Milwaukee Division, Chicago, Milwaukee & St. Paul R. R.** Runs northwest. *a*

m—**Evanston Division, Chicago, Milwaukee & St. Paul R. R.** Runs north. *a*

n —**Pittsburg, Cincinnati, Chicago & St. Louis R. R., Pennsylvania Line, "Pan - Handle."** Runs south. *b*

o —**Pittsburg, Ft. Wayne & Chicago R. R., Pennsylvania Line, "Fort Wayne."** Runs south. *b*

p —**Chicago, Rock Island & Pacific R.R.** Runs southwest. *a c* } Use Depot No. 4, cor. Van Buren

q —**Lake Shore & Michigan Southern Railroad.** Runs south and east. *a-c*

r —**New York, Chicago & St. Louis R. R., Nickel Plate."** Runs southeast. *a-d* } & Sherman streets.

s —**Baltimore & Ohio R. R.** Runs southeast. *c*

t —**Chicago & Northern Pacific R. R.** Runs northwest. *e* } Use Depot No 5, corner Harrison St.

u —**Chicago, St. Paul & Kansas City R. R., "Maple Leaf."** Runs northwest. *c*

v —**Wisconsin Central R. R.** Runs northwest. *e* } and Fifth Ave.

w—**Atchison, Topeka & Santa Fe R.R.** Runs southwest. *g*

x —**Chicago & Erie R. R.** Runs southeast. *g*

y —**Chicago & Eastern Illinois R. R.** Runs south. *a y*

z —**Chicago & Grand Trunk R. R.** Runs south and east. *d* } Use Depot No. 6, Polk street and Fourth Ave.

& —**Chicago & Western Indiana R. R.** Runs south.

* —**Louisville, New Albany & Chicago R. R., "Monon Route."** Runs southeast. *a d*

† —**Niagara Falls Short Line and Canadian Pacific.** *f*

‡ —**Wabash, St. Louis & Pacific R. R.** Runs southwest. *f b*

§ —**West Shore R. R.** Runs south and east. *d*

a Used by American Express; Office, 72 Monroe St. *b* Adams Express, 180 Dearborn St. *c* United States Express, 89 Washington St. *d* National Express, 138 Adams St. *e* Northern Pacific Express, 138 Adams St. *f* Pacific Express, 89 Washington St. *g* Wells, Fargo & Co. Express, 154 Dearborn Street.

Location of General Ticket Offices and Freight Depots in Chicago.

Railroad tickets may be obtained at passenger depot ticket windows, open 30 minutes before departure of each passenger train, and at general ticket offices, usually open from 7.30 A. M. to 6 P. M.,* located as follows, the name of each railway line being designated by small letters of the alphabet, as shown above:

R.R. Ticket Office.	Freight Depot.	R.R. Ticket Office.	Freight Depot.
.a— 67 Clark street.	193 Clark street.	..p—104 Clark St.	Polk and Sherman streets
.b—234 Clark St.	Foot of South Water St.	..q— 66 Clark St.	Polk St. and Pacific Ave.
..c—194 Clark St.	Foot of South Water St.	..r— 77 Clark St.	Taylor and Clark streets.
.d— 67 Clark St.	Foot of South Water St.	..s—193 Clark St.	Fifth avenue and Polk St.
..e—208 Clark St.	N. Water and Dearborn Sts.	..t—205 Clark St.	Fifth avenue and Polk St.
.f—208 Clark St.	N. Water and Dearborn Sts.	..u—188 Clark St.	Fifth avenue and Polk St.
.g—197 Clark St.	Canal and Kinzie streets.	..v—205 Clark St.	Harrison and Franklin Sts.
.h—208 Clark St.	Harrison and Canal streets.	..w—212 Clark St.	Twelfth and State streets.
..i—195 Clark St.	2 West Van Buren street.	..x—107 Clark St.	Clark and Fourteenth Sts.
..j—211 Clark St.	Harrison and Canal streets	.y—204 Clark St.	Twelfth and Clark Sts.
.k—207 Clark St.	74 North Union street.	.z—103 Clark St.	Twelfth St. and Third Ave.
..l—207 Clark St.	74 North Union street.	..&—General Offices, Polk street and Fourth Ave.	
m—207 Clark St.	74 North Union street.	..*— 73 Clark St.	Taylor and Fourth Ave.
·n— 65 Clark St.	Clinton St. and Carroll Ave.	† ‡—201 Clark St.	Third Ave. and Twelfth St.
..o—248 Clark St.	2 West Madison street.	..§—197 Clark St.	23 Pacific avenue.

* Ticket offices, except at depots, are closed, Sundays; and on Saturdays one hour earlier than usual.

For the purpose of being easily understood, the distances here shown, between depots, are given in round numbers of a mile and fraction of a mile, and are a little more than actual distance.

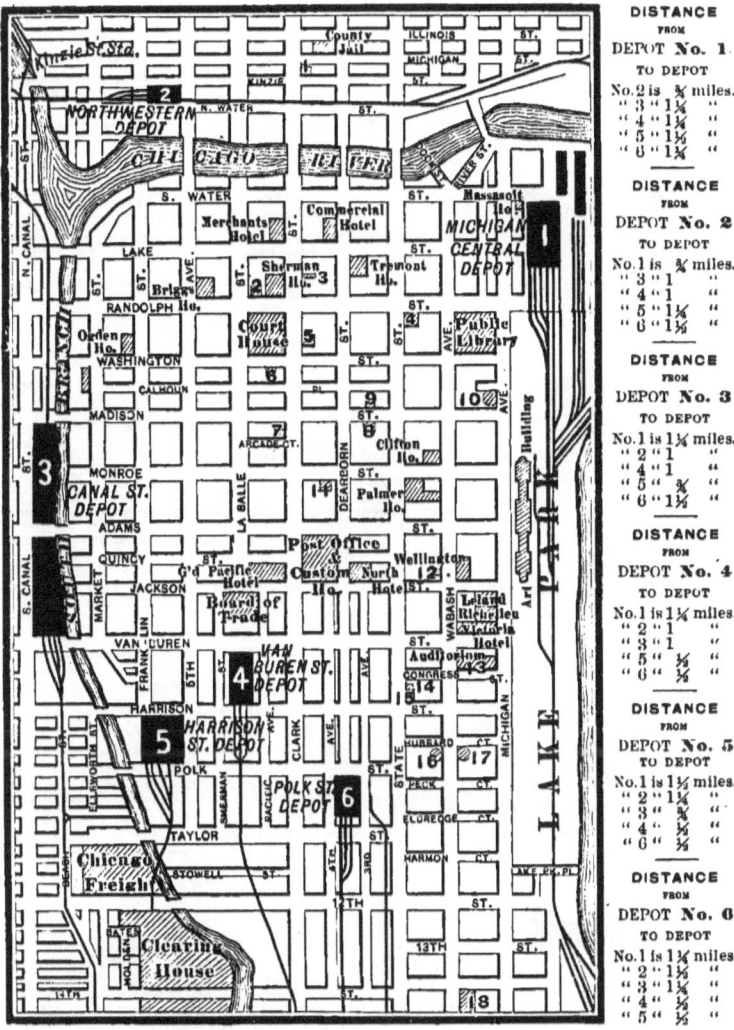

DISTANCE
FROM
DEPOT No. 1.
TO DEPOT
No. 2 is ¾ miles.
" 3 " 1¼ "
" 4 " 1¼ "
" 5 " 1½ "
" 6 " 1¾ "

DISTANCE
FROM
DEPOT No. 2
TO DEPOT
No. 1 is ¾ miles.
" 3 " 1 "
" 4 " 1 "
" 5 " 1¼ "
" 6 " 1½ "

DISTANCE
FROM
DEPOT No. 3
TO DEPOT
No. 1 is 1¼ miles.
" 2 " 1 "
" 4 " 1 "
" 5 " ¾ "
" 6 " 1½ "

DISTANCE
FROM
DEPOT No. 4
TO DEPOT
No. 1 is 1¼ miles.
" 2 " 1 "
" 3 " 1 "
" 5 " ½ "
" 6 " ½ "

DISTANCE
FROM
DEPOT No. 5
TO DEPOT
No. 1 is 1½ miles.
" 2 " 1¼ "
" 3 " ¾ "
" 4 " ½ "
" 6 " ½ "

DISTANCE
FROM
DEPOT No. 6
TO DEPOT
No. 1 is 1¾ miles
" 2 " 1½ "
" 3 " 1½ "
" 4 " ½ "
" 5 " ½ "

R. R. Passenger Depots, Large, Centrally Located Hotels, and Places of Amusement.

The principal places of general interest are easily found on the above map. The location of well-known places of public amusement are designated by figures, thus:

		This map represents an area of a little less than two miles in length and a little over one mile in width, being the center of retail trade.
1. Clark St. Theater.	7. Kohl & Middleton's.	13. Auditorium.
2. Hooley's Theatre.	8. McVicker's Theater.	14. Park Theater.
3. Olympic Theater.	9. Madison St. Theater.	15. People's Theater.
4. Central Music Hall.	10. Panorama of Fire.	16. Gettysburg.
5. Grand Opera House.	11. Columbia Theater.	17. Niagara Falls.
6. Chicago Opera House.	12. Eden Musee.	18. Libby Prison.

The clearing house, shown on the map, is the location of the proposed terminal of all freight lines entering Chicago. This space is to be occupied by a ten-story fire-proof warehouse, covering thirty-two acres, for transfer and storage purposes. This will abolish nearly all heavy teaming on the streets, as goods, heretofore hauled by teams to wholesale stores, and from one depot to another, will be transferred in this enclosure, under cover, directly from one railway to another.

No 1. Five-Glass Landau.
Well Lighted. Seats for Four.
Fine for Sight-seeing in All Kinds of
Weather.

Information about Omnibuses.

Before arrival in Chicago, an omnibus agent, carrying a large package of brass checks attached to leather straps, will call upon each traveler and afford the opportunity to purchase tickets for conveyance to the hotels, or transfer to other depots. The charges are, for each passenger, including trunk, 50 cents; for each additional trunk, 25 cents. Passengers should know definitely, and state clearly, where they are going. The agent, after receiving pay for the same, will give the passenger transportation tickets by omnibus, will take checks from the traveler, and make such record of the matter as will secure a very prompt delivery of baggage to the destination.

No. 2. Full-Front Hansom.
Well Lighted. Two Seats.
Private and Roomy for Satchel
and Hand Baggage.

City Ordinance Regulating Charges for the Use of Hacks and Cabs with Two Horses.

Between Depots. For conveying one or two passengers from one railroad depot to another depot—*one dollar.*

One Mile, One Dollar. For conveying one or two passengers not exceeding one mile—*one dollar.*

One Dollar and a Half. For conveying one or two passengers any distance, over one mile and less than two miles—*one dollar and fifty cents.* For each additional passenger—*fifty cents.* For one or two persons, any distance over two miles—*two dollars;* each additional passenger—*fifty cents.*

No. 3. Victoria Hansom.
Easy, Graceful. Two Seats.
Popular with Couples who Wish a
Driver in Front.

Charge for Children. Children between five and fourteen years of age, half above rates; children less than five years of age, no charge.

Charge per Day. For the use per day of any hackney coach or other vehicle, drawn by two horses or other animals, with one or more passengers—*eight dollars.*

Charge by the Hour. For the use of any such carriage or vehicle by the hour, with one or more passengers, with the privilege of going from place to place and stopping as often as may be required, as follows: For the first hour—*two dollars;* for each additional hour or part of an hour—*one dollar.*

No. 4. Hotel Omnibus.
From Railroad Stations to Different
Hotels, and from One Depot
to Another.

Rates for One-Horse Vehicles.

One Mile. One mile or fraction thereof, for each passenger, for the first mile—*twenty-five cents*

More than One Mile. One mile or fraction thereof for any distance after first mile, for one or more passengers—*twenty-five cents.*

Charge by the Hour. For the first hour—*seventy-five cents.* For each quarter-hour additional after first hour—*twenty cents.* For service outside of city limits and in the parks, for the first hour—*one dollar.*

No. 5. Side-Bar Buggy.
Livery—Seats for Two Persons.
Much Used in Private Riding about
the City.

Expressmen's Charges. Should there be only baggage to be conveyed, expressmen, generally in attendance near depots, will transport the same for *fifty cents.* ☞ Make record and keep number of express wagon until baggage is delivered.

No. 6. Coupe.
Livery—Used in Making Calls.
Quiet, Elegant. Much in Demand by
Fashionable People.

Where Hacks Are To Be Found.

Nos. 1, 2, 3, 4, herewith, and 9, 10, 11, and 12, on opposite page, are usually in waiting at depots, hotels, places of amusement, and designated places where hacks are allowed to stand, and charges are the same in each kind of vehicle, excepting omnibuses and where two horses are used.

No. 7. Phaeton.
Livery—Seats for Four Persons.
Comfortable. Roomy.
Used for Deliberate Sight-seeing.

No. 8. Later Style Omnibus.
Used in General Transportation to Hotels and Depots.
Accommodates Fourteen Persons, is Very
Genteel and Richly Furnished.

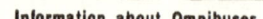

Information about Baggage.

Every passenger shall be allowed to have conveyed upon each vehicle, without charge, his ordinary traveling baggage, not exceeding in any case one trunk, and 25 pounds of other baggage. For every additional package, where the whole weight of baggage is over 100 pounds, if conveyed to any place within the business district, the driver shall be permitted to charge *fifteen cents*. Hacks and cabs also transport, without extra charge, the usual personal baggage. While the rates here given are explicit, and the distances to various parts of the city are clearly shown in this guide, it is usually safest to have an understanding, before entering a cab, as to what the charge is to be.

No. 9. Leather-Top Landau.
Private; Easy; Four Seats.
Much Used for Transportation and Funerals.

The Law Requires that the Following Information should be Posted in All One-Horse Cabs.

Twenty-five Cents. One mile or less, for each passenger—*twenty-five cents*. Each additional mile or fraction thereof, one or two passengers—*twenty-five cents*.

No Charge for Short Stops. For one stop or wait of not over five minutes no charge will be made. For over five minutes, or more than one stop or wait, *ten cents* will be charged for each ten minutes or part thereof.

No. 10. English Hansom.
Easy; Affords Fine View.
Convenient, Private, and Popular with the Public.

Charge for Packages. Packages too large to be carried inside will be charged *ten cents*.

Seventy-five Cents. For one or two persons, per hour, within four-mile limit—*seventy-five cents*. For each quarter-hour additional, or fraction thereof—*twenty cents*.

Outside Four-Mile Limit. For one or two persons per hour outside four mile limit, also Lincoln Park—*one dollar*. For each quarter-hour additional, or fraction thereof—*twenty-five cents*.

No. 11. Brougham.
Easy; Light; Stylish.
Private, Roomy, Comfortable and Much Used.

When Long Stops Are Made. When a continuous stop of more than fifteen minutes is made, the charge will be at the rate of *one dollar* per hour.

Definite Arrangement Should Be Made.

Must Be Understood. When service is desired by the hour, it must be so stated at the time of engaging the cab, otherwise the distance rate will be charged.

No. 12. Landaulet.
Popular in Fine Weather, and A Occasions when it is Desirable to See and Be Seen.

Hour Engagements. When the cab is discharged at a distance of over half a mile from the stand, the time necessary to return to the stand will be charged for.

Time Engagements. No time engagements will be made for less than the price for one hour.

In Case of Trouble. Should the driver overcharge, and be unwilling to settle amicably, the passenger should call one of the uniformed policemen, generally in the near vicinity of the depot, and explain circumstances. It is the duty of city officials to guard the interests of strangers while in the city. ☞Take number of hack driver and policeman.

No. 13. Top Surrey.
Livery—Seats for Four Persons.
Is Open, Light and Much in Demand for Family Use.

Where Special Carriages Are Obtained.

Nos. 5, 6 and **7** on the opposite page, and **Nos. 13, 14** and **16** herewith, are kept in readiness to let in the livery stables, in fine order, at prices similar, or slightly higher than hack rates, the terms being learned at the establishments where the carriages are for hire.

No. 14. Victoria.
Livery—Seats for Two Persons.
Is Graceful, Easy, Favorable for Sight-seeing.

No. 15. Palace Car.
Doors Open Out. Can Accommodate Five Persons. Fine, but yet Undergoing Trial.

No. 16. Tally-Ho.
Livery—Convenient for Twelve or more Persons. Delightful for Coaching, Picnicing and General Outing.

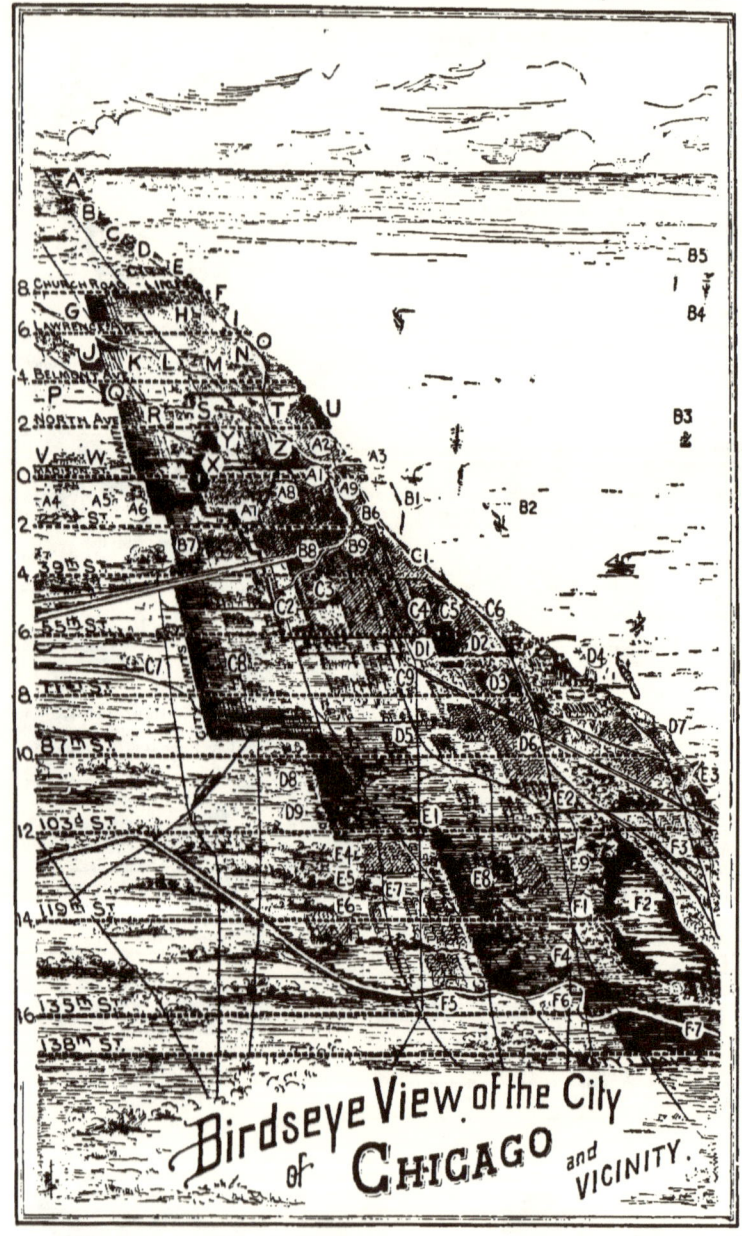

Showing Location of Principal Streets that are Two Miles Apart.

Beginning at Madison Street, on the left side of the page, will be found numbers indicating the streets that are two miles distant from each other, northward and southward from Madison Street. Letters and figures, in the above illustration, indicate important localities described on the opposite page.

The location of the following places, in or near the city of Chicago, is indicated by the letters seen in the bird's-eye view upon the opposite page.

A Highland Park.	X Garfield Park.	B6 Lake Front Park.	D6 Grand Crossing.
B Glencoe.	Y Humboldt Park.	B7 Lawndale.	D7 Cheltenham B'ach.
C Winnetka.	Z North Branch	B8 Ill. & Mich. Canal.	D8 St. Mary's Cemetery.
D Evanston.	Chicago River.	B9 South Branch Chicago River.	
E Calvary Cemetery.	A1 Wolf's Point.		D9 Evergreen Park.
F North City Limits.	A2 North Side.	C1 Douglas Mon'm'nt.	E1 Washington H'hts.
G Norwood Park.	A3 Chicago River.	C2 Western Avenue Boulevard.	E2 Burnside.
H Rosehill Cemetery.	A4 Waldheim Cemetery.		E3 Calumet Harbor.
I Edgewater.		C3 Chicago Stock Yards.	E4 Mount Greenwood Cemetery.
J Cook Co. Insane Asylum & Poorhouse.	A5 Altenheim.	C4 Grand Boulevard.	E5 Mt. Olivet Cemetery.
	A6 Grant Locomotive Works.	C5 Drexel Boulevard.	
K Irving Park.	A7 Douglas Park.	C6 Hyde Park.	E6 Mount Hope Cemetery.
L Avondale.	A8 Jefferson Park.	C7 Transfer Railway Yards.	
M Gross Park.	A9 Business Center of Chicago.		E7 Morgan Park.
N Graceland Cem'ery.		C8 Chicago Lawn.	E8 Roseland.
O Argyle Park.	B1 Government Pier.	C9 Englewood.	E9 Pullman.
P River Park.	B2 Lake Michigan.	D1 Washington Park.	F1 Kensington.
Q Mont Clair.	B3 Toward St. Joseph, Mich.	D2 Midway Plaisance.	F2 Lake Calumet.
R Galewood.		D3 Oakwoods Cemetery.	F3 South Chicago.
S Humboldt Boul.	B4 Toward Grand Haven, Mich.		F4 Gardner's Park.
T Deering.		D4 World's Fair Grounds.	F5 Blue Island.
U Lincoln Park.	B5 Toward Muskegon, Mich.		F6 Riverdale.
V Oak Park.		D5 Auburn Park.	F7 Calumet River.
W Austin.			

EARLY HISTORY OF CHICAGO.

On the opposite page is seen the general contour of the city. Originally settled near the mouth of the Chicago River (see locality on opposite picture, a little north of east end of Madison Street), its area has been extended until it includes a range of a little over 24 miles from north to south, and in some places a distance of 10 miles in width.

Of the aboriginal history of this region nothing is known. While groves of timber skirted the lake shore and the branches of the river, it is probable that for centuries the red men had lighted their fires and had annually carried devastation over great areas of land to such an extent that a general growth of trees, in this portion of the country, was impossible. Hence the boundless prairies of the Great

Original Site of Chicago, looking from the Lake.

West, over which roamed peacefully disposed Indians, up to the seventeenth century, at which time our history begins.

Jacques Marquette, a talented and devoted priest of the Roman Catholic faith, a native of Laön, in Picardy, and Louis Joliet, a native of Quebec, who was educated for the priesthood but afterwards became a fur-trader, discovered in 1673, while on a voyage of exploration, the Desplaines and Chicago Rivers. In the high waters of that period the rivers evidently seemed as one, and were named by them Checagou Portage, the name Checagou, in the language of the Illinois Indians, signifying strong smell, or onions, great numbers of the latter growing wild on the river banks at that time; the Chicago River and its banks at that period being supposed to resemble the above illustration. Marquette contracted a malarial fever, and died in 1675, after having established his religion among the Indians. La Salle was subsequently the most prominent explorer in the Northwest, and through his efforts and those of his successors, many Catholic missions were established throughout this region, among the different tribes of Indians.

The first permanent settler in Chicago was a fugitive slave from San Domingo, named Point De Sable, who engaged in profitable business near the mouth of the Chicago River, in the purchase of furs from the Indians, in 1779. De Sable sold his business to a Frenchman named Le Mai, and removed to Peoria, where he soon after died. Le Mai continued further trading with much profit to himself and the little hamlet, which was beginning to attain importance, up to 1804, at which time he sold his premises and his business.

The United States Government having, through previous purchase from the Indians, obtained six miles square of ground here, resolved to construct a fort at this point, and in accord with that purpose a sloop bearing provisions, ammunition, furniture, etc., arrived at the mouth of the river and discharged its cargo, July 4, 1803. At that time the Chicago settlement consisted of three rude huts, occupied by French fur-traders, their Indian wives, and a number of half-breed children, but the rumor of the arrival of the sloop having spread, nearly 2,000 Indians were present when the little belongings of the ship were transferred to small boats and rowed up the river, which was partially filled with sand, weeds and driftwood, to the elevated point where the fort was to be erected; the work was completed in 1804.

During the war between the English and the United States, in 1812, many tribes of Indians had been aroused to warfare against the white settlers. It was at that time that trouble began among the Indians surrounding Fort Dearborn. So serious became the danger that it was decided to evacuate the fort, which was done on the morning of August 15, 1812, at which time prior to leaving, the fort contained a garrison of about 65 men, several friendly Miami Indians, the wives and children of officers,

Old Fort Dearborn, Built in 1804, near corner River Street and Michigan Avenue.

soldiers and settlers—in all about 125 persons. Leaving the fort, which stood in the vicinity of the south end of Rush Street Bridge, the little band, headed by the Miamis, and led by Captain Wells, one of the bravest of the number, took their way southward along the beach of the lake, there being to the westward, a short distance back from the water, a range of sand hills. The hope of the fleeing whites was that they might escape the vigilance of the Indians and be able to reach Fort Wayne, Ind., where safety would be assured. As they went out from Fort Dearborn, however, their movements were closely watched by a large force of Indians, who kept even pace with them to the westward of the sand ridge, and, when nearly opposite what is now the foot of Twelfth Street, they were attacked by the savages and two-thirds of their number killed. Among those who escaped was John Kinzie, who returned to find his family, who were living outside of the fort, uninjured. The massacre broke up the settlement, the fort being completely destroyed and some of the homes of the settlers burned to the ground. The fort was rebuilt in 1816, on the site where the first had been, and was similar in appearance; we here give a view of it.

Four years after the destruction of the first fort, upon the rebuilding of the second, John Kinzie, with his family, returned. The home that he bought of Le Mai, improved and occupied in 1804, which he had surrounded with numerous ornamental trees prior to the destruction of the fort, still remained, and made a very comfortable home, much superior in

John Kinzie's House, First Family Residence in Chicago, 1810.

its accommodations to many homes of the pioneers in those days, and was the first habitation entitled to the name of dwelling built in Chicago.

This house was located near the forks of the river, on the north side, near the present Kinzie Street, and faced south towards the fort, a ferry-boat frequently plying between the north side and the fort, across the river, at that time.

Upon the rebuilding of the fort, in 1816, when a stronger garrison was established and greater security assured to the new settlers, the little Chicago hamlet thereafter began to grow, a favorite locality for settlement being Wolf's Point, on the south, west and north sides, at the junction of the north and south branches of the Chicago River. The growth was, however, very slow. Upon the arrival of Gurdon S. Hubbard, in 1818, besides the garrison, and Indians outside, there were only the Kinzie and Ouilmette families living in Chicago; and the white population did not exceed half a dozen families at any time up to 1827, when Congress made a grant of land to aid in the construction of the Illinois River and Lake Michigan Canal.

Fort Dearborn as Rebuilt in 1816, corner River Street and Michigan Avenue.

In 1821, Chicago and its environs were surveyed and laid out in government sections, each being one mile square, and containing 640 acres. In 1829, Chicago was surveyed and platted into village lots, and in 1830 the first map of the place was published—62 years ago at this writing, 1892. This was done at the expense of the state, for the purpose of selling lots and applying the proceeds in the building of the canal, an act for the construction of which had been secured in 1827, by Hon. Daniel P. Cook, from whom Cook County was named. This map, engraved on stone, was made at St. Louis, and was recorded at Peoria,

Sauganash Hotel, corner Lake and Market Streets, in 1833.

at that time the county seat of the region in which Chicago was located.

The earliest mention of Chicago in any official local records was in September 2, 1823, being an order for an election to be held at the house of John Kinzie, for the purpose of choosing a major and company-officers, probably for the military force here at that time.

The first justice of the peace was John Kinzie, appointed in 1825. It may be proper to remark here, that great credit is due to Mr. Kinzie and his family for the general peace and prosperity enjoyed by the little Chicago settlement, in the early years when difficulties with the Indians were common.

Chicago in 1833, showing Entrance to Chicago River.

Born in Quebec, in 1763, he was 41 years old, and a silversmith in Detroit, Mich., when he resolved to make Chicago his future home. Acting upon this resolution, he packed his earthly possessions upon three horses, his wife riding one, a daughter another, and he riding the third; baby John H. Kinzie, then six months old, being carried in a swaddling bag hung on the horn of the saddle. Thus equipped, the family followed an Indian trail from Detroit through Niles and St. Joseph, Mich., and around the southern extremity of Lake Michigan to the infant Chicago settlement, where they arrived in 1804. Soon after their arrival Mr. Kinzie purchased the cabin owned by Le Mai, and succeeded to his business as a dealer in furs, while he continued his trade as a silversmith, his patrons being the Indians, whose bows, arrows, guns, flint-locks and jewelry he kept in repair, endearing himself to his Indian neighbors by his even temper, his handicraft and his kindly advice. He died of apoplexy January 6, 1828, at the age of 65, in the brick building attached to Fort Dearborn and used as officers' quarters, while on a visit to his son-in-

Green Tree Hotel, Northeast corner Canal and Lake Streets, 1833.

law, Dr. Wolcott, who resided there at the time. He was buried in the military grounds south of the fort, from which place his remains were ultimately removed to Graceland, where they now lie. His son, John H. Kinzie, became an influential and honored citizen, who died on board the cars, near Pittsburg, June 21, 1865, very suddenly, while in the act of giving alms to a poor woman. John H. had one brother, Robert A., who became a paymaster in the army at Chicago, and died in 1873; a sister, Eleanor, who married Alexander Wolcott, an

Lighthouse and Block-house, last of Fort Dearborn, in 1857.

Indian agent; a sister, Maria, who married General Hunter, and a step-sister, who became Mrs. Helm.

In 1830, at the time of the issuance of the first Chicago map, the city limits were included within the territory bounded by the streets now known as Madison, State, Kinzie and Halsted. Cook County was organized in 1831. A severe visitation of cholera came in 1832. In that year Lake Street was laid out, and the first public religious worship was held in a log hut, constructed for that purpose. A post-office and weekly mail were established in 1833; and during the same year the Chicago Democrat, published by John Calhoun, came into existence. At that time the Sauganash Hotel, a log hut at the corner of Lake and Market Streets, had been enlarged by Mark Beaubien into a two-story building, with green blinds.

Drawbridge across Chicago River, at Dearborn Street, in 1834.

The primitive conditions, as late as 1834, may be understood when we are informed that, on July 11 of that year the schooner Illinois, the first large vessel that ever entered the Chicago River, sailed into the harbor amid great rejoicing, the sand-bar having been washed away by the freshet of the previous spring; and also that, in a grove of timber which stood at the corner of Market and Jackson Streets that year, a wild black bear was killed, and in the same neighborhood, in one day, a wolf hunt resulted in the killing of 40 of those animals, while wild ducks could be shot from the Tremont House on Dearborn Street. At this time, however, a drawbridge had been con-

Clark Street, with its Irregular Sidewalks, in 1867.

structed across the river at Dearborn Street, the first Tremont House had been built, and the village had had 1,200 people, three houses for public worship, an academy, infant school and other schools.

John Wentworth became the owner of the Democrat in 1836. At that time, and 12 years previously, Wolf's Point had been the principal place of settlement of Chicago residents.

The Green Tree, the first building constructed for hotel purposes, located at the corner of Lake and Canal Streets, was built by John H. Kinzie. It was subsequently known

as the Lake Street House, and was finally occupied as a saloon and private dwelling. The population of 200, in 1833, had now grown, in 1836, to 3,820, and during this year 450 vessels had arrived at this port.

The city was incorporated and the first city election held in 1837, John H. Kinzie being the Whig candidate for mayor, and William B. Ogden the Democratic candidate. The election was spirited, on purely political grounds, and resulted in the election of William B. Ogden

Cow kicking over a lamp, while being milked, in O'Leary's barn on DeKoven Street: alleged cause of the great Chicago Fire. This illustration is taken from Andreas' "History of Chicago."

by a vote of 469 to 237 for Mr. Kinzie. The total vote was 706, divided as follows: South Division, 405; North, 204; West, 97.

From 1837, through the successive decades, the growth of the city was rapid, increasing in number of inhabitants from 70, in 1830, to 4,853, in 1840. The Illinois & Michigan Canal was completed in 1848. The Galena & Chicago Union Railroad was completed to the westward as far as Elmhurst in 1849, and made the beginning of the immense railroad system now radiating widely in the West. The population had reached 29,963 in 1850. Preliminary work for the tunneling under the Chicago River was begun in 1853. The public schools were graded and classified in 1854. Arrangements were made in 1856 for raising the grade of the streets of the city eight feet. An iron swing bridge was placed at Madison Street in 1857. A street railroad on State Street, from Madison to Twenty-second Street, was opened in 1859. The population had increased to 112,172 in 1860; had reached 298,977 in 1870, and was rapidly augmenting when, on the evening of October 8, 1871, the great fire, originating in a cow stable on the north side of De Koven Street, a little east of Jefferson, and fanned by a terrific dry wind blowing from the west at the time, spread

Space Burned Over by the Great Chicago Fire.—From near Harrison Street to Fullerton Avenue. Area, 1x3¼ miles.

eastward and northward with such rapidity as to burn over, within a few hours, an area of 2,100 acres, thickly covered with buildings, causing 300 deaths, the destruction of 2,400 stores and factories, nearly 18,000 buildings, and rendering homeless 100,000 people, making a direct money loss of $192,000,000, and from stoppage of business and otherwise, a total loss of $290,000,000, which was partially repaid to the losers by $44,000,000 of insurance and $4,200,000 in contributions which came from all parts of the world. This immense conflagration and loss of property proved to be an untold blessing to the city, Chicago being soon fully restored, with the addition of all the modern improvements in architecture.

WILLIAM B. OGDEN.
1ST MAYOR.
Elected.....1837.
Democrat.

BUCKNER S. MORRIS.
2ND MAYOR.
Elected....1838.
Whig.

BENJ. W. RAYMOND.
3RD MAYOR.
First Elected..1839.
Whig.

ALEXANDER LOYD.
4TH MAYOR.
Elected....1840.
Democrat.

F. C. SHERMAN.
5TH MAYOR.
First Elected .1841.
Democrat.

ALSON S. SHERMAN.
7TH MAYOR.
Elected......1844.
Democrat.

Names, Places and Dates of Birth, and Politics of Mayors of Chicago.

NAME.	Where Born.	When Born.
William B. Ogden	Walton, N. Y....	June 15,1805
Buckner S. Morris	Augusta, Ky.....	Aug. 19,1800
Benj.W.Raymond	Rome, N. Y.. ...	... 1801
Alexander Loyd..	....	....
Fr'cis C. Sherman	Newton, Conn	 1805
Benj.W.Raymond	Rome, N. Y......	 1801
Augustus Garrett	New York, N. Y..	....
Alson S. Sherman	Barre, Vt........	Apr. 21, 1811
Augustus Garrett	New York, N. Y..	....
John P. Chapin..	....	....
James Curtiss....	New York, N. Y..	....
Jas. H.Woodworth	New York, N. Y..	....
James Curtiss....	New York, N. Y..	....
Walter S. Gurnee	Haverstraw,N.Y.	 1813
Charles M. Gray..	New York, N. Y..	....
Isaac L. Milliken.	....	....
Levi D. Boone...	Lexington, Ky...	Dec. 8, 1808
Thomas Dyer....	Canton, Conn....	Jan. 13, 1805
John Wentworth.	Sandwich, N. H..	Mar. 5, 1815
John C. Haines...	Deerfield, N Y...	May 26, 1818
John Wentworth.	Sandwich, N. H..	Mar. 5, 1815
Julian S. Rumsey	....	....
Fr'cis C. Sherman	Newton, Conn....	 1805
John B. Rice.....	Easton, Ind......	May 28, 1809
Roswell B. Mason	N'w Hartf'rd,N.Y	Sept.19,1805
Joseph Medill....	St. John's, N. B..	April 6, 1823
Harvey D. Colvin	Herkimer, N. Y..	Dec. 18, 1814
Monroe Heath...	Enfield Cen.,N H.	March.. 1827
C. H. Harrison...	Lexington, Ky...	Feb. 15, 1825
John A. Roche....	Utica, N. Y......	Aug. 12,1844
DeWitt C. Cregier	New York, N. Y..	June 1, 1829
H. Washburne...	Galena, Ill.......	Nov. 11, 1852

AUGUST. GARRETT.
6TH MAYOR.
First Elected..1843.
Democrat.

JOHN P. CHAPIN.
8TH MAYOR.
Elected....1846.
Whig.

J. H. WOODWORTH.
10TH MAYOR.
First Elected..1848.
Democrat.

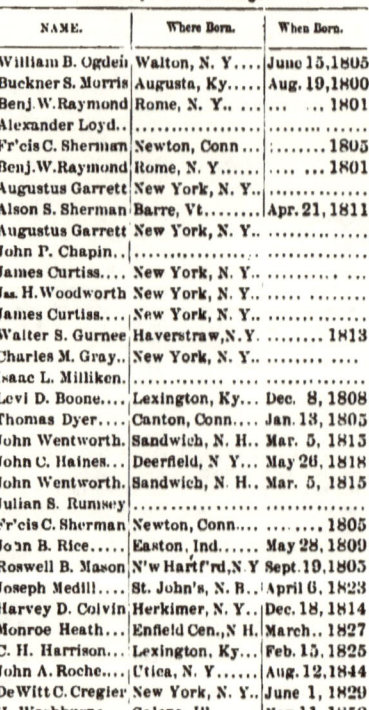

JAMES CURTISS.
9TH MAYOR.
First Elected..1847.
Democrat.

WALT. S. GURNEE.
11TH MAYOR.
First Elected..1851.
Democrat.

CHARLES M. GRAY.
12TH MAYOR.
Elected....1853.
Democrat.

ISAAC L. MILLIKEN.
13TH MAYOR.
Elected....1854.
Democrat.

LEVI D. BOONE.
14TH MAYOR.
Elected....1855.
American.

THOMAS DYER.
15TH MAYOR.
Elected....1856.
Democrat.

JOHN WENTWORTH.
16TH MAYOR.
First Elected..1857.
Republican.

JOHN C. HAINES.
17TH MAYOR.
First Elected..1858.
Republican.

JULIAN S. RUMSEY.
18TH MAYOR.
Elected....1861.
Republican.

JOHN B. RICE.
19TH MAYOR.
First Elected..1865.
Republican.

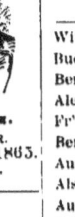

JOSEPH MEDILL.
21ST MAYOR.
Elected......1871.
Republican.

MONROE HEATH.
23RD MAYOR.
Elected....1876.
Republican.

Chicago Mayors; their Names, Occupations, Terms of Office, and Ages When Elected.

NAME.	Occupation.	Age When Elected.	No. of Years Served.
William B. Ogden	Real Estate.........	..31	.1..
Buckner S. Morris	Lawyer.............	.37	.1..
Benj.W.Raymond	Merchant	..38	.1..
Alexander Loyd..	Merchant & Builder		..1..
Fr'cis C. Sherman	Merchant & Builder	..36	..1..
Benj.W.Raymond	Merchant	..41	..1..
Augustus Garrett	Auctioneer, etc.		..1..
Alson S. Sherman	Cont'ctor & Builder	..32	..1..
Augustus Garrett	Auctioneer, etc.....		..1..
John P. Chapin..	Com'sion Merchant		..1..
James Curtiss....	Lawyer.............		..1..
Jas. H. Woodworth	Milling Business....		.2..
James Curtiss....	Lawyer.............		..1..
Walter S. Gurnee	Tanner, Merchant..	..38	.2..
Charles M. Gray..	Reaper Manuf'turer		..1..
Isaac L. Milliken.	Blacksmith.........		..1..
Levi D. Boone....	Physician	..47	.1..
Thomas Dyer....	General Trade......	..51	..1..
John Wentworth.	Editor	..42	..1..
John C. Haines...	Flour-maker	..40	.2..
John Wentworth.	Editor..............	..45	..1..
Julian S. Rumsey	....	....	.1..
Fr'cis C. Sherman	Merchant & Builder	.57	..3..
John B. Rice.....	Actor..............	..55	..4..
Roswell B. Mason	Civil Engineer......	..64	..2 .
Joseph Medill....	Editor..............	..48	..2..
Harvey D. Colvin	Supt.of U.S. Exp.Co	..58	..2..
Monroe Heath...	Paint Manufacturer	....	..2..
C. H. Harrison...	Real Estate.........	..54	..8..
John A. Roche....	Mech'nical Engine'r	...43	..2..
DeWitt C. Cregier	Mech'nical Engine'r	...50	..2..
H. Washburne...	Lawyer.	..38	....

ROSWELL B. MASON.
20TH MAYOR.
Elected....1869.
People's Party.

HARVEY D. COLVIN.
22ND MAYOR.
Elected....1873.
Democrat.

C. H. HARRISON.
24TH MAYOR.
First Elected..1879.
Democrat.

JOHN A. ROCHE.
25TH MAYOR.
Elected....1887.
Republican.

DeWITT C. CREGIER.
26TH MAYOR.
Elected....1889.
Democrat.

HEMPST'D WASHBURNE.
27TH MAYOR.
Elected....1891.
Republican.

This space is
reserved for the
28th Mayor of
Chicago.

Climatic Conditions—Geographical Position—The City's Possibilities.

When reviewing the history of Chicago and her wonderful growth, we are impressed with the daring achievements of her people. Only a brief time ago—and the city was prostrated under a holocaust of fire that laid waste nearly all the mercantile houses, great hotels, public buildings, and the large storehouse of wealth which her people had been gathering for a lifetime. Two decades more—and a new city stands where stood the old, immeasurably superior to the first city in all that is desirable in architecture and substantial buildings.

Evidently a people who can so quickly rise above misfortune, converting that misfortune into great blessing, must possess inherent energy and ability to accomplish; all of which is the result of peculiarly favorable conditions. Let us study for a little time the underlying causes which develop such energy and impel such progress in this city.

Primarily, the principal reason why Chicago is the home of a most energetic and progressive people is, that its inhabitants are themselves descendants of the world's best human energy. The Pilgrim Fathers represented the enterprise and the advancing spirit of the mother country. They had the courage and the will to emigrate to a new land, at a time when removal to an unknown country demanded much more courage and determination than it does now.

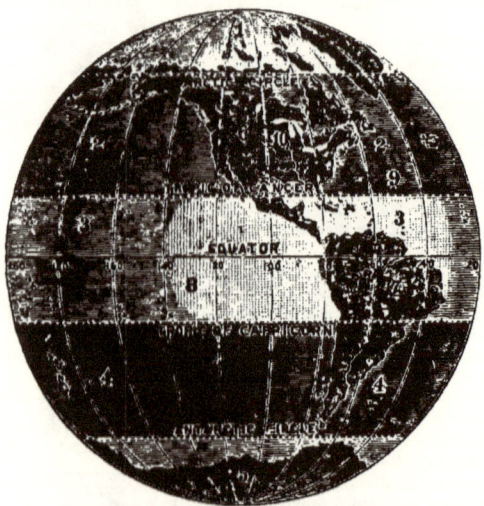

LOCATION OF CHICAGO IN THE TEMPERATE ZONE.

The above illustration represents the Zones of the Earth, Oceans and Divisions of the Western Hemisphere; No. 1 being the North Frigid Zone; 2, North Temperate; 3, Torrid; 4, South Temperate; 5, South Frigid; 6, North America; 7, South America; 8, the Pacific Ocean; 9, Atlantic Ocean; and 10, the location of Chicago in the North Temperate Zone.

The majority of the people of this city are descendants of the brave and resolute pioneers who have crossed the ocean, and braved the perils incident to settlement in a new and untried field. They are not only, therefore, descendants of a brave race, but they embody the best energy of Europe and the Eastern States, as shown in their departure from the pleasant Eastern home scenes, and resolute determination to acquire a livelihood and make for themselves a favorable position in the West.

The average of general intelligence and enterprise is much greater among the people of the West than is generally known by the people in the older countries. This is readily admitted when it is understood that this people not only had the courage to come west, but they brought with them the knowledge which they acquired in the East, to which has been added a western experience.

To an ancestry and surroundings in the Eastern States and in Europe, which have made these an energetic and progressive people, has been added a very favorable climatic condition, through the location of Chicago where it now stands. Had the same individuals who have wrought such marvels in architecture, and developed such enterprise in manufactures, agriculture, trade and commerce in the West, settled in a clime many degrees more frigid than Chicago, their efforts would have been absorbed in guarding themselves against cold. Had they located in a region much nearer the equator, their zeal would have been dissipated in perspiration, and their enterprise would have been lost to the world, in their effort to keep cool.

Examination of the Zones, in our illustration, shows that Chicago is situated in a temperate, invigorating climate, in the same latitude where the highest intellectual culture prevails in the Middle and the Eastern States. The winters are cold enough and long enough to cause the inhabitants to cultivate the prudential, saving quality which induces the individual to provide for a time of need. The summers are cool enough to keep the bodily activities toned up to their full energy, while the seasons are warm enough to reward, with bounteous harvests and excellent result, all those who put forth earnest effort.

Another cause of Chicago's success is its favorable geographical position. It is situated at the head of lake navigation, on the great fresh waters It lies in a section of the lowest elevation between the lakes and the Mississippi—a region most favorable for railroad building. It rests amid the most productive soil, and a highly intelligent and progressive rural population. Added to this, the map of the Western Hemisphere shows that this city is very nearly the exact center of the habitable portion of North America. With one point of the compass on Chicago, the other will include in the

CHICAGO THE CENTER.
The above circle incloses an area of more than 4,000 miles in diameter, Chicago being the exact center.

circle the whole of Mexico and Central America, Newfoundland, Labrador, Hudson Bay, all the settled portion of the Canadian Dominion and all the extreme Western States on the Pacific Coast.

As Chicago is the center of productive North America, so is it very nearly the center of population of the United States. It is thus easily seen why this city must ever be a great manufacturing center, having an immense population, for the following reasons:

First.—It is in the center of, and easily accessible to, the raw materials from which we manufacture—comprising hides, wool, cotton, wood and metals.

Second.—Two-thirds of the State of Illinois is underlaid with coal, with which to make steam or electric power, while great pipe lines from gas and oil fields contribute to supply the cheapest power for the propulsion of machinery.

Third.—The country directly tributary to Chicago is the most prolific food-growing region in the world; hence the low cost of living here.

Fourth.—As the Great West, tributary to Chicago, has the most fertile soil, so its inhabitants are destined to be a very rich people, as the most of all wealth comes from the soil.

Fifth.—With the raw material, the power and the food in readiness for the production of every manufacture, at the lowest cost; with a wealthy people ready to buy at a fair price, located in the center of population, Chicago is further assisted by unrivaled facilities for distribution, having over 30 leading railroad lines, which, with their branches, include over 60 railroads that bring in their freights and go out with manufactured productions to all parts of the country. These are balanced by a great number of lines of water transportation, communicating with all parts of the Northern Central States and all portions of the world.

Chicago for Health.

Not only is it thus shown that Chicago must be the great manufacturing center of the world, but the reasons exist why it will always be one of the healthiest regions in which to live. Originally located on low and swampy ground, a large portion of the business center of the city was filled in, and elevated several feet, in order to secure ready drainage. To obtain complete sewerage for all the city, whatever may be its size, for all time to come, a plan of drainage is in contemplation, which is to be located to the westward of Chicago, 10 miles from the Court House. It will consist of a grand canal, from 160 to 200 feet in width and 18 feet in depth. This canal is to extend from Joliet, northward up to and through the valley of the Desplaines River, intersecting Lake Michigan, possibly in the region of Evanston. This canal will be from 35 to 50 miles in length; will carry a large inflow of water from the lake, at the rate of

THE BOULEVARDS WHICH ARE TO BORDER THE CHICAGO DRAINAGE RIVERS.

one mile per hour, and all sewage lying to the westward of Chicago, for a distance of four and six miles on either side. It is expected that the current will be so rapid as to render the water comparatively pure; a portion of the stream from Joliet to the southern part of the city being a part of a ship canal system, extending from the Mississippi River to Chicago, along the banks of which may be built hundreds of manufactories.

In the near future, this canal will line the outer border of Chicago, and may form a feature of great attraction and beauty, having a charming boulevard on either side, a view of which we show herewith; the whole resembling the River Seine, as it winds through and encircles a portion of Paris, France.

Notwithstanding the large number of manufactories already in the city, which have hitherto besmeared the atmosphere with smoke, the record for health in this city stands very high, owing to good water obtained from several miles outward in Lake Michigan, a system of drainage that permits of no permanently stagnant water, and steadily prevailing winds from prairie and lake that purify the air. With the total abolition of smoke in residence and manufactory, through the incoming of oil, electricity and natural gas; with a smooth pavement from which all dirt can be removed by frequent washing, Chicago will become one of the most cleanly, as it is already one of the most beautiful, cities in the world. Such, in outline, is the city which the stranger is to visit, about which more specific details are given elsewhere.

Business Firms Employing 500 Persons and Over.

In a recent report of the Factory Inspector of the City Department of Health, numerous business firms and corporations are shown who give employment to the following number of persons:

Armour & Co., Packers.............. .. 7,775
Pullman Palace Car Company............5,450
Illinois Steel Company, South Chicago...5,200
Swift & Co., Packers................4,300
Chicago & Northwestern Railroad......3,741
Calumet Iron & Steel Company.........3,500
Nelson Morris & Co., Packers.........3,400
Wm. Deering & Co., Agri. Implements...3,000
Illinois Central Railroad.............2,847
Chicago, Milwaukee & St. Paul Railroad.2,750
Union Steel Co., 3179 S. Ashland Ave....2,500
Crane Manufacturing Company..........2,500
Chicago, Rock Island & Pacific Railroad.2,394
Illinois Steel Company................2,000
Pennsylvania Railroad Lines... 1,769
Wells & French Company, Car Works...1,600
McCormick Reaper Works...............1,600
Fraser & Chalmers, Machinery 1,550
Marshall Field & Co., Dry Goods........1,500
Fowler Bros., Meat Packers...........1,415
Libby, McNeill & Libby, Packers 1,410
Sailing vessels (ex. of freight handlers)..1,400
A. H. Andrews & Co., Furniture.......1,300
Anglo-American Packing & Provision Co.1,260
Western Union Telegraph Company....1,250
Chicago, Burlington & Quincy Railroad..1,164
Lake Shore & Michigan Southern R. R...1,105
Union Stock Yards & Transit Company..1,000
Chicago Packing & Provision Company.1,000
International Packing Company........1,000
Malleable Iron Works, 26th Street......1,000
Western Electric Works, S. Clinton St...1,000
C. & W. I. and Belt Railway Company....926
Chicago Sugar Refining Company........900
Adams & Westlake Company, Brass Wks...900
L. Wolff Manufacturing Co., Brass Wks...850
W.B. Conkey Co., Printers & Bookbinders..827
Western Wheel Works (Bicycles)..........800
U. S. Rolling Stock Company (Car Works).750
Northwestern Terra Cotta Company......750
Rand, McNally & Co., Publishers..........750
Chicago, St. Louis & Pittsburg Railroad...654
D. Bradley Manufacturing Company.......650
J. V. Farwell & Co., Dry Goods...........650
Norton Bros., Tinware..................610
John Cudahy, Packer...................600
Selz, Schwab & Co., Boots and Shoes......600
Maxwell Bros., Wooden Box Makers 600
J. S. Kirk & Co., Soap Makers............600
Brunswick, Balke & Collender Co.........600
Baltimore & Ohio Railroad...............581
Chicago, Alton & St. Louis Railroad.....552
J. M. W. Jones Co., Stationery & Printing..550
New York, Chicago & St. Louis Railroad..536
Car Wheel Foundry, Pullman.............530
Palmer House, Hotel....................525
Chicago & Eastern Illinois Railroad......525
Michigan Central Railroad...............525
Carson, Pirie, Scott & Co., Dry Goods......525
Armour & Co., Glue Works 525
Northern Pacific Railroad...... 519
Sam Allerton Packing Company...........500
Hibbard, Spencer, Bartlett & Co.,Hardware 500
Palmer, Fuller & Co., Sash, Doors & Blinds..500
Heywood & Morrill Rattan Company........500
Cribben, Sexton & Co., Stoves, Erie Street..500
Chicago Shipbuilding Company............500

City Valuation and Street Lighting.

Assessed Valuation of City......$219,354,368
Bonded Indebtedness of City.....$13,545,400
Accrued Indebtedness by Annexation.$983,900
Annual Cost of Street Lighting......$682,384
Total Number of Street Lamps........36,418
Number of Gas Lamps................26,236
Number of Gasoline Lamps........ 8,080
Number of Electric Lamps..............1,092
Number of Oil Lamps.................1,010
New Buildings Erected in 1891 11,805

Chicago's Increase in Area.

On February 11, 1835, the original plat showed the city of Chicago to be, in area, 2.55 square miles.
March 4, 1837, added 8.15 square miles, making a total of 10.70 square miles.
February 16, 1847, added 3.33 square miles, making a total of 14.03 square miles.
February 12, 1853, added 3.90 square miles, making a total of 17.93 square miles.
February 13, 1863, added 6.48 square miles, making a total of 24.41 square miles.
February 27, 1864, added 11.35 square miles, making a total of 35.79 square miles.
May 16, 1887, added 1.00 square miles, making a total of 36.79 square miles.
November and December, 1887, added 7.15 square miles, making a total of 43.94 square miles.
July 29, 1889, added 128.24 square miles, making a total of 172.18 square miles.
April 1, 1890, added 3.05 square miles, making a total of 175.23 square miles.
May 12, 1890, added 0.85 square miles, making a total of 176.08 square miles.
November 4, 1890, added 4.12 square miles, making a total of 180.20 square miles.

Growth of Chicago.

Date.	Population.	Date.	Population.
1830	70	1846	14,169
1832	600	1850	29,963
1837	4,170	1860	109,206
1840	4,479	1870	306,605
1843	7,580	1880	491,516
1845	12,088	1890	1,208,669

Nationality of People in Chicago in 1890.

Nationality.	Population.	Nationality.	Population.
United States	292,403	Holland	4,912
Germany	384,958	Hungary	4,827
Ireland	215,534	Roumania	4,350
Bohemia	54,209	Wales	2,966
Poland	52,756	Switzerland	2,735
Sweden	45,877	China	1,217
Norway	44,615	Greece	698
England	33,785	Belgium	682
France	12,963	Japan	407
Scotland	11,927	Spain	297
Russia	9,977	West Indies	37
Italy	9,921	Portugal	34
Denmark	9,891	Sandwich Islands	31
Canada	6,989	East Indies	28

Valuation of Chicago Property.

Water-works......................$50,000,000
Sewers.........................11,000,000
School Property...................11,000,000
Water Revenue..................2,267,900
Fire Department Property..........2,500,000
Electric-light Plant................2,000,000
Buildings........................2,000,000
Real Estate......................1,000,000
House of Correction................1,000,000
Police Department Property..........844,000
Public Library.....................232,000

Streets, Sidewalks, Bridges.

Miles of Streets.......................2,235
Miles of Sidewalk.....................2,968
Miles of Water Mains.................1,320
Miles of Sewers.......................784
Miles of Paved Streets................747
River Bridges.........................61
Viaducts.............................29
Miles of Water Tunnels...............13
Miles of Water Tunnels in Construction......8
River Tunnels.........................3
Miles of Wood Block Paving............471
Miles of Macadam Paving.............245
Miles of Stone Paving................24
Miles of Sheet Asphalt Paving........12
Miles of Asphalt Block Paving..........4

☞ Observe that black figures, in the Index, mean divisions of the city, and small figures mean sections. Study the following explanations carefully, as the plan is entirely new. Once understood, it will be easy to find the location of any street in the city without loss of time and the inconvenience of a folding map.

Explanation.—Following this index will be found a "Key Map to Location of All Sections and Streets in Chicago." Examination will show that the key map, which includes the entire area of Chicago, at the beginning of 1892, is divided into 13 divisions. Close examination shows each division to be divided into 18 parts, each part being a section of the city, and one mile square. On the 13 pages following the key map, are shown the several divisions of the key map, enlarged sufficiently to show the location of nearly every street in Chicago. To illustrate this index and the abbreviations, we will use the first line, thus:

A (N. S.) W, n, **3**, 17, Southport Av. 8.

The abbreviations should be read as follows: **A** is A Street; (N. S.) means North Side of the city; W means that this street extends west and the numbers grow larger in the direction the street goes; n means that even numbers are on the north side of the street; **3**, 17, means that this street is located in division **3**, section 17, in the key map, and is to be found in division **3** and section 17 of the division map; finally, that the number in A St., where it crosses Southport Av., is 8. The next line in the index reads as follows:

Abbott Ct.* (N. S.) N, **3**, 15. Bet. Hall and
Clark, fr. Diversey Av. north one block.

Abbott Ct. means Abbott Court; the star * means that this street is not shown on the map; its location, however, is between Hall Street and Clark Street, in division **3** and section 15, and it extends northward one block from Diversey Avenue. Next, in the index, is the following line:

Aberdeen (W. S.) S, e, **5**, 9, Harrison, 183.

This line indicates that Aberdeen Street is located on the West Side of the city; runs south; even numbers are on east side of the street; is in division **5**, section 9, and the street number, where it crosses Harrison Street, is 183. Next following in the index, is Aberdeen, on the South Side, which is in two divisions, extends through several sections, and reads as follows:

Aberdeen (S. S.) S, e, **8**, 6†, Fifty-first, 5100;
9, Fifty-ninth, 5900; 12, Sixty-seventh,
6700; 15, Seventy-fifth, 7500; 18, Eighty-
third, 8300; **11**, 3, Ninety-first, 9100.

The above is thus explained: Aberdeen, on the South Side, runs south; even numbers are on the east side of the street; is in division **8**, section 6†, the dagger indicating that the name of this street first appears in section 6; and, where it crosses Fifty-first Street, its number is 5100. It continues through section 9, and its number, at Fifty-ninth Street, is 5900. In section 12, where it crosses Sixty-seventh Street, its number is 6700; and so it continues to extend, through sections 15 and 18, into division **11**, section 3—the number of the street being given where it crosses another street, usually near the middle of each section. When a street extends through several sections, the dagger † indicates the section in which the name of the street first appears.

Explanation Concerning Street Numbers, Sections, and Dividing-Line Streets.

Streets mentioned in connection with the streets in the index, and the numbers that directly follow these streets thus mentioned, indicate the number of the street where this crossing is made.

The larger lines enclosing each section are streets on section lines; and the space enclosed is one mile square. This enables the reader to estimate the distances, from one portion of the city to another, and by knowing the number of a street at certain crossings, which is usually near the middle of the section, an approximate estimate can be made of the number on the street to which the person wishes to go.

Randolph Street, which runs westward from the center of the city to Ashland Avenue, and Lake Street, which extends from Ashland Avenue, westward, to West Fortieth Street, are dividing-line streets in the west division of the city, by which sections of streets, on the West Side, are located. Thus, Ada, North, is Ada Street on the north side of Randolph Street; and Ada, South, is Ada Street on the south side of Randolph Street. Western Av., North, is Western Avenue north of Lake Street, and Western Av., South, is Western Avenue south of Lake Street, numbers growing larger each way from Randolph and Lake Streets.

Some streets, running east and west, are divided by the Chicago River. Thus Adams, East, is Adams Street east of the river; Adams, West, is Adams Street west of the river.

Meaning of Abbreviations, Figures and Characters in Index.

(W. S.) West Side.	S Runs south.	e Even Nos. on east side of street.	Black figures, as **1, 2, 8,** indicate No. of division.
(N. S.) North Side.	N Runs north.	w Even Nos. on west side of street.	
(S. S.) South Side.	W Runs west.	n Even Nos. on north side of street.	Light figures, as 1, 2, 3, indicate No. of section.
* Not on the map.	E Runs east.	s Even Nos. on south side of street.	

Av. Avenue. Ter. Terrace. Ct. Court. Pl. Place. Sq. Square. Cres. Crescent. Boul. Boulevard.
Bet. Between. R.R. Railroad. N-W. Northwest. N-E. Northeast. S-W, Southwest. S-E, Southeast.

Fr. From. Ada, North, north of Randolph St. Adams, East, east of Chicago River. Rd. Road.
Pk. Park. Ada, South, south of Randolph St. Adams, West, west of Chicago River. Nr. Near.

† Indicates section where name of street first appears when street extends through several sections.

For Directions Concerning the Finding of All Streets See Explanation on Opposite Page.

A (N. S.) W, n, **3**, 17, Southport Av. 8.
Abbott Ct.* (N. S.) N, **8**, 15. Bet. Hall and Clark, fr. Diversey Av. north one block.
Aberdeen (W. S.) S, e, **5**, 9, Harrison, 183.
Aberdeen (S. S.) S, e, **8**, 6†, Fifty-first, 5100; 9, Fifty-ninth, 5900; 12, Sixty-seventh, 6700; 15, Seventy-fifth, 7500; 18, Eighty-third, 8300, **11**, 3, Ninety-first, 9100.
Aberdeen (N. S.) E, **8**, 5.
Aberdeen (S. S., in Calumet) S, **11**, 9.
Aberdeen Av. (S. S., in Hegewisch) S, **13**, 18.
Ada, North (W S.) N, w, **5**, 6, Kinzie, 142.
Ada, South (W. S.) S, e, **5**, 6†, Randolph, 2; **8**, 6, Fifty-first, 5100, 9, Fifty-ninth, 5900; 12, Sixty-seventh, 6700; 15, Seventy-fifth, 7500; 18, Eighty-third, 8300.
Adams, East (S. S.) W, s, **6**, 8, Michigan Av. 1; 7†, Market, 249.
Adams, West (W. S.) W, s, **6**, 7†. Canal, 27; **5**, 9, Centre Av. 367; 8, Robey, 743; 7, California Av. 1207; 4, 9, Central Park Av. 1677; 8, West Forty-fourth, 2247.
Adams (W. S.) W, **2**, 7.
Adams (S. S., in Calumet) S, **11**, 9.
Adams Av. (S.S.) S, **9**, 12, 15†; **12**, 3.
Addison (N. S.) E, n, **3**, 10†, Hoyne Av. 301; *Post Office, Adams, Jackson,* 11, Racine Av. 1201; *Clark and Dearborn Streets.* 12, Pine Grove Av. 1807.
Addison Av. (S. S.) S, **9**, 12.
Addison Av. (N. S.) W, **1**, 5.
Addison Ter. (N. S.) W, **13**, 1.
Adelaide Av. (N. S.) N, e, **3**, 10, Roscoe Boul. 70.
Adelaide Ct.* (W. S.) W. **4**, 14. First south of Twenty-fourth, fr. Fairmount to Butler.
Alaska—Name changed; see St. Michael's Ct.
Albany (S. S.) S, **8**, 10.
Albany Av. North*(W. S.) N, e, **5**, 4, Kinzie, 126; 1, Grand Av. 416.
Albany Av. South (W. S.) S, e, **5**, 4, Lake, 2; 7†, Harrison, 324; 10, Sixteenth, 801; 13, Twenty-sixth, 1227; 16, Thirty-sixth, 3600; **8**, 1, Fortieth, 4000.
Albert* (W. S.) S-W, e, **5**, 12, Eighteenth, 1. Bet. Loomis and Laflin, fr. W. Eighteenth southwest ½ block.
Aldine (N. S.) E, **3**, 12.
Aldine Pl.* (S. S.) S, w, **6**, 17, Aldine Sq. 3764. Bet. Stanton and Vincennes Avs., fr. Aldine Sq. to Thirty-ninth.
Aldine Sq. (S. S.) **8**, 17, Nos. 1 to 43.
Alexander * (S. S.) W, n, **6**, 13, Portland Av. 58. Bet. Twenty-second Pl. and Twenty-third, fr. Wentworth Av. to Stewart Av.
Alexander Av. (N. S.) N, e, **3**, 11; 8†, Buena Av. 1664.
Alice Av. (S. S.) S, **13**, 16.
Alice Ct.* (W. S.) **3**, 16.
Alice Pl. (W. S.) W, s, **2**, 18, Powell Av. 41.
Alice Pl.* (W. S.) W, s, **3**, 16, Leavitt, 83. Bet. North Av. and Columbia St., fr. Milwaukee Av. to Leavitt St.
Alice Pl. (S. S., in Morgan Park) **11**, 8.
Allen Av. (S. S.) S, **12**, 11.
Allen Av. (W. S.) N-E, **2**, 14.
Allport (W. S.) S, e, **3**, 12, Nineteenth, 780. *Eye and Ear Infirmary, Adams and Peoria Streets.*
Almond * (W. S.) S, e, **5**, 8, Ashland, 38. First east of Kendall, fr. Taylor to Ashland.
Alton (W. S., in Norwood Park) **1**, 1.
Ambrose (N. S.) W, n, **5**, 14†, Hoyne Av. 146; 13, California Av, 528.
Andrew Av. (W. S.) W, **2**, 8.
Andrews (S. S., in Worth) W, **11**, 7.
Andrews Av. (S. S., in Calumet) W, **12**, 13.
Ann, North (W. S.) N, w, **5**, 6, Fulton, 64.
Ann, South (W. S.) S, e, **5**, 6, Washington Boul. 32.

Ann (S. S., in Blue Island) S, **11**, 16.
Anna* (W. S.) W, n, **5** 13, Rockwell, 100. Bet. Twenty-ninth and Thirtieth, fr. Western Av. to Washtenaw Av.
Anna Av. (N. S.) N, e, **3**, 10, Roscoe Boul. 70.
Anna Pl. (S. S., in South Washington Heights) W and S, **11**, 11.
Anthony Av. (S. S.) S-E, n-e, **9**, 11†, 15; **10**, 16; **13**, 1; 2, Ninety-first, 9100.
Arbor Place (W. S.) W, s, **5**, 6, Sheldon, 44.
Arcade Ct.* (S. S.) W, **6**, 7. Bet. Madison and Monroe, fr. Clark to La Salle.
Arch (S. S.) S-E, w, **5**, 15, Bonaparte, 2930.
Archer Av. (S. S.) S-W, n, **6**, 10, State and Nineteenth, 1900; 13†, Butler, 2363; **5**, 15, Main, 2800; 17, Hoyne Av. and Thirty-fifth, 3500; 16; **8**, 1; **7**, 3, 6, 5, 4.
Archibald * (W. S.) E, **5**, 13. Bet. Douglas Park Boul. and Twenty-fifth, fr. Francisco east ¼ block.
Ardmore Av. (N. S.) E, **3**, 2.
Argyle (N. S.) E, n, **3**, 5.
Argyle Av. (S. S., in Hegewisch) S, **13**, 18.
Arlington Av. (W. S., in Morgan Park) W, **11**, 8.
Armida Av. (S. S., in Morgan Park) S, **11**, 5, 8†, 11.
Armitage Av. (W. S.) W, s, **3**, 17, Mendell, 22; 16†, Robey, 288; **2**, 18, California Av. 756; 17, Central Park Av. 1192; 16; **1**, 18, 17, 16.
Armitage Ct. (N. S.) E, **3**, 18, Clarkson Av. 2.
Armour (W. S.) N, e, **5**, 6, Ohio, 86.
Armour Av. (S. S.) S, w, **6**, 10, Sixteenth, 1600; 13, Twenty-sixth, 2600; 16†, Thirty-fifth, 3500; **9**, 1, Forty-third. 4300; 4, Fifty-first. 5100; 7, 13; **12**, 10.
Artesian Av. (W. S.) N, e, **5**, 4, Kinzie, 122.
Arthington (W. S.) W, s, **5**, 9, Lytle, 36.
Arthur (W. S.) S, e, **6**, 10, Seventeenth, 1702.
Arthur Av. (S. S.) S, w, **10**, 17 Eighty-second, 8200.
Ash (S. S.) S-E, w, **5**, 5, 16. Thirty-second, 42.
Ashford Av. (W. S.) W, **2**, 16.
Ashkum Av. (S. S.) S, w, **13**, 2†, Ninety-first, 9101; 5, Ninety - ninth, 9900.
Ashland * (W. S.) W, s, **8**, Cypress, 56. First north of Twelfth, fr. Robey to Olive.
Ashland Av. North (W. S.) N, e, **5**, 5, Kinzie, 100; 2, Division, 544; **3**, 16, Clybourn Pl. 957; 18,†Diversey Av. 1466; 10, Addison, 1994; 7, Montrose Boul. 2524; 4, North Fifty-ninth, 3058; 1.
Ashland Av. South (W. S. and S. S.) S; e, north of river, w, south of river; **5**, 5, Lake, 2; 8, Harrison, 312; 11†, Sixteenth, 752; 14, the river, 1135; 17, Thirty-fifth, 3500; **8**, 2, Forty-third, 4300; 5, Fifty-first, 5100; 8, 11, 14, 17; **11**, 2, 5, 8, 11, 14, 17.
Ashland Ct.* (W. S.) W, s, **5**, 6, Ashland Av. 18. Bet. Indiana and Ohio, extending east half block fr. Ashland Av.
Ashton * (S. S., in Calumet) S, **11**, 3. Third west of Halsted, fr. Eighty-seventh to Nintieth.
Ashton (S. S., in Calumet) W, **11**, 2†, 1.
Astor (N. S.) N, w, **6**, 2, Banks, 73.
Asylum Pl. (W. S.) W, s, **3**, 16, Robey, 230.
Atlantic (S. S.) S, w, **9**, 1†, Forty-third, 4300; 4, Fifty-first, 5100; 7, Fifty-eighth, 5800; 16.
Atlantic Av. (S. S., in Chicago Lawn) W, **7**, 12.
Attica* (S. S.) W, **5**, 18. Bet. Thirty-second and Thirty-third, fr. Auburn to Laurel.
Attrill (W. S.) N-E, e, **2**, 18, Milwaukee Av. 40.
Auburn (S. S.) S, w, **5**, 18, Thirty-third, 3300.
Auburn Av. (S. S.) W, **9**, 16.

Augusta (W. S.) W, n to Crawford Av. and s
. beyond, **5**, 3, Centre Av. 24; 2†, Robey,
402; 1, California Av. 872; **4**, 3, Central
Park Av. 1342; 2, West Forty-fourth,
1885; 1, West Fifty-second, 2394.
Austin (W. S.) W, **1**, 10.
Austin (W. S., in Jefferson) N, 1, 8.
Austin Av. (W. S.) W, **s**, **6**, 4, Jefferson, 2;
5, 6, Centre Av. 288; 5†, Robey, 674; 4,
Seymour Av. 912.
Austin Av. North (W. S.) N, **1**, 17†, 14, 11, 8.
Avenue A (S. S.) S, **10**, 10.
Avenue A (S. S.) S, **13**, 12†, 13.
Avenue B (S. S.) S, **10**, 10, Seventieth, 7000.
Avenue B (S. S.) S, **13**, 6†, 9, 12, 15.
Avenue C (S. S.) S, w, **10**, 10.
Avenue C (S. S.) S, w, **13**, 6†, 9, 12, 15.
Avenue D (S. S.) S, w, **13**, 6†, 9, 12.
Avenue E (S. S.) S, w, **13**, 6†, 100th, 10000; 9,
106th, 10558; 12, 15.
Avenue F (S. S.) S, w, **13**, 6†, 9, 106th, 10558;
12, 15.
Avenue G (S. S.) S, w, **13**, 6†; 9, 106th, 10558;
12.
Avenue H (S. S.) S, w, **13**, 6†;
9,106th, 10558; 12.
Avenue I (S. S.) S, w, **13**, 9,
106th, 10558.
Avenue J (S. S.) S, w, **13**, 6†,
Ninety-ninth, 9900; 9,
106th, 10600; 12.
Avenue K (S. S.) S, w, **13**, 6†;
9, 106th, 10600; 12.
Avenue L (S. S.) S, w, **13**, 6†;
9, 106th, 10558; 12.
Avenue M (S. S.) S, w, **13**, 6†;
9, 106th, 10558; 12.
Avenue N (S. S.) S, w, **13**, 12.
Avenue O (S. S.) S, w, **13**, 12.
Avers Av. North (W. S.) N, e, **4**, 6†, Kinzie, 126;
3, Division, 604; **2**, 17, Dickens Av. 1162.
Avers Av. South (W. S.) S, e, **4**, 12, Nineteenth,
917; 15†, Twenty-sixth, 1265.
Avon Av. (S. S.) S, **8**, 7, 10†; **11**, 7.
Avon Av. (S. S.) S, **7**, 8.
Avon Pl. (W. S.) S, **6**, 8, Hoyne Av. 50.
Avondale Av.* (W. S.) N-W, **2**, 15, 11.   On
west side of C. & N. W. R. R., fr. Park Av.
to Warner Av.
Ayer's Ct.* (W. S.) S, e, **5**, 6, Huron, 49.   First
west of Centre Av., fr. Chicago Av. to
Huron.

B (N. S.) W, n, **8**, 17, Dominick, 44.
Baker (S. S.) W, n, **9**, 1, Wright, 600.
Baker (S. S.) W, **8**, 15.
Baldwin* (W.S.) N, e, **5**, 5, Austin Av. 32.   First
east of Robey, fr. Kinzie St. to Austin Av.
Baldwin Av. (S. S.) S, **10**, 13.
Ball Pl. (S. S.) W, **11**, 2.
Ballou Av. (W. S.) N, e, **2**, 17†, Armitage Av.
1076; 14.
Balmoral Av. (N. S.) E, n, **8**, 4†, Robey, 401; 5,
Evanston Av. 1207.
Baltimore Av. (S. S.) S-E, w, **10**, 17, Commer-
cial Av. 8462.
Banks (N. S.) E, s, **6**, 2, Ritchie Pl. 52.
Barber (W. S.) W, s, **6**, 10, Jefferson, 100.
Barclay (W. S.) N, e, **5**, 1, Thomas, 178.
Barklay Av. (S. S.) S, **13**, 8†, 11.
Barry (N. S.) E, n, **8**, 15, Waubun Av. 1901.
Bartlett Av. (W. S.) W, s, **4**, 3, Sheridan Av. 62.
Basil Av. (W. S.) N, e, **2**, 18, Wabansia Av.
896.
Batavia Av. (W. S.) N-W, **1**, 5.
Bates* (W. S.) W, s, **6**, 10, Holden, 59.   Bet.
Judd and Wilson, fr. Lumber St. to Stewart
Av.
Bauwans* (W. S.) N-W & N, e, **5**, 2, Elk, 43.
Bet. Milwaukee Av. and Blackhawk.
Baxter (N. S.) N, w, **8**, 14†, Wellington Av. 2;
11, Roscoe, 256.
Bayson (W. S.) W, s, **4**, 2, West Forty-third,
1827.

Beach * (W. S.) S, e, **6**, 7, Polk, 70.   First east
of Canal, fr. Harrison to Twelfth.
Beach Av. (W. S.) W, s, 4, 3, Homan Av. 127.
Beckwith Av. (S. S.) S,
11, 10.
Beethoven Pl. (N. S.) E,
s, **6**, 1, Sedgwick, 2.
Belden Av. (N. S.) E, n,
8, 17†, Racine Av.
160; 18, Cleveland
Av. 476.
Belden Av. (W. S.) W,
s, **2**, 17, Hancock
Av. 482.
Belden Pl.* (N. S.) N
and W, e, **8**, 18,
Belden Av. 2.   Bet.
Larrabee St. and
Cleveland Av.
Belder Av. (W. S.) W,
2, 16.

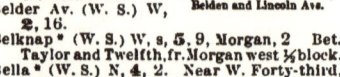
Epis. Church of Our Savior,
Belden and Lincoln Avs.

Belknap* (W. S.) W, s, **5**, 9, Morgan, 2   Bet.
Taylor and Twelfth, fr. Morgan west ½ block.
Bella * (W. S.) N, **4**, 2.   Near W. Forty-third,
fr. Thomas to Hirsch.
Belle Plaine Av. (N. S.) E, **8**, 7, Ravenswood
Park, 607.
Bellevue Pl. (N. S.) E, s, **6**, 2, Rush, 12.
Belmont Av. (N. S.) E, n, **2**, 12; **8**, 13†, Robey,
401; 11, Racine Av. 1201; 12, Waubun
Av. 1901.
Belmont Av. West (W. S.) W, s, **2**, 12, Elston
Av. 140; 11, 10†; **1**, 12, 11, 10.
Belmont Av. (S. S., in Calumet) S, **11**, 8.
Belmont Av. (W. S., in Montrose) N, **2**, 7.
Belt Line (W. S.) S, **4**, 5.
Bensley Av. (S. S.) S, **13**, 5, 8†, 11.
Benson * (S. S.) S, w, **5**, 18, James, 3133.   First
west of Broad, fr. Thirty-first to Waterville.
Benton Pl. (S. S.) E, **6**, 5.
Berg Pl. (W. S.) W, n, **8**, 18.
Berkley Av. (S. S.) S-E, w, **9**, 3, Forty-second,
4201.
Berkley Av. (S. S., in Morgan Park) W, **11**, 11.
Berkshire Av.* (S. S.) S, e, **11**, 7, 10.   The
same as Johnson Av., fr. 108th to 115th.
Berlin (W. S.) W, s, **8**, 16†, Oakley Av. 142;
2, 18, Cromwell, 45.
Berlin (S. S.) W, **8**, 11.
Bernard * (W. S.) N, **2**, 11.   First west of Ho-
man Av., fr. Henderson St. to Avondale Av.
Berrien (S. S., in Blue Island) S, **11**, 18.
Berteau Av. (N. S.) E, **8**, 7†, Ravenswood Park,
607; 8.
Berteau Av. (W. S.) W, **2**, 9†; **8**, 5, Evanston
Av. 1201.
Berwyn Av (N.S.) E, n, **8**, 5, Evanston Av. 1201.
Bessemer Av * (S. S.) S, **12**, 9.   First wes of
Lake Calumet, fr. 104th to 106th.
Best Av. (N. S.) N, e, **8**, 14, Marianna, 70.
Beta (N. S.) N, **8**, 11.
Bethuel (W. S.) S, e, **4**,
12, Nineteenth, 915.
Better * (W. S.) W, n,
5, 9, Aberdeen, 28.
Second south of
Polk, fr. Sholto to
May.
Beveridge Av. (S. S.)
S, **10**, 10, Sixty-
ninth, 6901.
Bickerdike (S. S.) N, w, **5**, 6, Erie, 70.
Bickerdike (S. S.) S, **10**, 16.
Bickerdike Sq.* (W. S.) W, s, **5**, 6, Armour,
402. Bet. Indiana and Ohio, fr. Bickerdike
to Armour.
Bingham (W. S.) N-W, s, **2**, 18, Armitage Av. 1.
Binzo (W. S.) N-E, s, **8**, 16, Lister Av. 16.
Birch * (W. S.) W, s, **5**, 8, Myrtle, 32. Bet.
Polk and Taylor, fr. Robey to Kendall.
Birch Av (S. S.) S, **13**, 16.
Birdsall (S. S., in Blue Island) W, **11**, 13.
Bishop (S. S.) S, w, **8**, 3, Forty-sixth, 4600; 6†,
Fifty-first, 5100; 9, 12, 15, 18; **11**, 3.

Fowler Hall, of McCormick
Theological Seminary,
1060 North Halsted Street,
bet. Belden and Fullerton Avs

. " n to Crawford Av. and s beyond," in the description of Augusta Street, means that even
numbers, on Augusta Street, are on the north side of the street, to Crawford Avenue; and beyond
Crawford Avenue, they are on the south side of the street.   On several of the streets, in the city,
even numbers thus change from one side of the street to the other, as the reader will observe.

Bishop Ct.* (W. S.) S, e, **5**, **6**, Washington Boul.
2. First west of Sheldon, fr. Washington
Boul. to Madison.
Bismarck (W.S.) W, n, **5**, 1, Washtenaw Av. 62.
Bismarck Av. (S. S., in Hegewisch) S, **13**, 18.
Bismarck Ct.* (W. S.) W, s, **5**, 6, Noble, 105.
Bet. Erie and Huron, fr. ½ block west of
Centre Av. to Noble.
Bissell (N. S.) N-W and N, e, **3**, 17, Centre, 224.
Bissell (S. S.) S, **10**, 16.
Bissell Av. (S. S.) S, **10**, 14, Seventy-fourth,
7400.
Bixby Pl.* (W. S.) N,
e, **5**, 6, Kinzie, 2.
First east of Ar-
mour, fr. Kinzie
St. to Austin Av.
Blackhawk (N. S.) N-
E and E, s, **3**†,
Hawthorn Av.
110; **6**, 1, Sedg-
wick, 366.
Blackhawk, West (W.
S.) W, s, **5**, 3†, Elston Av. 42; 2, Paulina,
290.

Entrance to Rosehill Cemetery,
about three blocks north of
Bryn Mawr Avenue.

Blackwell (S. S.) S, w, **6**, 10, Nineteenth, 1900
Blackwell* (S. S.) S, **8**, 6. Fifth west of Hal
sted, fr. Fiftieth to Fifty-first.
Blaine (W. S.) W, s, **5**, 13, Washtenaw Av. 62
Blair (W. S.) S, e, **6**, 10, Canalport Av. 2.
Blake* (S. **S.**) S-E, **5**, 17. Second west of
Leavitt, extending ½ block fr. Archer Av.
Blanchard Av. (S. S.) S, **5**, 16; **8**, 1†, 4, 7, 10;
11, 7, 10.
Blanchard Pl.* (S. S.) S, **6**, 14. Bet. Wabash
Av. and State, fr. an alley south of Twenty-
fourth to an alley north of Twenty-fifth.
Blanche (S. S.) W, **8**, 9.
Blanche (W. S.) W, s, **5**, 3, Elston Av. 79.
Bliss* (N. S.) N-E, s, **5**, 3, Hickory Av. 32.
Second south of Division, fr. North Branch
St. to North Branch Canal.
Block* (N. S.) N, e, **3**, 18, Eugenie, 56. Bet.
Mohawk St. and Cleveland Av., fr. North
Av. to Eugenie.
Bloom (S. S.) S, w, **5**, 17, Thirty-sixth, 3558.
Bloomingdale Rd. (W. S.) W, s, **3**, 17, Elston
Av. 38; 16, Robey, 300; **2**, 18, California
Av. 922; 17†, Central Park Av. 1357; 16.
Blucher (N. S.) N, **3**, 14, Nelson, 228.
Blucher* (W. S.) W, s, **5**, 2, Wood, 25. Second
north of Division, fr. Lull Place west to
Wood.
Blue Island Av. (W. S.) S-W, s, **5**, 9, Taylor,
164; 12†, Sixteenth, 478; 14 Robey,
1014.
Blue Island Rd. (S. S.) S-W, **12**, 16; **11**, 18†,
17.
Bluff (S. S., in Blue Island)
S, **11**, 17.
Boardman* (S. S.) S-E. **5**,
17, Archer Av. 3621.
Third west of Leavitt,
fr. C. A. & St. L. R. R.
to Archer Av.
Boardman Pl. (N. S.) W,
3, 14.

U. S. Marine Hospital,
on the Lake Shore, between
Buena and Graceland Avs.

Bonaparte* (S. S.) S-W, n, **5**, 15, Arch, 2950.
Bet. Archer Av. and Lyman, fr. Arch to
Lock.
Bond (S. S.) W, **7**, 15.
Bond* (W. S.) W, **2**, 10. First north of
Warner Av., fr. St. Charles Av. to Selwin
Avenue.
Bond Av. (S. S.) S-E, w, **10**, 14, Seventy-fifth,
7500; 17, Eighty-third, 8300.
Bonfield (S. S.) S-E, w, **5**, 15, Archer Av. 2900.
Bonney Av. (W. S.) S, e, 4, 9†, Harrison, 328;
12, Sixteenth, 788; 15, Twenty-sixth,
1236; **7**, 6.
Boomer (S. S.) S, **9**, 1. (Now vacated.)
Boone* (W. S.) W, s, **5**, 8, DeKalb, 1. First
south of Polk, fr. DeKalb to Leavitt.
Borso Pl. (S. S., in Morgan Pk.) W, **11**, 8.
Boston Av. (W. S.) W, s, **6**, 7, Desplaines, 1.
Bosworth Av. (N. S.) N, e, **3**, 11, Addison Av.
142.
Boulevard* (N. S.) N, w, **6**, 5, Ohio, 51. First
west of the lake, fr. Ohio to Ontario.

Boulevard* (S. S., in Calumet) S, **12**, 10. Bet-
Union and Jefferson, fr. Diana to west part
of Sharpshooters' Park.
Boulevard Pl. (S. S.) W, **9**, 2.
Boulevard Way* (W. S.) S, e, **5**, 13, Twenty
fifth, 38. First west of Francisco, fr.
Douglas Boul. to Twenty-fifth.
Boursault (N. S.) E, **3**, 7.
Bowen (S. S., in Calumet) S, **11**, 3†, 6.
Bowen Av. (S. S.) W, s, **9**, 3†, Ellis Av. 93. 2,
Vincennes Av. 441.
Bowery, The* (W. S.) S, e, **5**, 9, Tilden, 17.
Bet. Morgan and Aberdeen, fr. Van Buren
to Congress.
Bowman Av. (W. S.) N, **2**, 9.
Bowmanville Rd. (N. S.) N-E, **2**, 6; **3**, 4†.
Brackett (S. S.) W, **9**, 11.
Bradley* (W. S.) W, s, **5**, 3, Cleaver, 75. Bet.
Sloan and Ingraham, fr. Elston Av. to Holt.
Bradley Pl. (N. S.) E, **3**, 11.
Brand (W. S.) N and N-W, e, **8**, 13, Berg Pl. 42.
Brand Av. (W. S.) N, **2**, 14.
Breckenridge Av. (W. S.) W, s, **2**, 17, Summers
Av. 1467; 16†.
Bremen (W. S.) W, s, **2**, 18, Myrtle, 2.
Bremen Pl. (W. S.) W, s, **2**, 18, Powell Av. 41.
Breslau* (W. S.) N, e, **3**, 16, Hamburg. 2. Bet.
Oakley and Western Avs., fr. Hamburg to
Ems.
Briar Pl. (N. S.) E, n,
3, 13, Leavitt, 201.
Brigham* (W. S.) W, s,
5, 2, Paulina, 59.
Bristol (S. S.) W, n, **9**,
1, Sultan, 414.
Bristol Av. (W. S.) N,
4, 2.
Broad (S. S.) S-E, w,
5. 15, Archer Av.
3000.

St. Joseph's Hospital (old
building). Burling St. and
Garfield Avenue.

Broadway (S. S., in Blue Island) W, **11**, 17†, 16.
Brompton Av. (N. S.) E, **3**, 12, Halsted, 1604.
Bronson (S. S.) W, **8**, 6.
Brookes Av. (S. S., at Grand Crossing) S, **9**,
15†, Seventy-fifth, 7500; 18, Eighty-third,
8300.
Brooks Av. (S. S.) S, **9**, 16.
Broom (S. S.) N. e, **5**, 5, Indiana, 2.
Bross Av. (S. S.) S-W, n, **5**, 17, Robey,
3103; 16†.
Brown (W. S.) S, e, **5**, 9, Taylor, 2; 12†.
Sixteenth, 264.
Brunswick (W. S.) N, **2**. 14.
Bryan Pl.* (W. S.) N-W; Nos. odd, on north
side only; **5**. 6, Lake, 57. On northeast side
of Union Park, fr. West Randolph to Lake.
Bryant Av. (S. S.) N, e, **6**, 17, Stanton Av. 88.
Bryn Mawr Av. (N. S.) E, n, **3**, 4†; 2, Evanston
Av. 1199.
Buckingham Pl. (N. S.) E, n, **3**, 12, Evanston
Av. 1757.
Buena Av. (N. S.) E, **3**, 8†, 9.
Buena Park Ter. (N. S.) N-E, **3**, 8.
Buena Vista Pl. (S. S.) N-E, n, **6**, 13, Emerald
Av. 6.
Buffalo Av. (S. S., in South Chicago) S, w, **10**,
18†, Eighty-third, 8300; **13**, 3, Ninety-
first, 9100.
Buffalo Av. (S. S., in Hegewisch) S, **13**, 18.
Bunker (W. S.) W, s, **6**, 7, Clinton, 59.
Burchell Av. (W. S.) N, e, **2**, 15, Humboldt
Boulevard
1428.
Burchell Av.
(W. S.) W,
s, **2**, 17,
Ballou,
430.
Burling (N. S.)
N, e, **3**,
18†, Cen-
tre, 210;
15, Dewey
Ct. 716.
Burlington* (W. S.) S, e, **6**, 10, Sixteenth, 1.
Bet. Jefferson and Seward, fr. Sixteenth to
Eighteenth.
Burnett* (W. S.) W, **5**, 2, Hoyne Av. 170. Bet.
Thomas and Augusta, fr Robey to Leavitt.

St. Joseph's Hospital (new building),
Burling St. and Garfield Av.

Buruside Av. (S. S.) N-W, **12**, 2.
Burr Oak Av. (S. S., in Blue Island) W, **11**, 14.
Burtis (S. S.) Name changed; see Seeley Av.
Burton Pl. (N. S.) E, s, **6**, 1†, Clark, 2; 2, Lake Shore Drive, 100.
Bush Av. (S. S) S, **13**. next south of section 16.
Butler (S. S.) S, w, **6**, 13†, Twenty-sixth, 2600; 16, Thirty-fifth, 3500; **9**, 4, Fifty-first, 5100.
Butler Av. (W. S.) S, w, **4**, 14, Twenty-sixth, 2600.
Butterfield. Name changed; see Armour Av.
Byford Av. (W. S.) S, e, **4**, 12, Fifteenth, 743.
Byrne Av. (W. S.) N, **2**, 14.
Byron Av. (N. S.) E, n, **3**, 10†, Lincoln Av. 601; 11, Racine Av. 1205.
Byron Av. (W. S.) W, s, **2**, 18, Mozart, 31.
Byron Av. (W. S.) W, **2**, 12.

C (N. S.) W, n, **3**, 17, Dominick, 28.
Calhoun Av. (S. S., in South Chicago) S, **13**, 5, 8†, 11.
Calhoun Pl. (S. S.) W, **6**, 4.

California Av. North (W. S.) N, e, **5**, 4†, Kinzie, 126; 1, Division, 604; **2**, 18, Armitage Av. 1072; 15, Diversey Av. 1554.
California Av. South (W. S. & S. S.) S, e, **5**, 4†, Lake, 1; 7, Harrison, 323; 10, Sixteenth, 804; 13, Twenty-sixth, 1293; 16; **8**, 1, 4, 10, 16; **11**, 1, 4, 7, 10, 13, 16.
California Av. (S. S., in Blue Island) S, **11**, 13†, 16.
Calumet (S. S., in Blue Island) W, **11**, 18.
Calumet Av. (S. S.) S, w, **6**, 11, Eighteenth, 1800; 14†, Twenty - sixth, 2600; 17, Thirty-fifth, 3500; **9**, 2, Forty-third,4300; 5, Fifty-first, 5100; 8. Fifty-ninth, 5900; 11, Sixty-seventh, 6700; 14, Seventy-fifth, 7500; 17; **12**, 5, 8, 17.
Calumet Av.(S. S.) S, **13**, 11.
Calumet Av. (S. S.) S, **11**, 14.
Campbell * (S.S., in South Washington Heights) S-E, **5**, 17. Bet. Wood and Lincoln, fr. Thirty-first southeast about two blocks.
Campbell Av. North*(W. S.) N, e, **5**, 4, Kinzie, 126; 1. Division, 604; **2**, 18, Armitage Av. 1050.
Campbell Av. South (W. S. & S. S.) S, e, **5**, 4, Lake. 1, 7†, Harrison, 323; 10, Sixteenth, 801; 13, 16; **8**, 13.
Campbell Park * (W.S.) W, s, **5**, 8, Leavitt, 1. Bet. Polk and Flournoy, fr. Leavitt St. to Oakley Av.

Mercy Hospital, Calumet Av. and Twenty-Sixth St.

Campbell Pl.* (N. S.) E, **6**, 4. Bet. Indiana and Ohio, fr. La Salle Av. to Clark.
Canal, North*(W. S.) N, w, **6**, 4, Fulton, 73.
Canal, South (W. S.) S, e, **6**, 4, Randolph, 1; 7†, Harrison, 301; 10, Sixteenth, 976; 13; **12**, 1, 10.
Canal (S. S., in Blue Island) W, **11**, 17.
Canal Pl. (W. S.) W, **3**, 17.
Canalport Av. (W. S.) S-W, n, **6**, 10†, Canal, 2; **5**, 12, Morgan, 290.
Carl (N. S.) E, s, **6**, 1, Wells, 2.
Carl (W. S.) S, **4**, 14.
Carlin Av. (S. S.) S, w, **10**, 14, Seventy-seventh, 7700.
Carlson (S. S.) W, **12**, 14. :

Carlyle Pl.* (S. S.) W, **6**, 17. Bet. Thirty-fifth and Thirty-sixth, fr. Cottage Grove Av. west ¼ block.
Carm (S. S.) S, **11**, 1.
Carondelet (S. S.) S, **13**, 11.
Carpenter, North (W. S.) N, w, **5**, 6†, Kinzie, 115; 3, the river, 385.
Carpenter, South (W. S. and S. S.) S, e, **5**, 6†, Randolph, 1; **8**, 6, 9, 12, 15, 18.
Carpenter Rd. (W. S.) N and N-E, 1, 5, 2†, 3.
Carrington (S. S.) W, **11**, 1.
Carroll (W. S.) W, **2**, 14.
Carroll Av. (W. S.) W, s, **6**, 4, Canal, 1; **5**, 6†, Ann, 337; 5, Robey, 793; 4, Francisco, 1333; 4, 6, Central Park Av. 1769, 5, West Forty-fourth or Richmond Av. 2167.
Carse Av. (S. S., in South Chicago) S, **13**, 1.
Cass (N. S.) N, w, **6**, 5†, Kinzie, 1; 2, Rush, 244.
Cass (S. S., in Blue Island) S, **11**, 18.
Castello Av. (W. S.) W, **2**, 17†, 16.

Union Depot, Canal and Adams Streets.

Castello Av. (W. S.) N, **2**, 14.
Castle (W. S.) W, s, **4**, 2. Forty-fourth, 1885
Catalpa Pl.* (W. S.) N-W and W, **2**, 18, Follansbee, 16; 15, Kedzie, 144. First east of Kedzie Av., beginning at McGovern.
Catalpha * (N. S.) E, **3**, 8. First south of Berteau Av., fr. Perry to Clark.
Cedar (N. S.) E, s, **6**, 2, Lake Shore Drive, 76.
Cedar (S. S.) W, **9**, 7.
Cedar* (S. S.) S, **13**, 11. East of Calumet River, fr. 111th to 113th.
Cedar (S. S.) W, **7**, 15.
Cedar (S. S., in Lyons) S, **7**, 13.
Cedar Av. (W. S., in Norwood Pk.) **1**, 1.
Centennial Ct.* (W. S.) W, n, **5**, 5. Paulina. 50. Bet. Ohio and Erie,fr. Ashland Av.toPaulina.
Central Av.* (S. S.) S, **6**, 5. First east of Michigan, fr. South Water to Randolph.
Central Av. (S. S., in South Chicago) S, **10**, 16.
Central Av. (W. S., in Cicero) N, **4**, 7†, 4; 1, 11.
Central Av. (W. S., in Galewood) N, **1**, 16.
Central Av. (W. S., in Norwood Park) **1**, 1.
Central Boul. (W. S.) W, s, **5**, 4, Sacramento Av. 1238, **4**, 6†, Central Park Av. 1607.
Central Park Av. North (W. S.) N, e, **4**, 6, Kinzie, 126; 3†, Division, 604; **2**, 17, Armitage Av. 1090; 14, 11.
Central Park Av. South (W. S. & S. S.) S, e, **4**, 9, Harrison, 335; **12**, Sixteenth, 803; 15†, Twenty - sixth, 1253; 18; **7**, 3, 6, 9, 12, 15, 18.
Centre (N. S.) E, n, **3**, 17†, Racine Av. 31; 18, Lincoln Av. and Sedgwick, 393.

St. James Episcopal Church, Cass and Huron Streets.

Centre * (N. S.) N, **3**, 15. First east of Clark.
Centre * (N. S.) S, **3**, 11. First west of Clark, fr. Graceland Av. south about a block.
Centre (N. S.) E, **3**, 4†; 5, Evanston Av. 1117.
Centre (N. S.) W, **2**, 8†, 7.
Centre (W. S.) N, **1**, 9.
Centre (S. S., in Calumet) W, **11**, 9.
Centre Av. North (W. S.) N, w, **5**, 6†, Kinzie, 1; 3, Augusta, 314.
Centre Av. South (W. S.) S, e, **5**, 9†, Harrison, 179; 12, Sixteenth, 537; 15, Lumber, 835; **8**, 6, Fifty-first, 5100; 9, 12, 15, 18; **11**, 3, 6, 9, 12.
Centre Av. (S. S.) S, **13**, 8, 11†, 14.
Centre Av. (W. S., in Montrose) N, **2**, 7.
Centre Av. (W. S.) W, s, **2**, 15†, Elston Av. 215; 14.
Centre Av. (S. S., in Washington Heights) S and S-E, **1**, 18.
Centre Av. See Ashland Av., fr. 131st south.
Chadwick* (S. S., in Blue Island) S, **11**, 17.
Chalmers Pl*. (N. S.) W, **3**, 17. Bet. Belden and Fullerton Avs., fr. ¼ block west of Halsted St. to Sheffield Av.

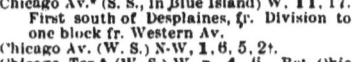

Chamberlain Av. (W. S.) S, **2**, 13.
Chambers (S. S.) S, **13**, 8, 11†, 14.
Champlain (S. S.) S, w, **5**, 17, Thirty-fifth. 3450.
Champlain (S. S., in Blue Island) S-E, **11**, 18.
Champlain Av. (S. S.) S, w, **9**, 2, Forty-third, 4258; 5†, Fiftieth,4958; 11, Sixty-seventh, 6700; 14, Seventy-fifth, 7500; **12**, 2.
Chanay (W. S.) N-E, **2**, 18.
Chapel Av. (S. S., in Worth) S, **11**, 4.
Chapin (W. S.) E, n, **5**, 3.
Chapin* (W. S.) N, **2**, 11. Second east of Central Park Av., fr. Henderson Av. to C. & N. W. R. R.
Chappell Pl. (S. S.) Name changed; see Berkley Av.
Charles (S. S.) S-E, **13**, 8, 11†.
Charles (W. S.) S, e, **6**, 7, Harrison, 313.
Charles (S. S., in Calumet) S-E, **11**, 5†, 6, 9.
Charles Ct. (S. S.) S, **11**, 9.
Charles Pl.* (S. S.) W, n, **6**. 7. Bet. Congress and Harrison, fr. Fifth Av. to Franklin.
Charlotte (W. S.) W, s, **4**, 9†, Central Park Av. 1857; 8, West Forty-fourth, 2357.
Charlotte Av. (W. S.) W, **1**, 18.
Charlton (N. S.) N, e. **3**, 2, Francis, 2766.
Charlton (S. S.) S, w, **5**, 18, Thirty-fourth, 3400.
Chase (W. S.) N, w, **5**, 3, Fry, 25.
Chase Av. (W. S.) N, e, **2**, 17, Breckenridge Av. 904.
Chase Ct.* (W. S.) S, e, **5**, 14, Coulter, 2. Bet. Oakley and Western Avs., fr. Coulter St. to Blue Island Av.
Chatham* (S. S., in Blue Island) S, **11**, 17. Bet. Chicago and Wabash, fr. 131st to Calumet River.
Chatham Ct. (N. S.) N, e, 6, 1, Elm, 38.
Chauncey Av. (S. S., at Grand Crossing) S, **9**, 15, 18†.
Cheltenham Av. (S. S.) S, **10**, 18, Eighty-fourth, 8400.
Cheltenham Pl. (S. S.) S-W, **10**, 14, Bond Av. 73.
Cheney (W. S.) W, **2**, 5, 4†.
Cherry (S. S.) W, **7**, 15.
Cherry (S. S., in Calumet) W, **11**, 11.
Cherry Av.* (N. S.) N-W and N, e, **5**, 3, Eastman, 148. Bet. North Branch and Hickory, fr. junction of Bliss and North Branch to North Av.
Cherry Pl. (W. S.) W, s, **2**, 18, Perry Av. 50.
Chester (N. S.) S-W, W and N, **3**, 16, Clybourn Av. 2.

Chicago Avenue Church, northwest corner Chicago and La Salle Avenues.

Chestnut (N. S.) E, s, **6**, 1†, Market, 146; 2, Pine, 460.
Chestnut* (S. S.) W, **8**, 4. Bet. Fifty-third and Fifty-fourth, fr. Sacramento Av. to Sheridan Av.
Chestnut (S. S., in Englewood) W, n, **9**, 7, Stewart Av. 500.
Chestnut (W. S., in Austin) W, **4**, 4.
Chestnut (W. S., in Montclair) N, **1**, 16.
Chestnut Pl.* (N. S.) N, w, **6**, 2, Delaware Pl. 23. First east of Rush, fr. Chestnut St. to Delaware Pl.
Chicago (S. S., in Blue Island) S. **11**, 17.
Chicago Av. East (N. S.) E, s, **6**, 4†, Market, 138; 2, the lake, 470.
Chicago Av. West (W. S.) W, n, **6**, 1, the river. 2; **5**, 3, Centre Av. 264; 2, Robey, 688; 4†, California Av. 1158; 4, 3, Central Park Av. 1654; 2, West Forty-fourth, 2176; 1, West Fifty-second, 2690.

Chicago Av.* (S. S., in Blue Island) W, **11**, 17. First south of Desplaines, fr. Division to one block fr. Western Av.
Chicago Av. (W. S.) N-W, **1**, 6, 5, 2†.
Chicago Ter.* (W. S.) W, n, **4**, 6. Bet. Ohio and Huron, fr. Harding Av. to West Fortieth.
Chippewa Av. (S. S.) S, e, **8**, 16.
Choctaw Av. (S. S.) S, e, **8**, 16.
Christiana Av. (W. S.) N, e, **4**, 3, Division, 100.
Church (S. S., in Morgan Park) S and S-W, **11**, 9, 8, 11†.
Church (W. S., in Jefferson) E and N-E, **1**, 0.
Church Pl.* (S. S.) S-E, w, **5**, 15, Archer Av. 2861. Second east of Lock, one block long, on north side of Archer Av.
Church Pl. (W. S.) W, s, **5**, 9, Aberdeen, 68.
Church Rd. (N. S., City Limits) E, **3**. 1†, 2.
Churchill (W. S.) W, s, **3**, 16, Hoyne Av. 51.
Cicero Ct. (W. S.) S, e, **5**, 7, Congress, 67.
Circle, East (W. S., in Norwood Park) **1**, 1.
Circle, West (W. S., in Norwood Park) **1**, 1.
Clara Pl. (W. S.) W, s, **2**, 18, Powell Av. 41.
Clare Av. (S. S., in Calumet) N W, **11**, 11.
Claremont (W. S.) W, **1**, 5.
Claremont Av. (N. S.) E, n, **3**, 5, Evanston Av. 1201.
Claremont Av.* (N. S.) N, **3**, 4. First east of Western Av., fr. Webster Av. to North Fifty-ninth.
Claremont Av. (W. S.) S, e, **5**, 8, Flournoy, 353.
Clarence (W. S.) W, **4**, 8.
Clarence Av. (N. S.) N, e, **3**, 11, Grace, 170
Clarinda (W. S.) W, n, **5**, 3, Holt, 2; 2†.
Clarinda (S. S., in Worth) S, **11**, 1.
Clark, North (N. S.) N and N-W, e, **6**, 4, Kinzie,40; 1†, Division, 4 4 8; **3**, 18, Centre, 879; 15, Diversey, 1382; 14, Noble Av. 1603; 11, Addison, 1990; 8, Montrose Boul. 3063; 3, North Fifty-ninth, 3594; 2.
Clark, South (S. S.) S, w, **6**, 4, South Water, 2; 7†, Harrison, 352; 10, Sixteenth, 1600; 13, 16; **9**, 1, 4, 7; **12**, 4, 10.
Clark (W. S.) W and S-W, **1**, 6.
Clark Av. (S. S., in South Chicago) S, **13**, 1.
Clarkson Av. (W. S.) N, e, **2**, 18, Armitage Av. 120.
Clarkson Ct* (W. S.) S, e, **5**, 4, Lake, 1. Bet. Francisco and California Avs., fr. Lake St. to Washington Boul.
Clay (N. S.) E and S-W, n, **3**, 17, Sheffield Av. 1.
Clay (N. S.) W, **2**, 6.
Clay Av. (N. S.) E, **3**, 4, Garfield Av. 337.
Claybourn Av. (W. S.) N, **2**, 5†. 2.
Clayton* (W. S.) W, s, **5**, 12, Morgan, 61. Bet. Twentieth and Twenty-first, fr. Johnson nearly to Centre Av.
Cleaver (W. S.) S, e, **5**, 3, Bradley, 108.
Clement Av.* (S. S.) S-E, **9**, 11. See Anthony Av.
Clement Av. (S. S.) S, **8**, 1.
Cleveland (S. S., in Englewood) W, n, **9**, 7, Wallace, 600.
Cleveland Av. (N. S.) N, e, **6**, 1†, Clybourn Av. 2; **3**, 18, Centre, 440.
Cleveland Av. (N. S.) E, **3**, 11. Name changed; see Newport Av.
Cleveland Av. (W. S.) N,4, 2, Iowa,400.
Clifton (W. S.) W, s, **4**, 14, Butler Av. 2169.
Clifton Av. (N. S.) N, e, **3**, 14†, Wellington, 2; 11, Roscoe or Knauer, 258.
Clifton Av. (W. S.) N, e, **2**, 15, Humboldt Boul. 1428.

Clifton Av. (S. S., in Worth) 8, **11**, 1†, 7, 10.
Clifton Park Av. (W. S.) 8, e. **4**, 12, Sixteenth, 804; 15†, Twenty-sixth, 1256.
Clinton, North (W. S.) N, w, **6**, 4, Kinzie, 137.
Clinton, South (W. S.) 8, e, **6**, 4†, Randolph, 1; 7, Harrison, 291; 10, Maxwell, 537.
Clinton (S. S., in Blue Island) S-E, **11**, 18.
Clinton (S. S., in Calumet) 8, **12**, 1, 4†.
Clinton (W. S., in Norwood Park) N-E, **1**, 1.
Clinton Av. (S. S.) 8, **9**, 4.
Cloud Av. (S. S., in South Chicago) 8, **13**, 1.
Cloud Ct. (S. S.) W, n, **9**, 7, Wentworth Av. 300.
Clybourn Av. (N. S.) N-W, e, **6**, 1†, Division, 2; **5**, 3, Weed, 278; **3**, 17, Racine Av. 552; 13, Diversey Av. and Robey, 1240.
Clybourn Pl. (N. S.) W, s, **3**, 17, Hawthorne Av. 41.
Clybourn Pl. West (W. S.) W, s, **3**, 17, Elston Av. 161; 16†, Robey, 359.
Clyde* (N. S.) N-E, e ,**3**, 17, Maude Av. 22. Bet. Willow St. and Wabansia Av., fr. Clybourn Av. to Centre.
Coblentz (W. S.) W, s, **3**, 16, Leavitt, 95.
Cochrane (S. S.) W, **11**, 13.
Coles Av. (S. S.) S-E, **10**, 14. Seventy-fifth, 7501.
Colfax Av. (S. S.) 8, w, **9**, 11, Sixty-sixth, 6600.
Colfax Av. (S. S.) 8, **13**, 7, 10†, 13.
Colfax Av. (S. S.) 8, **10**, 17†; **13**, 11, 14, 17.
College (S. S., in Calumet) 8, **11**, 2.
College (S. S., in Washington Heights) S, **11**, 8.
College Pl. (S. S.) W, n, **6**, 17, Rhodes Av. 54.
Collins* (W. S.) W, s, **5**, 10, Albany Av. 2. Bet. Douglas Boul. and Fifteenth, fr. Albany Av. to Kedzie Av.

First M. E. Church, 1834.
Clark and North Water Sts.

Collins (S. S., in Calumet) W, **11**, 13.
Collins Ct.* (W. S.) 8, w, **5**, 14, Coulter, 54. Bet. Oakley Av. and Leavitt, fr. Laughton to Coulter.
Cologne (S. S.) S-W, n, **5**, 15, Main, 2500.
Colonade Row (S. S., in Blue Island) 8, **11**, 17.
Colorado Av. (W. S.) S-W, s, **5**, 7†, Francisco, 71; **4**, 9, Central Park Av. 534; 8, West Forty-fourth, 1077.
Colton (S. S.) W, **9**, 17.
Columbia (W. S.) W, **3**, 16, Milwaukee Av. 2.
Columbia Av. (W. S., in Jefferson) N, **2**, 16.
Columbia Pl.* (W. S.) N, e, 4, 6, Fulton, 90. First west of Hamlin Av., fr. Lake to Kinzie.
Columbus Av. (W. S., in Jefferson) N-W, **2**, 7.
Columbus Av. (S. S.) S-W, **9**, 13; **7**, 18†.
Commercial (N. S.) N-W and N, e, **3**, 13†, Paulina, 2; 10, Byron, 2202; 7. Montrose Boul. 2532; 4, Webster Av. 2954.
Commercial (W. S.) N, e, **3**, 16, Clybourn Pl. 140.
Commercial Av. (S. S., in South Chicago) 8, w, **10**, 17†, Eighty-third, 8300; **13**, 2, Ninety-first, 9100; 5, Ninety-ninth, 9854.
Concord (S. S.) W, n, **9**, 4†, Stewart Av. 500; 8, 6.
Concord (S. S., in Blue Island) 8, **11**, 17.
Concord Pl. (N. S.) N, n, **3**, 17, Sheffield Av. 46.
Congress, East (S. S.) W, n, **6**, 8†, Michigan Av. 2; 7, Market, 223.
Congress, West (W. S.) W, n, **6**, 7†, Clinton, 69; **5**, 9, Centre Av. 330; 8, Robey, 746; 7, California Av. 1204; 4, 9, Homan Av. 1564; 8, West Forty-fourth, 2248.
Congress Pk.* (W. S.) 8, e, **5**, 7, Congress, 35. First east of Washtenaw Av., from Van Buren to Harrison.
Connors* (N. S.) E; Nos. on north side only; **6**, 1. First south of Blackhawk, fr. Cleveland Av. to Sedgwick.

Conrad* (W. S.) W, n, **6**, 10, Ruble, 2. Bet. Eighteenth and Canalport Av., fr. Ruble to Union.
Constance Av. (S. S.) 8, **10**, 16.
Cook (N. S.) E, **3**, 1.
Cook (S. S.) 8, **9**, 6†, 9.
Cook (W. S.) W, **2**, 12.
Cook (W. S.) W, **3**, 14.
Cook* (W. S.) S-W, n, **6**, 4, Dunn, 35. First north of Kinzie, fr. the river to Jefferson.
Coolidge* (W. S.) W, s, **6**, 10, Union, 60. Bet. Dussold and Kramer, fr. Jefferson to Halsted.
Cooper (N. S.) N, e, **3**, 17, Clybourn Av. 2.
Cooper (S. S.) 8, **9**, 11.
Cork* (W. S.) W, n, **5**, 5, Paulina, 50. Bet. Erie and Ohio, fr. Ashland Av. to Paulina.
Cornelia (N. S.) E, n, **3**, 10†, Wood, 601; 11, Racine Av. 1207; 12, Pine Grove Av. 1802.
Cornelia (W. S.) W, n, **5**, 3, Milwaukee Av. 6; 2†, Wood, 274; 1, Seymour Av. 646.
Cornelia (W. S.) N-E, e, **2**, 18†, Stave, 42.
Cornelia (W. S., in Jefferson) W, **2**, 11.
Cornelius (S. S., in Calumet) W, **12**, 7.
Cornell (W. S.) W, n, **5**, 3, Noble, 92.
Cornell Av. (S. S.) 8, e, **10**, 4†, Fifty-first, 5100; 7, Fifty-sixth, 5558.
Cortez (W. S.) W, n, **5**, 1, Francisco, 928.
Cortland (W. S.) W, s, **3**, 16, Hoyne Av. 51.
Cortland Av. (W. S.) W, s, **2**, 18, California Av. 461; 17†, Central Park Av. 883; 16; 1, 17, 16.
Cortland Ct. (W. S.) W, s, **2**, 17, Clarkson Av. 2
Corwin* (W. S.) 8, e, **5**, 11, Sixteenth, 49. Bet. Lincoln and Robey, fr. Fifteenth to Sixteenth.
Corwin Pl.* (W. S.) 8, w, **5**, 14, Moore, 2. Bet. Lincoln and Robey, fr. Moore south about ½ block.
Cosgrove Av. (N. S.) E, **3**, 7†, Ravenswood Park, 608; 8, Clark, 914.
Cossitt Av. (W. S., in Montrose) N, **2**, 7.
Costello Av. (W. S.) N, **2**, 14.
Cottage Grove Av. (S. S.) S-E and 8, w, **6**, 14†. Twenty-sixth St. and South Park Av. 2614; 17, Thirty-fifth St. and Vincennes Av. 3510; **9**, 2, Forty-third, 4300; 5, Fifty-first, 5101; 8, Fifty-ninth, or Midway Pleasance, 5901; 11, Sixty-seventh, 6700; 14, Seventy-fifth, 7500; 17; **12**, 2, 5, 8, 17.
Cottage Grove Av.* (S. S., in Pullman) N, w, **12**, 9, 106th, 701. Third west of Lake Calumet, fr. 107th to 104th.
Cottage Pl.* (W. S.) W, **5**, 9. Bet. Adams and Jackson, fr. Throop to Loomis.
Couch Pl. (S. S.) W, **6**, 4.
Coulter (W. S.) S-W and W, s, **5**, 14†, Robey, 1; 13, California Av. 487.

Presbyterian Hospital,
Congress and Wood Streets.

Court (S. S., in Calumet) W **11**, 9, 8†.
Court Pl. (S. S.) W, **6**, 4.
Court Pl. (S. S.) W, **9**, 10.
Coventry (W. S.) N-W, e, **3**, 17, Bloomingdale Rd. 120.
Craft (N. S.) N and N-E, **3**, 11.
Crandall Av.* (N. S.) N, **2**, 11. First west of Hamlin Av., fr. School St. to Cornelia Av.
Crawford* (S. S.) 8, w, **6**, 13, Crawford Ct. 2227. Second west of Stewart Av., fr. Twenty-second St. to Archer Av.
Crawford Av. North (W. S.) N, e. 4, 5, Kinzie, 126; 2†, Division, 604; **2**, 16, Armitage Av. 1104; 13.
Crawford Av. South (W. S.) 8, e, 4, 5, Lake, 2; 8, Harrison, 427; 11, Sixteenth, 912; 14, Twenty-sixth, 1390; 17†, **7**, 2, 5, 8, 11, 14, 17.
Crawford Av.* (S. S.) 8, **9**, 14. First west of St. Lawrence, near Seventy-seventh.

Crawford Ct.* (S.S.) **6**, 13. Bet. Twenty-second St. and Archer Av., and west of the Grand Trunk R. R.
Cregier Av. (S. S.) S, **10**, 13.
Crilly Pl.* (N. S.) N, e, **3**, 18, Eugenie, 2. Bet. Franklin and Wells, fr. Eugenie to Florimond.
Crimea (S. S.) S, w, **9**, 1, Bristol, 4528.
Crittenden* (W. S.) E, s, **5**, 3, Wade, 24. Second south of Division, fr. Noble to C. & N. W. R. R.
Crittenden Rd. (S. S.) S-E, **13**, 14, 17†.
Crocker Av. (S. S.) S, **8**, 9.
Cromwell (W. S.) N, c, **2**, 15, Rhine. 36. First east of California Av., fr. Milwaukee Av. to Fullerton Av.
Crooked (N. S.) E and S, n, **3**, 17.
Crosby (N. S.) N-W, e, **6**, 1, Elm, 116.
Cross (W. S.) S, e, **4**, 9, Harrison, 325.
Crossing (W. S.) W, s, **3**, 17, Mendell Ct. 24; 16†, Paulina, 111.
Crown Pl. (W. S.) S, e, **5**, 13, Twenty-sixth, 1.
Crystal (W. S.) W, n, **5**, 2, Hoyne Av. 124.
Currier* (W. S.) N, e, **5**, 3, Crittenden, 46. First east of Noble, fr. Augusta to Chapin.
Curtis, North (W. S.) N and N-W, w, **5**, 6, Austin Av. 143.
Curtis, South (W. S.) S, e, **5**, 6, Washington Boul. 31.
Curtis (S. S.) S, **8**, 18.
Custab Av. (W. S.) W, **2**, 10.
Custer Av. (S. S.) S, **8**, 16.
Custom House Pl.* (S. S.) S, w, **6**, 7, Harrison, 106; 10. Bet. Dearborn and Clark, fr. Jackson to Fourteenth.
Cuyler Av. (N.S.) E, **3**, 7.
Cynthia Ct.* (W. S.) S, e, **4**, 12, Ogden Av.907. First east of Central Park Av., fr. Ogden Av. to Twenty-second.
Union League Club House, Jackson St. and Fourth Av. or Custom House Pl.
Cypress* (W. S.) S, e, **5**, 8, Taylor, 39. First west of Myrtle. fr. Kendall to Twelfth.

Dakota Av. (S. S.) W, **8**, 11.
Dale Pl. (W. S.) S, e, **5**, 11, Twenty-second. 2. Bet. Wood and Paulina, fr. Twenty-second south about ½ block.
Daly (S. S.) S, **5**, 16.
Damon* (W. S.) W, n, **5**, 9, Aberdeen, 72. First north of Taylor, fr. Sholto to May.
Danford (S. S.) S, **13**, 8.
Danforth (W. S., in Jefferson) N-W, **1**, 6.
Dania Av. (W. S.) N, e, **5**, 1†, Division, 604; **2**, 18, Bloomingdale Rd. 954.
Daniels Pl. (W. S.) W, **4**, 2.
Dashiel Av. Name changed; see Union Av.
Dauphin Av. (S. S.) S-W, **12**, 3.
Davis (N. S.) N, **3**, 4.
Davis (S. S.) S, **8**, 8†, 11.
Davis (W. S.) N, e, **5**, 2†, Division, 600; **3**, 16, Wabansia Av. 894.
Davis Av. (S. S.) S, **12**, 10.
Davlin (W. S.) N, e, **4**, 6, Fulton, 90.
Davlin (W. S.) S-W and S, **2**, 14.
Davol (S. S., in South Washington Heights) S-W, **11**, 11.
Dawson Av. (W. S.) N-E, **2**, 14.
Day Av. (S. S.) S, **13**, 11, 14†.
Dayton (N. S.) N, e, **5**, 3, Recs. 2; **3**, 17†, Centre, 316.
Dean* (W. S.) N-W, w, **5**, 2, Paulina, 7. First north of Milwaukee Av., fr. Paulina to Brigham.
Dearborn (S. S.) S, w, **6**, 4, South Water. 2; 7†, Harrison, 368; 10, Sixteenth, 1600; 13, Twenty-sixth, 2600; 16, Thirty-fifth,

3500; **9**, 1, Forty-third, 4300 ; 4, Fifty-first, 5100; 7, Fifty-ninth. 5900; 10, Sixty-seventh, 6700; 13, Seventy-fifth, 7500; **12**, 4, 10.
Dearborn Av. (N. S.) N, w, **6**, 4, Kinzie, 35; 1†, Division, 421.
Dearborn Pl.* (S. S.) S, e, **6**, 5, Washington, 41. See Garland.
Deering (S. S.) S-E, w, **5**, 15, Archer Av. 2900.
DeKalb (W. S.) S-W, s, **5**, 8, Polk, 77.
DeKoven (W. S.) W, s, **6**, 7, Clinton, 121.
Delameter Pl. (W. S.) N, e, **2**, 17, Cortland, 1034.
Union Club House, Dearborn Av. and Washington Pl.
Delaware (W. S.) W, n, **4**, 1, West Forty-ninth, 2210.
Delaware Av. (W. S.) S, w, **4**, 14, Pearl, 2534.
Delaware Pl. (N. S.) E, s, **6**, 1, Dearborn Av. 2 ; 2†, Pine, 114.
Della (W. S.) W, s, **4**, 8, West Forty-seventh, 2581.
Deming (N. S.) E an_ N-E, n, **3**, 15, Clark, 1805.
Dempster Pl. (N. S.) E, **3**, 15.
Depot (W. S.) W, 1, 6.
Depot Pl. (W. S.) N, **2**, 10.
Depuyster (W. S.) W, s, **6**, 7, Desplaines. 1.
Desplaines, North*(W. S.) N, w, **6**, 4, Kinzie, 121.
Desplaines, South (W. S.) S, e, **6**, 4, Randolph, 1; 7†, Harrison, 279.
Desplaines (S. S.) S, **9**, 4, 7†, 16; **12**, 1, 4, 10.
Desplaines (S. S., in Blue Island) W, **11**, 17.
Detroit Av. (W. S.) N, **4**, 2.
Devon Av. (N. S., City Limits) E, **3**, 2.
Devonshire (S. S., in Blue Island) W, **11**, 17.
Dewey Ct. (N. S.) E, n, **3**, 15, Orchard, 1707.
Dewey Pl. (S. S.) W, 11, 2.
Dexter (S. S.) S, **8**, 9.
Dexter Av.* (W. S.) S-W, **5**, 14. Bet. the river and the Ill. and Mich. Canal, fr. Ashland Av. to Thirty-first.
Dexter Av. (S. S.) W, **3**, 1.
Diamond Av.* (W. S.) N, **4**, 2. See West Forty-fourth, fr. Division St. to North Av.
Diana (S. S., in Calumet) W, **12**, 10.
Diana Ter. (N. S.) N, **3**, 15. First east of Evanston Av., fr. Diversey Av. to Surf.
Dickens Av. (W. S.) W, s, **2**, 18†, California Av. 1; 17, Central Park Av. 481; 16.
Dickey (S. S.) S, w, **9**, 10†, Sixty-ninth, 6900; 13, Seventy-fifth, 7500; 16.
Dickey Av. (W. S.) W, s, **4**, 3, Homan Av. 127.
Dickson (N. S.) N, e, **5**, 3†, Division, 534; **3**, 17, Bloomingdale Rd. 898.
Dieden (W. S.) S-W, **5**, 3.
Diller (W. S.) N, e, **5**, 5, Austin Av. 70.
Diversey Av. East (N. S.) E, n, **3**, 13†, Claybourn Av. 401; 14. Racine and Lincoln Avs. 1207; 15, Lakeview Av. 1948.
Diversey Av. West (W. S.) W, s, **3**, 13†; **2**, 15, California Av. 384; 14, 13; 1, 15, 14, 13.
Division Street (N. S.) E, s, **5**, 3, the river, 2; **6**, 1†, Sedgwick, 318; 2, Lake Shore Drive, 633.
Division, West (W. S.) W, n, **5**, 3, the river. 8; 2†, Robey, 418; 1, California Av. 876; 4, 3, Central Park Av. 1362; 2, West Forty-fourth, 1886; 1.
Division (S. S., in Blue Island) S, **11**, 16.
Division (S. S., in Blue Island) S, **11**, 17.
Division Av. (W. S.) N-E, **2**, 7.
Dix* (W. S.) N and N-W, w, **5**, 3, Sangamon, 112. Second west of Halsted, fr. Chicago Av. to ½ block west of Sangamon.

Dobbins Av. (S. S.) S, **11**, **6**.
Dobson Av. (S. S.) S, **9**, 15†, Seventy-fifth, 7500; 18, Eighty-second, 8200.
Dock* (S. S.) N-W, **6**, 5. First west of Michigan Av., fr. River Street to the river.
Dodge (W. S.) S, e, **6**, 10, Maxwell, 79.
Dolton Av. (S. S., in Riverdale) S, **12**, 17.
Dominick (N. S.) N-W, e, **3**, 17, A St. 92.
Dor Pl. (W. S.) W, s, **4**, **3**, Springfield Av. 1.
Douglas (W. S.) W, **2**, 11†, 10.
Douglas Av. (S. S., in Calumet) S, **11**, 3†, **6**.
Douglas Av. (S. S.) S, **13**, 9, 12†.
Douglas Boul. (W. S.) S, E and S, **4**, 9†, 12; **5**, 10, 13.
Douglas Park Av. (S. S.) S, **6**, 13.
Douglas Park Pl. (W. S.) W, **5**, 10.
Dover* (W. S.) N, **2**, 7. First east of C. & N. W. R. R., fr. Irving Park Boul. to Centre.
Drake Av. (W. S.) N, e, **4**, 6, Ohio, 240.
Dresden (W. S.) W, **1**, 17.
Dresden Av. (W. S.) N, **2**, 14.
Drew (S. S., in Washington Heights) S, **11**, 8.
Drexel Av. (S. S.) S, w, **9**, 6, Fifty-second, 5200; 9†, Fifty-ninth, 5900; 12, Sixty-seventh, 6700; 15, Seventy-fifth, 7500; 18, Eighty-third, 8300.
Drexel Boul. (S. S.) S-E and S, **9**, 3, Forty-third, 4300; 6†, Fifty-first, 5100.
Dreyer (S. S.) S, **8**, 5†, 11.
Drummond Av.* (W. S.) N, **5**, 1. Bet. Central Park Boul. and Barclay, fr. Augusta to Division.
Duane (S. S., in Calumet) W, **11**, 11.
Duane (S. S., in Blue Island) S, **11**, 17.
Dudley (W. S.) N, e, **5**, 2†, Division, 542; **3**, 10, Armitage Av. 984.
Duncan Av. (S. S.) S, w, **10**, 14, Railroad Av. 7640; 17†, Eighty-second, 8161.
Dunham Av. (S. S., in Calumet) S, **12**, 10.
Dunn* (W. S.) N-W, w, **6**, 4, Kinzie, 1. First east of Jefferson, fr. Kinzie northwest about a block.
Dunning (N. S.) E, n, **3**, 13; 14†, Racine Av. 1201.
Durham Av. (W. S.) N, **2**, 16.
Dussold (W. S.) W, s, **6**, 10, Union, 59.
Dwight (W. S.) W, **1**, 6.
Dyer (S. S.) S, **11**, 3.
Dyer (W. S., in Jefferson) N-W, **1**, 6.

Eagle (W. S.) w, **6**, 4, Union, 53.
Earl (S. S.) W, n, **6**, 13, Shields Av. 2.
Earl Av. (S. S.) S, **10**, 13.
Early Av. (N. S.) S-E and E, **3**, 2, Swift, 1079.
East Av. (W. S., in Jefferson) N, **1**, 6.
East Circle (W. S., in Norwood Pk.) **1**, 1.
East Ct. (N. S.) S, **3**, 15.
East Crescent Av. (S.S., in Morgan Pk.) S, **11**, 8.
East End Av. (S. S) S, w, **10**, 4†, Fifty-first 5100; 7, Fifty-sixth, 5558.
Eastern Av. (S. S.) S, **8**, 10, 13†.
Eastern Av. (W. S.) N, **1**, 6†, 2.
Eastman (N. S.) N-E and E, s, **5**, 3, Hawthorne Av. 140.
Eastman* (W. S.) N-E. **1**, 6. From cor. of Maynard and Central Avs. to Milwaukee Av.
East River Av. (S. S.) S, **13**, 11.
Eastwood Av. (N. S.) E, **3**, 8.
Eberhard Av. (S. S.) S, **7**, 9, 12†.
Eberhardt Av. (W. S.) W, s, **4**, 3, Sheridan, 64.
Eberly Av. (W. S.) N, **2**, 14.

Ebuda Av. (S. S., in Morgan Pk.) W, **11**, 8.
Eda (S. S.) W, n, **6**, 17, Michigan Av. 28.
Edbrook Pl. (W. S.) W, s, **2**, 18, Powell Av. 41.
Eddy (N. S.) E, **3**, 11.
Edgar (W. S.) N, e, **3**, 16, Bloomingdale Rd. 122.
Edgecomb Ct. (N. S.) E, **3**, 8.
Edgerton Av. (S. S.) W, s, **9**, 9, Sixtieth, 6000.
Edgewater Av. (N. S.) E, **3**, 2.
Edgewater Pl. (N. S.) E, **3**, 2.
Edgewood Av.* (W. S.) W, s, **2**, 18, Milwaukee Av. 2. See McGovern.
Edith (W. S.) E, **4**, 3.
Edmond (N. S.) E, **3**, 11.
Edson Av. (N. S.) N, **3**, 14.
Edward (N. S.) N; Nos. odd and even, east side only; **3**, 18.
Edwards (W. S., in Jefferson) N and N-E, **1**, 6.
Edwards Av. (S. S., in South Chicago) S, w, **10**, 14, Seventy-eighth, 7800; 17†, Eighty-third, 8300.
Eighteenth, East (S. S.) W, n, **6**, 11†, Calumet Av. 1; 10, the river, 262.
Eighteenth, West (W. S.) W, n, **6**, 10†, Stewart Av. 26; **5**, 12, Centre Av. 450; 11, Robey, 906; 10, California Av. 1368; **4**, 12, Central Park Av. 1878; 11.
Eighteenth Pl. (W. S.) W, n, **5**, 12, Morgan, 96.
Eighth (S. S., in Pullman) S, **12**, 9.
Eightieth (S. S.) W, **10**, 17†, Reynolds Av. 341; 16; **9**, 18, 17, 16; **8**, 18, 17.
Eightieth Ct.* (S. S.) W, **10**, 17. First south of Eightieth, fr. Houston to I. C. R. R.
Eighty-first (S. S.) W, **10**, 17†, Reynolds Av. 361; 16; **9**, 18, 17, 16; **8**, 18, 17, 16; **7**, 18.
Eighty-first Pl.* (S. S.) W, **9**, 18. First south of Eighty-first, fr. Woodlawn Av. to I. C. R. R.
Eighty-second (S. S.) W, **10**, 17†, Reynolds Av. 371; 16; **9**, 18, 17, 16; **8**, 17, 16; **7**, 18.

Phaeton Station, Drexel and Oakwood Bouls.

Eighty-second Ct. (S. S.) W, **9**, 16.
Eighty-second Pl.* (S. S.) W, **9**, 18. First south of Eighty-second, fr. Woodlawn Av. west 2 blocks.
Eighty-third (S. S.) W, **10**, 18; Cheltenham Av. 2; 17†, Sherman Av. 426; 16; **9**, 18, 17, 16; **8**, 18, 17, 16; **7**, 18.
Eighty-third Ct. (S. S.) W, **9**, 16.
Eighty-third Pl.* (S. S.) W, **9**, 18. First south of Eighty-third, fr. Stony Island Av. to Jefferson.
Eighty-third Pl. (S. S.) W, s, **10**, 17, Arthur Av. 225.
Eighty-fourth (S. S.) W, **10**, 18†, Cheltenham Av. 3; 17, Sherman Av. 428; 16; **9**, 18, 17, 16; **8**, 18, 17.
Eighty-fifth (S. S.) W, **10**, 18†, Cheltenham Av. 2; 17, Sherman Av. 430; 16; **9**, 18, 17, 16; **8**, 18, 17.
Eighty-sixth (S. S.) W, **10**, 18†, the Strand, 1; 17, Sherman Av. 420; 16; **9**, 18, 17, 16; **8**, 18, 17.
Eighty-sixth Pl. (S. S.) W, **9**, 18.
Eighty-seventh (S. S.) W, **10**, 18, the Strand, 1; 17†, Sherman Av. 451; 16; **9**, 18, 17, 16; **8**, 18, 17, 16; **7**, 18, 17.
Eighty-seventh Pl. (S. S.) W, **12**, 3†, 2.
Eighty-eighth (S. S.) W, **13**, 3, the Strand, 1; 2, Muskegon Av. 413; 1†; **12**, 3, 2, 1; **11**, 3, 2.
Eighty-eighth Pl. (S. S.) W, **12**, 3, 2.
Eighty-ninth (S. S.) W, **13**, 3, the Strand, 1; 2, Muskegon Av. 413; 1†; **12**, 3, 2, 1; **11**, 3, 2.
Eighty-ninth Pl. (S. S.) W, **12**, 3, 2†.
Elaine (N. S.) N-W, **3**, 12.
Elbridge Av. (W. S.) E and N-E, **2**, 14.
Elburn Av.* (W. S.) W, **5**, 9, Loomis, 50. Formerly Nebraska, second north of Twelfth, fr. Throop St. to Ashland Av.
Elderkin (W. S.) W, **1**, 6.
Eldredge Ct. (S. S.) W, s, **6**, 8, Wabash Av. 33
Eldridge Av. (S. S.) S, **11**, 4.

Eleanor Av. (S. S., in South Chicago) S, **10**, 10†; **13**, 10, 13.
Eleventh, West* (W. S.) W, n, **5**, 9, Sholto, 102. First north of Twelfth, fr. Morgan to May.
Eleventh, West (W. S.) W, n, **5**, 9, Loomis, 50.
Elgin (S. S.) W, n, **6**, 10, Stewart Av. 72.
Elias Ct.* (S. S.) S-E, w, **5**, 15. Archer Av. 2900. First east of Deering, fr. Archer Av. to Lyman.
Elizabeth, North (W. S.) N, w, **5**, 6, Kinzie, 141.
Elizabeth, South (W. S.) S, e, **5**, 6†, Randolph, 1; **8**, 9, 12, 18; **11**, 3.
Elizabeth (S. S.) W, n, **9**, 4, Wright, 588.
Elizabeth (S. S., in Calumet) S-E, **11**, 6.
Elk* (W. S.) W, s, **5**, 2, Paulina, 27. First south of Blackhawk, about ¼ block long, on east side of Paulina.
Elk Grove Av. (W. S.) N-W and N, e. **5**, 2, Wood, 666; **8**, 16†, Armitage Av. 984.
Ellen (W. S.) S-W and W, s, **5**, 2, Macedonia, 68.
Ellery Av. (S. S.) S, **8**, 17.
Ellington Av. (S. S.) S, **10**, 13.
Elliott (S. S.) S-W and S, **10**, 16.
Ellis Av. (S.S.) S-E, w, **6**, 17, Thirty-fifth, 3500; 18†; **9**, 3, Forty-third, 4300; 6, Fifty-first, 5100; 9, Fifty-ninth, 5900 ; 12, Sixty-seventh, 6658; 15, 18.
Ellis Pk. (S. S.) S, w, **6**, 17, Thirty-sixth, 3600.
Ellsworth* (W. S.) S, e, **6**, 7, Mather, 52. First west of the river, fr. Harrison to Polk.
Elm (N. S.) N-E and E, s, **6**, 1†, Market, 214; 2, Lake Shore Drive, 488.
Elm (S. S.) W, **7**, 15.
Elm (W. S.) W, **1**, 6.
Elm (W. S.) W, **1**, 10.
Elm* (W. S., in Austin) W, **4**, 4. First north of Chestnut, fr. West Fifty-third west through Austin.
Elm (S. S., in Blue Island) W, **11**, 17.
Elm, East (W. S., in Norwood Pk.) **1**, 1.
Elm, West (W. S., in Norwood Pk.) **1**, 1.
Elm (S. S.) W, **11**, 9, 8†, 7.
Elmwood Pl.* (S. S.) S, w, **6**, 17, Thirty-eighth, 3800. Formerly Johnson Pl., bet. Langley and Vincennes Avs.
Elston Av. (W. S.) N-W, e, **5**, 3†, Division, 240; **8**, 17, Armitage Av. 772; 16, Asylum Pl. 945; 13; **2**, 15, Centre Av. 1801; 12, 11, 8, 7, 4; 1, 6, 3, 2, 1.

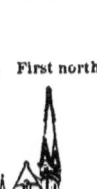

Church of the Holy Trinity (English Lutheran), Elm St. and La Salle Av.

Emerald (W. S.) W, **4**, 2.
Emerald Av. (S. S.) S, w, **6**, 13, Twenty-sixth, 2600; 16†, Thirty-fifth, 3500; **9**, 1, Forty-third, 4300; 4, Fifty-first, 5100; 7, Fifty-ninth, 5858; 10, Sixty-seventh, 6700; 13, Seventy-fifth, 7500; 16, Eighty-third, 8258.
Emerson Av. (W. S.) W, n, **5**, 5, Robey, 102.
Emery (W. S.) W, s, **4**, 3, Central Park Av. 233.
Emery Av.* (W. S.) W, **2**, 11. First north of Belmont Av., from Dresden to Brunswick.
Emily (W. S.) W, n, **5**, 2, Paulina, 58.
Emma (W. S.) W, n, **5**, 3, Milwaukee Av. 2.
Emmet (S. S.) S, **7**, 5.
Ems (W. S.) W, s, **3**, 16, Oakley Av. 143.
Englewood (S. S., in Chicago Lawn) W, **7**, 9.
Englewood Ct. (S. S., in Euglewood) W, n, **9**, 7, Stewart Av. 500.
Ericson Av.* (S. S., in Pullman) N, w, **12**, 9, 105th, 800. Second west of Lake Calumet, fr. 106th to 104th.
Erie, East (N. S.) E, s, **6**, 4†, Market, 114; 5, the lake, 438.
Erie, West (W. S.) W, s, **6**, 4†, Desplaines, 2; **5**, 6, Centre Av. 233; 5, Robey, 619; 4, Seymour, 892; **4**, 5, West Forty-sixth, 2305; 4, Hawkins, 2619.
Erie (W. S.) N, **2**, 11†, 8.
Erie Av. (S. S., in South Chicago) S, w, **13**, 2†, Ninety-first, 9100; 5, Ninety-eighth, 9754.
Erina (S. S.) S, **7**, 5.
Ernst Av. (N. S.) E, **3**, 2.

Escanaba Av. (S. S., in South Chicago) S, w, **10**, 17†, Eighty-fourth, 8400; **13**, 2, Ninety-first, 9100; 5, Ninety-ninth, 9858.
Esmond (S. S., i Morgan Pk.) S-W, **11**, 8†, 11.
Essex Av. (S. S., in South Chicago) S, **10**, 17†; **13**, 2.
Essex Av. (S. S.) S, **13**, 11, 14†, 17.
Euclid (S. S.) S, **8**, 9.
Euclid* (S. S.) S, **9**, 16. See Wright, fr. Seventy-ninth to Eighty-second.
Euclid Av. (W. S., in Norwood Pk.) **1**, 1.
Euclid Av. (N. S.) N, **3**, 2.
Euclid Av. (S. S., in Worth) S, **11**, 10.
Euclid Av. (S. S.) S, **10**, 13.

Grand Central Depot, Fifth Avenue and Harrison St.

Eugenie (N. S.) E, s, **3**, 18, Sedgwick, 82.
Evans Av. (S. S.) S, **9**, 2, Forty-third, 4300; 5†, Forty-ninth, 4859; 11, 14, 17; **12**, 2.
Evans Ct.* (W. S.) W, s, **6**, 10, Union, 1. First north of Eighteenth, fr. Union to Halsted.
Evanston Av. (N. S.) N and N-W, **3**, 15, Clark St. and Diversey Av. 4; 12, Addison Av. 558; 11; 8†, Montrose Boul. 1100; 5, North Fifty-ninth, 2324; 2, Ardmore Av. 2722.
Everett (W. S.) W, **2**, 10.
Everett (S. S.) W, **9**, 12.
Everett (W. S., in Jefferson) N, **1**, 6
Everett (S. S.) S, w, **10**, 4†; 7, Fifty-sixth, 5558.
Evergreen (W. S.) N-W, **2**, 14.
Evergreen Av. (W. S., in Norwood Pk.) **1**, 1.
Evergreen Av. (W. S.) S-W and W, s, **5**, 2, Robey, 123.
Evergreen Av. (W. S.) W, s, **2**, 15†, 659; 14.
Everts Av. (S. S.) S, **8**, 2†, 5, 11.
Ewing (W. S.) W, s, **6**, 7†, Beach, 29; **5**, 9, Blue Island Av. 263.
Ewing Av. (S. S., in South Chicago) S-E and S, w, **13**, 3†, Ninety-third, 9300; 6, Ninety-ninth, 9900; 9, 106th, 10600.
Ewing Pl. (W. S.) W, s, **5**, 2, Hoyne Av. 49.
Exchange Av. (S. S., in South Chicago) S, **10**, 17†, Baltimore Av. 8403; **13**, 2, Ninety-first, 9100; 5, Ninety-ninth, 9900.
Exchange Av. (S. S.) W, **9**, 3.
Exchange Pl.* (S. S.) S, **6**, 4. Bet. Clark and La Salle, fr. Washington to Madison.
Exeter (S. S., in Blue Island) S, **11**, 17.

Fairfax Av. (S. S., in Morgan Pk.) W, **11**, 8.
Fairfield Av. North (W. S.) N, e, **5**, 4†, Kinzie, 125; 1, Augusta, 480; **2**, 18, Armitage Av. 1036.
Fairfield Av. South (W. S.) S, e, **5**, 7, Harvard, 447; 10†, Sixteenth, 797.
Fairfield (S. S., in Morgan Pk.) S-W, **11**, 8, 11†.
Fairmount (S. S., in Blue Island) S, **11**, 17.
Fairmount Av. (W. S.) S, w, **4**, 14, Clifton, 2434.
Fairview (W. S.) W, **1**, 17.
Fairview Av. (S. S., in Worth) S, **11**, 7†, 10.
Fairview Av. (S. S.) N, e, **2**, 15, Humboldt Boul. 316.
Fairview Pl. (S.S., in Worth) S, **11**, 4.
Fake (S. S.) S-E, w, **5**, 6†, Bona parte, 39.
Falcon (W. S.) **2**, 8.

Western Theological Seminary, 1113 Washington Boul., bet. Fall St. and California Av.

Fall* (W. S.) S, e. **5**, 4, Washington Boul. 55. First west of Rockwell, fr. Lake St. to Warren Av.
Faraday Av.* (S. S., in Pullman) N, **12**, 9. First west of Lake Calumet, fr. 104th north one block.
Farmer (S. S., in Calumet) S, **11**, 12.
Farragut Av.* (S. S.) S, **10**, 13. Second west of Yates Av., fr. Seventy-fourth south about ¼ block.

Forty-first (S. S.) W; east of State, s, west of State, n; **9**, 3†, Lake Av. 59; 2, Grand Boul. 491; 1, Stewart Av. 500.

Forty-first, West (W. S.) See West Forty-first.

Forty-first Pl. West (W. S.) See West Forty-first Pl.

Forty-second (S. S.) W; east of State, s, west of State, n; **9**, 3†, Lake Av. 65; 2, Grand Boul. 541; 1, Stewart Av. 500; **8**, 2, 1.

St. Luke's Hospital, near Fourteenth Street, on Indiana Avenue.

Forty-second Ct. (S. S.) W, **9**, 1.

Forty-second Pl. (S. S.) W, s, **9**, 3†, Drexel Boul. 197; 2. Vincennes Av. 461.

Forty-second, West (W. S.) See West Forty-second.

Forty-second Pl. West (W. S.) See West Forty-second Pl.

Forty-third (S. S.) W; east of State, s, west of State, n; **9**, 3, Oakenwald Av. 23; 2†, Grand Boul. 555; 1, Stewart Av. 500; **8**, 2, 1; **7**, 3.

Forty-third, West (W. S.) See West Forty-third.

Forty-third Pl. West (W. S.) See West Forty-third Pl.

Forty-fourth (S. S.) W; east of State, s, west of State, n; **9**, 3†, Lake Av. 60; 2, Grand Boul. 587; 1, Stewart Av. 500; **8**, 2, 1; **7**, 3.

Forty-fourth Ct. (S. S.) W, **9**, 1.

Forty-fourth Pl. (S. S.) W, s, **9**, 2.

Forty-fourth, West (W. S.) See West Forty-fourth.

Forty-fourth Pl. West (W. S.) See West Forty-fourth Pl.

Forty-fifth (S. S.) W; east of State, s, west of State, n; **9**, 3, Woodlawn Av. 81; 2†, Grand Boul. 621; 1, Stewart Av. 500; **8**, 3, 2, 1; **7**, 3.

Forty-fifth Ct. (S. S.) W, n, **9**, 1.

Forty-fifth, West (W. S.) See West Forty-fifth.

Forty-fifth Pl. West (W. S.) See West Forty-fifth Pl.

Forty-sixth (S. S.) W; east of State, s, west of State, n; **9**, 3, Woodlawn Av. 117; 2†, Grand Boul. 655; 1, Stewart Av. 500; **8**, 3, 2, 1.

Forty-sixth Ct. (S. S.) W, **9**, 1.

Forty-sixth, West (W. S.) See West Forty-sixth.

Forty-sixth Pl. West (W. S.) See West Forty-sixth Pl.

Forty-seventh (S. S.) W; east of State, s, west of State, n; **9**, 3, Woodlawn Av. 151; 5†, Grand Boul. 691; 1, Stewart Av. 500; **8**, 3, 2, 1; **7**, 3, 2.

Forty-seventh Ct * (S. S.) E, **9**, 6. Bet. Forty-seventh and Forty-eighth, fr. Cottage Grove Av. east ½ block.

Forty-seventh Pl.* (S. S.) W and N, **8**, 5, 4. Bet. Forty-seventh and Forty-eighth, extending west and north fr. Leavitt.

Forty - seventh, West (W. S.) See West Forty-seventh.

Forty - seventh Pl. West (W. S.) See West Forty-seventh Pl.

Forty-eighth (S. S.) W; east of State, s, west of State, n; **9**, 6. Woodlawn Av. 187; 5†, Grand Boul. 727; 4, Stewart Av. 500; **8**, 6, 5; **7**, 5.

Temple Building, Franklin and South Water Sts. Here First Baptist Church held its first services, in summer of 1833.

Forty-eighth, West (W. S.) See West Forty-eighth.

Forty-ninth (S. S.) W; east of State, s, west of State, n; **9**, 6, Woodlawn Av. 215; 5†, Grand Boul. 763; 4, Stewart Av. 500; **8**, 6, 5, 4; **7**, 6, 5.

Forty-ninth Ct. (S. S.) W, **8**, 5.

Forty-ninth, West (W. S.) See West Forty-ninth.

Foster (N. S.) W, **2**, 6.

Foster Av.* (S. S.) S, **12**, 3. Second west of Adams Av., fr. Ninety-first to Ninety-fourth.

Fourteenth, East (S. S.) W, n, **6**, 11†, Indiana Av. 2; 10, Clark, 146.

Fourteenth, West (W. S.) W, s, **6**, 10†, Stewart Av. 85; **5**, 12, Blue Island Av. 455; 11, Robey, 875; 10; **4**, 12; 11, West Forty-fourth, 2289.

Fourth (S. S., in Calumet) S, **11**, 9, 12†.

Fourth Av. (S. S.) Name changed; see Custom House Pl.

Fourth Av. (S. S.) S, **13**, 18.

Fourth Av. (S. S., in Pullman) S, **12**, 8†, 11.

Fowler (W. S.) W, s, **5**, 2, Robey, 63.

Fox* (S. S.) S, w, **5**, 18, Thirty-second, 3200. First west of Ullman, fr. Thirty-first to railroad tracks.

Fox Pl. (W. S.) W, s, **5**, 3, Elston Av. 3.

Francis (N. S.) E, **3**, 2, Southport Av. 1003.

Francis Pl. (W. S.) S-W and W, s, **2**, 18, California Av. 44.

Francisco, North (W. S.) N, e, **5**, 4, Kinzie, 126; 1†, Division, 618.

Francisco, South (W. S.) S. e, **5**, 4. Lake, 1; 7†, Harrison, 323; 13, Twenty-sixth, 1251; **8**, 1, 4.

Francisco Av. (W. S.) N, e, **2**, 15, Centre Av. 1748.

Frank (N. S.) Name changed; see Piano Ter.

Frank* (W. S.) W, n, **5**, 12, Blue Island Av. 80. First north of Fourteenth, fr. Waller St. to Blue Island Av.

Frank Ct. (W. S., in Norwood Pk.) **1**, 1.

Frankfort (W. S.) W, s, **3**, 16, Leavitt, 95.

Frankfort (W. S.) W, **1**, 17.

Franklin, North (N. S.) N, w, **6**, 4†, Kinzie, 25; 1, Division, 387; **3**, 18. Menomonee, 685.

Franklin, South (S. S.) S, w, **6**, 4†, the river, 2; 7, Harrison, 358.

Franklin (W. S.) W, **2**, 7†; 1, 9.

Fullerton Avenue Presbyterian Church, Fullerton Av. and Larrabee Street.

Franklin (W. S.) W, **1**, 5.

Franklin (S. S., in Calumet) S, **11**, 6.

Franklin Av. (W. S.) W, s, **2**, 15†, Thomas Av. 397; 14.

Frederick Av. (W. S.) W, s, **4**, 3, Hamlin Av. 357.

Frederick Pl. (N. S.) E, n, **3**, 15, Larrabee, 1801.

Free (S. S.) N, **12**, 8.

Free (W. S., in Jefferson) N, **1**, 5, 8†.

Freeman (S. S.) W, 2.

Fremont (N. S.) N, e, **3**, 17, Centre, 146.

Fremont (W. S.) W, **1**, 2.

French Av. (S. S.) S, w, **10**, 14, Seventy-seventh, 7701.

Frink* (W. S., in Austin) W, **4**, 4. First south of Kinzie, fr. West Fifty-third west through Austin.

Front (N. S.) N, **3**, 1.

Front* (S. S.) E, **6**, 5. First south of the river, fr. Michigan Av. east three blocks.

Front (W. S.) W, n, **3**, 3, Carpenter, 106.

Front (S. S., in Calumet) S, **11**, 6.

Front (S. S., in Kensington) S, **12**, 11.

Fry (W. S.) W, n, **5**, 3†, Noble, 100; 1.

Fuller* (S. S.) E, s, **5**, 15, Short, 103. Fr. the river, near west end of Cologne, east to Archer Av.

Fullerton Av. East (N. S.) E, n, **3**, 13, the river, 1; 17†, Racine Av. 309; 15, Clark, 763.

Fullerton Av. West (W. S.) W, s, **3**, 13, Robey, 90; **2**, 15, California Av. 544; 14†, Central Park Av. 1057; 13; **1**, 13.

Fulton (W. S.) W, n, **6**, 4, Canal, 2; **5**, 6†, Ann, 332; 5, Robey, 732; 4, California Av. 1274, **4**, 6, Central Park Av. 1770; 5, West Forty-fourth, 2250; 4, West Fifty-second. 2766.

Fulton (S. S., in Blue Island) W, **11**, 17.

Fulton Av. (N. S.) E, **3**, 1.

Furlong* (W. S.) W, s, **4**, 3, Grand Av. 27. First south of McElroy, fr. Kedzie Av. to Grand Av.

Fyffe (W. S., in Cicero) W, **4**, 13.

Gage (S. S.) S, w, **5**, 18, Thirty-seventh, 3700.

Gage Park (S. S.) At junction of Garfield Boul. and Western Av. Boul. **8**, 4†, 5, 7, 8.

Galena (W. S.) W, **1**, 17.

Galt Av. (N. S.) E, **3**, 8, Hazel, 1501.

Gambrinus (W. S.) N, **2**, 12.

Gano Av. (S. S., in Calumet.) Name changed; see Dunham Av.

Garden* (W. S.) W, **5**, 9. Bet. Jackson and Van Buren, near Morgan and Aberdeen.

Garden (S. S., in Blue Island) S, **11**, 13, 16†.

Garden (W. S., in Galewood) N-E, and N, **1**, 17.

Garden Av. (W. S.) W, s, **2**, 15, California Av. 265; 14†.

Gardner (N. S.) W, n, **6**, 1, Vine, 2.

Gardner Av. (W. S.) N, **2**, 12.

Garfield Av. (N. S.) E, n, **3**, 17†, Racine Av. 165; 18, Sedgwick, 525.

Garfield Av. (N. S.) N, **3**, 4.

Garfield Av. (W. S.) W, s, **2**, 17, Hancock Av. 481.

Garfield Boul. (S. S.) W; east of State, s, west of State, n; **9**, 5, South Park Av. 941; 7†, Stewart Av. 500; **8**, 6; 5, Wood, 1858.

Garland Pl. (S. S.) S, e, **6**, 5, Washington, 41.

Garrett* (S. S.) N-E, **5**, 14. Second east of Wood, fr. Thirty-first northeast about two blocks.

Garvin Av. (S. S., in South Chicago) S, **13**, 1.

Gary Pl. (N. S.) N-E, **3**, 12.

Gault Pl.* (N. S.) N, w, **6**, 1, Hobbie, 159. Bet. Larrabee and Milton, fr. Oak to Division.

Augustana Hospital, near Garfield Av., on Lincoln Av.

Geary* (N. S.) N-W, w, **6**, 2. Second-west of the lake, fr. Chestnut St. to Walton Pl.

Gehrke Av. (N. S.) E, **3**, 14.

Genesee (W. S.) N, **2**, 9.

Genesee Av.* (W. S.) N, e, **4**, 9, Harrison, 2, First west of Central Park Av., fr. Harrison St. to Colorado Av.

Genesee Av. (S. S.) S, e, **4**, 18; **7**, 6†.

Geneva (S. S.) W, **5**, 16.

Geneva Av. (S. S.) W, **4**, 18.

Genevieve* (S. S.) S, **8**, 6. First east of Centre, fr. Fiftieth to Fifty-first.

Genevieve Av.* (W. S.) N, e, **2**, 17, Cortland Av. 1036. First west of Hamlin, fr. Bloomingdale Rd. to Armitage Av.

Genevra Av. (S. S., in Morgan Park) S, **11**, 8, 11†.

George (N. S.) E, n, **3**, 13†, Robey, 357; 14, Racine Av. 1201.

George* (W. S.) W, n, **5**, 3, Carpenter, 52. First north of Front, fr. the river to Elston Av.

George (W. S.) W, **2**, 10.

George Av. (N. S.) E, n, **3**, 15, Waubun Av. 1901.

George Av. (W. S.) N, **2**, 16.

George Pl.* (W. S.) N, e, **5**, 5, Kinzie, 2. First west of Robey, fr. Kinzie north ½ block.

Geraldine Av.* (W. S.) N, **2**, 10, 7. Fr. junction of Milwaukee Av. and Everett to Centre.

Germania Pl.* (N. S.) E, s, **6**, 1, La Salle Av. 2. Formerly Grant, first south of North Av., fr. La Salle Av. to Clark.

Giddings (N. S.) E, **3**, 7, Lyman Av. 327.

Gilbert Av. (S. S.) S, **9**, 16.

Gilbert Pl. (S. S.) S-E, **9**, 16,

Gillett Av. (S. S., in South Chicago) S, **13**, 5, 8†, 11.

Gilpin Pl. (W. S.) W, s, **5**, 9, Lytle, 28.

Girard (W. S.) N-E and N, e, **5**, 2, Milwaukee Av 698; **3**, 16†, Armitage Av. 984.

Girard (S. S.) S, **11**, 3.

Glenlake Av. (N. S.) E, **3**, 2.

Glenview Av. (W. S.) W, n, **4**, 3, Hamlin Av. 1084.

Glenwood (S. S.) S, **11**, 3.

Glenwood Av.* (W. S.) N, e, **5**, 2, Augusta, 424. Formerly Dudley, between Lincoln and Robey, fr. Chicago Av. to Division.

Entrance to Graceland Cemetery,* north of Graceland Avenue.

Glory Pl. (W. S.) N-E, e, **3**, 16, Elston Av. 24.

Goethe (N. S.) E, s, **6**, 1†, Sedgwick, 2; 2, Lake Shore Drive, 257.

Goethe Av. (S. S., in Hegewisch) S, **13**, 18.

Gold * (W. S.) S, e, **5**, 9, Harrison, 2. First east of Morgan, fr. Harrison to Gurley.

Gold (W. S.) N, **1**, 17.

Goldsmith Av. (S. S.) S-W, **9**, 13.

Good* (W. S.) W, s, **5**, 9, Aberdeen, 21, First south of Polk, fr. Sholto to May.

Goodman (W. S.) N-W, **1**, 5.

Goodspeed (S. S.) S, **8**, 2†, 5, 11.

Goodwin (W. S.) W, s, **4**, 12, St. Louis Av. 51.

Gordon (S. S.) W, n, **9**, 1, Stewart Av. 500.

Gordon Ter. (N. S.) E, **3**, 9.

Goshen (S. S.) W, n, **9**, 1, Sultan, 414.

Grace* (N. S.) N, e, **6**, 1, Division, 2. First east of Halsted, fr. Division to Vedder.

Grace (N. S.) E, **3**, 10†, Paulina, 701; 11. Racine Av. and Clark, 1201; 12, Pine Grove Av. 1701.

Grace Av. (S. S.) S, w, **9**, 9, Sixty-second, 6200; 12†, Jackson Park Ter. 6458.

Grace Av.* (S. S.) S, **9**, 14. Second east of South Park Av., near Seventy-seventh.

Grace Av. (W. S.) N, **2**, 9.

Graceland Av. (N. S.) E, **3**, 7†, Lincoln Av. and Robey, 401; 8, Racine Av. 1201; 9.

Graham (S. S.) S, **13**, 8.

Graham (W. S., in Jefferson) N, 1, 8. First east of Free, fr. Lawrence Av. to Perry.

Grand (S. S., in Blue Island) N W, **11**, 17.

Grand Av. (N. S.) E, **3**, 1†, Robey, 401; 2.

Grand Av. (S. S., in Calumet) S, **11**, 6†, 9, 12.

Grand Av. (S. S., in Worth) S, **11**, 7†, 10.

Grand Av. (W. S.) N-W, s, **5**, 4†, California Av. 255; 1, Albany Av. 432; **4**, 3, Central Park Av., 795; 2, Keeney Av. 1253; **2**, 16; 1, 18, 17, 16.

Grand Boul. (S. S.) S, w, **6**, 17, Thirty-fifth, 3500; **9**, 2, Forty-third, 4300; 5†. Fifty-first St. and Washington Park, 5058.

Grand Ter. (S. S.) W, **9**, 15.

Grant (N. S.) E, **6**, 1. Name changed; see Germania Pl.

Grant Av.* (S. S.) S, **5**, 16. First east of California Av., fr. Thirty-fifth to Thirty-ninth.

Grant Av. (W. S.) N, **4**, 2†; **2**, 16.

Grant Av. (W. S.) W, **1**, 5.

Grant Pl. (N. S.) W, n, **3**, 18, Cleveland Av. 48.

Michael Reese Hospital, Groveland Av. and Twenty-ninth St.

Grant Pl. (N. S.) E, **3**, 4, Garfield Av. 337.

Grant Pl. (S. S.) S, w, **9**, 10, Sixty-ninth, 6900.

Grassie Av. (S. S.) S, **8**, 1.

Graves Pl.* (S. S.) S, w, **6**, 17, Thirty-third, 3200, First east of Rhodes Av., fr. Cottage Grove Av. to Thirty-third.

Gray (W. S.) W, **1**, 6.

Graylock Av. (S. S.) W, e, **9**, 4, Stewart Av. 459.

Greeley Pl.* (W. S.) S, e, **5**, 3, George, 2. First east of Carpenter, near Front.

Green, North*(W. S.) N, w, **5**, 6, Kinzie, 111; 3, Front, 313.

Green, South (W. S.) S, **5**, 6, Randolph, 1; 9†, Harrison, 251; **8**, 9, 12, 15, 18; **11**, 6, 9.

Green Bay Av. (S. S., in South Chicago) S, w, **10**, 18†, Eighty-third, 8300; **18**, 3, Harbor Av. 9118; 18.

Greenwich (W. S.) W, s, **3**, 16, Hoyne Av. 51.

Greenwood (S. S., in Blue Island) S. **11**, 16.

Greenwood Av. (S. S.) S, w, **9**, 3, Forty-third, 4301; 6†, Fifty-first, 5100; 9, Fifty-ninth, 5900; 12, Sixty-seventh, 6700; 15, Seventy-fifth, 7500; 18, Eightieth, 8000.

Greenwood Av. (W. S.) W, s, **3**, 13, Oakley Av. 1; **2**, 15†, California Av. or Park Av. 321; 14, 13.

Greenwood Av. (W. S.) N, **2**, 10†, 7, 4.

Gregory (S. S., in Blue Island) S, **11**, 17.

Grenshaw (W. S.) W, s, **5**, 8, Oakley Av. 1060; 7†, Washtenaw Av. 1301; **4**, 9, Central Park Av. 1845.

Gresham Av. (W. S.) N-E, **2**, 14.

Griffin (W. S.) **1**, 5.

Griffin Av. (W. S.) W, **2**, 14.

Gross Av. (S. S.) S-W, **8**, 3.

Gross Av. (S. S.) S, **13**, 1.

Gross Av. (W. S.) N, w, **2**, 18, Cortland, 1017.

Gross Park (N. S.) E, **3**, 10.

Gross Park Av. (N. S.) N, **3**, 10, Roscoe. 510.

Gross Ter.* (W. S.) S, e, **5**, 7, Colorado Av. 49. First east of Albany Av., fr. Madison St. to Colorado Av.

Grove (S. S., in Calumet) W, **12**, 7; **11**, 9†, 8, 7.

Grove* (S. S.) S and S-W, w, **6**, 10, Sixteenth, 1600; 13, Archer Av. 2298. Along east side of the river, fr. Sixteenth St. to Archer Av.

Grove* (W. S., in Austin) W, **4**, 4, Robinson Av. 2426. Second north of Chestnut, fr. West Fifty-third west through Austin.

Grove (S. S., in Blue Island) W, **11**, 16.

Grove (W. S., in Galewood) N, **1**, 16.

Grove (W. S., in Jefferson) N-W, **1**, 6.

Grove (W. S., in Jefferson) N-W, **1**, 5.

Grove Av. (W. S.) W, **2**, 9†, 8.

Grove Ct. (N. S.) W, e, **3**, 18, Larrabee, 2.

Grove Pl. (S. S.) S, w, **9**, 10, Sixty-fourth, 6400.

Groveland Av. (S. S.) S-E, w, **6**, 14†, Twenty-eighth, 2800; 17, Thirty-third, 3268.

Groveland Av. (W. S.) W, **2**, 13.

Groveland Ct. (S. S.) S-E, **9**, 16.

Groveland Ct. (S. S., in Washington Heights) S and S-E, **11**, 8.

Groveland Park (S. S.) E, s, **6**, 17.

Grunewald (S. S., in Worth) W, **11**, 13.

Gurley (W. S.) W, s, **5**, 9, Sholto, 99.

Gutenberg (W. S.) N, e, **2**, 17. Name changed; see Genevieve Av.

Haddock Pl.* (S. S.) W, **6**, 5, 4. An alley bet. South Water and Lake, fr. Wabash Av. to Franklin.

Haines* (N. S.) N-E, s, **5**, 3, Hickory Av. 12. Second south of Division, fr. the river north-east to Halsted.

Hale (S. S.) W, **11**, 9.

Hall (N. S.) N, **3**, 15.

Halsted, North* (W. S. & N. S.) N, w, **5**, 6, Kinzie. 123; 3, Division St. and Hawthorne Av. 493; **3**, 17, Centre, 881, 14, Diversey Av. 1360; 11, Addison Av. 1890; 8.

Halsted, South (W. S. & S. S.) S, e; to Thirty-ninth, w, south of Thirty-ninth, **5**, 6, Randolph, 1; 9†, Harrison St. and Blue Island Av. 269; 12, Sixteenth, 669, 15, Twenty-sixth,2600; 18, Thirty-fifth,3500;

8, 3, Forty-third, 4300; 6, Fifty-first, 5100; 9, Fifty-ninth, 5900; 12, Sixty-seventh, 6700; 15, Seventy-fourth, 7400; 18, Eighty-third, 8300; **11**, 3, 6, 9, 12, 15, 18.

Hamburg (W. S.) W, s, **3**, 16, Leavitt, 95

Hamilton (N. S.) N, **3**, 1.

Hamilton Av. (W. S.) S, w, **5**, 8, Adams, 34.

Hamilton Av. (W. S.) N, **2**, 16.

Hamlin Av. North (W S.) N, e, **4**, 6†, Kinzie, 126; 3, Division, 604; **2**, 17, Armitage Av. 1096; 11.

Hamlin Av. South (W.S) S. **4**, 6†; 12, Sixteenth, 100; 15, Twenty-sixth, 585; 18; **7**, 3.

Hammond* (N. S.) N, w, **3**, 18, Menomonee, 65. First east of Sedgwick, fr. Eugenie, at intervals, to Wisconsin.

Hammond Av. (W. S.) N, e, **2**, 15†, Diversey Av. 770; 12.

Hampden Ct.* (N. S.) N-W **3**, 15. First east of Clark, fr. Deming northwest about two blocks.

Hancock Av. (W. S.) N, e, **2**, 17, Armitage Av. 1076.

Hanover (S. S.) S. Name changed; see South Canal.

Harbor Av.* (S. S.) S-W, w, **13**, 3, the Strand, 9100; 2, South Chicago Av. 9400. On west side of Calumet River, fr. the Strand to S. Chicago Av.

McCormick Hall, of McCormick Theological Seminary, 1060 North Halsted Street.

Harding Av. (W. S.) N, **2**, 8.

Harding Av. (W. S.) N, **2**, 5.

Harding Av. North (W. S.) N, e, **4**, 6†, Kinzie, 126; 3, Division, 603.

Harding Av. South (W. S.) S, e, **4**, 6†; 15, Twenty-sixth, 1265.

Harmon Ct. (S. S.) W, s, **6**, 7, Wabash Av. 33.

Harriet Av. (S. S.) S, **9**, 10.

Harrison, East (S. S.) W, s, **6**, 8, Michigan Av. 1; 7†, the river, 211.

Harrison, West (W. S.) W, s, **6**, 7†, the river, 1; **5**, 9, Centre Av. 441; **8**, Robey, 889; 7, California Av. 1379; **4**, 9, Central Park Av. 1877; 8, West Forty-fourth, 2389; 7.

Harrison Av. (S. S.) S, **12**, 3.

Hart (S. S.) S, **5**, 16; **8**, 1†, 4, 7.

Hart* (W. S.) N, e, **5**, 5, Kinzie, 2. First west of Lincoln, fr. Kinzie St. to Austin Av.

Hartwell Av. (S. S.) S, w, **9**, 11, Sixty-seventh, 6658.

Harvard (W. S.) W, s, **5**, 7†, California Av. 1371; **4**, 9, Douglas Boul. 1991; 8, West Forty-third, 2309.

Harvard (S.S.) S. Name changed; see Shields Av.

Harvey Av. (S. S.) S. Name changed; see Francisco.

Hastings* (W. S.) W, n, **5**, 12, Centre Av. 18; 11†, Robey, 456.

Hathaway (W. S.) W, **2**, 10.

Haugan (N. S.) N, **3**, 11.

Haven (S. S.) W, n, **6**, 13, Stewart Av. 22.

Hawhe Av. (S. S.) S, **13**, 16.

Hawkins (W. S.) N, **4**, 4.

Hawkinson Av. (S. S.) S, **13**, 14.

Hawthorne Av. (N. S.) N-W, e, **6**, 1, Elm, 190, **5**, 3†, Eastman, 370; **3**, 17, Lewis, 804.

Hawthorne Av.* (S. S.) S-W, **9**, 13. Fr. Stewart Av., near Seventy-sixth, southwest to Goldsmith, near Seventy-ninth.

Hawthorne Av. (W. S., in Cicero) N, **4**, 13, 16†

Hawthorne Pl. (N. S.) E, **3**, 12, Evanston Av 1

Hayes Av. (S. S.) W, **13**, 6.

Hayes Boul.* (W. S.) W, **2**, 13. First south of Wyoming, fr. West Forty-fourth to Jefferson Av.

Haynes Ct. (S. S.) S-E, w, **5**, 15, Archer Av. 2900.

Hazel (N. S.) N, **3**, 8.

Hazel (S. S., in Calumet) W, **11**, 5

Hazelton Av. (W. S., in Jefferson) N, **1**, 6.

Hazle (S. S., in Calumet) W, **11**, 9.

Heald (S. S.) S, w, **9**, 7, Fifty-ninth, 5900.

Heffton (S. S., in Washington Heights) W, **11**, 8.

Hegewisch Av. (S. S., in Hegewisch) S, **13**, 17.

Heine (W.S.) N, e, **2**, 18, Bloomingdale Rd. 120.
Heine (W. S.) N, **2**, 12, 9†.
Heine Pl.* (N. S.) N-E and E, s, **6**, 1, Sedgwick, 66. Fr junction of Clybourn and Cleveland Avs. to Sedgwick.
Henderson (W, S.) W, **2**, 11.
Henderson* (N. S.) N, **3**, 13. Fr. Wrightwood Av. to Diversey Av., a few blocks west of Ashland Av.
Henry (W. S.) N-W, e, **3**, 17, Rawson, 42.
Henry (W. S.) W, s, **6**, 10, Stewart Av. 2; **5**, 12, Centre Av. 98; 11†, Robey, 519.
Henry (S. S., in Blue Island) S, **11**, 16.
Henry Ct. (W. S.) N-E, e, **2**, 18, Point, 2.
Herbert Av. (N. S.) N, **2**, 5.
Hermitage Av. (W. S.) S, e, **5**, 8†, Harrison, 310; **8**, 5, 8.
Herndon (N. S.) N-E and N, e, **3**, 17†, Webster Av. 102; 14; 11, Addison Av. 970.
Hervey (W. S.) W, s, **3**, 16, Elkgrove Av. 235.
Hesing Av. (W. S.) W, **2**, 12.
Hewes Av. (S. S., in South Chicago) S, **13**, 4, 7†, 10.
Hewitt Av. (S. S.) S, **13**, next south of section 16.
Hibbard Av. (S. S.) S, w, **9**, 6, Fifty-second, 5200.
Hicking Av. (S. S.) W, **9**, 6.
Hickory (S. S.) S-W, n, **5**, 15, Deering, 2800.
Hickory Av. (N. S.) N-W, e, **5**, 3, Division, 144.
Hickory Av. (S. S., in Calumet) W, **11**, 5.

College of Physicians and Surgeons, 813 West Harrison St., cor. of Honore St.

High (N. S.) N, e, **3**, 17†, Webster Av. 2; 14.
High (S. S.) S, **9**, 10.
High (W. S.) N, **2**, 10.
High (S. S., in Blue Island) W, **11**, 17, 16†.
High (S. S., in Calumet) S, **11**, 9.
High (S. S., in Calumet) W, **11**, 9.
High (W. S., in Galewood) N, **1**, 16.
High Av. (S. S.) S, w, **13**, 9†, 106th, 10554; 12, 18.
Highland Av. (W. S.) N, 4, 2.
Highland Av. (S. S., in Calumet) S, **11**, 8.
Hill (W. S., in Galewood) N, **1**, 16.
Hill (N. S.) E, s, **6**, 1, Franklin, 58.
Hilliard (S. S.) S-W, **11**, 2.
Hilliard Av. (S. S., in Calumet) S, **11**, 9, 12†.
Hillside (S. S., in Calumet) S, **11**, 3.
Hinkley Av. (W. S.) N, **2**, 11.
Hinkley Av. (W. S.) N, **2**, 16†. 13.
Hinman (W. S.) W, s, **5**, 12†, Throop, 459; 11, Robey, 871; 10, California Av. 1281.
Hinsche* (N. S.) N-E, e, **6**, 1, Blackhawk. 36. Bet. Clybourn Av. and Larrabee, fr. Clybourn Av. to Blackhawk.
Hirsch (W. S.) W, n, **5**, 2, Leavitt, 2; 1†, California Av. 340; **4**, 2, West Forty-fourth, 1885.
Hobbie (N. S.) N-E and E, s, **6**, 1, Milton Av. 102.
Hoey* (S. S.) S-W, **5**, 15. First south of Archer Av., fr. Mary southwest ½ block.
Hoffman Av. (W. S.) N, e, **2**, 18†, Milwaukee Av. 2; 15, Diversey Av. 438.
Holden (W. S.) S, e, **6**, 10, Maxwell, 79.
Holden Pl. (S. S.) S, **6**, 5†, 8, 11.
Holland Rd. (S. S.) S-E, **9**, 16†; **12**, 1.
Hollowell (W. S., in Jefferson) N, **1**, 6.
Hollywood Av. (N. S.) E, **2**, 2.
Holmes (S. S.) S, **9**, 9.
Holstein Park (W. S.) **3**, 16.
Holt (W..S.) N, e, **5**, 3†, Division, 534; **2**, 17, Wabansia Av. 832.
Homan Av. North (W. S.) N, e, 4, 6†, Kinzie, 126; 3; Division, 604; **2**, 14, 11.
Homan Av. South (W. S. & S. S.) S, e, **4**, 6†, Lake, 1; 9, Harrison, 323; 12, Sixteenth, 803; 15, Twenty-sixth, 1255; 18; **7**, 6, 9, 12.
Homer (W. S.) W, s, **3**, 16†, Robey, 1; **2**, 18, Washtenaw Av. 393.
Homer Av. (N. S.) E, **2**, 2.
Honore (W. S.) S, e, **5**, 8†, Harrison, 319; 17, Thirty-fifth, 3500; **9**, 11; **11**, 2, 14.
Honore (S. S.) S, **9**, 10†, 13, 16.

Hood Av. (N. S.) E, **3**, 1.
Hooker (N. S.) N-W, e, **5**, 3, Division, 140.
Hope (W. S.) W, s, **5**, 9, Morgan, 57.
Hope Av. (S. S.) S, w, **9**, 12, Sixty-fifth Ter. 6534.
Hopkins* (S. S.) S, **9**, 1. Second west of Wentworth Av., fr. Thirty-ninth to Forty-first.
Hopkinson (S. S.) S-W, **11**, 2.
Horton Ct.* (S. S.) W, **11**, 2. Bet. Ninety-third and Ninety-fourth, fr. Ashland Av. to C., St. L. & P. R. R.
Hosmer Av. (W. S.) N, **1**, 18.
Hough (S. S., in Calumet) S, **11**, 3†, 6.
Hough Pl.* (S. S.) N-W, **5**, 15. First east of Quarry, fr. Archer Av. northwest about one block.
Houssen Ct. (W. S.) S-W, **2**, 14.
Houston (S. S., in South Chicago) S, w, **10**, 17†, Eighty-third, 8300; **13**, 2, Ninety-first, 9100; **13**, 5, Ninety-eighth. 9756; 17.
Howard (S. S., in Kensington) S, **12**, 11.
Howard (S. S., in Calumet) S, **11**, 5.
Howard Av. (W. S.) N, 4, 2; **2**, 16†, 13.
Howard Av. (S. S.) S, **13**, next south of section 16.
Howard Av. (S. S., in Hegewisch) S-E, **13**, 17.
Howard Ct. (W. S.) W, s, **5**, 1, Central Park Boul. 1001.
Howe (N. S.) N, e, **3**, 18, Centre, 136.
Hoxie Av. (S. S.) S, **13**, 5, 8†, 11.
Hoyne Av. North (W. S. & N. S.) N, e, **5**, 5, Kinzie, 98; 2†, Division, 534; **3**, 16, Armitage Av. 962; 13, Clybourn Av. and George, 500; **3**, Addison Av. 1010.
Hoyne Av. South (W. S. & S. S.) S; e, in West Side, and w, in South Side; **5**, 5, Lake, 1; 8†, Harrison, 323; 11, Sixteenth, 805; 14, Blue Island Av. 1185; 17, Thirty-fifth St. and Archer Av. 3458; **8**, 5, 11; **11**, 5.
Hubbard (W. S.) W, s, **4**, 5, West Forty-sixth, 2223; 4†, Hawkins, 2545.
Hubbard Ct. (S. S.) W, s, **6**, 8, Wabash Av. 33.
Huber* (N. S.) E, n, **3**, 17, Racine Av. 57. Bet. Belden and Fullerton Avs., fr. Herndon St. to Racine Av.
Huck Av. (N. S.) N, **3**, 4, Grant Pl. 68.
Hudson (S. S.) W, **5**, 16.
Hudson Av. (N. S.) N, w, **6**, 1†, Sigel, 57; **3**, 18. Centre, 369.
Hull* (N. S.) N, w, **3**, 18, Menomonee, 51. Bet. Cleveland and Hudson Avs., fr. Eugenie to Menomonee.

National Bichloride of Gold Institute, corner of Hoyne Avenue and Monroe Street.

Hull* (W. S.) S, **5**, 7. First west of California Av., fr. Fillmore to Twelfth.
Humboldt (W. S.) N, e, **2**, 18, Armitage Av. 238.
Humboldt (W. S.) N, e, **2**, 15†, Diversey Av. 770; **2**, 12.
Humboldt (W. S.) W, **4**, 2.
Humboldt Av. (W. S.) W; n, east of California Av., and s, west of California Av.; **2**, 18, California Av. 874; 17, Central Park Av. 523; 16†, West Forty-fourth, 1885.
Humboldt Av. (W. S.) W, n, **5**, 1, Washtenaw Av. 818.
Humboldt Boul. (W. S.) W, s, **2**, 15, California Av. 267.
Humboldt Boul., or Humboldt Park Boul. (W. S.) N, e, **2**, 18†, Armitage Av. 238; 15.
Hunting Av. (W S., in Irving Pk.) N, **2**, 7.
Huntington (W. S.) W, **1**, 6.
Hurlburt Av. (W. S., in Cicero) W, **4**, 13.
Huron, East (N. S.) E, s, **6**, 4†, Market, 114, 5, the lake, 442.
Huron, West (N. S.) W, n, **5**, 6, Centre Av. 102; 5†, Robey, 486; 4, Washtenaw Av. 858; **4**, 6, Central Park Av. 1412; 5, West Forty-sixth, 2050; 4, Hawkins, 2362.

Huron (W. S.) N, **2**, 11.
Huron (S. S., in Blue Island) S-E, **11**, 18.
Hutchinson (W. S.) W, **2**, 8.
Hydraulic Pl.* (S. S.) W, **6**, 7.   An alley bet.
  Monroe and Adams, fr. State to Clark.
Hyman Av. (S. S.)   See West Forty-eighth.

Ida (W. S.) W, **4**, 8.
Iglehart Pl. (S. S.) S-E, w, **6**, 14,   Twenty-
  seventh, 2700.
Illinois (N. S.) E,
  s, **6**, 4†. Mar-
  ket, 50; 5, the
  lake, 486.
Illinois (S. S.,
  in Blue Island) S,
  11, 18.
Illinois Av. (S. S.)
  S, w, **5**, 18,
  Thirty - third,
  3252.
Illinois Av. (S. S.)
  S-E, **10**, 17,   St. James Episcopal Church,
  Eighty - third   First Building, 1837,
  Pl. 8300.   Illinois and Cass Streets.
Illinois Av. (S.S., in Calumet) S-W, **11**, 11,
Indiana, East (N. S.) E, s, **6**, 4†, Market, 86;
  5, the lake, 500.
Indiana, West (W. S.) W, s, **6**, 4†, Jefferson,
  1; **5**, 6, Centre Av. 281; 5, Robey, 679;
  4, 6, Lawndale Av. 1639; 5, West Forty-
  sixth, 2223; 4, Hawkins, 2545.
Indiana Av. (S. S.) S, w, **6**, 8; 11, Sixteenth,
  1600; 14†, Twenty-sixth, 2600; 17, Thirty-
  fifth, 3500; **9**, 2, Forty-third, 4300; 5,
  Fifty-first, 5100; 8, Fifty-ninth, 5900;
  11, Sixty-seventh, 6700; 14, 17; **12**, 5, 8,
  11, 14, 17.
Indiana Boul. (S. S.) S-E, w, **13**, 6†, Ewing
  Av. 10062; 9, 106th, 10600.
Ingleside Av. (S. S.) S, w, **9**, 6, Fifty-first,
  5100; 9†, Fifty-ninth, 5900; 12, Sixty-
  seventh, 6658.
Ingraham (W. S.) W, n, **5**, 3, Elston Av. 2.
Inkerman (S. S.) S, w, **9**, 1, Forty-sixth,
  4600.
Iowa (W. S.) W, n, **5**, 2, Robey, 88; 1†, California Av. 558; 4, 2, West Forty-fourth,
  1892; 1, West Fifty-second, 2394.
Iron (S. S., in Kensington) W, **12**, 11.
Irvine Av. (N. S.) N, **3**, 7.
Irvine Av. (W. S.) N, e, **2**, 17, Armitage Av.
  1090.   Name changed; see Lawndale Av.
Irving (W. S.) W, **1**,
  10.
Irving Av. (W. S.) S,
  e, **5**, 8†, Harrison,
  321; 11, Four-
  teenth, 683.
Irving Av. (S. S.) S,
  7, 5.
Irving Av. (W. S.) N,
  2, 10, 7†.
Irving Pl.* (W. S.) N,
  e, **5**, 5, Kinzie,
  45.   Bet. Oakley
  Av. and Leavitt,
  fr. Fulton to   Sinai Temple, cor. Indiana Av.
  Kinzie.   and Twenty-first St.
Irving Park Boul. (W.
  S.) W, **2**, 9, 11†, 7; **1**, 9, 8, 7.
Isabella (W. S.) E, **4**, 3.

Jackson, East (S. S.) W, s, **6**, 8, Michigan Av.
  1; 7†, Market, 255.
Jackson, West (W. S.) W, s, **6**, 7†, the river,
  2; **5**, 9, Centre Av. 383; 8, Robey, 783;
  7, California Av. 1235; 4, 9, Central
  Park Av. 1685; 8, West Forty-fourth,
  2247; 7.
Jackson* (S. S.) W, **9**, 4.   Bet. Fifty-third and
  Fifty-fourth, fr. Wentworth Av. to railroad
  crossing.
Jackson (S. S., in Blue Island) W, **11**, 17.
Jackson (W. S.) W, **1**, 6.
Jackson (W. S.) W, **2**, 5.
Jackson Av. (S. S.) S, w, **9**, 6, Fifty-fourth,
  5400; 9†, Fifty-ninth, 5858.

Jackson Park Ter. (S. S.) W, s, **9**, 12, Hope Av.
  267
James* (S. S.) W, **8**, 5.   First north of Fifty-
  second, fr. Hoyne Av. to C., St. L. & P.
  R. R.
James (N. S.) E, **3**, 1.
James (S. S., in Blue Island) W, **11**, 16.
James (S. S., in Calumet) S, **11**, 12.
James Av. (S. S.) W, n, **5**, 18, Ullman, 974.
Janiot (N. S.) E, n, **3**, 7, Wright Av. 285.
Jane (W. S.) S-W & W, s, **5**, 3, Milwaukee Av.
  1; 2†, Robey, 279; 1, California Av. 707.
Jan Huss Av. North*(W. S.) N, e, **4**, 6, Kinzie,
  126; 3, Division, 604; **2**, 17, Armitage
  Av. 1096; 14.
Jan Huss Av. South (W. S.) S, e, **4**, 9†, Harri-
  son, 265; 12, Sixteenth, 787; 15, Twenty-
  sixth; 1267; **7**, 3, 9.
Jansen (N. S.) N, e, **3**, 11, Addison Av. 140.
Jasper (S. S.) S, **5**, 18.
Jasper (W. S.) W, **4**, 2.
Jay* (N. S.) N, e, **3**, 17, Webster Av. 138. Bet.
  Racine and Seminary Avs., from Centre St.
  to Fullerton Av.
Jefferson, North*(W. S.) N, w, **6**, 4, Kinzie,
  123.
Jefferson, South (W. S.) S, e, **6**, 4, Randolph,
  1; 7†, Harrison, 275; 10, Sixteenth, 643;
  9, 16; **12**, 1, 4, 7;
  10, 13.
Jefferson (S. S.) S, **8**,
  10, 13†.
Jefferson (W. S.) N, **1**,
  17.
Jefferson Av. (S. S.) S,
  w, **9**, 6†, Fifty-first,
  5100; 9, Fifty-
  seventh, 5658; 12,   First Rush Medical College
  Sixty-eighth, 6800;   (1844), Indiana St. and
  15, Seventy - fifth,   Dearborn Av.
  7500; **12**, 3.
Jefferson Av. (S. S.) N, 1, 18†, 15, 12, 9, 6, 3.
Jefferson Ct. (W. S.) W, s, **2**, 18, Perry Av. 93.
Jeffery Av. (S. S.) S, **10**, 10, 13†, 16; **13**, 1.
Jessamine Av. (W. S.) S, **4**, 13, 16†.
Jesse Pl.* (N. S.) N, e, **5**, 5, Kinzie, 2.   First
  east of Hoyne Av., fr. Kinzie north ½ block.
Joan Pl. (S. S., in Calumet) S-W, **11**, 11.
John (S. S., in Calumet) S, **11**, 12.
John Pl.* (W. S.) W, s, **5**, 15, Halsted, 2. First
  south of Twenty-second, fr. Halsted west
  about one block.
Johnson (W. S.) S, e, **5**, 9, Taylor, 1; 12†, Six-
  teenth, 267.
Johnson Av.* (S. S.) S, w, **6**, 14,   Twenty-
  seventh, 2700. Second east of Cottage
  Grove Av., fr. ¼ block north of Twenty-
  seventh to Twenty-eighth.
Johnson Av. (S. S.) S, e, **7**, 3, 6, 9†, 12, 15, 18;
  11, 1, 4, 7, 10, 13.
Johnson Pl. (S. S.) **6**, 17.   Name changed; see
  Elmwood Pl.
Johnston Av. (W. S.) W, s, **2**, 18, Thomas Av.
  127.
Jones (W. S., in Jefferson) N, **1**, 6.
Jordan Av. (S. S.) S, **10**, 16.
Joseph (S. S.) W, **5**, 16†; 4, 18.
Joseph* (S. S.) S-E, w, **5**, 15, Archer Av. 2636.
  First west of Mary, fr. Hickory St. to
  Archer Av.
Joseph Av. (W. S.) N, **2**, 11.
Josephine Av. (W. S., in Nor-
  wood Pk.) S, **1**, 1.
Judd (S. S.) W, **13**, 8.
Judd (W. S.) W, s, **6** 10,
  Canal, 47.
Judson* (N. S.) N-W, e, **5**, 3,
  Eastman, 2. First east of
  Hawthorne Av., fr. East-
  man to Blackhawk.
Julia Ct.* (W. S.) N-E, e, **2**,
  18, Stave, 20. Bet. Henry
  Ct. and Attrill, near Mil-   Old First Regiment
  waukee Av.   Armory, 22 to 26
Julian (W. S.) W, s, **5**, 2,   Jackson St.
  Paulina, 57.
Julius* (W. S.) S, e, **5**, 9, Eleventh, 2. Bet.
  Sholto and Aberdeen, fr. Eleventh St. to
  Blue Island Av.

Junction Av. (S. S.) W, **7**, 9.
Junction Av. (S. S., in Calumet) W, **11**, 9.
Juniata (W. S.) W, **2**, 8.
Justine (S. S.) S, **8**, 6†, 9, 12.

Kedzie Av. North (W. S.) N, e, **4**, 6†, Kinzie, 126; 3, Division, 604; **2**, 17, Armitage Av. 1063; 14. Logan Sq. 1434; 11.
Kedzie Av. South (W. S.) S, e, **4**, 6†, Lake, 1; 9, Harrison, 323; 12, Sixteenth, 803; 15, Twenty-sixth, 1253; 18; **7**, 3, 6, 9, 12, 15, 18.
Keefe Av. (S. S.) S-W, **9**, 11.
Keeley (S. S.) S-E, w, **5**, 15, Lyman, 3000.
Keeney Av. (W. S.) N, **4**, 2†; **2**, 16, 13.
Keenon (W. S.) W, s, **5**, 2, Paulina, 57.
Keith* (W. S.) S, e, **5**, 6, Huron, 47. Second west of Centre Av., fr. Chicago Av. to Huron.
Kellogg Av. (W. S.) S, w, **4**, 14, Twenty-fifth, 2500.
Kellogg Av. (S. S., in Worth) S, **11**, 1.
Kemper Pl. (N. S.) E, n, **3**, 18, Larrabee, 57.
Kendall (W. S.) S-W, s, **5**, 8, Birch, 56.
Kenmore Av. (N. S.) N, **3**, 5†. North Fifty-ninth, 512; 2, Ardmore Av. 914.
Kensington Av. (S. S.) W, **12**, 11.
Kenwood Av. (S. S.) S, w, **9**, 6, Forty-eighth, 4800.
Kenwood Av. (W. S.) W, **2**, 11.
Kenwood Pl.* (S. S.) W, **9**, 2. Bet. Forty-fifth and Forty-sixth, fr. Vincennes Av. to Grand Boul.
Kenwood Ter.* (S. S.) W, **10**, 13. Bet. Seventy-second and Seventy-third, fr. Ellington Av. to Euclid Av.
Kerney (S. S.) S, **7**, 15.
Kidder Ct. (S. S.) W, **9**, 15.
Kimball (S. S., in Calumet) W, **11**, 5.
Kimball Av. (W. S.) N, e, **2**, 17†, Armitage Av. 1114; 14.
Kimbark Av. (S. S.) S, w, **9**, 6, Fifty-first, 5100; **9**, 6, Fifty-ninth, 5858.
King Pl. (N. S.) E, **3**, 13, Oakley Av. 51; 14†, Racine Av. 1155.
Kingsbury* (N. S.) N-W and N, w, **6**, 4, Ohio, 89. First east of the river, fr. Kinzie St. to Chicago Av.
Kingston (W. S., in Norwood Pk.) N-E, **1**, 1.
Kingston Av. (W. S., in Norwood Pk.) N, **1**, 1.
Kingston Av. (S. S.) S, **10**, 17†; **13**, 2.
Kingston Av. (S. S.) S, **13**, 11, 14†, 17.
Kinkade Av. (S. S.) S, **8**, 1†, 10.
Kinkaide Av. (S. S.) S, **7**, 8.
Kinzie, East (N. S.) E, s, **6**, 4†, Market, 50; 5, North Water and Rush, 299.
Kinzie, West (W. S.) W, s, **6**, 4†, Canal. 4; **5**, 6, Centre Av. 357; 5, Robey, 735; 4, California Av. 1151; **4**, 6; 5, West Forty-fourth, 2248; 4, West Fifty-second, 2763.
Kleinman Av. (S. S.) S, **13**, 11.
Knauer* (N. S.) E, **3**, 11. Same as Roscoe, fr. Racine Av. to Sheffield Av.
Koenig Av. (W. S.) N, e, **2**, 15.
Kohlsaat Av.* (N. S.) N-E, **3**, 12. Fr. junction of Evanston Av. and North Halsted to Sheridan Rd.
Kosciusko (W. S.) W, s, **3**, 16, Hoyne Av. 53.
Kossuth (W. S.) W, **1**, 17.
Kramer (W. S.) W, s, **3**, 10, Union, 59.
Kroll* (W. S.) S, **5**, 14. Bet. Robey St. and Hoyne Av., fr. Moore south ½ block.
Kruse Av. (S. S.) S. Name changed; see Florence St.

Kuehl Pl. (W. S.) N-E, e, **3**, 16, Elston Av. 28.
Kuhn's Ct.* (W. S.) W and N, **2**, 18. Bet. Maple Pl. and Powell Pk., fr. Western Av. west ½ block, then north ½ block.
Kuyper (S. S., in Calumet) W, **12**, 7.

Lafayette (S. S.) S, w, **9**, 7, 13†.
Lafayette Pl. (N. S.) Name changed; see Walton Pl.
Lafayette Parkway (N. S.) E, **3**, 5.
Laflin (W. S.) S, e, **5**, 9, Harrison, 149; 12†, Sixteenth, 507; 15, the river, 976; 18, Thirty-fifth, 3459; **8**, 3, Forty-fifth. 4500; 6, Fifty-first, 5100; 9, 12, 15, 18; **11**, 3.
Lake, East (S. S.) W, n, **6**, 5, Michigan Av. 4; 4†, South Water and Market, 252.
Lake, West (W. S.) W, n, **6**, 4†, the river, 2; **5**, 6, Ann, 366; 5, Robey, 774; 4, California Av. 1274; **4**, 6, Central Park Av. 1752; 5, West Forty-fourth, 2250; 4, West Fifty-second, 2766.
Lake (S. S.) S-E, w, **6**, 18†, Thirty-seventh, 3700; **9**, 3, Forty-third, 4300; 6, Fifty-first, 5100; 9, Fifty-seventh, 5658; **10**, 14, Seventy - fifth, 7500.
Lake Av. (S. S., in Riverdale) S, **12**, 18.
Lake Park Av. (S. S.) S-E, w, **6**, 14†, Twenty-fifth, 2450; 17, Thirty-third, 3266.
Lake Park Pl.* (S. S.) W; Nos. odd and even, on south side only; **6**, 8, Michigan Av. 11. First north of Twelfth, fr. the lake to Michigan Av.
Lake Shore Drive (N. S.) N, **6**, 2, Goethe, 73.
Lakeside Av. (N. S.) E, **3**, 8.
Lakeside Av. (S. S.) S, **13**, 10, 13†.
Lake View Av.* (N. S.) N, e, **3**, 15, Diversey Av. 264. At west side of Lincoln Pk., fr. next south of Roslyn Pl. to Diversey Av.
Lakewood Av. (N. S.) N, **3**, 5.
Lane Pl. (N. S.) N, e, **3**, 18, Centre, 2.
Langdon* (N. S.) S-W, s, **6**, 1, Clybourn Av. 10. Second north of Rees, fr. Clybourn Av. to Uhland.
Langley Av. (S. S.) S, w, **6**, 17†, Thirty-seventh, 3700; **9**, 2, Forty-third, 4300; 5, Fiftieth. 4859; 11, Sixty-seventh, 6700; 14, Seventy-fifth, 7500; **12**, 2.
Langley Ter.* (S. S.) **9**, 2. North side of Forty-second, fr. Langley Av. west one block.
Larmon Av. (S. S.) S, **9**, 13.
Larrabee (N. S.) N, e, **6**, 1†, Division, 204; **3**, 18, Centre, 634; 15, Deming, 922.
La Salle (S. S.) S, w, **6**, 4, South Water. 2; 7†, Van Buren, 284; 10, Sixteenth, 1600; 13, Twenty-sixth, 2600; 16, Thirty-fifth, 3500; **9**, 1, Gordon, 4330; 4, Fifty-first, 5100; 7; **12**, 4, 10.
La Salle (S. S., in Calumet) S, **11**, 9.
La Salle Av. (N. S.) N, w, **6**, 4, Kinzie, 35; 1†, Division. 419; **3**, 18, Clark St. and Lincoln Park, 698.
Laughton (W. S.) W, s, **5**, 14, Hoyne Av. 1; 13†, California Av. 415.
Laurel (S. S.) S, w, **5**, 18, Thirty-fifth, 3500.
Laurel (S. S., in Calumet) S, **11**, 2.
Laurel (S. S., in Calumet) W, **11**, 5.
Laurel Av. (W. S.) N, e, **2**, 15, Humboldt Boul. 284.
Laurel Av. (S. S., in Blue Island) S-E, **11**, 16.
Law Av. (W. S.) S, e, **6**, 7, Harrison, 67.
Lawndale Av. North (W. S.) N, e, **4**, 6†, Kinzie, 126; 3, Division, 602; **2**, 17, Humboldt Av. 1210.

Zouave Armory, Centre Av., bet. Jackson and Van Buren Sts.

Epworth M. E. Church, Kenmore and Berwin Avenues.

La Salle Street Tunnel.

First Baptist Church (1844), Washington and La Salle Streets.

Luce* (W. S.) N-W, e, **5**, 3, Blackhawk, 2. Ret, Elston Av. and C. & N. W. R. R., fr. Blackhawk St. to Fox Pl.
Luella Av. (S. S.) S, **10**, 13†, 16; **13**, 1, 10, 13.
Lull Pl.* (W. S.) S and W, e, **5**, 2, Blucher, 47. Ret. Division St. and Milwaukee Av., fr. Milwaukee Av. to Wood St.
Lumber (W. S.) S and S-W. e, **6**, 10†, Sixteenth, 1603; 13, Union, 2309; **5**, 15, Centre Av. 2642; 13.
Lundy's Lane (S. S.) S, w, **5**, 17, Thirty-fifth, 3500.
Lunu Ct. (W. S.) W, s, **5**, 10, Western Av. 1.
Luther* (W. S.) W, s, **5**, 13, Washtenaw Av. 60. Ret. Martin and Coulter, fr. Rockwell St. to Washtenaw Av.
Luz Pl. (N. S.) E, **6**, 1.
Lydia (W. S.) W, n, **6**, 4, Union. 25.
Lydiard (W. S.) N, e, **4**, 4†, Kinzie, 22; 1, Augusta, 410.
Lyman (S. S.) S-W, n, **5**, 15, Deering, 3000.
Lyman Av. (N. S.) N, e, **3**, 7, Wilson Av. 1308.
Lynch Pl.* (S. S.) S, **5**, 18. First east of Ashland Av., fr. Thirty-second to Thirty-third.
Lyndale Av. (W. S.) W, **2**, 16.
Lyon Av. (S. S.) W, **11**. 14. Same as 119th, fr. Ashland Av. to Western Av.
Lyons Av. (S. S.) N-W, **12**, 2.
Lytle (W. S.) S, e, **5**, **9**, Gilpin Pl. 65.

McAllister Pl.* (W. S.) W, s, **5**. 9, Lytle, 29. At north side of Vernon Pk., fr. Centre Av. to Loomis.
McAlpine (S. S.) S, **5**, 17, Thirty-fourth, 3400.
McAuley Av. (W. S.) N, e, **4**, 2†, Hirsch, 766; **2**, 16.
McChesney Av. (S. S.) S, w. **9**, 11, Sixty-fifth, 6500.
McDermott* (S. S.) S-E, w. **5**, 15, Archer Av. 2938. First east of Lock, fr."C. A. & St. L. R. R. to Archer.Av.
McDowell* (W. S.) W, **5**, 13. First south of Coulter, fr. Washtenaw Av. west ¼ block.
Macedonia* (W. S.) N, e, **5**, 2, Division, 2. First west of Wood, fr. Division to Ellen.
McElroy (W. S.) W, s, **4**, 3, Sheridan, 48.
McGlashen* (S. S.) S, e, **6**, 13, Archer Av. 2242 Ret. Stewart Av. and Hanover, fr. Twenty-second St. to Archer Av.
McGovern (W. S.) W, s, **2**, 18, Milwaukee Av. 2.
McHenry (W. S.) N & N-W, e, **5**, 3, Blanche, 2; **3**, 17†, the river, 205.
Mack (W. S.) S, **4**, 14.
McKibbon Av. (S. S.) S, **8**, 1.
Mackinaw Av. (S. S.) S, w, **10**, 18†, Eighty-third, 8300; **13**, 3, Ninety-first, 9100; 18, 131st, 13100.
Maclay Av. (S. S.) S, **7**, 6.
McLean Av. (W. S.) W, s, **2**, 17†, Central Park Av. 482; 16.
McMaster (W. S.) W, **2**, 11.
McMullen Ct. (W. S.) W, s, **5**, 12, May, 36.
McReynolds (W. S.) W, s, **5**, 2, Paulina, 58.
McTartane Av. (S. S.) S, **13**, 1.
Madison, East (S. S.) W, s, **6**, **5**, Michigan Av. 1; 7†, Market, 269.

Madison,West (W. S.) W, s, **6**, 7†, the river, 1; **5**, 6,
Hospital of the Alexian Brothers, 569 North Market Street.
Centre Av. 384; 5," Robey, 785; 4, California Av. 1249; **4**, 6, Central Park Av. 1736; 5, West Forty-fourth, 2247; 4, West Fifty-second, 2765.
Madison (W. S.) W, **2**, 7†; **1**, 9.
Madison (S. S.) S, **11**, 6.

Madison Av. (S. S.) S, w, **9**, 6, Fifty-first, 5100; 9†, Fifty-ninth, 5900; 12, Sixty-fifth, 6500; 15, Seventy-fifth, 7500; 18.
Madison Ct.* (S. S.) S-W, **9**, 12. First east of I. C. R. R., fr. Sixty-sixth to Sixty-seventh.
Madison Pk. (S. S.) W, s, **9**, 6, Woodlawn Av. 235.
Magazin (W. S.) W, **1**, 17.
Magnolia Av. (N. S.) N, **13**, 5.
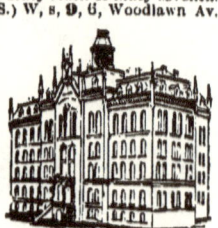
Malier (W. S.) W, s, **4**, 8, West Forty-fifth, 2457.
Main (S. S.) S-E, w. **5**, 15, Archer Av. 2800.
Main (W. S.) W, **1**, 17.
Manistee Av. (S. S.) S, w, **13**, 2†, Ninetieth, 9001; 5, Ninety-ninth, 9900; 8, 105th, 10500.
St. Ignatius College, May and Twelfth Streets.
Maple (N. S.) E, s, **6**, 1, Clark, 30.
Maple (W. S.) W, **1**, 6.
Maple (S. S.) W, **7**, 15.
Maple (S. S., in Calumet) S-E, **11**, 5, 6†.
Maple (S. S., in Worth) S, **11**, 1†, 4.
Maple Av. (S. S.) W, **7**, 9.
Maple Av. (S. S.) S, **7**, 12.
Maple Av.* (W. S., in Montclair) N, **1**, 16, 13. Second east of Washington Av., fr. Prospect to Lexington.
Maple Av. (S. S., in Worth) S, **11**, 13.
Maple Pl. (W. S.) W, s, **2**, 18, Powell Av. 41.
Maplewood (W. S.) S, **4**, 5.
Maplewood Ave. North (W. S.) N, e, **5**, 4, Fulton, 68; 1†, Division, 604; **2**, 18, Bloomingdale Rd. 954; 15, Diversey Av. 1294.
Maplewood Av. South (W. S.) S, e, **5**, 16, Thirty-second, 42.
Maplewood Pl. (W. S.) S, e, **5**, 10, Fourteenth, 12.
Mars Av. (N. S.) N, e, **3**, 10, Roscoe, 74.
Marble Pl. (S. S.) W, **6**, 7. An alley bet. Monroe and Adams, fr. State St. to Fifth Av.
Marble Pl. West (W. S.) W, **6**, 7, Desplaines, 94.
Marcy (N. S.) N-W, e, **3**, 17, Wabansia Av. 184.

Margaret* (W. S.) S, e, **5**, 12, Henry, 23. First east of Centre Av., fr. Fourteenth to Fifteenth.
Margaret Pl. (W. S.) S, **4**, 12. Name changed; see Jan Huss Av.
Marianna (N. S.) E, n, **3**, 14, Racine Av. 1201.

Former Interior of Immanuel Baptist Church, Michigan Avenue, near Twenty-third Street.
Marina (S. S., in Worth) S, **11**, 1.
Marion Pl.* (W. S.) N, e, **5**, 2. Ellen, 78. First east of Lincoln, fr. Division to Ellen.
Mark (W. S.) W, **2**, 10.
Mark (W. S.) W, n, **6**, 10, Union, 2.
Market, North (N. S.) N, w, **6**, 4†, Kinzie, 33; 1, Division, 381.
Market, South (S. S.) S, w, **6**, 4†, Lake, 2; 7, Congress, 269.
Market (S. S., in Blue Island) W, **11**, 17.
Market (S. S., in Riverdale) W, **12**, 17.
Market Sq.* (S. S.) S-E, w, **5**, 17, Archer Av. 3132. First east of Wood, fr. Thirty-first St. to Ashland Av.
Marlin Pl. (W. S.) W, **4**, 2.
Marquette Av. (S. S.) S, w, **13**, 2†, South Chicago Av. 8954; 5, Ninety-ninth, 9854; 8, 105th, 10500.
Marshfield (S. S., in Calumet) S, **11**, 14.

Montrose Boul. West (W. S.) W, **2**, 9, 8, 7†; **1**, 9.
Moore* (N. S.) 8, e, **6**, 1, Division, 1. Bet. Market and Franklin, fr. Division to Elm.
Moore (W. S.) W, s, **5**, 14, Robey, 97; 13†, California Av. 527.
Moore (W. S.) N, **2**, 10, 13†. Second west of West Forty-sixth, fr. Belmont Av. to Warner Av.
Moore Pl. (W. S.) 8, e, **4**, 12, Eighteenth, 847.
Moorman* (W. S.) S-E, s, **5**, 2, Lull Pl. 9. First south of Milwaukee Av.,fr. Ellen to Paulina.
Morgan, North*(W. S.) N, w, **5**, 6, Kinzie, 117.
Morgan, South (W. S.) 8, e, **5**, 6, Randolph, 1; 9†, Harrison, 251; 12, Sixteenth, 633†

15, Lumber, 931; **8**, 6, Fifty-first, 5100; 9, 12, 15, 18; **11**, 6, 9, 12.
Morgan Av. (S. S., in Calumet) W & N-W, **11**, 12†, 11, 7.
Morgan Pl. (W. S.) W, s, **5**, 9, Aberdeen, 57.
Morgan Pl.* (S. S.) W, s, **9**, 3, Sidney Av. 68. Bet. Forty-fourth and Forty-fifth, fr. Lake Av. to Greenwood Av.
Morris (S. S.) W, **9**, 4.
Morrison Av. (W. S.) N, **2**, 9, 12†. Same as Kedzie Av., north of Irving Park Boul.
Morton (W. S.) **1**, 5.
Mosspratt (S. S.) 8, w, **5**, 18, Thirty-second, 3200.
Mound Av. (S. S.) W, n, **9**, 4, Stewart Av. 459.
Mound Av. (S. S., in Calumet) 8, **11**, 9.
Mountain Av. (S. S., in Calumet) 8, **11**, 2.
Mountain Av. (S. S.) 8, **12**, 10. Name changed; see Canal St.
Mowry Av. (S. S.) 8, **7**, 9. Name changed; see Hamlin Av.
Mozart (W. S.) N, e, **2**, 18, Armitage Av. 238.
Mozart (W. S.) N, **2**, 9.
Mulberry Av. (W. S., in Norwood Pk.) **1**, 1.
Murray (S. S., in Calumet) 8, **12**, 4†, 7.
Murray Av. (W. S., in Jefferson) N, **1**, 6.
Muskegon Av. (S. S.) 8, w, **10**, 17†, Baltimore Av. 8316; **13**, 2, Ninety-first, 9100; 5, Ninety-ninth, 9900; 8, 108th, 10600; 11.
Muspratt (S. S) See Mosspratt.
Mynon Av. (S. S.) W, **11**, 8.
Myrtle (W. S.) 8, e, **5**, 8, Taylor, 39.
Myrtle (W. S., in Galewood) N, **1**, 17.
Myrtle* (N. S.) N, **3**, 2. First east of Clark, fr. Bryn Mawr Av. to Olive.
Myrtle Av. (S. S.) S-W and 8, w, **9**, 12, Sixty-sixth, 6600.
Myrtle Av. (S. S.) W, **9**, 3, Lake Av. 46.
Myrtle Av. (S. S.) 8, **12**, 10. Name changed; see Scanlan Av.
Myrtle Av. (W. S.) N, e, **2**, 18, Milwaukee Av. 2; 15†, Diversey Av. 395.
Myrtle Av. (W. S.) N, **4**, 1.
Myrtle Av. (W. S., in Cicero) N, **4**, 16†, 13.

Napoleon Pl. (S. S.) W, **6**, 13. Name changed; see Twenty-eighth Pl.
Nassau* (W. S.) S, e, **5**, 7, Van Buren, 45. Bet. Francisco St. and Sacramento Av., fr. Jackson to Van Buren.
Nassau (S. S., in Blue Island) W, **11**, 17.
Nebraska (W. S.) W, **5**, 9. Name changed; see Elburn Av.
Nebraska Av. (W. S.) N, e, **2**, 18, Armitage Av. 120.
Nellie Av. (N. S.) E, n, **3**, 10; 11†, Racine Av. 1201; 12, Pine Grove Av. 1803.
Nelson (N. S.) E, **3**, 13†, 14. Name changed; see King Pl.
Nelson Av. (W. S.) W, **4**, 1.
Nestledown Av. (S. S.) 8, **13**, 1.
Nevada (N. S.) E, **3**, 12, Evanston Av. 1801.
Nevada Av. (W. S.) W, **2**, 13.

New (S. S., in Blue Island) W, **11**, 17, 16†.
Newberry Av. (W. S.) 8, e, **5**, 9, Taylor, 1; 12†, Sixteenth, 265.
Newport Av. (N. S.) E, s, **3**, 11†, Racine Av. 1201; 12, the lake. 98.
Newton (W. S.) N, w, **5**, 2, Augusta, 61.
Niagara (W. S.) W, n, **4**, 2; 1†, West Fiftieth, 2268.
Nicholls* (W. S.) N, e, **5**, 4, Kinzie, 129. Bet. Albany and Sacramento Avs., fr. Kinzie St. to Central Park Boul.
*Nieman Av. (W. S., in Norwood Pk.) N-E, **1**, 1.
Nineteenth, East (S. S.) W, n, **6**, 10, Wentworth Av. 210.
Nineteenth, West (W. S.) W, n, **6**, 10, Union, 2; **5**, 12†, Centre Av. 367; 11, Robey, 891; 10, California Av. 1348; **4**, 12, Homan Av. 1695.
Nineteenth Pl.* (W. S.) W, n, **5**, 12, Brown, 94. Bet. Nineteenth and Twentieth, fr. Johnson west one block.
Ninth Av. (S. S., in Pullman) S-W, **12**, 9.
Ninetieth (S. S.) W, **13**, 3, the Strand, 1; 2†, Escanaba Av. 377; 1; **12**, 3, 2, 1; **11**, 3, 2.
Ninetieth Pl. (S. S.) W, **12**, 3, 2†.
Ninety-first (S. S.) W, **13**, 3, Green Bay Av. 37; 2, Escanaba Av. 377; 1†; **12**, 3, 2, 1; **11**, 3, 2, 1.
Ninety-first Ct. (S. S.) W, **12**, 3.
Ninety-first Pl.* (S. S.) W, **12**, 2. Bet. Ninety-first and Ninety-second, fr. Cottage Grove Av. to South Park Av.
Ninety-first Pk. (S. S., in Calumet) W, **11**, 2.
Ninety-second (S. S.) W, **13**, 3, Harbor and Mackinaw Avs. 75; 2, South Chicago Av. 351; 1†; **12**, 3, 2, 1; **11**, 3, 2, 1.
Ninety-second Ct. (S. S.) W, **12**, 3.
Ninety-second Pl. (S. S.) W, **13**, 1†; **12**, 2.
Ninety-third (S. S.) W, **13**, 3, Harbor Av. 131; 2, Anthony Av. 385; 1†; **12**, 3, 2, 1; **11**, 3, 2, 1.
Ninety-fourth (S. S.) W, **13**, 2, Muskegon Av. 417; 1†; **12**, 3, 1; **11**, 3, 2, 1.
Ninety-fifth (S. S.) W, **13**, 3, Ewing Av. 113; 5†, Muskegon Av. 619; 1; **12**, 3, 2, 1; **11**, 3, 2, 1.
Ninety-sixth (S. S.) W, **13**, 6†, Ewing Av. 117; 5, Muskegon Av. 661; 4; **12**, 6, 5, 4; **11**, 6, 5.
Ninety-seventh (S. S.) W, **13**, 6†, Ewing Av. 147; 5, Muskegon Av. 693; **12**, 5, 4; **11**, 6, 5.
Ninety-eighth (S. S.) W, **13**, 6†, Ewing Av. 173; 5, Muskegon Av. 719; **12**, 5, 4; **11**, 6, 5.
Ninety-ninth (S. S.) W, **13**, 6†, Ewing Av. 199; 5, Muskegon Av. 749; 4; **12**, 6, 5, 4; **11**, 6, 5, 4.
Nixon (W. S.) 8, e, **5**, 9, Polk, 1.
Noble (W. S.) N, w, **5**, 6†, Kinzie, 141; 3, Division, 581.

Noble Av. (N. S.) E, n, **3**, 13†, Hoyne Av. 257; 14, Racine Av. 1201.
Noble Ct. (S. S., at Grand Crossing) 8, **9**, 15.
Normal Parkway, North* (S. S.) W, **9**, 10. Bet. Sixty-seventh and the Cook County Normal School, fr. C., R. I. & P. R. R. to Wright.

Normal Parkway, South* (S. S.) W, **9**, 10. Bet. Cook County Normal School and Sixty-ninth, fr. C., R. I. & P. R. R. to Wright.
Norman Av. (W. S.) N, e, **2**, 18, Wabansia Av. 896.
North (N. S.) E, **3**, 4.
North Av. East*(N. S.) E, s, **3**, 17, the river, 2; 18, Sedgwick, 356; **6**, 2, Lake Shore Drive, 616.

North Av. West (W. S.) W, s, **3**, 17, the river,
1; 16†, Robey St. and Milwaukee Av. 471;
2, 18, California Av. 915; 17, Central
Park Av. 1375; 16, Tripp Av. 1796; **1**,
18, 17, 16.
North Av. (N. S.) E, **3**, 1.
North Av. (S. S., in Blue Island) W, **11**, 13.
North Ct. (N. S.) E, **3**, 5.
North Branch (N. S.) N-W and N, n, **6**, 1, Haw-
thorne Av. 6; **5**. 3†, Division and Rees,
362.
North Fifty-ninth, (N. S.) See Fifty-ninth,
North.
North Grove Ct. (N. S.) See Grove Ct.
North Normal Parkway (S. S.) See Normal
Parkway, North.
North Park Av. (N. S.) N, w, **3**, 18, Centre, 778.
North Pier (N. S.) E, **6**. 5.
North Pl. (W. S.) N-W, e, **3**, 16, Armitage
Av. 4.
North Water (N. S.) E, s, **6**, 4†, Wells, 98; 5,
St. Clair, 378.
Norton (W. S.) S, e, **5**. 9, Polk, 71.
Norwood* (W. S., in Norwood Pk.) W, **1**, 1.
First north of Vine, fr. Willow Av. to
East Circle.
Norwood Av. (W. S.) W, s, **4**, 3, Sheridan,
61.
Norwood Park Av. (W. S., in Norwood Pk.) W,
1, 4.
Norwood Park Rd. (W. S.) N-W, **1**, 5†, 2.
Notre Dame Av. (S. S.) S-W, **13**, 5†, 8.
Nursery (N. S.) N-W. e, **3**, 17, Herndon, 50.
Nutt* (W. S.) S, e, **5**, 12, Sixteenth, 1. First
west of Morgan, fr. Sixteenth to Eight-
eenth.
Nutt Av. (S. S.) S, **9**, 15†, Seventy-fifth, 7500;
18.
Nutt Ct.* (W. S.) S, e, **5**, 12, Nineteenth, 1.
First west of Morgan, fr. Nineteenth to
Twentieth.

Oak (N. S.) N-E and E,
s, **6**, 1†, Market,
162; 2, Pine, 448.
Oak (S. S.) W, n, **9**, 4,
Stewart Av. 549.
Oak (S. S.) W, **7**, 15.
Oak (W. S.) W, **2**, 5, 4†.

Newberry Library.
Oak and State Streets.

Oak (W. S.) W, s, **4**, 1, West Fiftieth, 2269;
2†. First north of Augusta, fr. West Forty-
eighth to West Fiftieth.
Oak (W. S., in Montclair) N, **1**, 16.
Oak (S. S., in Calumet) S, **11**, 5.
Oak (S. S., in Calumet) S-E, **11**, 5, 6†.
Oak Av. (S. S.) S-W, **12**, 11.
Oak Av. (S. S.) W, n, **6**, 17, Stanton Av. 82.
Oak Av. (S. S.) S†, **13**, 10.
Oak Pl. (N. S.) N, e, **3**, 11.
Oakdale Av. (N. S.) E, n, **3**, 13†, Leavitt, 201;
14, Racine Av. 1201; 15, Lake View Av.
2001.
Oakenwald Av. (S. S.) S-E and S-W, w, **9**, 3,
Forty-third, 4301.
Oak Grove Av. (N. S.) E, **3**, 11.
Oakland Pl.* (N. S.) N, **3**, 14. First east of
Sheffield Av., fr. George St. to Wellington
Av.
Oakley Av. North (W. S. & N. S.) N, e, **5**, 5,
Kinzie, 124; 2†, Division, 604; **3**, 16,
Armitage Av. 1052; 13, Oakdale Av. 1524;
16, Cornelia. 1878; 7.
Oakley Av. South (W. S. & S. S.) S; north of
Ill. & Mich. Canal, e,
south of the Canal,
w; **5**, 5, L a k e, 2;
8†, Harrison. 323; 11.
Sixteenth, 803; 14.
Coulter, 1195; 17.
Thirty-fifth, 3500; **8**.
2, 5, 8, 11, 17.
Oak Park Av. (W. S.) N, **1**,
16.

Washingtonian Home,
Ogden Avenue and
Madison Street.

Oakwood Av. (S. S.) W, s,
6, 18, Lake Av. 12;
9, 3†, Drexel Boul. 117; **8**. 1.
Oakwood Boul. (S. S.) W, s, **9**, 2, Vincennes
Av. 307.

O'Brien* (W. S.) W, s, **6**, 10, Union, 59. Bet.
Dussold and Kramer, fr. Jefferson to
Halsted.
O'Brien Av. (W. S.) N, **2**, 16.
Odell Pl. (S. S., in Calumet) W, **12**, 4.
Ogden Av. (W. S.) S-W, s, **5**, 6, Randolph. 2;
8†, Harrison, 369; 10. Fifteenth, 1015;
4, 12, Clifton Park Av. 1501; 14, Kellogg
Av. 2047; 13.
Ogden Av. (S. S.)
S, **8**, 4†, 10;
11. 1, 4, 7,
10.
Ogden Boul.* (W.
S.) S-W, **8**, 11;
10, Rockwell,
887. Same as
Ogden Av., fr.
Twelfth St. to
Douglas Pk.
Ogden Pl.* (W. S.)
W, n, **5**, 8,
Paulina, 48.
Bet. Madison
and Monroe,
fr. Ogden Av.
to Wood.
Oglesby* (W. S.)
N, **2**, 17. Fifth
street west of
Kedzie Av., fr. North Av. to Armitage Av.
Oglesby Av. (S. S.) S, **10**, 10, Sixty-ninth,
6900.
Oglesby Av. (S. S.) S, w, **9**. 9, Sixtieth, 6000;
12†, Sixty-seventh, 6658.
Oglesby Av. (S. S., in Calumet) S, **11**, 6.
Ohio, East (N. S.) E, s, **6**, 4†, Market, 86; 5,
the lake, 484.
Ohio, West (W. S.) W, s, **6**, 4†, Desplaines, 1;
5, 6, Centre Av. 243; 5, Robey, 631; 4,
California Av. 1089; 4, 6, Central Park
Av. 1587; 5, West Forty-sixth, 2223; 4,
Hawkins, 2545.
Olga (N. S.) N, **3**, 11.
Olive (W. S.) S, e, **5**, 8, Ashland, 46.
Olive (N. S.) E, n, **3**, 2, Southport Av. 961.
Olive (S. S., in Blue Island) W, **11**, 14.
Olive (S. S., in Lyons) S, **7**, 13.
Olive Ct.* (N. S.) N, **3**, 5. First east of Clark,
fr. Rome Av. to Argyle.
Omer (W. S.) N, **2**, 8.
100th (S. S.) W, **13**, 6†, Ewing Av. 261; 5, 4;
12, 4; **11**, 6.
101st (S. S.) W, s, **13**, 6†, Ewing Av. 295; 5,
4; **12**, 4; **11**, 6, 5.
102nd (S. S.) W, **13**, 6†, Ewing Av. 295; 5,
4; **12**, 4.
103rd (S. S.) W, **13**, 6,
Ewing Av. 301; 5†, 4;
12, 6, 5, 4; **11**, 6,
5, 4.
103rd Pl.* (S. S.) W, **12**.
8. Bet. 103rd and
104th, fr. Michigan
Av. to State.
104th (S. S.) W, **13**, 9†,
Ewing Av. 301; 8, 7;
12, 9, 8, 7; **11**, 9,
8, 7.

Temple of Zion Congregation,
Ogden Av. and Washington Boul.

Third Presbyterian Church,
Ogden and South
Ashland Ave.

105th (S. S.) W, **13**, 9†, Ewing Av. 301; 8, 7;
12, 9, 8, 7; **11**, 9, 8, 7.
106th (S. S.) W, **13**, 9†, Avenue I, 301; 8, 7;
12, 9, 8; **11**, 9, 8, 7.
107th (S. S.) W, **13**, 9†, 8, 7; **12**, 8; **11**, 9,
8, 7.
107th Pl. (S. S., in Calumet) W, **11**, 9.
108th (S. S.) W, **13**, 9†, 8, 7; **12**, 8; **11**,
9, 7.
108th Pl. (S. S., in Calumet) W, **11**, 9.
109th (S. S.) W, **13**, 9†, 8, 7; **11**, 9, 7.
109th Pl. (S. S., in Calumet) W, **12**, 8, 7†;
11, 9.
110th (S. S.) W, **13**, 9, 8, 7†; **12**, 8, 7; **11**, 9,
8, 7.
110th Pl. (S. S., in Calumet) W, **12**, 7†;
11, 9.
111th (S. S.) W, **13**, 9, 8†, 7; **12**, 8, 7; **11**,
9, 8, 7.
111th Pl. (S. S.) W, **12**, 11, 10†.

112th (S. S.) W, **13**, 12†, 11, 10; **12**, 11, 10; **11**, 10.
112th Pl. (S. S.) W, **12**, 11, 10†.
113th (S. S.) W, **13**, 12, 11†, 10; **12**, 11, 10; **11**, 10.
113th Pl. (S. S.) W, **12**, 11, 10†.
114th (S. S.) W, **13**, 12†, 11, 10; **12**, 11, 10; **11**, 10.
114th Pl.* (S. S.) W, **13**, 12.
Bet. 114th and 115th, fr. Avenue E to Avenue F.

Wesley Hospital, 355 Ohio Street.

115th (S. S.) W, **13**, 12†, 11; **12**, 11, 10; **11**, 12, 11, 10.
115th Pl.* (S. S.) W, **13**, 12. Bet. 115th and 116th, fr. Avenue E to Avenue F.
116th (S. S.) W, **13**, 12†, 11, 10; **12**, 11, 10; **11**, 12, 10.
117th (S. S.) W, **13**, 12†, 11, 10; **12**, 11, 10; **11**, 12, 10.
118th (S. S.) W, **13**, 12†, 11, 10; **12**, 11, 10; **11**, 12, 10.
119th (S. S.) W, **13**, 15†, 11, 10; **12**, 11, 10; **11**, 12, 10.
120th (S. S.) W, **13**, 15†, 14, 13; **12**, 14; **11**, 14.
121st (S. S.) W, **13**, 13†; **12**, 14; **11**, 14.
122nd (S. S.) W, **13**, 14, 13†; **12**, 14; **11**, 14.
123rd (S. S.) W, **13**, 14, 13†; **12**, 14, 13; **11**, 14, 13.
124th (S. S.) W, **13**, 14, 13†; **12**, 14, 13.
125th (S. S.) W, **13**, 14, 13†; **12**, 14, 13.
126th (S. S.) W, **13**, 14, 13†; **12**, 13.
127th (S. S.) W, **13**, 14†; **12**, 13; **11**, 14, 13.
128th (S. S.) W, **13**, 17.
130th (S. S.) W, **13**, 18, 17†; **12**, 18, 17.
131st (S. S.) W, **13**, 18, 17†; **12**, 18, 17.
132nd (S. S.) W, **13**, 18†, 17; **12**, 18, 17.
133rd (S. S.) W, **13**, 18, 17†; **11**, 18, 17.
134th (S. S.) W, **13**, 18†, 17, 16; **12**, 18, 17.
135th (S. S.) W, **13**, 18, 17, 16†.
136th (S. S.) W, **13**, south of sections 18† and 16; **12**, south of section 17.
137th (S. S.) W, **13**, south of sections 17 and 16†; **12**, south of section 17.
138th (S. S.) W, **13**, south of sections 17 and 16†; **12**, south of sections 17 and 16.
O'Neil* (W. S.) W, s, **5**, 15, Halsted, 1. Second south of Twenty-second, fr. Halsted west one block.
Ontario (N. S.) E, s, **6**, 4†, Market, 104; 5, the lake, 478.
Ontario, West (W. S.) W, s, **4**, 5, West Forty-sixth, 2233; 4†, Robinson Av. or West Fifty - second, 2609.

Chicago Historical Society Library, near Ontario Street, on Dearborn Avenue.

Ontario (W. S.) N, **2**, 11.
Ontario (S. S., in Blue Island) S-E. **11**, 18.
Ontario Av. (S. S.) S, w, **10**, 17†, Eighty-third, 8300; **13**, 2, Ninety-first, 9100.
Orange (S. S., in Blue Island) W, **11**, 17.
Orchard (N. S.) N-E and N. e. **6**. 1, Clybourn Av. 2; **8**, 18†, Centre, 262; 15, Dewey Ct. 710.
Orchard (S. S.) W, s, **9**, 3, Oakenwald Av. 21.
Orchard (W. S., in Galewood) N, **1**, 17.
Orchard (S. S., in Worth) W, **11**, 13.
Osborne* (W. S.) N, e, **5**, 5, Indiana. 2. First west of Paulina, fr. Indiana to Ohio.
Osgood (N. S.) N, e, **8**, 17, Garfield Av. 150.
Oswego* (W. S.) N, e, **5**, 5. Kinzie. 2. First east of Paulina, fr. Kinzie north ½ block.
Oswell (S. S.) S, **9**, 4.
Otis* (N. S.) N, e, **6**, 1, Division, 2. Second west of Larrabee, fr. Division to Vedder.
Otto (N. S.) E, n, **8**, 11, Herndon, 1101.
Our (W. S., in Jefferson) N-W, **1**, 6.
Owasco (W. S.) W, s, **5**, 7†, California Av. 249; 4, 8, West Forty-fourth, 2247.
Oxford Ct. (S. S.) W, **6**, 17.

Pacific Av. (S. S.) S, e, **6**, 7, Harrison, 97, **11**, 10.
Pacific Av. (S. S.) W, **7**, 12.
Packers' Av. (S. S.) S, **8**, 3.
Page, North (W. S.) N, e, **5**, 5, Austin Av. 26
Page, South (W. S. & S. S.) S, e, **5**, 5†, Lake, 1; **8**, 11; **11**, 2, 14.
Page (S. S., in Calumet) S, **11**, 14.
Palace Pl.* (S. S., in Morgan Pk.) S, **11**, 8. First east of Western Av., fr. 107th to the Circle.
Palasaide Av. (S. S.) W, **7**, 9.
Palatine (W. S.) W, s, **4**, 12, St. Louis Av. 61.
Palm Av. (S. S.) W, **7**, 12.
Palmer (N. S.) N, e, **8**, 7†, Montrose Boul. 1174; 4, North Fifty-ninth, 1710.
Palmer Av. (S. S.) S, w, **10**, 10, Sixty-ninth, 6900.
Palmer Av. (W. S.) W, s, **2**, 18, Mozart, 40.
Palmer Sq.* (W. S.) W, s, **2**, 18, Nebraska Av. 176. First south of Johnson Av., fr. Thomas Av. to Kedzie Av.
Park* (W. S.) N-W, e, **5**, 2, Evergreen Av. 68. First west of Milwaukee Av., fr. Wood to Lincoln, and fr. Evergreen Av. to Robey.
Park (S. S., in Calumet) W and N-W, **11**, 12†, 11, 8.
Park Av.* (N. S.) N, **8**, 15. First west of Sheridan Rd., fr. Diversey Av. to Surf.

Hospital for Women and Children, Paulina and Adams Streets.

Park Av. (S. S.) S, **7**, 5.
Park Av. (S. S.) N, **7**, 8.
Park Av. (S. S.) W, **7**, 9.
Park Av. (W. S.) W, s, **5**, 5†, Robey, 191; 4, California Av. 685; **4**, 6, Homan Av. 1047; 5, West Forty-fourth, 1679; 4, West Fifty-second, 2195.
Park Av. (W. S.) N, **2**, 14.
Park Av. (W. S.) N, **2**, 10†, 7.
Park Av. (S. S., in Calumet) S, **12**, 4.
Park Cres. (S. S., in Morgan Pk.) **11**, 8. A semi-circle, with ends at Prospect Av.
Park Ct. (S. S.) W, **9**, 6.
Park Ct. (W. S., in Norwood Pk.) N-E, **1**, 1.
Park Pl. (W. S.) N, **2**, 14.
Park Pl. (S. S., in Calumet) W, **11**, 6, 5†.
Park End Av. (S. S.) S, **9**, 8.
Park Front* (N. S.) E, **8**, 18. First north of Menomonee, fr. Wells to Clark.
Parker Av. (W. S.) W, **2**, 13.
Parmelee (W. S.) W, s, **5**, 14, Hoyne Av. 1; 13†, Washtenaw Av. 349.
Parnell Av. (S. S.) S, w, **6**, 13, Twenty-ninth, 2900; 16†, Thirty-fifth, 3500.
Parnell Av. (S. S.) S, **13**, 17.
Paulina, North (W. S. & N. S.) N, e, **5**, 5†, Kinzie, 100; 2, Division, 544; **3**, 16, Armitage Av. 1020; 13, Wrightwood Av. 1318; 10, Addison Av. 2008; 7, Montrose Boul. 2532; 4, Tuttle Av. 2906.
Paulina, South (W. S. & S. S.) S; in South Side, e, in South Side, **5**, 5†, Lake, 1; 8. Harrison, 309; 11, Sixteenth, 751; 14, the river, 1247; 17, Thirty-fifth, 3500; **8**, 2, 5, 11; **11**, 2, 14.

Fourth Baptist Church, Paulina St. and Washington Boul.

Paus (N. S.) N, **8**, 14.
Paxton Av. (W. S.) N, **1**, 5.
Paxton Av. (S.S.) S, **10**, 13†, 16; **13**, 7, 10, 13.
Pearce (W. S.) W, s, **6**, 7, Desplaines, 1.

Pearl (N. S.) N; Nos. odd and even, on west side only; 3, 18, Garfield Av. 1.

Pearl* (N. S.) N, 3. 2. Second east of Clark, fr. Bryn Mawr Av. to Olive.

Pearl (S. S.) W, 11, 6.

Pearl (S. S.) S, 7, 15.

Pearl (S. S., in Calumet) S-W, 11, 5.

Pearl (W. S.) W, s, 4. 14, Butler Av. 2169.

Pearl (W. S.) W, 1, 16.

Pearson, East (N. S.) E, s, 6, 1†; 2, the lake. 154.

Pearson, West (N. S.) E, s, 6, 1, Market, 18.

Peck Ct. (S. S.) W, s, 6, 8, Wabash Av. 33.

Pedro Pl. (S. S., in Morgan Pk.) S-E, 11, 11.

Penn* (N. S.) N, e, 6, 1, Division, 2. Second east of Halsted, fr. Division to Vedder.

Penn Pl. (W. S.) W, 4, 5.

Pennock Boul. (W. S.) W, 2, 12.

Pennsylvania Av. (S. S.) S, 13, south of section 16.

Pennsylvania Av. (W. S.) N, 2, 16.

Pensacola Av.* (N. S.) E, 3, 7. First south of Montrose Boul., fr. Lincoln Av. to Robey.

Peoria, North*(W. S.) N, w, 5, 6, Kinzie. 113.

Peoria, South (W. S. & S. S.) S, e, 5, 6, Randolph, 1; 9†, Harrison, 257; 6, 6. Fiftieth Ct. 5034; 9, 12, 15, 18; 11, 3, 6, 9, 12.

Pepper Av. (W. S., in Austin) N, 4, 4.

Perry (N. S.) N, e, 3, 17, Clybourn Av. 2; 14†, Diversey Av. 326; 11, Addison Av. 890; 8, Montrose Boul. 1422.

Perry Av. (S. S.) S, 9, 10†, 13.

Perry Av. (W. S.) N, e, 2, 18, Bremen, 114.

Perry Av. (W. S.) W, 1, 5.

Peterson* (W. S.) W, s, 3, 16, Robey, 1. Second north of Wabansia Av., fr. Robey St. to Hoyne Av.

Peterson Av. (N. S.) W, 2, 3, 2†.

Peterson Av. (N. S.) E, 3, 1†, 2.

Pharo Av. (S. S.) S, 8, 4†, 7.

Philadelphia Pl. (W. S.) W, 4, 5.

Phillips* (W. S.) W, 5, 6, Fay, 51. Bet. Erie and Pratt, fr. Halsted west to Sangamon.

Phillips Av. (S. S.) S, 10, 17.

Phillips Av. (S. S.) S, 13, 9, 12, 18†.

Phillips Av. (S. S.) S, 13, south of section 17.

Phillips Av. (W. S.) W, 2, 8.

Phinney Av. North (W. S.) N, e, 4, 6, Huron, 306.

Phinney Av. South (W. S.) N, e, 4, 9, Van Buren, 2.

Piano Ter.* (N. S.) N, 3, 15. First east of Evanston Av., fr. Diversey Av. to Surf.

Pier (S. S.) E, 6, 18.

Pierce (S. S.) W, 8, 17.

Pierce St. or Forty-second Pl. (S. S.) W, 9, 2.

Pierce Av. (W. S.) W, s, 4, 3, Homan Av. 127.

Pierce Pl. (S. S.) W, n, 9, 7, Wright. 601.

Pierson Av. See Albany Av.

Pigdon (W. S.) W, 2, 8, 7†.

Pine (N. S.) N, w, 6, 5†, North Water, 1; 2, Oak, 255.

Pine (N. S.) E, n, 3, 4, West Ravenswood Park, 607.

Pine (S. S.) S, 11, 2.

Pine (S. S.) W, 7, 15.

Pine (W. S.) W, 2, 14.

Pine (W. S.) W, 1, 10.

Pine (S. S., in Calumet) W, 11, 11.

Pine Av. (S. S.) W, 7, 4, 5.

Pine Av. (W. S., in Austin) N, 4, 4†, 1.

Pine Grove Av. (N. S.) N-W, n, 3, 15; 12†, Addison Av. 554.

Pitney Ct.* (S. S.) S-E, w, 5, 15, Archer Av. 3000; 18, James, 3127. First west of Broad, fr. C., A. & St. L. R. R. to James.

Pittsburg Av. (S. S.) S, 13, 14.

Pittsfield Av. (S. S.) S, 7, 9†, 12.

Pleasant* (N. S.) N, e, 6, 1, Division, 2. Third east of Halsted, fr. Division to Vedder.

Pleasant (W. S.) N, 2. 8.

Pleasant Av. (N. S.) N, e, 3, 1, Grand Av. 136.

Pleasant Av. (S. S.. in Calumet) S-E, 11, 2.

Pleasant Pl. (W. S.) W, s, 3, 16, Oakley Av. 141.

Pleasant Pl. (W. S.) S, e, 4, 4, Randolph, 153.

Plum* (W. S.) W, s, 5, 9, Loomis, 1. First south of Harrison, fr. Loomis to Laflin.

Plymouth Pl.* (S. S.) S, w, 6, 7, Harrison, 98; 10, Fourteenth, 1356. First west of State, fr. Jackson to Fourteenth.

Poe (W. S.) N-E and N-W, e, 3, 17, Maud Av. 2.

Point (W. S.) N-W, w, 2, 18, Francis Pl. 64.

Polk, East (S. S.) W, s, 6, 7, Pacific Av. 75.

Polk, West (W. S.) W, s, 6, 7†, Ellsworth. 19; 5, 9, Centre Av. 413; 8, Robey, 829; 7, California Av. 1285; 4, 9, Central Park Av. 1777; 8.

Poplar (S. S.) W, 7, 15.

Poplar Av. (S. S.) S-E, w, 5, 15, Stearns. 2900.

Portland (S. S., in Blue Island) S, 11, 17.

Portland Av. (S. S.) S, w, 6, 13†, Twenty-sixth, 2600; 16, Thirty-fifth, 3500; 12, 7, 10.

Portland Av. (W. S.) W, 4, 2, West Forty-sixth, 2022.

Post* (S. S.) S-E, w, 5, 15, Levee. 2728. Near south side of river, fr. Ashland Av. to the Ill. & Mich. Canal.

Potomac Av. (W. S.) W, n, 5, 2†, Robey, 63; 1, California Av. 508.

Potwyme Pl. (W. S.) E, 3, 7.

Street View in Pullman.

Poucher Av. (S. S.) S, 8, 9.

Powell Av. (S. S.) S, 13, 4, 7†.

Powell Av. (W. S.) N, e, 2, 18, Edbrook Pl. 118; 15†.

Powell Park (W. S.) W, n, 2, 18, Powell Av. 42.

Prairie (S. S.) W, 11, 9.

Prairie Av. (S. S.) S, w, 6, 11, Sixteenth, 1600; 14†, Twenty-sixth, 2600; 17, Thirty-fifth, 3508; 9, 2, Forty-third, 4300; 5. Fifty-first, 5100; 8, Fifty-ninth, 5900; 11, Sixty-seventh, 6700; 14, Seventy-fifth, 7500; 17; 12, 5, 8, 17.

Prairie Av. (W. S.) N, 1, 5.

Prairie Av. (S. S., in Blue Island) W, 11, 16.

Prairie Av. (S. S., in Calumet) S and S-W, 11, 6.

Prairie Av. (W. S., in Norwood Pk.) W, 1, 1.

Pratt (W. S.) W, n, 5, 6, Fay, 47.

Pratt Av. (S. S., in South Washington Heights) S, 11, 14.

Pratt Pl. (W. S.) W, n, 5, 8. Hamilton Av. 36.

Prescott (S. S.) W, 2, 9†, 8, 7.

Primrose (N. S.) N, 3, 1.

Primrose Av. (S. S.) S, 13, 1.

Prince Av. (W. S.) W, s, 4, 3†, Central Park Av. 253; 2.

Princeton (W. S.) W, 1, 13.

Prindiville (W. S.) N-E, e, 2, 18, Milwaukee Av. 40.

Prospect Av. (S. S.) S-E and S-W, 11, 2†, 5, 8, 11, 14.

Prospect Av. (W. S.) W, 1, 16.

Prospect Pl. (S. S.) N, e, 6, 17, Vincennes Av. 124. Name changed; see Thirty-sixth.

Providence Pl. (W. S.) W, 2, 9.

Public Square (S. S., in Blue Island) 11, 17.

Pulaski (W. S.) W, s, 3, 16, St. Hedwigs, 34.

Root (S. S.) W, n, **9**, 1, Stewart Av. 500.
Rosalie Ct. (S. S.) S, **9**, 9.
Roscoe (N. S.) E, n, **3**, 10, Robey, 401; 11†, Racine Av. 1201; 12, Evanston Av. 1757.
Roscoe (W. S.) W, **2**, 12.
Roscoe Boul. (N. S.) See Roscoe, fr. Western Av. to Robey.
Rose* (W. S.) N, w, **5**, 3, Cornell, 57. First west of Noble, fr. Chicago Av. to Cornell.
Rosebud (W. S.) N-W, n, **3**, 16, Bloomingdale Rd. 2.
Rosemont Av. (N. S.) E, **3**, 2.
Rosenmerkel (S. S.) W, n, **9**, 7, Wright, 600.
Roslyn Pl. (N. S.) N-E, **3**, 15.
Ross (W. S.) S, **4**, 14.
Ross Av. (S. S.) W, **9**, 8.

Fourth Presbyterian Church, Rush and Superior Streets.

Rubeus Av. (N. S.) N, **3**, 2.
Ruble (W. S.) S, e, **6**, 10, Eighteenth, 65.
Rudolph* (N. S.) **3**, 13.
Rumsey (W. S.) N, e, **5**, 5†, Indiana, 2; 2, Division, 296.
Rundell Pl. (W. S.) W, **5**, 9. See Church Pl.
Kupp Av. (S. S.) S, **13**, 1.
Rush (N. S.) N & N-W, w, **6**, 5†, the river, 1; 2, State and Elm, 369.
Russell (S. S.) W, **9**, 15.
Russell Av. (S. S.) S, **13**, 8, 11†, 14, 17.
Rutledge Av. (W. S.) N, **2**, 8.

Sackett Av. (S. S.) S, **8**, 1†, 4.
Sacramento (W. S.) N, **2**, 9.
Sacramento Av. North (W. S.) N, e, **5**, 4, Fulton, 70.
Sacramento Av. South (W. S. & S. S.) S, e, **5**, 4, Lake, 1; 7†, Harrison, 323; 13, Twenty-sixth, 1231; 16; **8**, 1, 4, 7; **11**, 1.
Sacramento Sq.* (W. S.) **5**, 4. At the junction of Sacramento Av. and Central Boul.
Saginaw Av. (S. S., in South Chicago) S, w, **13**, 2, Ninety-first, 9100.
St. Charles (W. S.) W, **1**, 17.
St. Charles Av. (W. S.) N, **2**, 10†, 7.
St. Clair (N. S.) N, w, **6**, 5, Ontario, 76.
St. Clair (S. S., in Blue Island) S-E, **11**, 18.
St. Elmo (N. S.) E, **3**, 10.
St. Francis (W. S.) W, **1**, 17.
St. George's Ct. (W. S.) N-E, e, **2**, 18, Milwaukee Av. 40.
St. Hedwig's (W. S.) N, e, **3**, 16, Kosciusko, 44.
St. Helens (W. S.) N-E, e, **2**, 18, Stave, 20.
St. James Pl.* (N. S.) N-E, n, **3**, 15, Clark, 1904. First north of Fullerton Av., fr. Clark St. to Lincoln Pk.
St. Joe Av.* (W. S.) W, **2**, 6. First north of Foster, fr. Western Av. to Lincoln Av.
St. John Av. (W. S.) N, **2**, 11.
St. John's Av. (W. S., in Montrose) N, **2**, 7.
St. John's Pl.* (W. S.) N, e, **5**, 6, Fulton, 33. First east of Ashland Av., fr. Lake St. to Arbor Pl.
St. Lawrence Av. (S.S.) S, w, **9**, 2, Forty-third, 4300; 5†, Fifty-first, 5058; 11, Sixty-sixth, 6558; 14, 17; **12**, 2, 8.
St. Louis Av. North (W. S.) N, e, **4**, 6†, Kinzie, 128; **3**, Weage Av., 724.
St Louis Av. South (W. S.) S, e, **4**, 9†, Jackson, 205; 12, Sixteenth, 803; 15, Twenty-sixth, 1253; 18; **7**, 6.

St. Stephen's Church, North Sangamon and West Ohio Streets.

St. Mary's Ct.* (W. S.) N-E, e, **2**, 18, Stave, 20. Bet. St. George's Ct. and Prindiville Ct., near California Av.
St. Michael's Ct.* (N. S.) W, s, **6**, 1, Larrabee, 1. Formerly Alaska, bet. Luz Pl. and Blackhawk, fr. Larrabee west one block.

St. Paul Av. (W. S.) E, **3**, 16.
St. Phillips Av. (W. S.) S, **4**, 5.
Sampson (W. S.) See Thirteenth, West, west of Blue Island Av.
Sampson Av. (W. S., in Jefferson) N, **1**, 9.
Samuel (W. S.) N, e, **5**, 2, Augusta, 94.
Sangamon, North*(W. S.) N, w, **5**, 6, Kinzie, 111; 3, the river, 373.
Sangamon, South (W. S. & S. S.) S, e, **5**, 6, Randolph, 1; 9†, Harrison, 247; **8**, 6, 9, 12, 15, 18; 6, 9, 12.
Sanger (S. S.) S-E, w, **6**, 13, Twenty-fifth, 2501.
Saratoga (W. S.) W, **1**, 13.
Sawyer Av. (W. S. & S. S.) S, e, **4**, 12, Sixteenth, 790; 15†, Twenty-sixth, 1253; **7**, 3, 6.
Sawyer Av. (S. S., in Kensington) W, **12**, 11.
Sayers Av. (W. S., in Montclair) N, **1**, 16†, 13.
Scanlan Av. (S. S.) S, **12**, 10.
Schell Av. (S. S.) See Shell Av.
Schick Pl. (N. S.) See Shick Pl.
Schiller (N. S.) E, s, **6**, 1†, Sedgwick, 82; 2, Lake Shore Drive, 332.
Schiller Av. (N. S., in Calumet) S, **11**, 11.
School (N. S.) E, n, **3**, 10†, Robey, 401; 11, Racine Av. 1201; 12, Evanston Av. 1761.
School (S. S.) S, w, **9**, 1†, Forty-third, 4300; 4, Fifty-first, 5100; 7, Fifty-ninth, 5900.
School (S. S., in Kensington) S, **12**, 11.
School* (W. S.) W, **6**, 7, Jefferson, 40. Bet. Madison and Monroe, fr. Canal to ½ block west of Desplaines.
School (W. S.) W, **2**, 11.
School (S. S., in Calumet) S, **11**, 6.
Schorling Av. (S. S.) See Shoerling Av.
Schuyler (W. S.) **2**, 15. Now known as Linden Pl. or First Av.
Scott (N. S.) E, n, **6**, 2, Lake Shore Drive, 59.
Scott (W. S.) W, **4**, 9.
Scovel Av. (S. S.) S, **13**, 4, 7†, 10.
Scudder (S. S., in Calumet) W, **12**, 4; **11**, 6†.
Sebor (W. S.) W, s, **6**, 7, Clinton, 95.
Second* (W. S.) W, **6**, 4. Board of Trade Building, First north of Erie, fr. Sherman St., Pacific Av. the river to Halsted. and Jackson St.
Second Av. (S. S.) S, **13**, 18.
Second Av. (S. S., in Pullman) S, **12**, 11.
Second Av. (S. S.) See Avenue K.
Second Av. (W. S.) N-W, e, **2**, 15, Leddy St. and Fullerton Av. 58.
Section Av. (S. S.) W, **12**, 13.
Sedgwick (N. S.) N-w, **6**, 4, Erie, 1; 1†, Division, 255; **3**, 18, Lincoln Av. and Centre, 657.
Sedgwick Ct.* (N. S.) S, e, **6**, 1, Division, 1. First east of Sedgwick, fr. Division to Elm.
Seeley Av. (W. S.) S, e, **5**, 8, Adams, 65.
Seeley Av. (S. S.) S, **8**, 5, 11†.
Seipp Av. (S. S.) S, **10**, 13.
Selden (W. S.) W, s, **5**, 8, Wood, 1.
Selwin Av. (W. S.) N, **2**, 10†, 7.
Selwyn Av. (S. S.) S, **7**, 5.
Seminary Av. (N. S.) N, e, **3**, 17†, Centre, 64; 14, Diversey Av. 658; 11, Cornelia, 1130.
Seminary Pl. (N. S.) E, n, **3**, 14, Racine Av. 1201.
Semple (S. S.) S, **8**, 9.
Seneca* (N. S.) N, w, **6**, 5, Illinois, 22. First east of St. Clair, fr. Illinois to Indiana.
Seneshall (S. S.) S, **9**, 1.
Sennott Pl. (S. S.) W, **11**, 2.
Seress (S. S.) E, **13**, 8.
Seventeenth, East (S. S.) W, n, **6**, 10, Clark, 172.
Seventeenth, West (W. S.) W, n, **6**, 10†, Canal, 62; **5**, 12, Centre Av. 448; 11, Robey, 906; 10, Washtenaw Av. 1316.
Seventh Av. (S. S.) See Avenue G.
Seventieth (S. S.) W, **10**, 10†, **9**, 12, 11; 10, Stewart Av. 500; **8**, 12, 11, 10.
Seventieth Ct. (S. S.) E, **9**, 11.
Seventy-first (S. S.) W, **10**, 11, Lake Av. 16; 13†; **9**, 12, 11; 10, Stewart Av. 500; **8**, 12, 11, 10; **7**, 12, 11, 10.

Seventy-first Ct. (S. S.) W, **8, 14.**
Seventy-first Pl. (S. S.) W, **9**, 15.
Seventy-first, North (N. S., City Limits) **2**, 3.
Seventy-second (S. S.) S-W and W, **10**, 14,
  Bond Av. 72; 13†; **9**, 15, 14, 13; **8**, 15.
Seventy-second Ct. (S. S.) W, **8**, 14.
Seventy-second Pl. (S. S.) W, **9**, 15.
Seventy-third (S. S.) S-W and W, **10**, 14, Lake
  Av. 19; 13†; **9**,
  15, 14, 13; **8**, 15.
Seventy-fourth (S. S.)
  S-W and W, **10**,
  14, Lake Av. 17;
  13†; **9**, 15, 14,
  13; **8**, 15.
Seventy-fourth Pl. (S.
  S.) W, **10**, 13†;
  9, 15.
Seventy-fifth (S. S.)
  S-W and W, **10**,
  14, Lake Av. 29;
  13†; **9**, 15, 14,
  13; **8**, 15, 14, 13;
  7, 15, 14.

Rock Island Depot.
Sherman and Van Buren Streets.

Seventy-sixth (S. S.) S-W and W. **10**, 14†,
  Coles Av. 121; 13; **9**, 15, 14, 13; **8**, 15.
Seventy-sixth Ct. (S. S.) S-W, s, **10**, 14, Coles
  Av. 121.
Seventy-seventh (S. S.) S-W and W, **10**, 14†,
  Duncan Av. 189; 13; **9**, 15, 14, 13; **8**,
  15.
Seventy-seventh Ct. (S. S.) S-W, s, **10**, 14,
  Coles Av. 121.
Seventy-eighth (S. S.) S-W and W, **10**, 14†.
  Duncan Av. 241; 13; **9**, 15, 14, 13; **8**,
  15.
Seventy-eighth Pl. (S. S.) S-W, s, **10**, 14, Coles
  Av. 122.
Seventy-ninth (S. S.) W, **10**, 15; 14†, Duncan
  Av. 351; 13; **9**, 15, 14, 13; **8**, 15, 14,
  13; **7**, 15, 14.
Seventy-ninth Ct. (S. S.) W, **10**, 17.
Seward (W. S.) S, e, **6**, 10, Eighteenth St.
  and Canalport Av. 65.
Seymour Av. (W. S.) Name changed; see
  Campbell Av., North.
Seymour Av. (S. S.) S, **13**, 7, 10†.
Shakespeare Av. (W. S.) W, s, **2**, 18, Cali-
  fornia Av. 1.
Shaughnessy* (N. S.) N,
  e, **6**, 1. First east
  of Sedgwick, fr.
  Goethe to Sigel.
Sheffield Av. (N. S.) N,
  e, **5**, 3, Hawthorne
  Av. and Weed, 2;
  3, 17†, Centre, 220;
  14, Diversey Av.
  718; 11, Addison
  Av. 1250; 8, Mon-
  trose Boul. 1768;
  5, North Fifty-
  ninth, 2309; **2**,
  Ardmore Av. 2708.
  (Called Sheridan
  Rd., fr. Byron north
  to City Limits.)

Cathedral of the Holy Name,
North State and Superior Sts.

Shelby Ct.* (W. S.) S, e,
  5, 12, Nineteenth, 2. First east of Morgan,
  fr. Nineteenth to Twentieth.
Sheldon (N. S.) N, e, **3**, 11, Byron, 70.
Sheldon, North (W. S.) N, w, **5**, 6, Fulton, 75.
Sheldon, South (W. S.) S, e, **5**, 6, Randolph, 1.
Sheldon Av. (N. S.) N. **3**, 10.
Sheldon Av. (W. S) N, **2**, 10†, 7.
Shell Av. (S. S.) S, **9**, 15†, Seventy-fifth, 7500;
  18, Eighty-third, 8300.
Shepard (S. S., in Morgan Pk.) S-W & S, **11**, 11.
Shergold Ct. (S. S.) W, **9**, 15.
Sheridan (W. S.) N, e, **4**, 6†, Kinzie, 126; 3,
  Division, 604; **2**, 17, Armitage Av. 1076.
Sheridan (W. S., in Norwood Pk.) N-E, **1**, 1.
Sheridan Av. (S. S.) S, w, **9**, 9, Sixtieth, 6000;
  12†, Sixty-seventh, 6658.
Sheridan Av. (S. S.) S, **10**, 17.
Sheridan Av. (S. S.) S, **13**, 11, 14†, 17.
Sheridan Av. (W. S. & S. S.) S, e, **5**, 7, Fill-
  more, 1; **8**, 1†, 4, 7.
Sheridan Av. (W. S.) N, **2**, 14.

Sheridan Av. (W. S., in Norwood Pk.) N, **1**, 1.
Sheridan Av.* (S. S.) W, n, **6**, 10, Wentworth
  Av. 2. Bet. Twentieth and Twenty-first, fr.
  Wentworth Av. west about two blocks.
Sheridan Rd. (N. S.) N, W and N, **3**, 15, 12†,
  11, 8, 5, 2.
Sherman (S. S.) S, w, **6**, 7, Harrison, 98.
Sherman (S. S.) S, **9**, 1†, Forty-third, 4300; 4,
  Fifty-first, 5100; 7, Fifty-ninth, 5858;
  10, Sixty-seventh, 6700; 13, Seventy-
  second, 7158; 16, Eighty-sixth, 8600.
Sherman (S. S., in Calumet) S, **11**, 2.
Sherman Av. (S. S.) S, **10**, 17, Eighty-fifth,
  8500.
Sherman Av. (S. S.) W, **8**, 17.
Sherman Av. (S. S.) S, **13**, 7, 10†.
Sherman Av. (S. S., in Worth) S, **11**, 10.
Sherman Av. (W. S., in Jefferson) N, **2**, 13.
Sherman Av. (W. S.) N, **1**, 9.
Sherman Pl.* (N. S.) W, **6**, 5. Bet. Superior
  St. and Chicago Av., fr. Pine west ¾ block.
Sherman Pl. (N. S.) E, n, **3**, 15, Clark, 1765.
Shick Pl.* (N. S.) N-E, **6**, 1. First east of Mo-
  hawk, fr. Clybourn Av. to Cleveland Av.
Shields Av. (S. S.) S, w, **6**, 13. Twenty-sixth,
  2600; 16†, Thirty-fifth, 3500; **9**, 1, 4, 7,
  16; **12**, 1.
Shober (W. S.) N, e, **5**, 2†, Division, 604; **3**,
  16, Wabansia Av. 894.
Sholto (W. S.) S, e, **5**, 9, Polk, 63.
Short* (S. S.) S-E,
  w, **5**, 15, Hick-
  ory, 2800.
  First west of
  Haynes, fr. Co-
  logne south-
  east about two
  blocks.
Short (S. S., in Cal-
  umet) S-W,
  11, 11.
Short Pl. (S. S., in
  South Wash-
  ington H'ghts)
  S. **11**, 11.
Shurtleff Av. (S.S.)
  S, **9**, 1†; **12**,
  10.

Grace Episcopal Church,
near Sixteenth St., on Wabash Av.

Sibley* (W. S.) S, e. **5**, 9, Harrison, 1. First
  east of Loomis, fr. Harrison to Taylor.
Sidney Av. (S. S.) S, w, **9**, 3, Forty-fourth,
  4416.
Sidney Ct.* (N. S.) N-W, **3**, 15. About a block
  west of Lincoln Pk., fr. Wrightwood Av.
  to Diversey Av.
Siebens Pl.* (N. S.) N-W, **6**, 1. Bet. Clybourn
  Av. and Blackhawk, fr. Larrabee north-
  west one block.
Siegel Av. (W. S.) N, **2**, 12.
Sigel (N. S.) E, s, **6**, 1, Sedgwick, 76.
Silva (S. S., in Calumet) S, **11**, 6.
Silver* (W. S.) S, e, **5**, 9, Harrison, 2. First
  west of Blue Island Av., fr. Harrison to
  Gurley.
Silverman Av. (W. S., in Jefferson) N, **1**, 9.
Simons Av. (W. S.) See Kedzie Av., North.
Sinnott Pl.* (W. S.) W, s, **5**, 6, Centre Av. 2.
  Bet. Indiana and Ohio, fr. Centre Av. to
  Elizabeth.
Sioux Av. (S. S.) S, **8**, 16.
Sixteenth, East (S. S.) W, n, **6**, 11†, Prairie Av.
  13; 10, the river, 304.
Sixteenth, West (W. S.) W,
  n. **6**, 10†, Stewart Av.
  24; **5**, 12, Centre Av.
  414; 11, Robey, 860;
  10, California Av.
  1336; **4**, 12, Central
  Park Av. 1802; 11,
  West Forty-fourth,
  2320.
Sixth Av. (S. S.) S, **13**, 3,
  6. See Avenue H.
Sixth Av. (S. S., in Pullman) S, **12**, 8.
Sixtieth (S. S.) W, **9**, 9;
  8†, South Park Av.
  966; 7, Stewart Av. 500; **8**, 9; **7**, 9, 8.

First Baptist Church,
South Park Avenue and
Thirty-first Street.

Sixtieth Ct. (S. S.) W, n, **9**, 7, Stewart Av. 500.

Sixty-first (S. S.) W, **9**, 9†, Woodlawn Av. 459;
  8, South Park Av. 1003; 7, Wright,
  600; **8**, 9; **7**, 9.
Sixty-first Ct.* (S. S.) W, **9**, 7. First south of
  Sixty-first, fr. Wallace to Halsted.
Sixty-first Pl. (S. S.) W, **9**, 9, Madison Av. 324.
Sixty-second (S. S.) W, **9**, 9, Woodlawn Av.
  459; 8†; 7, Stewart Av. 500; **8**, 9; **7**, 9.
Sixty-second Pl. (S. S.) W, s, **9**, 9, Madison
  Av. 325.
Sixty-third (S.
  S.) W, **9**, 9,
  Woodlawn
  A v. 459;
  11†, South
  Park Av.
  9 9 7;   7,
  StewartAv.
  500; **8**, 9,
  8, 7; **7**, 9,
  8.
Sixty-third Ct.
  (S.S.) W, **9**,
  10.
Sixty-third Pl.*
  (S. S.) W,
  9, 12. First
  s o u t h o f
  Sixty-third,
  fr. Drexel Av. west about one block.

South Park Av. M. E. Church,
South Park Av. and Thirty-third St.

Sixty-fourth (S. S.) W, **9**, 12, Woodlawn Av.
  469; 11†; 10, Stewart Av. 500; **8**, 12, 11,
  10; **7**, 12.
Sixty-fifth (S. S.) W, **9**, 12, Woodlawn Av.
  469; 11†; 10, Stewart Av. 500; **8**, 12, 11,
  10; **7**, 12.
Sixty-fifth Ct. (S. S.) W, **9**, 10.
Sixty-fifth Ter. (S. S.) W, **9**, 12, Hope Av. 292.
Sixty-sixth (S. S.) W, **9**, 12, Woodlawn Av.
  469; 11†; 10, Stewart Av. 500; **8**, 12, 11,
  10; **7**, 12.
Sixty-sixth Pl. (S. S.) W, **9**, 12†, Hope Av.
  267; 10.
Sixty-seventh (S. S.) W, **10**, 10†; **9**, 12, Woodlawn Av. 471; 11; 10, Stewart Av. 500;
  8, 12, 11, 10; **7**, 12, 11.
Sixty-eighth (S. S.) W, **10**, 11, 10†; **9**, 12,
  11; 10, Wentworth Av. 300; **8**, 12, 11,
  10; **7**, 12.
Sixty-ninth (S. S.) W, **10**, 10†; **9**, 12, 11; 10,
  Stewart Av. 500; **8**, 12, 11, 10; **7**, 12.
Sixty-ninth Ct. (S. S.) W and S-W, **9**, 11.
Sixty-ninth Pl. (S. S.) W, **9**, 12.
Slade* (S. S.) N-W, **5**, 14. Second west of Ash-
  land Av., fr. Thirty-first northwest about
  two blocks.
Slater Av. (S. S.) W,
  13, 8.
Sloan (W. S.) W, s, **5**,
  3, Elston Av. 1.
Slocum Av. (W. S.)
  W, **2**, 10.
Smart* (W. S.) N, e,
  5, 5, Kinzie, 2.
  Bet. Wood and
  Lincoln, fr. Kinzie
  St. to Austin Av.
Smith (S. S.) W, **5**,
  16.
Smith Av.* (N. S.) N,
  e, **5**, 3, Black-
  hawk, 32. Second
  west of Halsted,
  fr. Blackhawk St.
  to North Av.

Masonic Temple,
State and Randolph Streets.

Snell* (W. S.) S, e, **5**, 6, Huron, 47. First east
  of Noble, fr. Chicago Av. to Huron.
Snow (W. S.) N-E, **3**, 13.
Snyder (S. S.) W, n, **9**, 1, Wallace, 700.
Sobieski* (W. S.) N, e, **3**, 16, Kosciusko, 44.
  Bet. Robey St. and Hoyne Av., fr. Asylum
  Pl. to Fullerton Av.
Soult (N. S.) N, e, **3**, 14, Wellington, 2.
South Av. (N. S.) E, **3**, 1.
South Chicago Av. (S. S.) S-E, **9**, 11†, St.
  Lawrence Av. and Sixty-ninth, 6859; 15,
  Greenwood Av. and Seventy-fourth, 7359;
  10, 16; **13**, 2, Muskegon Av. 9180.
South Chicago Av. (S.S.,In Hegewisch)S,**13**,17.

South Ct. (N. S.) E, **3**, 5.
South Ct. (W. S., in Norwood Pk.) S-W, **1**, 1.
South Normal Parkway (S. S.)   See Normal
  Parkway, South.
South Park Av. (S. S.; S, w, **6**, 14†, Cottage
  Grove Av. and Twenty-sixth, 2600; **6**,
  17, Thirty-fifth, 3458; **9**, 5, Fifty-first,
  5100; 8, Fifty-ninth, 5900; 11, Sixty-
  seventh, 6700; 14, 17; **12**, 2, 5, 8, 17.
South Park Ct. (S. S.) S, w, **9**, 9, Sixtieth, 6000.
Southport Av. (N. S.) N, e, **3**, 17†, Webster Av.
  160; 14, Diversey Av. 540; 11, Addison
  Av. 1080; 8, 5, 2.
South Water (S. S.) W and S-W, n, **6**, 5, Michi-
  gan Av. 22; 4, Franklin, 242.
Southwest Boul. (W. S. & S. S.) S and E, **5**, 13,
  Twenty-sixth, 2600.
·Spaulding Av. (W. S. & S. S.) S, e, **4**, 9†, Har-
  rison, 321; 12, Sixteenth, 793; 15, Twenty-
  sixth, 1253; 18; **7**, 3, 6, 9, 12.
Spears Av. (S. S.) S-E & S, **8**, 1.
Spencer (S. S., in Calumet) W, **11**, 9.
Spencer Av. (S. S.) S, **8**, 1.
Spencer Av. (S. S.) S, **8**, 9.
Spencer Av. (S. S.) S, **10**, 13, 16†; **13**, 10, 13.
Spencer Pl. (S. S., in Calumet) W, **11**, 9.
Spring (S. S.) W, n, **6**, 13, La Salle, 84.
Spring (S. S., in Calumet) W, **11**, 11.
Spring* (S. S., in Worth) W, **11**, 1. Same as
  Ninety-fifth, extending west fr. Warner
  Av. or Western Av.
Springer Av. (S. S.) W, n, **5**, 18, Ullman, 974.
Springfield Av. North (W. S.) Name changed;
  see Jan Huss Av., North.
Springfield Av. South (W. S.) Name changed;
  see Jan Huss Av., South.
Spruce (S. S., in Calumet)
  S, **11**, 2.
Spruce* (W. S.) W, s, **5**, 9,
  Loomis, 1. First north
  of Polk, fr. Loomis to
  Laflin.
Spruce (W. S.) W, **1**, 10.
Stanley (S. S.) W, **11**, 12.
Stanton Av. (S. S.) S, w, **6**,
  17†, Thirty - seventh,
  3700; **9**, 2, Forty-
  fourth, 4359.
Stanwood Av. (S. S.) W, **12**, 11, 10†.
Star Av. (S. S.) S, **9**, 12, Sixty-fourth, 6400.
Starr (N. S.) E, s, **3**, 18, Sedgwick, 2.
State, North (N. S.) N, w, **9**, 4†, Kinzie, 21; 1,
  Division, 383.

St. Mary's Church (1833),
State and Lake Streets.

State, South (S. S.) S, w, **6**, 4†, Lake, 30; 7,
  Harrison, 356; 10, Sixteenth, 1600; 13,
  Twenty-sixth, 2600; 16, Thirty-fifth,
  3500; **9**, 2, Forty-third, 4300; 4, Fifty-
  first, 5100; 7, Fifty-ninth, 5900; 10,
  Sixty-seventh, 6700; 13, Seventy-fifth,
  7500; 16, Eighty-third, 8301; **12**, 1, 4,
  7, 10, 13, 16.
State (S. S., in Blue Island) S, **11**, 17.
State Ct.* (N. S.) N, **3**, 15. Bet. Halsted St.
  and Evanston Av., fr. ½ block south of
  Fletcher Av. north to Belmont Av.
Station (W. S.) N-W, w, **3**, 13, Oakley Av. 83.
Stave (W. S.) N-W, w, **2**, 18, Armitage Av. 1.
Stearns (S. S.) W and S-W, n, **5**, 15, Poplar Av.
  2922.
Stein* (W. S.) N-W, e, **3**, 17, Redfield, 2. First
  east of Elston Av., fr. Redfield northwest
  about a block.
Stella Pl. (N.
  S.) N, **3**,
  8.
Stephens (S.
  S.) S, **13**,
  8.
Stephens* (W.
  S.) S, e, **5**,
  7, Jackson,
  1. Bet.
  Francisco
  S t. a n d
  California
  A v., f r.
  Jackson to Van Buren.

Proposed Depot for Chicago Elevated
Railway Company, State and Twelfth Sts.

Stephenson (W. S.) S, e, **6**, 10, Maxwell, 81.
Steuben (S. S., in Calumet) N-W, **11**, 11.

Thirty-fourth, West (W. S.) W, 4, 16.
Thirty-fourth Ct. (S. S.) W, n. 5, 18†, Laurel, 964; 17. Lincoln, 1492.
Thirty-fifth, East (S. S.) W, n, 6, 17. South Park Av. 188; 16†. Stewart Av. 636; 5, 18, Ullman, 1112; 17, Robey, 1592; 16.
Thirty-fifth, West (W. S.) W, 4, 17†, 16.
Thirty-fifth Ct. (S. S.) W, n, 5, 18†, Laurel, 984; 17, Oakley Av. 1772.
Thirty-sixth (S. S.) W, n, 6, 17†, Stanton Av. 206; 16, Butler, 700; 5, 18, Laurel, 984; 17, Robey, 1600; 16.

Calumet Club House, Twentieth St. and Michigan Av.

Thirty-sixth Pl.* (S. S.) W; Nos. on south side only; 6, 17, Stanton Av. 22. Bet. Thirty-sixth and Thirty-seventh, fr. Vincennes Av. west ½ block.
Thirty-seventh (S. S.) W, n, 6, 18, Lake Av. 18; 17†, Grand Boul. 276; 16, Stewart Av. 678; 5, 18, Laurel, 998; 17, Robey, 1590; 16; 4, 18.
Thirty-seventh Ct. (S. S.) W, n, 6, 17†, Indiana Av. 360; 16, Butler, 736; 5, 18, Laurel, 978; 17, Robey, 1598.
Thirty-eighth (S. S.) W, n, 6, 17†, Grand Boul. 276; 16, Stewart Av. 678; 5, 18, Laurel, 998; 17, Robey, 1598; 16; 4, 18.
Thirty-eighth Ct. (S. S.) W, n, 6, 16†, Portland Av. 618; 5, 18, Laurel, 998; 17, Wood, 1480.
Thirty-ninth (S. S.) W, n, 6, 18, Lake Av. 2; 17, Grand Boul. 306; 16†, Stewart Av. 728; 5, 18, Ullman, 1180; 17, Robey, 1662; 16; 4, 18, 17.
Thirty-ninth Pl.* (S. S.) W, s, 9, 2. First south of Thirty-ninth, fr. Wabash Av. east ½ block.
Thomas (W. S.) W, n, 5, 2, Robey, 110; 1†, California Av. 594; 4, 2, West Forty-fourth, 1885; 1, West Fiftieth, 2260.
Thomas Av. (W. S.) N, e, 2, 18, Humboldt Boul. 390; 15†, Diversey Av. 770; 12.
Thome Av. (N. S.) E, 3, 2.
Thompson (W. S.) Name changed; see Lemoyne.
Thompson Av. (W. S.) W, 4, 1.
Thompson Av. (S. S.) S, 7, 6.
Thorndale Av. (N. S.) E, 3, 2.
Thorndike (W. S.) W, s, 4, 2, West Forty-second, 1754.
Thornton Av. (S. S., in Riverdale) S, 12, 18.
Throop (W. S. & S. S.) S; in West Side, e, in South Side, w; 5, 9†, Harrison, 183; 12, Sixteenth, 549; 15, the river, 945; 8, 6, Fifty-first, 5100; 9, 12, 15, 18; 11, 3.

First Presbyterian Church, Twenty-first St. and Indiana Av.

Tilden (W. S.) W, n, 5, 9, Aberdeen, 64.
Tilton Av. (W. S.) S, 4, 5.
Todd* (S. S.) N-W, 6, 10. First north of Twenty-second, beginning near west end of Elgin and extending about ½ block to the river.
Tolman Av.* (S. S.) S, 8, 4. First east of Washtenaw Av., fr. Forty-seventh south about one block.
Tompkins Pl. (S. S.) Name changed; see Ridgewood Ct.
Torrence Av. (S. S., in South Chicago) S, 13, 5†, Ninety-ninth, 9854; 8, 11, 14.
Tower Pl.* (N. S.) N, w, 6, 2, Pearson, 168. First east of Rush, fr. Chicago Av. to Pearson.
Town* (N. S.) N, e, 6, 1, Blackhawk, 2. Second west of Larrabee, fr. Blackhawk St. to North Av.
Towner (W. S.) W, 4, 8.
Townes Ct.* (N. S.) S, 6, 1. Second east cf Halsted, fr. North Av. south ½ block.

Townsend* (N. S.) N, w, 6, 4, Erie, 23; 1†, Division, 257.
Tracy Av. (S. S.) 9, 4, 7. Name changed; see Shields Av.
Tracy Av. (S. S.) W. See 103rd, fr. State west.
Transit (S. S.) S-W, 10, 16.
Transit Av. (S. S.) W, 8, 3.
Tremont (W. S.) W, 4, 9. Name changed; see Van Buren.
Tremont (S. S.) W, n. 9, 7, Wright, 600.
Tremont Av. (S. S.) S, 11, 17.
Tremont Av. (S. S.) S, 8, 10†; 11, 7, 10.
Tremont Av. (S. S., in Calumet) S-E, 11, 5.
Tripp Av. (W. S.) N, 4, 2†; 2, 16, 13.
Troy, North (W. S.) N, e, 5, 4, Ohio, 238.
Troy, South (W. S.) S, e, 5, 7†, Van Buren, 87; 13, Twenty-sixth, 1179.
Trumbull Av. North (W. S.) N, e, 4, 6, Ohio, 240.
Trumbull Av. South (W. S.) S, e, 4, 9†, Harrison, 321; 12, Sixteenth, 803; 15, Twenty-sixth, 1253; 7, 6.
Trumbull Av. (S. S., in Calumet) S, 11, 3, 6†.
Truro* (W. S.) W, s, 5, 10, Kedzie, 62. First north of Sixteenth, fr. Douglas Pk. to Kedzie Av.
Trustee* (W. S.) N, e, 5, 5, Austin Av. 26. First west of Ashland Av., fr. Kinzie St. to Austin Av.
Tucker (S. S.) S, w, 5, 18. Thirty-seventh, 3700.
Turner (N. S.) E, 6, 10.
Turner (S. S.) S, 8, 9.
Turner Av. (W. S.) S, e, 4, 12, Sixteenth, 793; 15†, Twenty-fourth, 1131; 7, 6.
Tuscola (N. S.) 3, 7. Name changed; see Oakley Av.
Tuttle Av. (N. S.) E, n, 3, 4†, Ravenswood Pk. 601; 5.
Twelfth, East (S. S.) W, n, 6, 8, Indiana Av. 2; 10†, the river, 238.
Twelfth, West (W. S.) W, s, 6, 10†, Stewart Av. 80; 5, 9, Centre Av. 467; 8, Robey, 895; 7, California Av. 1379; 4, 9, Central Park Av. 1867; 8, West Forty-fourth, 2371.
Twelfth Street Boul.* (W. S.) 5, 11. West Twelfth, fr. Ashland Av. west to Ogden Av.
Twentieth, East (S. S.) W, n, 6, 11, Calumet Av. 24; 10†, Wentworth Av. 220.
Twentieth, West (W. S.) W, s, 6, 10†. Jefferson, 26; 5, 12, Centre Av. 373; 11, Robey, 871; 10, California Av. 1283.
Twenty-first, East (S. S.) W, n, 6, 11, Calumet Av. 24; 10†, Stewart Av. 344.
Twenty-first, West (W. S.) W, s, 6, 10†, Jefferson, 33; 5, 12, Centre Av. 369; 11, Robey, 831; 10, California Av. 1293; 4, 12, St. Louis Av. 1687.
Twenty-second, East (S. S.) W, n, 6, 11†, Calumet Av. 34; 10, Stewart Av. 428.

Church of the Messiah, Twenty-third St. and Michigan Av.

Twenty-second, West (W. S.) W, s, 6, 10, Lumber and Jefferson, 31; 5, 12, Centre Av. 399; 11†, Robey, 871; 10, California Av. 1347; 4, 12, Central Park Av. 1787; 11, Kellogg Av. 2332.
Twenty-second Av.* (S. S.) S, 9, 18. First west of Woodlawn Av., fr. Eighty-first to Eighty-third.
Twenty-second Pl. (S. S.) E, n, 6, 13, Portland Av. 31.

Standard Club Building, Twenty-fourth St. and Michigan Av.

Twenty-third, East (S. S.) W, n, 6, 14, South Park Av. 10; 13†, Stewart Av. 426.
Twenty-third, West (W. S.) W, s, 4, 15†, Central Park Av. 1801; 13.

Twenty-third Pl. (S. S.) W, n, **6**, 13, Stewart Av. 190.
Twenty-fourth, East (S. S.) W, n, **6**. 14, South Park Av. 26; 13†, Stewart Av. 396.
Twenty-fourth, West (W. S.) W, s, **4**, 15†, Central Park Av. 1801; 14, Fairmount Av. 2115; 13.
Twenty-fourth Pl. (S. S.) E, n, **6**, 13, Stewart Av. 145.
Twenty-fifth, East (S. S.) W, n, **6**. 14, South Park Av. 46; 13†, Stewart Av. 470.
Twenty-fifth, West (W. S.) W, s, **5**. 13, California Av. or Southwest Boul. 489; **4**. 15, Central Park Av. 913; 14†. Richmond Av. or West Forty-fourth, 2289.
Twenty-fifth Ct. (W. S.) W, s, **5**,13, Francisco, 539.
Twenty-fifth Pl. (S. S.) E, n, **6**,13, Butler, 123.
Twenty-sixth, East (S. S.) W, n. **6**. 14, Cottage Grove and South Park Avs. 2; 13†, Stewart Av. 392.
Twenty-sixth, West (W. S.) W, s, **5**. 13†, California Av. or Southwest Boul. 211; **4**, 15, Central Park Av. 637; 14, Richmond Av. or West Forty-fourth, 2289; 13.
Twenty-seventh, East (S. S.) W, n, **6**, 14†, South Park Av. 130; 13, Stewart Av. 522; **5**, 15, Quarry, 786.

Plymouth Congregational Church, near Twenty-sixth St., on Michigan Avenue.

Twenty-seventh, West (W. S.) W, n, **5**, 13, Sacramento Av. 2111; **4**, 15†, Central Park Av. 2454; 14, 13.
Twenty-eighth, East (S. S.) W, n, **6**, 14, Cottage Grove Av. 52; 13†, Stewart Av. 460.
Twenty-eighth, West* (W. S.) W, n, **5**, 13, Sacramento Av. 2112; **4**, 14, Forty-third, 2850. Fr. Sacramento Av. to Whipple, and fr. West Fortieth to West Forty-third.
Twenty-eighth Pl.* (S. S.) W, n, **6**,13, Stewart Av. 104. First south of Twenty-eighth, fr. Wentworth Av. to Wallace.
Twenty-ninth, East (S. S.) W, n, **6**. 14†, South Park Av. 90; 13, Stewart Av. 460.
Twenty-ninth, West (W. S.) W, n, **5**. 13, California Av. or Southwest Boul. 1984; **4**, 14†, West Forty-third, 2859; 13.
Twomey* (N. S.) W and N, n, **6**. 1, Sedgwick, 2. First north of Division, fr. Sedgwick west ½ block, thence north ½ block.
Tyson Av.* (N. S.) N, e, **3**, 10, Roscoe, 70. First west of Robey, fr. School to Cornelia.

Uhland (N. S.) N-W, **6**. 1. Rees, 42.
Ullman (S. S.) S, w, **5**, 18. Thirty-fifth, 3500.
Unadilla (S. S., in Morgan Pk.) W, **11**, 11.
Underwood Av. (S. S.) S, **8**. 1.
Union, North (W. S.) N, w, **6**, 4, Kinzie, 115.
Union, South (W. S. & S.S.)S, e, **6**,4†,Randolph, 1; 10, Sixteenth, 589; 13, Lumber, 839.
Union Av. (S. S.) S, w. (Formerly Dashiel Av. and Winter). **6**, 13, Twenty-sixth, 2600; 16, Thirty-fifth, 3500; **9**, 14, Forty-third, 4300; 4. Fifty-first, 5100; 7, Fifty-ninth. 5900; 10, Sixty-seventh. 6700; 13, Seventy-fifth, 7500; 16, Eighty-first, 8100; **12**, 1, Ninety-first, 9100; 4, 7.
Union* (S. S.) W, **12**, 8. Bet. 110th and 111th, fr. Michigan Av. to State.
Union (S. S., in Blue Island) W, **11**, 17, 16†.

Chicago Theological Seminary. Union Park and Ashland Boulevard.

Union Pl. (W. S.) S-W, c, **6**, 13, Twenty-second, 1.
Union Pl.* (W. S.) S, e, **5**, 7, Congress, 2. First west of Campbell Av., fr. Congress to Harrison.

Union Park Pl.* (W. S.) N, w, **5**, 6, Fulton, 27. First west of Sheldon, fr. Lake St. to Arbor Pl.
University Pl. (S.S.) W; Nos. odd, on south side only; **6**, 17, Rhodes, 71.
Upland (S. S.) W, **12**, 14.
Upton (W. S.) S-W and W, s, **3**, 16, Milwaukee Av. 1.
Utica* (W. S.) S, e, **5**, 7, Fillmore, 2. Bet. Albany Av. and Sacramento Av., fr. Fillmore St. to Douglas Pk.

Vail (S. S.) S, **8**, 8, 11, 14†.
Van Buren, East (S. S.) W, s, **6**, 8, Michigan Av. 1; 7†, Market, 239.
Van Buren, West (W. S.) W, s, **6**, 7†, the river, 1; **5**, 9, Centre Av. 379; 8, Robey, 745; 7, California Av. 1213; **4**, 9, Homan Av. 1571; 8, Forty-fourth, 2247; 7.
Van Buren (N. S.) N, **3**, 1.
Van Buren (W. S.) W, **2**, 7.
Van Horn (W. S.) W, n, **5**, 12, Laflin, 616; 11†, Robey, 906; 10, Washtenaw Av. 1324.

Chicago Athenæum. 18-26 Van Buren Street.

Vaunatta Av. (W. S.) N, **2**, 16.
Vedder (N. S.) E and S-E, s, **6**, 1, Larrabee, 120.
Vermont (S. S.) W, **11**,17,16†. Same as 131st.
Vermont Av. (S. S.) S, w, **5**, 17, Thirty-fifth, 3502.
Vernon (S. S., in Blue Island) W, **11**, 14.
Vernon Av. (S. S.) S, w, **6**, 14†. Twenty-ninth, 2900; 17, Thirty-fifth, 3500; **9**, 2, 8, 11, 14.
Vernon Av. (W. S.) N, **2**, 10.
Vernon Park Pl. (W. S.) W, s, **5**, 9, Centre Av. 1.
Verona Av. (S. S., in Blue Island) W, **11**,17.
Victor (S. S.) S, **8**, 6.
Victor (N. S.) S-E and E, n, **3**, 2, Charlton, 1121.
Victoria Av. (S. S.) S, **10**,13†, 16.
Vilas Av. (N. S.) E, n, **3**,7.
Vincennes Av. (S. S.) S-W and S, w, **6**, 17†, Cottage Grove Av. and Thirty-fifth, 3500; **9**, 2, Forty-third, 4300; 5, Fifty-first, 5100; 8, Sixtieth, 6000; 11, Sixty-seventh, 6700; 14;**12**, 2.

Church of Notre Dame, Vernon Park Pl. and Sibley St.

Vincennes Av. (S. S.) S-W, w, **9**, 10, Seventieth, 7000; 13, Seventy-sixth, 7600; 16†, Eighty-third, 8300; **11**, 3, 6, 9, 8, 11, 14.
Vincennes Pl. (S. S.) W, **9**, 5.
Vine (N. S.) N, e, **6**, 1, Division, 2; **3**, 18†, Willow, 262.
Vine (W. S., in Montclair) N, **1**, 16†, 13.
Vine, East (W. S., in Norwood Pk.) **1**. 1.
Vine, West (W. S., in Norwood Pk.) **1**, 1.
Virginia* (W. S.) S-W and S, **5**, 12. Bet. Throop and Loomis, beginning south of Fifteenth and ending at Sixteenth.

Wabansia Av. East*(N. S.) N-E, n, **3**, 17, Clybourn Av. 41.
Wabansia Av. West (W. S.) S-W and W, s, **3**, 17, the river, 2; 16†, Robey, 381; **2**, 18, California Av. 823; 17, Central Park Av. 1241; 16; **1**, 18, 17, 16.
Wabash (S. S., in Blue Island) S, **11**, 17.
Wabash (S. S.) W, **6**, 15.

Wabash Av. (S. S.) S; north of Twelfth, e,
south of Twelfth. w; **6**, 5, South Water, 1;
8†, Harrison, 363; 11, Sixteenth, 1600;
14, Twenty-sixth, 2600; 17, Thirty-fifth,
3500; **9**, 2, Forty-third, 4300; 5, Fifty-
first, 5100; 8, Fifty-ninth, 5900; 11,
Sixty-seventh, 6700; 14, Seventy-fifth,
7500; 17; **12**, 5, 8.
Wabash Av. (W. S., in Norwood Pk.) N-W,
1, 1.
Wabash Av. (S. S., in Worth) S, **11**, 1.

Academy of St. Francis Xavier,
Wabash Avenue and Twenty-ninth Street.

Wade* (W. S.) W & N-W, n, **5**, 3, Elston Av. 2.
First north of Augusta, fr. Elston Av. west about ½
block. and northwest about ½ block.
Walden Parkway (S. S., in Calumet) S, **11**, 5.
Waldo Pl. (W. S.) W, s, **6**, 4, Union, 33.
Waldon* (S. S.) S, **13**, 11. West of Grand
Calumet River, fr. 114th to 115th.
Walker (S. S., in Morgan Pk.) N-W, **11**, 8, 11†.
Walker Ct.* (W. S.) N, e, **5**, 12. First east of
Blue Island Av., fr. Eighteenth north ½
block.
Wall (S. S.) S, w, **5**, **18**, Thirty-second, 3200.
Wallace (S. S.) S, w, **6**, 13, Twenty-sixth,
2600; 16†, Thirty-fifth, 3500; **9**, 1,
Forty-third, 4300; 4, Fifty-first, 5100; 7,
Fifty-ninth, 5900; 10. Sixty-seventh,
6700; 13, Seventy-fifth, 7500; 16, Eighty-
third, 8300; **12**, 1, 4.
Wallace (W. S.) W, s, **4**, 2, West Forty-second,
1761.
Wallace Av. (W. S.) N, e, **2**, 15†, Diversey Av.
770; 12.
Walleck Pl.* (W. S.) S, w, **5**, 11, Eighteenth,
24. Bet. Hoyne Av. and Leavitt, fr. C., B.
& Q. R. R. to Eighteenth.
Wallen (W. S.) S, e, **5**, 12, Maxwell, 65.
Walnut (S. S.) W, **13**, 11.
Walnut* (S. S.) W, **8**, 4. Bet. Fifty-fourth and
Fifty-fifth, fr. Sacramento Av. to Sheridan
Av.
Walnut (S. S., in Blue Island) W, **11**, 17, 16†.
Walnut (S. S., in Calumet) S, **11**, 5†, 8.
Walnut (S. S., in Calumet) W, **12**, 4; **11**, 6†, 5.

Home for the Friendless,
Wabash Av. and Twentieth St.

Walnut (N. S.) E, n, **3**, 4†, Robey, 401; 5.
Walnut (W. S.) W, n. **5**, 5†, Robey, 196; 4,
California Av. 574; **4**, 6, Homan Av. 942.
Walnut (W. S., at Dunning) N, **1**, 10.
Walnut (W. S.) W, **1**, 18.
Walnut (W. S., in Cicero) S, **4**, 7.
Walnut (W. S., in Norwood Pk.) W, **1**, 1.
Walsh (N. S.) **3**, 15. Name changed; see Surf.
Walsh Ct. (W. S.) W, n, **5**, 12. Centre Av. 28.
Walter (S. S.) **9**, 2. Name changed; see Ver-
non Av.
Walton Pl. (N. S.) E, s, **6**, 1†, Dearborn Av. 2;
2, Pine, 122.
Ward (N. S.) N-E and N, e, **3**, 17†, Webster Av
50; 14, Diversey Av. 398.
Ward Av. (S. S.) S, **5**, 16†, **8**, 1.
Ward Ct.* (W. S.) W, s, **6**, 10, Jefferson, 27.
First south of Twentieth, fr. Lumber to
Jefferson.
Warner Av. (N. S.) E, **3**, 7.
Warner Av. (W. S.) W, **2**, 12, 11†, 10; **1**, 12,
11, 10.
Warren (S. S., in Calumet) N-W, **11**, 11.
Warren Av. (W. S.) W, s, **5**, 6, Robey, 196; 4,
Robey, 257; 4†, California Av. 751; **4**, 6,
Homan Av. 1113.
Warren Av. (W. S., in Norwood Pk.) N-W, **1**, 1.

Warsaw Av. (W. S.) W and N-W, s, **2**, 15,
Francisco, 331.
Washburn (S. S.) W, **8**, 15.
Washburne Av. (W. S.) W, n, **5**, 12, Centre
Av. 90; 11†, Robey, 518; 10.
Washington, East (S. S.) W, s, **6**, 5, Michigan
Av. 1; 4†, Market, 239.
Washington, West (W. S.) W. s, **6**, 4†, the
river, 1; **5**, 6, Ann, 347; 5, Robey, 677;
4, California Av. 1157; **4**, 6, Homan Av.
1519; 5, Richmond or West Forty-fourth,
2149; 4, West Fifty-second, 2666.
Washington (W. S., in Jefferson) W, **2**, 7†; **1**,
9.
Washington (W. S., in Cicero) S, **4**, 16.
Washington (W. S., in Norwood Pk.) N-E, **1**, 1.
Washington Av. (N. S., in Lake View) W, **3**,
4†, Robey, 401; **2**, 6.
Washington Av. (S. S., in Hyde Park) S, w, **9**,
6†, Fifty-first, 5100; 9, Fifty-ninth, 5858;
15; **12**, 3.
Washington Av. (S. S.) S, **8**, 10†, 16.
Washington Av. (W. S., in Jefferson) N, **2**,
10†, 7.
Washington Av. (W. S., City Limits) N, **1**, 16†,
13, 10.
Washington Av. (S. S., in Morgan Pk.) S-W,
11, 5, 8†, 11, 14.
Washington Av. (S. S., in South Washington
Heights) S, **11**, 14.
Washington Boul. (W. S.) See Washington,
West, fr. Halsted
west to Garfield
Pk.
Washington Pl.* (N.
S.) E: Nos. on
south side only;
6, 1, Clark, 1.
First north of
Chestnut, fr.
Clark St. to Dear-
born Av.
Washington Park
Av.* (W. S.) N,
2, 4. First east
of Elston Av., fr.
Lawrence Av.
to Foster.

First Catholic Cathedral (1843),
Wabash Av. and Madison St.

Washington Sq.* (N. S.) **6**, 1. Bet. Clark St. and
Dearborn Av., on south side of Walton Pl.
Washtenaw Av. North (W. S.) N, e, **5**, 4†,
Kinzie, 124; 1, Division, 604; **2**, 18,
Armitage, 1086.
Washtenaw Av. South (W. S. & S. S.) S, e, **5**,
7, Harrison, 323; 10†, Sixteenth, 803;
13, Twenty-sixth, 1266; **8**, 1, 10.
Water, North (N. S.) See North Water.
Water, South (N. S.) See South Water.
Water, West (W. S.) See West Water.
Water* (S. S.) S-E, **5**, 15. Bet. the river and
Ill. & Mich. Canal, fr. Ashland Av. south-
east one block.
Water, North (S. S., in Blue Island) S-W, **11**,
18†, 17.
Water, South (S. S., in Blue Island) S-W, **11**,
18, 17†.
Waterside Av. (S. S.) S-E, **13**, 18.
Waterville* (S. S.) S-E, w, **5**, 18, Springer Av.
3257. First east of the river, fr. Thirty-
second to Thirty-
third.
Watson Av. (S. S.) S,
13, 11.
Waubun Av. (N. S.) N,
e, **3**, 15, Welling-
ton Av. 208.
Waver* (S. S.) W, **6**,
13. First south of
the river, fr. Arch-
er Av. west about
1½ blocks.
Waverly Pl.* (W. S.) N, e, **5**, 6, Washington
Boul. 42. Bet. Elizabeth and Ada, fr.
Madison St. to Washington Boul.
Wayman (W. S.) W, n, **6**, 4, Desplaines, 41.
Wayne Av. (N. S.) N, **3**, 5.
Weage Av. (W. S.) W, s, **4**, 3, Homan Av. 127.
Webber Av. (N. S.) E, **3**, 1.
Webster (W. S.) W, **2**, 11.

South Division High School,
Wabash Av. and Twenty-sixth St.

Webster Av. (N. S.) E, n, **3**, 17†, Racine Av. 165; 18, Sedgwick, 523.

Webster Av. West (W. S.) **3**, 16. Name changed; see Asylum Pl.

Webster Av. (N. S., in Lake View) E, n, **3**, 4†, Robey, 401; 5, Evanston Av. 1119.

Webster Av. (S. S.) S, **9**, 10, Sixty-ninth, 6900; 13†, Seventy-fourth, 7358; 16, Eighty - second, 8200; **12**, 1.

Weddel (S. S.) W, **8**, 15.

Weed (N. S.) N-E and E, s, **5**, 3, Hawthorne and Sheffield Avs. 52.

Weed Ct. (N. S.) N-E, e, **6**, 1, Clybourn Av. 2.

Tabernacle Baptist Church (1843), bet. Washington and Randolph Sts., on La Salle St.

Weld (W. S.) W, **1**, 6.

Wellington Av. (N. S.) E, n, **3**, 13†, Paulina or Commercial, 701; 14, Racine Av. 1201; 15, Sheridan Rd. 2001.

Wellington Av. (W. S., in Jefferson) W, **2**, 11.

Wellington Av. (W. S.) W, **1**, 14.

Wells (N. S.) N, e, **6**, 4, Kinzie, 36; 1†, Division, 396; **3**, 18, Clark St. and Lincoln Pk. 757.

Wendell (N. S.) E, s, **6**, 1, Franklin, 52.

Wendell Av. (S. S.) S, **10**, 17.

Wentworth Av. (S. S.) S, w, **6**, 10, Sixteenth, 1600; 13, Twenty-sixth, 2600; 16†, Thirty-fifth, 3500; **9**, 1, Forty-third, 4300; **4**, Fifty-first, 5100; 7, Fifty-ninth, 5900; 10, Sixty-seventh, 6700; 13, Seventy-fifth, 7500; 16, Eighty-fourth, 8400; **12**, 4, 7, 10, 13.

Werder (W. S.) W, n, **5**, 1, Washtenaw Av. 62.

Wescott Ct.* (S. S.) S, **9**, 16. First west of Vincennes Av., fr. Eightieth south ½ block.

Wesson (N. S.) N, w, **6**, 1, Oak, 133.

West* (S. S.) W, **13**, 11. First south of 113th, fr. Grand Calumet River to Day Av.

West (W. S., in Jefferson) N, **1**, 17.

West (W. S., in Cicero) S, **4**, 7.

West Ct. (N. S.) S, **5**, 12†, 15. First east of Evanston Av., fr. Belmont Av. south ½ block.

West Circle (W. S., in Norwood Pk.) **1**, 1.

West Crescent Av. (S. S., in Morgan Pk.) **11**, 8.

Western Av. North (W. S. & N. S.) N, e, **5**, 4†, Kinzie, 124; 1, Division, 604; **2**, 18, Armitage Av., 1052; 15, Diversey and Elston Avs. 1587; 12, Cornelia, 1878; 9, 6, 3.

Cathedral of St. Peter and St. Paul, Washington Boul. and Peoria St.

Western Av. South (W. S. & S. S.) S; north of the river, e, south of the river, w; **5**, 4†, Lake, 1; 7, Harrison, 323; 10, Sixteenth, 803; 13, Twenty-sixth, 1253; 16, Thirty-fifth, 3500; **8**, 1, Forty-third, 4300; 4, Fifty-first, 5100; 7, 10, 13, 16; **11**, 1, 4, 7, 10, 13, 16.

Western Av. Boul. (W. S.) See Western Av., fr. Thirty-fifth south to Fifty-fifth.

West Fiftieth, North (W. S.) N, e, **4**, 4†, Kinzie, 28; 1, Thomas, 470.

West Fiftieth, South (W. S.) S, e, **4**, 4, Lake, 1.

West Fiftieth Pl. (W. S.) N, **1**, 18.

West Fifty-first, North* (W. S.) N, **4**, 1, Iowa, 351.

West Fifty-first, South (W. S.) S, **4**, 4†, Randolph, 149.

West Fifty-first Pl. (W. S.) N, **1**, 18.

West Fifty-second (W. S.) S, e, **4**, 4, Park Av. 106; 7†.

West Fifty-third (W. S.) N, **4**, 4.

West Fifty-third Pl. (W. S.) N, **1**, 18.

West Fifty-fourth (W. S.) N, **1**, 18.

West Fortieth St., North (W. S.) N, e, 4, 5, Kinzie, 126; 3†, Division, 604; **2**, 16, Armitage Av. 1104; 13. Same as Crawford Av.

West Fortieth St., South (W. S.) S, e, **4**, 5, Park Av. 33; 8; 11, Sixteenth, 1601; 14, 18†. Same as Crawford Av.

West Fortieth Pl. North*(W. S.) N, e, **4**, 2, Prince Av. 800.

West Fortieth Pl. South (W. S.) S, e, **4**, 5, Park Av. 33; 11†, Sixteenth, 1601; 14.

West Forty-first, North*(W. S.) N, **4**, 5, Lake, 2; 2, Division, 604.

West Forty-first, South (W. S.) S, e, **4**, 5, Lake, 1; 8†, Harrison, 431; 11, Sixteenth, 1601; 14, Twenty-sixth, 2601.

West Forty-first Pl. (W. S.) S, **4**, 11†, Fourteenth, 1401; 14, Twenty-sixth, 2601.

West Forty-second, North (W. S.) N, e, **4**, 5†, Kinzie, 62; 2, Division, 604.

West Forty-second, South (W. S.) S, e, **4**, 5†, Lake, 1; 8, Harrison, 443; 11, Sixteenth, 1601; 14, Twenty-sixth, 2601.

West Forty-second Pl.* (W. S.) S, **4**, 11, Fourteenth, 1358; 14, Twenty-sixth, 2601. First west of West Forty-second, fr. Twelfth to Fourteenth, and fr. Twenty-sixth to Thirty-first.

West Forty - third, North (W. S.) N, **4**, 5, Kinzie, 58; 2†, Division, 604.

West Forty - third, South (W. S.) S, e, **4**, 5, Lake, 1; 8†, Harrison, 449; 11, 14.

West Forty-third Pl. (W. S.) S, w, **4**, 11, Thirteenth, 1300.

Building now occupying Site of Old Fort Dearborn, South Water St. and Michigan Av.

West Forty-fourth, North *(W. S.) N, e, **4**, 5, Kinzie, 52; 2, Division, 604.

West Forty-fourth, South (W. S.) S, e, **4**, 5, Lake, 1; 8, Harrison, 449; 11†, Sixteenth, 1601.

West Forty-fourth Pl. (W. S.) S, **4**, 8†; 11, Sixteenth, 1600.

West Forty-fifth, North (W. S.) N, e, **4**, 5†, Kinzie, 46; 2.

West Forty-fifth, South (W. S.) S, e, **4**, 5†, Lake, 1; 8, Harrison, 449; 11, Sixteenth, 1559.

West Forty-fifth Pl. (W. S.) S, e, **4**, 8†, Harrison, 463; 11, Sixteenth, 1559.

West Forty-sixth, North (W. S.) N, e, **4**, 5†, Kinzie, 49; 2, Division, 548.

West Forty-sixth, South (W. S.) S, e, **4**, 5†, Lake, 1; 8, Harrison, 463; 11.

West Forty-sixth Pl.* (W. S.) S, e, **4**, 8, Van Buren, 397. First west of West Forty-sixth, fr. Jackson to Harrison.

West Forty-seventh, North (W. S.) N, e, **4**, 5†, Kinzie, 46; 2, Division, 542.

West Forty-seventh, South (W. S.) S, e, **4**, 5†, Lake, 1; 8, Harrison, 473.

West Forty-seventh Pl. (W. S.) N, **4**, 2.

West Forty-eighth, North*(W. S.) N, e, **4**, 4, Kinzie, 38; 1, Division, 540.

West Forty-eighth, South (W. S.) S, e, **4**, 4, Lake, 1; 7, Harrison, 482; 10†.

West Forty-ninth, North (W. S.) N, e, **4**, 4†, Kinzie, 38; 1, Thomas, 474.

West Forty-ninth, South (W. S.) S, e, **4**, 4, Park Av. 87.

Westminster Av. (W. S.) S, **3**, 4, 14.

Weston (N. S.) E, **3**, 14.

Weston (S. S., in Calumet) W and N-W, **11**, 12†, 11.

Northwestern Depot, Wells and Kinzie Streets.

Weston Pl. (S. S., in Calumet) S-W, **11**, 2.

West Water, North* (W. S.) N and N-W, w, **6**, 4. Kinzie, 78. First west of the river, fr. Randolph to Fulton, and fr. Kinzie to Indiana.

West Water, South* (W. S.) S, w, **6**, 4, Washington, 38. First west of the river, fr. Randolph to Madison.

Wharf* (W. S.) S-E, **6**, 10. Bet. Stewart Av. and Canal, fr. Lumber to the river.
Wharton Av. (S.S.) S, **9**, 6, Fifty-first. 5100; 9†, Sixtieth, 6000; 12, Sixty-seventh, 6658.
Wheaton (W. S.) W, s, **4**, 3, Sheridan, 47.
Wheelock Av. (S. S.) S, **9**, 13.
Whipple (W. S.) S, e, **5**, 7†, Van Buren, 111; 13, Twenty-sixth, 1231.
Whitehouse (W. S.) W, n, **4**, 15, Central Park Av. 2488.
Whitehouse Pl. (S. S.) W, n, **6**, 13, Portland Av. 476.
Whiting* (N. S.) E, s, **6**, 1, Franklin, 50. Bet. Locust and Oak, fr. ¼ block west of Market to ¼ block east of Wells.
Whitney Av. (S. S., in Worth) S, **11**, 4.
Wieland (N. S.) N, e, **6**, 1, Schiller, 487.
Wilbur Av. (S. S., in Calumet) S, **11**, 8.
Wilcox (S. S.) See Ninety-ninth, fr. Centre Av west to Wood, **11**, 6.
Wilcox Av. (W. S.) W, s, **5**, 8, Oakley Av. 901; 7†, California Av. 1209; **4**, 8, West Forty-fourth, 2247.
Will (W. S.) N, w, **5**, 3, Milwaukee Av. 1.
Will (W. S.) S, **4**, 14.
Willard Pl.* (W. S.) N, w, **5**, 6, Washington, 1. Bet. Elizabeth and Ann, fr. Washington Boul. to Randolph.
Willett Av. (S.S.) S, **13**, 4†, 7, 10.
William (S. S.) W, **5**, 16†; **4**, 18.

Chicago Homeopathic College, Wood and York Streets.

William (S. S.) S, **7**, 15.
William (S. S.) S, **9**, 1.
William (S. S., in Calumet) S, **11**, 12.
William Av. (W.S.) W, s, **4**, 3, Lawndale Av. 307.
Williams (W. S., in Jefferson) N, 1, 6.
Williard (S. S., in Calumet) W, **11**, 9.
Willis (W. S., in Jefferson) W, **2**, 8†, 7.
Willis Ct.* (W. S.) S, e, **5**, 11. First west of Oakley Av., fr. Thirteenth to R.R. Crossing.
Willow (N. S.) W and S-W, n, **3**, 18, Larrabee, 2; 17†, Hawthorne Av. 120.
Willow (S. S., in Calumet) W, **11**, 11.
Willow (W. S., in Lyons) S, **7**, 13.
Willow Av. (W. S., in Austin) N, 4, 4†, 1.
Willow Av. (W. S., in Norwood Pk.) N, **1**, 1.
Wilmont Av. (W. S.) N, **1**, 18.
Wilmot Av. (W. S.) W and N-W, s, **3**, 16, Leavitt, 123.
Wilmot Av.* (W. S.) N-W, w, **2**, 15, Thomas Av. 652. First north of Milwaukee Av., fr. Thomas Av. to Humboldt Boul.
Wilson (W. S.) W, s, **6**, 10, Canal, 47.
Wilson Av. (N. S., in Lake View) N, e, **3**, 7†, Robey, 401; 8, Sheridan Rd. 1407.
Wilton Av. (N. S.) W, **3**, 11.
Winchester Av. (W. S. & S. S.) S, e, **5**, 8†, Harrison St. and Ogden Av. 319; **8**, 5, 11, 17; **11**, 2.
Windett Av. (N. S.) E, n, **3**, 8.
Windsor* (S. S.) S-W, **10**, 14. Bet. Seventy-fifth and Seventy-sixth, fr. Coles Av. to I. C. R. R.
Windsor Av. (N. S.) E, n, **3**, 8, Sheffield Av. or Sheridan Rd. 1401.
Winfield (S. S.) W, **11**, 11.
Winneconna* (S. S., in Calumet) S-W, **9**, 13. Fr. cor. of Stewart Av. and Seventy-seventh to cor. of Goldsmith and Seventy-ninth.
Winston (S. S.) S-E, **11**, 6.
Winter (S. S.) S. Name changed; see Union Av.
Winthrop Av. (N. S.) N, e, **3**, 5†, North Fifty-ninth, 512; 2, Ardmore Av. 914.
Winthrop Pl.* (W. S.) S, s, **6**, 11, 1. Bet. Loomis and Laflin, fr. Polk to Taylor.
Wisconsin (N. S.) W, n, **3**, 18, Sedgwick, 74.
Wisner Av. (W. S.) N-E, **2**, 14.

Wolcott (N.S.) N, e, **3**, 10, Roscoe, 500; 7†, Montrose Boul. 1174; 4, North Fifty-ninth, 1710.
Wolcott Av. (S. S.) S, **8**, 1.
Wolf (W. S., in Cicero) W, **4**, 13.
Wolfram (N. S.) E, n, **3**, 14, Racine Av. 1201.
Wolfram (W. S.) W, **2**, 14.
Wood, North (W. S.)
  N, e, **5**, 5†, Kinzie,
  98; 2, Division,
  550; **3**, 16, Armitage Av. 1028.
Wood, South (W. S.
  & S. S.) S, e, **5**, 5†,
  Lake, 1; 8, Harrison, 309; 11, Sixteenth, 751; 14,
  the river, 1247;
  17, Thirty-fifth,   Rush Medical College, Wood and West Harrison Sts.
  3500; **8**, 2, 5, 8,
  11; **11**, 2, 5, 8, 14.
Wood* (S. S.) W, **13**, 11. First north of 114th, fr. Waldon St. to Day Av.
Wood (S. S.) W, **13**, 11.
Wood (W. S., in Galewood) N, **1**, 16.
Wood (S. S., in South Washington Heights) S, **11**, 14.
Woodard (W. S. N-E, **2**, 14.
Woodbine Av. (W. S.) N, **4**, 1.
Woodbine Av. (W. S., in Cicero) N, 4, 16†, 13.
Woodburn Av. (W. S.) S, **4**, 5.
Woodbury Av. (S. S.) S, **11**, 1.
Woodland (S. S., in South Washington Heights) S-W, **11**, 11.
Woodland Av. (W. S., in Jefferson) W, **2**, 12.
Woodland Av. (W. S.) See Millard Av., fr. Douglas Boul. south to West Sixteenth, 4, 12.
Woodland Park (S. S.) E, **6**, 17.
Woodlawn Av. (S. S.) S, w, **9**, 3, Lake Av. 4447; 6, Fifty-first, 5100; 9†, Fifty-ninth, 5900; 12, Sixty-seventh, 6700; 15, 18.
Woodlawn Av. (S. S., in Worth) W, **11**, 4.
Woodside Av. (N.S.) N, e, **3**, 10, Addison Av. 206.
Woodward (W. S.) See Woodard.
Work (W. S.) S, **4**, 8, Harvard, 555.
Work Av. (S. S.) W, n, **9**, 4, State, 100.
Worthen Av.* (W. S.) S, e, **5**, 10, Nineteenth, 97. First west of Albany Av., fr. Ogden Av. to Twenty-first.
Wright (N. S., in Lake View) N, **3**, 4, Pine, 40.
Wright (S. S.) S, w, **9**, 1†, Forty-third, 4300; 4, Fifty-first, 5100; 7, Fifty-ninth, 5900; 10, Sixty-seventh, 6700; 13, Seventy-fifth, 7500; 16, Eighty-fourth, 8400.
Wright (W. S.) N-W, **3**, 17. Name changed; see Henry.
Wright(W.S.)W, **6**, 10;
  5, 12. Name changed; see Henry.
Wright Av. (N. S., in Lake View) N, e, **3**, 7, Sunnyside Av. 1240.
Wright Pl.* (W. S.) N, e, **5**, 4. Bet. Rockwell   Western Av. M. E. Church, St. and Washtenaw   Western Av. and West Av., fr. Grand Av.   Monroe Street. to Huron.
Wrightwood Av. (N. S.) E and N-E, n, **3**, 13, Commercial, 637; 14†, Racine Av. 1201; 15, Lake View Av. 1981.
Wyoming (W. S.) W, **2**, 13.

Yale (S. S.) S, w, **9**, 10, Sixty-seventh, 6700; 13†, Seventy-fourth St. and Vincennes Av. 7400; 16, Eighty-second, 8200; **12**, 1.
Yale (S. S., in Calumet) W, **11**, 9.
Yates Av. (S. S.) S, w, **10**, 10; 13, Seventy-fifth, 7454; 16†.
Yeaton (W. S.) W, s, **5**, 8, Lincoln, 53.
York (W. S.) W, s, **5**, 9, Laflin, 1; 8†, Wood, 159.
York (S. S., in Blue Island) W, **11**, 17, 16†.
York Pl. (N. S.) E, n, **3**, 15, Clark, 1706.
Yorktown (S. S.) S, **5**, 17, Thirty-fourth, 3400.

Zero Pk. (N. S.) **3**, 5.
Zion Pl. (W. S.) W, n, **5**, 12, Throop, 2.

8

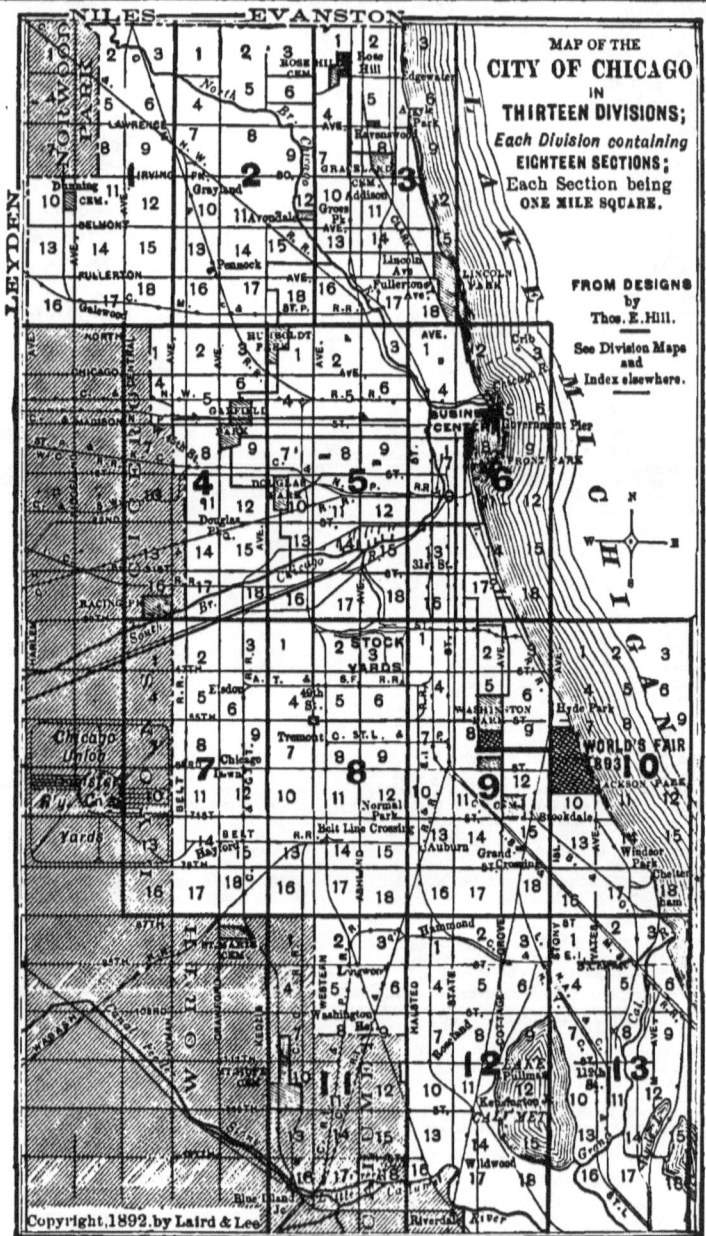

MAP OF THE

CITY OF CHICAGO

IN

THIRTEEN DIVISIONS;

Each Division containing

EIGHTEEN SECTIONS;

Each Section being
ONE MILE SQUARE.

FROM DESIGNS
by
Thos. E. Hill.

See Division Maps
and
Index elsewhere.

Copyright, 1892, by Laird & Lee

Plan Showing Part of the City in which Any Street is Located.

Use **Irving Street** as an illustration. The Index says: "Irving (W. S.) W, 1, 10," which means that Irving Street is on the West Side, runs west, is in Division 1, and Section 10.

Above we see that that Division and Section are in the northwest part of the city. In Section 10, Division 1, enlarged, we find Irving Street, as seen on the opposite page.

See page 80 for explanation of " Index to All Chicago Streets."

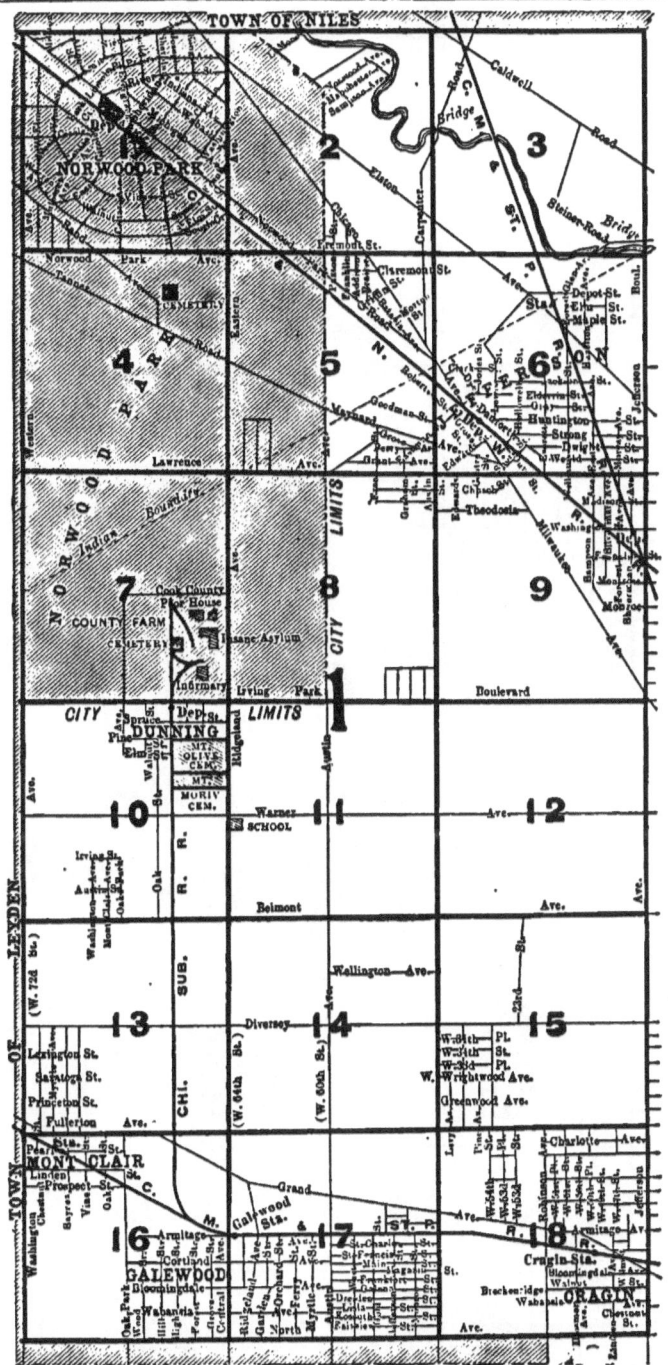

Northwestern Portion of City, Showing Location of County Buildings at Dunning.

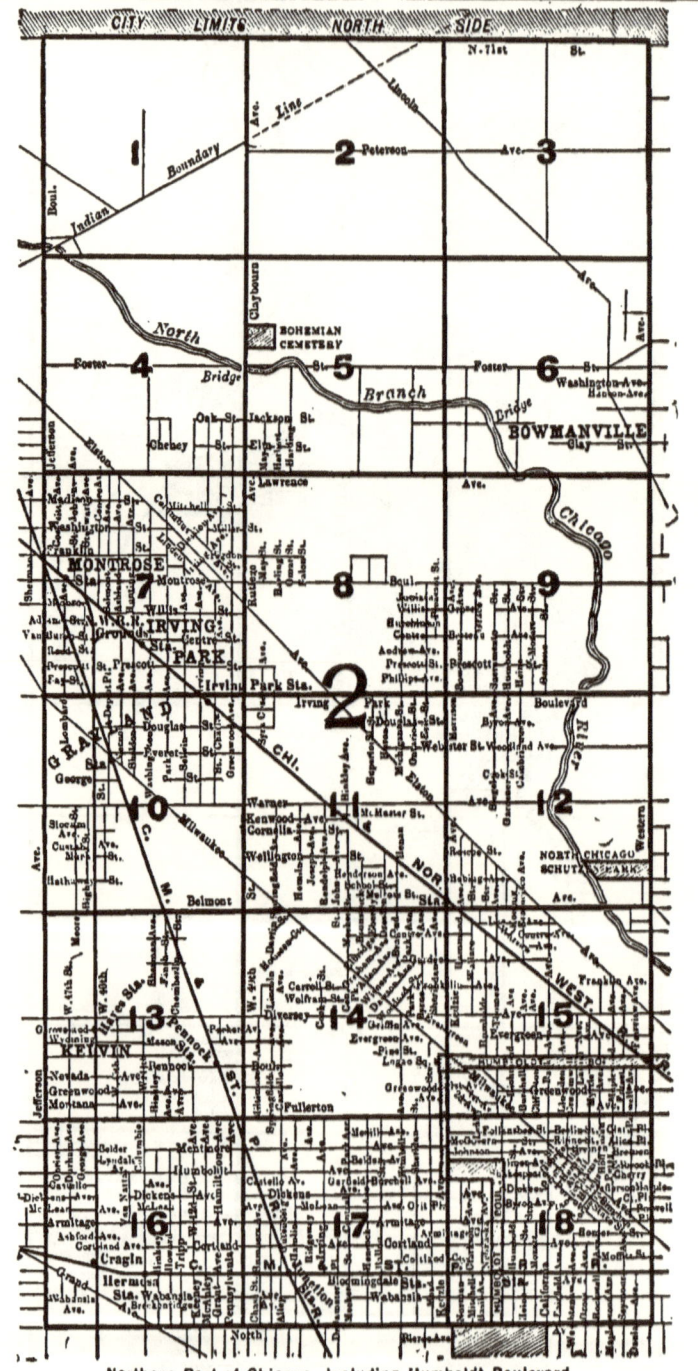

Northern Part of Chicago, Including Humboldt Boulevard.

Northeastern Part of Chicago, Including Rosehill and Graceland Cemeteries.

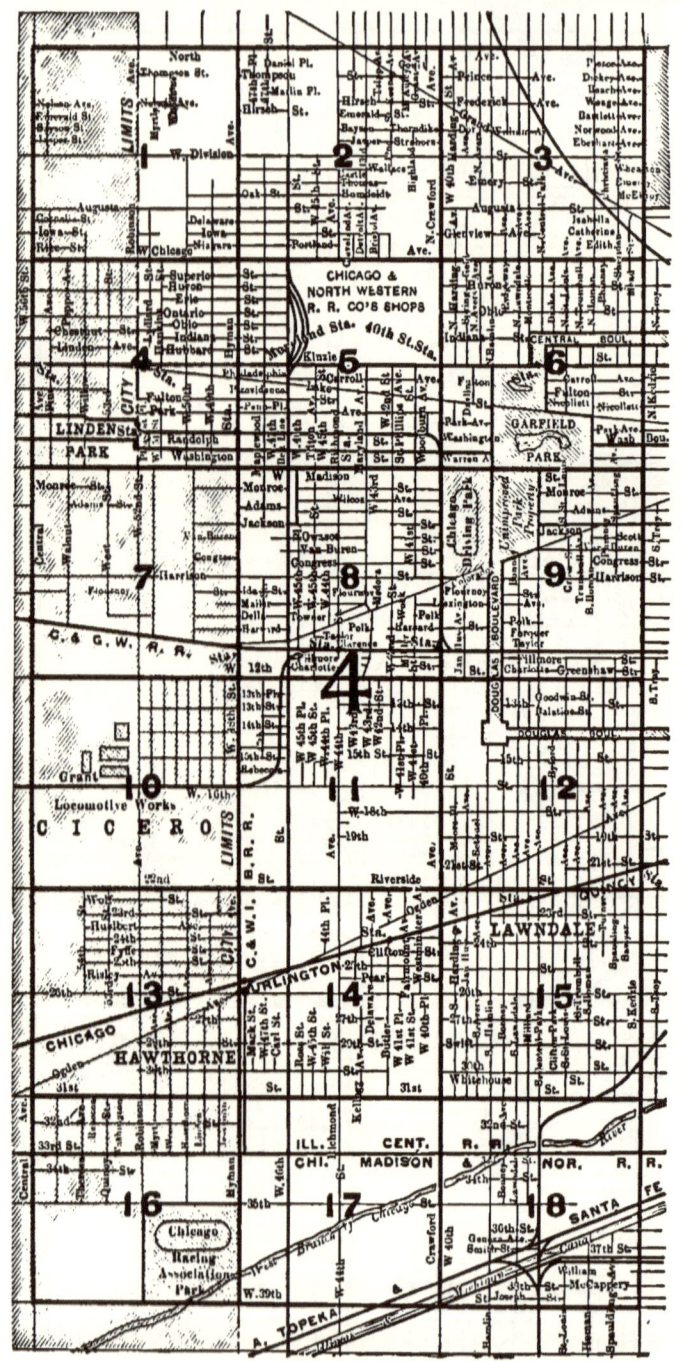

Western Part of Chicago, Including Garfield Park and Douglas Boulevard.

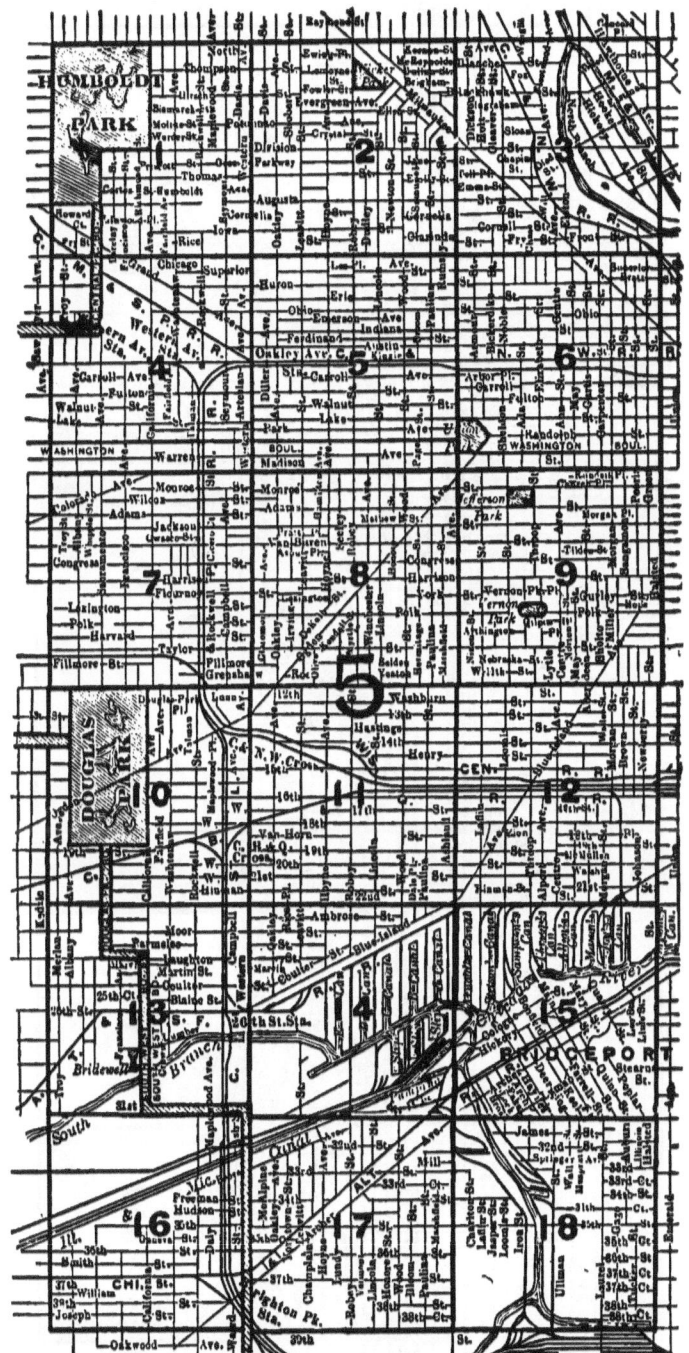

Central Part of Chicago, Including Humboldt and Douglas Parks.

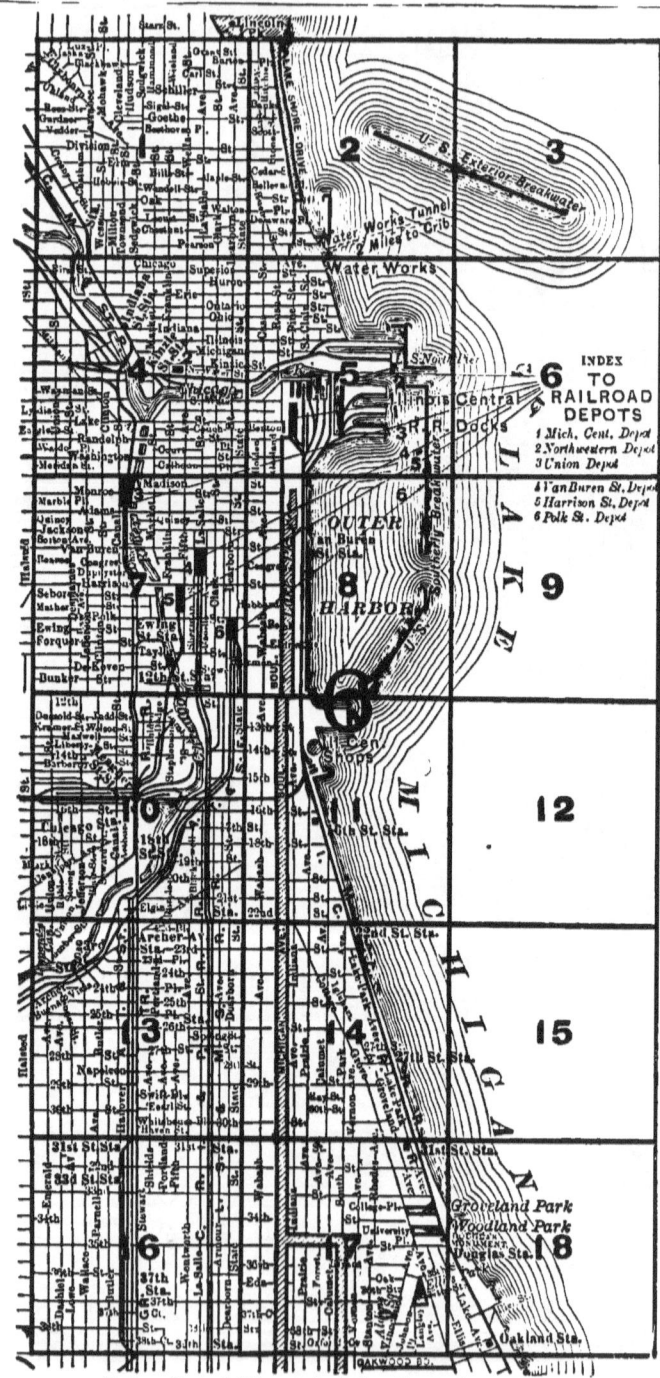

Eastern Part of Chicago, Including the Business Center.

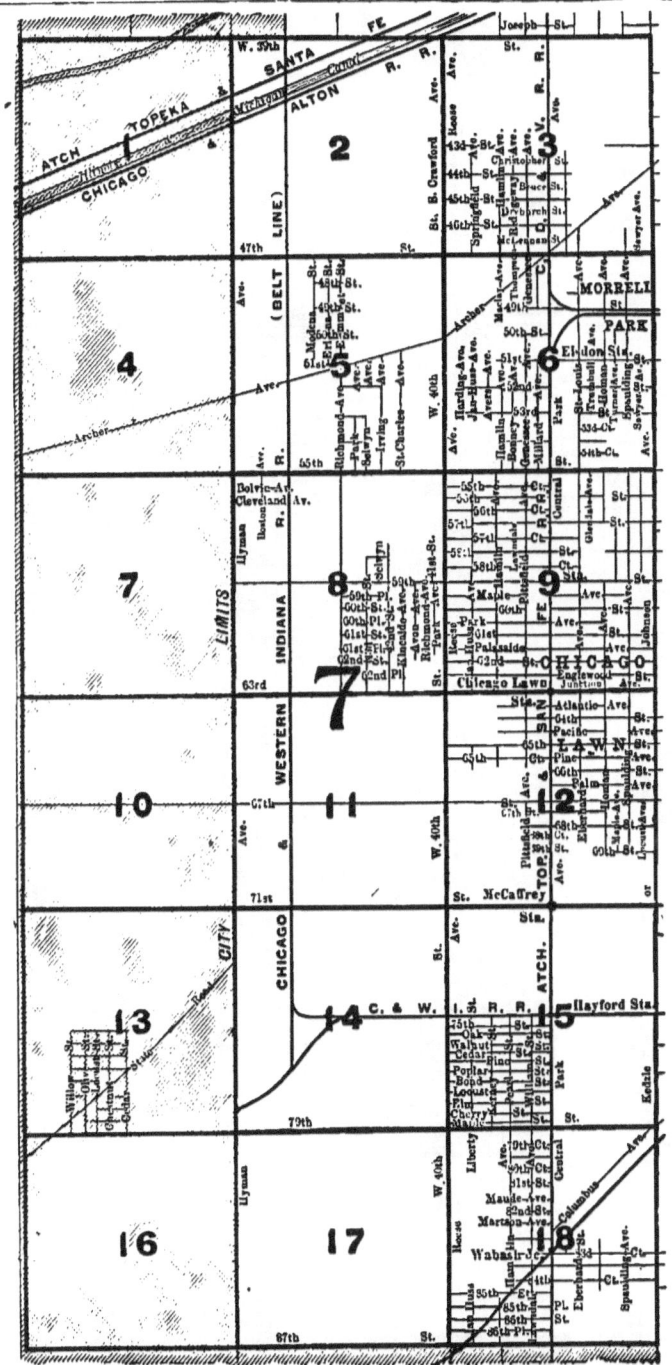

Southwestern Chicago, Extending to Eighty-seventh Street.

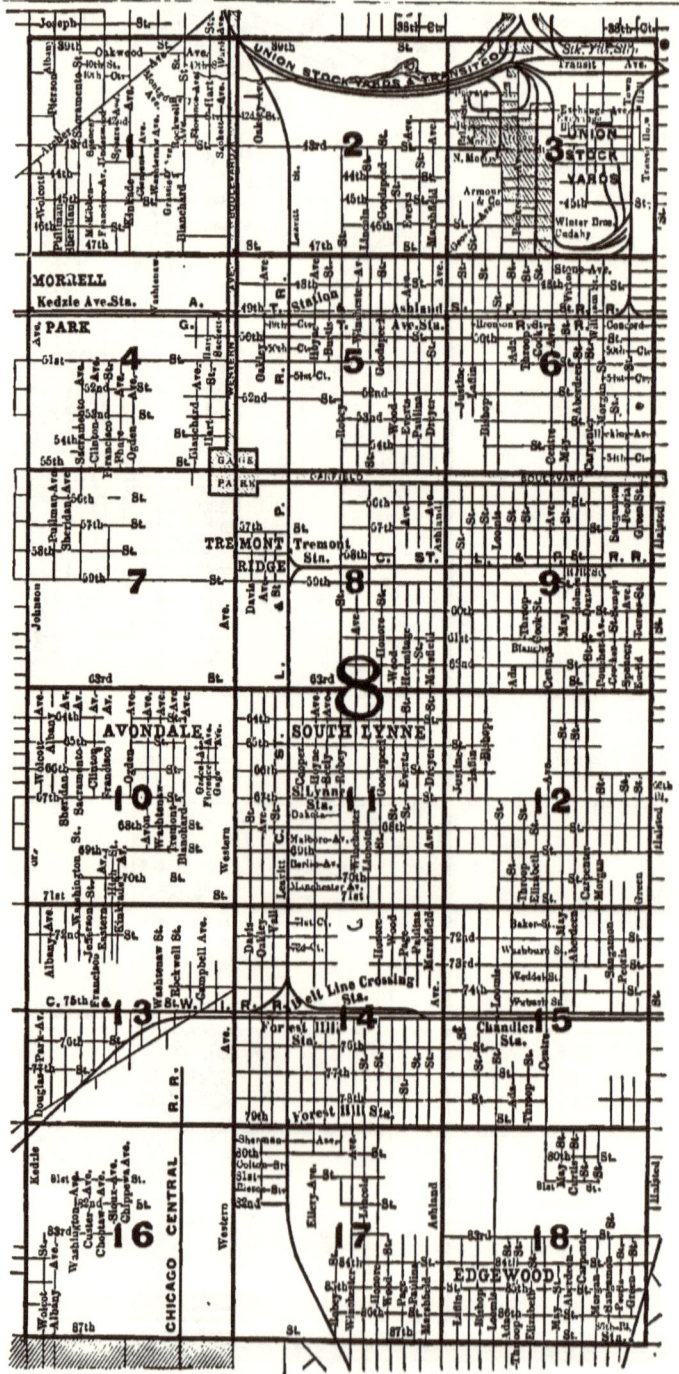

Southern Part of Chicago, Including Morrell Park and the Stock Yards.

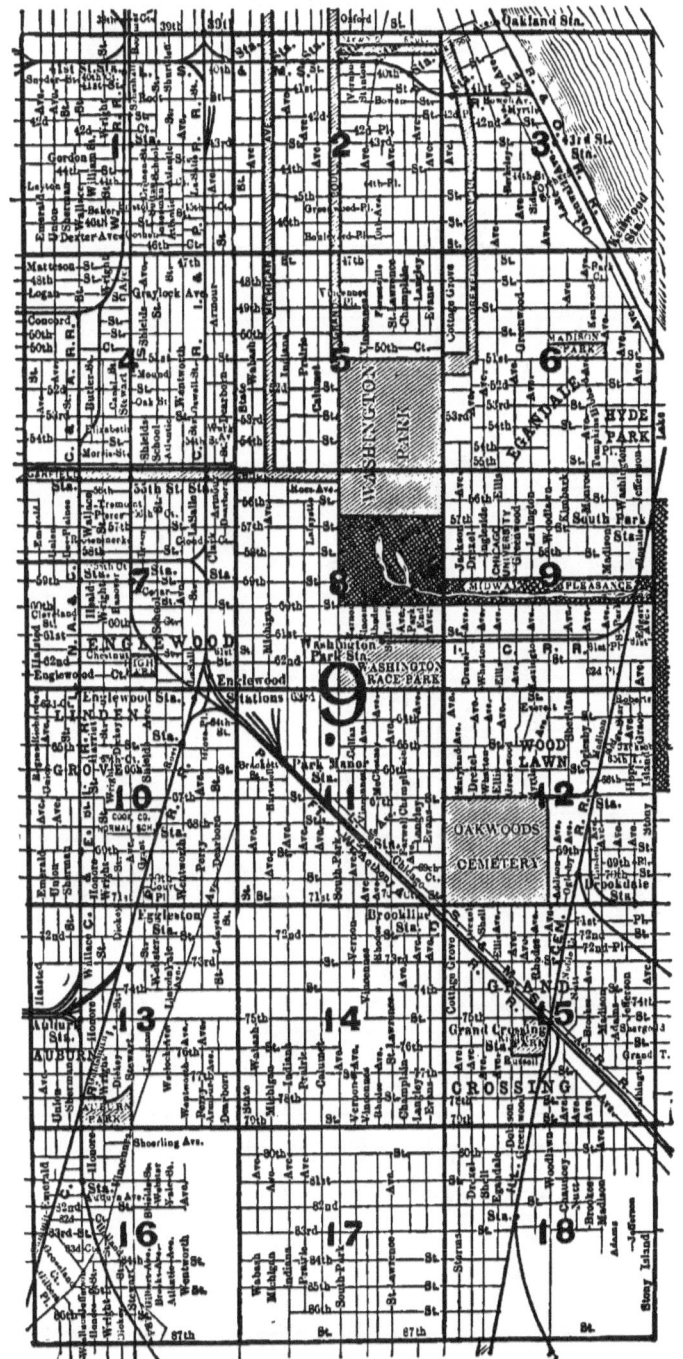

Southern Part of Chicago, Including Washington Park.

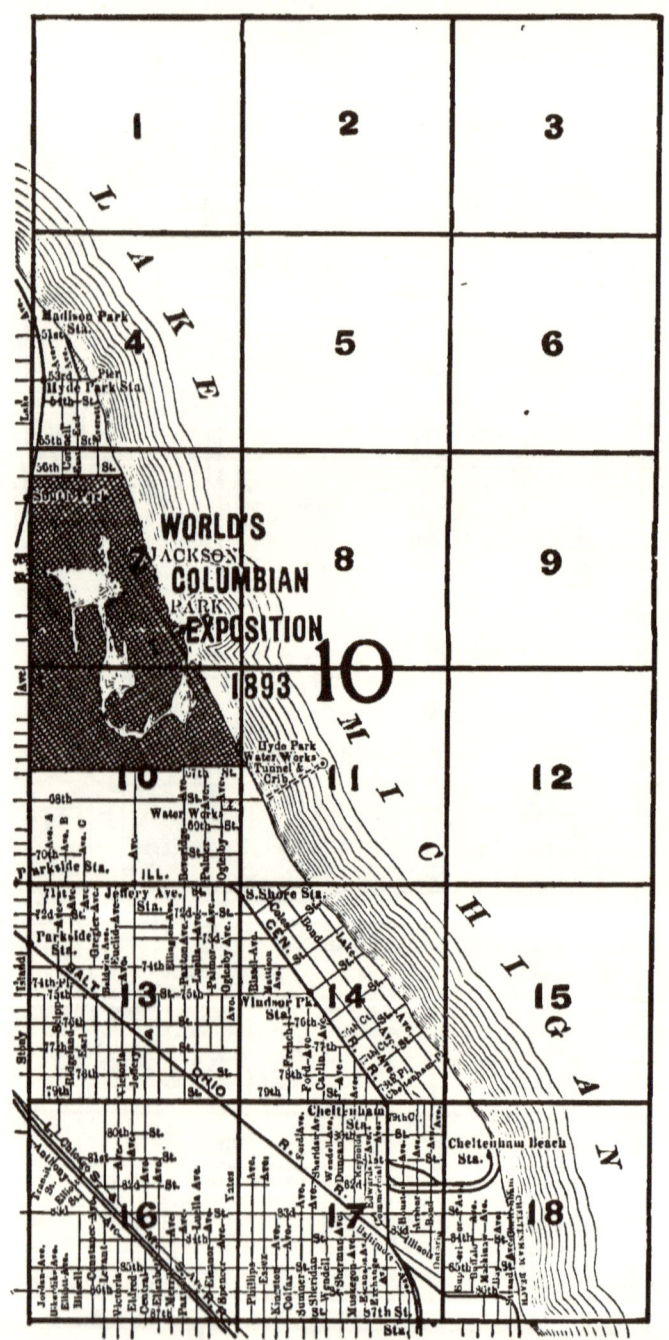

Southern Part of Chicago, Including the Greater Part of the World's Fair Grounds.

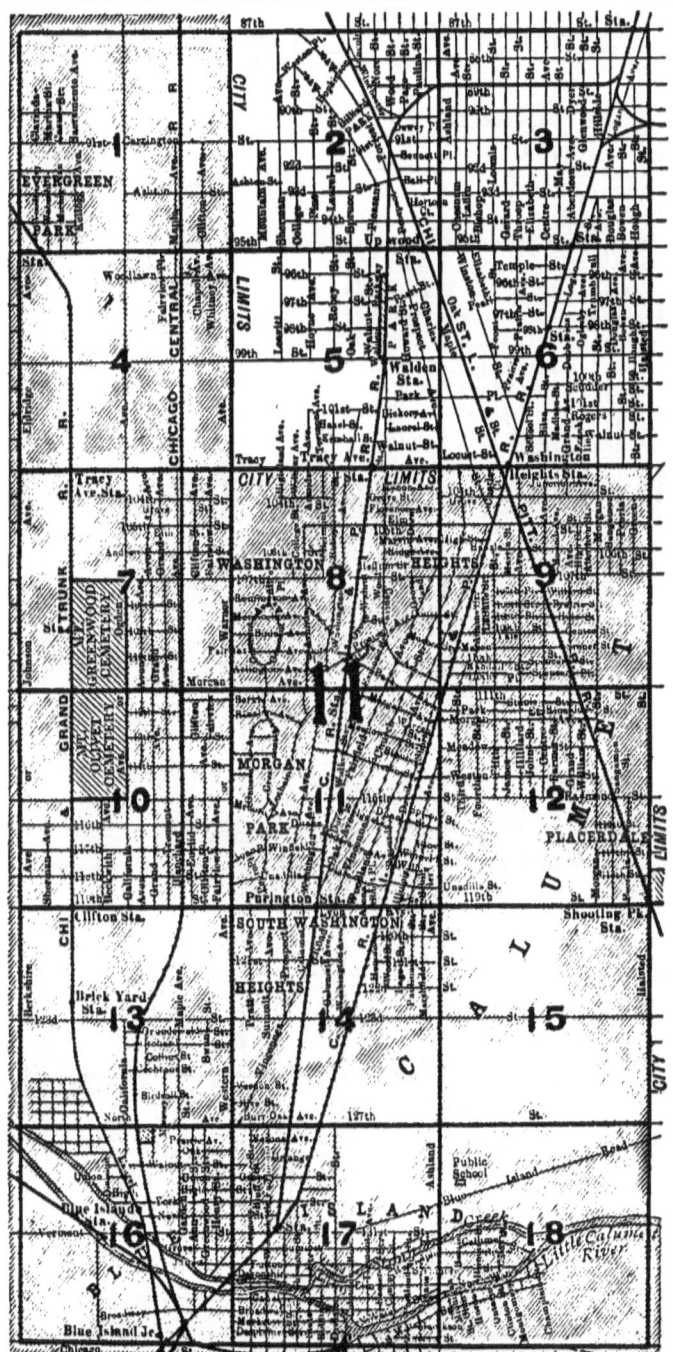

Southwestern Part of Chicago, Including Washington Heights.

Southern Part of Chicago, Including Pullman and Lake Calumet.

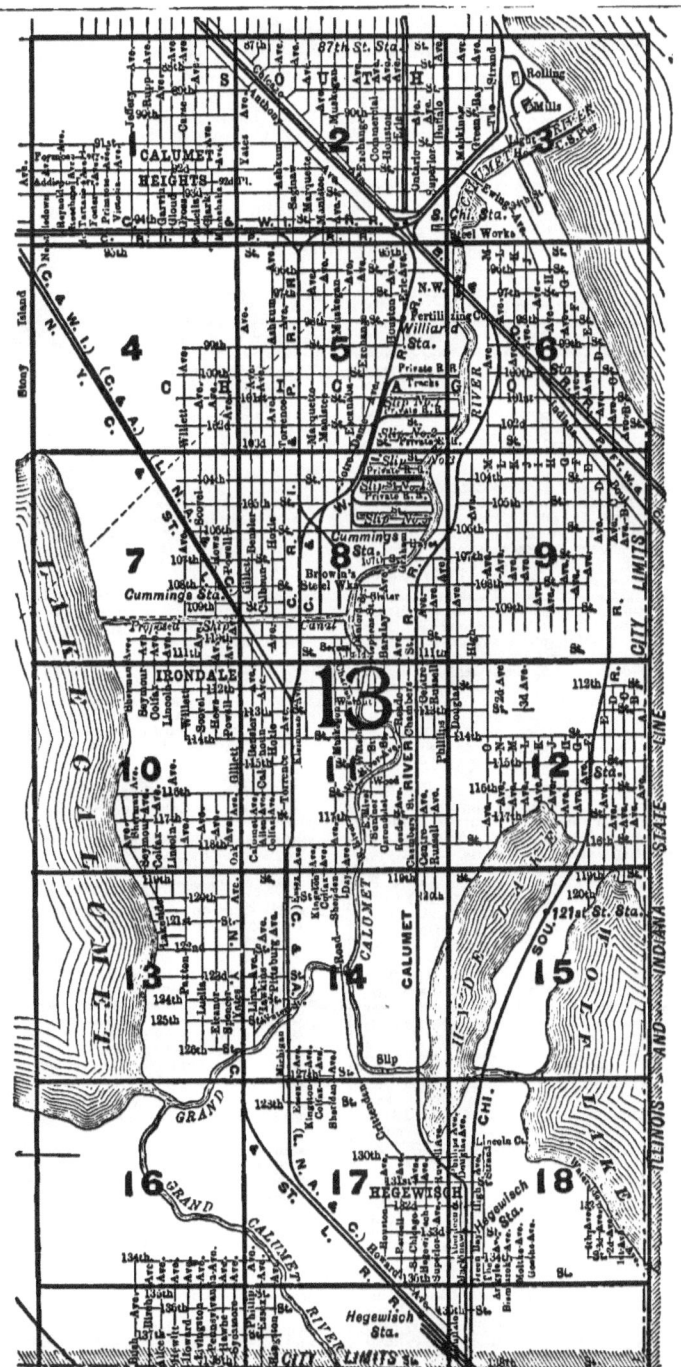

Extreme Southeastern Part of Chicago, Including South Chicago.

INCLUDING
STEAM RAILWAYS,
ELEVATED ROADS
AND
COMPRESSED
AIR LINES.

INCLUDING
CABLE LINES.
ELECTRIC, MOTOR,
AND
HORSE-CAR LINES.

Explanation.—All fullface figures designate the number of the division of the city, and small figures that follow designate the number of the section in ∴ at division. Thus, in the following, the words "Archer Av., **6**, 13," mean Arc Avenue in division **6**, and section 13 in division **6**.

(No. 1)—CHICAGO, ALTON & ST. LOUIS R. R.— Trains leave the Union Depot, at corner of Canal and Adams Sts., and run south, crossing the south branch of the river and stopping at Twenty-third St., near Archer Av., **6**, 13. Thence they run southwest, on a line nearly parallel with Archer Av., stopping at Brighton Park Station, which is located at Thirty-seventh and Hart Sts., in **5**, 16; west on Thirty-seventh St. to Illinois & Michigan Canal, and southwest along the south side of canal.

(No. 2)—CHICAGO & EASTERN ILLINOIS R. R.— Trains leave Dearborn Station, at the corner of Polk St. and Fourth Av., and run south, stopping at the following stations: **6**, 13, Archer Av. Station, near Twenty-third St.; 16, Thirty-third St.; **9**, 1, Forty-first St.; 4, Forty-ninth St.; 7, Fifty-fifth St.; 7, Fifty-ninth St.; 10. Englewood, at Sixty-third St.; 10, Normal Park, at Sixty-eighth St.; 13, Seventy-second St., 13, Auburn Junction, at Seventy-fifth St.; 13, Auburn Park, near Seventy-eighth St.; 16, Eighty-first St.; 16, Eighty-third St.; **12**, 1, Oakdale, near Ninetieth St.; 1, Euclid Park, at Ninety-fifth St.; 4, Fernwood, at 103rd St.; 7, Roseland, at 111th St., 10, Kensington, near 116th St.; 17, Riverdale, at 133d St.; 17, Dolton, at 138th St. About twenty-three trains each way daily.

(No. 3)—CHICAGO & GRAND TRUNK R. R.— Trains leave Dearborn Station, at corner of Polk St. and Fourth Av., and run south to Forty-ninth St., then west, stopping at the following stations: **9**, 4, Halsted St., **8**, 6, Centre Av.; 5, Ashland Av.; 5, Oakley Av.; 4, Morrell Park, at Kedzie Av.; **7**, 6, Elsdon, at Fifty-first St. and Central Park Av. Thence the route runs south, with stations as follows: **7**, 6, Fifty-fifth St.; 9, Fifty-ninth St.; 9, Chicago Lawn, at Sixty-third St.; 12, Sixty-seventh St.; 12, McCaffrey, at Seventy-first St.; 15, Hayford, at Seventy-fifth St.; 18, Clarkdale, near Eighty-third St.; St. Maria, near Eighty-ninth St. (outside of map); **11**, 1, Evergreen Park, at Ninety-fifth St.; 7, Tracy Av. or 103rd St.; 7, Mt. Greenwood or Mt. Olivet, at 109th St.; 10, Mt. Hope, near 117th St.; 13, Clifton, at 119th St.; 13, Brick Yard Station, north of 123rd St.; 13, Wireton, between 123rd and 127th St.; 16, Blue Island, near 131st or Vermont St.; 16, Blue Island Junction, at Chicago St. About fifteen trains each way daily.

(No. 4) — CHICAGO & NORTHERN PACIFIC R. R.—Trains leave the Grand Central Depot, at corner of Harrison St. and Fifth Av., and run south, across the river, to Meagher St., **6**, 10, then west, stopping at the following stations: **6**, 10, Halsted St.; **5**, 12, Blue Island Av.; 11, Ashland Av.; 10, Ogden Av.; 7, Douglas Park, at California Av.; **4**, 9, West Fortieth St. Junction; 8, Crawford Av.; 8, West Forty-fifth St.; 7, West Forty-eighth St.; 7, Central Av. At West Fortieth St. Junction a branch of the road turns north, with a station at Colorado Av., **4**, 9, and at Madison St., 9,

Then it turns west, with stations as follows: 4, 5, Marvin, at Richmond Av. o West Forty-fourth St.; 4, Moreland, at Hyman Av. or West Forty-eighth St., 4. Linden Park, at West Fifty-second St. About twenty-three trains each way daily. At West Forty-sixth St. a branch turns south to Hyman Av. Station, at Sixteenth St., **4** 11; thence west to Grant Works Station, near Robinson Av., 10, and Donald or Central Av. Station, 10.

(No. 5)—CHICAGO & NORTHWESTERN R. R. (GALENA DIVISION).—Trains leave depot at corner of Wells and Kinzie Sts., and run west along Kinzie St., stopping at the following stations: **5**, 5, Oakley Av.; 4, Sacramento Av.; 4, 6, Central Park Station, at north side of Garfield Park; 5, West Fortieth St.; 5, Moreland, at West Forty-seventh St.; 4, Linden Park, near West Fifty-second St.; 4, Austin, at Central Av. or West Fifty-sixth St. About twenty-nine trains each way daily.

(No. 6)—CHICAGO & NORTHWESTERN R. R. (MILWAUKEE DIVISION). — Trains leave depot at corner of Wells and Kinzie Sts., and run west across the river; thence northwest and north, stopping at the following stations: **3**, 16, Clybourn Junction, between Clybourn Pl. and Armitage Av.; 13, Deering, at Fullerton Av.; 10, Gross Park, between School St. and Roscoe Boul.; 7, Cuyler, at Graceland Av.; 7, Ravenswood, between Wilson and Sunnyside Avs.; 4, Summerdale, at North Fifty-ninth St.; 1, Rose Hill, at east side of Rose Hill Cemetery; 1, High Ridge, near Grand Av. About thirty-seven trains each way daily.

(No. 7)—CHICAGO & NORTHWESTERN R. R. (WISCONSIN DIVISION).—Trains leave depot at corner of Wells and Kinzie Sts., and run west across the river; thence northwest, stopping at the following stations: **2**, 15, Maplewood, at Humboldt Boul.; 11, Avondale, at Belmont and Kedzie Avs.; 10, Irving Park, near Irving Park Boul.; 7, Hunting Av.; 7, Montrose, at Montrose Boul.; 4, 6, Jefferson Park, at Milwaukee Av.; 1, Norwood Park. About twenty-two trains each way daily.

(No. 8)—CHICAGO, BURLINGTON & QUINCY R. R.—Trains leave the Union Depot, at corner of Canal and Adams Sts., and run south, stopping at Ewing St., **6**, 7, and Chicago Station, near Fifteenth St., 10. Thence they run west, stopping at Blue Island Av., **5**, 12, and Western Av., 11; then southwest, stopping at the following stations: **5**, 10, Douglas Park, near Kedzie Av.; **4**, 15, Millard Av.; 14, Crawford, at Butler Av.; 14, Hawthorne, at Hyman Av. About fourteen trains each way daily.

(No. 9)—CHICAGO, MILWAUKEE & ST. PAUL R. R. (COUNCIL BLUFFS DIVISION).—Trains leave the Union Depot, at corner of Canal and Adams Sts., and run north, crossing the river at Kinzie St.; then northwest along the east side of the river and North Branch Canal, to Clybourn Pl., **3**, 17;

then west, crossing the river again, and stopping at the following stations: **8**, 16, Milwaukee Av.; **2**, 18, Humboldt, at Humboldt Boul.; 17, Elsmere, at Kimbell Av.; 17, Pacific Junction, between Hamlin and Gutenberg Avs.; 16, Hermosa, at West Forty-fourth St.; **1**, 18, Cragin, near Grand Av.; 17, Galewood, near West Sixty-fourth St.; 16, Mont Clair, near Fullerton Av. About eight trains each way daily. West of West Sixty-fourth St. a branch of the railroad turns north, and extends to Dunning, **1**, 10, and the Cook County Poor House and Insane Asylum, 7.

(NO. 10)—CHICAGO, MILWAUKEE & ST. PAUL R. R. (EVANSTON DIVISION).—Trains leave Union Depot, at the corner of Canal and Adams Sts., and run north, crossing the river at Kinzie St., then northwest, along east side of river and North Branch Canal, to Clybourn Pl., **3**, 17. Thence they run north, stopping at the following stations: **3**, 17, Fullerton Av.; 14, Lincoln Av.; 14, Belmont Av.; 11, Addison St.; 8, Buena Park or Graceland, at Buena Av.; 5, Argyle Park, at Argyle St.; 5, Edgewater, at Bryn Mawr Av. About seventeen trains each way daily.

(NO. 11)—CHICAGO, MILWAUKEE & ST. PAUL R. R. (MILWAUKEE DIVISION).—Trains leave the Union Depot, at corner of Canal and Adams Sts., and run north to Kinzie St., **6**, 4; then west, along Kinzie St., to Western Av., **5**, 4. Thence they run northwest, stopping at the following stations: **2**, 13, Pennock, at Pennock Boul.; 10, Grayland, at Milwaukee Av.; **1**, 9, Montrose, at Washington St.; 6, Forest Glen, near Elston Av. About four trains each way daily.

(NO. 12)—CHICAGO, ROCK ISLAND & PACIFIC R. R.—Trains leave the Van Buren St. Depot, at corner of Van Buren and Sherman Sts., and run south, stopping at the following stations: **6**, 10, Twenty-second St.; 16, Thirty-first St.; 16, Thirty-ninth St.; **9**, 1, Forty-fourth St.; 4, Forty-seventh St; 4, Fifty-first St.; 7, Fifty-fifth St.; 7, Fifty-ninth St.; 7, Englewood, at Sixty-second St. Thence the trains turn southwest, stopping at the following stations: **9**, 10, Sixty-fifth St.; 10, Normal Park, at Sixty-eighth St.; 13, Eggleston, at Seventy-first St.; 13, Seventy-fifth St.; 13, Auburn Park, at Seventy-eighth St.; **1**, **3**, South Englewood, at Eighty-seventh St.; 3, Ninety-fifth St.; 6, Ninety-ninth St.; 6, Washington Heights, at 103rd St.; 9, Given, near 109th St.; 11, Morgan Av. Near Eighty-ninth St. the "Dummy Track" turns west from the main track and stops at Brainerd, corner of Eighty-ninth and Loomis Sts., **11**, 3; then it turns south, stopping at the following stations: **11**, 2, Beverly Hill, near Ninety-first St.; 5, Longwood, at Ninety-fifth St.; 5, Walden, at Ninety-ninth St.; 5, Tracy Av.; 8, Belmont, at 107th St.; 8, Morgan Park, at 111th St.; 11, Raymond St. or 115th St.; 11, Purington, at 119th St.; 14, Burr Oak, at Burr Oak Av. or 127th St.; 17, Blue Island, at 131st St. About twenty-four trains each way daily.

(NO. 13)—ILLINOIS CENTRAL R. R.—Trains leave depot at the east end of Lake St., and run southeast along the lake shore, stopping at the following stations: **6**, 8, Van Buren St.; 11, Sixteenth St.; 11, Twenty-second St.; 14, Twenty-seventh St.; 14, Thirty-first St.; 18, Douglas, at Thirty-fifth St.; 18, Oakland, at Thirty-ninth St.; **9**, 3, Forty-third St.; 3, Kenwood, at Forty-seventh St.; 6, Madison Park, near Fiftieth St.; **10**, 4, Hyde Park, at Fifty-third St. Thence they run southwest, stopping at the following stations: **9**, 9, South Park, at Fifty-seventh St.; 9, Sixtieth St.;

9, Woodlawn Park, at Sixty-third St.; 12, Oakwoods, at Sixty-seventh St.; 12, Brookdale, at Seventieth St.; 15, Grand Crossing, at Seventy-fifth St; 18, Fordham, at Eighty-second St.; **12**, 3, Dauphin Park, at Eighty-ninth St.; 3, Burnside Crossing, at Ninety-fifth St.; 8, 104th St.; 8, Pullman, at 111th St.; 11, Kensington, at 115th St.; 14, Gardner's Park, at 123rd St.; 17, Wildwood, at 130th St.; 17, Riverdale, at 134th St. About sixty-two trains each way daily. From Sixty-seventh St. one branch of the road turns southeast, in **9**, 12, to Parkside, at Seventy-first St.; thence east, on Seventy-first St., to Jeffery Avenue Station, **10**, 13, and South Shore Station, at Seventy-first and State Sts., 14; thence southeast, stopping at the following stations: **10**, 14, Windsor Park, at Seventy-fifth St.; 14, Cheltenham, at Seventy-ninth St.; 17, Eighty-sixth St; 17, Eighty-seventh St.; **13**, 2, South Chicago, at Ninety-fourth St. About twenty-six trains each way daily.

(NO. 14)—LAKE SHORE AND MICHIGAN SOUTHERN R. R.—Trains leave the Van Buren St. Depot, corner of Van Buren and Sherman Sts., and run south, stopping at the following stations: **6**, 10, Twenty-second St.; 13, Twenty-sixth St.; 16, Thirty-first St.; 16, Thirty-ninth St.; **9**, 1, Forty-third St.; 4, Fifty-first St.; 7, Fifty-fifth St.; 7, Fifty-ninth St.; 7, Englewood, at Sixty-second St.; 11, Park Manor, at Sixty-sixth St.; 14, Brookline, at Seventy-first St.; 15, Grand Crossing, at Seventy-fifth St.; **10**, 16, Constance, near Eighty-third St.; **13**, 2, South Chicago, at Ninety-fourth St.; 6, 100th St.; 9, Colehour, at 104th St. About ten trains each way daily. At Fortieth St. there are two branch roads, one extending west to the Union Stock Yards, and the other east to the lake shore. On the latter branch the stations are as follows: **9**, 2, State St., Michigan Av., Prairie Av., Grand Boul., Vincennes Av., Langley Av.; 3, Cottage Grove Av., Drexel Boul., Lake Av.

(NO. 15)—NEW YORK, CHICAGO & ST. LOUIS R. R., "NICKEL PLATE."—Trains leave the Van Buren St. Depot, corner Van Buren and Sherman Sts., and run south, stopping at the following stations: **6**, 10, Twenty-second St.; **9**, 7, Englewood, near Sixty-third St.; 15, Grand Crossing, at Seventy-fifth St.; **12**, 6, Stony Island; **13**, 11, Irondale, at 112th St. About two trains each way daily.

(NO. 16)—PITTSBURG, CINCINNATI, CHICAGO & ST. LOUIS R. R., "PAN-HANDLE."—Trains leave the Union Depot, corner Canal and Adams Sts., and run south, crossing the river near Twenty-first St.; then southwest, on a line nearly parallel with Archer Av., stopping at Brighton Park Station, which is located at Thirty-seventh and Hart Sts., in **5**, 16. Thence they run south and south-east, stopping at the following stations: **8**, 11, South Lynne, at Sixty-seventh St.; 14, Forest Hill, at Seventy-ninth St; **11**, 2, Fairview Park (formerly Upwood) at Ninety-fifth St.; 9, Washington Heights, at 103rd St.; 15, Shooting Park, at 119th St.; **12**, 13, Blue Island Road, at 127th St.; 13, Riverdale, at 135th St. About six trains each way daily.

(NO. 17)—PITTSBURG, FT. WAYNE & CHICAGO R. R., "FORT WAYNE."—Trains leave the Union Depot, at corner of Canal and Adams Sts., and run south, stopping at the following stations: **6**, 13, Archer Av.; **8**, 3, Union Stock Yards; **9**, 1, Forty-first St.; 4, Fifty-first St.; 7, Fifty-fifth St.; 7, Sixty-first St.; 10, Englewood, at Sixty third St. Thence they run southeast, stopping at the following stations; **9, 11** Park Manor, at Sixty-sixth St.; **14,** Brook line, at Seventy-first St.; **15,** Grand Crossing, at Seventy-fifth St.; **10,** 16, Constance, near Eighty-third St.; **13,** 2, South Chicago, at Ninety-fourth St.; **5,** Willards, at Ninety-eighth St.; **5,** West 100th St.; **8,** Cummings, at 106th St.; **6,** 106th St.; **9,** Colehour, at 104th St; **12,** 115th St.; **15,** 121st St.; **18,** Hegewisch, at 133rd St. About twenty trains each way daily.

(**No. 18**)—WABASH, ST. LOUIS & PACIFIC R. R.—Trains leave Dearborn Station, at corner of Polk St. and Custom House Pl. or Fourth Av., and run south, stopping at the following stations: **6,** 13, Archer Av., near Twenty-third St.; **9,** 1, Forty-first St.; 4, Forty-ninth St.; **10,** Englewood, at Sixty-third St.; **13,** Auburn Junction, at Seventy-fifth St. Thence the trains run west, stopping at Forest Hill, between Leavitt St. and Western Av., **8, 14;** thence they run southwest. About four trains each way daily.

NORTH SIDE STREET CAR LINES

Explanation.—The words "Time, 20 minutes," "Time, 15 minutes," etc., in the description of street car lines, mean that the time consumed in going from the starting point to the terminus of any line, is 20 minutes or 15 minutes, as the case may be.

(**No. 19**)—ASHLAND AV. HORSE LINE (NORTH SIDE).— From Belmont Av. and Gross Pk. north on Ashland Av. to Graceland High School. Car leaves every 20 minutes. Last car leaves Belmont Av. at 10 : 30 P. M.; leaves Graceland High School at 8 P. M. *Red light.*

CABLE GRIP CAR,
PROPELLED BY UNDERGROUND WIRE ROPE.

to Fullerton Av. Time, 45 minutes. Last car leaves Fullerton Av. at 11 : 24 P. M.; leaves Monroe and La Salle at 12 : 09 A. M. *Red light.*

(**No. 20**)—CITY LIMITS CABLE LINE VIA CLARK ST. (NORTH SIDE).—From Monroe and La Salle to North Clark St. and Diversey Av. Car leaves every 3 minutes. Runs east on Monroe to Dearborn, north on Dearborn to Randolph, west on Randolph to La Salle, north (through tunnel) to Illinois, east on Illinois to Clark, north on Clark to Diversey Av. Time, 31 minutes. Last car leaves Diversey Av. at 11 : 46 P. M.; leaves Monroe and La Salle at 12 : 22 A. M. *Green light. Sign on car, "Clark Street."*

(**No. 21**) CITY LIMITS CABLE LINE VIA WELLS ST. (NORTH SIDE).—From Monroe and La Salle to North Clark St. and Diversey Av. Car leaves every 6 minutes. Runs to Illinois by same route as line (No. **20**), then west on Illinois to Wells, north on Wells and Clark to Diversey Av. Time, 32 minutes. Last car leaves Diversey Av. at 11 : 38 P. M.; leaves Monroe and La Salle at 12 : 10 A. M. *Red light. Sign on car, "Wells Street."*

(**No. 22**)—CLARK ST. AND LAWRENCE AV. HORSE LINE (NORTH SIDE).—From Diversey Av. northwest on Clark St. to Lawrence Av. Time, 28 minutes. Car leaves every 15 minutes. Last car leaves Diversey Av. at 11 : 15 P. M.; leaves Lawrence Av. at 11 : 45 P. M. *Green light.*

(**No. 23**)—CLARK ST., FULLERTON AND WEBSTER AVS. CABLE AND HORSE LINE (NORTH SIDE).— From Monroe and La Salle to Racine and Webster Avs. Car leaves every 6 minutes. Runs to Clark by same route as line (No. **20**), then north on Clark St. and Lincoln Av. to intersection of Lincoln and Fullerton Avs., west on Fullerton Av., by horse power, to Racine Av., south on Racine Av. to Webster Av. Time, 37 minutes. Last car leaves Webster Av. at 11 : 35 P. M.; leaves Monroe and La Salle at 12 : 12 A. M. *Green and red light.*

(**No. 24**)—CLYBOURN AV. CABLE AND HORSE LINE (NORTH SIDE).—From Monroe and La Salle to Clybourn and Fullerton Avs. Car leaves every 6 minutes. Runs to Illinois by same route as line (No. **20**), then west on Illinois to Wells, north on Wells to Division, west on Division to Clybourn Av., northwest on Clybourn Av.

(**No. 25**)—CLYBOURN AV. TO BELMONT AV. HORSE LINE (NORTH SIDE).—From Fullerton Av. northwest on Clybourn Av. to Belmont Av. Time, 20 minutes. Car leaves every 15 minutes. Last car leaves Fullerton Av. at 10 : 40 P. M.; leaves Belmont Av. at 10 : 25 P. M. *Red light.*

(**No. 26**)—DEARBORN ST. HORSE LINE (NORTH SIDE).—From Northwestern Depot to Polk St. Depot. Car leaves every 10 minutes. Runs east on Kinzie St. to Dearborn Av., south on Dearborn to Polk. Time, 20 minutes. Last car leaves Northwestern Depot at 9 : 32 P. M.; leaves Polk St. Depot at 9 : 52 P. M. *Light, white diamond.*

(**No. 27**)—DIVISION AND MARKET STS. HORSE LINE (NORTH SIDE). — From Clark and Washington to Division St. and Milwaukee Av. Car leaves every 12 minutes. Runs north on Clark St. to Chicago Av., west on Chicago Av. to Market, north on Market to Division, west on Division to Milwaukee Av. Time, 36 minutes. Last car leaves Milwaukee Av. at 11 : 14 P. M.; leaves Clark and Washington at 11 : 50 P. M. *Green and white light.*

(**No. 28**)—GARFIELD AV. AND CENTRE ST. CABLE AND HORSE LINE (NORTH SIDE).— From Monroe and La Salle to Racine and Garfield Avs. Car leaves every 4 minutes. Runs to Clark by same route as line (No. **20**), then north on Clark to Centre, west on Centre St. to Lincoln Av., northwest on Lincoln Av. to Garfield Av., west on Garfield Av. to Racine Av. Time, 37 minutes. Last car leaves Racine Av. at 11 : 35 P. M.; leaves La Salle and Monroe at 12 : 12 A. M. *Orange light, with red star in center.*

(**No. 29**)—GRACELAND AV. LINE (NORTH SIDE). —From North Clark St. and Diversey Av. to Graceland and Alexander Avs. Car leaves every 10 minutes. Runs north on Evanston Av. to Graceland Av., west on Graceland Av. to Alexander Av. Time, 20 minutes. Last car leaves Clark St. and Diversey Av. at 11 : 45 P. M.; leaves Graceland and Alexander Avs. at 11 : 24 P. M. *Red light.*

(**No. 30**)—GROSS PARK HORSE LINE (NORTH SIDE).—From Wrightwood Av. northwest on Lincoln Av. to Belmont Av. Time, 10 minutes. Car leaves every 4 minutes. Last car leaves Wrightwood Av. at 11 : 45 P. M.; leaves Lincoln and Belmont Avs. at 12 midnight. *Purple light.*

No. 31)—HALSTED ST. CROSSTOWN HORSE LINE (NORTH SIDE).—From Twenty-second north on Halsted St. to Fullerton Av. Time, 54 minutes. Car leaves every 8 minutes. Last car leaves Fullerton Av. at 10:50 P. M.; leaves Twenty-second at 11:54 P. M. *Red light.*

No. 32)—HALSTED AND MARKET STS. HORSE LINE (NORTH SIDE).—From Fifth Av. and Randolph to Halsted St. and Evanston Av. Car leaves every 9 minutes. Runs north over Wells St. bridge to Illinois, west on Illinois to Market, north on Market to Division, west on Division to Clybourn Av., northwest on Clybourn Av. to Halsted, north on Halsted to Evanston Av. Time, 48 minutes. Last car leaves Evanston Av. at 11:06 P. M.; leaves Fifth Av. and Randolph at 11:54 P. M. *Purple light.*

No. 33)—HIGH RIDGE HORSE LINE (NORTH SIDE).—From Lawrence Av. north on Clark to High Ridge. Time, 28 minutes. Car leaves every 15 minutes. Last car leaves Lawrence Av. at 10 P. M.; leaves High Ridge at 10:30 P. M. *Green light.*

No. 34)—LARRABEE ST. HORSE LINE (NORTH SIDE).—From Clark and Washington to Lincoln and Webster Avs. Car leaves every 7 minutes. Runs to Chicago Av. by same route as line (No. 40), then west on Chicago Av. to Larrabee, north on Larrabee to Lincoln and Webster Avs. Time, 34 minutes. Last car leaves Lincoln and Webster Avs. at 11:22 P. M.; leaves Clark and Washington at 11:56 P. M. *White light.*

No. 35)—LINCOLN AV. CABLE LINE VIA CLARK ST. (NORTH SIDE).—From Monroe and La Salle to Lincoln and Wrightwood Avs. Car leaves every 2¼ minutes. Runs to Clark by same route as line (No. 20), then north on Clark to Centre, west on Centre to Lincoln Av., northwest on Lincoln Av. to Wrightwood Av. Time, 32 minutes. Last car leaves Wrightwood Av at 11:52 P. M.; leaves Monroe and La Salle at 12:24 A. M. *Purple light. Sign on car, "Clark Street."*

No. 36)—LINCOLN AV. CABLE LINE VIA WELLS ST. (NORTH SIDE).—From Monroe and La Salle to Lincoln and Wrightwood Avs. Car leaves every 12 minutes. Runs to Illinois by same route as line (No. 20), then west on Illinois to Wells, north on Wells and Clark to Centre, west on Centre to Lincoln Av., northwest on Lincoln Av. to Wrightwood Av. Time, 33 minutes. Last car leaves Wrightwood Av. at 11:40

P. M.; leaves Monroe and La Salle at 12:12 A. M. *Red light. Sign on car, "Wells Street."*

No. 37)—NORTH AV. HORSE LINE (NORTH SIDE).—From Lincoln Park to Humboldt Park. Car leaves Clark every 10 minutes. Runs west on North Av. to California Av. Time, 36 minutes. Last car leaves Clark at 10:30 P. M.; leaves California Av. at 11:06 P. M. *White light.*

No. 38)—NORTHWESTERN DEPOT HORSE LINE (NORTH SIDE).—From Depot at Wells and Kinzie to Madison and State. Car leaves every 6 minutes. Runs south on Wells St. and Fifth Av. to Lake, east on Lake to State, south on State to Madison, west on Madison to Fifth Av., north on Fifth Av. and Wells to depot at Kinzie. Entire time for round trip, 24 minutes. Last car leaves Madison and State at 11:40 P. M. *White light.*

No. 39)—ROSCOE BOULEVARD HORSE LINE (NORTH SIDE).—From Lincoln and Belmont Avs. to Roscoe Boul. and Western Av. (Sharpshooters' Park). Car leaves every 20 minutes. Runs west on Belmont Av. to Robey, north on Robey to Roscoe Boul., west on Roscoe Boul. to Western Av. Time, 22 minutes. Last car leaves Lincoln and Belmont Avs. at 11:50 P. M.; leaves Roscoe Boul. and Western Av. at 9:45 P. M. *Purple light.*

No. 40)—SEDGWICK ST. HORSE LINE (NORTH SIDE).—From Clark and Washington to Sedgwick and Centre. Car leaves every 7 minutes. Runs north on Clark to Kinzie, west on Kinzie to Market, north on Market to Chicago Av., west on Chicago Av. to Sedgwick, north on Sedgwick to Centre. Time, 30 minutes. Last car leaves Centre at 11:24 P. M.; leaves Clark and Washington at 11:54 P. M. *Red light, with white diamond in center.*

No. 41)—SHEFFIELD AV. HORSE LINE (NORTH SIDE).—From Wrightwood and Lincoln Avs. north on Sheffield Av. to Belmont Av. Time, 10 minutes. Car leaves every 10 minutes. Last car leaves Lincoln Av. at 11:32 P. M.; leaves Belmont Av. at 11:42 P. M. *Red light.*

No. 42)—STATE AND DIVISION STS. HORSE LINE (NORTH SIDE).—From State and Lake to Division and North Clark. Car leaves every 3 minutes. Runs north on State to Division, west on Division to Clark. Time, 14 minutes. Last car leaves Clark at 11:50 P. M.; leaves State and Lake at 12:10 A. M. *Red light.*

SOUTH SIDE STREET CAR LINES.

(No. 43)—ARCHER AV. CABLE AND HORSE LINE (SOUTH SIDE).—From State and Madison to Archer and Kedzie Avs. Car leaves for Pitney Av. every 3 minutes; for Kedzie Av. every 9 to 12 minutes. Runs south on State, by cable, to Nineteenth; thence southwest on Archer Av., by horse power, to Kedzie Av. Time, 62 minutes. *Return* by same route to State; thence same as line (No. 58). Last day car leaves Madison and State at 12:10 A. M.; leaves Archer and Kedzie Avs. at 11:04 P. M. *Yellow car, with dark yellow dash. White light.*

(No. 44)—ASHLAND AV. HORSE LINE (SOUTH SIDE).—From Archer Av. south on Ashland Av. to Sixty-ninth. Time, 62 minutes. Car leaves every 12 to 15 minutes. Last car leaves Archer Av. at 11:52 P. M. *Red car. Ruby light.*

(No. 45)—CLARK AND VAN BUREN STS. HORSE LINE (SOUTH SIDE).—From Clark and Washington to Van Buren St. and Wabash

Av. Car leaves every 6 minutes. Runs south on Clark to Van Buren, east on Van Buren to Wabash Av. Time, 10 minutes. Last day car leaves Clark and Washington at 10:24 P. M. *Drab car, with dark drab dash. Orange light.*

(No. 46)—HALSTED ST. HORSE LINE (SOUTH SIDE).—From O'Neil south on Halsted to Thirty-ninth. Time, 23 minutes. Car leaves every 3 to 6 minutes. Last car leaves O'Neil at 12:21 A. M.; leaves Thirty-ninth at 12 midnight. *Yellow car, with dark yellow dash. Ruby light.*

(No. 47)—FORTY-THIRD ST. HORSE LINE (SOUTH SIDE).—From the Illinois Central tracks to Stock Yards. Car leaves every 5 to 10 minutes. Runs west on Forty-third to State, north on State to Root, west on Root to Stock Yards. Time, 39 minutes. Last car leaves Illinois Central tracks at 11:40 P. M.; leaves Stock Yards at 11:09 P. M. *Blue car.*

(No. 48)—FORTY-SEVENTH ST. HORSE LINE (SOUTH SIDE).—From Cottage Grove Av. west on Forty-seventh St. to Ashland Av. Time, 40 minutes. Car leaves every 10 minutes. Last car leaves State at 11:46 P. M.; leaves Ashland Av. at 12:07 A. M. *Red car. Red light.*

(No. 49) — FIFTY-FIRST ST. HORSE LINE (SOUTH SIDE).—From State east on Fifty-first to Washington Park. Time, 8 minutes. Last car leaves State at 7:28 P. M.; leaves Washington Park at 7:23 P. M.

(No. 50)—HALSTED ST., TOWN OF LAKE, HORSE LINE (SOUTH SIDE).—From Fortieth south on Halsted to Sixty-ninth. Time, 40 minutes. Car leaves every 7 to 10 minutes. Last car leaves Fortieth at 12:01 A. M.; leaves Sixty-ninth at 11:27 P. M. *Yellow car, with dark yellow dash. Ruby light.*

(No. 51)—HYDE PARK CABLE LINE (SOUTH SIDE).—From Wabash Av. and Madison to Fifty-fifth St. and Lake Av. (Jackson Park). Car leaves every 1 to 2½ minutes. Route to Thirty-ninth same as line (No. 66); thence south on Cottage Grove Av. to Fifty-fifth, east on Fifty-fifth to Lake Av. Time, 53 minutes. Last car leaves Wabash Av. and Madison at 11:34 P. M.; leaves Fifty-fifth St. and Lake Av. at 11:29 P. M. *Car has dark blue dash. Blue light; white lantern in grip car.*

(No. 52)—INDIANA AV. CABLE AND HORSE LINE (SOUTH SIDE). — From Wabash Av. and Madison to Thirty-ninth St. and Indiana Av. Car leaves every 3 to 5 minutes. Route to Eighteenth by cable, same as line (No. 66); thence east on Eighteenth by horse power to Indiana Av., south on Indiana Av. to Thirty - ninth. Time, 39 minutes. *Return* by same route to Madison; thence same as line (No. 66). Last car leaves Wabash Av. and Madison at 12:16 A.M.; leaves Thirty-ninth St. and Indiana Av. at 11:36 P. M. *Green car, with dark green dash. Green light.*

(No. 53)—OAKWOODS CABLE LINE (SOUTH SIDE).—From Wabash Av. and Madison to Seventy-first (Oakwoods Cemetery). Car leaves every 1 to 2½ minutes. Route to Thirty-ninth same as line (No. 66); thence south on Cottage Grove Av. to Seventy-first. Time, 55 minutes. *Return,* north on Cottage Grove Av. to Thirty-ninth; thence same as line (No. 66). Last car leaves Wabash Av. and Madison at 11:25 P. M.; leaves Seventy-first at 11:20 P. M. *Sign on car, "To 71st."* *Red lantern in grip car.*

(No. 54)—SIXTY-FIRST AND SIXTY-THIRD STS. HORSE LINE (SOUTH SIDE).—From State and Sixty-first to Sixty-third and the Illinois Central tracks. Car leaves every 12 minutes. Runs east on Sixty-first St. to Cottage Grove Av., south on Cottage Grove Av. to Sixty-third, east on Sixty-third to Illinois Central tracks. Time, 22 minutes. Last car leaves State and Sixty-first at 11 P. M.; leaves Illinois Central tracks at 11:20 P. M. *Yellow car. Green light.*

(No. 55) — SIXTY-NINTH ST. HORSE LINE (SOUTH SIDE).—From State and Sixty-fourth to Sixty-ninth and Cooper. Car leaves every 9 to 18 minutes. Runs south on State to Sixty-ninth, west on Sixty-ninth to Cooper. Time, 37 minutes. Last car leaves State and Sixty-fourth at 11:18 P. M.; leaves Ashland Av., going east to depot, at 11:44 P. M.

ELEVATED RAILWAY.

(No. 56)—SOUTH CHICAGO AV. HORSE LINE (SOUTH SIDE).—From Cottage Grove Av. and Seventy-first southeast on South Chicago Av. to Grand Crossing. Time, 7 minutes. Last car leaves Cottage Grove Av. and Seventy-first at 11:32 P. M.; leaves Grand Crossing at 11:40 P. M.

(No. 57)—SOUTH PARK HORSE LINE (SOUTH SIDE).—From Indiana Av. and Thirty-ninth St. to Washington Park. Car leaves every 17 minutes. Runs south on Indiana Av. to Fifty-first, east on Fifty-first to Washington Park. Time, 21 minutes. Last car leaves Indiana Av. and Thirty-ninth at 7:06 P. M.; leaves Washington Park at 7:33 P. M. *Green car, with dark green dash. Green light.*

(No. 58)—STATE AND THIRTY-NINTH STS. CABLE LINE (SOUTH SIDE).—From State and Madison to Thirty-ninth and State. Car leaves every 1 to 2½ minutes. Runs south on State to Thirty-ninth. Time, 30 minutes. *Return,* north on State to Madison, east on Madison to Wabash Av., north on Wabash Av. to Lake, west on Lake to State, south on State to Madison. Last car leaves Madison at 12:26 A. M.; leaves Thirty-ninth at 11:54 P. M. *Light red car, with dark red dash. Ruby light; white lantern on grip car.*

(No. 59)—STATE AND SIXTY-THIRD STS. CABLE LINE—ENGLEWOOD—(SOUTH SIDE).—From State and Lake to Sixty-third and State. Car leaves every 1 to 2½ minutes. Runs south on State to Sixty-third. Time, 46 minutes. *Return,* north on State to Madison, east on Madison to Wabash Av., north on Wabash Av. to Lake, west on Lake to State. Last car leaves Madison, going south, at 12:10 A. M.; leaves Sixty-third at 11:38 P. M. *Light red car, with dark red dash. Ruby light; green lantern on grip car. Sign on car, "To 63rd."*

(No. 60)—THIRTY-FIRST ST. AND BRIGHTON PARK HORSE LINE (SOUTH SIDE).—From the lake west on Thirty-first to the river. Time, 38 minutes. Car leaves every 9 to 12 minutes. Last car leaves the lake at 11:44 P. M.; leaves the river at 11:12 P. M. *Red car, with dark red dash. Green light.*

(No. 61)—THIRTY-FIFTH ST. AND STANTON AV. HORSE LINE (SOUTH SIDE). — From Cottage Grove Av. and Thirty-fifth to Stanton Av. and Thirty-ninth. Car leaves every 9 minutes. Runs west on Thirty-fifth St. to Stanton Av., south on Stanton Av. to Thirty-ninth. Time, 6 minutes. Last car leaves Cottage Grove Av. and Thirty-fifth at 7:26 P. M.; leaves Stanton Av. and Thirty-ninth at 7:34 P. M. *Green car. Green light.*

(No. 62)—THIRTY-FIFTH AND ULLMAN STS. HORSE LINE (SOUTH SIDE).—From State and Thirty-fifth to Ullman and Thirty-first. Car leaves every 12 minutes. Runs west on Thirty-fifth to Ullman, north on Ullman to Thirty-first. Time, 25 minutes. Last car leaves State and Thirty-fifth at 11:21 P. M.; leaves Ullman and Thirty-first at 11 P. M.

(No. 63) — THIRTY-NINTH ST. AND STOCK YARDS HORSE LINE (SOUTH SIDE).—From Cottage Grove Av. and Thirty-ninth to Stock Yards. Car leaves every 6 to 8 minutes. Runs west on Thirty-ninth St. to Wentworth Av., south on Wentworth Av. to Root, west on Root to Stock Yards. Time, 30 minutes. Last car leaves Cottage

Grove Av. and Thirty-ninth at 12 midnight; last through car leaves Stock Yards at 11:31 P. M. *Blue car, with dark blue dash. Blue light.*

(NO. 64)—TWENTY-SECOND ST. HORSE LINE (SOUTH SIDE).—From Cottage Grove Av. west on Twenty-second to the river. Time, 12 minutes. Car leaves every 24 minutes. Last car leaves the river at 7:12 P. M.; leaves Cottage Grove Av. at 7 P. M.

(NO. 65)—TWENTY-SIXTH ST. HORSE LINE (SOUTH SIDE).—From Cottage Grove Av. west on Twenty-sixth to Halsted. Time, 18 minutes. Car leaves every 8 to 14 minutes. Last car leaves Cottage Grove Av. at 11:23 P. M.; leaves Halsted at 11:06 P. M.

(NO. 66)—WABASH AND COTTAGE GROVE AVS. CABLE LINE (SOUTH SIDE).—From Wabash Av. and Madison to Thirty-ninth St. and Cottage Grove Av. Car leaves every 1 to 2¼ minutes. Runs south on Wabash Av. to Twenty-second, east on Twenty-second to Cottage Grove Av., southeast on Cottage Grove Av. to Thirty-ninth. Time, 33 minutes. *Return* by same route to Madison; thence east on Madison to Michigan Av., north on Michigan Av. to Randolph, west on Randolph to Wabash Av., south on Wabash Av. to Madison. Last car leaves Wabash Av. and Madison at 12:23 A. M.; leaves Thirty-ninth St. and Cottage Grove Av. at 11:48 P. M. *Blue car, with dark blue dash. Blue light.*

(NO. 67)—WALLACE, HANOVER AND BUTLER STS. CABLE AND HORSE LINE (SOUTH SIDE). —From State and Madison to Butler and Thirty-ninth. Car leaves every 10 minutes. Runs south on State, by cable, to Archer Av.; thence southwest on Archer Av., by horse power, to Hanover, south on Hanover to Thirtieth, west on Thirtieth to Butler, south on Butler to Thirty-ninth. Time, 40 minutes. *Return* by same route to State; thence same as line (No. 58). Last day car leaves State and Madison at 11:43 P. M.; leaves Butler and Thirty-ninth at 11 P. M. *Green car. Green light.*

(NO. 68) — WENTWORTH AV. AND THIRTY-NINTH ST. HORSE LINE (SOUTH SIDE).— From Washington and Clark to Wentworth Av. and Thirty-ninth. Car leaves every 6 minutes. Runs south on Clark St. to Archer Av., southwest on Archer Av. to Wentworth Av., south on Wentworth Av.

to Thirty-ninth. Time, 44 minutes. Last car leaves, Clark and Washington at 11:48 P. M.; leaves Wentworth Av. and Thirty-ninth at 11:04 P. M. *Amber-colored car. Orange light.*

(NO. 69)—WENTWORTH AV. AND SIXTY-THIRD ST. LINE (SOUTH SIDE).—From State and Thirty-ninth to Wentworth Av. and Sixty-third. Car leaves every 12 minutes. Runs west on Thirty-ninth St. to Wentworth Av., south on Wentworth Av. to Sixty-third. Time, 36 minutes. Last car south from Thirty-ninth at 11:24 P. M.; last car north from Sixty-third at 10:48 P. M. *Wine-colored car. Orange light.*

(NO. 70)—WENTWORTH AV. AND SEVENTY-NINTH ST. CABLE AND HORSE LINE—AUBURN PARK — (SOUTH SIDE). — From State and Madison to Seventy-ninth and Halsted. Car leaves every 8 to 12 minutes. Runs south on State to Sixty-third, west on Sixty-third to Wentworth Av., south on Wentworth Av. to Vincennes Rd. and Seventy-third, southwest on Vincennes Rd. to Seventy-ninth, west on Seventy-ninth to Halsted. Time, 75 minutes. Last car leaves State and Madison at 12:06 A. M. *Wine-colored car. Orange light.*

(NO. 71) — SOUTH SIDE ALLEY ELEVATED RAILROAD (SOUTH SIDE).—Trains leave the station at Congress St. and run south, in the alley between Wabash Av. and State, to Fortieth, thence east, on the south side of Fortieth, to the alley between Prairie and Calumet Avs., and south in this alley to Forty-third. The stations are located at Congress St., Hubbard Ct., Twelfth, Eighteenth, Twenty-second, Twenty-sixth, Twenty-ninth, Thirty-first, Thirty-third, Thirty-fifth, Thirty-ninth, Indiana Av. and Fortieth, and Forty-third St. Time required to go from Congress St. to Forty-third St., 17¼ minutes. Fare for the whole distance, or any shorter distance, 5 cents. It is expected that before the opening of the World's Fair, in 1893, the road will be extended southward, between Prairie and Calumet Avs., to Sixty-third St., and thence eastward, along the middle of Sixty-third St., to Jackson Park. Stations will be erected at the following streets: Forty-Seventh, Fifty-first, Fifty-fifth, Fifty-eighth, Sixty-first, Sixty-third St. and South Park Av., Cottage Grove Av., Lexington Av., Madison Av., Stony Island Av., Jackson Park. The fare for the entire distance will be 5 cents.

WEST SIDE STREET CAR LINES.

(NO. 72) — ASHLAND AV. AND SANGAMON ST. HORSE LINE (WEST SIDE).—From Michigan Av. and Adams St. to Clybourn Pl. Car leaves every 7 to 8 minutes. Runs west on Adams to Sangamon, north on Sangamon to Austin, west on Austin to Ann, north on Ann to Erie, west on Erie to Ashland Av., north on Ashland Av. to Clybourn Pl. Time, 55 minutes. Last car leaves Clybourn Pl. at 11:05 P. M.; leaves Michigan Av. and Adams at 12 midnight. *Green car, with blue and white platform. Blue and white light.*

(NO. 73) — BLUE ISLAND AV. HORSE LINE (WEST SIDE).—From State and Washington Sts. to Blue Island and Western Avs. Car leaves every 2½ to 5 minutes. Runs south on State to Madison, west on Madison to Clinton, south on Clinton to Adams, west on Adams to Halsted, south on Halsted to Blue Island Av., southwest on Blue Island Av. to Western Av. Time, 40 minutes. Last car leaves Western Av. at 11:15 P. M.; leaves State and Washington at 12:06 A.M. *Car has blue dash. Green light.*

(NO. 74) — CANALPORT AV. HORSE LINE (WEST SIDE).—From State and Randolph to Halsted and O'Neil. Car leaves every 6 minutes. Runs west on Randolph to Clinton, south on Clinton to Harrison, east on Harrison to Canal, south on Canal to Canalport Av., southwest on Canalport Av. to Halsted, south on Halsted to O'Neil. Time. 40 minutes. Last car leaves O'Neil at 11:16 P. M.; leaves State and Randolph at 12 midnight. *Yellow car, with green dash. White light.*

(NO. 75) — CENTRE AV. AND ADAMS ST. LINE (WEST SIDE).—From Michigan Av. and Adams to Twenty-first St. and Western Av. Car leaves every 8 minutes. Runs west on Adams St. to Centre Av., south on Centre Av. to Twenty-first, west on Twenty-first to Western Av. Time, 50 minutes. Last car leaves Western Av. at 11:08 P. M.; leaves Michigan Av. and Adams at 12 midnight. *White sign. White light.*

(No. 76)—CHICAGO AV. HORSE LINE (WEST SIDE).—From State and Randolph to West Chicago Av. and Leavitt. Car leaves every 4 to 8 minutes. Runs west on Randolph to Clinton, north on Clinton to Milwaukee Av., northwest on Milwaukee Av. to West Chicago Av., west on Chicago Av. to Leavitt. Time, 36 minutes. Last car leaves Chicago Av. and Leavitt at 10:16 P. M.; leaves State and Randolph at 10:56 P. M. *Yellow car, with red letter-board and dash. Yellow light.*

(No. 77)—CHICAGO AV. AND HUMBOLDT PARK HORSE LINE (WEST SIDE).—From State and Randolph to California Av. and Division. Car leaves every 8 minutes. Runs east to Chicago Av. and Leavitt by same route as line (No. 76), west on Chicago Av. to California Av., north on California Av. to Division. Time, 50 minutes. Last car leaves California Av. and Division at 11:15 P. M.; leaves State and Randolph at 12:08 A. M. *Yellow car, with red letter-board and dash. Yellow light.*

(No. 78) — CLINTON AND JEFFERSON STS. HORSE LINE (WEST SIDE).—From State and Randolph to Jefferson and Meagher. Car leaves every 70 minutes. Runs west on Randolph to Clinton, south on Clinton to Twelfth, west on Twelfth to Jefferson, south on Jefferson to Meagher. Time, 33 minutes. Last car leaves State and Randolph at 6:09 P. M. *Brown car. Orange light.*

(No. 79)—DIVISION ST. CABLE AND HORSE LINE (WEST SIDE). — From La Salle and Madison to West Division St. and California Av. Car leaves every 6 to 7 minutes. Runs to West Division by same route as line (No. 89), then west on Division, by horse power, to California Av. Time, 42 minutes. Last car leaves Division St. and California Av. at 11:20 P. M.; leaves La Salle and Madison at 12 midnight.

CHICAGO STREET CAR,
PROPELLED BY ELECTRICITY.

(No. 80)—EIGHTEENTH ST. HORSE LINE (WEST SIDE).—From State and Randolph to Leavitt St. and Blue Island Av. Car leaves every 7¼ minutes. Runs west on Randolph to Halsted, south on Halsted to Eighteenth, west on Eighteenth to Leavitt, south on Leavitt to Blue Island Av. Time, 58 minutes. Last car leaves Blue Island Av. at 11:04 P. M.; leaves State and Randolph at 12:02 A. M. *Car has red and white dash, divided vertically. Green and white light, divided vertically.*

(No. 81)—HARRISON AND ADAMS STS. LINE (WEST SIDE).—From Michigan Av. and Washington to Harrison St. and Western Av. Car leaves every 4 to 8 minutes. Runs south on Michigan Av. to Adams, west on Adams to Centre Av., south on Centre Av. to Harrison, west on Harrison to Western Av. Time, 40 minutes. Last car leaves Western Av. at 11:18 P. M.; leaves Michigan Av. and Washington at 12 midnight. *Red sign. Red light.*

(No. 82)—HARRISON AND WASHINGTON STS. HORSE LINE (WEST SIDE).—From Michigan Av. and Washington to Harrison St. and Western Av. Car leaves every 4 to 8 minutes. Runs west on Washington to Franklin, south on Franklin to Adams, west on Adams to Centre Av., south on Centre Av. to Harrison, west on Harrison to Western Av. Time, 40 minutes. Last car leaves Western Av. at 11:10 P. M.; leaves State and Washington at 11:52 P. M. *Green sign. Green light.*

(No. 83)—INDIANA ST. HORSE LINE (WEST SIDE). — From State and Washington to West Indiana St. and Western Av. Car leaves every 3 to 6 minutes. Runs west on Washington St. to Fifth Av., north on Fifth Av. to Randolph, west on Randolph to Halsted, north on Halsted to Indiana, west on Indiana to Western Av. Time, 38 minutes. Last car leaves Western Av. at 11:21 P. M.; leaves State and Washington at 12:01 A. M. *Green car. Violet light.*

(No. 84)—LAKE STREET HORSE LINE (WEST SIDE).—From State and Randolph to West Lake and West Fortieth. Car leaves every 4 to 8 minutes. Runs north on State to Lake, west on Lake to West Fortieth. Time, 50 minutes. Last car leaves West Fortieth at 11:18 P. M.; leaves State and Lake at 12:10 A. M. *Yellow car. Yellow light.*

(No. 85)—MADISON ST. CABLE LINE (WEST SIDE).—From La Salle and Madison to Madison and West Fortieth. Car leaves every 1¼ to 3 minutes. Runs north on La Salle to Randolph, west on Randolph to Fifth Av., south on Fifth Av. to Washington, west on Washington (through tunnel) to Jefferson, south on Jefferson to Madison, west on Madison to West Fortieth. Time, 35 minutes. Last car leaves West Fortieth at 1¼ midnight; leaves Madison and La Salle at 12:35 A. M. *Yellow car. Red light.*

(No. 86)—MADISON ST. HORSE LINE (WEST SIDE)—Night Cars.—From State and Washington to Madison and West Fortieth. Car leaves every 20 minutes. Runs south on State to Madison, west on Madison to West Fortieth. Time, 55 minutes. First night car leaves State and Washington at 12:30 A. M. *Yellow car, red light.*

(No. 87) — NOBLE ST. CABLE AND HORSE LINE (WEST SIDE). — From La Salle and Madison to Clybourn Pl. and Wood. Car leaves every 14 minutes. Runs to Noble by same route as line (No. 89), then north on Noble, by horse power, to Blackhawk, west on Blackhawk to Holt, north on Holt to North Av., west on North Av. to Ashland Av., north on Ashland Av. to Clybourn Pl., west on Clybourn Pl. to Wood. Time, 40 minutes. Last car leaves Clybourn Pl. and Wood at 10:18 P. M.; leaves La Salle and Madison at 11 P. M. *Brown car. Red light.*

(No. 88)—OGDEN AV. CABLE AND HORSE LINE (WEST SIDE).—From La Salle and Madison to Ogden and Millard Avs. Car leaves every 2 to 4 minutes. Runs to Ogden Av. by same route as line (No. 85), then southwest on Ogden Av. to Millard Av. Time, 52 minutes. Last car leaves Western Av. at 11:36 P. M.; leaves La Salle and Madison at 12:38 A. M. *Yellow car. Yellow light.*

(No. 89) — MILWAUKEE AV. CABLE LINE (WEST SIDE).—From La Salle and Madison Sts. to Milwaukee and Armitage Avs. Car leaves every 3 minutes. Runs north on La Salle to Randolph, west on Randolph to Fifth Av., south on Fifth Av. to Washington, west on Washington (through tunnel) to Desplaines, north on Desplaines to Milwaukee Av., northwest on Milwaukee Av. to Armitage Av. Time, 40 minutes. Last car leaves Armitage Av. at 12 midnight; leaves La Salle and Madison at 12:35 A. M. *Yellow car, with blue dash. Green light.*

(No. 90) — MILWAUKEE AND NORTH AVS. CABLE AND HORSE LINE (WEST SIDE).— From La Salle and Madison Sts. to North and California Avs. Car leaves every 3 minutes. Runs to North Av. by same route as line (No. 89), then west on North Av., by horse power, to California Av. Time, 43 minutes. Last car leaves California Av. at 11:18 P. M.; leaves La Salle and Madison at 12 midnight. *Yellow car, with blue dash. Green light.*

(No. 91)—MILWAUKEE AV. NIGHT LINE (WEST SIDE).—From State and Randolph to Milwaukee and Armitage Av. Car leaves once an hour. Runs north on State to Lake, west on Lake to Milwaukee Av., northwest on Milwaukee Av. to Armitage Av. Time, 45 minutes. First night car leaves State and Randolph at 12:45 A. M. *Yellow car, with blue dash. Green light.*

(No. 92)—RANDOLPH ST. HORSE LINE (WEST SIDE).—From State and Randolph to Western Av. and Lake. Car leaves every 3 to 6 minutes. Runs west on Randolph to Bryan Pl. (Union Park), northwest on Bryan Pl. to Lake, west on Lake to Western Av. Time, 32 minutes. Last car leaves Western Av. at 11:24 P. M., leaves State and Randolph at 11:57 P. M. *Yellow car. Red light.*

(No. 93)—SOUTH HALSTED ST. HORSE LINE (WEST SIDE).—From State and Randolph to Halsted and O'Neil. Car leaves every 3 to 6 minutes. Runs west on Randolph to Halsted, south on Halsted to O'Neil. Time, 41 minutes. Last car leaves O'Neil at 11:14 P. M.; leaves State and Randolph at 11:57 P. M. *Yellow car, with red dash. Red light, with white star in center.*

(No. 94)—TAYLOR ST. LINE (WEST SIDE).— From Michigan Av. and Washington to Taylor St. and Western Av. Car leaves every 8 minutes. Runs south on Michigan Av. to Adams, west on Adams to Fifth Av., south on Fifth Av. to Harrison, west on Harrison to Canal, south on Canal to Taylor, west on Taylor to Western Av. Time, 40 minutes. Last car leaves Western Av. at 11:08 P. M.; leaves Michigan Av. and Washington at 11:52 P. M. *Yellow car, with blue and red platform. Blue and red light.*

(No. 95)—TWELFTH ST. HORSE LINE, No. 1 (WEST SIDE).—From State and Randolph to Lawndale. Car leaves every 6 minutes. Runs south on State to Madison, west on Madison to Fifth Av., south on Fifth Av. to Twelfth, west on Twelfth to Ogden Av.; transfer to Ogden Av. for Lawndale. Time, 56 minutes. Last car leaves Ogden Av. at 11:16 P. M.; leaves State and Randolph at 12:05 A. M. *Yellow car, with red dash. Green light.*

(No. 96)—TWELFTH ST. HORSE LINE, No. 2 (WEST SIDE).—From State and Van Buren to Twelfth St. and Kedzie Av. Car leaves every 6 minutes. Runs west on Van Buren to Jefferson, south on Jefferson to Twelfth, west on Twelfth to Kedzie Av. Time, 50 minutes. Last car leaves Kedzie Av. at 11:11 P. M.; leaves State and Van Buren at 12:01 A. M. *Yellow car, with red dash. Green light.*

(No. 97)—VAN BUREN ST. HORSE LINE, No. 1 (WEST SIDE).—From State and Randolph to Western Av. and Van Buren. Car leaves every 2½ to 5 minutes. Runs west on Randolph St. to Fifth Av., south on Fifth Av. to Van Buren, west on Van Buren to Western Av. Time, 39 minutes. Last car leaves Western Av. at 11:02 P. M.; leaves State and Randolph at 11:50 P. M. *Yellow car. Pink light.*

(No. 98)—VAN BUREN ST. HORSE LINE, No. 2 (WEST SIDE).—From State west on Van Buren to Kedzie Av. Time, 41 minutes. Car leaves every 2½ to 5 minutes. Last car leaves Kedzie Av. at 11.10 P. M.; leaves State and Van Buren at 11:51 P. M. *Yellow car. Pink light.*

(No. 99) — CICERO & PROVISO ELECTRIC STREET RAILWAY (WEST SIDE). — From West Fortieth St. or Crawford Av. west on West Madison to Forest Home Cemetery. Fare, 5 cents. Cars every 15 or 20 minutes, until 12 midnight.

(No. 100)—CALUMET ELECTRIC ROAD (SOUTH SIDE).—From the South Chicago Rolling Mills, on the lake shore, south on Eighty-ninth St. to Mackinaw Av., south on Mackinaw Av. to Harbor Av., southwest on Harbor Av. to Ninety-third, west on Ninety-third to Stony Island Av., south on Stony Island Av. to Ninety-fifth. Fare, 5 cents.

Including All Steam and Elevated Roads and All Street Car Lines of Whatever Kind.

Explanation.—To know how to reach any portion of the city by street car line, first find, on the map, the street where you wish to go, which is done by the aid of the Street Index. Then find by this "Index No. 2" the car lines that run nearest to that street. For full description of the lines, which are designated by (No. 18), (No. 22), etc., see "Index No. 1 to All Railway Lines," page 128.

With the introduction of elevated railways and motor lines, the time required to go from any section to the business center will be greatly lessened. On the average, horse cars now consume 13 minutes in going a mile; cable cars, 7 minutes; steam railways, 4 minutes, and elevated roads, 4 minutes. All sections in these Guide Maps being one mile square, a close estimate may thus be made of

the time required to go anywhere in the city by the various lines of transportation.

"Division 1," "Division 2," etc., which make separate head-lines through this Index, refer to the Map Divisions on pages 115, 116 and following pages, the sections herein mentioned corresponding with the 18 sections in each Division shown by map.

EXAMPLE.—To understand this Index, observe the following: On this page, just below "Division 2," are the words, "Section 1.—(No. 11), Forest Glen Station, near Elston Av., in Div. 1, Sec. 6." The full meaning is as follows: Into Section 1 line (No. 11), which we learn, by Street Car Index No. 1, to be the Chicago, Milwaukee & St. Paul Railroad, the nearest station for this Section being at Elston Avenue, in Division 1, Section 6.

Railway Lines in—DIVISION 1—See Map on Page 115.

This Index gives all street car lines and most convenient railroad stations in each Section. Each Division contains 18 Sections, each one mile square. See "Explanation" on this page. ABBREVIATIONS: Div., Division; Sec., Section; cor., corner. Other abbreviations found on page 80.

SECTION 1.—(No. 7), Norwood Park Station, at Central Av.

SEC. 2.—(No. 7), Norwood Park Station, at Central Av., in Sec. 1; Jefferson Park Station, at Milwaukee Av., in Sec. 6. (No. 11), Forest Glen Station, near Elston Av., in Sec. 6.

SEC. 3.—(No. 11), Forest Glen Station, near Elston Av., in Sec. 6.

SEC. 4.—(No. 7), Norwood Park Station. at Central Av., in Sec. 1; Jefferson Park Station, at Milwaukee Av., in Sec. 6.

SEC. 5.—(No. 7), Jefferson Park Station, at Milwaukee Av., in Sec. 6.

SEC. 6.—(No. 7), Jefferson Park Station. at Milwaukee Av. (No. 11), Forest Glen Station, near Elston Av.

SEC. 7.—(No. 9), Dunning Station, at Irving Park Boul. (City Limits).

SEC. 8.—(No. 7), Jefferson Park Station, at Milwaukee Av., in Sec. 6. (No. 9), Dunning Station, at Irving Park Boul. (City Limits), in Sec. 7.

SEC. 9.—(No. 7), Montrose Station, at Montrose Boul., in Div. 2, Sec. 7. (No. 11), Montrose Station, at Washington St.

SEC. 10.—(No. 9), Dunning Station, at Irving Park Boul. (City Limits).

SEC. 11.—(No. 9), Dunning Station, at Irving Park Boul (City Limits), in Sec. 10.

SEC. 12.—(No. 11), Grayland Station, at Milwaukee Av., in Div. 2, Sec. 12.

SEC. 13.—(No. 9), Mont Clair Station, near Fullerton Av., in Sec. 16; Galewood Station, near West Sixty-fourth St., in Sec. 16.

SEC. 14.—(No. 9), Galewood Station, near West Sixty-fourth St., in Sec. 17.

SEC. 15.—(No. 9), Cragin Station, near Grand Av., in Sec. 18. (No. 11), Pennock Station, at Pennock Boul., in Div. 2, Sec. 13.

SEC. 16.—(No. 9), Mont Clair Station, near Fullerton Av.; Galewood Station, near West Forty-sixth St.

SEC. 17.—(No. 9), Galewood Station, near West Sixty-fourth St.; Cragin Station, near Grand Av., in Sec. 18.

SEC. 18.—(No. 9), Cragin Station, near Grand Av.

Railway Lines in—DIVISION 2—See Map on Page 116.

This Index gives all street car lines and most convenient railroad stations in each Section. Each Division contains 18 Sections, each one mile square. See "Explanation" on this page. ABBREVIATIONS: Div., Division; Sec., Section; cor., corner. Other abbreviations found on page 80.

SECTION 1.—(No. 11), Forest Glen Station, near Elston Av., in Div. 1, Sec. 6.

SEC. 2.—(No. 11), Forest Glen Station, near Elston Av., in Div. 1, Sec. 6.

SEC. 3.—(No. 6), High Ridge Station, near Grand Av., in Div. 3, Sec. 1; Rose Hill Station, at east end of Rose Hill Cemetery, in Div. 3, Sec. 1.

SEC. 4.—(No. 7), Montrose Station. at Montrose Boul., in Sec. 7. (No. 11), Forest Glen Station, near Elston Av., in Div. 1, Sec. 6; Montrose Station, at Washington St., in Div. 1, Sec. 9.

SEC. 5.—(No. 6), Summerdale Station, at North Fifty-ninth St., in Div. 3, Sec. 4; Ravenswood Station, between Wilson and Sunnyside Avs., in Div. 3, Sec. 7. (No. 7), Montrose Station, at Montrose Boul., in Sec. 7. (No. 11), Forest Glen Station, near Elston Av., in Div. 1, Sec. 6; Mon-

trose Station, at Washington St., in Div. 1, Sec. 9.

SEC. 6.—(No. 6), Summerdale Station, at North Fifty-ninth St., in Div. 3, Sec. 4; Ravenswood Station, between Wilson and Sunnyside Avs., in Div. 3, Sec. 7.

SEC. 7.—(No. 7), Montrose Station, at Montrose Boul.; Hunting Av. Station; Irving Park Station, near Irving Park Boul. (No. 11), Montrose Station, at Washington St.; Grayland Station, at Milwaukee Av., in Sec. 10.

SEC. 8.—(No. 7), Montrose Station, at Montrose Boul., in Sec. 7; Hunting Av. Station, in Sec. 7; Irving Park Station, near Irving Park Boul., in Sec. 7; Avondale Station, at Belmont and Kedzie Avs., in Sec. 11.

SEC. 9.—(No. 6), Ravenswood Station, between Wilson and Sunnyside Avs., in Div. 3, Sec. 7; Cuyler Station, at Graceland Av., in Div. 3, Sec. 7. (No. 7), Irving

Railways in—DIVISION 2—Continued.

Park Station, near Irving Park Boul., in Sec. 7; Avondale Station, at Belmont and Kedzie Avs., in Sec. 11.

SEC. 10.—(No. 7), Irving Park Station, near Irving Park Boul. (No. 11), Grayland Station, at Milwaukee Av.

SEC. 11.—(No. 7), Irving Park Station, near Irving Park Boul., in Sec. 10; Avondale Station, at Belmont and Kedzie Avs.

SEC. 12.—(No. 7), Avondale Station, at Belmont and Kedzie Avs. (No. 25), at cor. of Belmont and Western Avs.; connects with (No. 24). (No. 39), at cor. of Roscoe Boul. and Western Av.; connects with (No. 30), and (No. 35) or (No. 36).

SEC. 13.—(No. 11), Pennock Station, at Pennock Boul.

SEC. 14.—(No. 7), Avondale Station, at Belmont and Kedzie Avs.; Maplewood Station, at Humboldt Boul., in Sec. 15. (No. 11), Pennock Station, at Pennock Boul., in Sec. 13.

SEC. 15.—(No. 7), Avondale Station, at cor. of Belmont and Kedzie Avs.; Maplewood Station, at Humboldt Boul.

SEC. 16.—(No. 9), Hermosa Station, at West Forty-fourth St.

SEC. 17.—(No. 9), Pacific Junction, between Hamlin and Gutenberg Avs.; Elsmere Station, at Kimbell Av.

SEC. 18.—(No. 9), Humboldt Station, at Humboldt Boul. (No. 89), at cor. of Milwaukee and Armitage Avs. (No. 90), on North Av., fr. California Av. to Western Av.

Street Car Lines in—DIVISION 3—See Map on Page 117.

This Index gives all street car lines and most convenient railroad stations in each Section. Each Division contains 18 Sections, each one mile square. See "Explanation" on page 136. ABBREVIATIONS: Div., Division; Sec., Section· cor., corner. Other abbreviations found on page 80.

SECTION 1.—(No. 6), High Ridge Station, near Grand Av.; Rose Hill Station, at east side of Rose Hill Cemetery. (No. 33), on Clark St., fr. City Limits to Bryn Mawr Av.; connects with (No. 22), and (No. 20) or (No. 21).

NORTH SIDE CABLE GRIP CAR.

(No. 20) or (No. 21). (No. 32), on Halsted St., fr. Evanston Av. to Belmont Av. (No. 41), at cor. of Belmont and Sheffield Avs.; connects with (No. 35) or (No. 36).

SEC. 2.—(No. 10), Edgewater Station, at Bryn Mawr Av. (No. 33), on Clark St., fr. City Limits to Bryn Mawr Av.; connects with (No. 22), and (No. 20) or (No. 21).

SEC. 4.—(No. 6), Summerdale Station, at North Fifty-ninth St.

SEC. 5.—(No. 10), Edgewater Station, at Bryn Mawr Av.; Argyle Park Station, at Argyle St. (No. 33), on Clark St., fr. Bryn Mawr Av. to Lawrence Av.; connects with (No. 22), and (No. 20) or (No. 21).

SEC. 7.—(No. 6), Ravenswood Station, between Wilson and Sunnyside Avs.; Cuyler Station, at Graceland Av.

SEC. 8.—(No. 10), Buena Park Station, at Buena Av. (No. 22), on Clark St., fr. Lawrence Av. to Graceland Av.; connects with (No. 20) or (No. 29), on Graceland Av., fr. Alexander Av. to Evanston Av.; connects with (No. 20) or (No. 21).

SEC. 10.—(No. 6), Cuyler Station, at Graceland Av.; Gross Park Station, between School St. and Roscoe Boul. (No. 19), on Ashland Av., fr. Graceland Av. to Belmont Av.; connects with (No. 30), and (No. 35) or (No. 36). (No. 39), on Roscoe Boul. fr. Western Av. to Robey St., on Robey St. fr. Roscoe Boul. to Belmont Av., on Belmont Av. fr. Robey St. to Ashland Av.; connects with (No. 30), and (No. 35) or (No. 36).

SEC. 11.—(No. 10), Addison St. Station; Belmont Av. Station. (No. 19), on Ashland Av., fr. Graceland Av. to Belmont Av.; connects with (No. 30), and (No. 35) or (No. 36). (No. 22), on Clark St., fr. Graceland Av. to Belmont Av.; connects with (No. 20) or (No. 21). (No. 29), on Graceland Av. fr. Alexander Av. to Evanston Av., on Evanston Av. fr. Graceland Av. to Grace St.; connects with

SEC. 12.—(No. 29), on Evanston Av., fr. Graceland Av. to Belmont Av.; connects with (No. 20) or (No. 21). (No. 32), on Halsted St., fr. Evanston Av. to Belmont Av.

SEC. 13.—(No. 6), Deering Station, at Fullerton Av. (No. 25), on Clybourn Av., fr. Belmont Av. to Fullerton Av.; connects with (No. 24). (No. 39), on Belmont Av., fr. Robey St. to Ashland Av.; connects with (No. 30), and (No. 35) or (No. 36).

SEC. 14.—(No. 30), on Lincoln Av., fr. Belmont Av. to Wrightwood Av.; connects with (No. 35) or (No. 36). (No. 32), on Halsted St., fr. Belmont Av. to Fullerton Av. (No. 35), on Lincoln Av., fr. Wrightwood Av. to Fullerton Av. (No. 41), on Sheffield Av., fr. Belmont Av. to Wrightwood Av.; connects with (No. 35) or (No. 36).

SEC. 15.—(No. 20), on Clark St., fr. Diversey Av. to Fullerton Av. (No. 21), on Clark St., fr. Diversey Av. to Fullerton Av. (No. 22), on Clark St., fr. Halsted St. to Diversey Av.; connects with (No. 20) or (No. 21). (No. 29), on Evanston Av., fr. Belmont Av. to Diversey Av.; connects with (No. 20) or (No. 21). (No. 32), on Halsted St., fr. Belmont Av. to Fullerton Av.

SEC. 16.—(No. 6), Clybourn Junction, between Clybourn Pl. and Armitage Av. (No. 9), Milwaukee Av. Station. (No. 72), on Ashland Av., fr. Clybourn Pl. to North Av. (No. 87), on Clybourn Pl., fr. Wood St. to Ashland Av., on Ashland Av. fr. Clybourn Pl. to North Av. (No. 89), on Milwaukee Av., fr. Western Av. to North Av. (No. 90), on North Av., fr. Western Av. to Milwaukee Av.

SEC. 17.—(No. 6), Clybourn Junction, between Clybourn Pl. and Armitage Av. (No. 10), Fullerton Av. Station. (No. 23), on Racine Av. fr. Webster Av. to Fullerton Av., on Fullerton Av. fr.

Car Lines in—DIVISION 3—Continued.

Racine Av. to Lincoln Av. (No. 24), on Clybourn Av., fr. Fullerton Av. to North Av. (No.28), on Garfield Av., fr. Racine Av. to Halsted St. (No. 32), on Halsted St., fr. Fullerton Av. to North Av. (No. 72), on Ashland Av., fr. Clybourn Pl. to North Av. (No. 87), on Ashland Av., fr. Clybourn Pl. to North Av.

Sec. 18.—(No. 20), on Clark St., fr. Fullerton Av. to North Av. (No. 21), fr. Fullerton Av. to North Av., via Clark and Wells Sts. (No. 23), fr. Fullerton Av. to North

Av., via Lincoln Av., Centre and Clark Sts. (No. 28), fr. Halsted St. to North Av., via Garfield Av., Lincoln Av:, Centre and Clark Sts. (No. 32), on Halsted St., fr. Fullerton Av. to North Av. (No. 34), on Larrabee St., fr. Lincoln Av. to North Av. (No. 35), fr. Fullerton Av. to North Av., via Lincoln Av., Centre and Clark Sts. (No. 36), fr. Fullerton Av. to North Av., via Lincoln Av., Centre, Clark and Wells Sts. (No. 40), on Sedgwick, fr. Centre St. to North Av.

Street Car Lines in—DIVISION 4—See Map on Page 118.

This Index gives all street car lines and most convenient railroad stations in each Section. Each Division contains 18 Sections, each one mile square. See "Explanation" on page 136. ABBREVIATIONS: Div., Division; Sec., Section; cor., corner. Other abbreviations found on page 80.

SECTION 1.—(No. 5), Linden Park Station, near West Fifty-second St., in Sec. 4; Moreland Station, at West Forty-seventh St., in Sec. 5. (No. 9), Cragin Station, near Grand Av., in Div. 1, Sec. 18; Hermosa Station, at West Forty-fourth St., in Div. 2, Sec. 16.

HORSE CAR, NOW BEING LARGELY SUPERSEDED BY ELEVATED, ELECTRIC AND CABLE CARS.

SEC. 2.—(No. 5), Moreland Station, at West Forty-seventh St., in Sec. 5; West Fortieth St. Station, in Sec. 5. (No. 9). Hermosa Station, at West Forty-fourth St., in Div. 2, Sec. 16; Pacific Junction, between Hamlin and Gutenberg Avs., in Div. 2, Sec. 17.

SEC. 3.—(No. 5), West Fortieth St. Station, in Sec. 5; Central Park Station, at north side of Garfield Park, in Sec. 6; Sacramento Av. Station, in Div. 5, Sec. 4. (No. 9), Pacific Junction, between Hamlin and Gutenberg Avs., in Div. 2, Sec. 17; Elsmere Station, at Kimball Av., in Div. 2, Sec. 17.

SEC. 4.—(No. 4), Linden Park Station, at West Fifty-second St.; Moreland Station, at West Forty-eighth St. (No. 5), Austin Station, at West Fifty-sixth St.; Linden Park Station, near West Fifty-second St.; Moreland Station, at West Forty-seventh St., in Sec. 5. (No. 99), on West Madison St., fr. Central Av. or West Fifty-sixth St., to Hyman Av. or West Forty-eighth St.; connects with (No. 4) or (No. 85), for the business center.

SEC. 5.—(No. 4), Moreland Station, at West Forty-eighth St.; Marvin Station, at West Forty-fourth St.; Madison St. Station. (No. 5), Moreland Station, at West Forty-seventh St.; West Fortieth St. Station. (No. 84), at cor. of West Fortieth and Lake Sts. (No. 99), on West Madison St., fr. Hyman Av. or West Forty-eighth St., to Crawford Av. or West Fortieth St.; connects with (No. 4) or (No. 85), for the business center.

SEC. 6.—(No. 4), Madison St. Station. (No. 5), West Fortieth St. Station; Central Park Station, at north side of Garfield Park; Sacramento Av. Station, in Div. 5, Sec. 4. (No. 84), on Lake St., fr. West Fortieth St. to Kedzie Av. (No. 85), on Madison St., fr. West Fortieth St. to Kedzie Av.

SEC. 7.—(No. 4), Central Av. Station; West Forty-eighth St. Station. (No. 4, north track), Linden Park Station, at West Fifty-second St., in Sec. 4; Moreland Station, at

West Forty-eighth St., in Sec. 4. (No. 99), on West Madison St., fr. Central Av. or West Fifty-sixth St., to Hyman Av. or West Forty-eighth St.; connects with (No. 4) or (No. 85), for the business center.

SEC. 8.—(No. 4), West Forty-eighth St. Station; West Forty-fifth St. Station; Crawford Av. Station. (No. 4, north track), Moreland Station, at West Forty-eighth St., in Sec. 5; Marvin Station, at West Forty-fourth St., in Sec. 5; Madison St. Station, in Sec. 5; Colorado Av. Station, in Sec. 9. (No. 85), at cor. of West Fortieth and Madison Sts. (No. 99), on West Madison St., fr. Hyman Av. or West Forty-eighth St., to Crawford Av. or West Fortieth St.; connects with (No. 4) or (No. 85), for the business center.

SEC. 9.—(No. 4), Madison St. Station; Colorado Av. Station; West Fortieth St. Junction. (No. 85), on Madison St., fr. West Fortieth St. to Kedzie Av. (No. 95), on Twelfth St., fr. Millard Av. to Kedzie Av. (No. 96), at cor. of Twelfth St. and Kedzie Av. (No. 78), at cor. of Kedzie Av. and Van Buren St.

SEC. 10.—(No. 4), Central Av. Station, in Sec. 7; West Forty-eighth St. Station, in Sec. 7. (No. 4, south track), Donald Station or Central Av. Station; Grant Works Station, near Robinson Av.; Hyman Av. Station, in Sec. 11. (No. 8), Hawthorne Station, at Hyman Av., in Sec. 14.

SEC. 11.—(No. 4), Hyman Av. Station; West Forty-eighth St. Station, in Sec. 8; West Forty-fifth St. Station, in Sec. 8; Crawford Av. Station, in Sec. 8; West Fortieth St. Junction, in Sec. 9. (No. 8), Hawthorne Station, at Hyman Av., in Sec. 14; Crawford Station, at Butler Av., in Sec. 14; Millard Av. Station, in Sec. 15.

SEC. 12.—(No. 4), West Fortieth St. Junction, in Sec. 9; Douglas Park Station, at California Av., in Div. 5, Sec. 7. (No. 8), Millard Av. Station, in Sec. 15; Douglas Park Station, near Kedzie Av. Station, in Div. 5, Sec. 10. (No. 88), on Ogden Av., fr. Millard Av. to Kedzie Av. (No. 95), on Twelfth St., fr. Millard Av. to Kedzie Av. (No. 96), at cor. of Twelfth St. and Kedzie Av.

SEC. 13.—(No. 8), Hawthorne Station, at Hyman Av.

SEC. 14.—(No. 8), Hawthorne Station, at Hyman Av.; Crawford Station, at Butler Av.

Car Lines in—DIVISION 4—Continued.

Street Car Lines in—DIVISION 5—See Map on Page 119.

This Index gives all street car lines and most convenient railroad stations in each Section. Each Division contains 18 Sections, each one mile square. See "Explanation" on page 136. ABBREVIATIONS: Div., Division; Sec., Section; cor., corner. Other abbreviations found on page 80.

Car Lines in—DIVISION 5—Continued.

SEC. 12.—(No. 4), Ashland Av. Station; Blue Island Av. Station; Halsted St. Station. (No. 8), Blue Island Av. Station. (No. 73), on Blue Island Av., fr. Twenty-second St. to Twelfth St. (No. 74), on Halsted St., fr. Twenty-second St. to Canalport Av. (No. 75), fr. Ashland Av. to Twelfth St., via Twenty-first St. and Centre Av. (No. 80), fr. Ashland Av. to Twelfth St., via Eighteenth and Halsted Sts. (No. 93), on Halsted St., fr. Twenty-second St. to Twelfth St. (No. 95), on Twelfth St., fr. Ashland Av. to Halsted St. (No. 96), on Twelfth St., fr. Ashland Av. to Halsted St.

SEC. 13.—(No. 8), Douglas Park Station, near Kedzie Av., in Sec. 10; Western Av. Station, in Sec. 10. (No. 73), at cor. of Western and Blue Island Avs.

SEC. 14.—(No. 73), on Blue Island Av., fr. Western Av. to Ashland Av. (No. 80), on Leavitt St., fr. Blue Island Av. to Twenty-second St.

SEC. 15.—(No. 43), on Archer Av., fr. Ashland Av. to Halsted St. (No. 46), on Halsted St., fr. Thirty-first St. to O'Neil St.; connects with (No. 74) or (No. 93). (No. 60), on Thirty-first St., fr. the river to Halsted St.; connects with (No. 51), (No. 52), (No. 53), (No. 67) or (No. 68), in Div. 6, Secs. 13 and 14, for the business center. (No. 73), on Blue Island Av., at cor. of Ashland Av. and Twenty-second St. (No. 74), on Halsted St., fr. O'Neil St. to Twenty-second St. (No. 93), on Halsted St., fr. O'Neil St. to Twenty-second St.

SEC. 16.—(No. 1), Brighton Park Station, at Thirty-seventh and Hart Sts. (No. 16), Brighton Park Station at Thirty-seventh and Hart Sts. (No. 43), on Archer Av., fr. Thirty-ninth St. to Western Av.

SEC. 17.—(No. 1), Brighton Park Station, at Thirty-seventh and Hart Sts., in Sec. 16; (No. 16), Brighton Park station, at Thirty-seventh and Hart Sts., in Sec. 16. (No. 43), on Archer Av., fr. Western Av. to Ashland Av. (No. 44), on Ashland Av., fr. Thirty-ninth St. to Thirty-first St.; connects with (No. 43).

SEC. 18.—(No. 14), Union Stock Yards Station, in Div. 8, Sec. 3. (No. 43), on Archer Av., at cor. of Ashland Av. and Thirty-first St. (No. 44), on Ashland Av., fr. Thirty-ninth St. to Thirty-first St.; connects with (No. 43). (No. 46), on Halsted St., fr. Thirty-ninth St. to Thirty-first St.; connects with (No. 74) or (No. 93). (No. 60), on Thirty-first St., fr. the river to Halsted St.; connects with (No. 51), (No. 52), (No. 53), (No. 58), (No. 67) or (No. 68), in Div. 6, Secs. 16 and 17, for the business center. (No. 62), fr. Thirty-first St. to Halsted St., via Ullman and Thirty-fifth Sts.; connects with (No. 58), (No. 67) or (No. 68), in Div. 6, Sec. 16, for the business center.

Street Car Lines in—DIVISION 6—See Map on Page 120.

This Index gives all street car lines and most convenient railroad stations in each Section. Each Division contains 18 Sections, each one mile square. See "Explanation" on page 136. ABBREVIATIONS: Div., Division; Sec., Section; cor., corner. For other abbreviations see page 80.

SECTION 1.—This section is crossed by the following street car lines, which are fully described in Index No. 1: (No. 20), (No. 21), (No. 23), (No. 24), (No. 27), (No. 28), (No. 32), (No. 34), (No. 35), (No. 36), (No. 40) and (No. 42).

SEC. 2.—(No. 42), on State St., fr. Division St. to Chicago Av. To reach points in the northern part of Sec. 2, use (No. 20), (No. 28) or (No. 35), which run on Clark St., in Sec. 1.

SEC. 4.—This section is crossed by all street car lines that run to the business center. For full description of these lines see Index No. 1.

SEC. 5.—(No. 42), on State St., fr. Chicago Av. to Lake St.

SEC. 7.—This section is crossed by the following South Side street car lines: (No. 43), (No. 58), (No. 59), (No. 67), (No. 68) and (No. 70). It is crossed also by the following West Side lines: (No. 72), (No. 75), (No. 81), (No. 82), (No. 94), (No. 96) and (No. 98). For full description of these lines see Index No. 1.

SEC. 8.—(No. 13), Van Buren St. Station. (No. 43), (No. 58), (No. 59), (No. 67) and (No. 70), on State St., fr. Twelfth St. to Madison St. (No. 51), (No. 52), (No. 53) and (No. 66), on Wabash Av., fr. Twelfth St. to Madison St., on Madison St. fr. Wabash Av. to Michigan Av. (No. 71), in alley between Wabash Av. and State St., fr. Twelfth St. to Congress St.

SEC. 10.—This section is crossed by the following South Side street car lines: (No. 43), (No. 58), (No. 59), (No. 67),

(No. 68) and (No. 70). It is crossed also by the following West Side lines: (No. 74), (No. 78), (No. 80), (No. 93), (No. 95) and (No. 96). For full description of these lines see Index No. 1. (No. 4), Halsted St. Station. (No. 8), Chicago Station. (No. 12), Twenty-second St. Station. (No. 14), Twenty-second St. Station.

SEC. 11.—(No 13), Twenty-second St. Station; Sixteenth St. Station. (No. 43) and (No. 67), on State St., fr. Nineteenth St. to Twelfth St. (No. 51) and (No. 53), fr. Indiana Av. to Twelfth St., via Twenty-second St. and Wabash Av. (No. 52), fr. Twenty-second St. to Twelfth St., via Indiana Av., Eighteenth St. and Wabash Av. (No. 58), (No. 59) and (No. 70), on State St., fr. Twenty-second St. to Twelfth St. (No. 64), on Twenty-second St., fr. Indiana Av. to State St.; connects with the following lines for the business center: (No. 51), (No. 52), (No. 53), (No. 58), (No. 59), (No. 66) and (No. 70), in Sec. 11; (No. 43), (No. 67) and (No. 68), in Sec. 10. (No. 66), fr. Cottage Grove Av. to Twelfth St., via Twenty-second St. and Wabash Av. (No. 71), in alley between Wabash Av and State St., fr. Twenty-second St. to Twelfth St.

SEC. 13.—(No. 1), Twenty-third St. Station. (No. 12), Thirty-first St. Station; Twenty-second St. Station. (No. 14), Thirty-first St. Station; Twenty-sixth St. Station; Twenty-second St. Station. (No. 17), Archer Av. Station. (No. 18), Archer Av. Station. (No. 58) and (No. 59), on State St., fr. Thirty-first St. to Twenty-second St. (No. 60), on Thirty-first St., fr. Halsted St. to State St.; connects with (No. 51), (No. 52), (No. 53), (No. 58), (No. 67) and (No. 68),

Street Car Lines in—DIVISION 6—Continued.

in Secs. 13 and 14, for the business center. (No. 64), on Twenty-second St., fr. State St. to the river; connects with the following lines, for the business center: (No. 43), (No. 67) and (No. 68), in Sec. 13; (No. 51), (No. 52), (No. 53), (No. 58), (No. 59), (No. 66) and (No. 70), in Sec. 14. (No. 65), on Twenty-sixth St., fr. State St. to Halsted St.; connects with the following lines, for the business center: (No. 58), (No. 67) and (No. 68), in Sec. 13; (No. 51), (No. 52), (No. 53), (No. 59), (No. 66) and (No. 70), in Sec. 14. (No. 67), fr. Thirty-first St. to Twenty-second St., via Butler St., Thirtieth St., Hanover St. and Archer Av. (No. 68), on Wentworth Av., fr. Thirty-first St. to Twenty-second St.

SEC. 14.—(No. 13), Thirty-first St. Station; Twenty-seventh St. Station. (No. 51) and (No. 53), fr. Thirty-first St. to Wabash Av., via Cottage Grove Av. and Twenty-second St. (No. 52), on Indiana Av., fr. Thirty-first St. to Twenty-second St. (No. 58), (No. 59) and (No. 70), State St., fr. Thirty-first St. to Twenty-second St. (No. 60), on Thirty-first St., fr. State St. to the lake; connects with (No. 51), (No. 52), (No. 53), (No. 58), (No. 67) and (No. 68), in Secs. 13 and 14, for the business center. (No. 64), on Twenty-second St., fr. Cottage Grove Av. to State St.; connects with the following lines, for the business center: (No. 51), (No. 52), (No. 53), (No. 58), (No. 59), (No. 66) and (No. 70), in Sec. 14; (No. 43), (No. 67) and (No. 68), in Sec. 13. (No. 65), on Twenty-sixth St., fr. Cottage Grove Av. to State St.; connects with the following lines, for the business center: (No. 51), (No. 52), (No. 53), (No. 58), (No. 59), (No. 66) and (No. 70), in Sec. 14; (No. 67) and (No. 68), in Sec. 13. (No. 66), fr. Thirty-first St. to Wabash Av., via Cottage Grove Av. and Twenty-second St. (No. 71), in alley between Wabash Av. and State St., fr. Thirty-first St. to Twenty-second St.

SEC. 16.—(No. 2), Thirty-third St. Station. (No. 12), Thirty-ninth St. Station; Thirty-first St. Station. (No. 14), Thirty-ninth St. Station; Thirty-first St. Station.

(No. 58) and (No. 59), on State St., fr. Thirty-ninth St. to Thirty-first St. (No. 60), on Thirty-first St., fr. Halsted St. to State St.; connects with (No. 51), (No. 52), (No. 53), (No. 58), (No. 67) and (No. 68), in Secs. 16 and 17, for the business center. (No. 62), on Thirty-fifth St., fr. State St. to Halsted St.; connects with (No. 58), (No. 67) and (No. 68), for the business center. (No. 63), on Thirty-ninth St., fr. Wentworth Av. to State St.; connects with the following lines, for the business center: (No. 58) and (No. 68), in Sec. 16; (No. 51), (No. 52), (No. 53), (No. 58), (No. 59), and (No. 70), in Sec. 17. (No. 67), on Butler St., fr. Thirty-ninth St. to Thirty-first St. (No. 68), on Wentworth Av., fr. Thirty-ninth St. to Thirty-first St.

SEC. 17.—(No. 13), Oakland Station, at Thirty-ninth St., in Sec. 18; Douglas Station, at Thirty-fifth St.; Thirty-first St. Station. (No. 51) and (No. 53), on Cottage Grove Av., fr. Thirty-ninth St. to Thirty-first St. (No. 52), on Indiana Av., fr. Thirty-ninth St. to Thirty-first St. (No. 58), (No. 59) and (No. 70), on State St., fr. Thirty-ninth St. to Thirty-first St. (No. 60), on Thirty-first St., fr. State St. to the lake; connects with (No. 51), (No. 52), (No. 53), (No. 58), (No. 67) and (No. 68), in Secs. 16 and 17, for the business center. (No. 61), fr. Thirty-ninth St. to Cottage Grove Av., via Stanton Av. and Thirty-fifth St.; connects with (No. 51), (No. 53) and (No. 66). (No. 63), on Thirty-ninth St., fr. State St. to Cottage Grove Av.; connects with the following lines, for the business center: (No. 58) and (No. 68), in Sec. 16; (No. 51), (No. 52), (No. 53), (No. 58), (No. 59), (No. 66) and (No. 70), in Sec. 17. (No. 66), on Cottage Grove Av., fr. Thirty-ninth St. to Thirty-first St. (No. 71), in alley between Wabash Av. and State St., fr. Thirty-ninth St. to Thirty-first St.

SEC. 18.—(No. 13), Oakland Station, at Thirty-ninth St.; Douglas Station, at Thirty-fifth St. (No. 51) and (No. 53), at cor. of Cottage Grove Av. and Thirty-ninth St. (No. 66), at cor. of Cottage Grove Av. and Thirty-ninth St.

Street Car Lines in—DIVISION 7—See Map on Page 121.

This Index gives all street car lines and most convenient railroad stations in each Section. Each Division contains 18 Sections, each one mile square. See "Explanation" on page 136. ABBREVIATIONS: Div., Division; Sec., Section; cor., corner. Other abbreviations found on page 80.

SECTION 1.—(No. 3), Elsdon Station, at Fifty-first St., in Sec. 6. (No. 8), Hawthorne Station, at Hyman Av., in Div. 4, Sec. 14.

SEC. 2.—(No. 1), Brighton Park Station, at Thirty-seventh and Hart Sts., in Div. 5, Sec. 16. (No. 3), Elsdon Station, at Fifty-first St., in Sec. 6. (No. 8), Hawthorne Station, at Hyman Av., in Div. 4, Sec. 14; Crawford Station, at Butler Av., in Div. 4, Sec. 14. (No. 16), Brighton Park Station, at Thirty-seventh and Hart Sts., in Div. 5, Sec. 16.

SEC. 3.—(No. 1), Brighton Park Station, at Thirty-seventh and Hart Sts., in Div. 5, Sec. 16. (No. 3), Elsdon Station, at Fifty-first St., in Sec. 6; Morrell Park Station, at Kedzie Av., in Sec. 6. (No. 16), Brighton Park Station, at Thirty-seventh and Hart Sts., in Div. 5, Sec. 16.

SEC. 4.—(No. 3), Elsdon Station, at Fifty-first St., in Sec. 6.

SEC. 5.—(No. 3), Elsdon Station, at Fifty-first St. in Sec. 6.

SEC. 6.—(No. 3), Elsdon Station, at Fifty-first St.; Morrell Park Station, at Kedzie Av.

SEC. 7.—See Sec. 9.

SEC. 8.—See Sec. 9.

SEC. 9.—(No. 3), Chicago Lawn Station, at Sixty-third St.; Fifty-ninth St. Station; Fifty-fifth St. Station.

SEC. 10.—See Sec. 12.

SEC. 11.—See Sec. 12.

SEC. 12.—(No. 3), McCaffrey Station, at Seventy-first St.; Sixty-seventh St. Station; Chicago Lawn Station, at Sixty-third St.

SEC. 13.—See Sec. 15.

SEC. 14.—See Sec. 15.

SEC. 15.—(No. 3), Hayford Station, at Seventy-fifth St.; McCaffrey Station, at Seventy-first St.

SEC. 16.—See Sec. 18.

SEC. 17.—See Sec. 18.

SEC. 18.—(No. 3), Clarkdale Station, near Eighty-third St.

Street Car Lines in—DIVISION 8—See Map on Page 122.

This Index gives all street car lines and most convenient railroad stations in each Section. Each Division contains 18 Sections, each one mile square. See "Explanation" on page 136. ABBREVIATIONS: Div., Division; Sec., Section, cor., corner. For other abbreviations see page 80.

SECTION 1.—(No. 1), Brighton Park Station, at Thirty-seventh and Hart Sts., in Div. 5, Sec. 16. (No. 3), Morrell Park Station, at Kedzie Av., in Sec. 4; Oakley Av. Station, in Sec. 5. (No. 16), Brighton Park Station, at Thirty seventh and Hart Sts., in Div. 5, Sec. 16. (No. 43), on Archer Av., fr. Kedzie Av. to Thirty-ninth St.

SEC. 2.—(No. 1), Brighton Park Station, at Thirty-seventh and Hart Sts., in Div. 5, Sec. 16. (No. 3), Oakley Av. Station, in Sec. 5; Ashland Av. Station, in Sec. 5. (No. 16), Brighton Park Station, at Thirty-seventh and Hart Sts., in Div. 5, Sec. 16. (No. 44), on Ashland Av., fr. Forty-seventh St. to Thirty-ninth St.; connects with (No. 43). (No. 48), at cor. of Ashland Av. and Forty-seventh St.; connects with the following lines, for the business center: (No. 59), (No. 69) and (No. 70), in Div. 9, Sec. 1; (No. 51) and (No. 53), in Div. 9, Sec. 2.

SEC. 3.—(No. 14), Union Stock Yards Station, at Fortieth St. (No. 17), Union Stock Yards Station. (No. 44), on Ashland Av., fr. Forty-seventh St. to Thirty-ninth St.; connects with (No. 43). (No. 46), at cor. of Halsted and Thirty-ninth Sts.; connects with (No. 74) or (No. 93). (No. 47), on Root St., at entrance to Stock Yards; connects with the following lines, for the business center: (No. 59) and (No. 70), in Div. 9, Sec. 1; (No. 51) and (No. 53), in Div. 9, Sec. 2. (No. 48), on Forty-seventh St., fr. Ashland Av. to Halsted St.; connects with the following lines, for the business center: (No. 59), (No. 69) and (No. 70), in Div. 9, Sec. 1; (No. 51) and (No. 53), in Div. 9, Sec. 2. (No. 63), on Root St., at entrance to Stock Yards; connects with the following lines, for the business center: (No. 58), (No. 68), and (No. 70), in Div. 9, Sec. 1; (No. 51), (No. 52), (No. 53) and (No. 66), in Div. 9, Sec. 2.

SEC. 4.—(No. 3), Morrell Park Station, at Kedzie Av.; Oakley Av. Station, in Sec. 5.

SEC. 5.—(No. 3), Oakley Av. Station; Ashland Av. Station. (No. 44), on Ashland Av., fr. Fifty-fifth St. to Forty-seventh St.; connects with (No. 43). (No. 48), at cor. of Ashland Av. and Forty-seventh St.; connects with the following lines, for the business center: (No. 59), (No. 69) and (No. 70), in Div. 9, Sec. 1; (No. 51) and (No. 53), in Div. 9, Sec. 2.

SEC. 6.—(No. 2), Fifty-fifth St Station, in Div. 9, Sec. 4; Forty-ninth St. Station, in Div. 9, Sec. 4. (No. 3), Ashland Av. Station; Centre Av. Station; Halsted St. Station. (No. 18), Forty-ninth St Station, in Div. 9, Sec. 4. (No. 44), on Ashland Av., fr. Fifty-fifth St. to Forty-seventh St.; connects with (No. 43). (No. 48), on Forty-seventh St., fr. Ashland Av. to Halsted St.; connects with the following lines, for the business center: (No. 59), (No. 69) and (No. 70), in Div. 9, Sec. 1; (No. 51) and (No. 53), in Div. 9, Sec. 2.

SEC. 7.—(No. 3), Chicago Lawn Station, at Sixty-third St., in Div. 7, Sec. 9; Fifty-ninth St. Station, in Div. 7, Sec. 9; Fifty-fifth St. Station, in Div. 7, Sec. 9; Morrell Park Station, at Kedzie Av., in Div. 8, Sec. 4; Oakley Av. Station, in Div. 8, Sec. 5.

SEC. 8.—(No. 2), Englewood Station, at Sixty-third St., in Div. 9, Sec. 7; Fifty-ninth St. Station, in Div. 9, Sec. 7; Fifty-fifth St. Station, in Div. 9, Sec. 7. (No. 3), Oakley Av. Station, in Sec. 5; Ashland Av. Station, in Sec. 5. (No. 16), South Lynne Station, at Sixty-seventh St., in Sec. 11. (No. 44), on Ashland Av., fr. Sixty-third St. to Garfield Boul.; connects with No. 43).

SEC. 9.—(No. 2), Englewood Station, at Sixty-third St., in Div. 9, Sec. 7; Fifty-ninth St. Station, in Div. 9, Sec. 7; Fifty-fifth St. Station, in Div. 9, Sec. 7. (No. 3), Ashland Av. Station, in Sec. 6; Centre Av. Station, in Sec. 6; Halsted St. Station, in Sec. 6. (No. 18), Englewood Station, at Sixty-third St., in Div. 9, Sec. 7. (No. 44), on Ashland Av., fr. Sixty-third St. to Garfield Boul.; connects with (No. 43).

SEC. 10. —(No. 3), McCaffrey Station, at Seventy-first St., in Div. 7, Sec. 12; Sixty-seventh St. Station, in Div. 7, Sec. 12; Chicago Lawn Station, at Sixty-third St., in Div. 7, Sec. 12. (No. 16), South Lynne Station, at Sixty-seventh St., in Sec. 11.

SEC. 11.—(No. 16), South Lynne Station, at Sixty-seventh St. (No. 44), on Ashland Av., fr. Sixty-ninth St. to Sixty-third St.; connects with (No. 43). (No. 55), on Sixty-ninth St., fr. Cooper St. to Ashland Av.; connects with (No. 70).

SEC. 12.—(No. 2), Seventy-second St. Station, in Div. 9, Sec. 13; Normal Park Station, at Sixty-eighth St., in Div. 9, Sec. 10; Englewood Station, at Sixty-third St., in Div. 9, Sec. 10. (No. 12), Seventy-fifth St. Station, in Div. 9, Sec. 10; Eggleston Station, at Seventy-first St., in Div. 9, Sec. 10; Normal Park Station, at Sixty-eighth St., in Div. 9, Sec. 10. (No. 18), Englewood Station, at Sixty-third St., in Div. 9, Sec. 10. (No. 44), on Ashland Av., fr. Sixty-ninth St. to Sixty-third St.; connects with (No. 43). (No. 55), on Sixty-ninth St., fr. Ashland Av. to Halsted St.; connects with (No. 70).

SEC. 13. — (No. 3), Hayford Station, at Seventy-fifth St., in Div. 7, Sec. 15; McCaffrey Station, at Seventy-first St., in Div. 7, Sec. 12. (No. 16), Forest Hill Station, at Seventy-ninth St., in Sec. 14; South Lynne Station, at Sixty-seventh St., in Sec. 11. (No. 18), Forest Hill Station, at Seventy-fifth St., in Sec. 14.

SEC. 14.—(No. 16), Forest Hill Station, at Seventy-ninth St.; South Lynne Station, at Sixty-seventh St., in Sec. 11. (No. 18), Forest Hill Station, at Seventy-fifth St.

SEC. 15.—(No. 2), Auburn Park Station, near Seventy-eighth St., in Div. 9, Sec. 13; Auburn Junction, at Seventy-fifth St., in Div. 9, Sec. 13; Seventy-second St. Station, in Div. 9, Sec. 13. (No. 12), Auburn Park Station, at Seventy-eighth St., in Div. 9, Sec. 13; Seventy-fifth St. Station, in Div. 9, Sec. 13. (No. 18), Auburn Junction, at Seventy-fifth St., in Div. 9, Sec. 13. (No. 70), at cor. of Halsted and Seventy-ninth Sts.

SEC. 16.—(No. 3), Clarkdale Station, near Eighty-third St., in Div. 7, Sec. 18. (No. 16), Forest Hill Station, at Seventy-ninth St., in Sec. 17.

SEC. 17.—(No. 12), Beverly Hill Station, near Ninety-first St., in Div. 11, Sec. 2;

Car Lines in—DIVISION 8—Continued.

Brainerd Station, at cor. of Eighty-ninth and Loomis Sts., in Div. **11**, Sec. **3**; South Englewood Station, at Eighty-seventh St., in Div. **11**, Sec. **3**. (**No. 16**), Forest Hill Station, at Seventy-ninth St.

SEC. **18.**—(**No. 2**), Eighty-third St. Station, in Div. **9**, Sec. **16**; Eighty-first St. Station, in Div. **9**, Sec. **16**; Auburn Park Station, near Seventy-eighth St., in Div. **9**, Sec.

13. (**No. 12**), Brainerd Station, at cor. of Eighty-ninth and Loomis Sts., in Div. **11**, Sec. **3**; South Englewood Station, at Eighty-seventh St., in Div. **11**, Sec. **3**; Auburn Park Station, at Seventy-eighth St., in Div. **9**, Sec. **13**. (**No. 16**), Forest Hill Station, at Seventy-ninth St., in Sec. **17.** (**No. 70**), at cor. of Halsted and Seventy-ninth

Street Car Lines in—DIVISION 9—See Map on Page 123.

This Index gives all street car lines and most convenient railroad stations in each Section. Each Division contains 18 Sections, each one mile square. See "Explanation" on page 136. ABBREVIATIONS: Div., Division; Sec., Section; cor., corner. Other abbreviations found on page 80.

SECTION **1.**—(**No. 2**), Forty-first St. Station. (**No. 12**), Forty-seventh St. Station; Forty-fourth St. Station. (**No. 14**), Station at cor. of State and Fortieth Sts.; Forty-third St. Station; Thirty-ninth St. Station. (**No. 17**), Forty-first St. Station.

OMNIBUS LINE, FROM DEPOTS TO LEADING RETAIL STORES. FARE, 5C.

(**No. 18**), Forty-first St. Station. (**No. 46**), at cor. of Halsted and Thirty-ninth Sts.; connects with (**No. 74**) or (**No. 93**). (**No. 47**), fr. Halsted St. to Forty-third St., via Root and State Sts.; connects with the following lines, for the business center: (No **59**) and (No. **70**), in Sec. **1**; (**No. 51**) and (No. **53**), in Sec. **2**. (**No. 48**), on Forty-seventh St., fr. Halsted St. to State St.; connects with the following lines, for the business center: (**No. 59**), (**No. 69**) and (**No. 70**), in Sec. **1**; (**No. 51**) and (**No. 53**), in Sec. **2**. (**No. 58**), at cor. of State and Thirty-ninth Sts. (**No. 59**), on State St., fr. Forty-seventh St. to Thirty-ninth St. (**No. 63**), fr. the Stock Yards to Thirty-ninth St., via Root St. and Wentworth Av.; connects with the following lines, for the business center: (**No. 58**), (**No. 59**), (**No. 68**) and (**No. 70**), in Sec. **1**; (**No. 51**), (**No. 52**), (**No. 53**) and (**No. 66**), in Sec. **2**. (**No. 67**), at cor. of Butler and Thirty-ninth Sts. (**No. 68**), at cor. of Wentworth Av. and Thirty-ninth St. (**No. 69**), fr. Forty-seventh St. to State St., via Wentworth Av. and Thirty-ninth St.; connects with (**No. 58**), (**No. 59**), (**No. 68**) and (**No. 70**), for the business center. (**No. 70**), on State St., fr. Forty-seventh St. to Thirty-ninth St.

SEC. **2.**—(**No. 12**), Forty-seventh St. Station; Forty-fourth St. Station. (**No. 14**), Cottage Grove Av. Station; Langley Av. Station; Vincennes Av. Station; Grand Boul. Station; Prairie Av. Station; Michigan Av. Station; State St. Station; Forty-third St. Station, in Sec. **1**. (**No. 47**), on Forty-third St., fr. State St. to Cottage Grove Av.; connects with the following lines, for the business center: (**No. 59**) and (**No. 70**), in Sec. **1**; (**No. 51**) and (**No. 53**), in Sec. **2**. (**No. 48**), on Forty-seventh St., fr. State St. to Cottage Grove Av.; connects with the following lines, for the business center: (**No. 59**), (**No. 69**) and (**No. 70**), in Sec. **1**; (**No. 51**) on Cottage Grove Av., fr. Forty-seventh St. to Thirty-ninth St. (**No. 52**), at cor. of Thirty-ninth St. and Indiana Av. (**No. 53**), on Cottage Grove Av., fr. Forty-seventh St. to Thirty-ninth St. (**No. 57**), on Indiana Av., fr. Forty-seventh St. to Thirty-ninth St.; connects with (**No. 52**). (**No. 58**), at cor. of State and Thirty-ninth Sts. (**No. 59**), on State St., fr. Forty-seventh St. to Thirty-

ninth St. (**No. 63**), on Thirty-ninth St., fr. Cottage Grove Av. to State St.; connects with the following lines, for the business center: (**No. 58**), (**No. 59**), (**No. 68**) and (**No. 70**), in Sec. **1**; (**No. 51**), (**No. 52**), (**No. 53**) and (**No. 66**), in Sec. **2**. (**No. 66**), at cor. of Cottage Grove Av. and Thirty-ninth St. (**No. 71**), north from Forty-third St., in the alley between Prairie and Calumet Avs., to Fortieth St., west on Fortieth St. to alley between Wabash Av. and State St., north in this alley to Thirty-ninth St.

SEC. **3.**—(**No. 13**), Kenwood Station, at Forty-seventh St.; Forty-third St. Station; Oakland Station, at Thirty-ninth St. (**No. 14**), Lake Av. Station; Drexel Boul. Station; Cottage Grove Av. Station. (**No. 47**), on Forty-third St., fr. the Illinois Central tracks to Cottage Grove Av.; connects with the following lines, for the business center: (**No. 59**) and (**No. 70**), in Sec. **1**; (**No. 51**) and (**No. 53**), in Sec. **2**. (**No. 53**), on Cottage Grove Av., fr. Forty-seventh St. to Thirty-ninth St. (**No. 66**), at cor. of Cottage Grove Av. and Thirty-ninth St.

SEC. **4.**—(**No. 2**), Fifty-fifth St. Station; Forty-ninth St. Station. (**No. 3**), Halsted St. Station. (**No. 12**), Fifty-fifth St. Station; Fifty-first St. Station; Forty-seventh St. Station. (**No. 14**), Fifty-fifth St. Station; Fifty-first St. Station. (**No. 17**), Fifty-fifth St. Station; Fifty-first St. Station. (**No. 18**), Forty-ninth St. Station. (**No. 48**), on Forty-seventh St., fr. Halsted St. to State St.; connects with the following lines, for the business center: (**No. 59**), (**No. 69**) and (**No. 70**), in Sec. **1**; (**No. 51**) and (**No. 53**), in Sec. **2**. (**No. 59**), on State St., fr. Fifty-fifth St. to Forty-seventh St. (**No. 69**), on Wentworth Av., fr. Fifty-fifth St. to Forty-seventh St.; connects with (**No. 58**), (**No. 59**), (**No. 68**) and (**No. 70**), for the business center. (**No. 70**), on State St., fr. Fifty-fifth St. to Forty-seventh St.

SEC. **5.**—(**No. 12**), Fifty-fifth St. Station, in Sec. **4**; Fifty-first St. Station, in Sec. **4**; Forty-seventh St. Station, in Sec. **4**. (**No. 14**), Fifty-fifth St. Station, in Sec. **4**; Fifty-first St. Station, in Sec. **4**. (**No. 48**), on Forty-seventh St., fr. State St. to Cottage Grove Av.; connects with the following lines, for the business center: (**No. 59**), (**No. 69**) and (**No. 70**), in Sec. **1**; (**No. 51**) and (**No. 53**), in Sec. **2**. (**No. 49**), on Fifty-first St., fr. State St. to Washington Park; connects with (**No. 59**). (**No. 51**), on Cottage Grove Av., fr. Fifty-fifth St. to Forty-

Car Lines in—DIVISION 9—Continued.

seventh St. (No. 53), on Cottage Grove Av., fr. Fifty-fifth St. to Forty-seventh St. (No. 57), fr. Washington Park to Forty-seventh St., via Fifty-first St. and Indiana Av.; connects with (No. 52). (No. 59), on State St., fr. Fifty-fifth St. to Forty-seventh St.

Sec. 6.—(No. 13), Hyde Park Station, at Fifty-third St.; Madison Park Station, near Fiftieth St.; Kenwood Station, at Forty-seventh St. (No. 51), fr. Lake Av. to Forty-seventh St., via Fifty-fifth St. and Cottage Grove Av. (No. 53), on Cottage Grove Av., fr. Fifty-fifth St. to Forty-seventh St.

Sec. 7.—(No. 2), Englewood Station, at Sixty-third St.; Fifty-ninth St. Station; Fifty-fifth St. Station. (No. 12), Englewood Station, at Sixty-second St.; Fifty-ninth St. Station; Fifty-fifth St. Station. (No. 14), Englewood Station, at Sixty-second St.; Fifty-ninth St. Station; Fifty-fifth St. Station. (No. 17), Englewood Station, at Sixty-third St.; Sixty-first St. Station; Fifty-fifth St. Station. (No. 18), Englewood Station, at Sixty-third St. (No. 54), at cor. of State and Sixty-first Sts.; connects with (No. 53), (No. 59) and (No. 70), for the business center. (No. 59), on State St., fr. Sixty-third St. to Fifty-fifth St. (No. 69), on Wentworth Av., fr. Sixty-third St. to Fifty-fifth St.; connects with (No. 58), (No. 59), (No. 68) and (No. 70), for the business center. (No. 70), fr. Wentworth Av. to Fifty-fifth St., via Sixty-third and State Sts.

Sec. 8.—(No. 12), Englewood Station, at Sixty-second St., in Sec. 7; Fifty-ninth St. Station, in Sec. 7; Fifty-fifth St. Station, in Sec. 7. (No. 14), Englewood Station, at Sixty-second St., in Sec. 7; Fifty-ninth St. Station, in Sec. 7; Fifty-fifth St. Station, in Sec. 7. (No. 51), at cor. of Cottage Grove Av. and Fifty-fifth St. (No. 53), on Cottage Grove Av., fr. Sixty-third St. to Fifty-fifth St. (No. 54), fr. State St. to Sixty-third St., via Sixty-first St. and Cottage Grove Av.; connects with (No. 53), (No. 59) and (No. 70), for the business center. (No. 59), on State St., fr. Sixty-third St. to Fifty-fifth St.

Sec. 9.—(No. 13), Woodlawn Park Station, at Sixty-third St.; Sixtieth St. Station; South Park Station, at Fifty-seventh St. (No. 51), on Fifty-fifth St., fr. Lake St. to Cottage Grove Av. (No. 53), on Cottage Grove Av., fr. Sixty-third St. to Fifty-fifth St. (No. 54), fr. Sixty-first St. to the Illinois Central tracks, via Cottage Grove Av. and Sixty-third St.; connects with (No. 53), (No. 59), and (No. 70), for the business center.

Sec. 10.—(No. 2), Seventy-second St. Station, in Sec. 13; Normal Park Station, at Sixty-eighth St.; Englewood Station, at Sixty-third St. (No. 12), Eggleston Station, at Seventy-second St.; Normal Park Station, at Sixty-eighth St.; Sixty-fifth St. Station; Englewood Station, at Sixty-second St., in Sec. 7. (No. 14), Englewood Station, at Sixty-second St., in Sec. 7. (No. 17), Englewood Station, at Sixty-third St. (No. 18), Englewood Station, at Sixty-third St. (No. 55), fr. Sixty-fourth St. to Halsted St., via State and Sixty-ninth Sts.; connects with (No. 70). (No. 59), at cor. of State and Sixty-ninth Sts. (No. 69), at cor. of Wentworth Av. and Sixty-third St.; connects with (No. 58), (No. 59), (No. 68) and (No. 70), for the business center.

(No. 70), fr. Seventy-first St. to State St., via Wentworth Av. and Sixty-third St.

Sec. 11.—(No. 14), Brookline Station, at Seventy-first St.; Park Manor Station, at Sixty-sixth St.; Englewood Station, at Sixty-second St., in Sec. 7. (No. 17), Brookline Station, at Seventy-first St.; Park Manor Station, at Sixty-sixth St.; Englewood Station, at Sixty-third St., in Sec. 10. (No. 53), on Cottage Grove Av., fr. Seventy-first St. to Sixty-third St. (No. 54), at cor. of Cottage Grove Av. and Sixty-third St.; connects with (No. 53), (No. 59) and (No. 70), for the business center. (No. 55), on State St., fr. Sixty-fourth St. to Sixty-ninth St.; connects with (No. 70). (No. 59), at cor. of State and Sixty-third Sts.

Sec. 12.—(No. 13), Park Side Station, at Seventy-first St.; Brookdale Station, at Seventieth St.; Oakwoods Station, at Sixty-seventh St.; Woodlawn Park Station, at Sixty-third St. (No. 14), Brookline Station, at Seventy-first St., in Sec. 14; Park Manor Station, at Sixty-sixth St., in Sec. 11. (No. 17), Brookline Station, at Seventy-first St., in Sec. 14; Park Manor Station, at Sixty-sixth St., in Sec. 11. (No. 53), on Cottage Grove Av., fr. Seventy-first St. to Sixty-third St. (No. 54), on Sixty-third St., fr. the Illinois Central tracks to Cottage Grove Av.; connects with (No. 53), (No. 59) and (No. 70), for the business center.

Sec. 13.—(No. 2), Auburn Park Station, near Seventy-eighth St.; Auburn Junction, at Seventy-fifth St.; Seventy-second St. Station. (No. 12), Auburn Park Station, at Seventy-eighth St.; Seventy-fifth St. Station; Eggleston Station, at Seventy-first St. (No. 18), Auburn Junction, at Seventy-fifth St. (No. 70), Halsted St. to Seventy-first St., via Seventy-ninth St., Vincennes Rd. and Wentworth Av.

Sec. 14.—(No. 2), Auburn Park Station, near Seventy-eighth St., in Sec. 13; Auburn Junction, at Seventy-fifth St., in Sec. 13. (No. 12), Auburn Park Station, at Seventy-eighth St., in Sec. 13; Seventy-fifth St. Station, in Sec. 13; Eggleston Station, at Seventy-first St., in Sec. 13. (No. 13), Fordham Station, at Eighty-second St., in Sec. 18; Grand Crossing Station, at Seventy-fifth St., in Sec. 15. (No. 14), Grand Crossing Station, at Seventy-fifth St., in Sec. 15; Brookline Station, at Seventy-first St.; Park Manor Station, at Sixty-sixth St., in Sec. 11. (No. 17), Grand Crossing Station, at Seventy-fifth St., in Sec. 15; Brookline Station, at Seventy-first St.; Park Manor Station, at Sixty-sixth St., in Sec. 11.

Sec. 15.—(No. 13), Grand Crossing Station, at Seventy-fifth St.; Park Side Station, at Seventy-first St. (No. 14), Grand Crossing Station, at Seventy-fifth St.; Brookline Station, at Seventy-first St. (No. 17), Grand Crossing Station, at Seventy-fifth St.; Brookline Station, at Seventy-first St. (No. 53), at corner of Seventy-first St. and Cottage Grove Av. (No. 56), on South Chicago Av., fr. Grand Crossing to corner of Cottage Grove Av. and Seventy-first St.; connects with (No. 53).

Sec. 16.—(No. 2), Eighty-third St. Station; Eighty-first St. Station; Auburn Park Station, near Seventy-eighth St., in Sec. 13. (No. 12), South Englewood Station, at Eighty-seventh St.; Auburn Park Station, at Seventy-eighth St., in Sec. 13. (No. 70), on Seventy-ninth St., fr. Halsted St. to Vincennes Rd.

Car Lines in—DIVISION 9—Continued.

Street Car Lines in—DIVISION 10—See Map on Page 124.

This Index gives all street car lines and most convenient railroad stations in each Section. Each Division contains 18 Sections, each one mile square. See "Explanation" on page 136. ABBREVIATIONS: Div., Division; Sec., Section; cor., corner. O abbreviations found on page 80.

Railway Lines in—DIVISION 11—See Map on Page 125.

This Index gives all street car lines and most convenient railroad stations in each Section. Each Division contains 18 Sections, each one mile square. See "Explanation" on page 136. ABBREVIATIONS: Div., Division; Sec., Section; cor., corner. Other abbreviations found on page 80.

Railways in—DIVISION 11—Continued.

SEC. 7. — (No. 3), Mt. Greenwood or Mt. Olivet Station, at 109th St.; Tracy Av. Station, (103rd St.) (No. 12), Morgan Park Station, at 111th St., in Sec. 8; Belmont Station, at 107th St., in Sec. 8; Tracy Av. Station, at 103rd St., in Sec. 8.

SEC. 8.—(No. 12). Given Station, near 109th St., in Sec. 9; Washington Heights Station, at 103rd St., in Sec. 9; Morgan Park Station, at 111th St.; Belmont Station, at 107th St.; Tracy Av. Station (103rd St.) (No. 16), Washington Heights Station, at 103rd St., in Sec. 9.

SEC. 9.—(No. 2), Roseland Station, at 111th St., in Div. 12, Sec. 7; Fernwood Station, at 103rd St., in Div. 12, Sec. 7. (No. 12), Given Station, near 109th St.; Washington Heights Station, at 103rd St. (No. 16), Washington Heights Station, at 103rd St.

SEC 10.—(No. 3), Clifton Station, at 119th St.; Mt. Hope Station, near 117th St.; Mt. Greenwood or Mt. Olivet Station, at 109th St., in Sec. 7. (No. 12), Purington Station, at 119th St., in Sec. 1; Raymond or 115th St. Station, in Sec. 11; Morgan Park Station, at 111th St., in Sec. 11.

SEC. 11.—(No. 12), Morgan Av. Station; Purington Station, at 119th St.; Raymond or 115th St. Station; Morgan Park Station, at 111th St.

SEC. 12.—(No. 2), Roseland Station, at 111th St., in Div. 12, Sec. 7. (No. 12), Morgan Av. Station; Given Station, near 109th

St., in Sec. 9; Purington Station, at 119th St., in Sec. 11; Raymond St. Station, in Sec. 11. (No. 16), Shooting Park Station, at 119th St.

SEC. 13.—(No. 3), Wireton Station, between 123rd and 127th Sts.; Brick Yard Station, north of 123rd St.; Clifton Station, at 119th St. (No. 12), Burr Oak Station, at 127th St.; Purington Station at 119th St.

SEC. 14.—(No. 12), Burr Oak Station, at 127th St., Purington Station, at 119th St.

SEC. 15.—(No. 12), Burr Oak Station at 127th St., in Sec. 14; Purington Station, at 119th St., in Sec. 14. (No. 16), Bine Island Road Station, at 127th St., in Div. 12, Sec. 13; Shooting Park Station, at 119th St.

SEC. 16.—(No. 3), Blue Island Junction, at Chicago St.; Blue Island Station, near 131st St.; Wireton Station, between 123rd and 127th Sts., in Sec. 13. (No. 12), Blue Island Station, at 131st St., in Sec. 17; Burr Oak Station, at 127th St., in Sec. 17.

SEC. 17.—(No. 3), Blue Island Junction, at Chicago St., in Sec. 16; Blue Island Station, near 131st St., in Sec. 16. (No. 12), Blue Island Station, at 131st St.; Burr Oak Station, at 127th St.

SEC. 18.—(No. 12), Blue Island Station, at 131st St., in Sec. 17; Burr Oak Station, at 127th St., in Sec. 17. (No. 16), Blue Island Rd. Station, at 127th St., in Div. 12, Sec. 13.

Railway Lines in—DIVISION 12—See Map on Page 126.

This Index gives all street car lines and most convenient railroad stations in each Section. Each Division contains 18 Sections, each one mile square. See "Explanation" on page 136. ABBREVIATIONS: Div., Division; Sec., Section; cor., corner. Other abbreviations found on page 80.

SECTION 1.—(No. 2), Euclid Park Station, at Ninety fifth St.; Oakdale Station, near Ninetieth St. (No. 12), Ninety-fifth St. Station, in Div. 11, Sec. 3; South Englewood Station, at Eighty-seventh St., in Div. 11, Sec. 3.

SEC. 2.—(No. 2), Euclid Park Station, at Ninety-fifth St., in Sec. 1; Oakdale Station, near Ninetieth St., in Sec. 1. (No. 13), Burnside Crossing, at Ninety-fifth St., in Sec. 3; Dauphin Park Station, at Eighty-ninth St., in Sec. 3.

SEC. 3.—(No. 13), Burnside Crossing, at Ninety-fifth St.; Dauphin Park Station, at Eighty ninth St. (No. 15), Stony Island Station.

SEC. 4.—(No. 2), Fernwood Station, at 103rd St.; Euclid Park Station, at Ninety-fifth St. (No. 12), Ninety-fifth St. Station, in Div. 11, Sec. 3.

SEC. 5.—(No. 2), Fernwood Station, at 103rd St., in Sec. 4; Euclid Park Station, at Ninety-fifth St., in Sec. 4. (No. 13), 104th St. Station, in Sec. 8; Burnside Crossing, at Ninety-fifth St.

SEC. 6.—(No. 13), 104th St. Station, in Sec. 8; Burnside Crossing, at Ninety-fifth St. (No. 15), Stony Island Station.

SEC. 7.—(No. 2), Roseland Station, at 111th St.; Fernwood Station, at 103rd St.

SEC. 8.—(No. 2), Roseland Station, at 111th St., in Sec. 7; Fernwood Station, at 103rd St., in Sec. 7 (No. 13), Pullman Station, at 111th St.; 104th St. Station.

SEC. 9.—(No. 13), Pullman Station, at 111th St., in Sec. 8; 104th St. Station, in Sec. 8.

SEC. 10.—(No. 2), Kensington Station, near 116th St.; Roseland Station, at 111th St. (No. 16), Shooting Park Station, at 119th St.

SEC. 11.—(No. 2), Kensington Station, near 116th St.; Roseland Station, at 111th St., in Sec. 10 (No. 13), Kensington Station, at 115th St.; Pullman Station, at 111th St.

SEC. 13.—(No. 2), Kensington Station, near 116th St., in Sec. 10. (No. 13), Wildwood Station. at 130th St., in Sec. 17; Gardner's Park Station, at 123rd St., in Sec. 14. (No. 16), Blue Island Road Station, at 127th St.; Shooting Park Station, at 119th St., in Div. 11, Sec. 15.

SEC. 14.—(No. 2), Kensington Station, near 116th St., in Sec. 10 (No. 13), Wildwood Station, at 130th St., in Sec. 17; Gardner's Park Station. at 123rd St.; Kensington Station, at 115th St., in Sec. 11.

SEC. 16.—(No. 13), Riverdale Station, at 134th St., in Sec. 17; Wildwood Station, at 130th St., in Sec. 17. (No. 16), Riverdale Station, at 135th St.; Blue Island Road Station, at 127th St.

SEC. 17.—(No. 2), Dolton Station, at 138th St.; Riverdale Station, at 133rd St. (No. 13), Riverdale Station, at 134th St., in Sec. 17; Wildwood Station, at 130th St., in Sec. 17. (No. 16), Riverdale Station, at 135th St.

SEC. 18.—(No. 2), Dolton Station, at 138th St., in Sec. 17; Riverdale Station, at 133rd St., in Sec. 17. (No. 13), Wildwood Station, at 130th St., in Sec. 17.

Railway Lines in—DIVISION 13—See Map on Page 127.

This Index gives all street car lines and most convenient railroad stations in each Section. Each Division contains 18 Sections, each one mile square. See "Explanation" on page 138. ABBREVIATIONS: Div., Division; Sec., Section; cor., corner. Other abbreviations found on page 80.

148

ALL ABOUT CHICAGO.

IMPORTANT FACTS CONCERNING THE CITY.

A Stroll among the Places of Interest and
Unusual Attraction.

THE stranger in Chicago, having become acquainted with the geography of its streets and the means of reaching any part of the city through the various modes of transportation, is now in readiness to make the general acquaintance of this metropolis. For that purpose he will take at first

A Brief View of the City.

The maps, which we have examined in our study of the location of streets, give a general view of the entire area of Chicago, the business portion of which, in the older district of the city, is confined within comparatively narrow limits, the great bulk of the exchange business of the city being within the area shown in the map on page 67, the manufacturing, and largely the mercantile, establishments being within the lines shown in Division 6, on page 114. Many smaller stores are, however, gradually being established in various central parts outside of these limits, and, with the establishment of rapid transit, the business district will doubtless be yet much more widely spread.

We will walk for a little time in the business center and study the

Architecture of the New Buildings.

Travelers who have been in all parts of the civilized world, tell us that in architectural grandeur, within the space of one mile square, this city surpasses all their highest expectations.

There is a very good reason why this should be so. Following the great fire, which devastated the entire business district, came the rebuilding of the city, with the introduction of every modern building appliance, in the era immediately following the fire of 1871.

Chicago thus became a new city, presenting to the stranger the most advanced ideas in building. But architectural improvement did not stop there. The rapid enhancement in the value of real estate at the business center has given the inducement to remove the business blocks of fifteen years ago, and cover the space they have occupied with a yet vastly better class of structures than those that were the best known in architecture so short a time ago. We are thus in the fifth era of building in Chicago, the first being the primitive dwellings of the early settlers; the second, the better structures that succeeded them in the next era; the next, the large, substantial and noble edifices of the third era that went down in the fire; then the improved and vastly better buildings that arose in the fourth era out of the ashes of those that were swept away in the great conflagration, and now, lastly, in the fifth era, we witness the immense fireproof structures that raise their giant forms in various parts of the business center, their interior fittings supplied with every modern device for health and comfort which has been invented in the last few years of rapid advance in architectural knowledge.

New Architectural Era.

The beginning of the fifth era of building in Chicago came with the construction of the nine-story fireproof Montauk block on Monroe Street.

This was a remarkably tall edifice in its time. When completed, it was one of the sights of the city. Then came the Opera House block, on Washington Street, the Rookery, Calumet, Home Insurance and other ten-story buildings on South La Salle Street, and the Montauk was forgotten.

It was then that the architect and builder resolved to surpass the previous record, and the twelve-story Tacoma building arose at the northeast corner of Madison and La Salle Streets. This carried the prize for tall structures for a time, until Hannah, Lay & Co. bought the old Chamber of Commerce block, at the southeast corner of La Salle and Washington Streets, and went up with their new building so high as to throw the Tacoma into the shade.

Then followed in quick succession several sixteen-story buildings, among them being the Ashland Block, opposite the Sherman House, on Clark Street, the Unity building, on Washington Street, and the Monadnock and Manhattan, on South Dearborn Street.

It was then that the late Norman T. Gassette and several of his fellow Masons resolved to surpass all previous efforts in high building, and the result was the creation of the twenty-story edifice, known as the Masonic Temple, at the corner of Randolph and State Streets.

Famous Buildings.

In the meantime, other public-spirited business people were planning great edifices that should remain as benefactions to the public in the present and in the future.

Realizing the imperative necessity for a great audience hall, Ferdinand W. Peck conceived the plan of the Auditorium, largely consecrated to music, oratory and art, which stands as a grand memorial where formerly stood his father's residence, on Michigan Avenue. A few earnest women in temperance work have caused the erection of the great Temperance Temple, at the corner of Monroe and La Salle Streets, while the Great Northern Hotel, on Dearborn Street, the Post Office, The Fair, the Le'er building, occupied by Siegel, Cooper & Co., the Columbus, the Marshall Field building and other great fireproof edifices stand out, at this writing, in conspicuous relief.

What the future of building is to be 'n the business center, it is impossible to predict. It is probable, however, that a large number of the structures of the fourth era will come down, to give place to twelve and fourteen story edifices, with all the modern conveniences. Not all of them will come down, however. A few of the centrally located buildings that went up directly after the fire were so well built that their architecture and general equipment can hardly be improved to day. The Palmer House was grand in the beginning. It yet stands a model in architecture. The City Hall and Court House, the Board of Trade building, the Marshall Field retail store, at the corner of State and Washington Streets, the Pullman building, on Adams Street, the Rialto, on Van Buren Street, and others, will long endure as edifices of a very high grade, no probability existing of their being greatly surpassed in architecture or superior interior embellishment for many years to come.

Interior Finish of Buildings.

Having given general attention to the great structures that greet the eye in the business center, let us enter some of these buildings and inpect their interiors.

Passing down State Street, look in, for a little while, upon the Masonic Temple, 265 feet high, and see the sixteen elevators, as they float up and down, with a carrying capacity of 40,000 passengers per day. It will be entertaining to go to the observation parlors on the roof, and view the city below while you partake of refreshments there.

Resuming our walk, we go into Marshall Field's and leisurely walk through. Like several other stores in this vicinity, this is a great exposition of itself. Returning to the street and continuing our stroll southward, we wend our way, in the midst of a great throng of people, down to the Palmer House. See this rotunda inside. Observe how it is broken into many little niches. What an ideal place in one corner here to meet a friend in the evening and perfect a trade, or arrange with the committee for the plan of a campaign. Everybody appreciates this, and hence the appointments to meet at the Palmer House. The rotunda is crowded. You think there is a convention being held in the city, and that the delegates are all stopping here. Not so. This is simply the everyday condition in the hotel office. This is a popular hotel. It has many guests, and it is a centrally located and desirable place to meet a friend.

You see those pictures upon the wall at the southern side of the rotunda. Those are views of numerous great business blocks which Mr. Potter Palmer, the proprietor of this hotel, formerly owned and lost in the great fire. We pass on through reading-room, wash-rooms, toilet-rooms, and look for a little time into billiard-rooms—all conveniently arranged—all finished to perfection. We go up to the parlors, accessible through broad halls, all superbly furnished. Continue our investigation and look in upon the palatial dining-room. Return to the rotunda, glance in upon one of the most elegantly furnished barber shops in the world, resplendent in sparkling glass and artistic decoration. Pass out and down State Street; go in and through portions of the great retail store known as The Fair, which extends from State Street to Dearborn Street; return to State Street and continue southward, visiting the great store building occupied by Siegel, Cooper & Co., radiant in one portion of the interior with a sparkling fountain, reflecting many-colored electric lights. It is but a brief step from State Street over to the Auditorium Hotel, with its attractive office, finished in many-colored marbles, its beautifully furnished parlors, and its unique dining-room in the upper part of the building, from which the guests look down to the eastward upon the many craft sailing on the quiet blue of Lake Michigan.

Pause in one of the guest-rooms of these modern hotels and see the lately invented mechanism for the use of guests, found in many rooms. Do you see that dial upon the wall? You see several spaces upon the same. In one is marked "cold water," in another, "newspapers," in another, "stationery," etc. Turn that hand upon the dial to the name of the article required, and in a very brief time a waiter will rap at your door, bearing the article you desired.

Earthquake Proof.

In going eastward to La Salle Street, we will go in and examine the lower rooms of the Great Northern Hotel. Like most of the other modern hotels of Chicago, this one is made to be absolutely fireproof. You wonder, as you look at this massive structure, which is fourteen stories high, what the result would be to guests if an earthquake should occur in this city. That has been anticipated in these tall buildings. All these immense edifices are constructed of a framework of steel, riveted together in the most substantial manner. A first-class earthquake might start occasionally a brick on some outer portion of the building, but it could no more shake this building down than it could shake a bird-cage to pieces.

We go northward on Dearborn Street to Adams Street, and westward to the Rookery building, at the corner of Adams and La Salle Streets. This is not the tallest of the new buildings, but its architecture, you observe, is very pleasing on the exterior. Go into the interior. See that magnificent court open through to the top of the building, with its beautifully arching roof protecting the lower floors.

Oh, no, that is not the finest interior office building in the city. We have many beautiful interiors, and opinion is divided as to which is the most elegant. We will go northward on La Salle Street, and, at the corner of La Salle and Washington Streets, examine the interior of the Chamber of Commerce building. Again look up. See the bronze balustrades rising one above another—up—up—fourteen stories. Let us go up in one of the elevators, and look down from over one of the balustrades in one of the upper stories, on the people moving below. Queer sight. You will not forget it.

You are getting tired of looking at buildings. You are willing to take our word for the remainder as to the beauty of the interiors. Very well. You will stay here a few weeks, and, during that time, you will see other hotels equally elegant in their interior furnishings. You will see audience rooms in theaters, churches and halls that have been fitted, decorated and furnished in a great variety of styles, regardless of expense, and these will be supplemented by interiors yet much more charming, on account of beautiful furnishings, in the clubrooms and in many of the private residences.

FACILITIES FOR OBTAINING FOOD FROM ALL PARTS OF THE EARTH.

If you have any doubts about being able to get a sufficiency to eat in Chicago, we take this early occasion to assure you that your fears are unfounded.

Turn back to page 77. Do you see that Chicago is in the exact center of the habitable portion of the North American Continent? It is, and is more accessible to all kinds of food products than any other city on earth. From the lakes at the north, come the speckled trout and the great variety of fresh-water fish. From the Atlantic coast, come all the kinds of salt-water and shell fish; from the east, all the fruits peculiar to the region in their season; from the south, the sugars, the syrups and all the fruits and vegetables of the tropics; from the Pacific coast, the fruits and wines of California; and from the wonderfully prolific soil of the States surrounding this city, come all the grains, the vegetables and fruits in their season which it is possible to raise.

For proof of this, we will go down to Water Street, where an entire thoroughfare, for several blocks, is lined on each side with food productions from all parts of the American Continent.

EXPENSE OF BOARD AND RENTAL OF ROOMS.

1. At the large hotels, from $2 to $5 per day, or more, according to room.

2. At boarding houses, from $4 to $10 per week.

3. Handsomely furnished rooms for one or two persons can be had in hotels for $1 to $2 per day, meals to be taken elsewhere.

4. Single rooms can be had in private houses for $3 to $6 per week. Meals taken elsewhere.

5. Large, fine parlors in private houses, elegantly furnished, can be obtained for $10 or $15 per week. Meals taken elsewhere.

6. Regular meals can be obtained at the first-class hotels at from 75 cents to $1.50 per meal.

7. Meals can be obtained at the restaurants, with good attendance, clean table cloths, napkins, and excellently prepared food at from 20 to 50 cents per meal.

COST OF LIVING IN CERTAIN CHICAGO RESTAURANTS.

BILL OF FARE.

The following are the prices charged at one of the first-class, old established and leading restaurants in Chicago, during the year 1892. Tables are supplied with clean table-cloths and napkins; one or two waiters to each table of eight persons. Toilet rooms, news rooms and waiting rooms are also attached to the restaurant.

COLD MEATS AND SALADS.

	CENTS.		CENTS.		CENTS.
Beef, Cold Corned	25	Lambs' Tongues, Pickled	25	Potato Salad	15
Beef, Cold Roast	25	Lobster Salads	25	Sardines, per plate	25
Beef Tongue, Cold	25	Mutton, Cold Roast	25	Tripe, Pickled	25
Chicken Salad	25	Pigs' Feet, Pickled	20	Turkey, Cold Roast	30
Ham, Cold Boiled	25	Pork, Cold Roast	25	Veal, Cold Roast	25
Lamb, Cold Roast	30	Pork and Beans, Cold	20		

SOUP.

Beef Soup	10	Bouillon	10	Codfish Chowder	10
		With Bread and Butter, 15 cents.			

FISH.

Bass, Black, Fried	25	Mackerel, Salt, Boiled	20	Trout, Lake, Fried	20
Codfish Balls, Fried	20	Mackerel, Salt, Broiled	20	Whitefish, Baked, Stuffed	20
Crabs, Soft Shell	35	Sardines, per plate	25	Whitefish, Broiled	20
Lobster, Fresh (half)	25	Trout, Boiled, with Egg		Whitefish, Fried	20
Lobster, Fresh (whole)	50	Sauce	20		

EGGS.

Boiled Eggs (Three)	15	Omelet, Ham	20	Scrambled Eggs	15
Dropped Eggs (Two)	15	Omelet, Jelly	25	Scrambled Eggs on Toast	20
Dropped Eggs (Three)	20	Omelet, Plain	15	Shirred Eggs	20
Fried Eggs (Two)	15	Poached Eggs on Toast(Two)	20		

ROAST OR BOILED.

Beef	25	Mutton	25	Turkey, with Cranberry	
Beef, Corned, and Spinach	25	Mutton, Leg of, with Caper		Sauce	30
Ham	25	Sauce	25	Veal, Stuffed	25
Lamb, Spring, Mint Sauce	35	Pork, with Apple Sauce	25		

BILL OF FARE—CONTINUED.

TO ORDER.

	CENTS.		CENTS.		CENTS.
Bacon, Fried or Broiled	20	Mutton Chops, Tomato		Steak, Tenderloin	35
Chicken, Fried, with Cream		Sauce	30	Steak, Tenderloin, with	
Sauce	30	Pigs' Feet, Fried	20	French Peas	45
Chicken, Spring, Broiled		Pigs' Feet, Pickled	20	Steak, Tenderloin, with	
(half)	40	Pork, Salt, Fried	20	Mushrooms	55
Ham, Broiled	20	Pork Chops, Fried	20	Sweet Breads, Fried	30
Ham and Eggs	35	Steak, Porterhouse	60	Tripe, Fried	20
Hash, Corned Beef	20	Steak, Porterhouse, with		Veal Cutlet, Breaded	25
Hash, Corned Beef, with		French Peas	70	Veal Cutlet, Breaded, with	
Poached Egg	25	Steak, Porterhouse, with		Tomato Sauce	30
Hash, Stewed Corned Beef	25	Mushrooms	80	Veal Cutlet, Plain	20
Kidneys, Broiled, on Toast	25	Steak, Sirloin	30	Veal Cutlet, Plain, with	
Liver and Bacon, Fried	25	Steak, Sirloin, with Fried		Tomato Sauce	25
Mush, Corn Meal, Fried	10	Onions	35	Welsh Rarebit	20
Mutton Chops	25	Steak, Small	20		

ENTREES.

Beef a la Mode	20	Corn Fritters, Cream Sauce	20	Mutton Pot Pie	20
Beefsteak Pie, Baked	20	Irish Stew	20	Pork and Beans, Baked	20
Chicken Pot Pie	30	Macaroni, Baked, with		Veal, Fricassee of, Gar-	
Codfish, Stewed in Cream	20	Cheese	20	nished with Vegetables	20

VEGETABLES.

Asparagus on Toast	10	Lettuce	10	Potatoes, Lyonaise	5
Beans, Baked (side dish)	5	Macaroni (side dish)	10	Potatoes, Minced, Fried	5
Beans, String	5	Mushrooms, Stewed	20	Potatoes, New, Boiled	5
Beets, Pickled	5	Onions, Boiled	5	Potatoes, New, in Cream	5
Cauliflower, Cream Sauce	10	Onions, Fried	5	Radishes	10
Celery, New	10	Onions, Young	10	Spinach	5
Corn, Sweet, Stewed	5	Peas, French	10	Tomatoes, Sliced	10
Cucumbers, Sliced	10	Peas, Green	5	Tomatoes, Stewed	5
		Potatoes, German, Fried	5		

RELISHES.

Beets, Pickled	5	Pickles, Imported English		Sauce, Apple	5
Cheese	5	Mixed	5	Sauce, Chili	5
Olives, Queen	10	Pickles, Sweet Mixed	5	Sauce, Cranberry	5
Pickles, Imported English		Pickles, Sweet Mixed, Chop-		Sauce, Rhubarb	5
Chow Chow	5	ped	5		

DAIRY DISHES.

Bread and Milk	10	Corn Meal Mush and Milk	10	Rice and Milk	10
Corn (Hulled) and Milk	10	Oatmeal Porridge and Milk	10	Soda Crackers and Milk	10

Any of the above, with Cream, 10 cents extra.

CAKES AND TOAST.

Cakes, Indian	10	Toast, Butter	5	Toast, Dry	5
Cakes, Wheat	10	Toast, Cream	15	Toast, Milk	10
		Toast, Dipped	5		

PUDDINGS, FRUITS, ICE CREAM, CAKE, PASTRY, ETC.

Apple Sauce	10	Custard, Cup	10	Pound Cake	10
Blackberries and Cream	10	Fruit Cake	10	Pudding, Cornstarch	10
Blueberries and Cream	10	Honey, White Clover	10	Pudding, Rice	10
Cake, Assorted	10	Ice Cream	10	Raspberries (Red) and	
Cantaloupe	15	Jelly Roll	10	Cream	10
Charlotte Russe	10	Macaroons	10	Raspberry Jam	10
Cheese	5	Peaches and Cream	15	Strawberries and Cream	10
Cranberry Sauce	5	Peaches, Preserved	10	Strawberry Short Cake	10
Currant Jelly	10	Pies, all kinds, per cut	5	Watermelon	10

TEA, COFFEE, ETC.

Beef Tea, per Bowl	15	Cocoa, per Pot	15	Milk, per Glass	5
Beef Tea, per Cup	10	Coffee, per Cup	5	Tea, per Cup	5
Buttermilk, per Glass	5	Coffee, per Pot	10	Tea, per Pot	10
Chocolate, per Cup	10	Coffee, Iced	5	Tea, Black, per Cup	5
Chocolate, per Pot	15	Cream, per Glass	10	Tea, Iced	5
Cocoa, per Cup	10	Lemonade, per Glass	5		

OYSTERS—NEW YORK COUNT AND SELECT.

Blue Points, ½ doz. on shell	25	Fried, per ½ doz	25	Roast, per ½ doz. on shell	35
Broiled, per ½ doz	25	Patties	25	Rockaways, ½ doz. on shell	25
Dry Stew	25	Raw, per ½ doz	15	Stew	25

No Tips Necessary for Waiters.

The practice of giving fees to table waiters, except at Christmas or other holidays, is not common in the United States, and it is not encouraged in Chicago. Patrons of hotels and restaurants prefer to pay their bills to the cashier and let the restaurant or hotel proprietor pay for the service of the waiter. Were the habit of giving fees to waiters to become common, the proprietor would reduce the wages of his waiters in proportion to the amount received in "tips" from guests, and hence waiters would not be the gainers.

The following necessaries are found to be as light in cost as in any city of this size:

Cost, First-Class for One Person.

For gentleman, board and room in private family, per week.............$10.00
Laundry, per week.........................1.00
Clothing, per week........................4.00
Papers, amusements, etc., per week.......2.00

Total, per week...................$17.00

COST OF LIVING ECONOMICALLY.

Board for gentleman, per week.... ... $5.00
Laundry, per week 50
Clothing through the year, per week.....1.00

Total........................ ....$6.50

COST OF LIVING AT CHEAP LODGING-HOUSES.

Lodging, per night, 10 cents; per week..$0.70
Food, per meal, 10 cents; per week..v....2.10
Clothing, per week, ...50
Laundry, per week..... 25

Total cost per week..............$2.85

Incidental Expenses (Average).

Shaving, one time.........................15c.
Hair-Cutting, one time ....30c.
Blacking Boots, one time............ .....10c.
Street Car Fare, each ride.................5c.
Newspapers, each copy...............1c., 2c.
Cigars, each....................5c., 10c., 15c.
Theater, one admission.......50c., 75c., $1 00
Suit of Clothing, average...............$30 00
Overcoat, average.......................$20 00
Hat, average............................$3 00
Shoes, one pair $3 00
Underclothing, one suit $4 00

CHARGE FOR USE OF HOUSES.

Per Month.

Rent of large house, furnished.......$150 00
Rent of large house, unfurnished......100 00
Rent of 12-room house, furnished.......80 00
Rent of 12-room house, unfurnished.....60 00
Rent of 6-room flat, first-class, unfur'd.40 00
Rent of 6-room flat, unfurnished.... ..30.00
Rent of cottage homes in suburbs.......20.00
Rent of small homes in suburbs.........10.00

MEDICAL ATTENDANCE—CHARGES MADE BY PHYSICIANS.

Ordinary visit during the day..........$2.00
Each additional patient, in the same household............................1.00
Visit between 10 P. M. and 6 A. M.......5.00
Rising at night (but not leaving office)....2.00
Visit as consulting physician....5.00 to 15.00
Each subsequent visit (as consulting physician).... ....3 00 to 10 00
If detained for unusual length of time, the charge per hour is.................2.00
Office consultation, according to importance of case.....................1.00 to 10 00
Letter of advice, or written opinion.
.............................5.00 to 25 00
Examination for life insurance...2.00 to 5.00
Certificate as family physician....2.00 to 3.00

Examination involving question of law, in case in which physician may be subpœnaed................$10.00 to 100.00
Visit to small-pox patient (in addition to regular charge)................ 1.00 to 3.00
Post-mortem, in case of legal investigation....................50.00 to 100 00
Attendance at court, per day..50.00 to 100.00
Services to distant patient, in addition to expense of travel, per day..50.00 to 100 00
Vaccination......................1 00 to 3 00
Surgical operations, according to degree of responsibility and skill required.
.............................3.00 to 500 00
Expense of nurse, per week....12.00 to 15.00

EXPENSE OF CARRIAGES ON FUNERAL OCCASIONS.

The following list, though not strictly adhered to by all undertakers, gives a sufficiently accurate idea of what are the usual charges for each carriage, each time, at funerals going to the various cemeteries:

CEMETERIES.	From North and South Sides.	From West Side.
Bohemian Cemetery..........	$6.00	$5.00
Boniface Cemetery...........	5.00	5 00
Calvary Cemetery......	6.00	6 00
Concordia Cemetery.........	7.00	5.00
Forest Home Cemetery........	7.00	5.00
Free Sons Cemetery..........	7.00	5 00
Graceland Cemetery........	5.00	5 00
Mt. Greenwood Cemetery....	8 00	8.00
Mt. Olive Cemetery.........	6.00	5.00
Mt. Olivet Cemetery.........	8.00	8 00
Oakwoods Cemetery...	6.00	6 00
Rosehill Cemetery..........	6.00	6.00
St. Stanislaus Cemetery.......	7.00	6 00
Waldheim Cemetery........	7.00	5 00

NOTE.—In cases where a funeral is from any point south of Twenty-second Street to any cemetery on the North or West Side, South Side undertakers usually add one dollar or

more to the above charges, according to the distance traveled.

CHARGE FOR HEARSE.—The charge for a hearse is generally two dollars more than for a carriage.

Charge for Hearse from home to depot, $5. Charge for Carriage from home to depot, $3.

COST OF COFFINS.—From $15 to $125. The latter sum should be sufficient to procure a good hardwood, cloth-covered casket; but, if a very elegant casket is wanted, the price may be $425 or more.

COST OF DEATH NOTICE IN PAPERS. — In Tribune—First insertion, free; subsequent insertions, first five lines, 50 cents, each additional line, 35 cents. In Inter Ocean—First insertion, free; each subsequent insertion, 25 cents, the notice not exceeding five lines in length. In Herald or Times—First insertion, free; subsequent insertions, 50 cents. In News Record—Two insertions, free; each subsequent insertion at the rate of 12½ cents a line.

COST OF BURIAL LOTS AT THE VARIOUS CEMETERIES.

Calvary, $25 to $100 per lot, according to size and location, the smallest lots being 10 feet by 16 feet.
Cemetery of the Congregation of the North Side, 50 cents per square foot.
Concordia, $35 and upwards per lot.
Forest Home, 35 to 45 cents per square foot.
Free Sons of Israel, $20 to $40 per lot; lots 12 feet by 16 feet.
Graceland, 65 cents to $1 per square foot.

Mt. Greenwood, 30 cents and upwards per square foot.
Mt. Olive, 30 to 40 cents per square foot.
Mt. Olivet, $25 to $100 per lot.
Oakwoods, 50 cents to $2 per square foot.
Rosehill, 50 cents per square foot.
St. Maria, 25 cents, 45 cents, 65 cents and 85 cents per square foot.
Waldheim, 45 cents to $1 per square foot.

The following are the average prices of food products, subject to some fluctuation.

Meaning of Abbreviations.—bbl., barrel; bl'k, black; bu., bushel; Cal., California; can'd, canned; cr'm'ry, creamery; dom., domestic; dz., doz., dozen; e'h, each; Fla., Florida; gal., gallon; gr'n, green; Ind., Indian; N. O., New Orleans; pkg., package; qt., quart; sm'd, smoked.

NAME OF ARTICLE.	Cost in Cents
Almonds, Cal., per lb.	35
—Princess, per lb.	40
—Shelled Jordan, per lb.	60
Apple Butter, 5-lb. pail	55
Apples, Baldwin, per bu.	$1.50
—Greenings, per bu.	1.50
—Jonathan, per bu.	2.25
—Pound Sweets, per bu.	1.75
Apricots, per doz.	10 to 20
Asparagus, Fresh, per bunch	35
Bananas, per doz.	25 to 40
Barley, Coarse, per lb.	7
—Fine, per lb.	8
Beans, Black Turtle, per lb.	5
—N. Y. Navy, per lb.	5
—Norwegian, per lb.	7
Beef, Roast, Fresh, per lb.	8-15
—Corn'd, Can'd, 1-lb. can	13
—Roast, Can'd, 1-lb. can	13
—Smoked, per lb.	13
Beefsteak, Round, per lb.	10
—Porterhouse, per lb.	12 to 18
—Sirloin, per lb.	12½ to 15
—Tenderloin, per lb.	35 to 40
Blackberries, Fresh, per box	15
Blueberries, 2-lb. can	11 to 16
Buckwheat Flour, per lb.	4
—Self-rising, 2-lb package	11
Bullfrogs' Legs, per doz.	$1.50
Butter, Cr'm'y, per lb.	23 to 35
Butterine, Dairy, 8-lb pail	$1.10
—Creamery, 8-lb. pail	1.50
Butternuts, per peck	35
Canary Seed, per lb.	6
Catsup, Cucumber, per pint	35
—Mushroom, per pint	40
—Tomato, per quart	50
—Walnut, per pint	40
Celery, Fresh, per doz.	40 to 45
Celery Salt, per bottle	15
Cheese, Imported, per lb.	30-70
—Full Cream, per lb.	15 to 20
—Half Cream, per lb.	10
Cherries, Fresh Cal., per lb.	20
—Dried, Pitted, per lb.	20 to 25
Chestnuts, French, per lb.	30
Chickens, Fresh, per lb.	13
—Prairie, each	50 to 60
—Spring, per lb.	16
Chili Sauce, per pint	30
Chocolate, per lb.	24 to 80
Cider, Apple, per qt.	25 to 35
—Apple, per gal.	80
—Sweet, per gal.	30
Clams, per 100	$1.00
—Canned, 2-lb. can	20 to 25
Cocoanuts, Fresh, each	10
Cooked Ham, 5-oz tin	15
Corn, per bu.	50 to 55
—Gr'n. in Ear, per doz.	18 to 20
Corn Meal, per lb.	2
Cracked Wheat, per lb.	5
Crackers, Butter, per lb.	10
—Graham, per lb.	11
—Oatmeal, per lb.	11
—Pretzels, per lb.	15
Crawfish, per 100	$1.00
Cucumbers, Fresh, each	3 to 5
Dates, Dried, per lb.	10 to 25
Ducks, Domestic, per lb.	16
Eggs, per doz.	15 to 18
Entire Wheat Flour, per lb.	5
Figs, Dried, per lb.	20 to 30
Fish, Bass, Black, per lb.	20
—Bass, White, per lb.	11
—Bluefish, per lb.	15
—Brook Trout, 3-lb can	25
—Bullheads, per lb.	13
—Catfish, per lb.	13
Fish, Cod, Dried, per lb.	10 to 12
—Eels, per lb.	10 to 14
—Flounders, per lb.	13
—Herring, Smoked, per dz.	35
——Saltw'ter, Fr'sh, per lb.	10
—Macker'l, Fr'sh, e'h.	20 to 35
—Perch, Fresh, per lb.	11
—Pickerel, Fresh, per lb.	13
—Pike, Fresh, per lb.	13
—Porgies, per lb.	15
—Salmon, Fresh, per lb.	30
——Canned, per 2-lb. can	40
—Sardines, Large, per tin	50
——Medium, per tin	35
—Sturgeon, Sm'd, 1-lb. can	30
—Trout, Lake, Fresh, per lb.	13
—Weakfish, per lb.	20
—Whitefish, Fresh, per lb.	13
Flour, Buckwheat, per lb.	4
—Entire Wheat, ⅛-bbl.	$1.00
—Gluten, ⅛-bbl.	1.80
—Graham, ⅛-bbl.	65
—Minn. Patent, ⅛-bbl.	63 to 69
—Rye, per ⅛-bbl.	85
—Winter Wheat, ⅛-bbl.	65
Fowl, per lb.	13
Frogs' Legs, Small, per doz.	35
Grapes, Concord, per basket	50
—Hothouse, per lb.	$1.25
—Malaga, per lb.	25 to 30
—White Niagara, per lb.	20
Green Turtle, 2-lb can	30 to 35
Ham, Cooked, per lb.	30 to 35
Ham, Cured, per lb.	12 to 16
Hickory Nuts, per quart	5
Horse Radish, pint bottle	15
Hominy, Akron Pearl, per lb.	3
Honey, in combs, per lb.	20
—in quart jars, each	30
Huckleberries, Fresh, per qt.	15
Lamb, Spring, qu'rt'r	1.50-3.00
Lard, 3-lb. gross-weight tin	35
Lemons, Fla., per doz.	40 to 60
—Malaga, per doz.	20
—Palermo, per doz.	35
Lobsters, per lb.	25
Macaroni, 1-lb pkg.	10 to 15
Maple Syrup, quart bottle	40
Milk, in summer, per quart	5
—in winter, per quart	6
—Condensed, per can	12-18
Molasses, Bl'k Strap, per gal.	30
—Extra N. O., per gal.	60
—New Orleans, per gal.	50
Muskmelons, each	5 to 35
Mustard, Colman's, 1-lb. can	40
Mutton Chops, per lb.	12 to 16
Mutton, Leg of, per lb.	13
Nectarines, per doz.	15
Nutmeg Melons, each	5 to 10
Oatmeal, Akron, per lb.	3
Oats, per bu.	40
—Rolled, per lb.	4
Olives, pint bottle	45
Onions, Fresh, Red, per quart	5
—Fresh, White, per qt.	8-10
Oranges, California, per doz.	35
—Florida, per doz.	30
—Fla., Ind. River, per doz.	50
—Fla., Tangerines, per dz.	60
—Russets, per doz.	40
Oysters, per 100	$1.00
Partridges, each	50 to 60
Peach Butter, 5 lb. pail	70
Peaches, Fresh, per box	50-75
Peach Plums, per doz.	20
Pea Meal, per lb.	10
Peanuts, Raw, per lb.	8
—Fresh Roasted, per lb.	10
Pears, Green, per doz.	30 to 60
Peas, Green, Fresh, per peck	40
—Split, per lb.	4
Pecans, Extra Large, per lb.	30
Pickles, Cauliflower, per qt.	60
—Mixed, per pint	25
—Onions, per quart	30 to 35
—Stuffed Mangoes, per qt.	75
—Stuffed Peppers, per qt.	65
—Walnuts, per pint	35
Pineapple, Fresh, each	40
—Cheese, each	65c. to $1.50
Plum Butter, 5-lb. pail	70
Plums, Fresh, per doz.	20
Pomegranates, Cal., per doz.	60
Pop Corn, Shelled, per lb.	10
Pork, Fresh, per lb.	12
Potatoes, Burbanks, per bu.	60
—New, per peck	40
—Sweet, per peck	60
Prunes, Bosnia, per lb.	9
—Double Prepared, per lb.	20
Quails, each	25
Quinces, Preserved, 5-lb pail	90
Rabbits, each	15 to 25
Raisins, 4 Crown, per lb.	40
—5 Crown, per lb.	50
—Ondara, per lb.	10
—Sultana, per lb.	20
Raspberries, Fresh, per pint	7
Rice, Carolina Head, per lb.	9
—Extra Louisiana, per lb.	7
—Louisiana, per lb.	5
Rice Flour, 1-lb. package	12
Rolled Wheat, 20-lb. pkg.	88
Rye, per bu.	80
Rye Flour, per ⅛ barrel	85
Rye Meal, Akron, per lb.	4
Sago, East India, per lb.	6
Salt, New York, per lb.	1
—Genesee, 7-lb. sack	12
—Genesee, 14-lb sack	20
Sausage, Frankfort, 6 in tin	50
—Armo'r's Oxf'rd, 1-lb. can	35
Shrimps, per quart	40
—Gordon's, pint bottle	70
Squirrels, each	10 to 25
Steamed Oats, 2-lb. pkg.	15
Strawberries, Fresh, per qt.	8-12
Sugar, Cut Loaf, per lb.	5½
—Golden C., per lb.	4
—Granulated, per lb.	5
—Off A., per lb.	4¼
—Powdered, per lb.	6
—Standard A., per lb.	4¼
—White Ex. C., per lb.	4¼
Syrup, C'nfec'ers' A, per gal.	70
—Can. Sap Maple, per gal.	1.00
—Rock Candy Drips, "	80
—Vt. Maple, per qt.	35 to 40
Tomatoes, Fresh, per lb.	10
Truffles, Fr., ½ bot., peeled	85
—French, ½ bot., brushed	80
Turkey, Fresh, Dom., per lb.	15
Turnips, Yellow, per bu.	$1.75
Venison, per lb.	14 to 20
Veal Cutlets, Rib, per lb.	15
—Shoulder, per lb.	13
—Leg of, per lb.	16
—Loin of, per lb.	15
—Stew, per lb.	8 to 16
Vinegar, Alden Cider, per gal.	30
—Claret, per gal.	60
—White Wine, per gal.	20-25
—Malt, per quart	25
—Raspberry, per pint	35
Walnuts, Black, per peck	35
Watermelons, each	25 to 40
Wheat, per bu.	70c. to $1.10

What Are My Chances for Getting Employment?

It should be understood that, with the rapid introduction of labor-saving machinery, population is fast gathering in great centers. Where ten persons were formerly necessary upon the farm during the period of planting and gathering the harvest, only two or three are required at the present time.

Time was, within the distinct recollection of middle-aged people to-day, when the hoe, the scythe, the cradle, the common rake and a pitchfork were the farm tools, and all the children of the household and numerous hired men could depend upon having work on the farm the year round. To-day the farmer and his youngest son, with the aid of the riding plow, planter, cultivator, mowing machine, hay loader, self-binding reaper and thrashing machine, can do all the outdoor farm work.

Having no further use for the elder boys on the farm, they have gone off with the hired men to the city to find work. And the girls, who used to braid hats and weave and spin, and make butter and cheese, have gone away to the city also.

The boys and girls come home occasionally, to visit the old people, and they wear hats and clothing and dress goods made in the great city factories, and they eat butter which the father, though a farmer, buys at the creamery. They go down to the village, and all is changed. The old saw-mill is idle, and the woolen mills and the wagon shops are all closed; and the workmen who used to be there have all gone to the great central cities to find employment.

A few days of vacation and visit, and they will return to the metropolis to continue their labors or seek other places where they may find work.

This is preliminary to what we wish to say, which is, that Chicago, like other great cities, is constantly crowded with individuals who arrive from the rural districts and from foreign cities to find employment. With the steady stream of incoming applicants seeking opportunity to work, it is sometimes difficult to readily find opportunity with which at first to pay expenses. Under these circumstances, unless a definite understanding exists as to where work will be had, people should not come here without sufficient means of support for a few weeks, until the time when employment may be obtained.

WAGES THAT ARE PAID TO THOSE WHO ARE EMPLOYED.

One of the first persons you see upon arrival is the gentleman in a blue coat, known as a policeman. He is on the patrol department of the police, his duty being to guard people from danger at street crossings, depots, bridges, etc. He receives for his services $1,000 per year. Other patrolmen get $720 per year. All other persons in the employ of the police department get salaries varying in amount from $1,000 per year up to that of the general superintendent, who receives $5,500 per annum.

You enter a vehicle or car, which will convey you to some point of destination in Chicago. The driver of the cab gets from $10 to $15 per week. If a street car, the driver of the horses, the conductor, and the gripman on the cable car get each 21 cents per hour, and work from 10 to 12 hours per day. In some portions of the city, with different companies, the pay is about $3 per day.

Wages of Employes in a Few of the Vocations.

Actors, theatrical, per week	$25.00 to $75.00
Barbers, with Commission, per week	13.00
Bill Posters, per sheet	0.03
Brakemen, R. R., per month	50.00
Bricklayers, per day	4.00*
Bricklayers, Pressed Brick, per day	5.00*
Carpenters, per day	2.80*
Cash Girls and Boys, per week	2.50
Clerks, Dry Goods, per week	10.00
Clothing Cutters, per week	30.00 to 50.00
Compositors, Book, per thousand ems	0.40
Compositors, Job, per week	18.00
Compositors, Evening Papers, per thousand ems	0.42
Compositors, Morning Papers, per thousand ems	0.46
Cooks, Head, per week	20.00 to 30.00
Cooks, Second, per week	10.00 to 15.00
Cornice Makers, per day	2.50
Elevator Conductors, per mth	40.00 to 65 00
Engineers, Stationary, per day	2.00 to 3.50
Florists, per week	12.00
Gasfitters, per day	3.50*
Gate Tenders, R. R., per month	25.00 to 30.00
Hod Carriers, per day	2 00*
Laborers on Buildings, per day	1.75*
Packers, Goods, etc., per week	10.00 to 15.00

Painters, per day	$2.50 to $3.00*
Paperhangers, per roll	0.25 to 0.40
Plasterers, per day	4.00 to 5.00*
Plumbers, per day	3.75*
Salesmen, Average, per week	12.00
Salesmen, Superior, per week	20.00 to 30.00
Sewer Diggers, per day	2.50*
Ship Carpenters, per day	3 00*
Steamfitters, per day	3.00
Street Sweepers, per day	1.75*
Stone Cutters, per day	4.00*
Stone Setters, Building, per day	4.00*
Switchmen, R. R., per month	60.00
Teachers, Public. Primary—	
Principals, per year	1,050.00 to 1.600.00
Assistants, per year	400.00 to ..950.00
Teachers, Public, Grammar Schools—	
Principals, per year	1,050.00 to 2.500.00
Assistants, per year	500.00 to 1,000.00
Teachers, Public, High Schools—	
Principals, per year	1,800.00 to 2 800.00
Assistants, per year	500.00 to 2,000.00
Teamsters, per week	9.00 to 12.00
Teamsters, one horse, per week	18.00
Teamsters, two horses, per week	25.00
Tinsmiths, per day	2.50 to 3.00*
Waiters, Restaurant, per week	10.00

* Work eight hours per day and are generally organized into Unions.

The Influence of its Operations on the Markets of the World.

Turning aside, for a time, from the details in the cost of living and the expense of disappearing from the earth, as explained on the preceding pages, we will go from the retail quarter of the city over to La Salle Street, a thoroughfare largely devoted to insurance, banking, and exchange transactions, and while here we will turn our attention to

The Board of Trade Building,

which faces northward, at the southern end of La Salle Street, and is the largest institution of the kind in the world.

The building is constructed of gray granite, is 175 feet in width, and 225 feet in depth. The ceiling of the main room is 80 feet in height. It is 237 feet up to the look out balcony, and 322 feet to the top of the ship, which, though it seems like a toy boat floating up there in the air, is 15 feet long.

Height of Building.

That tiny vessel up there was the highest above ground of any object in the city in 1892, the Auditorium tower being 270 feet high, the Masonic Temple, 265 feet, and the Monadnock, 204 feet, which latter figure is about the general height of the 16-story buildings, 169 feet being the height of the Great Northern Hotel, which is the average elevation of the 14-story buildings.

We go up to the visitors' gallery and look down upon the multitude of men who are shouting, many of them at the top of the voice, in order that they may be heard by the individuals with whom they are dealing, who may be a few feet distant from the person who is speaking.

This Board of Trade organization was formed in 1850, although an incipient organization, having 82 members, was in existence in 1848. Its early meetings were convened in a building at the corner of South Water and La Salle Streets. Subsequently it went into its own building, at the corner of La Salle and Washington Streets, which was burned down and replaced by a substantial building after the fire. This building was sold, and the present edifice, begun in 1882, was completed in 1885 at a cost of $1,800,000. In 1860 the number of members was 625. To-day the membership includes about 2,000 names: the nominal price of a membership is $10,000, but certificates of membership can easily be bought for $1,000 to $1,500 from retiring members. The session begins at 9:30 A. M. and closes at 1.15 P. M.

Purpose of the Board of Trade.

The purpose of this organization is to afford an opportunity for dealers in the staple articles of food, especially grains, to meet each other and effect an exchange, either by buying or selling. An examination of the floor below shows several circular stairways called "pits," in different parts of the room, so arranged that individuals may stand at different elevations and see and hear each other. These pits are occupied by different classes of buyers and sellers, one being devoted to wheat, another to corn, another to oats, etc. No purchases of less than 5,000 bushels of grain or 250 packages of pork or lard are allowed by the rules of the board. The exchanges effected here in 1890 reached the sum of $86,617,157.

With these men money comes quickly, and it may go as soon. Some of the members, after a few years of the excitement, retire rich. Many, who come on to the board in independent circumstances, lose all and retire poor. It is all a bet as to what the future supply and the price of grain will be. At this writing, an earnest effort is being made to induce Congress to enact such a law as will prevent all dealing in grain unless the person actually has the grain in possession. Should such a law go into effect, the excitement we see on the board to-day will largely disappear.

MARKET REPORTS—SUGGESTIONS AS TO FORM FOR WORDING TELEGRAMS.

The transactions on the board to-day will affect the prices of breadstuffs throughout all the civilized world to-morrow. The willingness of a single individual to risk large money that grain will be much higher in the future, and to prove that fact by buying freely and advancing prices, may compel the people of London and Berlin, New York and Paris to pay hundreds of thousands of dollars more for bread in the next few days. All dealers in breadstuffs throughout the world are, therefore, anxious concerning the news from the Chicago Board of Trade.

To furnish that news the telegraph lines do a most important work. They do so great a work in the furnishing of news in general, it is well to observe the following directions:

1. Condense your message, if possible, into ten words, unless you are willing to pay more for a longer message.

2. Write very plainly, so that the operator may not mistake your meaning.

3. Give sufficient thought to your message to so frame it that it will absolutely serve its purpose when you send it. The following will serve as samples of unsatisfactory telegrams:

FIRST: "*Meet me at station in Chicago on Thursday morning.*"

Three questions immediately arise: What station! What Thursday morning! What hour Thursday morning!

You improve a little by sending the following:

SECOND: "*Meet me at Northwestern Depot, in Chicago, next Thursday morning.*"

The message is yet indefinite and unsatisfactory. Think a little while, and word your telegram in ten words explicitly, so that your friend may know when and where to meet you, as follows:

THIRD: "*At Northwestern Depot, Chicago, next Thursday morning, nine till twelve.*"

The telegraph companies have instituted regulations, whereby the individual can deposit a certain amount of money in a telegraph office, pay a certain sum for the transmission, and the person to whom the telegram is sent receives the money at the telegraph office where the message is received, when certain conditions, which are explained at the telegraph office, are complied with.

Form of Telegram Authorizing Payment of Money.

CHICAGO, ILL.,.........189

THE WESTERN UNION TELEGRAPH COMPANY,

Pay to.............................
.........................*Dollars for me,*
subject to the terms and conditions, which are agreed to.

Signature,..................
Address,..................

Amount of Transfer, $......
Telegraph Service,..........
Other Service,.............
Total,... ....$——

Relieving the Telegraph Company from Certain Liability.

THE WESTERN UNION TELEGRAPH COMPANY.

CHICAGO, ILL.,.........189

*As the within named.........
may not be able to produce proper evidence of personal identity, I hereby authorize and direct the Western Union Telegraph Company to pay the within named sum of.................
.....................Dollars,
at my risk, to such person calling for the same, as the proper officer, manager or agent of said Company shall believe to be said.............*
....

Signature,...................

TIME IN VARIOUS PARTS OF THE WORLD WHEN IT IS NOON, OR 12 M., IN CHICAGO.

The following table will serve to inform the individual as to what is the best hour to send the telegram to any of the cities herein mentioned, this being solar time.

Albany, N. Y......12.56 p. m.	Hamburg, Germany.6.31 p. m.	Paris, France........6.00 p. m.
Amsterdam, Holland.6.11 p. m.	Hamilton, Ont....12.32 p. m.	Pekin, China......1.37 a. m.
Angra, Azores.......4.02 p. m.	Hannibal. Mo.....11.50 a. m.	Pensacola, Fla.....12.02 p. m.
Annapolis, Md......12.45 p. m.	Harrisburg, Pa....12.44 p. m.	Philadelphia, Pa...12.50 p. m.
Antwerp, Belgium...6.09 p. m.	Hartford, Conn.....1.00 p. m.	Pittsburg, Pa.....12.31 p. m.
Atchison, Kan......11.30 a. m.	Havana, Cuba.....12.21 p. m.	Pittsfield, Mass....12.57 p. m.
Athens, Greece.....7.26 p. m.	Hong Kong, China..1.28 a. m.	Port Huron, Mich..12.17 p. m.
Atlanta, Ga......12.13 p. m.	Houston, Tex.....11.27 a. m.	Portland, Me......1.10 p. m.
Auburn, N. Y.....12.45 p. m	Indianapolis, Ind..12.07 p. m.	Portland, Ore......9.39 a. m.
Auckland, N. Z....5.34 a. m	Jacksonville, Ill...11.50 a. m.	Portsmouth, Va....12.46 p. m.
Augusta, Me......1.12 p. m	Jefferson City, Mo..11.42 a. m.	Poughkeepsie, N.Y.12.55 p. m.
Baltimore, Md....12.45 p. m	Kalama, Wash.....9.41 a. m.	Providence, R. I....1.05 p. m.
Bangor, Me.........1.16 p. m	Kansas City, Mo...11.32 a. m.	Quebec, Can......1.06 p. m.
Bath, Me............1.12 p. m	Keokuk, Ia.......11.45 a. m.	Quincy, Ill......11.50 a. m.
Berlin, Germany....6.45 p. m	Key West, Fla.....12.24 p. m.	Raleigh, N. C......12.33 p. m.
Bombay, India.....10.43 p. m	Knoxville, Tenn...12.15 p. m.	Richmond, Va.....12.41 p. m.
Boston, Mass.......1.07 p. m,	Laramie, Wyo....10.55 a. m.	Rio de Janeiro.....2.58 p. m.
Bremen, Germany...6.26 p. m.	Leavenworth, Kan.11.32 a. m.	Rochester, N. Y...12.38 p. m.
Bridgeport, Conn..12.58 p. m,	Lima, Peru......12.43 p. m.	Rome, Ga......12.15 p. m.
Brooklyn, N. Y...12.55 p. m,	Lincoln, Neb.....11.24 a. m.	Rome, Italy......6.41 p. m.
Brussels, Belgium...6.08 p. m	Lisbon, Portugal...5.14 p. m.	Sacramento, Cal....9.45 a. m.
Buenos Ayres, S. A...1.57 p. m.	Little Rock, Ark...11.42 a. m.	St. John, N. B......1.27 p. m.
Buffalo, N. Y.....12.35 p. m.	Liverpool, Eng....5.39 p. m.	St. Johns, Newfo'l'd.2.20 p. m.
Burlington, Ia......11.46 a. m.	London, Eng......5.50 p. m.	St. Joseph, Mo.....11.33 a. m.
Burlington, Vt.....12.58 p. m.	Louisville, Ky.....12.09 p. m.	St. Louis, Mo.....11.50 a. m.
Cairo, Egypt.......7.56 p. m.	Lowell, Mass........1.05 p. m.	St. Paul, Minn.....11.39 a. m.
Calcutta, India....11.44 p. m.	Macon, Ga......12.20 p. m.	St. Petersburg, Rus.7.52 p. m.
Cambridge, Mass...1.12 p. m.	Madrid, Spain.....5.36 p. m.	Salt Lake City....10.23 a. m.
Canton, China.....1.24 a. m.	Melbourne, Aus....3.31 a. m.	San Antonio, Tex..11.18 a. m.
Cape Town, Africa..7 05 p. m.	Memphis, Tenn....11.51 a. m.	San Francisco, Cal..9.41 a. m.
Charleston, S. C....12 26 p. m.	Meridian, Miss....11.57 a. m.	Santa Fe, N. M....10.47 a. m.
Cincinnati, Ohio...12.13 p. m.	Mexico City, Mexico 11.15 a. m.	Savannah, Ga......12.27 p. m.
Cleveland, Ohio...12.24 p. m.	Milledgeville, Ga...12.18 p. m.	Selma, Ala......12.03 p. m.
Columbia, S. C....12.27 p. m.	Milwaukee, Wis...11.59 a. m.	Sioux City, Ia.....11.25 a. m.
Columbus, Ohio....12.19 p. m.	Minneapolis, Minn.11.38 a. m.	Springfield, Ill....11.53 a. m.
Concord, N. H......1.05 p. m.	Mobile, Ala......11.59 a. m.	Springfield, Mass...1.00 p. m.
Constantinople......7.47 p. m.	Moncton, N. B......1.31 p. m.	Syracuse, N. Y....12.46 p. m.
Council Bluffs, Ia...11.29 a. m.	Montgomery, Ala..12.06 p. m.	Terre Haute, Ind..12.01 p. m.
Danville, Va......12.33 p. m.	Montreal, Can.....12.57 p. m.	Toledo, Ohio......12.17 p. m.
Davenport, Ia.....11.48 a. m.	Moscow, Russia....8.21 p. m.	Toronto, Can......12.34 p. m.
Dayton, Ohio......12.14 p. m.	Nashville, Tenn...12.04 p. m.	Trenton, N. J.....12.52 p. m.
Denver, Colo......10.51 a. m.	Newark, N. J.....12.54 p. m.	Troy, N. Y......12.53 p. m.
Des Moines, Ia.....11.36 a. m.	Newburgh, N. Y...12.55 p. m.	Utica, N. Y......12.51 p. m.
Detroit, Mich......12.19 p. m.	Newburyport, Mass..1.07 p. m.	Valparaiso, Chili...1.04 p. m.
Dublin, Ireland....5.26 p. m.	New Haven, Conn..12.59 p. m.	Vera Cruz, Mexico,11.26 a. m.
Dubuque, Ia......11.48 a. m.	New Orleans, La...11.51 a. m.	Vicksburg, Miss...11.48 a. m.
Easton, Pa......12.50 p. m.	Newport, R. I......1.06 p. m.	Vienna, Austria....6.57 p. m.
Edinburgh, Scotland.5.38 p. m.	New York, N. Y...12.55 p. m.	Virginia City, M. T.10.23 a. m.
Elmira, N. Y......12.44 p. m.	Norfolk, Va......12.48 p. m.	Washington, D. C.12.43 p. m.
Evansville, Ind....12 02 p. m.	Northampton, Mass.1.00 p. m.	Wheeling, W. Va..12.28 p. m.
Fort Wayne, Ind..12.10 p. m.	Norwich, Conn.....1.02 p m.	Wilmington, Del...12.49 p. m.
Frankfort, Ky.....12.12 p. m.	Ogdensburg, N. Y.12.49 p. m.	Wilmington. N. C..12.41 p. m.
Galveston, Tex....11.32 a. m.	Omaha, Neb......11.27 a. m.	Worcester, Mass...1.06 p. m.
Geneva, Switzerl'nd.6.16 p. m.	Ottawa, Can......12.48 p. m.	Yankton, S. Dak..11.21 a. m.
Halifax, N. S........1.37 p. m.	Panama, S. A.....12.33 p. m.	Yokohama, Japan...3.10 a. m.

Population of Foreign Cities; Telegraph Rates to Them from Chicago. 157

Ten letters constitute a word. If a word contains more than ten letters it will be charged for as two words. The address, signature and date are all charged for. Messages repeated at half-rates.

Cities.	Countries.	Population of City.	Cost of Telegrams Per Word.	Cities.	Countries.	Population of City.	Cost of Telegrams Per Word.
Aberdeen	Scotland*	105,189	$ .31	Lille	France	188,272	$ .31
Agra	India*	165,340	1.29	Lima	S. America	101,488	1.72
Alexandria	Egypt	227,064	.62	Lisbon	Portugal*	253,496	.45
Allahabad	India	176,770	1.29	Liverpool	England	604,562	.31
Altona	Prussia*	104,717	.31	London	England	4,221,452	.31
Amritsar	India	151,896	1.29	Lucknow	India	272,590	1.29
Amsterdam	Holland*	417,539	.38	Lyons	France	376,613	.31
Antwerp	Belgium	215,779	.36	Madras	India	449,950	1.29
Athens	Greece	114,335	.44	Madrid	Spain	472,228	.46
Bahia	Brazil	140,000	1.89	Malaga	Spain	134,016	.46
Bangalore	India	155,857	1.29	Mandalay	India	187,910	1.33
Bangkok	India	600,000	1.29	Manila	Ind. Arch'pg'o	160,000	2.51
Barcelona	Spain	272,481	.44	Manchester	England	506,469	.31
Barcilly	India	109,844	1.29	Marseilles	France	376,143	.31
Barmen	Germany*	103,666	.31	Melbourne	Australia	491,378	3.23
Baroda	India	101,818	1.29	Messina	Italy	126,497	.38
Belfast	Ireland*	207,671	.31	Mexico	Mexico	350,000	† *2.85
Benares	India	222,420	1.29	Milan	Italy	321,839	.38
Berlin	Germany	1,609,536	.31	Montevideo	Uruguay*	120,000	2.00
Birmingham	England*	429,000	.31	Montreal	Canada	140,747	††
Blackburn	England	120,496	.31	Moscow	Russia	753,469	.49
Bologna	Italy*	123,274	.38	Munich	Bavaria*	135,715	.31
Bolton	England	115,253	.31	Nagoya	Japan	150,000	1.78
Bombay	India	804,470	1.29	Nanking	China	349,000	2.45
Bordeaux	France*	240,582	.31	Nantes	France	127,482	.31
Bradford	England	216,938	.31	Naples	Italy	494,314	.38
Bremen	Germany	118,615	.31	Newcastle	England	187,502	.31
Breslau	Germany	299,405	.31	Nottingham	England	212,602	.31
Brighton	England	115,606	.31	Odessa	Russia	270,643	.49
Bristol	England	222,049	.31	Oldham	England	132,010	.31
Brussels	Belgium	482,158	.36	Oporto	Portugal	105,830	.45
Bucharest	Roumania*	221,000	.42	Osaka	Japan	432,005	1.73
Buda Pesth	Aust.-Hung	513,010	.40	Palermo	Italy	244,991	.38
Buenos Ayres	S. America	350,000	1.82	Paris	France	2,344,550	.31
Cairo	Egypt	374,838	.67	Patna	India	170,654	1.29
Calcutta	India	466,459	1.29	Pekin	China	1,648,800	2.45
Canton	China	1,600,000	2.15	Pernambuco	S. America	130,000	1.69
Cardiff	England	130,283	.31	Poonah	India	160,460	1.29
Cawnpore	India	182,310	1.29	Portsmouth	England	160,128	.31
Charkow	Russia	159,660	.49	Prague	Aus-Hung	310,485	.40
Christiania	Norway*	150,400	.41	Preston	England	107,864	.31
Cologne	Germany	161,266	.31	Rangoon	India	181,210	1.29
Colombo	Ceylon*	120,000	1.31	Riga	Russia	175,332	.49
Con'nople	Turkey	871,561	.43	Rio de Janeiro	S. America	357,332	1.89
Copenhagen	Denmark*	320,000	.41	Rotterdam	Holland	209,136	.38
Danzig	Germany	114,822	.31	Rome	Italy	427,684	.38
Damascus	Turkey-Asia	200,000	.55	Rouen	France	107,163	.31
Delhi	India	193,580	1.29	Sainagar	India	132,681	1.29
Dhar	India	100,000	1.29	Salford	England	198,717	.31
Dresden	Germany	276,523	.31	Santiago	S. America	225,000	2.25
Dublin	Ireland	347,312	.31	Seville	Spain	133,938	.46
Dundee	Scotland	140,463	.31	Seoul	Corea	250,000	2.62
Edinburgh	Scotland	261,970	.31	Shanghai	China	355,000	2.02
Elberfeld	Prussia	106,499	.31	Sheffield	England	325,304	.31
Florence	Italy	167,001	.38	St. Etienne	France	117,875	.31
Foochow	China	630,000	2.02	Smyrna	Turkey'Asia	200,000	.53
Frankfort	Germany	154,513	.31	Stockholm	Sweden*	245,317	.45
Genoa	Italy	179,515	.38	St. Petersburg	Russia	956,226	.49
Ghent	Belgium	150,656	.36	Strasburg	Germany	111,987	.31
Glasgow	Scotland	507,143	.31	Stuttgart	Germany	125,906	.31
Hague	Holland	153,340	.38	Sunderland	England	131,302	.31
Hakodate	Japan	112,494	1.78	Surat	India	113,417	1.29
Hamburg	Germany	305,690	.31	Sydney	Australia	220,420	3.25
Hanover	Germany	139,746	.31	Tabris	Persia	165,000	.68
Hongkong	China	221,441	2.02	Teheran'	Persia	210,000	.68
Hull	England	200,934	.31	Tiflis	Russia'Asia	160,000	.55
Hyderabad	India	354,692	1.29	Tioto	Japan	255,403	1 78
Jeypore	India	142,578	1.29	Tokio	Japan	1,378,132	1.78
Jondpore	India	150,000	1.29	Toulouse	France	147,617	.31
Kagoshima	Japan	200,000	1.78	Trieste	Aus.-Hung	144,844	.40
Kanagawa	Japan	108,263	1.78	Tunis	Africa	120,000	.39
Kesho	India	150,000	1.29	Turin	Italy	252,832	.38
Kingston	England	154,250	.31	Valencia	Spain	170,763	.46
Kioto	Japan	229,810	1.78	Valparaiso	Chili	104,000	2.25
Kishineff	Russia	120,074	.49	Venice	Italy	159,100	.38
Konigsberg	Germany	151,151	.31	Victoria	China	221,141	2.45
Lahore	India	176,720	1.29	Vienna	Aus.-Hung	1,378,530	.40
Leeds	England	369,099	.31	Warsaw	Russia	450,000	.49
Leicester	England	142,581	.31	West Ham	England	128,692	.31
Leipzig	Germany	170,076	.31	Yagoya	Japan	126,898	1.78
Lemberg	Aus.-Hung	122,000	.40	Yokohama	Japan	115,012	1.78
Liege	Belgium	142,657	.36	Zanzibar	Africa	100,000	2.21

* Same price charged to all parts of the country. See "Code" of telegraph words elsewhere.
† * Price for ten words; 24c. each additional word. †† See telegraph rates elsewhere.

Suggestions to Senders of Telegrams to Foreign Countries.

If you expect to send many telegrams while in Chicago, it may be well to adopt a code of words which may be understood by your friend and yourself, and thus your business be unknown to the telegraph operators, and you save much money and time in sending telegrams. You may formulate a code and agree with your friend or business correspondent what it shall be, or you may adopt the words and phrases herewith, through understanding with your correspondents. In the preparation of your code, observe these suggestions:

1. No code-word should contain more than ten letters.

2. Each code-word should be enough different from the others, in spelling, to prevent confusion in the transmission of the telegraphic characters.

3. A message may sometimes be composed partly of code-words and partly of words used in their ordinary sense. The code words, therefore, should not be such words as are frequently used in business correspondence, but should be so peculiar in their nature as to be readily distinguished from the other words of a message.

The following sentences are such as are in frequent use when sending telegrams. The words in fullface type may each represent an entire sentence.

Securing Passage.

Abstruse..What is the fare for passage to—!
Adamant..Please send list of sailings for—
Affinity....Please secure accommodation on steamship—— for self and wife.
Agnostic..Please secure accommodation on Anchor Line for self, wife and family.
Alembic...Secure state-room on the —— and advise number.
Amnesty..My passage is not engaged.
Antelope..Inside berths preferred.
Antimony.Outside berths preferred.
Aquatic....Adjoining rooms preferred.
Arterial...As near amidships as possible.
Athletic...Your passage is secured.
Auditor...We have secured the rooms by steamer sailing ——
Autocrat..Cannot secure the desired berth.
Avarice...We cannot secure rooms by that steamer.

Departure.

Bachelor..On what date do you leave!
Balcony...I (we) sail to-day.
Balloon...I (we) sail Monday.
Baluster..I (we) sail Wednesday.
Bandit.....I (we) sail per —— on ——
Barbecue.——is better, and we expect to leave here on the ——
Baritone..Cannot sail (or leave) to-day.
Barnacle..Cannot sail (or leave) to-morrow.
Basilisk....Cannot sail (or leave) till Monday.
Bastile....Cannot sail (or leave) till Friday.
Bedizen....Will not be ready to leave until—
Benefice...Departure delayed on account of-
Benzine...Urgent business prevents my leaving by ——
Betrayal..I (we) think it best to postpone departure.
Beverage..Do not delay your departure.
Biology....I (we) think it best to postpone departure until ——; I may further advice, shall sail on that date per steamship ——
Bismuth...We are detained here by illness, and cannot say when we shall be able to leave.
Bitumen..Cannot sail by ——; will come next steamer.
Bivouac...Departure postponed; will wire you date I leave.

Letters and Telegrams.

Blockade..Any mail for me or my party!
Blowpipe.Any telegrams or cables for me!
Bobolink..Have you any letters for me! If so, please forward to ——
Bombast..Have you a registered letter on hand!
Boniface..Have no registered letter for you.

Botany....Have the following mail matter on hand for ——
Brigadier.Have important letters for you.
Brocade...Have nothing on hand for you.
Buffoon...We have telegram for you; shall we forward!
Cactus......We have inquired at post office; no letters there.
Cadet.......Please send letters to this place till otherwise directed.
Caitiff......Please send letters to- until the—
Caldron...Please send letters to this place till the ——
Calomel...In consequence of the illness of —— we are detained here for the present; please send our letters here accordingly.
Campaign.If you wish to communicate with me by telegraph, do so at —— before ——
Cannibal..Forward no more mail here, after ——
Canticle...Please hold my letters till further advice.
Capricorn.Have you forwarded mail matter according to instructions?
Cardinal..Have forwarded your mail matter as desired.
Category..Mail matter was sent to——
Cavalier...Have not forwarded mail matter.
Cayenne...Mail matter duly received.
Centurion.Mail matter not received.
Cerement.Telegram received; have done as requested.
Chalice....Don't understand instructions; please repeat.
Chancery.Please advise by letter.
Charade...Please advise by telegraph.
Cherubim.Please make inquiries at the post office.

Hotel Accommodation.

Daffodil....Can you accommodate a party of ——!
Darksome.Please reserve rooms for self and friends to-night.
Decimate.Can you accommodate self, wife and maid!
Denizen....Please reserve rooms for self and friend to-morrow.
Deponent.Please reserve good room; shall be in to-night.
Dewdrop..Please reserve good room; shall be in to-morrow.
Diadem....Please reserve rooms for me at the —— hotel.
Diagnose..Reserve my rooms; shall be with you on ——
Didactic...We can accommodate your party.
Digital.....Unable to accommodate your party; house full.
Diocese....We have reserved rooms.
Diploma...Rooms reserved for you at hotel named in letter.

Telegraph Code Words—Continued.

DormouseCannot get accommodations for you at hotel named, but have got nice rooms for you at the—

Dynasty...Cannot get rooms for you at the hotel named; shall I take them at the ——?

Express, Storage, Etc.

Eclipse.....Forward goods to care of ——

Effigy......Forward goods so as to reach here by ——

Emissary..Please pay all charges and debit me.

Endemic..Have forwarded your goods to—

Epigram..Have you anything in storage for me?

Evangel...Have nothing in storage for you.

Exodus.....Goods detained at customs.

Remittances.

Festoon...Are you in need of money?

Flotilla....Money almost exhausted.

Fossil......If you do not remit, shall be in trouble.

Fragile....Remit immediately,by telegraph.

Fulcrum..Impossible to remit before——

Return.

Galaxy.....Is it necessary for us to return at once?

Gallop. ....Telegraph if it is necessary I should return.

Galvanic...If agreeable, will remain another week.

Garland...Return by first steamer.

Gazelle. ...Return at once.

Gelatine...Return as soon as possible.

Geology...Advise you to hurry home.

Geranium.Return at once; important matters require your presence here.

Gewgaw...You must be here by the ——

Grenade... —— is dangerously ill, and the doctors think you should return at once.

Hectic......No necessity for you to return yet.

Hemlock..You need not return till ——

Hydrant...No need to hasten home; everything going on well.

Hyphen...Nothing here requiring your return.

Icicle......Please prepay my passage, and telegraph me name of steamer.

Jasmine...Have prepaid your passage, as requested.

Jubilee..... I have prepaid your passage per ——

SUGGESTIONS TO THE STRANGER IN THE CITY CONCERNING THE BOULEVARDS AND PARKS.

After being settled in your home in Chicago and becoming acquainted with the central part of the city, you will wish to go out to one of the numerous parks which abound in Chicago.

By a little study of the Key Map on page 114 you will find a line indicating a continuous street, extending from the north end of Lincoln Park, in Division 3, westward into Division 2; thence southward to Humboldt Park, in Division 5; thence south and west into Division 4, to Garfield Park; thence south and east to Douglas Park, in Division 5; thence south to Gage Park, on Fifty-fifth Street, in Division 8; thence eastward to Washington Park, in Division 9, from the south end of which communication is had with Jackson Park and the World's Fair grounds. From Washington Park this line extends northward to the business center, in Division 6, where it is proposed to enter a subway, under Lake Michigan, a little to the eastward of the end of Monroe Street, which subway, will connect with the Lake Shore Drive, on the north side of the Chicago River.

This is known as the boulevard system of Chicago, all the great parks being connected by a beautifully kept, broad avenue, lined on either side with grand elm trees and palatial residences. At an early opportunity you should, in company with congenial friends, be carried in a roomy, easy carriage. on some fine day. over this connecting system of boulevards.

If time permits, it is best to take this journey in two separate days, the first being occupied in going to Lincoln Park, Humboldt and Garfield Parks, returning to the business center, from Garfield Park, by way of Washington Boulevard.

On the second day, go out to Garfield Park and southward to Douglas and Washington Parks, returning to the business center by way of Michigan Avenue, Drexel or Grand Boulevard.

This is only a beginning of your visit to these interesting places. You have yet had no time to carefully and fully visit the great Chicago parks. Either by carriage or otherwise you should go to each again, and a day spent at each will be amply rewarded in the pleasure derived in a study of its beauties.

After a deliberate examination of the animals, the birds, conservatories, lakes, broad lawns, shrubs, trees and flowers, scattered over them all, each having its peculiar attractions, you will be always inclined to declare the last one visited the most attractive.

To see the parks to the best advantage, it is well to visit them with a company of three or four persons, in a sufficiently open carriage to see in all directions. The party should be accompanied by a guide, who is a ready talker—one who is familiar with all the attractive features of the grounds, and is ready, clear and full in explanation.

If the stranger cannot go thus in a carriage, conveyance to the parks may be had by street cars, the charge to any one of them, from the center of the city, being 5 cents, the line leading to each park being given on page 161. Upon arrival in the park, at central locations may be found park phaetons, which carry passengers at a charge of 25 cents per hour for each adult, the driver giving a description of points of interest in passing.

The Cemeteries of the City

Are also places of great beauty, being filled with marble sculpture of immense cost and great variety. . On the following pages we give in miniature some of the views and monuments you will see in these parks, also important facts as to parks and how to reach parks and cemeteries. Remember that the street car lines are designated by numbers, and are explained in **Index No. 1,** beginning on page 128.

The following Tables contain important information concerning size, and distance from center of the city.

Parks in Chicago.

For Location, in Divisions and Sections, see Maps, Pages 114–127.

PAVILION,
HUMBOLDT PARK.

POLICE MONUMENT,
(Haymarket Square),
Erected 1889,
BY
CITIZENS OF CHICAGO.
Cost, $5,000.

NAME OF PARK.	Where Located.		Number of Acres in Park.
	Divi-sion.	Sec-tion.	
Aldine Square........	.6	.17	....1.44
Campbell Park ‡.....	..5	..8	....0.05
Congress Park ‡.....	5	..7	....0.07
Douglas Park........	..5	.10	.179.79
Douglas Mon'm'nt Sq.	..6	.17	....2.02
Ellis Park..........	..6	.17	....3.38
Gage Park..........	..8	..4	...20.00
Garfield Park........	..4	..6	.185.87
Groveland Park......	..6	.17	....3.40
Holstein Park.......	..3	.16	....2.30
Humboldt Park......	..5	..1	.200.62
Jackson Park ‖......	10	..7	.586.00
Jefferson Park.	..5	..9	....5.50
Lake Front Park.....	..6	..8	...41.00
Lincoln Park........	..3	.18	.250.00
Logan Square ‡......	..2	.15	....4.25
Midway Plaisance ‖..	..9	..9	...80.00
Union Park.........	..5	..6	..14.03
Vernon Park........	..5	..9	....4.00
Washington Park....	..9	..8	.371.00
Washington Square ‡..	..6	..1	....2.25
Wicker Park........	..5	..2	....4.00
Woodlawn Park......	..6	.17	....3.86

‡ Location of these parks described in Street Index.
‖ Grounds selected for the location of the World's Columbian Exposition.

VIEW IN HUMBOLDT PARK.

LINCOLN MONUMENT,
(Lincoln Park).
Erected..October 22, 1887,
BY
ELI BATES.
Cost, $40,000.

Cemeteries in the City and in the Vicinity of Chicago.

VIEW IN DOUGLAS PARK.

OTTAWA INDIAN GROUP,
(Lincoln Park),
Erected 1886
BY
MARTIN RYERSON.
Cost, $14,000.

NAME OF CEMETERY.	Where Located.		Number of Acres.	Miles Distant from City Hall.
	Divi-sion.	Sec-tion.		
Anshe Maariv.....	..1	.10	......	12..
Austro-Hungarian..	..*	..*	....2..	11..
Beth Hamedrash..	..9	.12	....½	..9..
B'nai Abraham....	..*	..*	......	11..
B'nai Sholom......	..3	.11	......	..6..
Bohemian Cem'ry..	..2	..5	......	..7½
Calvary..	..†	..†	.100..	10..
Cong'ation of N. S.	..3	..1	....⅜	..8..
Concordia.........	..*	..*	...80..	11..
Fores' Home Cem.	..*	..*	...86..	10½
Free Sons of Israel	..*	..*	....7½	11..
German Lutheran	..3	.11	..14½	..6..
Graceland	..3	..8	.128..	..6..
Kebr'w Ben'vol'nt	..3	.11	....2..	..6..
Moses Montefiore..	..*	..*	....1..	11..
Mt. Greenwood....	11	..7	..30	16½
Mt. Hope Cemet'ry	11	.10	......	17..
Mt. Olive Cemet'ry	..1	.10	...41..	12..
Mt. Olivet Cemet'y	11	..7	...80..	16½
Oakwoods.........	..9	.12	.182..	..9..
Ohavey Emunah...	..*	..*	....⅜	11..
Ohavey Sholom...	..9	.12	....1..	..9..
Rosehill	..3	..1	.500..	..8..
St. Boniface	..3	..5	...30..	..6..
St. Maria.	..¶..	..¶.	.102..	13..
Sinai Congr'g'tion	..3	..1	....2..	..8..
Waldheim	..*	..*	...80..	11..
Zion Congreg'tion ..	..3	..1	....4..	..8..

* Located west of City Limits, near Maywood.
† Located north of City Limits, on Lake Shore.
¶ Locat'ed south of City Limits, near Eighty-seventh Street.

CONSERVATORY,
JACKSON PARK.

GRANT MONUMENT,
(Lincoln Park).
Erected..October 17, 1891,
BY
CITIZENS OF CHICAGO.
Cost, $65,000.

VIEW IN DOUGLAS PARK.

VIEW IN DOUGLAS PARK.

These Tables give information, concerning lines of railway, time and expense of going to Parks and Cemeteries from City Hall.

Parks and How to Reach Them.†

The time required and expense of going to Cemeteries liable to change.

ARTESIAN WELL,
GARFIELD PARK.

NAME OF PARK.	Street Car Lines that Go There.*	Time in Min- utes.
Aldine Square........	(No. 66)	..33
Campbell Park ‡....	(No. 82)	..38
Congress Park ‡.....	(No. 98)	..35
Douglas Park........	(No. 88)	..42
Douglas Mon'm'nt Sq.	(No. 66)	..30
Ellis Park........ ...	(No. 66)	..31
Gage Park...........	(No. 3)	..27
Garfield Park.......	(No. 85)	..32
Groveland Park......	(No. 66)	..28
Holstein Park.......	(No. 89)	..40
Humboldt Park......	(No. 79)	..42
Jackson Park ‖......	(No. 51)	..54
Jefferson Park.......	(No. 85)	..15
Lake Front Park.....	(No. 82)	...5
Lincoln Park........	(No. 20)	..20
Logan Square ‡......	(No. 89)	..40
Midway Plaisance ‖..	(No. 53)	..46
Union Park..........	(No. 85)	..17
Vernon Park.........	(No. 75)	..24
Washington Park....	(No. 53)	..41
Washington Square ‡	(No. 20)	..14
Wicker Park........	(No. 89)	..31
Woodlawn Park......	(No. 66)	..29

LA SALLE STATUE,
(Lincoln Park),
Erected..October 12, 1889,
BY
LAMBERT TREE.

† The charge by street cars to any park in the city is usually 5 cents.
* Street car numbers found, and lines described, on pages 128-135.
‡ Location of these parks described in Street Index.
‖ Grounds selected for the location of the World's Columbian Exposition.

DREXEL FOUNTAIN,
DREXEL BOULEVARD.

VIEW IN GARFIELD PARK.

Cemeteries in Chicago, and Street Car Lines That Go There.

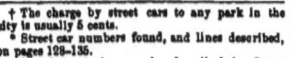

VIEW IN JEFFERSON PARK.

NAME OF CEMETERY.	Roads that Go There from Center of the City.	Time Re- quired to Go There in Min- utes.	Cost of Going There in Cents.
Anshe Maariv.....	(No. 9)	..50	..25
Austro-Hungarian	(No. 4)	..32	..28
Beth Hamedrash..	(No. 13)	..36	..27
B'nai Abraham....	(No. 4)	..32	..28
B'nai Sholom.....	(No. 10)	..22	..17
Bohemian Cem'ry	(No. 7)	..24	..23
Calvary, ...	(No. 6)	..32	..30
Cong'ation of N. S.	(No. 6)	..25	..23
Concordia.	(No. 4)	..32	..28
Forest Home Cem.	(No. 4)	..37	..30
Free Sons of Israel	(No. 4)	..32	..28
German Lutheran	(No. 10)	..22	..17
Graceland	(No. 10)	..22	..17
Hebr'w Ben'vol'nt	(No. 10)	..22	..17
Moses Montefiore..	(No. 4)	..32	..28
Mt. Greenwood....	(No. 3)	..56	..39
Mt. Hope Cemet'ry	(No. 3)	..69	..39
Mt. Olive Cemet'ry	(No. 9)	..50	..25
Mt. Olivet Cemet'y	(No. 3)	..56	..39
Oakwoods...	(No. 13)	..36	..27
Ohavey Emunah..	(No. 4)	..32	..28
Ohavey Sholom. .	(No. 13)	..36	..27
Rosehill	(No. 6)	..25	..23
St. Boniface ..	(No. 6)	..21	..17
St. Maria. .	(No. 3)	..47	..30
Sinai Congr'g'tion	(No. 6)	..25	..23
Waldheim	(No. 4)	..32	..28
Zion Congreg'tion	(No. 6)	..25	..23

DOUGLAS MONUMENT,
(Thirty-fifth St., near the lake).
Erected 1876,
BY
STATE LEGISLATURE.
Cost, $75,000.

SCHILLER MONUMENT,
(Lincoln Park),
Erected .. ..May 15, 1886,
BY
GERMAN SOCIETIES OF
CHICAGO.
Cost, $8,000.

GARFIELD PARK PAVILION.

CLUB HOUSE,
WASHINGTON PARK.

Location, Seating Capacity and Charge for Use of the Same.

NAME OF HALL.	LOCATION.	No. of Seats.	Rent for Single Entertainment. For General Entertainment.	For Dancing.
Accordia Hall........ a	112 and 114 Randolph St.............	.150	.........$5	....
Alhambra Theater......	State St. and Archer Av.......... ...	2,660		
Apollo Hall............b	2726-2730 State St.................	.200	$5..or...$6	....
Apollo Hall............c	69 State St., 5th floor.............	.250	$20,$25,$50	....
Apollo Hall............	252-256 Blue Island Av.............	.800	.........$5	........$65
Arbeiter Hall	368 W. Twelfth St.................	.300		$10..or. $25
Arbeiter Hall ....a	Sedgwick and Blackhawk Sts........	.125		
Arlington Hall.....	3032 Indiana Av. (large hall)......	.600	$15. to $20	........$25
Arlington Hall.........	3032 Indiana Av. (small hall)......	.150	.........$5	....
Athenæum Hall..,....d	18-26 Van Buren St........	.400	.........$25	....
Attfield Hall...........	465 State St......................	.600		
Auditorium..........	Wabash Av. and Congress St........	4,050	.........$600	....
Aurora Turner Hall.....	Milwaukee Av. and W. Huron St.....	.600	$45..to..$75	....
Battery D Armory	Michigan Av., N. of Lake Front Park.	5,000	.........$100	........$300
Bohemian Hall.........	106 and 108 De Koven St. (large hall).	.450	$5.. .to..$10	$25..to.. $35
Bohemian Hall.. ......a	106 and 108 De Koven St. (small hall).	.150	.........$2	....
Bohemian Turner Hall...	74 and 76 W. Taylor St. (large hall).	.600	.........$5	$25..to.. $50
Bohemian Turner Hall...	74 and 76 W. Taylor St. (small hall).	.200	.........$2	........$10
Bowman's Hall........ e	120 Chicago Av....................	.100	.........$8	....
Brand's Hall..........	160-170 N. Clark St...............	.800		
Brewster Hall.........	787 W. North Av..................	.600		........$30
Bricklayers' Hall.......f	Peoria and W. Monroe Sts..........	.380	.........$12	$25. to .$40
Carpenter Hall.........g	221 W. Madison St................			
Casino	227 Wabash Av...................	.600		
Castle's Hall............h	619-627 W. Lake St...............	.550		
Central Hall...........	2139 Wabash Av..................	.500		
Central Music Hall......i	State and Randolph Sts............	1,800	.........$125	....
Chicago Opera House....	Clark and Washington Sts..........	2,100		
Chickering Music Hall...	241 Wabash Av...................	.350	.........$25	....
Clark Street Theater.....	Kinzie and N. Clark Sts............	1,800		
Columbia Theater.......	104-110 Monroe St................	2,200		
Concordia Hall.........	235 and 237 Milwaukee Av.........	.600	$3. .to...$5	$15..to.. $25
Corinthian Hall........j	187 Kinzie St.....................	.100		
Criterion Theater......	274 Sedgwick St...........	1,700		
Curran's Hall..........k	350 Blue Island Av...............	.600	$15..or..$25	...... $55
Davies' Hall...........	Torrence Av. and 106th St..........			
Douglas Hall...........	Thirty-fifth St., near Indiana Av.....	.650	.........$12	$20.. or..$25
Douglas Hall.........m	South Park Av. & Twenty-seventh St..	.150		
Eden Musee...........	227 Wabash Av...................	.600		
Eigenmann's Hall......	South Chicago Av. & Ninety-third St..			
Englewood Opera House.n	315 Englewood Av................	1,000	$25..or..$35	....
Epstean's Museum......	111 Randolph St..................	.246		
Excelsior Hall ....a	107 Clark St......................	.150		
Farwell Hall...........	148 Madison St..........	1,800	$50..to ..$75	....
Finucane's Hall........o	2901 Archer Av...................			
First Cavalry Armory...	Michigan Av., N. of Lake Front Park.	4,800	$75 to..$100	....
Fitzgerald's Halls......p	182 W. Adams St..................	.300		
Folz's Hall............q	267 and 269 North Av.............	1,000	$10..or..$15	$30,$35,$40
Franchere's Hall.......r	188 Blue Island Av................	.400		
Freiheit Turn Hall......	3607-3611 Halsted St..............	.100		........$20
Garfield Hall..........a	Lincoln and Garfield Avs...........	.150		
Germania Hall..........a	62 N. Clark St....................	.600		
Grand Opera House.....	87 Clark St.......................	1,800		
Greenbaum Hall........	72-82 Fifth Av....................	.450	.........$10	........$25
Greif's Hall............s	54 W. Lake St....................	.350	$2...or...$3	....
Halsted St.Opera House.t	255 S. Halsted St.................	.300		
Havlin's Theater........u	1840 Wabash Av..................	2,000	.........$175	....
Haymarket Theater.....	161-169 W. Madison St............	2,356		
Hoefer's Hall...........a	227 North Av.....................	.150		
Hooley's Theater........	149 Randolph St..................	1,500		
Independence Hall......	180 Twenty-second St..............			
Jacobs' Academy	83 S. Halsted St..................	1,400		
Janssen's Hall..........a	786 W. Lake St...................	.150		
Jefferson Hall.........	48 and 50 Throop St...............	.450	.........$20	$50..to.. $75
Kastner's Hall	3001 Archer Av...................			
Kawalinski Hall v	709 Milwaukee Av................	..75		....
Kimball Hall..........	243-253 Wabash Av...............	.500	.........$40	....
Klare's Hall...........	72 N. Clark St....................	.500		$15..to .$60

NAME OF HALL.	LOCATION.	No. of Seats.	Rent for Single Entertainment. For General Entertainment.	For Dancing.
Kohl & Middleton's Mus'm	150 Clark St..........................	.325		
Kohl & Middleton's Mus'm	292 State St..........................	.325		
Landmark Hall..........	Cottage Grove Av.& Thirty-seventh St.			
Lanyon's Opera Block....	Englewood and Wentworth Avs.....			
Lehman's Hall..........a	366 W. Twelfth St..................	.100		
Lyceum Theater...........	54 S. Desplaines St................	1,800		
McVicker's Theater	78–84 Madison St..................	1,900		
Madison Hall..........b	142–148 W. Madison St..........	.400		$65..or. $75
Madison St. Opera House.	83 Madison St....................	1,400		
Martine's Hall..........c	55 S. Ada St....................	.600		$50..to. $60
Maskell Hall..........	173 S. Desplaines St.............,....			
Masonic Temple........ .*.	State and Randolph Sts............			
Meridian Hall..........	97 and 99 W. Randolph St...........			
Mueller's Hall..........	356–364 North Av...............	1,000	....$25	$40..to. $65
National Hall..........	Centre Av. and W. Eighteenth St.....	.250	...$20	$25,$35,$40
Oakley Hall..........	989 W. Polk St...................			
Odd Fellows' Hall......d	406 and 408 Milwaukee Av.....			
Olympic Theater........	49 Clark St...................	1,800		
O'Neill Hall..........	681 and 683 W. Lake St...........	.250	$5..or..$10	...$10
Oriental Hall..........e	122 La Salle St...............	.300	....$12.50	
Orpheus Hall...	49 La Salle St..............	.150	....$5	
Owsley's Hall..........	785–789 W. Madison St.....	.200	....$10	...$12
Park Theater..........	335 State St..............	1,200		
People's Theater........	339 State St..............	1,800		
Phelan's Hall..........	541 W. Indiana St..........	.200	....$10	$10..to. $12
Pilsen Hall..........	Brown and W. Twentieth Sts.....	.300		
Plasterers' Hall..........	192 Washington St.............	.500		
Pleiades Hall ....e	220 S. Halsted St.............	.200		
Princess Opera House...f	558 W. Madison St.............	.700		...$50
Prosperity Hall..........a	1735 State St.................	.300		
Recital Hall..........g	Auditorium Building.............	.500	...$40	
Rochester Hall..........h	220–224 W. Twelfth St...........	.300	$5..or..$10	$25..or. $35
Rosalie Music Hall.......	Rosalie Court and Fifty-seventh St.			
Schlotthauer's Hall.....	328 and 330 Sedgwick St.......	.200	$4...or.. $5	
Schoenhofen's Hall......	Milwaukee and N. Ashland Avs..	2,000	$20..or..$25	$45,$65,$75
Schoenhofen's Hall......	Milwaukee and N. Ashland Avs...	.400		$25..or. $30
Schoenhofen's Hall......	Milwaukee and N. Ashland Avs...	.250	....$5	
Sivore's Hall........	4300 State St..................	.250	$12. to..$15	$20..to. $40
Smrz Hall..........n	100 and 102 Wade St..............	.90		
Standard Theater	Halsted St.. S-W. cor. Jackson St.....	1,800		
Svea Hall..........	Chicago Av. and Larrabee St......			...$35
Temperance Temple...i	La Salle and Monroe Sts...........	.584	...$50	
Thirty-first St.Audit'r'm.j	77 Thirty-first St................	1,500	....$25	$50 ..or.$75
Thirty-first St. Hall......	77 Thirty-first St	.500		
Tibbitts Hall..... ....k	1033 Millard Av..................	.225	$5...or...$6	
Timmerman Opera House	Sixty-third St. and Stewart Av.....	1,150		
Turner Hall..........l	257 N. Clark St................	1,500	$50,$60,$90	
Turner Hall..........	253 W. Twelfth St.............	2,000	$25..or..$30	$50..or. $65
Uhlich Hall..........m	19–37 N. Clark St.............	.500	$10. to..$15	$35..to. $45
Union Hall..........	181 Clark St..............	.300	$6...or..$10	
Union Park Hall........	517 W. Madison St...........	.800	$10..or..$15	
Weiner's Hall..........a	3001 S. Halsted St...........	.100		
Windsor Theater........s	466 and 468 N. Clark St......	2,200		
Wolff's Hall..........a	432 Milwaukee Av.............	.100		
Workingmen's Hall......	368 W. Twelfth St.............	.300		$10..or. $25

a For lodges; usually rented by year or month.   b Used for dances and concerts.   c Two halls, each seating 600 people.   d Three halls, for lodges.   e Masonic lodge.   f Also a club-room, seating 100 people. The main hall is now used entirely by the Salvation Army.

g Rent during day, $30.   h Also small hall, seating 100, for lodges.   i Rent during day: forenoon, $25; afternoon, $35.   j Also three lodge halls here.   k Rent by week, $20.   l Rent by week, $350.   m Two halls, each seating 400 or 500 people.

.*. The Masonic Temple contains the following halls, at the rentals herewith given: The seventeenth, eighteenth and nineteenth floors are fitted up for Blue Lodges, Chapters, Councils and Commanderies as follows:—Blue Lodge Rooms, 32x46 feet, at $12.50 per night; also 40x62 feet, at $15 per night; there is a parlor, 30x54 feet, which is to be used in common with both rooms. The drill room on the same floor is 46x98 feet, with a gallery which has a seating capacity of 250 people, and can be used as a banquet, drill and dance hall at $25 per night. There is a Commandery Hall, 42x60 feet, with a gallery which will seat 100 people, with a Red Cross Room, 36x42 feet, for $1,200 per year (or 52 nights), this to include the use of the Drill Hall for as many nights as the halls are rented by the Commandery, together with the use of the armory, furnished with suitable lockers and all other requirements, including parlors, reception rooms, etc. The Consistory Hall is 46x108 feet, with a stage 25x46 feet, and a gallery that will seat 500 people. This has dressing rooms, candidates' rooms, committee rooms, parlors and armory. The large Blue Lodge Hall and the Commandery Hall will be fitted up for the use of the Chapters, and all necessary requirements will be added for their work.

In each case these prices include light, heat and janitor service.

A Selection Made from Each of the Several Denominations.

The schools for moral and spiritual instruction, in this city, include between five and six hundred churches. To give them all here would require seven pages of this volume. Of the entire number we select a few from each denomination, which are centrally located and easy of access for strangers, no effort being made to select those that are widely known or especially popular.

The numbers in parentheses attached to each church mentioned, refer to the street car line which runs nearest to each church, these numbers being explained on page 128. Those churches where no car line is mentioned are usually those located in the business district, to which it is an easy walk from the hotels.

Services are usually held in each church on Sunday mornings and evenings, beginning promptly at 10:30 A. M. and 7.30 P. M. Sunday schools are usually in session soon after the morning service, or later in the Sunday afternoon. Prayer meetings are generally held at churches on Wednesday evenings.

As a rule, the churches of the city are all supplied with a high order of music, their pulpits being filled by clergymen who have passed the ordeal in other cities for moral worth, oratorical ability and superior fitness for these high positions. We can assure the strangers within our gates that a Sabbath service in any of our churches will be found to be entertaining, generally instructive and spiritually beneficial. To these services all strangers and citizens are ever cordially welcomed.

CHURCHES AND THE LINES OF RAILWAY THAT LEAD TO THEM.

Baptist.

BELDEN AVENUE CHURCH, Belden Av. and N. Halsted St. Pastor, Rev. H. H. Barbour....................(No. 32)
CENTENNIAL CHURCH, Jackson and Lincoln Sts. Pastor, Rev. Alonzo K. Parker. ....(No. 88)
FIRST CHURCH, South Park Av. and Thirty-first St. Pastor, Rev. P. S. Henson......(No. 51), (No. 53) or (No. 66)
FIRST GERMAN CHURCH, Superior and Paulina Sts. Pastor, Rev. J. L. Meier................(No. 72) or (No. 76)
FOURTH CHURCH, Ashland Boul. and Monroe St. Pastor, Rev. J. Wolfenden............(No. 85) or (No. 88)
IMMANUEL CHURCH, Michigan Av., near Twenty-third St. Pastor, Rev. O. P. Gifford....(No. 51) or (No. 53)
LA SALLE AVENUE CHURCH, La Salle Av., near Division St. Pastor, Rev. H. O. Rowlands.......(No. 20) or (No. 21)
MEMORIAL CHURCH, Oakwood Boul., near Cottage Grove Av. Pastor, Rev. L. A. Crandall....(No. 51) or (No. 53)
SECOND CHURCH, Morgan and West Monroe Sts. Pastor, Rev. W. M. Lawrence............. ....(No. 85)

Christian.

CENTRAL CHURCH, Indiana Av. and Thirty-seventh St. Pastor, Rev. W. F. Black....................(No. 52)
WEST SIDE CHURCH, Jackson Boul., near Western Av. Pastor, Rev. John W. Allen.......(No. 97) or (No. 98)

Congregational.

FIRST CHURCH, Washington Boul. and Ann St. Pastor, Rev. E. P. Goodwin......... ....(No. 85) or (No. 88)
LINCOLN PARK CHURCH. Garfield Av. and Mohawk St. Pastor, Rev. David Beaton... . ...(No. 35) or (No. 36)
NEW ENGLAND CHURCH, Dearborn Av. and Delaware Pl. Pastor, Rev. James G. Johnson. ....(No. 20)
PLYMOUTH CHURCH, Michigan Av., near Twenty-sixth St. Pastor, Rev. Frank W. Gunsaulus........ ....(No. 52), (No. 58), (No. 59) or (No. 70)
SOUTH CHURCH, Drexel Boul. and Fortieth St. Pastor, Rev. W. Scott. ....(No. 13), (No. 51), (No. 53) or (No. 66)
TABERNACLE CHURCH, Morgan and W. Indiana Sts. Pastor, Rev. A. Monroe ......(No. 83), (No. 89) or (No. 90)
UNION PARK CHURCH, S. Ashland Av. and Washington Boul. Pastor, Rev. Frederick A. Noble..........
............(No. 85), (No. 88) or (No. 92)

Dutch Reformed.

FIRST HOLLAND REFORMED CHURCH, May and W. Harrison Sts. Pastor, Rev. R. Bloemendal.............
...(No. 75), (No. 81), (No. 82) or (No. 97)
HOLLAND CHRISTIAN REFORMED CHURCH, 525 W. Fourteenth St. Pastor, Rev. H. Doustra..........(No. 73)

Episcopal.

CATHEDRAL OF SS. PETER AND PAUL, Washington Boul. and Peoria St. Bishop, Rt. Rev. William E. McLaren......(No. 85), (No. 88) or (No. 92)
CHURCH OF OUR SAVIOR, Lincoln and Belden Avs. Rector, Rev. William J. Petrie...(No. 23), (No. 35) or (No. 36)
CHURCH OF THE ASCENSION, La Salle Av. and Elm St. Rector, Rev. Edward A. Larrabee.....(No. 20) or (No. 21)
CHURCH OF THE EPIPHANY, Ashland Boul. and W. Adams St. Rector, Rev. T. N. Morrison..............(No. 88)
GRACE CHURCH, 1445 Wabash Av. Rector, Rev. Clinton Locke.......
............(No. 51), I(No. 53) or (No. 66)
ST. ANDREW'S CHURCH, Washington Boul. and Robey St. Rector, Rev. W. C. Dewitt.(No. 84), (No. 85) or (No. 92)
ST. JAMES' CHURCH, Cass and Huron Sts. Rector, Rev. Floyd Tomkins.(No. 42)
ST. MARK'S CHURCH, Cottage Grove Av. and Thirty-sixth St. Rector, Rev. W. W. Wilson.............
............(No. 51), (No. 53) or (No. 66)
ST. STEPHEN'S CHURCH, Johnson St., near W. Taylor St. Pastor, Rev. C. N. Moller..... .....(No. 73) or (No. 94)
TRINITY CHURCH, Michigan Av. and Twenty-sixth St. Rector, Rev. John Rouse....................(No. 52)

Episcopal (Reformed).

CHRIST CHURCH, Michigan Av. and Twenty-fourth St. Rector, Rt. Rev. Charles E. Cheney..........(No. 52)
ST. PAUL'S CHURCH, Winchester Av. and W. Adams St. Rector, Rt. Rev. Samuel Fallows........ . ...(No. 85)

Evangelical Association of North America (German).

FIRST CHURCH, Thirty-fifth and Dearborn Sts. Pastor, Rev. C. Ott.. .
... .(No. 58), (No. 59) or (No. 70)
HUMBOLDT PARK CHURCH, Wabansia Av. and N. Rockwell St. Pastor, Rev. P. Wingert............ ......(No. 90)

Evangelical Lutheran.

ENGLISH.

CHURCH OF THE HOLY TRINITY, 398
La Salle Av. Pastor, Rev. Chas.
Koerner..............(No. 20) or (No. 21)
GRACE CHURCH, Belden Av. and Lar-
rabee St. Pastor, Rev. Lee M.
Hellman....(No. 20), (No. 21) or (No. 23)
WICKER PARK CHURCH, Le Moyne St.
and N. Hoyne Av. Pastor, Rev.
H. W. Roth............(No. 89) or (No. 90)

GERMAN.

CHRIST CHURCH, Humboldt and Byron
Avs. Pastor, Rev. E. Werfelmann.
....................(No. 9) or (No. 89)
EMANUEL CHURCH, Twelfth St. and
Ashland Av. Pastor, Rev Louis
Hoelter..............(No. 95) or (No. 96)
GETHSEMANE CHURCH, 4407 Went-
worth Av. Pastor, Rev. J. G.
Huetzel........................(No. 70)
NAZARETH CHURCH, Forest Av., near
Fullerton Av. Pastor, Rev. J. L.
Neve..............(No. 7) or (No. 89)

NORWEGIAN.

BETHANIA CHURCH, Carpenter and W.
Indiana Sts. Pastor, Rev. John Z.
Torgersen........................(No. 83)
EMANUEL CHURCH, Perry Av. and
Cherry Pl. Pastor, Rev. J. I.
Breidablick............(No. 9) or (No. 89)
TRINITY CHURCH, Peoria and W. In-
diana Sts. Pastor, Rev. C. O.
Broehaugh........................(No. 83)

SWEDISH.

GETHSEMANE CHURCH, May and W.
Huron Sts. Pastor, Rev. Matthew
C. Ranseen............(No. 89) or (No. 90)
IMMANUEL CHURCH, Sedgwick and
Hobbie Sts. Pastor, Rev. C. A.
Evald ....(No. 40)
SALEM CHURCH, Portland Av., between
Twenty-eighth and Twenty-ninth
Sts. Pastor, Rev. L. G. Abraham-
son..................... ...... (No. 68)

Evangelical Lutheran (Separatists).

CHURCH OF PEACE, Iowa and N. Wood
Sts. Pastor, Rev. G. W. Lechler..(No. 76)
FIRST CHURCH, 270 Augusta St.
Pastor, Rev. Freidag............
..............(No. 72), (No. 76) or (No. 79)

Evangelical Reformed.

FIRST GERMAN CHURCH, 177 and 179
Hastings St. Pastor, Rev. A.
Heinemann............(No. 95) or (No. 96)
THIRD FRIEDENS CHURCH, 1330 Well-
ington St. Pastor, Rev. O. J.
Accola................(No. 35) or (No. 36)

Evangelical United.

EMANUEL'S CHURCH, Forty-sixth and
Dearborn Sts. Pastor, Rev. W.
Haltendorf...................... (No. 59)
FIRST GERMAN ST. PAUL'S CHURCH,
Ohio St. and La Salle Av. Pastor,
Rev. R. A. John ....(No. 20) or (No. 21)
MARKUS CHURCH, Thirty-fifth St. and
Union Av. Pastor, Rev. G. Klein.(No. 67)
TRINITY CHURCH, S. Robey and W.
Twenty-fourth Sts. Pastor, Rev.
Julius Kircher.....................(No. 73)

Free Methodist.

FIRST CHURCH, 16 N. May St. Pastor,
Rev. O. V. Ketels......(No. 84) or (No. 92)
SECOND CHURCH, 447 Ogden Av.
Pastor, Rev. S. K. J. Chesbrough..(No. 88)

Independent.

CENTRAL CHURCH, Central Music Hall,
State and Randolph Sts. Pastor,
Rev. David Swing.
CHICAGO AVENUE CHURCH, Chicago
and La Salle Avs. Pastor, Rev.
T. B. Hyde............(No. 20) or (No. 21)
PEOPLE'S CHURCH, McVicker's Thea-
ter, 82 Madison St. Pastor, Rev.
H. W. Thomas.

Jewish.

ANSHE K'NESSETH ISRAEL, Judd and
Clinton Sts. Minister, Rev. B.
Bernstein......... ....
...(No. 74), (No. 78), (No. 95) or (No. 96)
KEHILATH ANSHE MAARIV (Congrega-
tion of the Men of the West),
Indiana Av. and Thirty-third St.
Minister, Rev. Isaac S. Moses.....(No. 52)
KEHILATH B'NAI SHOLOM (Sons of
Peace), Twenty-sixth St. and Indi-
ana Av. Minister, Rev. Dr. J. A.
Messing..........................(No. 52)
SINAI CONGREGATION, Indiana Av. and
Twenty-first St. Lecturer, Dr. E.
G. Hirsch............. ......(No. 52)
ZION CONGREGATION, Ogden Av. and
Washington Boul. Minister, Rev.
Jos. Stolz....(No. 85), (No. 88) or (No. 92)

Methodist Episcopal.

CENTENARY CHURCH, 295 W. Monroe
St., near Morgan St. Pastor, Rev.
H. W. Bolton.(No. 72), (No. 85) or (No. 88)
FIRST CHURCH, Methodist Church
Block, Clark and Washington Sts.
Pastor, Rev. William Fawcett.
GRACE CHURCH, La Salle Av. and
Locust St. Pastor, Rev. R. S.
Martin...............(No. 20) or (No. 21)
OAKLAND CHURCH, Oakwood Boul. and
Langley Av. Pastor, Rev. P. H.
Swift.................(No. 51) or (No. 53)
PARK AVENUE CHURCH, Park Av. and
Robey St. Pastor, Rev. W. W.
Painter..........................(No. 92)
SOUTH PARK AVENUE CHURCH, South
Park Av. and Thirty-third St.
Pastor, Rev. J. M. Caldwell......
...(No. 51), (No. 52), (No. 53) or (No. 66)
TRINITY CHURCH, Indiana Av., near
Twenty-fourth St. Pastor, Rev.
F. M. Bristol......................(No. 52)
WABASH AVENUE CHURCH, Wabash
Av. and Fourteenth St. Pastor,
Rev. O. E. Murray................
..........(No. 51), (No. 53) or (No. 66)
WESLEY CHURCH, 1003-1009 N. Hal-
sted St. Pastor, Rev. N. H. Axtell.
...(No. 23), (No. 32), (No. 35) or (No. 36)
WESTERN AVENUE CHURCH, Western
Av. and W. Monroe St. Pastor,
Rev. W. A. Phillips..............(No. 85)

GERMAN.

ASHLAND AVENUE CHURCH, 485 N.
Ashland Av. Pastor, Rev. Ernest
Fitzner......(No. 72), (No. 89) or (No. 90)
CENTRE STREET CHURCH, Centre and
Dayton Sts. Pastor, Rev. C. A.
Loeber..............(No. 28) or (No. 32)
EBENEZER CHURCH, Ullman & Thirty-
first Sts. Pastor, Rev. F. G. Wrede
..........................(No. 43);
or take (No. 58) and transfer to (No. 60)

New Jerusalem (Swedenborgian).

NEW CHURCH TEMPLE, Van Buren St.,
near Wabash Av. Pastor, Rev. L.
P. Mercer....(No. 51), (No. 53) or (No. 66)

Presbyterian.

CHURCH OF THE COVENANT, Belden
Av. and N. Halsted St. Pastor,
Rev. David R. Breed..............
....(No. 23), (No. 32), (No. 35) or (No. 36)
EIGHTH CHURCH, Washington Boul.
and Robey St. Pastor, Rev. Thos.
D. Wallace..(No. 84), (No. 85) or (No. 92)
FIFTH CHURCH, Indiana Av. and
\Thirtieth St. Pastor, Rev. Henry
T. Miller.......................(No. 52)
FIRST CHURCH, Indiana Av. and
Twenty-first St. Pastor, Rev. John
H. Barrows.......................(No. 52)
FORTY-FIRST STREET CHURCH, Grand
Boul. and Forty-first St. Pastor,
Rev. Thos. C. Hall...............
....(No. 14), (No. 52), (No. 53) or (No. 59)
FOURTH CHURCH, Rush and Superior
Sts. Pastor, Rev. M. Wolsey
Stryker.........................(No. 42)
JEFFERSON PARK CHURCH, Throop and
W. Adams St. Pastor, Rev. Fred
Campbell....(No. 75), (No. 81) or (No. 82)
SECOND CHURCH, Michigan Av. and
Twentieth St. Pastor, Rev. Simon
J. McPherson.(No. 51), (No. 53) or (No. 66)
SIXTH CHURCH, Vincennes and Oak
Avs.........(No. 51), (No. 53) or (No. 66)
THIRD CHURCH, Ogden and S. Ash-
land Avs. Pastor, Rev. John L.
Withrow...............(No. 85) or (No. 88)

Roman Catholic.

CATHEDRAL OF THE HOLY NAME,
Superior and North State Sts.
Archbishop, Most Rev. Patrick
A. Feehan; Rector, Rev. M. J.
Fitzsimmons.....................(No. 42)
ALL SAINTS' CHURCH, Wallace St. and
Twenty-fifth Pl. Pastor, Rev. E.
J. Dunne..............(No. 43) or (No. 67)
CHURCH OF THE HOLY FAMILY, May
and W. Twelfth Sts. Rector, Very
Rev. T. S. Fitzgerald; Pastor, Rev.
E. D. Kelly...........(No. 95) or (No. 96)
ST. ALPHONSUS' CHURCH (German),
Lincoln and Southport Avs. Su-
perior and Rector, Rev. J. H.
Schagemann.....................(No. 35)
ST. ANTHONY OF PADUA (German),
Hanover St. and Twenty-fourth
Pl. Pastor, Rev. Peter Fischer...(No. 67)
ST. CECELIA'S CHURCH, Bristol St.,
near Wentworth Av. Pastor, Rev.
E. A. Kelly. ....(No. 69)
ST. COLUMBKILL'S CHURCH, N. Paulina
and W. Indiana Sts. Pastor, Rev.
Thomas Burke.... .... (No. 83)
ST. GABRIEL'S CHURCH, Forty-fifth
and Wallace Sts. Pastor, Rev. M.
J. Dorney...............(No. 2) or (No. 69)
ST. JAMES' CHURCH, Wabash Av. and
Twenty-ninth St. Pastor, Rev.
Hugh McGuire...................
..............(No. 58), (No. 59) or (No. 70)

ROMAN CATHOLIC—Continued.

ST. JOHN'S CHURCH, Clark and Eight-
eenth Sts. Rector, Very Rev.
Thaddeus J. Butler...............(No. 68)
ST. JOSEPH'S CHURCH (German
Priory), Hill and N. Market Sts.
Prior, Very Rev. C. Engelbrecht..(No. 27)
ST. MARY'S CHURCH, Wabash Av. and
Eldredge Ct. Rector, Rev. E. A.
Murphy.....(No. 51), (No. 53) or (No. 66)
ST. MICHAEL'S CHURCH (German),
Eugenie St. and Cleveland Av.
Rector, Rev. F. Luette.(No. 34) or (No. 40)
ST. PATRICK'S CHURCH, Desplaines
and W. Adams Sts. Pastor, Rev.
Thomas F. Galligan...(No. 73) or (No. 75)
ST. STANISLAUS KOSTKA'S CHURCH
(Polish), Noble and Ingraham Sts.
Superior, Very Rev. Simon Chas.
Kobrzynski; Rector, Rev. Vincent
Barzynski.......................(No. 87)

Unitarian.

ALL SOULS' CHURCH, Oakwood Boul.
and Langley Av. Pastor, Rev.
Jenkin Lloyd Jones...(No. 51) or (No. 53)
CHURCH OF THE MESSIAH, Michigan
Boul. and Twenty-third St. Pastor,
Rev. W. W. Fenn.................(No. 52)
THIRD UNITARIAN CHURCH, Monroe
and Laflin Sts. Pastor, Rev. Jas.
Vila Blake .... (No. 85) or (No. 88)
UNITY CHURCH, Dearborn Av. and
Walton Pl. Pastor, Rev. T. G.
Milsted................(No. 20) or (No. 42)

United Presbyterian.

FIRST CHURCH, W. Monroe and S.
Paulina Sts. Pastor, Rev. Wm.
T. Meloy................(No. 85) or (No. 88)

Universalist.

CHURCH OF THE REDEEMER, Warren
Av. and Robey St. Pastor, Rev.
M. H. Harris.....................(No. 85)
ST. PAUL'S CHURCH, Prairie Av. and
Thirtieth St. Pastor, Rev. A. J.
Canfield........................(No. 52)
THIRD UNIVERSALIST CHURCH, North
Clark St., near Wellington Av.
Pastor, Rev. L. J. Dinsmore......
....(No. 20) or (No. 21)

Miscellaneous.

ARMOUR MISSION, Thirty-third St. and
Armour Av. Pastor, Rev. Howard
H. Russell...(No. 58), (No. 59) or (No. 70)
FIRST SOCIETY OF SPIRITUALISTS,
Washington Boul. and Ogden Av.
President, Lewis Bushnell.......
.........................(No. 85) or (No. 88)
GERMAN ADVENT CHURCH, 274 Au-
gusta St. Pastor, Rev. Chas. M.
Koier......(No. 72), (No. 76) or (No. 79)
SCANDINAVIAN ADVENT CHAPEL, 269
W. Erie St.....................(No. 72)

Prominent Buildings for which Strangers Often Inquire.

Abbey Bldg., 251 and 253 Wabash Av.
Adams Express Bldg., 185 to 199 Dearborn.
Agricultural Ins. Co.'s Bldg., 544 W. Madison.
Allerton Bldg., S. Water, n. e. cor. State.
American Express Co.'s Bldg., 72-78 Monroe.
Andrews Bldg., 153 and 155 La Salle.
Arcade Bldg., 156 to 164 Clark.
Argyle Bldg., Jackson, n. w. cor. Michigan Av.
Ashland Blk., 53-65 Clark.
Athenæum Bldg., 18-26 Van Buren.
Atlas Blk., 45-61 Wabash Av.
Auditorium Bldg., Wabash Av. and Congress.
Ayer's Bldg., 166-172 State.
Batchelder Bldg., Clark, s. e. cor. Randolph.
Bay State Bldg., State, s. e. cor. Randolph.
Board of Trade, Jackson and La Salle.
Bonfield Bldg., 109-203 Randolph.
Borden Blk., Randolph, n. w. cor Dearborn.
Boylston Blk., 265-273 Dearborn.
Brother Jonathan's Bldg., 2 and 4 Sherman.
Bryan Blk., 160-174 La Salle.
Calumet Bldg., 187-191 La Salle.
Castle's Blk. and Hall, 619-627 W. Lake.
Caxton Bldg., 323-334 Dearborn.
Central Manf. Blk., 74-88 Market.
Central Music Hall, State, s. e. cor Randolph.
Central Union Blk., Market and Madison.
Chamber of Commerce, Washington & La Salle.
Chemical Bank Bldg., 85 and 87 Dearborn.
Chicago Herald Bldg., 154 & 156 Washington
Chicago Opera House, Washington and Clark.
Citizens' Bank Bldg., 119 and 121 La Salle.
City Hall, Washington and La Salle.
Cobb's Bldg., 120 to 128 Dearborn.
Columbus Memorial Bldg., State & Washington.
Commerce Bldg., 14 and 16 Pacific Av.
Commercial Nat. Bank, Dearborn and Monroe.
Como Bldg., 325 Dearborn.
Counselman Bldg., La Salle and Jackson.
County Bldg., Clark, cor. Jackson.
Crilly and Blair Bldg., 163-171 Dearborn.
Criminal Court, Michigan St. & Dearborn Av.
Custom House, Clark, cor. Adams.
Dale Bldg., 308-318 Dearborn.
Davison Blk., 147-153 Fifth Av.
De Soto Blk., 144 and 146 Madison.
Donohue & Henneberry, 407-425 Dearborn.
Dore Blk., State, n. w. cor. Madison.
Drake Blk., Wabash Av., s. e. cor. Washington.
Drexel Bldg., 80 and 82 Adams.
Ely Bldg., Wabash Av., s. w. cor. Monroe.
Empire Blk., 128 and 130 La Salle.
Equitable Bldg., 106 to 110 Dearborn.
Evening Journal Bldg., 162-164 Washington.
Ewing Block, 20-38 N. Clark
Exchange Bldg., Van Buren St. and Pacific Av.
Farwell Bldg., Arcade Ct., rear 159 La Salle.
First Nat. Bank Bldg., Dearborn and Monroe.
Foote Blk., Clark, s. w. cor Monroe.
Franklin Bldg., 341-349 Dearborn.
Fry Bldg., 84 and 86 La Salle.
Fuller Blk., 148-156 Dearborn.
Fullerton Blk., 90-96 Dearborn.
Gaff Bldg., 230-238 La Salle.
Gazzolo Bldg., 82 and 84 W. Madison.
Girard Bldg., 298-306 Dearborn.
Grand Opera House, 87 Clark.
Grannis Blk. (See Illinois Bank Bldg.)
Greenbaum Bldg. and Hall, 72-82 Fifth Av.
Grocers' Blk., 29-43 Wabash Av.
Hale Bldg., State, s. e. cor. Washington.
Hampshire Blk., La Salle, s. e. cor. Monroe.
Hausen Bldg., 116 and 118 Dearborn.
Harding's Bldg., 155 and 157 Washington.
Haymarket Theater, 161-169 W. Madison.
Home Insurance Bldg., La Salle and Adams.
Honore Bldg., 194 to 210 Dearborn.
Howland Blk., 174-192 Dearborn.
Hyman Bldg., 146 to 152 South Water.
Illinois Bank Bldg., 111-117 Dearborn.
Imperial Bldg., 252-260 Clark.
Ingal's Bldg., 190 and 192 Clark.
Insurance Exchange Bldg., La Salle and Adams.
Inter-Ocean Bldg., Madison and Dearborn.
Jarvis Blk., 124 Clark.
Journal Bldg., 159 and 161 Dearborn.

Kedzie's Bldg., 120 and 122 Randolph.
Kent Bldg., 151 and 153 Monroe.
Kentucky Blk., 195-203 Clark.
Kimball Hall, 245 State.
Lafayette Bldg., 68-74 La Salle.
Lakeside Bldg., Clark, s. w. cor. Adams.
Lenox Bldg., 88 and 90 Washington.
Lill's Blk., 613-617 W. Lake.
Lind Blk., Randolph, n. w. cor. Market.
Loomis Bldg., 2-6 Clark.
Lumber Exchange, S. Water and Franklin.
Lumberman's Exchange, 238 South Water.
Madison Blk., 230-238 W. Madison.
Major Blk., 139 to 151 La Salle.
Mailers Bldg., 226 and 228 La Salle.
Manhattan Bldg., 307 to 321 Dearborn.
Marine Bldg., 152-158 Lake.
Masonic Temple, State, n. e. cor. Randolph.
McCormick Blk., 67-73 Dearborn.
McCormick, L. J., Bldg., 15-27 Wabash Av.
McNeil Bldg., 128 and 130 Clark.
McVicker's Theater Bldg., 78-84 Madison.
Mentone Flats, 146 Dearborn Av.
Mercantile Bldg., 112-118 La Salle.
Merchants' Bldg., La Salle and Washington.
Methodist Church Blk., Clark & Washington.
Metropolitan Blk., 159 to 165 Randolph.
Monadnock Bldg., Dearborn and Jackson.
Monon Bldg., 320 to 326 Dearborn.
Montauk Blk., 111 to 117 Monroe.
Morrison Bldg., Clark and Madison.
National Life Ins. Bldg., 159-163 La Salle.
Nevada Blk., Franklin, s. w. cor. Washington.
Nixon Bldg., 169-175 La Salle.
Ogden Bldg., Clark, s. w. cor. Lake.
Oriental Bldg. and Hall, 122 La Salle.
Otis Bldg., Madison, s. w. cor. State.
Otis Blk., 138-158 La Salle.
Owings Bldg., 213 Dearborn.
Owings', F. P., Blk., 232-236 Fifth Av.
Owsley's Blk. and Hall, 785-789 W. Madison.
Oxford Bldg., 84 and 86 La Salle.
Parker Bldg., 95 and 97 Washington.
Phenix Bldg., 128-150 Jackson. (Ent. 138).
Pontiac Bldg., Dearborn, n. w. cor. Harrison.
Portland Blk., 103-109 Dearborn.
Powers Bldg., Monroe, n. w. cor. Michigan Av.
Pullman Bldg., Adams, s. w. cor. Michigan Av.
Purington Bldg., 298-304 Wabash Av.
Quincy Bldg., Clark, n. e. cor. Adams.
Quinlan Blk., 81 and 83 Clark.
Rand-McNally Bldg., 162-172 Adams.
Rawson Bldg., 149 and 151 State.
Real Estate Board Bldg., Dearborn & Randolph.
Reaper Blk., Clark, n. e. cor. Washington.
Rialto Bldg., 135-153 Van Buren.
Rookery Bldg., La Salle, s. e. cor. Adams.
Royal Insurance Bldg., 165-173 Jackson.
Ryerson Bldg., 45-49 Randolph.
St. Mary's Blk., Madison, s.w. cor. Wabash Av.
Schiller Blk., 103-109 Randolph.
Sears Bldg., 99 and 101 Washington.
Sheppard Bldg., Fifth Av., n. e. cor. Quincy.
Shepherd, Madison, bet. Fifth Av. & La Salle.
Sibley Bldg., 2-16 N. Clark.
Staats Zeitung Bldg., 91-99 Fifth Av.
Stewart Bldg., State, n. w. cor. Washington.
Stock Exchange Bldg., 167-171 Dearborn.
Tacoma Blk., La Salle, n. e. cor. Madison.
Taylor Bldg., 140-146 Monroe.
Telephone Bldg., 203 Washington.
Temperance Temple, La Salle and Monroe.
Temple Ct., 217-225 Dearborn.
Teutonia Bldg., Fifth Av., s.e. cor. Washington
Thompson Blk., 229-247 W. Madison.
Times Bldg., Washington, n. w. cor. Fifth Av.
Traders' Blk., 6-12 Pacific Av.
Tribune Bldg., Dearborn, s. e. cor. Madison.
Uhlich Blk., 19-37 N. Clark.
Unity Bldg., 78-81 Dearborn.
U. S. Express Co.'s Bldg., 87 & 89 Washington
Venetian Bldg., 34 and 36 Washington.
Wadsworth Bldg., 175-181 Madison.
Webber Music Hall, 241 Wabash Av.
Western Bank Note, Michigan Av. & Madison.
Willoughby Bldg., Franklin, n.w. cor. Jackson.

THE CITY HALL OCCUPIES
THE WEST HALF OF THE SQUARE
BOUNDED BY WASHINGTON, LA
SALLE, RANDOLPH AND CLARK
STREETS.

FACES WEST UPON LA SALLE ST.

THE COOK COUNTY COURT
HOUSE OCCUPIES THE EAST
PORTION OF THE BLOCK BOUND-
ED BY CLARK, WASHINGTON, LA
SALLE AND RANDOLPH STREETS.

FACES EAST UPON CLARK ST.

COUNTY COURT HOUSE AND CITY HALL.

Rooms Occupied by Heads of Several of the Principal Departments in City Hall.

Floor.	Room.	OCCUPANTS.	OCCUPANTS.	Floor.	Room.
2	45	Mayor.	Fire Marshal	B*	14
1	35	City Clerk.	Superintendent of Police	1	32
1	33	City Treasurer.	City Collector	1	24
3	63	City Attorney.	Special Assessments	2	50
3	61	Prosecuting Attorney.	Water Collections	1	23
2	41	Corporation Counsel.	Bureau of Streets	2	55
1	34	Comptroller.	Bureau of Sewers	2	47
2	54	Commissioner of Public Works.	City Engineer	3	64
B*	2	Commissioner of Health.	Superintendent of Schools	3	72
1	26	Commissioner of Buildings.	B* Basement.		

DIRECTORY TO EACH FLOOR IN CITY HALL.

NOTE.—The growing needs of the city make it necessary to sometimes change the location of some department; hence this directory is liable to change in future years.

Basement Floor.

No. of Room.	OCCUPANT.	OCCUPANT.	No. of Room.
1	Captain and Secretary of Police.	Commissioner of Health	2
3	Detectives' Private Office.	Department of Health.	4
5	Detectives' Public Office.	Central Detail, Department of Police	6
7	Assistant Superintendent of Police.	Medical Inspectors, Department of Health	8
9	Custodian of Stolen Property.	Police Printing Office	10
11	Police Store Room.	Fire Alarm Office	12
13	Engine Room.	Fire Department Office	14
15	Gas Inspector, Bureau of Light.		

First Floor.

21	Superintendent of Water Office—Private.	City Collector's Private Office	22
23	Bureau of Water Rate Collections.	City Collector's Public Office	24
25	Water Assessor's Office.	Building Department	26, 28, 30
27, 29, 31	Inspector of Weights and Measures.	Superintendent of Police	32
33	City Treasurer's Office.	Comptroller's Office	34
35, 36	City Clerk's Office.		

Second Floor.

41	Corporation Counsel.	Engineers of Bureau of Sewers	42
43	City Engineer's Private Office.	Drainage Plats Office	44
45	Mayor's General Office.	Bureau of Sewers	46
47, 49	Sewerage Department.	Bureau of Maps	48
51	Engineers of Bureau of Streets.	Bureau of Special Assessments	50
53	House Moving and Sidewalk.	Bookkeeper and Purchasing Agent, Department of Public Works	52
55	Bureau of Streets, General Office.	Department of Public Works, Secretary	54
57	Time-keeper of Bureau of Streets.	Commissioner of Public Works, Private	56
		Superintendent of Streets, Private	58

Third Floor.

61	Prosecuting Attorney.	City Engineer	62
63, 65	City Attorney.	City Engineer, General Office	64, 66
67, 69	Board Election Commissioners.	Chief Janitor	68
68	Water Inspector's Office.	Election Commissioners' Public Office	70

BOARD OF EDUCATION.

71	Business Manager.	Superintendent of Schools	72
73	Chief Engineer and Auditor.	Board Room and Special Teacher of Drawing and German	74, 76
75	Clerk of the Board.	Committee Room	77, 78
79, 80	Special Teacher of Music and Drawing.	Compulsory Education	78½

Fourth Floor.

89½	City Architect.	Council Chamber	86

LIBRARY.

81	Circulating Library.	Library Reference Room	82
87	Library Reading Room.	Law Institute	85
89	Patent Office Reports.		

At the City Hall may be found the managers of municipal affairs. In its various departments the city government is conducted. Their work concerns every citizen and every stranger. What is done there? How is it done? For the purpose of answering these questions we enter and proceed from room to room to the top of the building, our journey beginning at the

BASEMENT OF THE CITY HALL BUILDING.

Turning to the right, we are in room No. 1, which is the office of the

Captain and Secretary of Police.

His duties include the keeping of the records of the police court, an account of the pay rolls, publishing an annual report and having the general financial management of the police department, under the direction of the comptroller.

The magnitude of this branch of government is seen when we study for the past year the following facts concerning

THE POLICE FORCE.

Expenses for 1891..............$2,622,046.45
Total estimated value of prop-
  erty.......................$881,226.60
Fines collected during year........$76,558.14
Number of arrests during year........70,550

PARTIAL LIST OF PRESENT POLICE FORCE.

Superintendent of Police 1
Assistant Superintendent....................1
Inspectors....................6
Captain of Detectives..,....................1
Captains....................16
Lieutenant of Detectives.... 1
Sergeants of Detectives....................2
Detectives.... 60
Patrol Sergeants....................82
Desk Sergeants....................93
Lieutenants....................53
Private Secretary....................1
Clerks........6
Custodian of Stolen Property............. 1
Veterinary Surgeon....................1
-Printer....................1
Bailiffs....................11
Pound Keepers....................8
Patrolmen, 1st Class........ 1,918
Patrolmen, 2nd Class....................241
Stenographer....................1
Assistant Stenographers....................2
Superintendent of Bureau of Identification..1
Photographer....................1
Chief Clerk of Detectives....................1
Pensioners....................20

Fifty-three buildings, situated in different parts of the city, are occupied as police stations.

DUTIES OF POLICEMEN.

Each patrol policeman is supposed to traverse a certain assigned district, in which he is expected to protect the interests of the people, give information to strangers and citizens as to the location of objects and places; assist people across the street; respond to alarms, arrest violators of the law, attend fires; convey sick and injured persons to their homes, to the hospital or to the police station; take dead bodies to the residence, or to the morgue if unidentified; care for the insane and destitute; take prisoners to the county jail or police court; take children to their parents; kill mad or crippled animals; stop runaway horses; recover stolen horses and vehicles; take children to the Foundlings' Home or orphan asylums, rescue people from drowning; conduct needy people to the benevolent institutions or the County Agent's office, where charity is dispensed, suppress disturbances, if possible without arrest, and give necessary advice. It should be his further duty, as is done by policemen in foreign cities, to investigate the sanitary condition of each building in his district, give instruction to householders when necessary, and report infractions of the sanitary law to the health department.

POLICE ALARM BOXES.

There are 634 police alarm boxes distributed throughout the city, and an alarm can be responded to by 38 wagons.

HOW TO CALL A POLICEMAN.

Any reputable citizen thinking it may be necessary to have police assistance, may call at police headquarters and obtain a key that will unlock a police signal box. The name of the person getting the key, and the number of his key, are accurately recorded. When he unlocks and opens the signal box, he finds a dial with ten spaces, upon each of which is a word indicating for what

Police Patrol Wagon.

the policemen are to be called, as "accident," "drunkard," "fires," "murder," "riot," etc. Upon turning the indicator to any one of these words, and there allowing it to remain, an alarm and a similar indication is made on a dial at the nearest police station, and a patrol wagon, with one, two, or more policemen, will immediately respond to the call.

The individual who gave the alarm cannot remove the key from the signal box. It must remain in the lock until the arrival of policemen. Hence, if a useless call, the number of the key will indicate who gave such alarm.

Keys to signal boxes are also usually accessible in drug stores, and leading stores in the vicinity of police signal boxes.

This department is directed by a general superintendent, who is appointed by the Mayor. There is a central station and ten precincts, each in charge of a captain. The precincts are divided into thirty-four districts, each having a station, which is in command of

Police Alarm Box.

a lieutenant assisted by sergeants. Each district, according to its size and the necessities, has from ten to seventy policemen.

The business center is under the guardianship of about 250 picked officers, known as the "Central Detail," who have the care of the people in the heart of the city, much of their work consisting in answering questions and protecting people at street crossings.

DETECTIVE POLICE FORCE.

The detective police force includes over 200 men who are dressed in citizens' costume, and are held in readiness to be detailed to render service in case of robberies, murders, petty thefts, etc.

STOLEN GOODS AT PAWNSHOPS.

As much stolen property is taken to the pawnshops for sale, each pawnbroker is required to send a daily report of stuff taken in pawn. All watches and their numbers are among the articles reported.

HOW TO RECOVER STOLEN WATCHES.

The owner of a watch should know its number. Should the watch be stolen, report number and general description of the watch to the detective department of the City Hall, and in due time it may be recovered, sometimes a year after it was stolen.

Several members of the detective force give their entire attention to pawnshops. Seven watches on the average are reported stolen each day in Chicago. About one quarter of these are recovered and restored to their owners.

BUREAU OF IDENTIFICATION.

Persons arrested are given a preliminary hearing before a police magistrate, and, if the facts warrant, a photograph is made of the individual and measurements are taken of the size of head, length of arms, hands, fingers, feet, height of body, etc., together with a description of all marks, scars, etc., on the body. The expectation is that, by and by, all criminals in the United States will have their measurements taken and a record made of name, place of birth, and previous history, the whole to be kept at one central bureau. The advantage of this is that when a criminal is captured and his measurements again taken and sent to the central bureau, it may lead to the discovery of who he is if he has been measured before.

POLICE STORE-ROOM AND PRINTING OFFICE.

On this floor is a room devoted to the storing of small articles that have been recovered from thieves but not yet claimed by owners. These articles are kept a certain length of time, after which they are sold at auction. Here, also, in another room, are kept the general supplies required in the several police stations, and in another apartment is a small printing office, which turns out daily a bulletin, which is sent to all police officers, giving a description of thieves that are wanted, people lost, and matters that policemen should be on the watch for.

Basement, Room 2—Commissioner of Health.

This department has the care of the general health of the city, and is classified in five divisions, as follows: 1. Department of Vital Statistics. 2. Medical Department. 3. Sanitary Department. 4. Meat and Odor Department. 5. Tenement, Factory and Smoke Department. To perform the work in this branch of the city service an office force of 25 persons are employed, assisted by 83 inspectors for the outside work.

The duties of this department include the keeping of a meteorological record of the weather; record of deaths and causes of the same; inspection of sanitary condition of streets and alleys; furnishing of ash and garbage receptacles, and removal of their contents; inspection of factories, tenements and buildings in process of construction, with reference to their sanitary condition; inquiry as to the condition of factory employes, examination of buildings for the detection of sewer gas; preparation of an annual report of trades and occupations and number of persons employed in them; inspection of markets for discovery of diseased meats, vegetables or fruits; removal of dead animals; suggestions of measures to be taken for the prevention of epidemics, etc. For the abatement and removal of nuisances under the above head apply at the Health Department.

Basement, Room 13—Engine Room.

In this room are the engines and apparatus for furnishing heat and light to all parts of the City Hall, and water for balancing the eight elevators in the building, the whole attended by a chief engineer, three assistant engineers, three oilers, six firemen and three coal handlers.

The amount of hard coal used here varies from 500 tons per month in the winter months to 270 tons per month in the summer months. The power furnished from this room pumps 800,000 gallons of water per day, for use of the building and the elevators, runs eight elevators, furnishes steam for two electric-light engines, which supply, in winter time, 1,700 incandescent lights in the City Hall, many lights in the foot passageway of the La Salle St. tunnel, and provide heat for the City Hall building through the 180 radiators. For the furnishing of steam, water and electricity, there are six boilers, seven pumps and four dynamos.

Basement, Room 15—Bureau of Light.

This apartment in the City Hall is the point from which issues the management of all our street lighting. The gas inspector turns the leaves of his record book and informs us, from actual figures, that on the first day of May, 1892, there were 27,463 street gas lamps in the city, 590 kerosene lamps and 9,958 gasoline lamps, about one half of which are cared for by the city, and the other half by contract.

For the purpose of knowing the quantity and quality of gas that is being furnished, 22 test lamps, distributed in different parts of the city, are used, which, being lighted and extinguished daily at the right time, indicate the average consumption of gas.

COST OF STREET LIGHTING.

The cost per light, per year, of the three kinds, is as follows: Gas, $14; gasoline, $15; kerosene, $12.

On May 1, 1892, there were also 993 electric street lamps in use, at a cost of $100 each per light per year, each lamp displacing four gas lamps. The difference between gas and electricity, and the superiority of the latter, are shown in the fact that while gas gives the light of 20 candles, an arc electric lamp gives a light which equals in power 2,000 candles.

WHERE ELECTRIC STREET LIGHTS ARE USED.

The entire down-town business district is now lighted at night by electricity, as are also State St. to Twenty-second St., Madison St. to Western Av.; Milwaukee Av., from Desplaines St. to North Av., and Blue Island Av., from Harrison St. to Sixteenth St. If complaints or suggestions are to be made concerning street lights, the reader will know hereafter where the authorities are that have charge of this department of the city service.

Although only a commencement has been made in electric street lighting, the city now owns four electric plants, distributed in various streets, and gives employment in this department to about eighty workmen.

City Hall, Basement, Room 14—Fire Department.

Another and a very important branch of the city service, with headquarters on the basement floor of the City Hall, is the fire department. Opinions differ as to the desirability of possessing a superior fire department at all times. A great and widely devastating conflagration, in the opinion of some people, is like a revolution, out of which we come purified and into better conditions; whereas a highly efficient fire department may so thoroughly prevent the burning of even old and dilapidated shanties as to hinder for tens of years the growth and improvement of certain portions of a city. Concerning varying opinions upon this subject, however, the Chicago fire department has nothing to do. Its mission is to extinguish fires, and with that end in view the effort is continually being made to secure the greatest possible efficiency, including the prompt alarm of fire, quickly getting to it in any part of the city, and its rapid extinguishment. To accomplish this the city is aided by fire-alarm apparatus and thoroughly drilled firemen to handle ladders, hose, chemical extinguishers and steam fire engines.

Fire Engine at Work.

IF THERE SHOULD BE A FIRE.

The wise person provides for emergencies. It is not well to worry about crossing the bridge until you get there, but the cautious person will have provided means for crossing the stream if there is a great probability of the bridge being gone when the traveler reaches the river.

It is not wisdom to borrow trouble in anticipation of fire, but it is well to presume that it may appear at an unexpected time, and to make preparations for its extinguishment when it comes. With this thought in mind, every resident should investigate all the opportunities in the vicinity for giving an alarm. In most large cities the means existing, very near at hand, are private telephones in the neighborhood, which should each have, upon a card hanging near the telephone:

1st. The telephone number of the nearest police station.

2nd. The telephone number of the nearest fire-engine house.

3rd. A list of public telephones in the vicinity, which should also have upon a card the telephone numbers of persons connected with the fire department, liable to be suddenly called in emergencies.

4th. The nearest police alarm boxes, with a full understanding of how to use them.

5th. The nearest fire alarm boxes, with knowledge of how to give an alarm of fire.

WHEN A FIRE IS FIRST DISCOVERED,

Take three seconds to make yourself cool and self-possessed. Then call the nearest persons to assist you. If the fire cannot be smothered or extinguished by water or conveniently kept chemicals, hasten to the nearest fire alarm box, which, in Chicago, is a red iron box, attached to a lamp-post, telegraph pole or other standing object.

HOW TO GIVE THE ALARM OF FIRE.

Turn the handle that extends outside the box until the box opens. The turning will give an alarm on a shrill bell, which will call a policeman, if he is near, who may assist. When the box is opened, pull vigorously on a hook within and let go. This gives the alarm to the Central Station, and from that point the

Hook and Ladder Company.

alarm is sent to the nearest fire-engine house, and if these directions are followed it will be but a brief time before the firemen will be at the fire.

During the drill in 1891, Fire Engine Company No. 16, with men in bed, arose, hitched to apparatus, laid 300 feet of hose and connected with fire-plug in 1 minute and 55 seconds.

FIRE EXTINGUISHING EQUIPMENT.

The following constitutes the fire department force, its wealth and strength in Chicago, according to the last report, issued December 31, 1891:

Money invested in buildings, land
  and fire-extinguishing apparatus $2,135,709
Annual expense of maintenance...$1,376,249
Number of feet of hose in use.........117,322
Number of feet of hose in reserve......20,800
Number of fire hydrants...............13,411
Number of miles of wire for alarms....2,003
Number of miles of water mains.......1,336
Number of men on the force.............990
Number of fire-alarm boxes.............881
Number of police boxes that can be used..675
Number of horses in the service.........421
Number of engine companies..............68
Number of hose vehicles..................68
Number of hook and ladder companies.....11
Number of one-horse chemical engines......10
Number of trucks with chemical engines....7
Number of two-horse chemical engines......4
Number of hand-engines....................3
Number of hand chemical engines..........3
Number of fire-boats......................3

WORK OF THE HOOK AND LADDER COMPANIES.

The purpose of the hook and ladder companies is well illustrated in the accompanying picture, which shows the use made of the hook - ladders — the firemen ascending the ladder and rescuing the inmates of a dwelling, often in the face of a tremendous blaze rushing from the front of the building. The brave and daring acts of firemen in the saving of life thus, are very many.

A Rescue.

Among the later and better buildings which have been erected within the past few years, especially in Chicago, many have been made so absolutely fireproof as to render the services of the hook and ladder companies unnecessary. Others, not entirely proof against fire, have been provided with fire escapes, consisting of iron ladders on the outside of the buildings, the location of which it is well for every guest at the hotel and every inmate of the building to understand.

City Hall—First Floor, Room 21—Water Department.

Leaving the basement rooms of the City Hall, we ascend in one of the eight elevators to the next landing, on what is known as the First Floor, and enter the office of

THE SUPERINTENDENT OF WATER OFFICE,

Where we learn that the city, at the beginning of 1892, furnishes water to about 200,000 buildings, 160,000 of which pay a fixed price, while about 40,000 buildings have meters supplied to them, and pay for their water in proportion to the amount they use.

An inspection is intended to be made of each building once a year, and, after the first year, the tax for water is based on the inspector's report, the water tax being due every six months, the rule being that if the charge due is not paid within sixty days, the water will be shut off. There are about 5,000 "shut-offs" during the year, among delinquent water-tax payers, necessitating the employment of fifty men in this department.

In all new buildings the amount of water tax to be levied is determined from the architect's plans, when the building permit is issued, these plans showing the number of water faucets to be placed in the building.

OFFICE FORCE AT THE WATER OFFICE.

To manage this department of the city there are the following number of employes:

Water Office........................50
Meter Department....................25
Assessors...........................25
Shut-off Men........................50
Inspectors 50

CHICAGO WATER SUPPLY SYSTEM.

In 1834 the city paid $95 50 for digging a well at the corner of what is now Cass and Michigan Streets. The lake water coming into favor, water carriers entered upon the business of supplying the people until 1836, when the Chicago Hydraulic Company, a private corporation, was organized, and a plant put in at a cost of $25,000, to draw water from the lake, these works being first in operation in 1842, a pump station being located at the corner of Lake Street and Michigan Avenue, for supplying the South Side with water in case of fire.

In 1851 the Legislature passed an act whereby Chicago was empowered to erect her own waterworks, the first iron pipe for the distribution of water being laid on Clark St., in 1852.

The water supply being limited, and the quality bad from contact with sewage, it was determined to arrange for a greater and better supply, and in the spring of 1864 work was begun for the construction of the two-mile tunnel, into which the water was allowed to flow at the crib, and the work completed in the spring of 1867, at an expense of $458,000.

THE WATER WORKS DURING THE GREAT FIRE.

The fire of 1871 destroyed the buildings surrounding the water works and inflicted a damage to buildings and machinery of $75,000. The engines, however, were repaired and in working order after a delay of eight days.

The first two-mile tunnel was five feet in diameter. In 1872 work was begun on a second two-mile tunnel, seven feet in diameter, extending to the crib, which was completed in 1874. This tunnel has been extended to a pumping station at Ashland Av. and Twenty-second St.

In 1887 work was begun on a new tunnel eight feet in diameter, to extend four miles into the lake, beginning at a point eastward of Peck Court. This was completed in June, 1892, and, with the 25 pumping engines, gives a capacity of 320,000,000 gallons of water, which can be drawn in from the lake and supplied to the people every twenty-four hours when required, being 213 gallons per day for each person in a city of 1,500,000 people.

New tunnel, 4 miles; old tunnel, 2¼ miles; government breakwater inlet to crib, 1½ miles; connecting tunnels between main tunnels and the pumping works, 4 miles; tunnel at Hyde Park, 1¾ miles; tunnel at Lake View, 1¼ miles. Total length of tunnel, 14½ miles.

The new tunnel is 85 feet beneath the surface of the ground, the average depth below the bottom of the lake being 40 feet. Cost of new tunnel, with all its connections, $1,100-000. Total cost of water works to date, about $17,000,000, and had yielded an income, up to January, 1891, of $25,193,724, being over $8,000,000 in excess of the cost. During the year 1890 the collections from water consumers were $2,149,595.79.

There are over 1,200 miles of water mains within the city limits, and about 130 miles of water-pipes are laid each year, the pipe varying from 6 to 36 inches in diameter.

SPRINKLING LAWNS.

Although the capacity for water supply is ample, the city authorities find it always necessary to economize in its use. For that reason they charge extra for the use of any unusual amount, and the time for sprinkling lawns is restricted to the hours between 6 and 7 in the morning, and from 6 to 8 in the evening.

City Hall—First Floor, Room 22—The City Collector.

In room 22, on the first floor, the City Collector has a force of 17 clerks, who receive the city tax, not only upon real estate, but from various other sources. Thus the moneys taken for licenses yield the annual sum of over $3,000,000. Building permits bring in yearly about $48,500. The inspection of elevators turns in about $11,000, while the dog pound returns in the past year were $1,786.50, there being 33,000 dogs in the city, many of which stray away from home, are captured by the policemen, confined in the dog pound, and redeemed by their owners. The dog tax itself yields the city over $60,000.

During the month of May, August and December, when the saloon licenses are being paid, the amount of collections from all sources ranges from $60,000 to $70,000 per day, all moneys thus coming in passing at once into the hands of the City Treasurer, who deposits in banks of his own selection. As a matter of interest to people who contemplate the opening of certain lines of business in Chicago, we give herewith a list of the

LICENSE FEES, GOOD FOR ONE YEAR,

To be paid on the following kinds of business:

Amusements, 1st Class	$300.00
Amusements, 2nd Class	200.00
Auctioneers	300.00
Bakers	5.00
Baths, with massage	5.00
Billiards	10.00
Bill Posters (with Wagon)	100.00
Bill Posters (without Wagon)	25.00
Boats, Tug	25.00

LICENSE FEES—Continued.

Boats, Steam	$25.00
Boats, Row	2.00
Boats, Sail	5.00
Boats, Junk	27.00
Bowling Alleys	10.00
Brewers	500.00
Brokers	25.00
Butchers	15.00
Distillers	500.00
Dogs	2.00
Drays	2.50
Druggists (Permit)	2.00
Gunpowder	25.00
Hacks	5.00
Hacks (Livery)	2.50
Hacks, Coupe, Gurney, &c	2.50
Intelligence, Male	100.00
Intelligence, Female	25.00
Junk Dealers	50.00
Liquors, Wholesale	250.00
Liquors, Wholesale, Malt	500.00
Lumber Yards	100.00
Omnibus	5.00
Pawnbrokers	300.00
Peddlers (with Wagon)	25.00
Peddlers (without Wagon)	10.00
Pool Tables	10.00
Rendering	100.00
Runners	12.00
Saloons	500.00
Scales, Public	10.00
Scavengers	5.00
Second-Hand Dealers	50.00
Shooting Galleries	10.00
Soap Factories	100.00
Tanneries	50.00
Wagons, One-Horse	2.50
Wagons, Two-Horse	5.00
Wagons, Junk	10.00
Weapons (Concealed)	2.00

City Hall—First Floor, Rooms 26, 28 and 30—Building Department.

In the clerical force of the building department there are thirty-five employes, their work consisting of the issuing of permits for the erection of new buildings and the repairing of old ones. Within certain limits, the exteriors of new buildings must consist of stone, brick, and iron or steel. Outside of those limits, wooden buildings may be built, but whatever the material, a permit must be obtained before the building is erected anywhere in the city.

PRESENT CITY FIRE LIMITS.

The fire limits now include the World's Fair Grounds, on the south; Garfield Park, on the west, and Lincoln Park, on the north; the area covered being about one-quarter of the city, designated as follows:

West on Sixty-seventh St. from the lake to State St., north on State St. to Thirty-ninth St., west on Thirty-ninth St. to Western Avenue Boul., north on Western Avenue Boul. to the Illinois & Michigan Canal, southwest on the Illinois & Michigan Canal to Crawford Av., north on Crawford Av. to North Av., east on North Av. to Western Av., north on Western Av. to the river, southeast on the river to Fullerton Av., east on Fullerton Av. to Halsted St., north on Halsted St. to Belmont Av., east on Belmont Av. to the lake.

Number of building permits granted in 1891, 11,805. Frontage of the buildings erected, 282,672 feet, or a little more than 53 miles. Cost of buildings, as stated in application for permits, $54,100,000, to which estimate 25 per cent may be added with safety.

PERMITS FOR HIGH BUILDINGS.

Buildings erected in 1891, 6 stories or more in height:

6-story buildings..31 | 13-story buildings...2
7 story buildings...8 | 14-story buildings...2
8-story buildings...4 | 16-story buildings..11
9-story buildings...1 | 17-story buildings...2
10-story buildings...6 | 18-story buildings...1
12-story buildings...3 |

Full particulars concerning requirements are obtained upon application at the building department.

City Hall—First Floor, Rooms 27, 29 and 31—City Sealer.

These rooms are occupied by an official whose duty consists in an inspection once a year of all scales, weights and measures, and large scales twice a year, some twelve persons being employed in this work. The constant endeavor of those having the management of city affairs, is to make each department of the government yield a revenue by which its clerical force may be paid for its service. This department is largely self-supporting, because of the following fees paid for inspection:

CHARGES FOR EACH INSPECTION.

Track Scales.............................$3.50
Ten-ton Scales and over...............2.00
From 1 to 10-ton Scales...............1.00
Beef Runaway Scales.....................75
Platform Scales...........................35
Counter Scales.... 20
Spring Scales............................20
Liquid Measures, 1 gallon and over.......10
Liquid Measures, under 1 gallon...........5
Dry Measures, except bushel baskets.......5
Bushel Baskets..........................15

City Hall—First Floor, Room 33—City Treasurer.

At a certain time in the year the City Council makes an appropriation of money for the conduct and maintenance of each department in the city government, which amount so appropriated is known as the police fund, fire department fund, etc. The law makes it the

duty for the Treasurer to receive all moneys from the City Collector, assign the sums designated to the different departments, and pay out the same to the different departments in amounts not to exceed the appropriations.

City Hall—First Floor, Room 34—Comptroller.

The last annual report for 1891 shows that the receipts of the city for that year were $29,550,560.29, and the total expenditures were $28,115,931.83. The bonded debt of the city, January 1, 1892, was $13,530,350. In this room the clerical force numbers about twenty-five persons, many of whom retain their positions through all the various

political administrations, because of their special training and fitness for the positions they hold.

This department is the center of the financial management of the city, all accounts of receipts of moneys and disbursements being kept here. The Comptroller's position is one of great financial responsibility.

City Hall—First Floor, Room 32—Superintendent of Police.

While the duties of the police force are quite fully described elsewhere, the official head of the police department is vested in the Superintendent, who holds his appointment from, and is subject to the will of, the Mayor.

The duties of this official are many, and his responsibilities are great. He is expected to give full opportunity for free speech, and he is expected to restrain speakers from utterances that may breed riot and disturbance. He is expected to permit over 6,000 saloons to run wide open from early morn until 12 at night, and he is expected to restrain all drunkenness and lawlessness that may occur in consequence of intemperance. He is expected to grant personal liberty, and he is expected to restrain from too much liberty. He is expected to put

the right men in the right places on the police force, and he is expected to spend a large share of his time in listening to complaints concerning the men he has appointed as guardians of the peace. Standing continually between two contending forces—the selfish, riotous and unscrupulous on the one side, and the conservative, law-abiding on the other —he usually retires from office with a swarm of enemies so great as to politically bury him for some years afterward.

Leaving the head of this department to the mercies of a crowd of waiting people in the ante-room, some of whom crave leniency, some want promotion in the police ranks, some want positions for themselves or their friends, we go forward to other rooms.

City Hall—First Floor, Rooms 35 and 36—Office of the City Clerk.

The last city official we visit on the first floor. He is busy writing up the minutes of the last Council meeting, and filing away the petitions, resolutions, committee reports and ordinances which have been introduced into

the Council meetings heretofore. For information found in the ordinances, and the workings of the City Council, the questioner goes to the office of the City Clerk. We ascend from this to the second floor.

City Hall—Second Floor, Room 45—The Mayor.

The Mayor is assisted by two secretaries, one stenographer, one messenger and two special policemen.

His duties are widely extended, and as the city grows larger, his responsibilities are becoming greater. Like the Superintendent of Police, he must attempt to serve all classes, and the wishes of his constituents are so greatly at variance, he also, at the close of his official term, usually steps down and out of office with a host of enemies, who will forget their grievances as the years go by. Aside from receiving petitions, deputations wishing his influence, and reformers who make suggestions, he is expected to be present and make a first-class off-hand speech on all important occasions, whether it be a speech of welcome at a brewers' convention, or an address at the opening of a building under the control of the Women's Christian Temperance Union. And further, he is expected to be in close consultation with the heads of all the departments. He should thoroughly know the needs of the city, be able to make suggestions, point out the way for the aldermen, and carefully weigh and inspect every ordinance with the firm resolve of vetoing if it does not come up to the requirements.

City Hall—Second Floor, Room 41—Corporation Counsel.

The Mayor is much assisted by an official known as the Corporation Counsel, a gentleman of tried legal ability, whose advice is supposed to be of service in all the technical questions that arise, his duty being also to draft the various ordinances that may come before the Council.

The resident of the city who may be in doubt concerning the city's liability, or may have important suggestions to make, involving legal technical questions, or may have in mind certain matters that may and should become law, ought to consult the Corporation Counsel. While suits pertaining to personal damage come before the City Attorney, much matter relating to personal rights comes within the province of the City Corporation Counsel.

City Hall—Second Floor, Room 43—Engineer's Offices.

Here we get considerable statistical information, this department having much to do with: 1. Harbor. 2. Bridge and viaduct construction. 3. Bridge and viaduct repairs. 4. Main sewerage works. 5. Water pipe extension and maintenance of meter-service. 6. Water works operation and construction.

By the Engineer's report of February 15, 1892, it is learned that Chicago has in port 998 vessels, of which 496 are steam and 502 are sail, with an aggregate carrying capacity of 1,000,000 tons.

Number of vessels arrived in port during the season of 1891 was 8,956. Departures, 9,144. Total number of vessels that passed Rush Street bridge, 13,400. Average, per day, 59. Average time consumed per vessel in passing bridge, 1 minute 36 seconds. Average time open per day, 1 hour 32 minutes.

There are thirty-nine viaducts in the city, the first being constructed at the ends of the Madison Street bridge in 1866, at a cost of $12,675. The most expensive viaduct was that at Milwaukee Av. and Desplaines St., which is 680 feet long at one end and 472 feet at the other end, its cost being $296,043, the railroads paying $131,878. The total cost, to the city, of all these viaducts has been $1,419,086. Cost to the railroads, $2,169,208. The city has paid 39½ per cent of the cost, and the railroads have paid 60½ per cent.

City Hall—Second Floor, Rooms 47 and 49—Sewerage Department.

In this department a complete diagram is kept of the network of sewers which drain the city, their total length being 888,321 miles, of which 396,758 miles are constructed of brick, and 494,536 miles are of vitrified clay pipe. The total cost of sewers up to January 1, 1892, had been $12,498,660.

Sewers are in size all the way from 6 inches to 9 feet in diameter, there being about two miles of 8-foot sewer, and four miles of 9-foot sewer. The size of the sewer depends somewhat upon the petition to the Council calling for the sewer, but not wholly, the officials in the sewer department being thoroughly informed as to the capacity of sewers, the connections to be made, the size of other sewers in that region, and the needs of the locality where this sewer is to be laid.

City Hall—Second Floor, Room 58—Superintendent of Streets.

This is an interesting department of municipal government, an ever live subject being the question of kind of pavement which shall be laid. At the beginning of 1892 the following were the amounts of the various pavements then in use:

KINDS OF PAVEMENT IN CHICAGO.

Cedar block, 481 miles; macadam, 256 miles; stone, 23 miles; sheet asphalt, 9 miles; asphalt block, 3 miles; brick, ½ mile; burned clay, ¼ mile. Total, 774 miles of paved streets.

CEDAR BLOCK PAVEMENT.

Opinions differ as to the best pavement for ultimate adoption in Chicago. The cedar block has the merit of being easily obtained, can be quickly laid, will endure in very good condition for some years, is easy to ride on, can be easily taken up and replaced when repairing streets, and is almost noiseless. Its objections are that it will wear

Cedar Block.

through in a few years, becomes filthy through saturation, cannot long withstand the heavy teaming of business streets, will greatly shrink and the blocks become loose in a long period of dry weather. When tightened, after shrinkage, will swell in wet weather, and get out of place, and during a flood on the streets may float away and be lost.

MACADAM PAVEMENT.

The macadam is a pleasant street when first laid, and, when decently well cared for, continues in good condition for some time afterwards. If neglected, it, ere long, becomes rough and, even with the best of care, its surface grinds into a fine powder, which wafts away in clouds of dust, which dust, if not blown from the street, is converted into a thin mud in wet weather, which is very destructive to carriages.

GRANITE BLOCK PAVEMENT.

The granite block is the most durable of all pavements, will last for generations, is easily taken up and replaced when necessary, and will stand the heaviest teaming in the central wholesale districts. The objections to this stone, however, are that

Granite Block.

its hard surface reflects intense heat, is slippery in wet weather, is expensive and excessively noisy.

ASPHALT BLOCK PAVEMENT.

The asphalt block is a brick made of sand. Like all pavements, it should have a firm foundation; it is rapidly laid, may be easily taken up for repairs, and is almost noiseless. Its disadvantages are that no means has been devised whereby it can endure continuous heavy teaming for years and retain an even surface.

VITRIFIED BRICK PAVEMENT.

Vitrified brick as a paving material is rapidly coming into use. It resembles a common brick in color and size, and is burned so hard it almost equals granite in quality of endurance. It has

Brick.

the advantage of being easily obtained from soil in regions far remote from other paving material, is easily laid, can be readily repaired, and is reasonable in price. Its disadvantages are slight irregularities of surface, making it somewhat noisy and preventing its being easily cleaned.

SHEET ASPHALT PAVEMENT.

Sheet asphalt has passed the experimental stage, its merits and disadvantages being well understood. Its great advantages are cleanliness, comparative freedom from noise, and power of resisting the action of climate, whether the weather be excessively dry or the streets be inundated with water. The objections to its use are that its surface gradually, at frequent intervals, shows depressions that hold water. It is slippery in wet

Sheet Asphalt.

and frosty weather, and is difficult to perfectly repair when torn to pieces where street improvements are going forward.

COST OF STREET PAVEMENTS.

Cedar Block.....90c to $1.00 per square yard.
Macadam........90c to $1.50 per square yard.
Granite Block.$3.00 to $3.25 per square yard.
Vitrified Brick.$1.75 to $2.00 per square yard.
Sheet Asphalt.........$2.90 per square yard.

The writer has carefully studied pavements made of the Nicholson blocks, as they are laid on a concrete foundation in the streets of London, and has watched the frequent washings of the asphalt pavements as they exist in Paris, and, after a careful review of the whole subject, is of the opinion that when the last sewer has been completed, the last gas-pipe has been laid, the last conduit is in place and the last water-pipe is in position —when the surface of the street is no more to be disturbed—the coming pavement will be that which can be made perfectly clean by washing, and that shall be noiseless. These qualities the people will imperatively demand. Added to these virtues shall be the merit of long endurance—the whole being furnished at a reasonable price.

City Hall—Second Floor, Room 53—House Moving and Sidewalks.

The sidewalk is a necessity in every city. It must be built and paid for. How to get it is easy, but what its width should be, how it should be built, and of what materials constructed, is a little more difficult to determine.

Do you want a new sidewalk? How far do you wish to have it extend? Of what material do you wish it made? You have doubtless a ready answer to these questions. Nevertheless, it will be well for you to come down to the Department of Streets and Sidewalks and talk the subject over. The officials in charge are, as is the case in all departments of the city government, very affable and ready to impart all the information you may require as to how to get your walk, what materials to use, and what its cost will be.

COST OF BUILDING SIDEWALKS IN CHICAGO.

And, incidentally, if you wish to know what it costs, in 1892, to build a sidewalk in Chicago, you can judge the expense from the following figures:

Wooden sidewalk, 6 feet wide, 2-inch plank, 5 cents per square foot; cost per lot of 25 feet front, $7.50. Concrete walks, from 18 to 22 cents per square foot. Stone walks, 40 cents per square foot; in the business district, where stone must be eight inches thick, 70 cents to $1 per square foot.

Possibly, without consulting you, other parties have had an ordinance passed and have levied an assessment to have a walk built such as you and your friends do not approve. Go down to the City Hall and talk the matter over with the Commissioner of Streets and the officials in the Department of Special Assessments.

On the second floor of the City Hall is located all the managing power for the platting, opening, grading, sewering, sidewalks, paving, cleaning and keeping the streets of Chicago in repair. With thousands of miles in use, every rod of which has to be cared for, this is no small job.' We will not attempt to fill your head with many of the details, but let us suppose that

YOU WISH TO MOVE A HOUSE.

This is what will be necessary for you to do. First, you will apply to this department for an inspector, who will examine the house to see if it can be moved, and the route over which it is to go, with a view to obstructions that may be in the way. Cost of inspection, $2.50.

Second. You must obtain the consent of the majority of the property owners in the block to which you intend to move, and in the block immediately opposite. This must be proven by a petition signed by said property owners, which petition must be accompanied by a certificate from the building inspector that the house is in a fit condition to move.

Third. You must now obtain a permit from the authorities to move your house, the charge for which is $5. If, however, the building is to be only moved from one part of the lot to another, while a permit is necessary, the charge in that case is only $1, and the consent of adjoining property owners is not required. The removal of a frame house from one part of the fire limits to another part of the fire limits is permissible, but a frame house from the outside cannot be moved to the inside of the fire limits. The removal of buildings through the streets will largely cease after the elevated roads are built.

City Hall—Second Floor, Room 48—Bureau of Maps.

You are about to erect a new building, somewhat isolated, perhaps, from other houses, and are in doubt as to what its number shall be. In that case go into Room 48, Second Floor, where you will find 45 large volumes of maps, containing plats of every block, street and alley in the city. Your own block, lot and street are there, and the clerk in charge will tell you your street number, the size of your lot, and give you any further information concerning the map of any portion of the city.

City Hall—Second Floor, Room 50—Bureau of Special Assessments.

When it has been determined that it is necessary to construct a new sidewalk, to pave a street or make some special improvement in a certain portion of the city, which will directly benefit those living in that particular locality, an ordinance is passed providing for the making of the improvement, and a special assessment against the property supposed to be benefited. This assessment is made by officials who have had long experience in this kind of work, and are supposed to be competent to determine how much each property holder should pay in order to contribute his share to the improvement. The assessment is, therefore, generally entirely just, but the impression may prevail that it is exceedingly unjust. In that case the property-owner who feels himself aggrieved should call at Room 50, Second Floor, and obtain a clear understanding of the subject. If yet satisfied that injustice is being done, appeal may be had to the courts, the methods of which will be clearly pointed out here. Throughout this second floor of the City Hall nearly every room is devoted, in some form, to the subject of streets; the Commissioner of Public Works and the Purchasing Agent for all the supplies the city may need in repairs and otherwise, being also located on this floor.

City Hall—Second Floor, Room 52—Purchasing Agent.

Upon the Purchasing Agent devolves the responsible work of buying the material for sidewalks when not built by the owners; cement for sewerage department, pipe, brooms for the street department, stationery, furniture and appliances for all the city departments. As an illustration of the magnitude of this work, it may be mentioned that there are twenty central points in various parts of the city devoted almost wholly to the storage of lumber and drain pipe for city use.

A study of the directory of each floor of the City Hall shows a certain degree of classification. Thus, on the basement floor are the officials entrusted with the preservation of the city from harm through disease, fire or lawlessness. On the first floor are the offices devoted to the collection and disbursement of moneys. On the second floor are the rooms given up to the management of streets and their drainage. On the third floor are the managers who determine why and how the city shall be governed—this portion of the building being largely devoted to the educational, legal and engineering departments. The top floor is devoted wholly to the making of laws for the government of the city and the imparting of education to those who read.

City Hall—Third Floor, Room 78½—Office of Supt. of School Census.

Here we learn several things it is well to know, and among these is the fact that the State of Illinois annually appropriates $300,000 for school purposes, and that an annual census must be taken to know what portion of this money is due to each division of the State, the money being apportioned according to the number of children of school age.

The superintendent in charge is ready to prove that the school census taken in Chicago is more accurate than a government census can be, because of the constant experience of his 150 enumerators, who annually go over this ground, during a period of 20 days, in such a manner that all previous residents are known and counted, and all new-comers are readily found. Many of the enumerators are ladies, who are found to be among the best of census-takers.

CHICAGO SCHOOL CENSUS FOR 1892.

The following table gives the school census returns for 1892. It shows the population by divisions, including Hyde Park, Lake, Lake View and Jefferson, the total being 1,438,010.

DIVISION.	Males.	Females.	Total.
West Division..	340,998..	304,430..	..645,428
South Division.	138,163..	113,015..	..251,173
North Division.	102,626..	..92,383..	..195,009
Lake	73,424..	..68,575..	..141,999
Hyde Park......	63,714..	..58,845..	..122,559
Lake View......	33,584..	..33,551..	..67,135
Jefferson......	7,634..	..7,068..	..14,702
Grand Total....	760,143..	677,867..	1,438,010

Of persons over 21 years old there are 895,847, and under 21 there are 542,163.

City Hall—Second Floor, Room 78½—Supt. of Compulsory Education.

The principal duty of the managers in charge of this department is to see that all children between the ages of 7 and 14 who do not go to some private school, shall attend a public school, and to this end 18 inspectors are employed throughout the school year —9 females and 9 males—to see that the law is enforced.

The inspectors are instructed to exercise discretion in the enforcement of the law among the poorer classes, who are dependent upon the labor of their children, and the superintendent has been instrumental in persuading one of the large department stores in the city to open a school for the instruction of the younger clerks, cash girls and small boys in their store, with very beneficial results.

The superintendent of the school census complains of one defect in the law, which is the lack of penalty to be inflicted in case the child will not go to school. There are on the records the names of 3,528 incorrigible children in Chicago who cannot be made to attend school by their parents, and the law is powerless to compel them to do so.

City Hall—Second Floor, Room 72—Superintendent of Schools.

Passing from the rooms (No. 79 and 80) assigned to special teachers of vocal music and drawing, we are in the large and commodious rooms of the Superintendent of Public Schools, and Board of Education, consisting of 21 members, under whose supervision and management there are at the present time, in the Chicago Public Schools, 3,001 teachers, distributed throughout 231 school buildings.

The curriculum of study in the public schools of Chicago is designed to be eminently practical, and the student who graduates at a Chicago High School holds a certificate, in the diploma, which is a guarantee

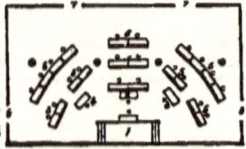

Board Room, Board of Education.

Seating Arrangement.
1. President of the Board.
2. Clerk of the Board.
3. Assistant Clerk.
4. Reporters.
5. Seats for Members.
6. Entrance to Superintendent's Office.
7. Entrance from Hall.
8. Entrance to Drawing Rooms.

of success so far as general education is concerned. The constant endeavor, however, is to make the course of study in every way adapted to the exigencies of the times, and with this object in view manual training is gradually being introduced, and will steadily be pushed forward as rapidly as circumstances will warrant.

The instruction in sewing is proving highly acceptable, while private cooking and kindergarten work are being studied, and the advantages they offer are given full attention.

CHICAGO PUBLIC SCHOOL STATISTICS FOR 1892.

Total expense of running Public Schools for past year...........$3,583,481
Expense for Salaries.............$2,298,782
Cost of teaching German in Schools...........................$116,311
Cost of teaching Drawing..........$21,904
Cost of teaching Music...........$17,073
Cost of teaching Physical Culture...$15,869
Number of Pupils enrolled in 1892...146,751
Number of Desks in School buildings.121,159
Number of Pupils that studied German....................................36,133
Number of Pupils of German parentage studying German........... ... 16,527
Number of Pupils in Evening Schools.12,000
Number of Pupils in School in excess of 1891........................11,210
Number of Desks in rented rooms.......7,628
Number of Teachers employed.........3,001
Number of Teachers in Evening Schools..256
Number of Male Teachers employed......190
Number of Grammar and Primary Schools combined......................167
Number of Primary Schools.............53
Number of Evening Schools.............45
Number of High Schools.................11
Percentage of Pupils in the Primary Grade....................................71.93
Percentage of Pupils in the Grammar Grade...............................24.48
Percentage of Pupils in the High Schools...............................3.59

CARE OF THE SCHOOL ROOMS.

Of the 231 school buildings, about one half are heated by steam; the balance, in about equal numbers, are heated by furnaces and stoves, the hard coal bill for the year being $35,971, and the cost of soft coal $81,119. Special attention is given to the sanitary condition of schools, the ventilation being so supplied as to give each pupil 1,800 cubic feet of fresh air per hour, or 30 cubic feet per minute.

The seating is so arranged, when possible, as to allow the light to come from the left side, and, while the recess has been abandoned, the school hours have been shortened, the forenoon session being from 9 to 11:45, and the afternoon session from 1:30 to 3:30.

City Hall—Third Floor, Room 71—Business Manager of Schools.

Experience has taught the necessity of having a manager to take charge of repair work on buildings and of the furnishing of supplies to pupils in the schools, the free list including drawing paper, tablets for mathematical work, lead pencils, slate pencils, pen holders and pens.

School books are furnished free to indigent children at the request of the principal of their school, the interest from a special fund being used for this purpose.

Other pupils buy their school books where they choose, the price being the same wherever they are purchased. the Board of Education stipulating with publishers, whenever a text book is adopted, that their books, wherever kept, shall be sold at a uniform price.

In some of the more wealthy districts second-hand clothing is collected from the pupils and distributed among the indigent children of other schools. This is as far as the school authorities have yet gone, in 1892, in the furnishing of clothing to pupils.

City Hall—Third Floor, Room 70—Board of Election Commissioners.

This is comparatively a new department in the city government, largely the result of the adoption of the Australian Ballot Law, which imposes such restrictions as are calculated to secure an honest election. About twenty men are here employed throughout the year, the number being increased to 150 during the fall election, these twenty permanent men becoming the instructors for the others, their active duties continuing until about the middle of November.

THE AUSTRALIAN BALLOT LAW requires that when there are more than 450 registered voters in any precinct the territory must be subdivided. The law also directs that after each presidential election the precincts must be rearranged so as to have, as nearly as possible, 300 voters in each. The first ward in Chicago, at a late election, was divided into eighteen precincts, and the printed notices resembled the form inserted here. The total number of voters at the last election in this city was 207,832. There were registered, just before election, between 42,000 and 43,000. Number of precincts, 560. About 60 or 70 will be added to that number this fall.

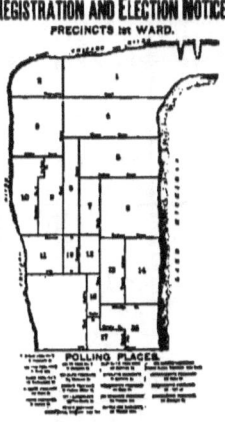

REGISTRATION AND ELECTION NOTICE.

PRECINCTS 1st WARD.

POLLING PLACES.

Ward Divided into Voting Precincts. Polling Places Published.

REQUIREMENTS OF THE NEW BALLOT LAW.

The Australian Ballot Law was enacted for the purpose of enabling all persons to vote as they may be inclined, without hindrance or interference at the time of election. To accomplish this, the law requires the appointment of three election commissioners by the county court, to be chosen from the different political parties. These commissioners divide the city into precincts, as shown herein, giving from 350 to 400 voters to each precinct, appoint judges and clerks of election, give them instructions as to methods of procedure, and have all tickets printed which voters may have occasion to use, the tickets to include only the names of those candidates who have been duly nominated in properly organized conventions.

It is made the duty of the judges of election to absolutely know that the persons who vote are entitled to vote, and are not intimidated at election time, are not influenced by ticket peddlers near the polls, and that no one can have knowledge of how they vote. To accomplish this, at a certain time prior to election, the names of all persons supposed to be entitled to vote in the precinct are recorded. Subsequently a thorough canvass is made of the precinct, to ascertain the names of all voters, and, after corrections and revisions are made, the names of all supposed voters are printed and hung in conspicuous places, in order that the general public may criticise and make any suggestions that are necessary to secure a correct list of those

PERSONS WHO ARE ENTITLED TO VOTE.

After waiting a certain number of days, the persons in charge meet again, for the last time before election, to revise the list, strike off names of those who should not vote, and add others who may be entitled to the privilege. At this last meeting the voting list is supposed to be completed, no one being allowed to vote except those who are duly registered.

Map Showing Ward and Congressional District Boundaries.

Explanation.—The heavy. black lines indicate ward boundaries. The largest figures (1, 2, 3, 4) designate location of Congressional Districts. The fine fringe lines, attached to the heavy black lines, give the boundaries of Congressional Districts. The smaller figures (1 to 34) indicate ward numbers.

THE THIRTY-FOUR WARDS OF CHICAGO AND THEIR BOUNDARIES. 181

Each Ward Entitled to Two Aldermen in the City Council. See Opposite Page for Map.

First Ward.—Bounded by the River, the Lake and 12th.

Second Ward.—Bounded on the north by 12th; on the south by 26th from the Lake to Clark, and by 16th from Clark to the River; on the west by the River from 12th to 16th, and by Clark from 16th to 26th.

Third Ward.—Bounded by 26th, 33rd, the Lake and Wentworth Av.

Fourth Ward.—Bounded by 33rd, 39th, the Lake and Stewart Av.

Fifth Ward.—Commencing at 16th and Clark, thence w. to the River, thence s. w. to S. Halsted, thence s. to 33rd, thence e. to Wentworth Av., thence n. to 26th, thence e. to Clark, thence n. to place of beginning.

Sixth Ward.—Commencing at S. Halsted and the South Branch of the River, thence n. along the River and the Ill. & Mich. Canal to Western Av., thence s. to 39th, thence e. to Stewart Av., thence n. to 33rd, thence w. to S. Halsted, thence n. to place of beginning.

Seventh Ward. — Commencing at the River and W. 12th, thence w. to Johnson, thence s. to W. 22nd, thence e. to S. Halsted, thence s. to the River, thence n. e. to the place of beginning.

Eighth Ward.—Commencing at W. 12th, cor. Johnson, thence w. to Throop, thence s. to the River, thence e. to S. Halsted, thence n. to W. 22nd, thence w. to Johnson, thence n. to place of beginning.

Ninth Ward.—Commencing at Centre Av., cor. W. Taylor, thence w. to S. Wood, thence s. to Ill. & Mich. Canal, thence n. e. along the Canal and the South Branch of the River to Throop, thence n. to W. 12th, thence e. to Centre Av., thence n. to place of beginning.

Tenth Ward.—Commencing at S. Wood, cor. W. Taylor, w. on W. Taylor to Campbell Av., thence s. to W. 12th, thence w. to W. 40th, thence s. to Egan Av., thence e. to Ill. & Mich. Canal, thence n. e. to S. Wood, thence n. to place of beginning.

Eleventh Ward. — Commencing at N. May, cor. W. Ohio, w. on W. Ohio to N. Paulina, thence s. to W. Taylor, thence e. to Sibley, thence n. to W. Harrison, thence e. to Throop, thence n. to W. Van Buren, thence e. to Centre Av., thence n. on Centre Av. and Ann to W. Lake, thence e. to N. May, thence n. to place of beginning.

Twelfth Ward.—Commencing at Washington Boul., cor. S. Paulina, w. on Washington Boul. to S. California Av., thence n. to W. Lake, thence w. to W. 48th, thence s. to W. 12th, thence e. to Campbell Av., thence n. to W. Taylor, thence e. to Paulina, thence n. to place of beginning.

Thirteenth Ward. — Commencing at Washington Boul., cor. S. Paulina, w. on Washington Boul. to California Av., thence n. to W. Lake, thence w. to W. 48th, thence n. to W. Chicago Av., thence e. to N. Paulina, thence s. to place of beginning.

Fourteenth Ward.—Commencing at W. Chicago Av., cor. N. Ashland Av., w. on W. Chicago Av. to W. 48th, thence n. to W. North Av., thence e. to N. Ashland Av., thence s. to place of beginning.

Fifteenth Ward.—Commencing at the River and W. North Av., w. on W. North Av. to N. Kedzie Av., thence n. to W. Belmont Av., thence e. to N. Western Av., thence s. to the River, thence s. e. to place of beginning.

Sixteenth Ward.—Commencing at N. May, cor. W. Ohio, w. on Ohio to N. Paulina, thence n. to W. Chicago Av., thence n. e. to N. Ashland Av., thence e. to the River, thence s. e. to N. Carpenter, thence s. to W. Chicago Av., thence w. to N. May, thence s. to place of beginning.

Seventeenth Ward.—Commencing at W. Lake and the River, w. on Lake to N. May, thence n. to W. Chicago Av., thence e. to N, Carpenter, thence n. to the River, thence s. e. to place of beginning.

Eighteenth Ward. — Bounded by W. Van Buren, W. Lake, the River, and on the west by Centre Av. and Ann.

Nineteenth Ward.—Commencing at W. Van Buren and the River, w. on Van Buren to Throop, s. on Throop to W. Harrison, w. on W. Harrison to Sibley, s. on Sibley to W. Taylor, e. on Taylor to Centre Av., s. on Centre Av. to W. 12th, e. on W. 12th to the River, and n. on the River to place of beginning.

Twentieth Ward.—Bounded by Division, Fullerton Av., N. Halsted and the River.

Twenty-first Ward. — Bounded by North Av., Fullerton Av., N. Halsted and the Lake.

Twenty-second Ward.—Bounded by Division, North Av., N. Halsted and the Lake.

Twenty-third Ward. — Bounded by Division, N. Wells and the River.

Twenty-fourth Ward. — Bounded by Division, N. Wells, the River and the Lake.

Twenty-fifth Ward.—Commencing at Fullerton Av. and Lake Shore, n. on Lake Shore to Church Road, thence w. to N. Clark, thence s. e. to Graceland Av., thence e to Racine Av., thence s. to Fullerton Av., thence e. to place of beginning.

Twenty-sixth Ward.—Commencing at Fullerton and Racine Avs., n. to Graceland Av., thence w. to N. Clark, thence n. w. to Church Road, thence w. to Western Av., thence s. to Chicago River, thence s. e. to Fullerton Av., thence e. to place of beginning.

Twenty-seventh Ward.—Commencing at Belmont and N. Western Avs., n. to City Limits, thence w. and s. on City Limits to N. North Av., thence e. to Kedzie Av., thence n. to Belmont Av., thence e. to place of beginning.

Twenty-eighth Ward.—Commencing at 39th St. and Western Av., n. to Ill. & Mich. Canal, thence s. w. to 39th St. and Crawford Av., thence n. to North Av., thence w. to City Limits, thence s. to 39th, thence e. to place of beginning.

Twenty-ninth Ward.—Commencing at 47th and State, n. to 39th, thence w. to City Limits, thence s. to 47th, thence e. to place of beginning.

Thirtieth Ward.—Commencing at 63rd and State, n. to 47th, thence w. to City Limits, thence s. to 63rd, thence e. to place of beginning.

Thirty-first Ward.— Commencing at 103rd and State, n. to 63rd, thence w. to City Limits, thence s. and e to place of beginning.

Thirty-second Ward.—Commencing at 55th and Lake Shore, n. w. to 39th, thence w. to State, thence s. to 55th, thence e. to place of beginning.

Thirty-third Ward.—Commencing at 136th and Indiana state line, n. to Lake Michigan, thence n. w. to 55th, thence w. to Stony Island Av., thence s. to City Limits, thence e. to place of beginning.

Thirty-fourth Ward.—Commencing at 136th and w. line Sec. 36, n. along Stony Island Av. to Fifty-fifth, thence w. to State, thence s. to 103rd, thence w. to Halsted, thence s. and e. to place of beginning.

Conditions under which Voting is Permitted.

Upon arrival at the voting place, if the challengers, who are seated beside the judges, are satisfied that the individual is entitled to vote, the voter is given, by one of the judges of election, one ballot, upon which are printed the tickets of all the regular candidates who are before the people to be voted for in that precinct, thus:

FORM OF BALLOT USED BY VOTERS.

O DEMOCRATIC.

For Governor.
☐ JOHN M. PALMER.
For Lieut.-Gov.
☐ ANDREW J. BELL.
For Secy. of State.
☐ NEWELL D. RICKS.

O REPUBLICAN.

For Governor.
☐ JOSEPH W. FIFER.
For Lieut.-Gov.
☐ LYMAN B. RAY.
For Secy. of State.
☐ I. N. PEARSON.

O PROHIBITION.

For Governor.
. ☐ DAVID H. HART.
For Lieut.-Gov.
☐ JOS. L. WHITLOCK.
For Secy. of State.
☐ JAMES R. HANNA.

With this ballot in hand the voter will retire to one of the booths, a cut of which we show herewith, and there, alone and unassisted. he can designate on the ballot the names of the candidates for whom he wishes to vote.

Booth in which to Mark Ballot.

To vote a straight party ticket he will mark in the circle, at the left of the party ticket of his choice, with a lead pencil, which he will find in the booth, a cross similar to the letter X.

To vote a split ticket, leave the circle blank and make a cross in the square to the left of your choice. Or you can write in the name of any candidate of your choice in the blank space on the ticket, making a cross opposite thereto.

In voting on any proposition submitted to vote and printed on the ballot, make a cross X mark in the column opposite the heading "Yes" or "No," and your ballot will be counted "for," if you mark opposite "Yes," and "against" if you mark opposite "No."

To illustrate, in the following the voter may designate his vote by a cross mark thus:

Proposed amendment to the constitution giving judges a life term of office and making them appointive.	YES.	X
	NO.	

OBSERVE FOLLOWING DIRECTIONS:

Do not erase or draw a line through the names printed on the ballot.

Before leaving the voting booth, fold your ballot so as to conceal the marks, and to expose the official endorsement on the back. Leave the booth and hand your ballot to the judge in charge of the ballot box, who, without marking it in any way, must deposit it in the box.

You will not be allowed to occupy a voting booth with another voter. You will not be allowed to occupy a booth more than five minutes, if others are waiting to vote. You will not be allowed to remain in the inclosed space more than ten minutes, and you must quit it as soon as you have voted. You will not be allowed to re-enter the inclosed space, after you have voted, during the election.

You will not be allowed to take a ballot from the polling place before the close of the election.

You will not be allowed to vote any ballot except the one you receive from the judges.

If you spoil a ballot in preparing it, you must return it and get another in place of it.

If you will declare upon oath that you cannot read the English language, or that by reason of physical disability you are unable to mark your ballot, upon request you will be assisted by two of the election officers, appointed for that purpose, of opposite political parties. These officers will mark your ballot as you direct.

Intoxication will not be regarded as physical disability, and if you are intoxicated you will receive no assistance in marking your ballot.

The polls will open at 6 o'clock in the morning and close at 4 o'clock in the evening. Between these hours you are entitled to absent yourself from your place of employment for a period of 2 hours, for the purpose of voting. You will not be liable to any penalty for your absence, nor shall any deduction be made from your wages or salary on that account; but you must ask for leave of absence before the day of election, and your employer may specify the hours during which you may be absent.

QUALIFICATIONS NECESSARY TO BE A VOTER.

Must be a male citizen above 21 years of age.

Must have lived in the state one year, county ninety days and voting precinct one month immediately preceding the time of voting.

Is entitled to vote, though born in a foreign country, if father took out naturalization papers before his children were 21 years old.

Is entitled to vote, though born on foreign soil, if born of American parents who were citizens of the United States at time of birth.

Is entitled to vote if born in the United States, even if parents are aliens, born out of the United States, and have never taken out naturalization papers.

Is entitled to vote if twenty-one years old on the day of election.

Is entitled to vote, though an alien and cannot produce naturalization papers, if the applicant makes oath that naturalization papers have been issued to him in due form, though he may not be able to name the court in which he was naturalized.

CONDITIONS UNDER WHICH CANNOT VOTE.

Is not entitled to vote, if born of alien parents on foreign soil, if father did not take out naturalization papers until after the applicant was 21 years old. Applicant must take out naturalization papers.

Is not entitled to vote, if born on foreign soil of alien parents, if father died before applicant was 21 years old, even though father had taken out first naturalization papers, but not the final papers. Applicant must take out naturalization papers.

Is not entitled to vote if the applicant has been convicted of bribery, felony or other infamous crime under the laws of the state, and has not received a pardon for the same from the officer entitled to grant such pardon.

Is not entitled to vote if an Indian and not taxed.

Is not entitled to vote if under 21 years of age, is an idiot, or if an alien, has not taken naturalization papers.

Is not entitled to vote, except in the state, county, town and precinct where the individual resides, and then only if he has complied with all the other conditions.

Each Congressional District Entitled to One Representative in Congress.

First Congressional District.

The First and Second Wards, and that part of the Third and Fourth Wards lying east of Clark Street, the Twenty-ninth, Thirtieth, Thirty-first, Thirty-second, Thirty-third and Thirty-fourth Wards of the City of Chicago, and the towns of Bloom, Bremen, Calumet, Lemont, Lyons, Orland, Palos, Rich, Riverside, Thornton and Worth, in the County of Cook.

Second Congressional District.

That part of the Third and Fourth Wards lying west of Clark Street, the Fifth, Sixth, Seventh and Eighth Wards, the Ninth Ward except that part lying west of Loomis Street and north of Twelfth Street, that part of the Tenth Ward lying south of Twelfth Street, that part of the Eleventh Ward lying south of Macalister Place and east of Loomis Street, and that part of the Nineteenth Ward lying south of Polk Street and Macalister Place, in the City of Chicago.

Third Congressional District.

That part of the Ninth Ward lying north of Twelfth Street and west of Loomis Street, that part of the Tenth Ward lying north of Twelfth Street, that part of the Eleventh Ward lying north of Macalister Place and west of Loomis Street, the Twelfth, Thirteenth and Fourteenth Wards, that part of the Fifteenth Ward lying east of Western Av., the Sixteenth, Seventeenth, Eighteenth, and that part of the Nineteenth Ward lying north of Polk St. and Macalister Pl., in the City of Chicago.

Fourth Congressional District.

That part of the Fifteenth Ward lying west of Western Avenue, the Twentieth, Twenty-first, Twenty-second, Twenty-third, Twenty-fourth, Twenty-fifth, Twenty-sixth, Twenty-seventh and Twenty-eighth Wards of the City of Chicago, and the towns of Cicero, Barrington, Elk Grove, Evanston, Hanover, Leyden, Maine, New Trier, Niles, Northfield, Norwood Park, Palatine, Proviso, Schaumberg and Wheeling, in the County of Cook.

COOK COUNTY SENATORIAL DISTRICTS.

Each Senatorial District Entitled to One Senator and Two Representatives in the State Legislature.

First Senatorial District.

That part of the Eleventh Ward lying north of Van Buren Street and east of Ashland Avenue, that part of the Seventeenth Ward lying south of Ohio Street, and the Eighteenth Ward of the City of Chicago.

Second Senatorial District.

That part of the Third Ward lying south of Twenty-ninth Street and east of Clark Street, and that part of the Fourth Ward lying east of Clark Street, the Twenty-ninth and Thirtieth Wards, and that part of the Thirty-first Ward lying north of Eighty-seventh Street, the Thirty-second and Thirty-third Wards and that part of the Thirty-fourth Ward lying east of State Street, in the City of Chicago.

Third Senatorial District.

The First and Second Wards, and that part of the Third Ward lying north of Twenty-ninth Street and east of Clark Street, in the City of Chicago.

Fourth Senatorial District.

That part of the Ninth Ward lying north of Twelfth Street and west of Loomis Street, that part of the Tenth Ward lying north of Twelfth Street, that part of the Eleventh Ward lying south and west of a line commencing at the intersection of Van Buren Street and Throop Street, thence west on Van Buren Street to Ashland Avenue, thence north on Ashland Avenue to Lake Street, thence west on Lake Street to Paulina Street, the Twelfth Ward, that part of the Thirteenth Ward lying south of Lake Street, and that part of the Nineteenth Ward lying north of Taylor Street, in the City of Chicago.

Fifth Senatorial District.

That part of the Seventh Ward lying north of Sixteenth Street, that part of the Eighth Ward lying north of Sixteenth Street, the Ninth Ward, except that part lying west of Loomis Street and north of Twelfth Street, that part of the Tenth Ward lying south of Twelfth Street and that part of the Nineteenth Ward lying south of Taylor Street, in the City of Chicago.

Sixth Senatorial District.

That part of the Twentieth Ward lying north of North Avenue, the Twenty-first Ward, that part of the Twenty-second Ward lying east of Sedgwick Street, that part of the Twenty-third

Ward lying east of Franklin Street, and the Twenty-fourth, Twenty-fifth and Twenty-sixth Wards, of the City of Chicago, and the town of Evanston, in the County of Cook.

Seventh Senatorial District.

That part of the Fifteenth Ward lying west of Western Avenue and the Twenty-seventh Ward, and that part of the Thirty-first Ward lying south of Eighty-seventh Street, and that part of the Thirty-fourth Ward lying west of State Street, in the City of Chicago, and the towns of Cicero, Barrington, Bloom, Bremen, Calumet, Elk Grove, Hanover, Lemont, Leyden, Lyons, Maine, New Trier, Niles, Northfield, Norwood Park, Orland, Palatine, Palos, Proviso, Rich, Riverside, Schaumberg, Thornton, Wheeling and Worth, in the County of Cook.

Ninth Senatorial District.

That part of the Eleventh Ward lying west of Ashland Avenue and north of Lake Street, that part of the Thirteenth Ward lying north of Lake Street, the Fourteenth Ward, that part of the Fifteenth Ward lying east of Western Avenue and west of Ashland Avenue, Clybourn Place and the Chicago River, that part of the Sixteenth Ward lying southwest of Milwaukee Avenue, and that part of the Seventeenth Ward lying north of Ohio Street and southwest of Milwaukee Avenue, in the City of Chicago.

Eleventh Senatorial District.

That part of the Third Ward lying west of Clark Street, that part of the Fourth Ward lying west of Clark Street, the Fifth and Sixth Wards, that part of the Seventh Ward lying south of Sixteenth Street and that part of the Eighth Ward lying south of Sixteenth Street, in the City of Chicago.

Thirteenth Senatorial District.

That part of the Fifteenth Ward lying east of Ashland Avenue and Clybourn Place, that part of the Sixteenth Ward lying north of Milwaukee Avenue, that part of the Seventeenth Ward lying north of Ohio Street from the Chicago River west to Milwaukee Avenue, thence northwest on Milwaukee Avenue to May Street, that part of the Twentieth Ward lying south of North Avenue, that part of the Twenty-second Ward lying west of Sedgwick Street, and that part of the Twenty-third Ward lying west of Franklin Street, in the City of Chicago.

City Hall—Third Floor, Room 61—Prosecuting Attorney.

Of the several thousand lawyers in Chicago, the city is compelled to employ several, who have had experience and have reputation for superior legal ability. Among these is the Prosecuting Attorney.

This official's duty is to prosecute those who violate the ordinances and commit offenses against the law. He has five regular assistants, besides clerks, stenographer, office boys, etc. The lawyer who decides to accept this position is certain to make enemies of two classes, the people who think he should be more vigilant in prosecuting offenders, and the violators of the law who think the prosecutor too severe in his prosecution. The importance of this office is understood when it is known that about 500 misdemeanors per day are reported to this department, and must in some manner be disposed of according to the offense.

Third Floor, Room 65—City Attorney, Special Assessment Attorney.

The City Attorney defends the city against prosecutions that come from various sources, there being about 450 cases pending against the city regularly. The complaints come mostly from injuries received on sidewalks, falling buildings, escaping gas in the streets, etc. On the average the complainants secure about three per cent of their claim. The City Attorney is aided by one assistant and five clerks.

The Special Assessment Attorney, also on the third floor, and closely associated with the other attorneys, finds it necessary to employ three assistant attorneys and three clerks to aid in the transaction of the business pertaining to this department.

The continual opening of new streets, construction of new sewers, etc., involve constant expense, which must be borne by those who are supposed to be most greatly benefited. To condemn land required for new streets, pay the owner a fair price, levy a just tax against those who must pay for the opening, etc., and carry the whole affair to a successful conclusion in a rapidly expanding city like Chicago, requires much attention, labor, experience and skill.

City Hall—Third Floor, Room 62—City Engineer.

In this department of the service there are about 2,000 workmen, including 50 clerks, the labor consisting of the construction of bridges and viaducts, the maintenance of the Chicago harbor, the operation of all bridges and the maintenance of the water tunnels. At this writing there are 39 viaducts in the city, and 52 bridges, 12 of which are turned by steam, and 40 by hand, the cost of operating, repairing and painting the bridges being $95,000 per year. The expense of harbor work amounts to $100,000 per year.

City Hall—Third Floor, Room 68—Chief Janitor.

This official is at the head of a force consisting of one assistant janitor, aided by seven men and eleven women, whose duty it is to attend to the opening, lighting and cleaning of the building, at the same time watching the condition of chairs, desks, etc., throughout the City Hall.

City Hall—Fourth Floor, Room 89½—City Architect.

In room 89½ we visit for a little time the gentleman who, with the exception of school plans, designs many of the city buildings. This official has one assistant, and gives special attention to planning the architecture for pumping stations and buildings required in the police and fire departments.

City Hall—Fourth Floor, Room 86—Council Chamber.

Probably the most interesting room in the City Hall building, to the general visitor, is that in which the aldermen assemble every Monday night to devise the ways and means by which the city shall be governed.

At the present time Chicago is divided into thirty-four wards, each being entitled to two aldermen in the Council, thus sending to the Chicago City Council sixty-eight aldermen to represent the city's interests. Of this number about fifty are, on the average, in attendance at each

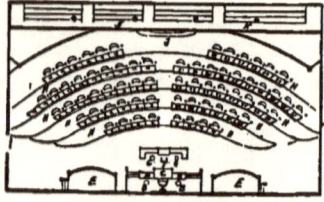

Chicago City Council Chamber.

Seating Arrangement.

A—Chairman.
B—Honored Visitors.
C D—Chairman's Desk.
E—Reporters.
F—Chief Clerk.
G—City Clerk and Assistant.
H—Seats for Aldermen.
I—Entrance to Anteroom.
J—Entrance from Hall.
K—Spectators' Gallery.

Council meeting, the number of visitors, who occupy a gallery assigned to spectators, being usually from thirty to fifty.

Formerly, the Mayor presided at the Council meetings. Latterly, the aldermen select one of their number as presiding officer, the Mayor reserving the right of affirmation or veto as heretofore in the passage of all ordinances.

The rules of the Council open the meeting at 7:30 P. M., close at 12 at night, no ordinance being permitted to pass, at any session, after that hour.

City Hall—Fourth Floor, Room 81—Chicago Public Library.

That portion of the City Hall building to which the greatest number of people ride in the several elevators is the one having the Public Library, which contained, June 1, 1892, the date of the last report, 177,178 volumes, being an increase of 10,703 volumes in the past year, costing the sum of $15,785.

The aggregate circulation, during the year, of books and periodicals in all departments of the library was 2,115,386, of which 1,014,341 were issued for home use.

The total number of visitors to the reading room in the main library, during the year, was 560,760, the average Sunday and holiday attendance being 760 per day. There are now in operation five branch reading rooms, the aggregate attendance at which was 134,914 persons. To perform the labor attendant upon this library there are, at present, 91 persons employed, to whom was paid in salaries during the past year, the sum of $57,717.09.

On June 1, 1892, having as resources the sum of $882,841, active measures were taken for the erection of a Public Library building on Dearborn Park ground, a miniature view of which edifice will be found among the public buildings mentioned in our Street Index.

There are **33** towns in Cook County; of these, **8** are included in the City of Chicago.

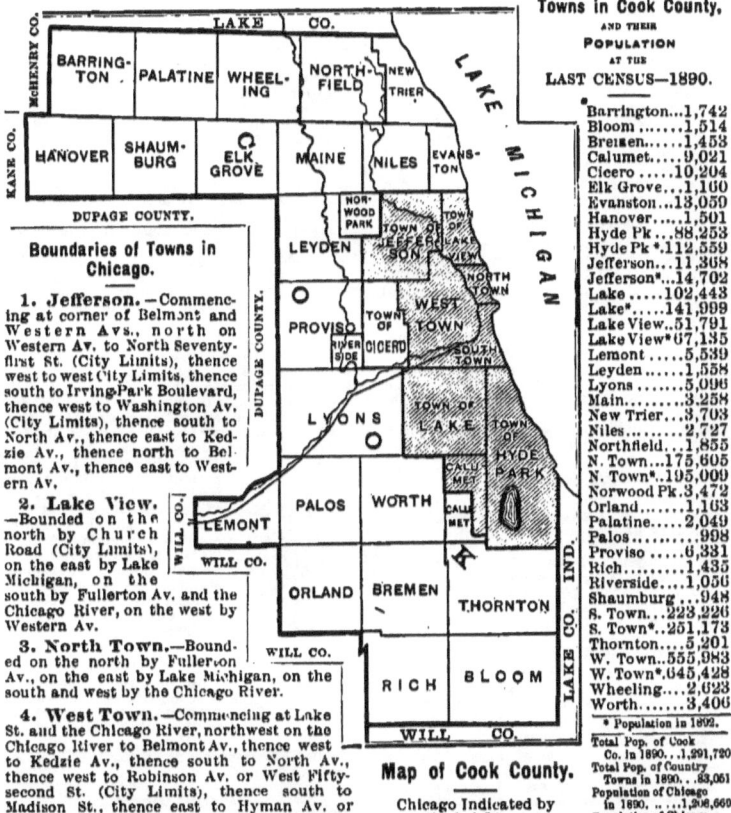

Boundaries of Towns in Chicago.

1. Jefferson.—Commencing at corner of Belmont and Western Avs., north on Western Av. to North Seventy-first St. (City Limits), thence west to west City Limits, thence south to Irving-Park Boulevard, thence west to Washington Av. (City Limits), thence south to North Av., thence east to Kedzie Av., thence north to Belmont Av., thence east to Western Av.

2. Lake View.—Bounded on the north by Church Road (City Limits), on the east by Lake Michigan, on the south by Fullerton Av. and the Chicago River, on the west by Western Av.

3. North Town.—Bounded on the north by Fullerton Av., on the east by Lake Michigan, on the south and west by the Chicago River.

4. West Town.—Commencing at Lake St. and the Chicago River, northwest on the Chicago River to Belmont Av., thence west to Kedzie Av., thence south to North Av., thence west to Robinson Av. or West Fifty-second St. (City Limits), thence south to Madison St., thence east to Hyman Av. or West Forty-eighth St., thence south to Twelfth St., thence east to West Forty-sixth St., thence south to Thirty-ninth St., thence east to Ill. & Mich. Canal, northeast on the Ill. & Mich. Canal to the Chicago River, northeast and north on the Chicago River to Lake St.

5. South Town.—Commencing at Thirty-ninth St. and the lake shore, north on the lake shore to the Chicago River, thence west, south and southwest, on the Chicago River, to the Ill. & Mich. Canal, southwest on the Ill. & Mich. Canal to Thirty-ninth St., east on Thirty-ninth St. to the lake shore.

6. Lake.—Bounded on the north by Thirty-ninth St., on the east by State St., on the south by Eighty-seventh St., on the west by Hyman Av. (City Limits).

7. Hyde Park.—Bounded on the north by Thirty-ninth St., on the east by the lake and the Indiana State line, on the south by 138th St. (City Limits), on the west by State St. and the Calumet River.

8. Calumet.—Commencing at the corner of State and Eighty-seventh Sts., west on Eighty-seventh St. to Western Av (City Limits), thence south to 107th St., thence east to Halsted St., thence south to Calumet River (near 131st St.), east on Calumet River to State St., thence north to Eighty-seventh St.

Map of Cook County.

Chicago Indicated by Shaded Lines.

Towns in Cook County,
AND THEIR
POPULATION
AT THE
LAST CENSUS—1890.

Barrington...	1,742
Bloom......	1,514
Bremen.....	1,453
Calumet.....	9,021
Cicero.....	10,204
Elk Grove...	1,160
Evanston...	13,059
Hanover....	1,501
Hyde Pk...	88,253
Hyde Pk*..	112,559
Jefferson...	11,368
Jefferson*..	14,702
Lake.....	102,443
Lake*.....	141,999
Lake View..	51,791
Lake View*	67,135
Lemont.....	5,539
Leyden.....	1,558
Lyons......	5,096
Main.......	3,258
New Trier..	3,703
Niles......	2,727
Northfield..	1,855
N. Town...	175,605
N. Town*..	195,009
Norwood Pk.	3,472
Orland......	1,163
Palatine....	2,049
Palos........	998
Proviso.....	6,331
Rich........	1,435
Riverside...	1,050
Shaumburg..	948
S. Town...	223,226
S. Town*..	251,173
Thornton....	5,201
W. Town..	555,983
W. Town*..	645,428
Wheeling...	2,623
Worth......	3,406

* Population in 1892.

Total Pop. of Cook Co. in 1890. .1,291,720
Total Pop. of Country Towns in 1890. .83,051
Population of Chicago in 1890. ...1,208,669
Population of Chicago in 1892. ...1,438,010

Rivers in Cook County.

The Desplaines rises in Wisconsin, crosses Lake County, runs south through the central northern part of Cook County, enters Will County from Lemont, and joins the Illinois River about 15 miles south of Joliet. The North Branch of the Chicago River runs from Northfield to the Chicago business center. The South Branch joins the Desplaines in the town of Lyons. The Calumet River, in Hyde Park, extends a distance of five miles, connecting Lake Calumet with Lake Michigan. The Ill. & Mich. Canal extends from La Salle, Ill., up through Lemont to the South Town, Chicago (see Map). The work of deepening the canal for drainage purposes was begun in . Lemont, in August, 1892.

Co. Commissioners' Room, Occupied as follows:
1. President.
2. Reading Clerk.
3. President's Desk.
4. Reporters' Table.
5. Reporters.
6. Commissioners.
7 and 9. Entrances.
8. Committee Room.

By examination of the Map of Cook County, and the statistics of population on the preceding page, it is seen that while Chicago covers only about one quarter of the area of the county, its population is fourteen times greater than that of all the country towns combined.

To have, therefore, a fairly suitable representation in the government of the county, Chicago is allowed to have ten out of the fifteen county supervisors, who meet weekly to consider the government of the county and its public institutions.

We enter the County Building from the Clark St. side, and first look in upon the office of the Recorder.

RECORDER'S OFFICE.

In this portion of the County Building, in the Record Department, there are 220 employes, of whom 120 are ladies engaged in copying deeds, mortgages and various legal papers, into the large volumes kept in the vaults here for future reference.

After paying the force of employes, the surplus turned into the County Treasury has latterly amounted to about $36,000 per year.

The number of instruments received here for record during 1891 was 194,896. Up to the present writing, October 1, 1892, since the fire, the number is 2,142,674, over 4,000 large volumes being necessary to contain them.

COUNTY CLERK'S OFFICE.

This is an important department in the management of County affairs, as shown by the fact that there are here employed 125 persons, at salaries varying from $4 per day to $3,000 per year, the total annual salaries amounting to $148,000.

Tax Collecting.

A SYSTEM PURSUED, WITH SOME VARIATION, IN ALL PARTS OF THE UNITED STATES.

A large portion of the work in the County Clerk's office consists in the collection of taxes. These become due about December 21 of each year, the town collector of each town making a vigorous effort, between that time and the 1st of March, to collect the amount to be paid by each property owner.

On the 10th of March, the several collectors close their books and send them to the County Treasurer, accompanied by a list of delinquent tax-payers.

During March and April the tax may be paid to the County Treasurer without additional expense.

PENALTY FOR NON-PAYMENT OF TAXES.

After the 1st of May, a penalty of one per cent a month is charged, together with the costs, which range from 6 to 18 cents per lot. On the second Monday of July, the County Treasurer makes application for judgment, and about the first or second Monday of August, the property on which the taxes are yet unpaid is offered for sale, the prices charged being the amount of tax. This sale is conducted by the town collector or his deputy, occurs between the hours of 10 A. M. and 4 P. M., and is continued from day to day, until all the tracts or lots in the delinquent list are sold or offered for sale. In other counties of the State the tax sales occur earlier in the year.

TIME IN WHICH PROPERTY SOLD FOR TAXES MAY BE REDEEMED.

Real estate sold for taxes may be redeemed at any time before the expiration of two years from the date of sale, on the following conditions:

First. By paying to the County Clerk the amount for which it was sold (which was the amount of tax), and 25 per cent additional, if redeemed at any time within six months from day of sale.

Second. Can be redeemed, between six and twelve months, upon payment of 50 per cent additional above the regular tax.

Third. Can be redeemed, between twelve and eighteen months, on payment of 75 per cent additional.

Fourth. Can be redeemed, between eighteen months and two years, on payment of 100 per cent, or twice the amount of tax, and the other taxes that have accrued in the meantime, with interest at ten per cent added thereto, from the time taxes were due. After the two years the purchaser, or the person who paid the tax, gets a tax title to the land, and the original owner of the land, in order to regain possession, must make such arrangement as he can with the owner of the tax title.

The great number of people who forget, or are unable to pay, their taxes when they become due, is shown in the fact that from 500 to 1,000 redemptions are made each month, largely by owners of suburban lots. In 1891 the tax sales numbered over 30,000, a large share of which may probably run one and two years before they are redeemed.

The inability to make prompt payment is the common fate of a great number of people throughout the country. The last United States census showed 9,000,000 of mortgages, resting on as many homes. Fewer foreclosures take place here than in most cities of like population, owing to rapidly advancing values.

MARRIAGE CEREMONY.

While the majority of marriages are solemnized at the private residence, many couples are married in the various court rooms, the scenes being similar to that shown above.

Marriage.

An interesting feature of this department of county government is that relating to the authorization of the privilege of getting married, about 53 licenses per day being issued, which read as follows:

MARRIAGE LICENSE.

State of)
Illinois, } ss. The People of the State of Illinois,
COOK CO.)

To ANY PERSON LEGALLY AUTHORIZED TO SOLEMNIZE MARRIAGE, GREETING:

Marriage may be Celebrated between Mr....
............of............, in the County of ....and State of............of the age of........years, and M..... ..... of............, in the County of............, and State of............, of the age of...... ......years.

Witness: HENRY WULFF, Clerk of the County Court of said Cook County, and the seal thereof, at my office in Chicago, this ....day of............A. D. 189..

....
Clerk of the County Court.

State of Illinois, } ss.
COUNTY OF COOK. } I................a............
hereby certify that Mr..........and M.........
were united in Marriage by me at.........., in the County of Cook and State of Illinois, on the ....day of.... ......, 189..

....

To obtain a license, it is only necessary that the male be 17 years old, and the female 14 years; and if the male be under 21, and the female under 18 years of age, that they have the written consent of parents or guardians. Marriage License fee is $1.50.

Naturalization Papers as Issued by the County Court.

According to the letter of the law, "no alien shall be admitted to become a citizen who has not, for the continued term of five years next preceding his admission, resided within the United States."

Any alien over eighteen years of age at the time of his arrival in the United States, who applies for admission as a citizen, must appear twice before a circuit or district court, or other suitable court of record, first, to declare his intention of becoming a citizen, and again, at least two years afterward, to take his oath of allegiance and receive his final naturalization paper.

He may declare his intention, and receive his first document, at any time after his arrival in the United States, and in this first step his own testimony will be considered sufficient. But when he applies for his second paper he must be accompanied by a witness, who shall declare on oath, and prove, to the satisfaction of the court, that the applicant has resided in the United States at least five years, and in the state where said court is at the time held, at least one year.

Any alien who, at the time of his arrival in the United States, had not passed his eighteenth birthday, will not be required to present two applications and procure two documents before being naturalized. As soon as he has reached the age of 21 years, and has resided 5 years in the United States, he may appear before the court and be admitted as a citizen, without having made any previous declaration of intentions. At the time of his admission, however, he must be accompanied by a witness, and must then, besides taking the oath of allegiance, "declare on oath that for two years next preceding, it has been *bona fide* his intention to become a citizen of the United States."

COURT ROOM.

Numbers designate the following officials and others generally in attendance:

1. Judge.
2. Clerk of Court.
3. Court Crier.
4. Witness.
5. Jurymen.
6. Lawyers.
7. Reporters.
8. Spectator.
9. Bailiff.
10. Lawyers.
11. Lawyers.
12. Waiting Jurors.

Form of First Paper in Being Naturalized.

UNITED STATES OF AMERICA.

State of Illinois, }
Cook County. } ss.

I,................ ....
do solemnly declare on oath, before HENRY WULFF, Clerk of the County Court of Cook County, in the State of Illinois, that it is bona fide my intention to become a citizen of the United States, and to renounce Forever all allegiance which I may in anywise owe to any foreign prince, potentate, state or sovereignty whatever, and particularly the allegiance which I may in anywise owe to the............
....whereof I was heretofore a Citizen or Subject.
Subscribed and sworn to before me this......
day of......A. D. 189.. ....
....
Clerk.

State of Illinois, }
Cook County. } ss.

I, HENRY WULFF, Clerk of the County Court of Cook County, in the State aforesaid, do hereby certify the above and foregoing to be a true, perfect and complete copy of an original Declaration of Intention now on file in my office.
Witness, HENRY WULFF, Clerk of said Court, and the Seal thereof, at Chicago, in said County, this..........day of..........
A. D. 189.. ....Clerk.

Final Certificate, or Last Paper, in Naturalization.

UNITED STATES OF AMERICA.

State of Illinois, }
County of Cook. } ss.

BE IT REMEMBERED, That on the ....day of.........., in the year of our Lord one thousand eight hundred and ninety ...., in the Circuit Court of Cook County, in the State of Illinois (the same being a Court of Record, having a Clerk and Seal), and of the................ term thereof, for the year aforesaid ....an alien, came into Court and applied to be admitted as a Naturalized Citizen of the United States, and it having appeared to the satisfaction of the Court that the said applicant has resided within the limits and under the jurisdiction of the United States for and during the full term of five years last past, and one year and upward immediately preceding the date hereof, in the State of Illinois, and that during said term of five years he has sustained a good moral character, and appeared to be attached to the principles contained in the Constitution of the United States, and well disposed to the good order, wellbeing and happiness of the same; and two years and upward having elapsed since the said applicant filed the declaration of his intention to become a citizen of the United States, according to the provisions of the several acts of Congress heretofore passed on that subject; and he having now here, in open Court, taken and subscribed the oath required by those laws to support the Constitution of the United States, and to renounce and abjure all allegiance and fidelity to every foreign prince, potentate, state or sovereignty whatever, and more particularly all allegiance which he may in anywise owe to........
....
of whom he was heretofore a subject.

It was Therefore Ordered and Adjudged by the Court, that the said ....
...................be and he was thereby admitted to all and singular the rights, privileges and immunities of a Naturalized Citizen of the United States, and that it be certified to him accordingly, which is done by these presents.
Witness, HENRY BEST, Clerk of said Circuit Court of Cook County, and the Seal thereof, at Chicago, in said Cook County, this..............day of..................
A. D. 189....

....
Clerk.

Fee for naturalization, 50 cents for each document.

Children who were under twenty-one years of age at the time of the naturalization of their parents, are, if living in the United States, considered as citizens thereof.

THE COURTS OF CHICAGO,

Several of which are in the County Building, include Police Court, Justice Court, Probate Court, Criminal Court, County Court, Circuit Court, Superior Court, Appellate Court, United States Circuit Court and United States District Court.

Places marked with a Star * have location designated in the Chicago City Directory, found in leading places of business. Places marked with two Stars ** are referred to elsewhere in this volume. See Index.

Argonaut Social Club.—Located in a curious building, resembling a ship, on the pier at the foot of Randolph St.

Art Institute.—East end of Monroe St. Large display of art works.

Athenæum.—26 Van Buren St. A popular place of intellectual entertainment and instruction. Gymnasium, parliamentary school and other departments open day and evening. Admission free to visitors.

Auditorium Hotel.—Cor. Congress St. and Michigan Av. Rotunda finished in elegant marble. Dining-room in tenth story.

Auditorium Tower.—Cor. Congress St. and Michigan Av., from top of which a good view may be had of the city. Admission, 25c.

Banks.—These institutions in Chicago are generally conducted by persons and corporations of large wealth, financial failure among them being a matter of very rare occurrence. A visit to one of these, and the depositing therein of all the money about the person, is one of the safeguards against loss which the stranger in the city would do well to observe soon after arrival.

Barber Shop.—Palmer House, cor. Monroe and State Sts. Very beautiful in decoration.

Billiard Halls.—Usually attached to all the leading hotels. Free to visitors. Fixed charge per hour to players.

Bird Stores.—Supplied with a large variety of living birds and pets, also a museum of stuffed birds and animals. Admission free.

Board of Trade.**

Book Stores.—Having the latest publications and rare collections of old, second-hand books.

Bridewell.—Cor. California Av. and Twenty-sixth St. Reached by Blue Island Av. street cars. An institution where offenders against the law are sent for short terms of confinement. About 9,000 persons are received here annually, the sexes being represented by about 19 males to 1 female on the average. Admission free, by applying to Supt.

Carlson Cottage.—No. 1872 Ashland Av., the place where Dr. Cronin was murdered, on the evening of May 4, 1889. Dr. Patrick Cronin was supposed to know too much about the Land League, a Fenian organization, and certain members of the Clan-na-Gael were appointed to "remove" him on the pretense that he was a British spy. Three persons were tried, convicted of his murder, and sentenced to prison for life. One of the number died in prison. The two remaining are now serving their sentence in the penitentiary at Joliet.

Cemeteries.**—Contain many fine monuments and works of art in sculpture. Very beautiful in landscape decoration. Among the oldest are Oakwoods, Calvary and Rosehill.

Chamber of Commerce Building.**—A stately and fine edifice, devoted to office purposes. Admission free to visitors' gallery.

Chinese Quarter.—Of the 1.500 Chinamen in this city, a large number may be found on Clark St., south of the Grand Pacific Hotel, engaged in laundry work and various avocations.

Concert Saloons.—Many of these are found on Clark St., north of the Chicago River. Admission free, but patrons are expected to each purchase a glass of beer, which costs 5 cents.

Consuls.—Foreigners in Chicago are entitled to advice from the person who represents their country in this city. It is well for newcomers to report to the Consul's office, where they will find those who speak their language, and will probably receive suggestions and information important for them to obtain upon coming to a new country. The locations of the several Consuls are as follows:

Argentine Republic, 83 Jackson St.
Austro-Hungarian, 78 and 80 Fifth Av.
Belgium, 167 Dearborn St.
Denmark, 209 Fremont St.
France, 70 La Salle St.
German Empire, Room 25, Borden Block, northwest cor. Randolph and Dearborn St.
Great Britain, Room 4, 72 Dearborn St.
Italy, Room 1, 110 La Salle St.
Mexico, Room 30, 126 Washington St.
Netherlands, 85 Washington St.
Russia, Room 62, 70 La Salle St.
Sweden and Norway, 153 Randolph St.
Switzerland, 167 Washington St.
Turkey, 167 Washington St.

Cook County Insane Asylum.—Located at Dunning, near the extreme northwest part of the city. (See Map, page 115.) Contains usually from 1,000 to 1,500 patients. Beautiful grounds; comfortable place for the insane. Admission free to visitors on application to the local superintendent.

Dancing Academies.—Several of these schools are in session most of the year, day and evening, the exercises being interesting to visitors. Admission free to visitors.

De Koven Street, No. 137.—Site of the origin of the great fire, which originated in a small stable, at this point, at nine o'clock on Sunday evening, October 8, 1871, extended eastward and northward, burned over about sixty-five acres an hour, and destroyed property at the rate of $125,000 worth per minute. Burned through Sunday night, and terminated on Monday, at midnight, four miles from where it began.**

Department Stores.—Of these there are several in the central portion of the city, which deal in a great variety of goods.

Depots or Railroad Stations.**—Several of these in Chicago are very elaborately fitted and furnished. A visit to them will well repay for the time thus expended.

Electric Fountain—In Lincoln Park; is an exhibition of rare beauty, an electric light being thrown upon the fountain so as to cause the water to appear in many colors. Admission free.

Elevated Railways.**—One of these begins on Congress St., between State St. and Wabash Av., and extends southward along the alleyway for several miles.

Employment Agencies.—Persons wishing to obtain work in Chicago for themselves or friends will find these desirable places to visit. A few of them, for men, are located as follows: 144 La Salle St., 135 Adams St., 389 S. Clinton St., 323 Dearborn St., 95 Fifth Av., 51 Market St., cor. Lake and South Water Sts., 400 Dearborn St., 97 Canal St., 21 W. Lake St., 121 S. Canal St., 79 S. Canal St., 209 Van Buren St., 2 Market St.

Fire Department Drill.**—By inquiry at the Fire Department, City Hall, information may be had as to when exhibitions take place; they are interesting. Admission free.

Fishing.—In one of the numerous small steamboats on the Lake Front, at the foot of Van Buren St., passage can be had for a few cents over to the Government pier and breakwater, where poles and bait can be secured, and from the side of the pier perch may be caught, to the amusement and profit of the fishermen. Boats also to the crib.**

Fort Sheridan.**—An encampment of Government soldiers will be found at this point, twenty-five miles north of Chicago, on the lake shore, a broad, beautiful driveway leading from the city to the grounds, which comprise about 500 acres. Also reached by Milwaukee Division of Chicago & Northwestern Railway. See "Suburban Villages and How to Go There."

Fox Lake.**—A beautiful resort 51 miles from Chicago, where a day can be delightfully passed amid the groves and charming grounds which surround the lake. See " Suburban Villages."

Glen Ellyn Springs.**—A delightful resort, reached in a forty-minute ride to the westward of Chicago.

Government Building. — The Post Office Building, bounded by Adams, Dearborn, Clark and Jackson Sts., occupies a square, and represents a value of about $6,000,000. Is three stories high, the first floor being used by the Post Office; the second is devoted to the use of the Collector of Customs, Internal Revenue Collector, Sub-Treasurer and Commissioner of Pensions. The third, by the various United States Courts. The building is too small to accommodate the departments for which it was designed, and as it has proven to be very defective in construction, it will, ere long, it is expected, be replaced by a larger and better edifice.

Government Offices. — The principal Government offices are in the Government Building. A few, however, are in quarters outside, because of lack of accommodation in this building. The location of the Government offices is designated below.

Custom House, Government Building, 2nd Floor, Rooms 2 to 14; night office, foot of River St.

Lighthouse Department, 138 Jackson St., Room 800.

Internal Revenue Department, Government Building, 2nd Floor, Rooms 21 to 28.

United States Treasury Department, Government Building, 2nd Floor, Room 15.

Office of Special Agent United States Treasury, Government Building, 4th Floor. Room 77.

United States Appraiser's office, 210 Market St.

United States District Attorney's office, Government Building, 3rd Floor, Room 40.

United States Circuit Court, Government Building, 3rd Floor, Room 31.

United States Commissioner's office, Government Building, 3rd Floor, Room 53.

United States Court of Claims, Government Building, 3rd Floor, Room 53.

United States District Court, Government Building, 3rd Floor, Room 39.

United States Engineer's office, 134 Van Buren St., Room 84.

Office of United States Inspector of Steam Vessels, 2 River St.

United States Marine Hospital, Government Building, 2nd Floor, Room 20.

United States Marshal's office, Government Building, 3rd Floor, Room 59.

United States Pension Agency, Government Building, 2nd Floor, Room 1.

United States Secret Service, Government Building, 4th Floor, Room 90.

United States Signal Office, Auditorium Building, 17th Floor.

Inspector Life Saving Station, Government Building, 4th Floor, Room 91.

Great Enterprises.*—(See page 79 of this volume). Many of these include mercantile establishments and manufactories, in which may be found the latest machinery and most approved methods for rapid production.

Haymarket Riot.—Locality, cor. West Randolph and Desplaines Sts., where, during an attempt by the police to disperse a meeting of laboring men, a bomb was exploded on the night of May 4, 1886. It killed eight policemen and wounded sixty-six. As instigators of this explosion, five of the leading labor agitators were hung.

Historical Society.—At 142 Dearborn Av. Contains a large and valuable collection of manuscripts, papers, books, relics, etc. Admission free.

Horse Exchange.-At Union Stock Yards. A general meeting place for sellers and buyers of horses at auction. Sales take place continually, about 100,000 horses being received here each year.

Horse Racing.—Adjoining Garfield Park and Washington Park; also at Hawthorne, about six miles southwest of the city, on the Chicago, Burlington & Quincy Railway. At Hawthorne and Garfield Park the races continue throughout pleasant weather, an adjournment being had for one month in midsummer, at which time the races take place at Washington Park. Admission usually 50 cents.

Humane Society.—Room 43,Auditorium Building; exhibits a large collection of implements of cruelty which have been taken from brutal drivers and others, gives suggestions for the suppression of cruelty, provides humane literature, etc. Visitors in the city are invited to visit the rooms.

Jail of Cook County, Michigan St., between Clark St. and Dearborn Av. Here the anarchists were confined, and in the jail yard hung, subsequent to the Haymarket riot; and here a number of prisoners are constantly confined, some held for trial, some waiting for transportation to the penitentiary. Visitors admitted by permission of the sheriff.

Lake Michigan lies to the eastward of Chicago, and affords outlet by water to all parts of the world. The importance of the city as a port of entry may be understood by a comparison with other cities that are supposed to have large commercial intercourse with all great cities on earth.

CHICAGO COMPARED WITH OTHER CITIES AS A PORT OF ENTRY.

In 1890 the following were the arrivals and clearances at the following cities :

NAME OF CITY.	Arrivals.	Clearances.	Total.
Baltimore, Md.	1,756	2,156	3,912
Boston, Mass.	3,171	3,389	6,560
New York, N. Y.	7,571	7,712	15,283
New Orleans, La.	1,040	987	2,027
Philadelphia, Pa.	1,806	1,943	3,740
Portland, Me.	2,758	698	3,456
San Francisco, Cal.	1,181	1,597	2,778
Total	19,283	18,482	37,756
Chicago, Ill.	9,188	9,284	18,472

From the above it is seen that the arrivals and clearances considerably exceed those of New York. They are nearly as many as those of New York and Baltimore, and exceed in number all the arrivals and clearances in Baltimore, Boston, Philadelphia and San Francisco together.

In 1891 fewer vessels came and went from Chicago, but vessels were larger and tonnage was greater.

Law Library is located in the upper part of the County Building, cor. Clark and Washington Sts.; is one of the largest and one of the most complete in the country, all reputable lawyers having access to it on the payment of a small fee.

Levee.—That portion of the city extending southward from Van Buren St. to Twenty-second St., lying between State St. and the river. As a great city is one of the safest places for a rascal to hide in, so this locality is the region over which many bad characters roam after nightfall, the probability being very strong that any tough who may be sought for in the city will be found, sooner or later, in "Cheyenne," alias the "Levee." Many respectable people, however, live in this section of the city, and numerous first-class business houses are here—so many that the character of the locality is rapidly changing for the better.

Libby Prison War Museum.— The celebrated old tobacco house at Richmond, Va., which, during the War of the Rebellion, was used by the Southerners as a prison for Union soldiers, was purchased by a company of capitalists and taken down, each brick being numbered in manner such as to rebuild the edifice exactly as it stood in Richmond. Contains a large collection of mementos of the war. Admission, 50 cents; children half-price.

Libraries and Reading Rooms.— Copies of nearly all the desirable books in the world may be found in the public libraries of Chicago, three of the largest of these now being on the way to further enlargement, namely, Chicago Public Library,* Crerar Library and Newberry Library. At the present time the general public can have access to the following

PUBLIC LIBRARIES IN CHICAGO.

Some of the libraries here mentioned represent each a collection of books worth several hundred thousand dollars. To all these libraries the general public is invited, under certain conditions:

ARMOUR MISSION LIBRARY, Thirty-third and Butterfield Sts.
ATHENÆUM LIBRARY, 26 Van Buren St.
CHICAGO PUBLIC LIBRARY, top floor, City Hall.
COBB'S LIBRARY, 91 Wabash Av.
CRERAR LIBRARY (plans being perfected for it).
HAMMOND LIBRARY, 81 Ashland Av.
HEBREW LIBRARY, 509 S. Canal St.
HISTORICAL SOCIETY LIBRARY, 142 Dearborn St.
HYDE PARK READING ROOM, 136 Fifty-third. St.
LAW INSTITUTE LIBRARY, Room 67, County Building.
LIBRARY M. E. CHURCH, cor. Lincoln and Ambrose Sts.
MISSION SOCIETY LIBRARY, 26 College Place.
NEWBERRY LIBRARY, northwest cor. Oak and State Sts.
NEW CHURCH UNION LIBRARY, 17 Van Buren St.
PULLMAN LIBRARY, 73 Arcade, Pullman.
RAVENSWOOD LIBRARY, cor. Commercial and Sulzer Sts.
SOUTH CHICAGO LIBRARY, Bowen School, cor. Ninety-third and Houston Sts.
UNION CATHOLIC LIBRARY, 94 Dearborn St.
WHEELER LIBRARY, 1113 Washington Boul.
Y. M. C. A. LIBRARY, 148 Madison St.

Life Saving Station.—The modes and appliances for saving life, established by the Government of the United States, are illustrated at the station at the northwest corner of the harbor.

Lighthouses.—Several of these are located in and about the Chicago Harbor. The "Chicago Light" is situated on the inner pier, on the north side of the river, and is visible for 16 miles.

Manual Training Schools are located as follows: For boys, at Glenwood; for boys, at Feehanville; for girls, at the Industrial School at Indiana Av. and Forty-ninth St., and Industrial School for Girls at South Evanston.

A high order of manual training is also conducted at the corner of Michigan Av. and Twelfth St., while beginnings in this work are being made in the Chicago Public Schools.

Manufactories.—(See page 79).

Military Headquarters.—The Illinois National Guard and the Military Division of the Missouri have separate headquarters in the Pullman Building, at the east end of Adams St. Armories occupied by various military organizations are located at 22 Jackson St., at Sixteenth St. and Michigan Av., and at Washington Boul. and Curtis St. It is estimated that 50,000 thoroughly drilled soldiers can be immediately called out here in a case of emergency, owing to the perfection of drill acquired in the Masonic and other secret societies.

Military Officers and Battalion.

Monuments.—(See partial description of these on pages 160 and 161). Many that are notable may be seen in the cemeteries.

Morgue.—Located near County Hospital, on West Polk St. Contains usually several bodies, on exhibition under glass, for the purpose of being identified. On the average, about ten bodies a day are picked up in Chicago, are taken here, placed on ice and kept for a certain time for identification. If not identified, they are buried in Potter's Field or turned over to a medical college. Clothes and other property are held indefinitely.

Museums.—Several of these are in the city, including Libby Prison, Anatomical and Dime Museums. Admission prices range from 10 cents to 50 cents.

Natatoriums. — Swimming schools for ladies and gentlemen are enjoyed by the swimmers and visitors who may be present. Among several, located in the city, those at 506 West Madison St. and 2323 Wabash Av. are accessible. Admission, 35 cents. Reduced rates to parties. Open days, evenings and Sundays.

Newspapers.—Many of the Newspaper Offices are most instructive places to visit.

Nurses' Training School, at 304 Honore St. The course of instruction here combines a certain amount of medical knowledge with information on the general subject of hygiene. It is a very popular school, the students having more or less hospital practice.

Palmer House.—Centrally located, at the corner of State and Monroe Sts. Its proprietor, Potter Palmer, was formerly a very successful dry goods merchant on Lake St. before the war, owned several large business blocks, which were burned in the great fire; survived the losses of that conflagration, erected this grand hotel, built a large castle residence on the North Side, secured the widening of State Street, erects several fine buildings each year, is in the prime of life, travels abroad a portion of each year, is very public-spirited, is a man of great force, has rendered in many ways great service to Chicago, being one of the prominent citizens who have largely contributed toward making this city what it is.

Parks and Boulevards.—(Parks described elsewhere). Among the most notable of the celebrated thoroughfares of Chicago are Grand and Drexel Boulevards, Michigan Avenue, Humboldt, Douglas, Ashland, Washington, Oakwood and Jackson Boulevards, besides Dearborn Avenue, the Lake Shore Drive, the Sheridan Road and others designated in our Street Index. The grand roadways leading from the center of the city to Fort Sheridan, to parks, and connecting parks with each other, extend nearly 100 miles.

Parliamentary Tactics.—Connected with the Soper School of Oratory, Athenæum Building. This department of instruction was established by the author of this volume, in 1891; is at present conducted by an ex-member of Congress. Class organized into upper and lower house of the Legislature, bills introduced and debates going forward as in the halls of legislation, the purpose being to give practice in extempore speaking and thorough training in parliamentary rules. Admission free to visitors.

Photograph Galleries.*—Those who would see the faces of distinguished people in the city, or would obtain views of the many beautiful residences and grounds of Chicago, should visit the photographic studios. Free exhibition.

Picnic Localities.—Desirable places for open air and picnicing near Chicago, are the following: Washington, Douglas, Garfield, Humboldt and Lincoln Parks; Cedar Lake, 40 miles southeast of the city, by the Louisville, New Albany & Chicago Railroad ; Willow Springs, 17 miles southwest on the Chicago & Alton Railroad; Glen Ellyn, 22 miles west on the Galena Division of the Chicago & Northwestern Railroad; Desplaines, 16 miles northwest on the Wisconsin Division of the Chicago & Northwestern Railroad ; Highland Park, 22 miles north, and Sheridan Grove, 24 miles north, on the lake shore; Ogden's Grove, 2½ miles northwest, at the northwest corner of Clybourn Av. and Willow St., reached by the Clybourn Av. street cars; Sharpshooters' Park, 5½ miles northwest, near the corner of Belmont and Western Avs., reached by the Clybourn Av. street cars or by the Wisconsin Division of the Chicago & Northwestern Railroad.

Power Houses.—Buildings in which the machinery for the propulsion of cable street cars may be seen, are located as follows: On the South Side of the city, at cor. of State and Twenty-first Sts., State and Fifty-second Sts., Cottage Grove Av. and Fifty-fifth St., Thirty-ninth and Wallace Sts., Archer Av. On the West Side, at cor. of Madison and Rockwell Sts., Milwaukee Av. and Cleaver St., Jefferson and Washington Sts., Desplaines and Washington Sts., Jefferson and Van Buren Sts., Twelfth St. and Blue Island Av. On the North Side, at cor. of La Salle Av. and Illinois St., Clark and Elm Sts., Lincoln and Wrightwood Avs.

CHICAGO STREET CAR TRAFFIC IN 1891.

Passengers carried during year	207,420,874
Gross amount of receipts	$10,259,838
Operating expenses	$6,223,903
Net profits	$4,035,935
Number of cars (cable and horse)	3,700
Number of grip-cars	753
Miles of street railway in Chicago	399
Miles of horse-car track	296
Cost of operation per mile, in cents, for each horse car	23.3
Average number of miles per horse, per day	12.9
Cost of operation per mile, in cents, for each cable car	9.3
Miles of cable track	9
Expense per passenger on horse cars	4.6
Expense per passenger on cable cars	2.6
Miles of electric road	9
Miles of elevated road (in use), Oct. 1892	5

Printing Presses.—Among the curiosities in the city are the rapid-running printing presses found in the press-rooms of the large daily papers. The type-setting machine, the electrotyping processes, the remarkably expeditious manner in which papers are printed and folded, ready for the newsboy to deliver to the customers, are all among the marvels of this age of wonderful invention. Admission free, upon application at newspaper counting rooms.

Public Schools.**—To those persons who are interested in educational matters the Public School system of this city is of especial interest. The private schools, which give instruction in every department of spiritual, intellectual and physical development, are also all of a high grade, as they must necessarily be, in order to successfully compete with the superior public schools.

Pullman is 13 miles south of Chicago City Hall; contains a population of about 15,000. Named after the founder of the town, George M. Pullman. Ground first broken here, for the building of the Pullman Palace Car Works, in the spring of 1880. Besides this manufactory, the place is the center of several other manufactories, including car-wheel works, knitting mills, terra cotta works, brick-making, etc. Many people visit the place to study the social and economic conditions of a town founded, built and governed with a view to securing the highest happiness of residents of the place and profit to the Pullman Palace Car Company. Take Illinois Central trains. Fare, round trip, 50 cents.

Retail Streets. — The central leading retail thoroughfares of the city are Lake, Randolph and Madison Sts., Wabash Av., State, Dearborn and Clark Sts.

Riding Schools.*—An elegant display of equestrianism is often made in the several riding schools of the city, among them being academies at 527 North Clark St. and 79 Sixteenth St. Admission free, except on certain occasions.

Rookery, Temperance Temple, Title & Trust Building, Monadnock, the Columbus and many other edifices are superior office buildings, and will repay a visit to them.

Safety Depositories.*—The vaults, massive doors, bars and bolts of the eighteen or twenty safety depositories of the city are an interesting study to those persons who wish a safe place for moneys, jewelry or valuable papers, they alone having access to them.

Shipbuilding Yard.—Located at South Chicago, on the Calumet River, about one mile from its entrance into Lake Michigan. (See page 17, Map, Division 13, Section 6). About 12 miles from City Hall. The works cover twenty acres, and ship construction in all its departments can be seen here.

Signal Service.—The rooms for this department of United States service are in the Auditorium tower, where a record is kept of thermometer, barometer, velocity of the wind, while telegraph reports, from 150 parts of the country, tell present conditions of the weather, and enable the superintendent in charge to predict the weather for the next 24 hours.

Stock Yards.—Located on South Halsted St., 5½ miles from City Hall. Reached by Halsted St. horse cars, State St. cable line, with transfer at Thirty-fifth St., Chicago & Rock Island R. R., Pittsburg & Fort Wayne R. R. or Illinois Central R. R. The Stock Yards grounds include 400 acres, 200 acres being devoted to yards, have 20 miles of streets, 20 miles of water troughs, 50 miles of feeding troughs, and several artesian wells, with an average depth of 1,230 feet. Packing property here worth about $10,000,000. Received at these yards in 1890, 3,485,292 cattle, 185-126 calves, 7,663,839 hogs, 2,183,768 sheep and 101,566 horses, the total value being $3,207,981,557. There are seventy-five packing companies here, employing 24,500 workmen, with a capital of $17,000,000. The yards can accommodate at one time 20,000 cattle, 120,000 hogs, 15,000 sheep. The rapidity with which animals are slaughtered and dressed here is one of the wonders of the world. Thus, a hog is caught by the leg and suspended from a pulley on a wire rope, glides along, head downward, to the individual who cuts the throat. By the time the animal is dead it is immersed in scalding water, passes directly on to the person who removes the entrails, goes forward to the individual who takes down the carcass, while another cuts it into pieces, distributing its several parts. Thus the movement of the animal, alive or dead, scarcely ceases, from the time it commences to move, until it is in the several receptacles, shoulders in one place, hams in another, and so on. Discard fine clothing when going to the Stock Yards, and, while admission is free on application to the superintendent at the yards, it is economy of time and greatly to the advantage of visitors to employ a guide when visiting this and various large manufacturing institutions, guides being paid from 50 cents to $2 per hour.

Towers.—Of these there are several, from which fine views of the city may be had, namely, the Water Works tower, on the North Side, Board of Trade Building,** Masonic Temple** and the Auditorium. Charges, 25 cents; free at the Water Works and Board of Trade.

Tunnels.—These go under the river, one being at La Salle Street and another at Washington Street. Were built, soon after the great fire, for carriages and pedestrians but, owing to the recent introduction of steam in the turning of bridges, have been transferred to the cable companies, pedestrians yet using the La Salle Street tunnel. Are lighted by electricity, and are best seen when riding through them in a cable car. Other tunnels are being constructed.

Water Street.—This is the wholesale market for the sale of fruits, vegetables, poultry and game. Instead of a market house, an entire thoroughfare for several blocks on each side of the street is here devoted to this purpose, the center of the street being crowded with teams, and the sidewalks filled with food products and buyers.

Water Works.—An interesting place to visit is the building containing the immense water works wheels and pumps, on the North Side, at the east end of Chicago Avenue. The experienced driver or guide will usually have the stranger call at the North Side Water Works on the way from the center of the city to Lincoln Park. The Water Works tower at this point is 175 feet high. Six engines are located here, furnishing a daily average of 50,000,000 gallons. The largest has a 1,200 horse-power, with fly-wheel 26 feet in diameter, and has a capacity for pumping 2,750 gallons at each stroke. Cost, $200,000.

Water Works Crib.—This edifice, which is used as an inlet for water into the original tunnel for water supply, is situated two miles northeast of the pier at the foot of Lake Street. The crib is an inclosure about 100 feet square, filled with stone, surrounding a nine-foot cylinder, which extends down 31 feet below the bottom of the lake, and 66 feet below the surface of the lake surrounding the crib, where it connects with two distinct tunnels, one 5 feet in diameter, the other 7 feet, leading to two different pumping works, the smaller connecting with the pumping works at the foot of Chicago Avenue, on the North Side, the larger extending under lake and city a distance of six miles, to the pumping works on the West Side, at corner of Ashland and Blue Island Avenues. On the top of the crib stands a residence occupied by the superintendent of the crib and his family, who have been there for the last eleven years. While, seemingly, this would be a lonely place, it is quite the contrary. Since its erection it has always been a point of interest for visitors and fishermen, quite a number of whom, on all pleasant days, come here, obtain bait and poles and while the hours away in catching perch. Fare, by numerous small steamers from the Lake Front, 25 cents.

Zoological Gardens.—These are located at Lincoln Park, and include a large variety of animals, the habits of which are a never-ceasing study of interest to the throngs of visitors.

Precautionary Measures for Strangers to Observe in Large Cities.

In proportion to the number of inhabitants less dangers exist in large cities than in thinly settled localities, but some dangers do exist, which all persons should try to avoid.

Beware of the stranger who proposes that you bet on any game.
Beware of the stranger who accosts you by name, and seemingly knows all about your family.
Beware of the stranger who proposes to show you about the city.
Beware of the man who proposes to give you something for nothing.
Beware of unsafe localities after nightfall.
Beware of material on unfinished buildings, and elsewhere, that may fall from overhead.

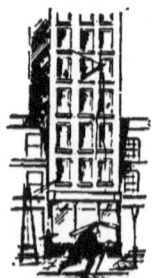

The timbers may not fall from the unfinished building, but it is safest to stay from under them.

team, thus coming immediately in front of another team, when crossing streets.
Beware of the man

Your pockets may not be picked in the crowd, but it is well to be guarded.

Beware of all crowds where pockets may be picked.
Beware who stops near you on the street, picks up something and afterwards proposes to sell you the article, rather than stop to find the loser.
Beware of standing on the outer edges of street cars, where you

The ropes may not break while the safe is being hoisted, but it is safest to keep from under it.

are liable to be hit by passing objects.
Beware of danger when crossing railroad tracks. While you are looking for a train one way, a train may be approaching from another direction.
Beware of being placed in positions where accidents may easily happen from fires, runaway teams, or falling buildings.
Beware of liquor drinking, dark streets and houses of ill repute. A "Mysterious Disappearance" seldom occurs with a prudent man.

Post Office, block bounded by Dearborn, Jackson, Clark and Adams Streets.
Open for General Delivery from 7:30 A. M. to 9 P. M., except Sunday, and from
11:30 A. M. to 12:30 P. M. on Sunday.

FOREIGN MAILS FROM CHICAGO.

GOING EAST.

For Great Britain and Ireland, Sundays, Mondays and Thursdays, via New York, close at 4 P. M.

For Denmark, Norway and Sweden, Sundays, Mondays and Thursdays, close at 4 P. M.

For Germany, Mondays and Thursdays.

For Canada—Provinces of Ontario and Quebec, close at 8:30 A. M. and 8 P. M. daily, except Sunday, and Sunday at 5 P. M. Hamilton (city), Ontario, Toronto (city), Ontario, special dispatch closes daily at 2:30 P. M. Mails for above points close on Sundays at 5 P. M.

For Nova Scotia, New Brunswick, Prince Edward's Island and Newfoundland, close daily at 8:15 and 11:30 A. M. and 8 P. M.

Gathering Mail from Street Letter Boxes.

FOREIGN MAILS FROM CHICAGO.

GOING WEST.

For China, Japan, New Zealand, Australia, Sandwich Islands, Fiji Islands, Samoa and specially addressed matter for Siam, close daily at 2 P. M., sent to San Francisco for dispatch, from that office.

NOTE.—Mails for countries, not named above, close daily at 4 P. M., and are sent to New York for dispatch from that office.

GOING NORTH.

For British Columbia and Manitoba, close daily at 2 A. M.

GOING SOUTH.

For Mexico, close daily at 8:15 A. M. and 8 P. M.

Office open for sale of Stamps, Envelopes, etc., at wholesale, from 9 A. M. to 7 P. M.
Retail Stamp window, on Clark Street side, open day and night.

General Information Relating to Postal Matters, and which Apply to All Parts of the United States.

United States Postal Money Order System.

FEES FOR MONEY ORDERS.

On orders not exceeding.....$	5....	5 cents.
Over $ 5 and not exceeding	10....	8 cents.
Over 10 and not exceeding	15....10 cents.
Over 15 and not exceeding	30....15 cents.
Over 30 and not exceeding	40....20 cents.
Over 40 and not exceeding	50....25 cents.
Over 50 and not exceeding	60....30 cents.
Over 60 and not exceeding	70....35 cents.
Over 70 and not exceeding	80....40 cents.
Over 80 and not exceeding	100,...45 cents.

No fraction of cents to be introduced in the order.

No single orders issued for more than $100.

Parties desiring to remit larger sums must obtain additional money orders.

No applicant, however, can obtain in one day more than three orders payable at the same office and to the same payee.

INTERNATIONAL MONEY ORDER SYSTEM.

Orders can be obtained upon any Money Order Office in Great Britain and Ireland, Germany, Austria, Belgium, Holland, Denmark, Sweden, Norway, Switzerland, Italy, Canada, France, Algeria, Japan, Portugal, the Hawaiian Kingdom, Jamaica, New Zealand, New South Wales, Hungary, Egypt and Hong Kong, India and Tasmania, Queensland, Cape Colony, the Windward Islands and the Leeward Islands, for any sum not exceeding $50 in United State. currency.

Parties desiring to remit larger sums must obtain additional money orders. There is no limit to the number of orders in the International Money Order System

FEES FOR ALL INTERNATIONAL MONEY ORDERS.

On orders not exceeding.....$10....10 cents.
Over $10 and not exceeding	20....20 cents.
Over 20 and not exceeding	30....30 cents.
Over 30 and not exceeding	40....40 cents.
Over 40 and not exceeding	50....50 cents.

POSTAL NOTES.

Postal notes for sums not exceeding $4.99 will be issued on the payment of a fee of 3 cents each. These notes are made payable to bearer at any Money Order Office in the United States.

REGISTRY DEPARTMENT.

Letters can be registered to all parts of the United States upon payment of a fee of 10 cents in addition to the regular postage.

CITY DELIVERY.

Free delivery of letters by faithful carriers will be secured by having the letters addressed to the street and number.

RAILWAY POST OFFICES.

Railway post offices are established on all lines from Chicago and other large cities. These offices run upon nearly all trains, and letters may be mailed at the cars up to the moment prior to the departure of the trains. Stamps of the denominations of two cents may be had at the cars.

POSTAL RATES TO FOREIGN COUNTRIES.

THE RATES OF POSTAGE to the countries and colonies composing the Universal Postal Union, which extends to nearly all parts of the civilized world, are as follows:

Letters (½ ounce)................................5 cents.
Postal cards, each ....2 cents.
Newspapers and other printed matter, per 2 ounces..........................1 cent.
Mer- ⎰ Packets not in excess of 4 oz..2 cents.
chan- ⎱ Packets in excess of 4 oz., for
dise. ⎰ each 2 oz. or fraction thereof.1 cent.
Registration fee on letters or other articles..........................10 cents.

Ordinary letters for countries of the Postal Union (except Canada and Mexico, which have the same postage on letters as United States, but special rates on certain third and fourth-class matter, explained at any post office) will be forwarded, whether any postage is prepaid on them or not. All other mailable matter must be prepaid, at least partially.

These Regulations Apply to All Parts of the United States.

First-class Mail Matter.

Letters, postal cards, and all matter wholly or partly in writing, as follows:

Accounts, whether partly or wholly in writing, whether in single sheets or book form.

Autograph albums, containing written signatures, or other miscellaneous written matter.

Bank books, with entries in writing therein.

Bank checks, when written, and whether canceled or uncanceled.

Bank notes, national or otherwise, on which there is writing.

Bills, when written or partly written, whether signed or unsigned.

Books, when presented for mailing with letters, and tied or fastened together in same package with letters.

Cartes de visite, or visiting cards, with written addresses thereon.

Checks, when partly written, whether signed or not, or canceled or uncanceled.

Contracts, wholly or partly in writing.

Copies, single or otherwise, when reproduced by other methods than ordinary type, plate or lithograph; copies made by type-writer or caligraph, or other similar process.

Copies of manuscript for publication, when not accompanied by proof-sheets or corrected proofs of same.

Correspondence, when actual and personal, whether the communication is wholly or partly in writing, or is prepared by type-writer, caligraph or other similar processes.

Deeds, wholly or partly in writing, whether executed or unexecuted.

FIRST-CLASS MAIL MATTER.

Cost of sending: **2 Cents** for each Ounce or Fraction thereof.

First-class Mail Matter.

Diaries, with entries in writing therein.

Drafts, wholly or partly in writing, signed or unsigned, canceled or uncanceled.

Drop letters deposited at offices having free delivery.

Envelopes, with written addresses thereon.

Insurance policies, wholly or partly in writing, and applications therefor.

Invitations, wholly or partly written.

Letters, whether written or printed (except circulars); and whether written by hand or type writer, caligraph or other similar process.

"Old letters," whether sent singly or in bulk.

Manuscript matter, music or other manuscript designed for publication, unless accompanied by proof-sheets or corrected proofs.

Mortgages, real or personal, and other deeds or contracts, wholly or partly in writing.

National bank notes, for they are partly written, requiring written signatures.

Packages, when sealed or sewed, or otherwise closed against inspection (except seeds).

Promissory notes, wholly or partly in writing, signed or unsigned.

Receipts, whether wholly or partly in writing, except receipts for subscription to, and inclosed with, second-class publications.

Signatures to personal communications, made by hand-stamp as well as handwriting.

Stenographic or short-hand notes.

Telegrams, offered for mailing, are letters, and not to be receipted for unless registered.

PUBLICATIONS WHICH CAN BE CIRCULATED AS SECOND-CLASS MAIL.

Second-class Mail Matter.

Newspapers and other periodical publications which are issued at stated intervals, and as frequently as four times a year; described as follows:

Second-class matter is of two kinds: First, that sent by publishers or news agents; second, that sent by others than publishers or news agents.

The conditions upon which a publication shall be admitted to the second class are as follows:

First. It must be issued at stated intervals, as frequently as four times a year, and bear a date of issue, and be numbered consecutively.

Second. It must be issued from a known office of publication.

Third. It must be formed of printed paper sheets, without board, leather, cloth, or other substantial binding such as distinguish printed books from periodical publications.

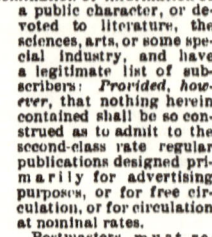

SECOND-CLASS MAIL MATTER.

Cost of sending: **1 Cent** for each Pound or Fraction thereof.

Second-class Mail Matter.

Fourth. It must be originated and published for the dissemination of information of a public character, or devoted to literature, the sciences, arts, or some special industry, and have a legitimate list of subscribers: *Provided, however,* that nothing herein contained shall be so construed as to admit to the second-class rate regular publications designed primarily for advertising purposes, or for free circulation, or for circulation at nominal rates.

Postmasters must require satisfactory evidence that publications offered for mailing at pound rates have a legitimate list of subscribers, by each of whom, or for each of whom, with the consent, expressed or implied, payment of the subscription price has been made or agreed to be made. Subscription price must be shown by the publication.

These Rates Applicable to All Parts of the United States.

Third-class Mail Matter.

Reproduction upon paper, by any process except that of hand-writing, of any words, letters, characters, figures or images, or of any combination thereof, not having the character of an actual and personal correspondence, as follows:

Reproductions from originals, not in the nature of personal correspondence, produced by the electric pen, metallograph, chirograph, copygraph or similar mechanical process easy of recognition. "Blue prints," so called, when they are reproductions not intended for other uses than as copies of the original, and are not in the nature of personal correspondence.

Photographs containing no writing other than the name of the sender.

Books (printed), circulars and other matter wholly in print.

Proofsheets and corrected proofsheets, and manuscript copy accompanying the same.

Valentines made wholly of paper, business and visiting cards, blank checks, drafts, and similar printed forms, printed blank check books, and books of blank drafts, deeds, insurance blanks, policies, shipping blanks or consignee blanks in book or tablet form, charters in blank for signature, etc., blue prints, photographs, engravings, heliotypes, hektograph prints, lithographs, address tags, labels not gummed, gummed labels and similar articles of print.

Seeds, scions, bulbs, roots, cuttings and plants.

THIRD-CLASS MAIL MATTER.

Cost of sending: **1 Cent** for each **2 Ounces** or Fraction thereof.

Third-class Mail Matter.

Seeds, or other articles not prohibited, which are liable from their form or nature to loss or damage unless specially protected, may be put up in sealed envelopes, if such envelopes are made of material sufficiently transparent to show the contents clearly without opening.

Proofs and corrected proofs may be accompanied by the original written manuscript.

Blank or printed postal cards or an envelope with printed address on it, may be inclosed for reply without subjecting the package to a higher rate. No written address can be placed thereon.

There is no limit of weight to single volumes of printed books, but other third-class matter is limited to four pounds.

For the protection of third-class matter, wooden or pasteboard rollers or sheets may be used.

Canvassing or prospectus books, containing sample chapters of, or other printed matter in relation to, the publication for which the books are used.

Corrected proofsheets, or printed maps, with or without manuscript copy, are entitled to be returned to the printer or engraver.

Printed matter sent through the mails as samples of the printing thereon, and for the purpose of securing orders for like printing to be done by the sender.

The words "please forward," "please send out," and other similar expressions, written upon a package of third or fourth class matter, will subject the same to letter postage.

MATTER WHICH CAN BE CARRIED IN THE UNITED STATES MAILS.

Fourth-class Mail Matter.

Merchandise of every kind that is not declared to be unmailable, described as follows:

Packages must not exceed four pounds in weight. There is no limit to *size* or *shape.*

Packages must be so wrapped that the contents may be easily and thoroughly examined by postmasters without injuring the wrappers. Sealed against inspection does not apply to merchandise such as canned goods (not liquids) hermetically sealed or sealed with internal revenue stamps, or proprietary articles sealed in their simplest commercial form, provided it is in other respects mailable.

In or on matter of the fourth class may be written any marks, numbers, names or letters for the purpose of description, as in the case of samples to indicate prices, etc. On the outside of the package, besides the address, may be written the names of articles contained

FOURTH-CLASS MAIL MATTER.

Cost of sending: **1 Cent** for each **Ounce** or Fraction thereof.

Fourth-class Mail Matter.

therein, and the sender's name, occupation and address, preceded by the word "from," with or without a request to return if undelivered. Any additional writing will subject it to letter postage, two cents per ounce.

Any printing, not personal correspondence, on the inside or outside of such matter, is allowable. Valuables should be registered; fee, 10 cents.

Sharp pointed instruments must have the points capped or inclosed so that they cannot cut through their inclosures; and if they have blades, the blades must be bound with wire to keep them within their sockets. Needles must be inclosed in metal or wooden cases.

Articles not liquid or liquefiable must be placed in a bag, box or removable envelope or wrapping made of paper, cloth or parchment. Such package must again be carefully secured.

Name, Location, When Founded, Whether Issued Morning or Evening.

In this city 325 papers are published—many of these the best of their kind. The following is a list of **30** *publications which are issued* daily:

Abendpost (German), 203 Fifth Av. First issued in December, 1890. An evening paper; independent in politics.

Afton Bladet (Swedish),192 Washington Street. An evening paper; independent in politics.

Arbeiter Zeitung (German), 28 Market St. Circulates largely among the German working classes. Publishes a Sunday edition called "**Die Fakel**," meaning in English "The Torch"; also a Wednesday edition, called the "Vorbote." Is socialistic and independent. Established 1877.

Argus, Room 62, 161 La Salle St. A morning paper; independent in politics.

Business, Room 509, 59 Dearborn St. An evening paper, devoted to finance.

Chicagske Listy (Bohemian). A morning independent paper, published at 362 West Eighteenth St. Also an extra Thursday edition, called "Amerika." Established 1883.

Denni Hlasatel (Bohemian), 611 Centre Av. A morning paper, devoted to labor interests. Established 1891.

Drovers Journal, Union Stock Yards. An evening paper, devoted to live stock interests. Also weekly and semi-weekly editions. Established 1871. Circulates among stockmen.

Dziennik Chicagoski (Polish), 141 West Division St. A morning paper; independent in politics. Established 1885.

Evening Journal, 161 Dearborn St. Oldest newspaper in Chicago. The "American," the first Chicago daily paper, was started in the spring of 1839. It was discontinued in 1842, and the "Express" immediately followed as its successor in the same year. The "Express" was merged into the "Journal," which was started as a Henry Clay paper in 1844. Republican.

Evening Post, 164 Washington St. Established in 1889. An evening paper; independent in politics.

Freie Presse (German), 94 Fifth Av. Established in 1871. Issues five daily editions. Its Sunday edition is known as the "Daheim," which means "At Home." Republican in politics.

Globe, 118 Fifth Av. A Democratic morning paper. Established 1888.

Herald, 158 Washington St. Founded in the spring of 1881. A morning paper; Democratic in politics.

NEWSBOY.

Illinois Staats Zeitung (German), northeast corner Washington St. and Fifth Av. Established in the spring of 1847. A morning paper; independent in politics.

Inter Ocean, northwest corner Madison and Dearborn Sts. Founded in 1872. A morning paper; Republican in politics.

Law Bulletin, 182 Monroe St. Interesting to lawyers.

Mail, 120 Fifth Av. Founded in 1882. An evening paper; Democratic in politics.

National Hotel Reporter, northwest corner Michigan Av. and Monroe St. Founded in 1871. A morning paper, devoted to the general interests of hotels throughout the country.

News Record, 123 Fifth Av. Founded in December 26, 1875. Publishes a morning, noon and evening edition, the evening issue being the Chicago Daily News. Independent in politics.

Polish Daily Telegraf, 32 Market St.

Real Estate and Financial Reporter, 125 Dearborn St. Devoted to the interests of those who are engaged in the sale of real estate.

Skandinaven (Norwegian), 187 North Peoria St. A morning paper; Republican in politics. Established, weekly, 1865; daily, 1871. Circulates also among Swedes.

Stockman, 819 Root St. Devoted to the interests of owners of live stock, particularly horses and cattle.

Sun, Union Stock Yards. An evening daily paper, devoted to news of special interest to dealers in live stock. Republican in politics. Established 1868.

Svornos (Bohemian), 150 West Twelfth St. An evening paper, independent in politics. Established in 1874.

Tageblatt (German), 83 Fifth Av. An evening paper. Established 1891.

Times, northwest corner Washington St. and Fifth Av. Founded in 1854. Morning paper; Democratic in politics.

Trade Bulletin, 28 Sherman St. Published in the interest of wholesale dealers in the produce trade.

Tribune, southeast cor. Madison and Dearborn Sts. Founded in 1847. Absorbed the "Democratic Press" in 1858. The Tribune is the oldest English morning daily. Republican in politics.

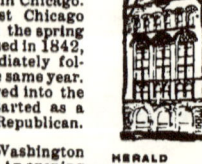

HERALD BUILDING.

TRIBUNE BUILDING.

STAATS ZEITUNG BUILDING.

INTER OCEAN BUILDING.

TIMES BUILDING.

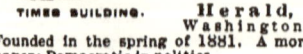

LUB life is a large factor in Chicago society. In the early history of a city very little occasion exists for the formation of society organizations. As years go by, however, and the population grows to such an extent that most of the people in the city are strangers to each other, it is found desirable to form organizations known as clubs, in which those persons who are congenial in tastes and have certain likes and ambitions in common, may frequently meet and exchange opinions with each other.

With the growth of population, these club organizations have rapidly multiplied in number, until to-day there are about six hundred clubs and societies in Chicago.

For the information of strangers and citizens of the city, we herewith give a partial list of the Clubs, their location, and the purposes to which they are devoted.

Social and Literary. Clubs---Their Location in 1892---Alphabetically Arranged.

For names of officers in following organizations see Chicago City Directory, found in all leading places of business.

Acacia Club, 105 Ashland Av.

Apollo Club (Musical), Apollo Hall, Central Music Hall Building, State and Randolph Sts.

Argonaut Club, Illinois Central Pier, Lake Michigan.

Ashland Club, 575 Washington Boul.

Bankers' Club.—President, E. G. Keith, 235 and 237 Adams St.

Beseda (Bohemian Reading Club), 74 W. Taylor St.

Bon Ami Club, of Wilmette, 14 miles north of the Court House.

Calumet Club, Michigan Av. and Twentieth Street.

Carleton Club, 3800 Vincennes Av.

Chicago Club, Michigan Av. and Van Buren Street.

Chicago Electric Club, 103 Adams St.

Chicago Literary Club, Michigan Av. and Van Buren St.

Chicago Woman's Club, Michigan Av. and Van Buren St.

Church Club, 103 Adams St.

Club Litteraire Français, 45 Randolph St.

Commercial Club, 159 La Salle St.

Conference Club of Evanston, 12 miles north of the Court House.

Cosmopolitan Club of Evanston, 12 miles north of the Court House.

Dearborn Club, 43 and 45 Monroe St.

Douglas Club, 3518 Ellis Av.

Douglas Park Club, 903 Sawyer St.

Evanston Club, Chicago Av. and Grove St., Evanston.

Fortnightly Club of Chicago, Michigan Av. and Van Buren St.

Germania Maennerchor, N. Clark St. and Germania Pl.

German Press Club, 106 Randolph St.

Girls' Mutual Benefit Club, 100 Cornelia St.

Grant Club, 111 Honore St.

Hamilton Club, 21 Groveland Park.

Harvard Club, Sixty-third and Harvard Sts., Englewood.

Harvard University Club.—President, Moses J. Wentworth, 45 La Salle St.

Hyde Park Suburban Club, Washington Av. and Fifty-first St.

Ideal Club, 531 and 533 Wells St.

Idlewild Club of Evanston, 12 miles north of the Court House.

Illinois Club, 154 S. Ashland Av.

Illinois Woman's Press Association, President, Mary Allen West, The Temple, La Salle and Monroe Sts.

Indiana Club, 3349 Indiana Av.

Irish-American Club, 40 Dearborn St.

Iroquois Club, Columbia Theater Building, 110 Monroe St.

Irving Club, Irving Park, 7 miles northwest of the Court House.

Ivanhoe Club, South Evanston, 11 miles north of the Court House.

John A. Logan Club 466 La Salle Av.

Kenwood Club, Forty-seventh St. and Lake Avenue.

La Grange Club, La Grange, 14 miles south-west of the Court House.

Lakeside Club, Indiana Av., between Thirty-first and Thirty-second Sts.

La Salle Club, 542 W. Monroe St.

Marquette Club, Dearborn Av. and Maple St.

Minnette Club, Campbell Av. and W. Monroe Street.

Nationalists' Club, meets at the Grand Pacific Hotel, Clark and Jackson Sts.

Newsboys' Club, Imperial Building, 252-260 Clark St.

North Shore Club, 1835 Wellington Av.

Oakland Club, Ellis and Oakland Avs.

Oaks, of Austin, 7 miles west of the Court House.

Palette Club.—A society of artists; gives exhibitions at the Art Institute.

Papyrus Club, Auditorium Building, Wabash Av. and Congress St.

Park Club, Fifty-seventh St. and Rosalie Ct.

Phœnix Club, Thirty-first St. and Calumet Avenue.

Practitioners' Club.—An association of physicians, meets at the Palmer House, State and Monroe Sts.

Press Club of Chicago, 131 Clark St.

Press League.—President, Mary H. Krout, 2719 Indiana Av.

Sheridan Club, 3532 Lake Av.

Single Tax Club, Gauntlet Hall, 206 La Salle Street.

Southern Society of Chicago, 425 Home Insurance Building, La Salle and Adams Sts.

Spanish-American Club, Tremont House, Dearborn and Lake Sts.

Standard Club, Michigan Av. and Twenty-fourth St.

Sunset Club.—Meets every Thursday evening, at 6:30 in one of the leading hotels.

Twentieth Century Club.—President, Chas. D. Hamill, 2126 Prairie Av.

Union Club, Washington Pl. and Dearborn Avenue

Union League Club, Jackson St. and Fourth Avenue.

University Club, Dearborn St. and Calhoun Place.

Washington Park Club, South Park Av. and Sixty-first St.

Whitechapel Club, at rear of 173 Calhoun Place.

Women's Suffrage Club, Sherman House, Clark and Randolph Sts.

Woodlawn Park Club, Sixty-fourth St. and Myrtle Av.

Hunting, Fishing and Gun Clubs.

Audubon Club, 110 La Salle St.

Chicago Cumberland Gun Club.—Grounds in Lake County, Ill. President, H. D. Nicholls, 75 W. Washington St.

Chicago Fly Casting Club.—President, A. H. Harryman, 175 Monroe St.

Chicago Rifle Club, 76 W. Monroe St.

Chicago Sharpshooters' Association, 49 La Salle St.

Chicago Shooting Club.—President, R. B. Organ, 4019 Indiana Av.

Cumberland Gun Club.—President, Charles K. Herrick, 81 Madison St.

Diana Hunting Club.—Club House at Thayer, Indiana. Secretary, J. A. Kreutzberg, Room 807, Home Insurance Building.

English Lake Hunting and Fishing Club, English Lake, Indiana. Secretary, A. W. Cobb, 41 River St.

Fox Lake Shooting and Fishing Club.—President, A. V. Hartwell, 907 Monadnock Building.

Fort Dearborn Shooting Club.—Secretary and Treasurer, C. K. Herrick, 81 Madison St.

Fox River Fish and Game Association.—President, George E. Cole, 86 Dearborn St.

Grand Calumet Heights Club.—President, W. L. Pierce, 145 La Salle St.

Gun Club.— President, F. C. Donald, Room 867, Rookery Building.

Lake George Sportsman's Association.—President, Jas. W. Sheahau. 385 Superior St.

Lake View Rifle Club, Rifle Range, Colehour.

Mak-Saw-Ba Shooting Club.—Club House at Davis Station, Indiana. President, T. Benton Leiter, 81 Clark St.

Minneola Fishing Club.—Club House at Fox Lake, Ill. President O H. Roche, 105 Rialto Building.

Mississippi Valley Amateur Rowing Association.—Secretary, D. R. Martin, Pullman, Ill.

North Chicago Schuetzen Verein, 267 North Avenue.

Sportsman's Club.—Secretary and Treasurer, A. W. Carlisle, Room 1051, Rookery Building.

Tolleston Club.—Grounds at Tolleston, Lake County, Indiana. Secretary, George P. Wells, 144 Ashland Boul.

Union Shooting and Fishing Club.—Club House at Fox Lake, Illinois. President, John G. Beazley, Room 602, Rialto Building.

Western Rifle Association.—Secretary and Treasurer, W. H. Chenoweth, 76 W. Monroe St.

Athletic and Sporting Clubs.

American Horse Show Association, 182 Monroe St.

Catlin Boat Club, east end of Pearson St.

Central Park Driving Association.— Secretary, W. H. Kane, 173 La Salle St.

Chicago Athletic Association, Michigan Av., between Madison and Monroe Sts.

Chicago Ball Club, 108 Madison St.

Chicago Canoe Club, east end of Thirty-seventh St.

Chicago City Base Ball League, 108 Madison St. and 145 Monroe St.

Chicago Cricket Association. — President, W. P. Griswold, 222 La Salle St.

Chicago Cricket Club, Room 5, 170 State St.

Chicago Curling Club, 83 Madison St.

Chicago Cycling Club, Lake Av. and Fifty-seventh St.

Chicago Fencing and Boxing Club, 106 Randolph St.

Chicago Tennis Club, 2901 Indiana Av.

Chicago Yacht Club. — Secretary, Harry Duvall, 655 Rookery Building.

Countess Yacht Club, Room 25, 6 Sherman St.

County Wheelmen.— Vice-Pres., A.B. McLean, 513 The Temple, La Salle and Monroe Sts.

Douglas Cycling Club, 586 W. Taylor St.

Evanston Boat Club, on Sheridan Road, Evanston.

Excello Tennis Club.—Secretary, E. U. Kimbark, 183 Monroe St.

Farragut Boat Club, 3016 and 3018 Lake Park Av.

Farragut Naval Association of Chicago.— Executive officer, C. B. Plattenberg, 1204 Masonic Temple.

Illinois Cycling Club, 1068 Washington Boul.

Lake View Cycling Club.—President, C. E. Wescott, 581 Diversey Av.

Lincoln Club, 1 Park Av.

Lincoln Cycling Club, 235 La Salle Av.

Lincoln Park Yacht Club.—Secretary, C. O. Andrews, 75 Lincoln Av.

North End Tennis Club.—Secretary, A. T. H. Brower, State St. and Burton Pl.

Oak Park Cycling Club.—Located at Oak Park, 9 miles west of the Court House.

Ogden Boat Club, at east end of Superior St.

Ontario Boat Club, east end of Ontario St.

St. George Cricket Club.—Secretary, W. Lovegrove, 710 N. Wells St.

Union Athletic Club, 52 State St.

Washington Cycling Club, 650 W.Adams St.

Missions, Societies, Unions, and Various Religious Organizations of Chicago.

Religious Societies—Where Located.

BAPTIST.

American Baptist Home Mission Society, 122 Wabash Av.

American Baptist Missionary Union, 122 Wabash Av.

American Baptist Publication Society, Department and Depository for the Northwest, 122 Wabash Av.

Baptist Missionary Training School, 2411 Indiana Av.

Baptist Pastors' Conference.—Meets every Monday at 122 Wabash Av., at 10:30 A. M.

Chicago Baptist City Mission Society, 40 Custom House Pl.

Chicago Baptist Social Union, 87 Metropolitan Block.

Northwestern Education Society. — Treasurer, Prof. I. M. Price, Morgan Park.

Women's Baptist Home Mission Society, 2411 Indiana Av.

Women's Baptist Home Mission Union, 2411 Indiana Av.

Women's Baptist Foreign Missionary Society of the West. 122 Wabash Av.

Women's Baptist Foreign Mission Quarterly, 122 Wabash Av.

CONGREGATIONAL.

American Board of Commissioners for Foreign Missions, 151 Washington St.

American Congregational Union, Room 26, 151 Washington St.

American Missionary Association, 151 Washington St.

Chicago City Missionary Society, Room 24, 151 Washington St.

Chicago Congregational Club. — Meetings thir Monday in each month, October to May inclusive, at the Grand Pacific Hotel.

Chicago Congregational Ministers' Union.— Meets Mondays at 10.30 A. M., at the Grand Pacific Hotel.

Congregational Sunday School and Publication Soc ety, 175 Wabash Av.

Illinois Home Missionary Society.—Office, 151 Washington St.

Illinois Woman's Home Missionary Union, Room 26, 151 Washington St.

New West Education Commission, 151 Washington St.

Western Education Society, 45 Warren Av.

Woman's Board of Missions of the Interior, Room 603, 59 Dearborn St.

Religious Societies—Continued.

EPISCOPAL.

Church Club of Chicago, 103 'Adams St.
Church Home for Aged Persons, 4327 Ellis Avenue.
Corporation for Relief of Widows and Orphans of Deceased Clergymen, 1701 Prairie Avenue.
Northern Deanery.—Meets every Monday at Church Club Rooms, 103 Adams St.
Sisters of St. Mary. — Mission houses at Cathedral, Washington Boul., cor. S. Peoria St.
Trustees of the Endowment Fund of the Diocese of Chicago, 104 Washington St.
Woman's Auxiliary of the Board of Missions. —President, Mrs. O. V. Wood, 1701 Prairie Av.

METHODIST.

Chicago Deaconesses' Home, 227 Ohio St.
Chicago Home Missionary and Church Extension Society, 57 Washington St.
Chicago Methodist Preachers' Meeting.—Sessions Mondays, at 10 : 30 A. M., in lecture room,

Methodist' Church Block, corner Clark and Washington Sts.
Chicago Training School for City, Home and Foreign Missions, Dearborn Av., cor. Ohio St.
Women's Foreign Missionary Society of the Methodist Episcopal Church, Northwestern Branch.—Meets 2nd and 4th Fridays of each month, at headquarters, 114 Dearborn Av.

PRESBYTERIAN.

Chicago Depository of Presbyterian Board of Publication and R. S. S. Work, 44 Madison Street.
Presbyterian Board of Aid for Colleges and Academies, Room 23, Montauk Block.
Presbyterian League, 150 Madison St.
Presbyterian Ministerial Association.—Meets Mondays, at 10 : 30 A. M., at Room 4,'Grand Pacific Hotel.
Woman's Presbyterian Board of Missions of the Northwest, Room 48, McCormick Block.

Chicago Exchanges—Meeting Places for the General Transaction of Business.

Anthracite Coal Association of Chicago, Room 203, 225 Dearborn St.
Builders' and Traders' Exchange, Rooms 12, 14 and 16, 159 La Salle St.
Chicago Board of Trade Clearing House, Board of Trade Building.
Chicago Clearing House, 103 Monroe St.
Chicago Coal Exchange, Room 635, 225 Dearborn St.
Chicago Flour and Feed Dealers' Association, 6-9 W. Madison St.
Chicago Fruit and Vegetable Shippers' Association, 144 South Water St.
Chicago Live Stock Exchange, Stock Yards.
Chicago Milk Exchange, meets Fridays at Sherman House.
Chicago Open Board of Trade, Open Board Building, 18-24 Pacific Av.
Chicago Open Board of Trade Clearing House, Open Board of Trade Building.

Chicago Real Estate Board, 59 Dearborn Street.
Chicago Stock Exchange, Stock Exchange Building, Dearborn and Monroe Sts.
Commercial Exchange (Wholesale Grocers), Room 11, 34 Wabash Av.
Gravel Roofers' Exchange, Room 99, 159 La Salle St.
Institute of Building Arts, 63 and 65 Washington St.
Lumbermen's Association of Chicago, Room 618, Chamber of Commerce.
National Butter, Cheese and Egg Association, 144 South Water St.
National Producers' and Shippers' Association.—Meets monthly, at 144 South Water St.
Produce Exchange, 144 South Water St., cor. Clark St.
Union Stock Yards and Transit Co., S. Halsted St., cor. Thirty-ninth St.

Asylums, Schools, Houses of Refuge and Homes for the Unfortunate.

Chicago Home For Incurables, Ellis Av. and Fifty-sixth St.
Chicago Industrial School for Girls, Forty-ninth St. and Indiana Av.
Chicago Nursery and Half Orphan Asylum, 175 Burling St. and 855 N. Halsted St.
Chicago Orphan Asylum, 2228 Michigan Av.
Cook County Insane Asylum, located at Dunning. Ill.
Cook County Poor House, Dunning Post Office.
Danish Lutheran Orphans' Home, Maplewood.
Erring Woman's Refuge, 5024 Indiana Av.
Foundlings' Home, 114 S. Wood St.
Franciscan Sisters House of Providence, Elm and Market Sts.
German Old People's Home, Harlem (Altenheim Post Office), Cook County, nine miles west of City Hall, on Wisconsin Central R. R.
Guardian Angel German (R. C.) Orphan Asylum, located at High Ridge.
Holy Family Orphan Asylum, Holt and Division Sts.
Home for the Aged, W. Harrison St., cor. Throop St. Branch, Sheffield Av., corner of Fullerton Av.
Home for the Friendless, 1926 Wabash Av.
House of Mercy (for young women), adjoining Mercy Hospital, Calumet Av., cor. Twenty-sixth St.
House of the Good Shepherd, N. Market St., cor. Hill St.
Illinois Industrial School for Girls, South Evanston.

Illinois Industrial Training School for Boys, Glenwood.
Illinois Masonic Orphans' Home, 447 Carroll Av.
Industrial Home for Girls, 1396 W. Van Buren St.
Martha Washington Home, Graceland Av., cor. Western Av., Lake View. Female department of the Washingtonian Home Association.
Newsboys' and Bootblacks' Home, 1418 Wabash Av.
Old People's Home, Indiana Av., corner Thirty-ninth St.
St. Joseph's Home for the Friendless, 409 S. May St.
St. Joseph's Orphan Asylum, 35th St., cor. Lake Av.
St. Joseph Provident Orphan Asylum, Crawford and Belmont Avs.
St. Mary's Training School for Boys, Feehanville, Cook County, Ill.
St. Vincent's Infant Asylum and Maternity Hospital, 191 La Salle Av.
School for the Deaf and Dumb, 409 S. May St.
Soldiers' Home.—Secretary, H. M. Bacon, Room 40, 107 Dearborn St.
Uhlich Evangelical Lutheran Orphan Asylum, 221 Burling St., corner Centre St.
Washingtonian Home, 566 to 572 W. Madison St.
Working Boys' Home and Mission of Our Lady of Mercy, 363 W. Jackson St.
Working Women's Home, 21 S. Peoria St.

Hospitals, Several of Which Are Free to the Needy.

Alexian Brothers' Hospital, 559 to 569 N. Market St.

Augustana Hospital, 151 Lincoln Av.

Bennett Hospital, Ada St., northwest corner Fulton St.

Chicago Emergency Hospital, 194 Superior Street.

Chicago Homœopathic Hospital, S. Wood St., southeast corner York St.

Chicago Hospital for Women and Children, W. Adams St., northwest corner Paulina St.

Cook County Hospital, W. Harrison St., cor. Wood St.

German Hospital, 754 and 756 Larrabee St.

Hahnemann Hospital, 2811 to 2815 Groveland Av.

Illinois Charitable Eye and Ear Infirmary, 227 W. Adams St.

Marine Hospital, N. Halsted St., nr. Graceland Av., five miles north of Court House, on lake shore. Office, Custom House Building, Room 20.

Maurice Porter Memorial Free Hospital for Children, 606 Fullerton Av.

Mercy Hospital, Calumet Av., cor. Twenty-sixth St.

Michael Reese Hospital, Twenty-ninth St., northeast cor. Groveland Av.

National Temperance Hospital, 3411 Cottage Grove Av.

Presbyterian Hospital, W. Congress St., southeast cor. S. Wood St.

Provident Hospital and Training School, 2900 Dearborn St.

St. Elizabeth's Hospital, Davis St., south east corner Thompson St.

St. Joseph's Hospital, 360 Garfield Av., northwest corner Burling St.

St. Luke's Free Hospital, 1420 to 1436 Indiana Av.

Wesley Hospital, 355 to 357 E. Ohio St.

Woman's Hospital of Chicago, Thirty-second St., northwest corner Rhodes Av.

Dispensaries, where Medicines are Supplied to Applicants.

Alexian Brothers' Hospital—Pharmacy, 559 N. Market St.

American College of Dental Surgery, 479 Wabash Av.

Armour Mission Dispensary, Thirty-third St., southeast corner Armour Av. Open daily (Sundays excepted), from 9 to 11 A. M.

Bennett Free Dispensary, Ada St., northwest corner Fulton St. Open daily (Sundays excepted), from 1:30 to 3 P. M.

Central Free Dispensary of West Chicago, Wood St., cor. W. Harrison St. Office hours, 9 to 12 A. M. and 1 to 6 P. M. Sundays, 9 to 10:30 A. M.

Central Homœopathic, S. Wood St., cor. York St. Open daily (except Sunday), from 9 to 12 A. M., and 2 to 4 P. M.

Chicago College of Dental Surgery, 102 Michigan Av. Open daily, from 9 A. M. to 4 P. M.

Chicago Hospital for Women and Children, Paulina St., cor. W. Adams St. Open every day, from 2 to 3 P. M., except Sunday.

Chicago Policlinic Dispensary, 176 Chicago Av. Open from 8:30 A. M. to 6 P. M. daily.

German Hospital, 754 and 756 Larrabee St. Hours, 9 to 12 A. M. and 2 to 4 P. M., except Sunday.

Hahnemann College Free Dispensary, 2813 Groveland Av. Open all day.

Illinois Eye and Ear Dispensary, 121 S. Peoria St. Open daily (except Sundays), from 2 to 3 P. M.

Lincoln Street Dispensary (Woman's Medical College), 333 and 335 S. Lincoln St. Open from 2:30 to 5 P. M.

Michael Reese Hospital, Free Dispensary, Groveland Av., northeast corner Twenty-ninth Street.

National Temperance Hospital, 3411 Cottage Grove Av. Open daily, from 2 to 4 P. M.

North Star, 192 Superior St. Open daily (except Sundays), from 1 to 2 P. M.

South Side Free Dispensary, Prairie Av., cor. Twenty-sixth St. Open daily, from 1 to 3 P. M.

St. Luke's Free Dispensary, 1420 to 1430 Indiana Av. Open daily, from 1 to 2:30 P. M.

West Side Free Dispensary, in College of Physicians and Surgeons, 815 Honore St., cor. W. Harrison St. Open daily (except Sunday), from 1 to 5 P. M.

Woman's Hospital of Chicago, Rhodes Av., northwest corner Thirty-second St. Open daily (except Sunday), from 2 to 4 P. M.

Convents, in which Principally Sisters of Charity Reside.

Franciscan Sisters, 353 N. Market St.

Good Shepherd, N. Market St., cor. Hill St.

Ladies of the Sacred Heart, 485 W. Taylor St. and 197 N. State St.

Little Sisters of the Poor, W. Harrison St., cor. Throop St.; Fullerton and Sheffield Avs.

Poor Handmaids of Jesus Christ, 212 Hudson Av.; 52 Newberry Av.; Forty-ninth and Laflin Sts.; Rosehill.

Religious of the Holy Heart of Mary, S. May St., cor. Eleventh St.

St. Benedict and St. Scholasticus, 333 N. Market St., cor. Hill St.

Servite Sisters of Mary, 1396 W. Van Buren St.

Sisters of Charity B. V. M., 210 Maxwell St.; 2954 Archer Av.; 892 S. Ashland Av.; 42 Commercial St.; W. Eighteenth and Johnson Sts.; 182 Osgood St.; 91 Cypress St.; 190 N. Paulina St.

Sisters of Christian Charity, Thompson and Davis Sts.; Lincoln and Taylor Sts.

Sisters of the Holy Nazareth, Seventeenth and Paulina Sts.; Southport and Belden Avs.

Sisters of Mercy, Wabash Av., cor. Twenty-ninth St.; Oakley Av., cor. Park Av.; Belmont Av.; Brighton Park; 4519 Wallace St.; South Chicago; Oakwood Boul., near Vincennes Av.; Wallace St. and Twenty-fifth Pl.

Sisters of Notre Dame, Lincoln Av., cor. Southport Av.; Vernon Park Pl., cor. Sibley St.; 190 Hudson Av.; 3908 Wentworth Av.; 124 Twenty-fourth Pl.; Noble St., cor. Bradley Street.

Sisters of St. Dominic, 226 Hermitage Av.

Sisters of St. Joseph, 186 N. Peoria St.

Sisters of St. Mary (Protestant Episcopal), 2406 Dearborn St.

Sisters of St. Vincent de Paul, 145 and 147 W. Adams St.

Third Order of St. Dominic, 511 N. Franklin St.; Hermitage Av and Jackson St., 5468 Kimbark Av.

Police Courts.

1st District, Harrison St. Station.
2nd District, Maxwell St. Station.
3rd District, Desplaines St. Station.
4th District, W Chicago Av. Station.
5th District, Chicago Av. Station.

6th District, Thirty-fifth St. Station.
7th District, Lake Av Station
8th District, Stock Yards Station.
9th District, Englewood Station.
10th District, Sheffield Av Station.

A Few of the Most Prominent Trades Unions.

BROTHERHOOD OF LOCOMOTIVE ENGINEERS.

Division No. 10, meets 2nd and 4th Sundays of each month, at 10:30 A. M., at State St., cor. Eighteenth St.
Division No. 111, meets Mondays, 7:30 P. M., at 4747 State St.

BROTHERHOOD OF LOCOMOTIVE FIREMEN.

Lodge No. 47, meets 1st Monday evening and 3rd Sunday afternoon, at Eighteenth and State Streets.

BROTHERHOOD OF RAILROAD TRAINMEN.

Local Subordinate Lodges.

Lodge No. 4, meets 1st and 3rd Sundays of each month. 1:30 P. M., at Wentworth Av., cor. Fifty-first St.
Lodge No. 70, meets 2nd and 4th Sundays of each month, 1:30 P. M., at Ogden Av., cor. Robey St.

ORDER OF RAILWAY CONDUCTORS.

Chicago Division, No. 1, meets 1st and 3rd Sundays of each month, at 10 A. M., at 83 Madison St.

SWITCHMEN'S MUTUAL AID ASSOCIATION OF NORTH AMERICA.

Headquarters, Rooms 77 and 78, 14 and 16 Pacific Av.

Local Subordinate Lodges.

Lodge No. 1, meets 2nd and 4th Sundays of each month, 7:30 P. M., at Plasterers' Hall, Washington St., near Franklin St.
Lodge No. 36, meets 1st and 3rd Sundays of each month, at Wentworth Av., cor. Fifty-first St.

BUTCHER AND GROCERY CLERKS' ASSOCIATION.

Supreme Council, meets at 73 Jackson St.
Success Council, No. 3, meets 1st and 3rd Mondays of each month, at 146 Twenty-second Street.
Garden City Council, No. 2, meets 2nd and 4th Thursdays of each month, at W. Adams St., cor. Halsted St.

IRON MOLDERS' UNION OF NORTH AMERICA.

Local Union, No. 239, meets Saturdays, at 8 P. M., at W. Madison St., cor. Jefferson St.

PRINTING TRADES' UNIONS.

Chicago Typographical Union, No. 16, meets last Sunday of each month, in Plasterers' new Hall, Washington St., near Franklin St.
Pressmens' Union, No. 3, meets 1st Saturday of each month, at Adams and La Salle Sts.

MISCELLANEOUS.

Brass Molders' Union, No. 1, meets Saturdays, 7 P. M., at Bricklayers' Hall, cor. Peoria and Monroe Sts.
Bricklayers' Union. meets at Monroe and Peoria Sts. every Friday evening.
Building Trades' Council, meets every Friday evening, at 167 Washington St.
Cigar Makers' Progressive International Union, No. 15, meets 1st and 3rd Mondays of each month, 8 P. M., at 54 W. Lake St.
Cigar Makers' Union, International, No. 14, meets 1st and 3rd Wednesdays of each month, at 31 N. Canal Street.
Central Labor Union, meets at 54 W. Lake St.
Engineers, Machinists, Smiths, Pattern Makers and Millwrights, Chicago Branch, No. 435, meets alternate Saturdays, at W. Adams St., cor. Halsted St.
Journeymen Horseshoers' Local Union, No. 4, meets 2nd and 4th Wednesdays of each month, at 208 La Salle St.
Knights of Labor, Central Council, meets 2nd Sunday of each month, at 36 La Salle St.
Seamen's Union, meets at 47 W. Lake St. every Tuesday.
Stair Builders' Union, meets every Wednesday, at 71 W. Lake St.
Tin and Sheet Iron Workers' Union, meets Tuesdays, at Bricklayers' Hall.
Trade and Labor Assembly of Chicago, Secretary, Thomas M. Campbell, 148 Monroe St.
United Carpenters' Council, headquarters Room 14, 163 Washington St.
United Carpenters' Council of Chicago, meets Thursdays, at 167 Washington St.
United Order of American Bricklayers and Stonemasons, meets Fridays, at S. Peoria St., cor. W. Monroe St.
United Order of Plasterers, meets Thursday evening, at 192 Washington St.
West Division Street Railway Employers' Benevolent Association, meetings 1st and 3rd Saturdays of each month, at 47 W. Lake St.

Some of the Most Centrally Located Secret and Benevolent Societies.

ANCIENT FREE AND ACCEPTED MASONS.

Grand Lodge of Illinois—Headquarters at Masonic Temple, northeast corner State and Randolph Sts.
Oriental, No. 33, meets Fridays, at 122 La Salle St.
Germania, No. 182, meets Thursdays, at 62 N. Clark St.

ANCIENT ORDER OF FORESTERS.

Grand Court of Illinois. Executive Council meets 1st and 3rd Thursdays of each month, at 8 P. M., in Room 20, Exchange Bldg
Chicago, No. 7365, meets 2nd and 4th Tuesdays of each month, at 85 Madison St.

GRAND ARMY OF THE REPUBLIC.

, Headquarters—United States Express Company's Bldg., Rooms 506 and 507, 87 and 89 Washington St.
George H. Thomas, No. 5, meets 2nd and 4th Fridays of each month, at 204 Dearborn St.
George A. Custer, No. 40, meets 2nd and 4th Wednesdays of each month, at 85 E. Madison Street.

INDEPENDENT ORDER OF FORESTERS.

High Court of Illinois.—Secretary, T. W. Saunders, Room 6, 53 Dearborn St.
Garden City, No. 1, meets at 112 Randolph St., 2nd and 4th Sundays of each month.
Chicago, No. 17, meets at 85 Madison St., 1st and 3rd Mondays of each month.

INDEPENDENT ORDER OF ODD FELLOWS.

Superior, No. 18, meets 1st and 3rd Wednesdays of each month, at 107 Clark St.
Cosmopolitan, No. 299, meets Thursdays, at 53 La Salle St.
Garden City, No. 389, meets Wednesdays, at 149 Randolph St.

KNIGHTS OF HONOR.

Illinois Grand Lodge—Grand Dictator, W. D. Dunning, 241 S. Robey St.
Chicago, No. 932, meets 1st and 3rd Tuesdays of each month, at 112 Randolph St.

KNIGHTS AND LADIES OF HONOR.

Grand Lodge of Illinois—Grand Protector, L. W. Kadlec, 179 W. Twelfth St.
Palestina, No. 89, meets at 106 Randolph St., on 1st and 3rd Tuesdays of each month.

KNIGHTS OF PYTHIAS.

Grand Lodge—G. Keeper of Records and Seal, H. P. Caldwell, Room 34, 126 Washington St.
Welcome, No. 1, meets Wednesdays, at 208 La Salle St.
Cosmopolitan, No. 6, meets Thursdays, at 116 Fifth Av.

ROYAL ARCANUM.

Grand Council of Illinois—Grand Secretary, H. B. Chandler, Room 35. Honore Blk.
Myrtle, No. 105, meets 2nd and 4th Mondays of each month, at 70 Adams St.

| RAILROADS AND THEIR CONNECTIONS IN ALL PARTS OF THE COUNTRY. | | LOCATION OF AGENTS WHO ARRANGE FOR TRANSPORTATION. |

LEADING RAILWAYS: REGIONS TO WHICH THEY EXTEND.

CANADIAN PACIFIC R. R., 232 Clark St.
Quebec, Can., to Montreal, Can.
Montreal and Ottawa, to Vancouver. B. C.

CENTRAL R. R. OF GEORGIA, 8 Rookery Bldg.
Savannah, Ga., to Atlanta, Ga.
Macon, Ga., to Montgomery, Ala.
Columbus, Ga., to Birmingham, Ala.
Columbus, Ga., to Greenville, Ga.
Griffin, Ga., to Chattanooga, Tenn.
Augusta, Ga., to Port Royal, S. C.

CHICAGO & WEST MICHIGAN R. R., 193 Clark St.
La Crosse, Ind., to Elk Rapids, Mich.
Allegan to Muskegon and Pentwater, Mich.
Muskegon to Big Rapids, Mich.

CLEVELAND, CINCINNATI, CHICAGO & ST. LOUIS
R. R., 234 Clark St. and 10 Pacific Av.
Cleveland, O., to St. Louis, Mo.
Cincinnati, O., to Chicago, Ill.
Peoria, Ill., to Springfield, O.
Benton Harbor, Mich., to Louisville, Ky.
Sandusky, O., to Cincinnati, O.

COTTON BELT ROUTE. (See St. Louis Southwestern R. R., 4 Rookery Bldg.)

DELAWARE, LACKAWANNA & WESTERN R. R.,
10 Rookery Bldg.
Binghampton, N. Y., to Junction, N. J.
New York to Danville, N. J.
Scranton, Pa., to Northumberland, Pa.
Owego, N. Y., to Ithaca, N. Y.
New York to Easton, Pa.
Binghampton to Utica and Syracuse, N. Y.
Oswego, N. Y., to Syracuse, N. Y.

DENVER & RIO GRANDE R. R., 236 Clark St.
Denver, Colo., to Pueblo, Colo.
Pueblo, Colo., to Grand Junction, Colo.
Pueblo, Colo., to Silverton, Colo.
Pueblo, Colo., to Trinidad, Colo.
Antonito, Colo., to Espanola, Colo.

DETROIT, LANSING & NORTHERN R. R., 193
Clark St.
Detroit, Mich., to Howard City, Mich.
East Saginaw to Howard City, Mich.
Detroit to Grand Rapids, Mich.

EAST TENNESSEE, VIRGINIA & GEORGIA R. R.,
193 Clark St.
Bristol, Tenn., to Chattanooga, Tenn.
Chattanooga, Tenn., to Brunswick, Ga.
Chattanooga, Tenn., to Memphis, Tenn.
Selma, Ala., to Mobile, Ala.

ELGIN, JOLIET & EASTERN R. R., 514 Royal
Insurance Bldg.
Spaulding, Ill., to McCool, Ind.
Aurora, Ill., to Joliet, Ill.
Waukegan, Ill., to Spaulding, Ill.

FITCHBURG R. R., 217 Royal Insurance Bldg.
Boston, Mass. to Troy, N. Y.
Boston, Mass., to Bellows Falls, N. H.
Worcester, Mass., to Winchendon, Mass.

GRAND TRUNK R. R., 307 Home Ins. Bldg.
Portland, Me., to St. Henri, Que.
Montreal, Que., to Toronto, Ont.
Toronto, Ont. to Sarnia, Ont.
Suspension Bridge, N. Y., to Windsor, Ont.
Toronto, Ont., to North Bay, Ont.

GREAT NORTHERN RAILWAY LINE, 132 Jackson St.
St. Paul, Minn., to Butte, Mont.
St. Paul, Minn., to Duluth, Minn.
St. Paul, Minn., to Gretna, Manitoba.
St. Paul, Minn., to Willmar, Minn.
Breckenridge, Minn., to Larimore, N. D.

G. N. R. L.—Continued.
Breckenridge, Minn., to Ellendale, N. D.
Sioux City, Ia., to Willmar, Minn.
Benson, Minn., to Huron, N. D.

HOUSTON & TEXAS CENTRAL R.R., 204 Clark St.
Houston, Tex., to Denison, Tex.
Austin, Tex., to Hempstead, Tex.
Austin, Tex., to Marble Falls, Tex.

INDIANA, ILLINOIS & IOWA R. R., 755 Rookery
Building.
Streator, Ill., to Knox, Ind.

LOUISVILLE & NASHVILLE R. R., 6 Rookery
Building.
Cincinnati, O., to New Orleans, La.
St. Louis, Mo., to Evansville, Ind.
Evansville, Ind., to Nashville, Tenn.
Louisville, Ky., to Jellico, Tenn.
Flomaton, Ala., to Pensacola, Fla.
Pensacola, Fla., to River Junction, Fla.
Cincinnati, O., to Livingston, Ky.
Attalla, Ala., to Calera, Ala.

LOUISVILLE, NEW ORLEANS & TEXAS R. R.
New Orleans, La., to Memphis, Tenn.
Memphis, Tenn., to Vicksburg, Miss.
Natchez, Miss., to Jackson Miss.

MEXICAN CENTRAL R. R., 236 Clark St.
El Paso, Tex., to City of Mexico, Mex.
Tampico, Mex., to Aguascalientes, Mex.
Irapuato, Mex., to Guadalajara, Mex.

MEXICAN INTERNATIONAL R. R., 204 Clark St.
Eagle Pass, Tex., to Torreon, Mex.
Torreon, Mex., to Durango, Mex.

MEXICAN NATIONAL R. R., 10 Rookery Bldg.
Laredo, Tex., to City of Mexico, Mex.
Laredo, Tex., to Corpus Christi, Tex.

MILWAUKEE, LAKE SHORE & WESTERN R. R.,
208 Clark St.
Milwaukee, Wis., to Ashland, Wis.

MISSOURI, KANSAS & TEXAS R. R., 12 Rookery
Building.
Hannibal, Mo., to Denison, Tex.
Parsons, Kan., to Junction City, Kan.
Denison, Tex., to Boggy Tank, Tex
Denton, Tex., to Dallas, Tex.

MISSOURI PACIFIC R. R., 199 Clark St.
St. Louis, Mo., to Omaha, Neb.
Pleasant Hill, Mo., to Joplin, Mo.
Sedalia, Mo., to Independence, Mo.
Myrick, Mo., to Boonville, Mo.
Ottawa, Kan. to Pueblo, Colo.
Chetopa, Kan., to Larned, Kan.
Ft. Scott, Kan., to Kiowa Kas.
Atchison, Kan., to Lenora, Kan.
Ft. Scott, Kan., to Topeka, Kan.
Kansas City, Mo., to Ottawa, Kan.

NASHVILLE, CHATTANOOGA & ST. LOUIS R. R.
194 Clark St.
Hickman, Ky., to Nashville, Tenn.
Nashville, Tenn., to Chattanooga, Tenn.
Chattanooga, Tenn., to Atlanta, Ga.
Decherd, Tenn., to Columbia, Tenn.

NEWPORT NEWS & MISSISSIPPI VALLEY R. R.,
204 Clark St.
Louisville, Ky., to Memphis, Tenn.
Evansville, Ind., to Princeton, Ky.

NEW YORK CENTRAL & HUDSON RIVER R. R.,
97 Clark St.
New York to Albany, N. Y.
Albany, N. Y., to Buffalo, N. Y.
Syracuse, N. Y., to Niagara Falls, N. Y.
New York to Chatham, N. Y.

NEW YORK, LAKE ERIE & WESTERN R. R., 802 Phœnix Bldg.
New York to Salamanca, N. Y.
Buffalo, N. Y., to Hornellsville. N. Y.
Corning, N. Y., to Rochester, N. Y

NORTHERN PACIFIC R. R., 210 Clark St.
St. Paul, Minn., to Portland. Ore.
Ashland, Wis., to Brainerd. Minn.
Winnipeg Junc., Minn., to Winnipeg, Man.

PHILADELPHIA & READING R. R.
Philadelphia to Pottsville, Pa.
Reading, Pa., to Harrisburg, Pa.
Port Clinton, Pa., to Williamsport, Pa.
Reading, Pa., to Quarryville, Pa.
Harrisburg, Pa., to Gettysburg, Pa.
Harrisburg, Pa., to Shippensburg. Pa.
Philadelphia, Pa., to Bound Brook, N. J.
Philadelphia to Bethlehem, Pa.
Camden, N. J., to Atlantic City, N. J.

QUEEN & CRESCENT ROUTE (Cincinnati, New Orleans & Texas Pacific R. R.), 193 Clark St.
Cincinnati, O., to Chattanooga. Tenn.
Louisville, Ky., to Burgin, Ky.
Chattanooga, Tenn., to Birmingham, Ala.
Birmingham, Ala., to New Orleans, La.
Meridian, Miss., to Vicksburg, Miss.

ROME, WATERTOWN & OGDENSBURG R. R., 95 Clark St.
Buffalo, N. Y., to Oswego, N. Y.
Oswego, N. Y., to Massena Springs, N. Y.
Utica, N. Y., to Ogdensburg, N Y.

ST. LOUIS, IRON MOUNTAIN & SOUTHERN R. R., 199 Clark St.
St. Louis, Mo., to Texarkana. Tex.
Cairo, Ill., to Poplar Bluff, Mo.
Memphis, Tenn., to Bald Knob. Ark.
Little Rock, Ark., to Ft. Smith. Ark.
Little Rock, Ark., to Arkansas City, Ark.
Knobel, Ark., to Helena, Ark.

ST. LOUIS SOUTH WESTERN R. R., 4 .Rookery Building.
Cairo, Ill., to Gatesville, Tex.
Mt. Pleasant, Tex., to Sherman, Tex.
Tyler, Tex., to Lufkin, Tex.

ST. LOUIS & SAN FRANCISCO R. R., 212 Clark Street.
St. Louis, Mo., to Sapulpa, Ind. Ter.
Monett, Mo., to Paris, Tex.
Pierce City, Mo., to Ellsworth, Kan.
Beaumont, Kan., to Anthony, Kan.

SOUTHERN PACIFIC COMPANY, 204 Clark St.
Ogden, Utah, to San Francisco, Cal.
San Francisco, Cal., to Portland, Ore.
San Francisco, Cal., to Los Angeles, Cal.
San Francisco, Cal., to Monterey, Cal.
Los Angeles, Cal., to El Paso, Tex.
El Paso, Tex., to New Orleans, La.
Sacramento, Cal., to Redding, Cal.
San Francisco to Santa Margarita, Cal.

TOLEDO, ST. LOUIS & KANSAS CITY, 204 Clark Street.
Toledo, O., to St. Louis, Mo.

TEXAS & PACIFIC R. R., 199 Clark St.
New Orleans, La., to Marshall, Tex.
Marshall, Tex., to Ft. Worth, Tex.
Texarkana, Tex., to Ft. Worth, Tex.
Ft. Worth. Tex., to El Paso, Tex.

UNION PACIFIC R. R., 191 Clark St.
Omaha, Neb., to Ogden, Utah.
Julesburg, Colo., to Denver, Colo.
Kansas City, Mo., to Denver, Colo.
Salina, Kan., to Oakley, Kan.
Denver, Colo., to Cheyenne, Wyo.
Denver, Colo., to Leadville, Colo.
Leavenworth, Kan., to Miltonvale, Kan.
Denver, Colo., to Ft. Worth, Tex.
Ogden, Utah, to Frisco, Utah.
Granger, Wyo., to Portland, Ore.
Ogden, Utah, to Silver Bow, Mont.
Pendleton, Ore., to Spokane, Wash.
Sioux City, Ia., to Columbus, Neb.
Valley, Neb., to Manhattan, Kan.
St. Joseph, Mo., to Grand Island, Neb.

WEST SHORE R. R., 199 Clark St.
New York to Albany, N. Y.
Albany, N. Y., to Buffalo, N. Y.

WILMINGTON & NORTHERN R. R., 62 Wabash Avenue.
Wilmington, Del., to Reading, Pa.

Railroad Fast Freight Lines---Their Offices in Chicago.

BLUE LINE (Bonded), to New York, Philadelphia, Boston and points East. Ship at Michigan Central Depot, foot of South Water St. Office, 209 La Salle St.

CANADA SOUTHERN LINE, via West Shore R.R., to New York and all points on the West Shore R. R. Ship at Michigan Central Depot, foot of South Water St. Office, 209 La Salle St.

CENTRAL STATES DISPATCH.—Ship by Illinois Central R. R., foot of South Water St. Office, 10 Pacific Av.

COMMERCIAL EXPRESS LINE, to New York, Boston, Philadelphia and points East. Ship at Chicago & Grand Trunk Depot, corner Twelfth St. and Third Av. Office, Room 111, Royal Insurance Bldg., 171 and 173 Jackson St.

EMPIRE LINE (Bonded), to New York, Philadelphia, etc. Ship at Lake Shore & Michigan Southern R. R. Depot, corner Polk St. and Pacific Av. Office, Room 27, southwest corner Van Buren Street and Pacific Avenue.

ERIE DISPATCH (Bonded).—Great Western Dispatch Division—Ship at Chicago & Erie Depot, corner Clark and Fourteenth Sts. South Shore Line Division—Ship at Pittsburg. Fort Wayne & Chicago Depot, Madison Street bridge. Erie & Pacific Dispatch Division—Ship at Pittsburg, Cincinnati, Chicago & St. Louis Depot, Halsted Viaduct. Office, 146 Jackson St.

GREAT EASTERN LINE (Bonded), to New York, Boston. Portland, Montreal, Philadelphia, etc. Ship at Chicago & Grand Trunk Depot, corner Twelfth St. and Third Av. Office, 25 Pacific Av.

GREEN LINE, via Cincinnati and Louisville, to all Southern points. Ship at Pittsburg, Cincinnati, Chicago & St. Louis Depot, cor. Canal and Fulton Sts. Office, 14 and 16 Pacific Av.

HOOSAC TUNNEL LINE (Bonded), to New York, Boston, Philadelphia and Eastern points. Ship at Wabash Depot, corner Twelfth St. and Third Av. Office, Rooms 103 and 104 Royal Insurance Bldg.

INTERSTATE DISPATCH (Bonded), to New York, Boston, Philadelphia, etc. Ship at New York, Chicago & St. Louis Depot, Clark and Taylor Sts. Office, 191 La Salle St.

KANAWHA DISPATCH, to points in Virginia, North and South Carolina, Eastern Seaboard points, etc. Ship at Illinois Central Depot, foot of South Water St. Office, 10 and 12 Pacific Av.

LACKAWANNA LINE, to New York, Boston, Philadelphia and other points East. Ship at New York, Chicago & St. Louis Depot, Clark and Taylor Sts. Office, 189 La Salle Street.

LEHIGH & WABASH DISPATCH, to New York, Philadelphia and Eastern points. Ship at Wabash Depot, Twelfth St. and Third Av. Office, 109 Royal Insurance Bldg.

MERCHANTS DISPATCH TRANSPORTATION CO. (Bonded), receives perishable freight only for New York, Philadelphia, Boston and other Eastern points. Ship at Michigan Central Depot, foot of South Water St., or Lake Shore & Michigan Southern Depot, corner Polk St. aud Pacific Av. Offices, 138 Jackson St.

NATIONAL DISPATCH (Bonded), to Boston and New England points. Ship at Chicago & Grand Trunk Depot, Twelfth St. and Third Av.   Office, 169 Jackson St.

NATIONAL LINE, to New York, Baltimore, Philadelphia, Pittsburg, Boston and other Eastern points. Ship at Pittsburg, Cincinnati, Chicago & St. Louis Depot, corner Carroll and Halsted Sts. Office, 16 and 18 Pacific Avenue.

NICKEL PLATE LINE, to New York, Boston, Philadelphia and points East. Ship at New York, Chicago & St. Louis Depot, corner Taylor and Clark Sts.   Office, 191 La Salle St.

ONTARIO DISPATCH.—Ship at Wabash Depot, corner Twelfth St. and Third Av. Office, 180 Jackson St.

RED LINE, to New York, Boston, Philadelphia, etc. Ship at Lake Shore & Michigan Southern Depot, corner Polk St. and Pacific Av. Office, 144 Van Buren St.

STAR UNION LINE (Bonded), to New York, Baltimore, Philadelphia, Pittsburg, Boston and other Eastern points. Red Star Department (high-class freights)—Ship at Pittsburg, Fort Wayne & Chicago Depot, near Van Buren Street bridge. Black Star Department (heavy freights) — Ship at Pittsburg, Fort Wayne & Chicago Depot, near Madison Street bridge, West Side. Office, southwest corner Jackson and Sherman Sts.

TRADERS DISPATCH (Bonded), to New York, Boston, Philadelphia, etc. Ship at New York, Chicago & St. Louis Depot, corner Clark and Taylor Sts. Office, 187 La Salle Street.

UNION DISPATCH.—Office, Market and Washington Sts.

WEST SHORE LINE (Bonded), to New York, Boston, Philadelphia, etc. Ship at Chicago & Grand Trunk Depot, corner Twelfth St. and Third Av.   Office, 23 Pacific Av.

Offices of the Various Ocean Steamship Lines.

Allan Line, 112 La Salle St.
Allan-State Line, 112 La Salle St.
American Line, 32 Clark St.
Anchor Line Mail Steamships, 70 La Salle St.
Baltic Line, 125 La Salle St.
Beaver Line, 52 Clark St.
Compagnie Generale Transatlantique, 166 Randolph St.
Cunard Line, 131 Randolph Street.
Dominion Royal Mail Line, 74 La Salle St.
Fabre Line, 62 Clark St.
Florio Rubattino Italian Line, 164 Randolph Street.
Furness Line, Room 217, 169 Jackson St.
Guion Line, 60 Clark St.
Hamburg-American Packet Co., 125 La Salle St.
Hamburg-Baltimore Line, 125 La Salle St.
Hansa Line, 92 La Salle St.

Inman Line, 32 Clark St.
Netherlands-American Steam Navigation Co., 86 La Salle St.
Norddeutscher Lloyd's Steamship Co., 80 and 82 Fifth Av.
Norddeutscher Lloyd's Steamship Co., Baltimore Line, 78 Fifth Av.
Pan American Transportation Co., Room 1341, 79 Dearborn St.
Red Star Line, 32 Clark St.
State Line, 112 La Salle St.
Thingvalla Line, 140 Kinzie St.
Union Direct Hamburg Line, 125 La Salle Street.
White Star Line, 54 Clark St.
Wilson Line of Steamers, Room 404, Rookery Building.
World's Fair Steamship Company, Rooms 1143 and 1145, Rookery Building.

Location of Offices Where Lost Articles May Be Claimed.

If articles are left upon incoming railroad trains, they are usually found by persons connected with the railroads, whose business it is to go through the cars immediately upon arrival of trains in the city. Information as to articles found on the trains may be obtained of the depot policeman. As a precaution, it is well to have name and address on every package which is taken upon the railroad train.

If the article has been lost or stolen on the streets, apply at once to the police department, at the City Hall.

If package or pocket-book was left or lost in a store, apply at the counter where the last purchases were made.

If the loss occurs upon a street car, application should be made at the street car offices, which are located as follows:

Offices of Street Railway Lines.

Calumet Electric Street Railway Co., Room 606, Tacoma Building.
Chicago City Railway Co., 2020 State St.
Chicago Passenger Railway Co., 89 W. Washington St.
Chicago West Division Railway Co., 89 W. Washington St.
Chicago & Edison Park Street Railway Co., Room 20, 173 La Salle St.
Chicago & South Side Rapid Transit Railroad Co., Room 627, Rookery Building.
Cicero & Proviso Street Railway Co., Room 601, Tacoma Building.

Grand Crossing & Windsor Park Railway Co., Room 50, 175 Dearborn St.
North Chicago Street Railroad Co., 444 N. Clark St.
South Chicago City Railway Co., Room 208, 164 Dearborn St.
West Chicago Street Railroad Co., 89 W. Washington St.
West Side Rapid Transit Co., Room 507, 84 La Salle St.
West & South Towns Street Railway Co., Room 513, Tacoma Building.

**Name of Place, Distance from Chicago, Rate of Fare, including Board, and Time Required.
to Go There. For Ticket Offices See Footnote at Bottom of Page.**

NAME OF TOWN.	NAME OF STEAMBOAT LINE.	Distance in Miles from Chicago.	Time in Days and Hours. Ds.	Hs.	FARE FROM CHICAGO. Single 1st Class.	Single 2nd Class.	Round Trip. 1st Class.
Abnapee, Wis	Goodrich's Menominee Line..........a	..202	1	..5	$..5.00	$..4.00	$10.00
Arcadia, Mich......	Goodrich's Ludington & Manistee Line a	..240	1	..1	..5.00	....	..10.00
Ashland. Wis......	Lake Mich. & Lake Superior Trans. Co.b	..939	5	...	..23.00	..8.00	..42.00
Bayfield, Wis......	Lake Mich. & Lake Superior Trans. Co.b	..959	5	...	..23.00	..8.00	..42.00
Benton Harbor,Mich	Graham & Morton Trans. Co..........c	63	..	..5	..1.00	...50	..2.00
Brockville, Canada.	Merchants' Line..................d	.....	7	..2	..18.00	..9.00	..34.00
Buffalo, N. Y........	Lackawanna Trans. Co...............d	.....	3	...	..13.00	..6.50	..25.00
Charlevoix, Mich..*	Northern Michigan Trans. Co..........e	..370	1	..2	..7.00	..4.00	..13.00
Cheboygan, Mich...	Northern Michigan Trans. Co..........e	..374	2	16	..8.00	..4.00	..15.00
Cornwall, Canada..	Merchants' Line..................d	.....	7	..8	..21.50	..10.75	..36 00
De Tour, Mich......	Lake Mich. & Lake Superior Trans. Co.b	..390	2	...	..9.00	..4.50	..17.00
Duluth, Minn......	Lake Mich. & Lake Superior Trans. Co.b	1,039	5	12	..24.00	..8.00	..43.00
Duncan City, Mich.	Northern Michigan Trans. Co..........e	..376	2	15	..8.00	..4.00	..15.00
Eagle Harbor,Mich.	Lake Mich. & Lake Superior Trans. Co.b	..794	4	12	..10.00	..8.00	.....
Egg Harbor, Wis...	Goodrich Menominee Line.............a	..365	1	12	..6.00	..4.00	..12.00
Elk Rapids, Mich..*	Northern Michigan Trans. Co..........e	..375	1	20	..6.50	..4.00	..12.00
Ephraim, Wis.....	Goodrich Menominee Line.............a	..351	1	12	..6.00	..4.00	..12.00
Escanaba, Mich.. ...	Goodrich Line......................a	..302	2	...	..7.00	..5.00	..13.00
Fayette, Mich......	Goodrich Line......................a	..444	2	12	..8.00	..5.50	..14.00
Frankfort, Mich ..*.t	Goodrich Line (via Milwaukee).... ...a	.....	1	...	..5.00	....	..9.00
Garden, Mich......	Goodrich Line......................a	..427	2	12	..8.00	..5.50	..14.00
Gladstone, Mich...	Goodrich Line......................a	..392	2	...	..7.50	..5.50	..13.50
Glen Haven, Mich..	Northern Michigan Trans. Co..........e	..240	1	..7	..5.50	..3.00	..10.00
Grand Haven, Mich.	Goodrich Line......................a	..110	..	..8	..3.00	..2.50	..5.00
Green Bay, Wis.....	Goodrich Line......................a	..280	1	14	..6.00	..4.00	..12.00
Hancock, Mich.....	Lake Mich. & Lake Superior Trans. Co.b	..681	4	...	..17.00	..7.00	..30.00
Harbor Sp'gs,Mich.t	Seymour Trans. Co ....f	..365	1	..4	..7.00	..4.00	..13.00
Holland, Mich.....	Graham & Morton Trans. Co..........c	..107	..	..7	..2.00	..1.00	..4.00
Holland, Mich.....	Michigan Fruit Line................e	.....	..	..8	..2.00	..1.00	..3.50
Houghton, Mich...	Lake Mich. & Lake Superior Trans. Co.b	..680	4	...	..17.00	..7.00	..30.00
Kewaunee, Wis...	Goodrich Line......................a	..190	1	..5	..5.00	..4.00	10.00
Kingston, Canada..	Merchants' Line..................d	1,208	6	14	..17.00	..8.50	..32.00
Lachine, Canada....	Merchants' Line..................d	.....	7	10	..22.00	..11.00	..38.00
Lake Linden, Mich..	Lake Mich. & Lake Superior Trans. Co.b	..719	4	...	..17.00	..7.00	..30.00
Ludington, Mich. t.*	Goodrich's Manistee Line...........a	..184	..	21	..4.50	..4.00	..8.50
Mackinaw, Mich.t.t	Seymour Trans. Co..................f	.....	1	..8	..8.00	..4.00	..15.00
Manistee, Mich...*.t	Goodrich Line (via Milwaukee).......a	..209	..	22	..4.50	..4.00	..8.00
Manistique, Mich...	Goodrich Line......................a	..510	3	...	..8.00	..5.50	..14.00
Manitowoc, Wis...t	Goodrich's West Shore Line.........a	..160	..	20	..4.00	..3.00	..7.00
Marinette, Wis......	Goodrich's Menominee Line.........a	..325	1	12	..6.00	..4.00	..12.00
Marquette, Mich...	Lake Mich. & Lake Superior Trans. Co.b	..610	3	12	..14.00	..6.00	..25.00
Menominee, Mich..	Goodrich Line......................a	..252	1	12	..6.00	..4.00	..12.00
Milwaukee, Wis..t.t	Goodrich's West Shore Line.........a	..90	..	..6	..2.00	..1.50	..3.50
Montreal, Canada..	Merchants' Line..................d	1,600	7	21	..22.00	..11.00	..38.00
Muskegon, Mich...	Goodrich Line......................a	..127	..	10	..3.00	..2.50	..5.00
Northport, Mich...t	Seymour Trans. Co..................f	.....	1	..6	..6.50	..3.50	..12.00
Ottawa Beach,Mich.	Michigan Fruit Line................e	..101	..	..8	..2.00	..1.00	..3.50
Petoskey, Mich....*	Northern Michigan Trans. Co.........e	..332	1	..4	..7.00	..4.00	..13.00
Pierport, Mich.......	Goodrich's Ludington & Manistee Line.a	..220	1	...	..5.00	..4.00	..10.00
Port Colborne, Ont.	Merchants' Line..................d	.....	4	18	..13.00	..6.50	..24.00
Prescott, Canada....	Merchants' Line..................d	1,313	7	..3	..18.00	..19.00	..34.00
Racine, Wis.......	Goodrich's West Shore Line ....a	..60	..	..4	..1.50	..1.00	..2.50
Sarnia, Canada.....	Merchants' Line..................d	..650	2	21	..9.00	..4.50	..16.00
Saugatuck, Mich....	O'Connor's Dock Co. Line.....c	..93	..	..8	..1.50	....	..2.50
Sault Ste Marie,Mich	Lake Mich. & Lake Superior Trans. Co.b	..450	2	...	..11.00	..5.00	..21.00
Sheboygan, Wis...	Goodrich's West Shore Line.........a	..140	..	18	..3.50	..2.50	..6.00
St. Catharines, Can.	Merchants' Line.........d	..700	3	19	..13.00	..6.50	..24.00
St. Helena, Mich....	Northern Michigan Trans. Co.........e	..461	2	12	..7.00	..3.50	..13.00
St. Ignace, Mich..t.t	Seymour Trans. Co..................f	.....	1	..8	..8.00	..4.00	..15.00
St. James, Mich.....t	Seymour Trans. Co..................f	.....	1	..4	..7.00	..4.00	..13.00
St. Joseph, Mich....	Graham & Morton Trans. Co c	..60	..	..5	..1.00	...50	..2.00
St. Joseph, Mich...	St. Joseph & Lake Mich. Trans. Co...b	..60	..	..4	..1.00	...50	..2.00
South Haven, Mich.	O'Connor's Dock Co. Line.........c	..75	..	..7	..1.50	...75	..2.50
Sturgeon Bay, Wis..	Goodrich's Menominee Line.........a	..227	1	12	..6.00	..4.00	..12.00
Suttons Bay, Mich..	Northern Michigan Trans. Co...... ..e	..370	1	15	..6.50	..4.00	..11.00
Thompson, Mich....	Goodrich Line......................a	..504	3	...	..8.00	..5.50	..14.00
Torch Lake, Mich...	Northern Michigan Trans. Co.........e	..338	1	..5	..6.50	..4.00	..12.00
Toronto, Canada....	Merchants' Line..................d	.....	5	18	..14.00	..7.00	..25.00
Traverse City,Mich.t	Seymour Trans. Co..................f	..291	1	..9	..6.50	..3.50	..12.00
Washburn, Wis....	Lake Mich. & Lake Superior Trans. Co.b	..944	5	...	..23.00	..8.00	..42.00
Wash. Harbor, Wis.	Goodrich's Menominee Line.........a	..385	2	12	..6.00	..4.00	..12.00
WhiteFish Pt.,Mich.	Lake Mich. & Lake Superior Trans. Co.b	.....	2	12	..12.00	..5.00	..22.00
Windsor, Canada...	Merchants' Line..................d	..700	3	..7	..9.00	..4.50	..16.00

* Seymour Transportation Line also runs to this point.

† Northern Michigan Transportation Line also comes to this place.

‡ Lake Michigan & Lake Superior Transportation Co. also runs to this point.

a Ticket Office, north end of Michigan Av.

b Ticket Office, cor. Rush and N. Water Sts.

c Ticket Office, 46 and 48 River St.

d Ticket Office, 127 and 129 Market St.

e Ticket Office, east end of Michigan St.

f Ticket Office, 432 to 448 Illinois St.

Where Shall We Go To-night?

The following are among the leading places of entertainment and amusement in this city, and their charges for admission.

Alhambra Theater, State St. and Archer Av., 1¾ miles south of City Hall. Open every night; also Wednesday and Saturday afternoons. Charge for admission: 25c., 35c., 50c., 75c. and $1.00.

Auditorium Theater, corner Congress St. and Wabash Av., ¾ mile southeast of City Hall. Devoted to opera, musical entertainments, conventions, lectures, spectacular plays, drama and theatricals. Open day or evening, according to advertisement. Prices of admission vary, according to entertainment.

Battle of Gettysburg Panorama, corner Wabash Av. and Panorama Pl., about one mile southeast of City Hall. Is a realistic picture, representing the Battle of Gettysburg and the buildings and scenery surrounding Gettysburg at the time of the battle. Open every day and evening. Admission: 50 cents; children, 25 cents.

Casino (formerly Eden Musee), west side of Wabash Av., near Adams St., ¾ mile southeast of City Hall. Principally devoted to an exhibition of wax works, representative of distinguished people, besides musical renditions by minstrel and concert troupes in the amusement hall. Admission: 25 cents; seats, 25 and 50 cents extra.

Central Music Hall, State and Randolph Sts., two blocks east of City Hall. Devoted largely to musical entertainments, lectures, conventions and exhibitions. Open, according to advertisement. Occupied each Sunday morning by religious service, led by Prof. David Swing. Admission to this service free.

Chicago Opera House, Clark and Washington Sts., opposite City Hall. Opera and general theatricals. Open every evening and Wednesday and Saturday afternoons. Admission: 50c., 75c., $1.00 and $1.50, according to location; boxes, $10, $12 and $15.

Columbia Theater, Monroe St., between Clark and Dearborn Sts., two blocks south of City Hall. Open every evening, and Wednesday and Saturday afternoons. Admission: 50c., 75c., $1 and $1.50; boxes, $10, $12 and $15.

Criterion Theater, corner Sedgwick and Division Sts., North Side, 1¾ miles from City Hall. Light comedies and burlesques. Open every evening. Admission: 25c., 50c. and 75c.

Epstean's New Dime Museum, north side of Randolph St., near Clark St. Admission, 10 cents.

Grand Opera House, Clark St., opposite Court House. Opera and general theatricals. Open every evening, and Wednesday and Saturday afternoons. Admission: 50c., 75c., $1, $1.50; boxes, $10 and $15.

Havlin's Theater, Wabash Av., between Eighteenth and Twentieth Sts., two miles south of City Hall. Devoted to general theatricals. Open every evening, and Thursday, Saturday and Sunday afternoons. Admission: 25c., 35c., 50c. and $1; boxes, $4, $6, $8 and $10; single seats in boxes, $1.

Haymarket Theater, 161 West Madison St., near Halsted St., ¾ mile from City Hall. Open every evening; also Wednesday and Saturday afternoons. Admission: 15c., 25c., 50c., 75c., $1 and $1.50; boxes, $5 to $10.

Hooley's Theater, 149 Randolph St., opposite the City Hall. Open every evening; also Wednesday and Saturday afternoons. Admission: 25c., 50c., 75c., $1 and $1.50; boxes, $6, $12 and $15.

Jacob's Academy of Music, 83 S. Halsted St., ¾ mile west of the City Hall. A comedy, drama and vaudeville theater. Open every evening; also Wednesday, Saturday and Sunday afternoons. Admission: 15c., 25c., 35c. and 50c.

Jacob's Clark St. Theater, 42 N. Clark St., six blocks north of the City Hall. A light comedy and vaudeville theater. Open every evening; also Thursday, Saturday and Sunday afternoons. Admission: 25c., 50c. and 75c.; boxes, $6; single seats in boxes, $1.

Kohl & Middleton's Museums.—South Side Museum, 146-152 S. Clark St., two blocks south of the City Hall. Open every day and evening. A similar establishment, called the Globe Museum, is located at 292 State St., about ¾ mile southeast of the City Hall. Admission to either museum, 10 cents.

Libby Prison War Museum.—(See page 190).

Lyceum Theater, 58 S. Desplaines St., ¾ mile west of the City Hall. A variety theater. Open every evening; also Tuesday, Thursday, Saturday and Sunday afternoons. Admission: 25c., 35c., 50c. and 75c.; boxes, $5; single seats in boxes, $1. Admission to matinees: 20c., 25c., 35c. and 50c.; box seats, 75c.; whole boxes, $4.

Madison Street Opera House, 85 Madison St., between State and Dearborn Sts., about three blocks southeast of the City Hall. A variety theater. Open every day, both afternoon and evening. Admission: matinee, 25c. and 50c.; evening, 25c., 50c., 75c. and $1.

McVicker's Theater, 82 Madison St., between State and Dearborn Sts., about three blocks southeast of the City Hall. Open every evening, and Saturday afternoon. Admission: 25c., 50c., 75c., $1 and $1.50; boxes, $10 and $12.

Olympic Theater, 46 Clark St., about ½ block north of City Hall. A variety theater. Open every afternoon and evening, Sunday included. Admission: 10, 20 and 30 cents.

Panorama of Chicago Fire, Michigan Av., near Madison St., about six blocks southeast of the City Hall. A representation of the great fire of 1871, which laid waste the entire business district of Chicago. Open daily; week-days, from 9 A. M. to 10 P. M.; Sundays, 2 to 10 P. M. Admission, 50 cents; children, 25 cents.

Park Theater, 335 State St., about ¾ mile southeast of the City Hall. Open every afternoon and evening. Admission: 10c., 15c., 25c., 50c. and 75c.; boxes, $4.

People's Theater, 339 State St., about ¾ mile southeast of the City Hall. A vaudeville and variety theater, presenting also an occasional drama. Open every evening; also Wednesday, Saturday and Sunday afternoons. Admission: 35c., 50c., 75c. and $1; boxes, $6 and $7; single seats in boxes, $1.50.

Schiller Theater, 105 Randolph St., about ½ block east of the City Hall. Open every evening; also Wednesday and Saturday afternoons. Occasional entertainments in the German language. Admission: 25c., 50c., 75c., $1 and $1.50; boxes, $10.

Standard Theater, 169 S. Halsted St., a little more than a mile southwest of the City Hall. Open every evening; also Wednesday, Saturday and Sunday afternoons. Admission: 25c., 35c., 50c. and 75c.; box seats, $1.

Windsor Theater, 468 N. Clark St., 1½ miles north of the City Hall. Open every evening; also Wednesday, Saturday and Sunday afternoons. Admission: 35c., 50c., 75c. and $1; matinees, 25c., 35c., 50c. and 75c.

EXPLANATION.

Star (*) means that this house is conducted only on the European plan, charging for rooms and paying for meals separately.

Dagger (†) indicates that this house is conducted both on the American and European plans; that is, the guest can pay for rooms and meals together, or for rooms separately.

Parallels (‖) mean that this hotel is large, centrally located and strictly first-class. Other hotels may be equally excellent.

Prices attached mean the price which is charged per day, and those here mentioned are about the average of prices charged by the many hotels of the city.

Alhambra Hotel, State St., cor. Archer Av.
Alma House, 520 Wabash Av.
American Hotel, 118 Kinzie St.
Arcade Hotel, 164 Clark St.
Arlington House, 34 and 36 W. Madison St.
Ashland European Hotel, 19 Clark St.
Atlantic Hotel, Van Buren and Sherman, $2.
Atlas House, 54 Custom House Pl.
Auditorium Hotel,† ‖ Michigan Av. & Congress.
Bartl's Hotel. 353 State St.
Bennett House, 71 Monroe St.
Bingham House, 134 and 136 Michigan St.
Bowen House, 47 N. Market St.
Bradford Hotel, 32 N. Wells St.
Brown's Hotel, 284 and 286 State St.
Burke's European Hotel, 140 Madison, $1 up.
Carleton House, 78 Adams St.
Central European Hotel, 13 S. Water St
Central House, 250 State St.
Chicago European Hotel, 154 & 156 Clark St.
City Hotel, State St., corner Sixteenth St.
Clarence House, 243 S. Canal St.
Clarendon Hotel, 152 N. Clark St., $2.
Clarendon Hotel, 479 Wabash Av.
Clifton, Monroe St. and Wabash Av., $2.50, $3.
Colombo Hotel, 66 N. Wells St.
Commercial Hotel, Lake and Dearborn Sts., $2.
Continental, Wabash Av. & Madison St., $2.
Crescent Hotel, 347 Fifth Av.
Currier's,* 17 Clark St., 50c., 75c., $1.
Damon Hotel, 86 N. Clark St.
Danmark Hotel, 128 Kinzie St.
Davenport House. 180 N. Clark St.
Dearborn Hotel, 398 to 404 State St.
Dearborn Park Hotel, 6 Washington St.
Deming European Hotel, 136 Madison St.
Ettna European Hotel, 163 & 165 Adams St.
Eureka House, 75 Jackson St.
Fifth Avenue European Hotel, 171 Fifth Av.
Garden City Hotel, 46 and 48 Sherman St.
Garden City House, 105 N. Wells St.
Garfield House, 83 N. Wells St.
Gault House, Madison and Clinton, $2, $2.50.
Geneva House, 276 Michigan St.
Germania House, 182 Randolph St.
Gibson House, 265 Clark St.
Golden Star House, 203 Plymouth Pl.
Goldston's Hotel, 286 Wabash Av.
Gore's Hotel,* 266 Clark St., $1 and upward.
Granada Hotel,† 76 Rush St.
Grand Central,* 19 W. Madison St., 50c.
Grand Central Hotel, 373 Fifth Av.
Grand Hotel, 230 State St.
Grand Pacific,‖ Clark and Jackson, $3 to $5.
Grand Palace, 97 N. Clark St., 50c. to $1.50.
Great Northern Hotel, * ‖ 237 Dearborn St.
Hamburg House, 186 Randolph St.
Hammond House, 7 N. Clark St.
Hotel Brevoort,* 143 Madison, $1, $1.50, $2.
Hotel Brewster, 292 Dearborn St.
Hotel Brunswick, Michigan Av. & Adams St.
Hotel Casino, 16 Madison St.
Hotel Columbia, 15 N. State St.
Hotel Cortland, 16 to 22 Adams St., $1.50, $2.
Hotel Crystal, 49 Fifth Av.
Hotel Fargo, 248 State St.
Hotel Grace,* Clark and Jackson, $1 and up.
Hotel Henrici * (German), 70 Randolph, $1 up.
Hotel Isaria, 10 W. Randolph St.
Hotel Kinzie, 44 N. Clark St.
Hotel Lafayette, W. Madison & Desplaines Sts.
Hotel Marquette, Dearborn and Adams Sts.
Hotel Meyer, 1 South Water St.
Hotel Midland, 167 Madison St.
Hotel Newport, 73 Monroe St.
Hotel Oxford, Canal and Adams Sts.
Hotel Park, 85 Clark St.
Hotel Parker, 25 Clark St.

Hotel Renner, 67 and 69 Randolph St.
Hotel Richelieu,*‖ 187 Michigan Av., $2.50 up.
Hotel Richmond,* 280 State St.,75c., $1, $1.50.
Hotel Rutland, 282 Indiana St.
Hotel Stockholm, 56 Chicago Av.
Hotel Willard, Wabash Av. and 18th St.
Hotel Willi, 186 Clark St.
Hotel Windham, 52 Rush St.
Howard European Hotel, 184 N. Clark St.
Imperial Hotel, 51 Clark St.
Inter Ocean Hotel, 268 State St.
Kimball Hotel, 262 Clark St.
Knickerbocker Hotel, 79 & 81 S. Jefferson St.
Kuhns' Hotel,* 165 Clark St., 75c. to $2.50.
Lalande Hotel, 321 Clark St.
Lansing, 135 Adams St.
La Salle House, 47 La Salle St.
Lauterbach's Hotel, 20 N. State St.
Leland Hotel,‖ Michigan Av. and Jackson St.
Lexington,‖ Michigan Av. & 22nd St., $3 to $6.
Libby Hotel,* 1414 Wabash Av., 75c. and up.
Lincoln Hotel, 70 Jackson St.
Lindell Hotel, 343 Fifth Av.
Loyal Hotel, 45 and 47 Michigan Av.
Madison House, 164 Madison St.
Mather House, 362 Wabash Av.
McCoy's,* Clark & Van Buren Sts., $1 and up.
McEwan's European Hotel, 95 W. Madison St.
Merchant's Exchange Hotel, 12 S. Water St.
Merchant's Hotel, 22 Clark St.
Metropolitan Hotel, 26 N. Wells St.
Muskegon House, 21 Michigan Av.
National Hotel, 228 and 230 Clark St.
Neef's European, N. Wells and Michigan Sts.
New Rockford Hotel, 224 Clark St.
Normandie House, 15 N. Clark St.
North City Hotel, 89 N. Wells St.
Northern Pacific Hotel, 62 & 64 Sherman St.
Ogden House, 100 Franklin St.
Old Metropolitan Hotel, 194 Randolph St.
Oxford Hotel, Canal and Adams Sts., $2.
Palmer House,†‖ State and Monroe Sts.
Panorama Hotel, 49 Hubbard Ct.
Plymouth Hotel, 45 and 47 Plymouth Pl.
Prince's European Hotel, 277 Clark St.
Randolph European Hotel, 102 Randolph St.
Rawnsley House, 499 State St.
Revere House,† N. Clark and Michigan Sts.
Ricardo Hotel, 168 Clark St.
Royal European Hotel, 37 Adams St.
Saratoga,* 161 Dearborn St., 75c. to $3.
Shelburne Hotel, 308,310 & 312 E. Chicago Av.
Sherman House,‖ Clark and Randolph, $3, $5.
Southern,† Wabash Av. and 22nd, $2.50, $4.
St. Benedict Hotel, 183 Cass St.
St. Bernard Hotel, 12 Madison St.
St. Lawrence House, 403 S. Clark St.
St. Mark's Hotel, 196 Washington St.
Stadt Hanover, 144 Michigan St.
Stafford's European Hotel, 131 Van Buren St.
Stanwix House, 1339 to 1341 State St.
Superior Hotel, 210 N. Clark St.
Teller's Hotel, 143 N. Clark St.
Thompson's European, 148-156 Dearborn St.
Tremont House,‖ Dearborn and Lake, $3, $5.
Underwriter's Hotel Company, 249 Clark St.
Union Hotel, 101 S. Canal St.
Victoria Hotel,‖ Michigan Av. & Van Buren St.
Virginia Hotel,‖ Rush and Ohio St., $3 to $5.
Washington Hotel, 15 W. Madison St., $2.
Waters European Hotel, 98 & 100 N. Clark St.
Wellington,*‖ Wabash Av. and Jackson, $2 up.
Wells St. House, 95 N. Wells St.
Westminster Hotel, 462 and 466 N. Clark St.
Wheeler's Hotel, 18 Quincy St.
Windsor,* 153 Dearborn St., 75c, $1, $1.50
Woodruff, Wabash Av. and 21st St., $3 to $4.
Woods Hotel, 30 Van Buren St.

Tier of Towns.	Township. 1	Township. 2	Township. 3	Township. 4	Township. 5	Township. 6	Township. 7	Township. 8	Township. 9

Suburban Towns, Cities and Villages in the Vicinity of Chicago.

Explanation.—The above map is divided into townships, shown by straight lines. Each tier is divided into townships numbering from left to right. To find any station observe in what tier and what township the same is located. Thus, to find Glen Ellyn, located in tier 8, township 5, see 8, in column of black figures, at left side of the map; then follow to the right and in the square containing the figure 5, is the name of this village. See table on succeeding pages. All suburban stations cannot be shown, for lack of space, but their location and direction from Chicago can be understood by this page. This map covers an area 84 miles in length by 54 miles in width; the whole including 4,536 square miles.

Each square, on the above map, indicates a township six miles square. The name of each township is given in the diagram at the end of the list of suburban stations.

See List of Suburban Towns on Following Pages.

As Suburban Villages grow rapidly, the Populations here given are hardly reliable.

The hope of many people, in a great city, is that the time may come when their families can be surrounded by the pure air, the green trees, the rustic life, the broad lawns, and the freedom which pertains to residence in the country. To rest in the shadow of the vine, to lie down in the welcome hammock, in the shade of the friendly tree, to be surrounded by happy, rosy children, to get away thus from the din, the dust, the grime, the contests, the pomp and the vanities, is the wish of many a weary man, is the dream of many a tired woman, whose home in the city is all that a city home can be.

When the time has come to make choice of a location for a residence in a suburb, many questions will suggest themselves, and among these will be: What is the population of that locality? what the distance from the city? what the time to get there? what the cost? what the direction? how near is the city depot from the place of business? For the purpose of answering these queries the following particulars are given, relating to over 400 suburban hamlets, villages and cities in the near vicinity of Chicago.

Facts For People Who Desire to Visit or Live in the Suburbs of Chicago.

The following list of suburban stations, villages and cities, gives the name of place, its population, distance from Chicago, name of railroad used and region where town is located; time required to get there by fastest trains, cost one way, round-trip, ten-ride, twenty-five ride and monthly tickets, and the depot used by trains going to that point. The time of running trains and rates of fares are liable to change.

NAME OF PLACE.	Popula- tion. in 1890.	Miles from Chicago.	Tier.	Town ship.	R.R.	Time in Hrs. and Minutes.	Cost One Way.	Cost of Round Trip.	Cost of 10 Rides.	Cost of 25 Rides.	Cost of Monthly. Ticket.	What De- pot.
Ainsworth	20	45.0	Ind.	Ind	.z.	2.31	$1.00	$1.60	$ 7.50	$	$11.40	0
Air Line Junction		29.3	Ind	Ind	n.	1.18	.75	1.35		7.90	8.60	3
Alden	100	89.0	1	1	h.	5.00	2.07					2
Alexander		37.5	9	3	j.		1.12					3
Algonquin	500	52.8	4	3	e.	1.43	1.40	2.45	10.00	12.50		2
Almora		40.4	6	3	k.	1.24	1.20					3
Alpine	21	26.5	11	7	.4.	1.14	.74	1.33	4.00	8.75		6
Altenheim	cc	800	10.9	8	7	.t.	.32	.28	.50	1.25	2.65	5.00	3
Antioch		303	54.0	1	5	v.	2.10	1.48	2.65	10.90	13.50	17.80	5
Aptakisic		10	34.0	4	6	v.	1.28	.81	1.40	5.55	8.20	12.00	5
Argyle Park	aa.City	6.9	7	9	m.	.25	.21	.35	1.40	2.00	4.00	3
Arlington Heights	1,424	22.4	5	6	h.	.52	.67	1.15	4.50	5.90	7.10	2
Auburn Park	City	9.0	9	9	p.	.33	.26	.50	1.10	2.75	4.60	4
Aurora	19,634	37.4	9	3	j.	1.06	1.12		9.00	13.00	10.00	3
Austin	cc	4,051	6 7	8	e.	.21	.20	.35	1.35	2.00	4.00	2
Avondale	City	5.1	7	8	h.	.19	.15	.25	1.05	1.75	3.55	2
Barr		300	17.4	5	7	l.	.43	.50	.90	3.50	4.15	6.25	3
Barrington		832	31.6	5	4	h.	1.10	.95	1.65	6.35	7.90	9.00	2
Bartlett		300	30.2	6	4	k.	1.03	.88	1.50	6.05	7.50	8.20	3
Batavia		3,543	39.0	8	3	.e.	1.11	1.12	1.90	7.10	8.90	9.70	2
Beecher		342	37.0	14	9	y.	1.55	1.13		7.50	15.00	9.85	0
Belmont	cc	City	13.2	10	9	p.	.49	.30	.75	1.60	3.70	5.20	4
Bensenville		295	17.3	7	6	k.	.41	.40	.90	3.50	4.50	6.25	3
Benton		350	40.0	1	7	f.	1.30	1.20	2.15	8.00	10.00	10.40	2
Berger	cc		23.3	11	9	n.	1.08	.55	1.00	2.50	6.25	7.75	3
Bernice	cc		26.7	11	9	u.	1.13	.70	1.25	4.00	7.80	8.50	3
Berwin	cc	250	9.5	8	j.	.30	.29	.43	1.90	2.65	4.75	3
Beverly Hill	cc	City	11.2	10	9	p.	.42	.34	.60	1.45	3.55	5.00	4
Big Rock		200	50.4	9	3	j.	1.40	1.53					3
Birchwood	cc		10.0	6	9	m.	.32	.30	.48	2.00	2.95	5.35	3
Bloom		314	27.0	12	9	y.	1.29	.81		4.00	9.00	8.35	0
Blue Island		2,521	16.3	10	8	p.	.55	.47	.80	2.00	4.25	5.85	4
Brainerd	cc	City	10.6	10	9	p.	.40	.32	.60	1.35	3.35	4.90	4
Bremen		89	23.5	11	8	p.	1.17	.68	1.00				4
Briar Hill			49.0	5	1	k.	1.55	1.53					3
Brighton Park	City	5.1	8	8	l.	.15	.15	.25	1.00	2.50		3
Brisbane			35.3	13	6	.t.	1.41	1.06	1.91	6.25	11.75		0
Bristol		300	46.0	10	2	j.	1.26	1.37					3
Brookdale	cc	City	8.7	9	9	c.	.36	.26	.30	1.30	2.75	4.80	1
Brookline	cc	City	9.1	9	9	o.	.28	.25	.30	1.30	2.75	5.00	3
Buena Park	cc	City	6.0	7	9	m.	.22	.17	.30	1.20	1.95	3.90	3
Burlington		1.658	81.3	w.	Wis	.l.		3.60	14.35	23.20			1
Burlington		100	53.0	6	1	c.	1.36	1.48					1
Burlington Heights	cc		29.0	9	4	j.	.43	.85		6.20	8.00	8.75	1
Burnham	cc	25	19.3	11	9	s.		.58	.85	2.75	6.60	8.50	3
Burnside Crossing	cc	City	10.7	9	9	.c.	.45	.35	.45	1.55	3.10	5.75	1
Burr Oak	cc		15.4	10	9	p.		.60	.65	1.95	4.15	5.75	4
Byrneville	cc		22.5	9	7	w.	.57	.58	1.00	3.00	6.00		6
Calumet	cc		19.0	11	9	y.	.57	.56		2.40	5.50	7.15	0
Calvary	cc	210	10.2	6	9	f.	.32	.30	.50	2.05	3.10	5.60	2
Camp Lake			60.0	Wis	Wis	v.	2.20	1.62	2.90	11.80	14.70		5

NAME OF PLACE.	Population in 1890.	Miles from Chicago.	Tier.	Township.	R.R. **	Time in Hrs. and Minutes.	CostOne Way.	Cost of Round Trip.	Cost of 10 Rides.	Cost of 25 Rides.	Cost of Monthly Ticket.	What Depot.
Camp McDonald....cc		26.8	.5	..6	. v.	.1.15	$..63	$1.05	..$3.85	$5.95	..$8.35	...5
Canfield......		11.1	.6	...7	.h.	35	37	...65	...2.50	..3.65	....6.00	...2
Carpentersville......	754	48.4	..5	...3	..e.		1.27	..2.20	..8.85	11.00		...2
Cary..........	161	38.3	..4	...3	.h.	1.31	1.15	..2.05	...7.70	..9.60	..10.10	..2
Caton Farm......		47.0	.11	...4	¶¶		1.66					...
Central Park cc	aa.City	.4.2	..8	..8	..e.	...15	...13	...20	85	..1.65	...3.35	..2
Chandler......cc	..City	.8.6	.9	..9	..t.	...32	...26	..47	.1.00	..2.25		..6
Cheltenham......cc	..City	11.4	..9	..9	..c.		...34	..35	.1.60	..3.40	...5.90	..1
Chicago Heights...cc	314	27.0	.12	..9	.y.	1.29	...81		..4.00	..9.00		..6
Chicago Lawn......cc	..City	10.1	..9	..8	..z.	...39	...20	..35	.1.50	..2.50	...3.25	..6
Chickering......		63.0	.14	...3	.w.	2.27	1.89					..6
Clarendon Hills......	212	18.3	..9	..6	.j.	...40	...55	..82	.3.50	..4.60	...6.75	..3
Clarkdale......cc	..City	12.6	..9	..8	..z.	...46	...28	..50	.1.75	..3.15	...4.00	..6
Clarke......	100	24.2	Ind.	Ind	..o.	1.12	...75	1.35	.4.00	..0.50	...9.50	..3
Clifton......cc		17.3	.10	..8	..z.	1.19	...42	..70	.2.00	..3.95	...5.25	..6
Clintonville......	900	39.0	..6	..3	..e.		1.07	1.00	.7.25	..8.75	...9.90	..2
Cloverdale......cc	15	29.0	..7	..5	..c.	...55	...78	1.25	.4.90	..6.15		..1
Clyde......	103	.8.4	.8	..8	.j.	...27	...25	..38	.1.75	..2.30	...4.30	..3
Coal Branch Junction		58.0	.14	...3	.w.	2.27	1.63					..6
Coal City......	1,672	59.0	.14	...3	.w.	2.27	1.66					..6
Colehour......cc	1,998	13.6	.10	..9	.q.	...46	...41	..50	.1.90	..4.45	...7.25	..4
Coleman......		39.0	..7	...3	.c.	1.12	1.06	1.90				..1
Conleys......		19.0	.10	..7	.t.	1.01	...53	..95	.2.50	..6.00		..6
Constance......cc	..City	11.0	..9	..9	..o.	...30	...32	..40	.1.60	..3.45	...6.35	..3
Conway Park...cc		11.7	..8	..7	.t.	...30	...28	..50	.1.25	..2.65	...5.00	..5
Cortland......	500	55.2	bb.	Ill.	..e.	2.02	1.66	3.10	12.50	21.25		..2
Corwith......cc	..City	.6.0	.8	..8	.w.	...32	...20					..3
Coynes......		40.5	.11	..5	.f.		1.06	2.00				..3
Coyne's......		72.0	.14	..1	¶¶	2.23	2.05					..
Cragin......cc	..City	.7.0	..7	..8	.k.	...23	...18	..35	.1.40	..2.15	...4.35	..3
Crawford......cc	..City	.6.1	..8	..8	.j.	...22	...18	..27	.1.25	..1.90	...3.25	..3
Crete	642	30.6	.13	..9	.y.	1.40	...91		.5.00	11.00	...8.85	..6
Crown Point......	2,600	41.2	Ind	Ind	..u.	1.41	1.05	1.90	.5.75	12.25	..14.50	..3
Crystal Lake......	781	42.9	..3	..3	.h.	1.32	1.29	2.35	8.60	10.75	..11.15	..2
Cummings......	..City	14.0	.10	..9	..o.	...47	...42	..50	.1.90	..4.50	...7.00	..3
Custer Park......cc	100	54.5	Ill.	Ill.	.t.	2.00	1.64	2.95	12.50	24.40		..6
Cuyler......cc	..City	.5.0	..7	..9	.f.	...19	...16	..30	.1.10	..1.75	...3.60	..2
Dauphin Park...cc	..City	10.2	..9	..9	..c.	...42	...33	..40	.1.50	..3.00	...5.50	..1
Deerfield	500	23.8	..4	..7	.i.	...55	...71	1.20	.4.80	..5.90	...6.95	..3
Deering......cc	..City	.3.0	..7	..9	.f.	...18	...10	..15	...65	..1.25	...3.00	..2
De Kalb......cc	3,450	58.5	Ill.	Ill.	..e.	2.07	1.70	3.15	12 75	21.25		..2
Del Abbey......		63.0	.14	...3	¶¶	2.27	1.89					..
Des Plaines......	1,000	16.6	..6	..7	.h.	...40	...50	..85	.3.35	..4.65	...6.35	..2
Diamond......	100	63.0	.14	...3	¶¶	2.27	1.89					..
Diamond Lake......	50	38.6	..4	..6	.v.	1.41	...98	1.75	.6.25	..9.30	..13.35	..5
Divine......		62.0	.14	...3	¶¶	2.03	1.89					..
Dolton......	1,110	.9.0	.11	..9	.n.	1.04	...50	..90	.2.00	..4.25	...7.45	..3
Donald cc		.8.7	..8	..8	.t.	...21	...20	..35	.1.25	..2.00	...4.00	..5
Douglas Park......	City	.4.4	..8	..9	.t.	...15	...08	..16	...80	..1.45	...3.00	..5
Downer's Grove......	960	21.2	..9	..6	.j.	...38	...64	..95	.4.00	..5.25	...7.25	..3
Drummond		48.0	.13	..4	.w.	1.52	1.37					..6
Dundee......	2,000	47.6	..5	..3	..e.		1.25	2.15	.8.50	10.65		..3
Dunning......	100	12.0	..7	..8	.k.	...50	...25	..45	.1.75	..2.65	...5.00	..3
Du Page......cc		30.2	..9	..4	.i.	...55	...91		.6.75	..8.75		..3
Dyer......	600	28.5	Ind	Ind	*	1.19	...90	1.60	.4.55	..9.00		..6
East Chicago......	1,200	23.7	Ind	Ind	..o.	1.10	...65	..95	.2.90	..6.75	...8.50	..3
East Grove......	60	20.4	..9	..6	.j.	...43	...61	..92	.3.90	..5.00	...7.10	..3
East Plato......	10	44.0	..6	..2	.c.	1.20	1.22	2.10				..3
East Roseland. cc	25	12.8	.10	..9	..c.	...48	...39	..50	.1.60	..3.25	...6.25	..1
Edgewater......	..City	.7.5	..7	..9	.m.	...27	...23	..40	.1.55	..2.15	...4.25	..3
Edison Park......cc		12.0	..6	..7	.h.	...35	...37	..65	.2.50	..3.65	...6.00	..2
Eggers......cc		19.0	.11	..9		...50						..
Eggleston......cc	..City	.7.7	..9	..9	.p.	...30	...23	..40	.1.10	..2.65	...4.25	..4
Elburn cc	584	44.0	..6	..3	..e.	1.57	1.32	2.40	10.00	13.25		..2
Elgin	17,429	42.5	..6	..3	..e.	1.20	1.10	1.90	.7.35	..8.75	..10.00	..2
Elmhurst......	1,050	15.8	..8	..6	..e.	...32	...47	..80	.3.20	..4.50	...6.30	..2
Elsdon......cc	..City	.8.5	..8	..8	.z.	...35	...15	..25	.1.15	..2.15	...3.00	..6
Elsmere......cc	..City	.5.6	..7	..8	.k.	...15	...14	..23	.1.00	..1.90	...3.85	..3
Elwood......	312	45.8	.13	..5	.i.	1.50	1.37	2.55				..3
Englewood......cc	..City	..6.5	..9	..9	.p.	...26	...20	..30	.1.00	..2.15	...3.75	..4
Englewood on Hill..cc	..City	11.7	..9	..9	.n.	...31						..3
Eola......	20	33.5	..9	..4	.j.	1.09	1.01		.7.75	10.00	...9.50	..3
Erwin cc		..9.6	..8	..8	.t.	...29	...22	..40	.1.25	..2.15	...4.45	..5
Euclid Park......cc	..City	10.7	.10	..9	.y.	...48	...32		.1.00	..2.50	...4.90	..6
Evanston......	8,000	11.8	..6	..7	.f.	...32	...35	..60	.2.40	..3.55	...6.00	..2
Evergreen Park....cc		14.2	.10	..8	..z.	...50	...33	..60	.1.80	..3.55	...5.00	..6
Fairmount Park...cc		..9.2	..8	..8	.t.	...29	...22	..40	.1.25	..2.10	...4.25	..5
Fairview......cc		17.9	..6	..7	.v.	...53	...42	..80	.3.00	..4.30	...6.35	..5
Fairview Park......cc	..City	15.1	.10	..9	.n.	...33	...35	..60	.1.45	..3.55	...5.00	..3
Feehanville......		24.8	..5	..6	.v.	1.11	...67	..95	.3.75	..5.70	...7.80	..5
Fernwood......	818	12.0	.10	..9	.y.	...50	...35		.1.20	..3.00	...5.00	..6
Fields......		17.8	.10	..9	..o.	...54	...50	..60	.2.50	..5.70	...9.45	..3

aa "City," in the city limits of Chicago. | "Ind.," in Indiana. ¶ "Wis.," in Wisconsin.
bb "Ill.," in Illinois, outside of the map. cc Name does not appear on the map. ** R. R., Railroads. ¶¶ Not on a line of railway going to Chicago.

NAME OF PLACE.	Population in 1890.	Miles from Chicago	Tier.	Township	R.R	Time in Hrs. and Minutes.	Cost One Way	Cost of Round Trip.	Cost of 10 Rides.	Cost of 25 Rides.	Cost of Monthly Ticket.	What Depot.
Fordham ...cc ...City		10.4	.9	.9	c.	.40	$.30	$.35	$1.40	$2.85	$5.25	1
Forest Glen ...City		10.2	.7	.8	l.	.30	.27	.50	2.05	2.65	5.30	3
Forest Hill ...cc ...City		12.9	.9	.9	n.	.37	.30	.55	1.45	3.50	5.00	3
Forest Home ...cc		10.5	.8	.7	t.	.37	.28	.50	1.25	2.65	5.00	5
Fort Sheridan ...cc	451	24.5	.4	.7	f.	.53	.73	1.25	4.85	6.05	7.50	2
Fox ...				1	j.	2.03	1.59					3
Fox Lake ...92		50.9	.2	.4	v.	2.02	1.35	2.45	10.05	12.45	16.45	5
Frankfort Station...	431	36.0	.12	.7			1.07					2
Franklin Park ...cc	30	15.1	.7	.7	t.	.50	.34	.65	2.00	3.60	6.00	5
Freeman		52.0	.5	.2	e.	1.57						2
Frontenac		37.0	.9	.4			1.12					
Galewood ...City		8.7	.7	.8	k.	.30	.23	.44	1.70	2.40	4.70	3
Gardner's Park ...cc ...City		15.3	.10	.9	c.	.57	.46	.55	1.85	4.10	6.90	1
Gary		15.0	.9	.7	w.	.51	.40	.50	2.25	5.00		6
Geneva	1,692	35.0	.8	.3	e.	1.05	1.07	1.90	7.10	8.90	9.70	2
Gilberts	250	50.0	.5	.2	e.	1.31	1.35					2
Given ...cc		12.8	.10	.9	p.	.49	.38	.70	1.55	3.65	5.15	4
Glencoe	560	19.0	.5	.8	f.	.55	.57	.95	3.80	5.25	6.65	2
Glen Ellyn	550	22.5	.8	.5	e.	.43	.68	1.15	4.50	5.90	7.10	2
Glenwood	200	23.6	.12	.9	y.	1.22	.71		3.30	8.00	7.90	6
Globe ...cc		25.1	.11	.9	n.	1.10	.65	1.15		7.50	8.10	3
Goodenow	175	34.2	.13	.9	y.	1.46	1.03	..	6.50	14.00	9.35	6
Graceland ...City		5.8	.7	.9	m.	.22	.17	.30	1.20	1.95	3.90	3
Grade Siding		32.5	.3	.7	f.	1.15	.96	1.61				2
Grand Crossing ...City		9.4	.9	.9	c.	.38	.27	.30	1.30	2.75	5.00	1
Granger ...cc		33.0	.7	.4	c.	.59	.89	1.50	6.05	7.50		1
Grant Park	450	44.7	Ill.	Ill.	y.	2.12	1.34		9.50	20.00	10.80	6
Grant Works ...cc		8.2	.8	.4	t.	.35	.19	.35	1.25	1.95	3.90	5
Grayland ...cc ...City		8.0	.7	.8	l.	.24	.21	.35	1.40	2.15	4.35	3
Gray's Lake	375	45.5	.2	.5	v.	1.52	1.19	2.10	7.85	11.05	15.00	2
Greenwood ...cc	137	22.2	.11	.9	n.							3
Gregg's		19.4	.9	.6	l.	.46	.58	.87	3.75	4.85	7.00	3
Griffith		35.8	Ind	Ind	z.	2.01	.85	1.55	5.00	10.50	9.65	6
Grossdale		12.1	.8	.7	j.	.27	.36	.55	2.25	3.45	5.25	3
Gross Park ...City		4.5	.7	.9	f.	.17	.13	.25	.90	1.65	3.35	2
Gurnee	178	38.6	.2	.6	l.	1.23	1.16	1.95	7.75	8.90	9.70	3
Hammond	5,700	20.8	Ind	Ind	*.	1.00	.60					6
Hammond's		34.2	.6	.4	k.	1.19	1.00	1.70	6.85	8.50	9.75	3
Hampshire	696	51.0	.5	.1	k.	1.52	1.53					3
Hampton		47.8	.13	.5	l.	1.55	1.43	2.65				3
Handee ...cc		42.4	.3	.5	v.	1.44	1.09	1.90	7.15	10.25	14.20	5
Harlem		11.2	.8	.7	t.	.29	.27	.50	1.25	2.60	5.00	5
Hartland		55.0	.2	.1	h.	2.10	1.66					3
Hartsdale		33.0	Ind	Ind	n.	1.26	.85	1.50		10.75	9.65	3
Harvey ...cc	1,500	19.6	.11	.9	c.	1.13	.59	.75	2.20	4.50	7.20	1
Hawthorne ...cc		6.9	.8	.8	j.	.24	.21	.31	1.50	2.15	3.50	3
Hayford ...cc	50	11.6	.9	.8	z.	.35	.25	.40	1.70	2.90	3.80	6
Hebron	300	67.0	.1	.2	h.	4.25	2.03					3
Hegewisch ...City		18.5	.10	.9	o.	.55	.70	2.25	5.50	7.50		3
Helmes ...cc		25.8	.5	.6	v.	1.12	.60	1.00	3.80	5.85	8.05	5
Hermosa ...City		5.9	.7	.8	k.	.20	.16	.30	1.25	2.00	4.20	3
Hessville	25	23.4	Ind	Ind	r.	1.30	.75	1.05				4
Highland Park	2,163	22.9	.4	.7	f.	.50	.69	1.15	4.60	5.90	7.10	2
Highlands		16.3	.9	.6	j.	.38	.49	.73	3.15	4.30	6.15	3
High Ridge ...cc		8.2	.6	.9	f.	.27	.25	.40	1.65	2.45	4.65	2
Highwood	1,451	24.2	.4	.7	f.	.53	.73	1.25	4.85	6.05	7.50	2
Hills ...cc		22.0	.8	.6	c.	.38	.65	1.15	4.50	5.75	7.50	1
Hinsdale	1,500	16.9	.9	.6	j.	.31	.51	.76	3.25	4.40	6.25	3
Hobart	1,000	33.4	Ind	Ind	o.	1.21	1.00	1.80	8.00		12.00	3
Homewood	500	23.4	.11	.9	c.	1.20	.70	.90	2.35	4.05	7.40	1
Humboldt ...cc ...City		4.9	.7	.8	k.		.13	.22	.85	1.80	3.75	3
Huntley	500	55.0	.4	.2	e.	1.37	1.50					2
Hyde Park Center ...City		6.5	.9	.9	c.	.26	.19	.25	1.00	2.15	3.80	1
Ingleton	50	30.8	.7	.4	u.	1.10	.90	1.55	6.00	7.50		5
Irondale ...cc ...City		17.0	.10	.9	r.							4
Irving Park ...City		6.5	.7	.8	h.	.20	.20	.35	1.35	2.00	4.00	2
Itasca	333	21.0	.7	.6	k.	.46	.61	1.05	4.25	5.75	7.00	3
Jefferson Park ...City		8.7	.7	.8	h.	.27	.26	.45	1.75	2.65	5.00	2
Johnstone ...cc		10.4	.10	.8	t.	.54	.43	.77				6
Joliet	23,264	37.0	.12	.5	l.	1.20	1.06	2.00	8.50	10.00		3
Kenilworth ...cc		17.5	.5	.8	f.	.39	.45	.75	3.00	4.35	6.30	2
Kenosha	6,532	51.5	Wis	Wis	f.	1.33	1.54	2.05	10.30	12.75	13.40	2
Kensington ...City		14.5	.10	.9	c.	.54	.41	.50	1.80	4.00	6.85	1
Kenwood ...cc ...City		5.7	.8	.9	c.	.22	.17	.25	.90	1.85	3.25	1
Kirwin ...cc		9.4	.8	.8	f.	.24	.24	.45	1.25	2.45	4.65	5
Kolz...		16.9	.6	.7	v.	.52	.39	.75	2.60	4.20	6.85	5
Lacton ...cc		22.6	.9	.5	j.	.59	.68		4.50	6.25	7.75	3
La Fox	155	40.0	.8	.2	e.	1.50	1.22	2.20	8.60	11.40		2
La Grange ...cc	2,314	13.7	.9	.7	j.	.29	.41	.62	2.50	3.75	5.50	3
Lake	250	36.0	Ind	Ind	d.	1.33	1.05	1.90				1
Lake Bluff	100	30.2	.3	.7	f.	1.05	.90	1.55	6.05	7.50	8.40	2
Lake Forest	1,203	28.0	.3	.7	f.	1.00	.84	1.45	5.60	7.00	8.00	2
Lake Side	100	17.5	.5	.8	f.	.43	.53	.90	3.50	4.85	6.50	2
Lake Villa	92	50.9	.1	.5	v.	2.02	1.35	2.45	10.05	12.45	16.45	5
Lake Zurich	200	31.6	.4	.5	h.	1.10	.95	1.65	6.35	7.90	9.00	2
Lancaster		28.0	.4	.7	l.	1.04	.84	1.40	5.60	6.05	7.40	3

NAME OF PLACE.	Population in 1890.	Miles from Chicago.	Tier.	Township.	R.R.	Time in Hrs. and Minutes.	Cost One Way.	Cost of Round Trip.	Cost of 10 Rides.	Cost of 25 Rides.	Cost of Monthly Ticket.	What Depot.
Lansing	218	28.1	11	9	n.	1.16	$.75	$1.35	$4.00	$7.85	$8.50	3
La Vergne........cc		9.1	8	8	j.	.29	.27	.41	1.80	2.50	4.00	3
Lawndale......cc	City	5.4	8	8	j.	.22	.16	.24	1.00	1.70		3
Leithon		37.9	4	5	v.	1.37	.96	1.70	6.20	6.10	13.20	5
Lemont	6,000	25.5	10	6	J.	1.10	.71	1.35	5.00	10.00		3
Libertyville	550	35.0	3	6	l.	1.35	1.00	1.80	7.10	8.25	9.25	3
Lily Lake	100	45.5	7	2	u.	1.35	1.37	2.50	10.25	13.50		5
Linden Park......cc		6.2	8	8	e.	.23	.18	.30	1.20	1.85	3.75	2
Lisle	62	24.4	9	5	J.	.44	.73		5.00	7.00	8.25	3
Liverpool		30.5	Ind	Ind	o.	1.37	.90	1.00	7.00		11.25	3
Llewellyn Park...cc		14.1	5	8	m.	.45	.40	.05	2.65	3.95	6.10	3
Lockport	2,400	32.0	11	5	l.	1.22	.93	1.75	6.25	10.00		3
Lombard	515	20.0	8	6	e.	.39	.00	1.00	4.00	5.40	6.65	2
Longwood	City	11.7	10	9	p.	.43	.35	.40	1.45	3.55	5.00	4
Loon Lake......cc		53.0	1	4	v.	2.10	1.41	2.55	10.45	12.95	17.10	5
Lorenzo	10	53.0	14	4	w.	2.02	1.51					0
Lowry........cc		9.7	8	8	t.		.23	.45	1.25	2.40	4.60	5
McCaffrey......cc	City	11.1	9	8	s.	.43	.23	.40	1.65	2.75	3.75	6
McHenry	979	50.2	2	3	h.	1.51	1.52	2.45	10.05	12.55		2
McQueen		42.5	6	2	e.	1.30	1.37					2
Madison Park...cc	City	6.1	8	8	c.	.24	.18	.25	.95	2.00	3.50	1
Manhattan	250	39.6	13	6	i.	1.38	1.19	2.14	7.75	14.50		6
Mannheim	50	14.1	7	7	k.	.41	.39	.70	2.85	4.10	6.20	3
Maple Park	382	50.0	7	1	e.	1.50	1.52	2.80	11.50	18.25		2
Maplewood	City	4.1	7	8	h.	.16	.12	.20	.85	1.65	3.35	2
Marengo	1,500	66.0	3	1	e.	1.54	1.85					2
Marley	62	29.9	12	6	i.	1.27	.84	1.51	5.00	10.00		3
Marvin........cc	City	7.2	8	8	t.	.21	.16	.30	1.00	1.75	3.60	5
Mason		37.3	4	5	v.	1.37	.94	1.65	6.15	8.95	13.10	5
Mather		24.1	8	5	e.		.72	1.25	5.00	6.25	7.50	2
Matteson	323	28.0	12	8	c.	1.15	.84					1
Maynard		29.9	Ind	Ind	l.	1.19	.75	1.35	4.00	7.00	8.70	3
Maywood	1,200	10.4	8	7	e.	.35	.31	.55	2.10	3.15	5.65	2
Meacham	100	23.1	7	5	k.	.50	.66	1.15	4.65	5.90	7.20	3
Melrose	25	11.3	8	7	e.	.47	.34	.00	2.30	3.45	5.90	2
Millbrook	150	55.0	11	1	*	2.10	1.00					4
Millers	100	30.0	Ind	Ind	q.	1.14	.90	1.50				4
Millsdale		46.3	13	4	w.	1.47	1.32					0
Minooka	360	51.0	13	3	p.	1.41	1.43					4
Mokena	364	29.7	12	7	p.	1.28	.86	1.00				4
Momence	2,000	49.9	Ill.	Ill.	y.	2.23	1.50		11.00	25.00	11.50	6
Monee	445	34.1	13	8	c.	1.27	1.02					1
Montclare	City	9.6	7	8	k.	.27	.26	.50	1.95	2.85	5.45	3
Montgomery	300	40.0	9	3	j.	1.28	1.21					3
Montrose	City	7.5	7	8	h.	.24	.23	.40	1.55	2.25	4.50	2
Moreland......cc	City	5.6	8	8	e.	.21	.17	.30	1.10	1.80	3.65	2
Morgan Park ... cc	1,027	13.7	10	9	p.	.50	.40	.75	1.65	3.75	5.25	4
Morrell Park...cc	City	8.0	9	8	z.	.30	.15	.25	1.15	2.00	3.00	6
Morris	3,653	62.0	14	2	p.	2.03	1.74					1
Morton	81	14.3	6	8	l.	.37	.40	.70	2.90	3.25	6.00	3
Morton Park......cc		7.5	8	8	j.	.25	.23	.34	1.60	2.50	3.75	3
Mount Forest	148	16.5	9	7	l.	.55	.50	.90	2.50	5.50		3
Mount Greenwood .cc	100	16.2	10	8	z.	.50	.39	.60	2.00	3.75	5.65	6
Mount Olivet......cc		16.2	10	8	z.	.56	.39	.60	2.00	3.75	5.65	6
Mount Hope......cc		16.2	10	8	z.	1.09	.39	.60	2.00	3.75	5 65	6
Mount Prospect	75	19.9	6	6	k.	.56	.59	1.00	3.95	5.40	6.65	2
Naperville	2,216	28.4	9	5	j.	.51	.85		6.20	8.00	8.75	3
New Chicago......cc		18.4	11	9	c.	1.10	.55	.70	2.10	4.40	7.10	1
New Lennox	220	33.1	12	6	i.	1.28	.99	1.78	5.75	10.00		6
Normal Park......cc	City	7.3	9		p.	.28	.22	.35	1.10	2.60	4.10	4
North Aurora	200	41.6	9	3	e.	1.18	1.12	2.10	8.00	10.50	10.00	2
North Edgewater...cc	City	8.3	7	9	m.	.28	.25	.45	1.70	2.45	4.65	3
North Evanston...cc	140	13.0	6	9	f.	.35	.39	.65	2.65	3.95	6.10	2
North Oswego		41.0	10	3	j.	1.41	1.31					3
North Wayne		33.0	7	4	c.	.30	.94	1.60	6.30	7.80	8 95	1
Norwood Park	616	11.1	7	8	h.	.32	.33	.55	2.25	3.15	5.70	2
Oakdale......cc	City	10.2	10	9	y.	.40	.31			2.25		6
Oak Glen	300	17.4	5	7	l.	.43	.50	.90	3.50	4.15	6.25	3
Oak Glen		28.4	11	5	z.	1.45	.70	1.25	3.60	7.90		0
Oakland......cc	City	4.6	8	9	c.	.18	.13	.25	.70	1.50	2.70	1
Oak Lawn	400	14.0	10	8	l.	.48	.35		1.75	3.75		6
Oak Park	5,000	8.0	8	8	e.	.27	.25	.45	1.70	2.50	4.75	2
Oakwoods......cc	City	9.2	9	9	c.	.36	.27	.30	1.30	2.75	4.90	1
Ontarioville	125	28.5	6	4	k.	1.00	.82	1.45	5.70	7.15	7.95	3
Orchard Place	125	20.1	6	7	v.	1.00	.48	.85	3.00	4.40	6.35	5
Orison........cc		10.7	7	7	k.		.29	.55	2.15	3.15	5.70	3
Orland	175	23.2	11	7	t.	1.12	.64	1.15	3.25	8.00		6
Oswego	641	43.0	10	3	j.	1.42	1.31					3
Pacific Junction...cc	City	5.3	7	8	k.	.18	.15	.25	1.05	1.95	4.00	3
Palatine	891	26.1	5	5	h.	1.06	.78	1.35	5.25	6.55	8.00	2
Park Manor......cc	City	8.3	9	9	o.	.20	.23	.30	1.15	2.50	4.50	3
Park Ridge	987	13.1	6	7	h.	.37	.39	.65	2.65	3.95	6.10	2
Park Side	City	9.0	9	9	c.	.36	.27	.30	1.30	2.75	4.90	1
Patterson		45.0	12	5	w.	1.45	1.10	2.20				0
Pennock......cc	City	6.4	7	8	l.	.20	.16	.30	1.25	2.00	4.20	3
Pine		30.0	Ind	Ind	q.		.70	1.15				4

NAME OF PLACE.	Population in 1890.	Miles from Chicago.	Tier.	Township.	R.R.	Time in Hrs. and Minutes.	Cost One Way.	Cost of Round Trip.	Cost of 10 Rides.	Cost of 25 Rides.	Cost of Monthly Ticket.	What Depot.
Pingree Grove	100	.44.4	..5	..2	.k.	1.47	$1.34	$....	$....	$....	$....	...3
Plainfield	852	.48.5	..11	..4	¶¶		...1.55					...3
Plano	2,728	.52.0	..10	..1	.j.	1.45	.1.55		...\			...3
Plato Center	25	.45.0	..6	..2	.c.	1.25	.1.30					...3
Prairie View	50	.34.4	..4	..6	.v.	1.30	..85	.1.45	..5.65	.8.25	.12.05	..5
Prospect Park....cc	473	.22.5	..8	..5	.e.	..43	..68	.1.15	..4.50	.5.90	..7.10	..2
Pullman	City	.13.9	..10	..9	.c.	..51	..40	..50	..1.75	.3.75	..6.75	..1
Purington....cc		.14.7	..10	..9	.p.	..53	..44	..80	..1.80	.3.95	..5.50	..4
Racine	21,014	.61.7	Wis	Wis	.f.	1.50	.1.85	.3.55				..2
Ranney		.51.6	Wis	Wis	.l.	1.51	.1.55		.10.35	12.75	.13.50	..3
Ravenswood	City	..5.8	..7	..9	.f.	..21	..17	..30	..1.20	.1.80	..3.65	..2
Itavinia		.21.5	..4	..7	.f.	1.01	..64	.1.10	..4.30	.5.60	..6.90	..2
Redesdale	10	.39.2	Ind	Ind	.z.	2.09	..95	.1.60	..6.00		.10.25	..6
Rhodes....cc		.13.6	..8	..7	.v.	..48	..34	..65	..2.25	.3.55	..5.85	..5
Richardson	40	.51.4	..7	..1	.u.	1.45	.1.54	.2.85	.11.60	18.50		..5
Richmond	415	.60.4	..1	..3	.h.	1.44	.1.82	.3.10	.12.00	20.00		..2
Richton....cc	203	.29.2	.12	..8	.c.	1.30	..87					..1
Ridgefield	300	.45.7	..3	..2	.h.	1.48	.1.37	.2.50	..9.20	12.25		..2
Ridgeland....cc	270	..7.7	..8	..8	.e.	..23	..23	..40	..1.55	.2.30	..4.50	..2
Ringwood	300	.54.0	..2	..3	.h.	2.33	.1.62	.2.70	.10.85	15.30		..2
Ritchie	75	.53.0	Ill.	Ill.	.l.	1.57	.1.59	.2.86	.12.00	23.50		..6
Riverdale	City	.20.8	.10	..9	.n.	1.02	..50	..90	..2.00	.4.25	..7.10	..3
River Forest		..9.8	..8	..7	.e.	..31	..28	..50	..1.90	.2.85	..5.50	..2
River Park	15	.15.4	..7	..7	.t.		..34	..65	..2.00	.3.60	..6.00	..5
Riverside	1,000	.11.1	..8	..7	.j.	..24	..33	..50	..2.00	.3.10	..5.00	..3
Riverview....cc		.21.4	..6	..7	.v.	..40	..50	..85	..3.35	.4.65	..6.35	..5
Rockefeller	150	.40.0	..3	..6	.v.	1.41	.1.02	.1.80	..6.75	.9.60	.13.55	..5
Rogers Park	1,708	..9.0	..6	..9	.f.	..28	..27	..45	..1.85	.2.75	..5.00	..2
Rollins	50	.48.2	..2	..5	.v.		.1.27	.2.25	..8.95	11.80	.15.20	..5
Romeo		.29.5	.11	..5	.w.	1.18	..82	.1.55				..6
Rondout	100	.32.3	..3	..6	.l.	1.11	..97	.1.65	..6.50	.7.50	..8.35	..3
Rosehill	City	..7.8	..6	..9	.f.	..25	..23	..40	..1.55	.2.25	..4.50	..2
Roseland....cc	City	.13.5	.10	..9	.y.	..53	..38		.1.50	.3.50	..5.50	..6
Roselle	450	.24.5	..7	..5	.k.	..53	..70	.1.25	..4.90	.6.15	..7.50	..3
Russell	80	.47.0	..1	..6	.l.	1.42	.1.41	.2.35	..9.40	11.75	.11.90	..3
Nag Bridge	217	.21.6	.10	..6	.l.	1.05	..65	.1.00				..3
St. Charles....cc	1,690	.38.0	..7	..3	.e.	1.15	.1.07	.1.90	..7.10	.8.90	..9.70	..2
St. Maria....cc		.13.0	.10	..8	.z.	..47	..30	..55	..1.80	.3.40	..4.50	..6
Salt Creek	120	.19.2	..7	..6	.k.	..50	..55	..95	..3.85	.5.35	..6.60	..3
Sedley	65	.50.1	Ind	Ind	.z.	2.47	.1.10	.1.80	..8.50		.12.40	..6
Schererville	200	.34.7	Ind	Ind	.n.	1.30	..95	.1.65		.11.75	.10.50	..3
Shermerville	125	.20.9	..5	..7	.l.	..50	..60	.1.05	..4.20	.5.00	..6.50	..3
Shooting Park....cc	City	.18.3	.10	..9	.n.	..54	..40	..70	..2.00	.4.25	..6.00	..3
Silver Lake		.61.6	Wis	Wis	.v.	2.23	.1.67	.3.00	.12.15	15.05		..5
Sollitt	100	.41.0	Ill.	Ill.	.y.	2.03	1.23		.8.50	17.50		..6
South Addison		.20.0	..7	..6	.c.	..42	..57	.1.00	..4.00	.5.40	..7.00	..1
South Chicago	City	.12.9	..9	..9	.e.	..49	..30	..45	..1.75	.3.90	..6.75	..1
South Elmhurst		.19.0	..8	..6	.u.	..43	..47					..5
South Englewood....cc	800	..9.7	.10	..9	.p.	..37	..20	..55	..1.25	.3.10	..4.75	..4
South Evanston	2,500	.10.8	..6	..9	.f.	..28	..32	..55	..2.20	.3.25	..5.90	..2
South Holland....cc	1,005	.16.9	.11	..9	.y.	1.03	..59		.2.50	.6.00	..7.25	..6
South Lynne....cc	City	.11.2	..9	..9	.n.	..27	..30	..55	..1.45	.3.50	~.5.00	..3
South Oak Park....cc		..9.9	..8	..8	.t.	..35	..25	..45	..1.25	.2.50	..4.75	..5
South Park....cc	City	..7.1	..9	..9	.c.	..28	..21	..25	..1.10	.2.35	..4.05	..1
South Ridgeland....cc		..8.9	..8	..8	.t.	..23	..23	..40	..1.25	.2.30	..4.50	..5
South Shore....cc	City	.10.1	..9	..9	.c.	..41	..30	..30	..1.40	.3.00	..5.40	..1
Spaulding		.32.8	..6	..4	.k.	1.17	..95	.1.65	..6.60	.8.20	..9.50	..3
Spencer	275	.33.6	.12	..6	¶¶	2.18	.1.01	.1.82				
Spring Bluff	170	.45.0	..1	..7	.f.	1.40	.1.35	.2.45	..9.00	11.25	.11.70	..2
Starks	175	.29.0	..7	..5	.c.	..55	..78	.1.25	..4.90	.6.15		..1
Steele		.33.6	.12	..6	.l.	2.18	.1.01	.1.82	..6.00	11.25		..6
Stough....cc		.17.8	..9	..6	.j.	..38	..53	..80	..3.40	.4.50		..3
Sturgis....cc		.10.2	..8	..8	.t.		..24	..45	..1.25	.2.45	..4.75	..5
Sugar Grove	100	.46.0	..9	..2	.j.	1.30	.1.36					..3
Summerdale	City	..6.5	..7	..9	.f.	..23	..20	..35	..1.35	.2.00	..4.00	..2
Summit	272	.11.9	..9	..7	.i.	..45	..35	..65	..2.00	.4.75		..3
Sunset		.47.0	..5	..2	.k.	1.52	.1.50					..3
Sycamore	2,987	.60.0	Ill.	Ill.	.e.		.1.70	.3.15	.12.75	21.25		..3
Symerton	32	.47.0	.14	..5	.l.	1.48	.1.41	.2.54	.10.00	19.50		..6
Tamarack	30	.48.0	.10	..4	¶¶		.1.47					..3
Tedens....cc		.22.0	.10	..6	.w.	1.07		.1.30				..6
Terra Cotta	25	.45.7	..3	..3	.h.		.1.37	.2.45	.10.00	12.50		..2
Thatcher's....cc		.31.6	..9	..4	.j.		..95		.7.25	.9.25		..5
Thatcher's Park....cc		.12.3	..8	..7	.t.	..42	..31	..60	..1.45	.3.05	..5.75	..5
Thornton	450	.22.2	.11	..9	.y.	1.18	..65		.2.90	.7.25	..7.70	..6
Tinley Park....cc	89	.23.5	.11	..8	.p.	1.17	..68	.1.00				..4
Tolleston	300	.22.0	Ind	Ind	.o.	1.17	..80	.1.45	..5.00	12.50	.10.00	..3
Tracy....cc		.12.7	.10	..9	.p.	..46	..37	..70	..1.55	.3.65	..5.15	..4
Tremont....cc	City	.12.7	.10	..9	.n.							..9
Trevor		.58.3	Wis	Wis	.v.	2.17	1.57	.2.80	.11.50	14.25	.31.40	..5
Turner	1,506	.30.0	..8	..4	.e.	1.00	..90	.1.55	..6.00	.7.50	..8.40	..2
Turner Park....cc		.11.5	..7	..7	.k.	..25	..32	..60	..2.30	.3.40	..5.05	..3
Union		.62.0	..4	..1	.e.	1.54	.1.75					..2
Valparaiso	5,090	.43.9	Ind	Ind	.o.	1.30	.1.30	.2.35	.10.00			..3
Wadsworth	150	.42.9	..1	..6	.l.	1.32	.1.29	.2.15	..8.60	10.00	.10.40	..3
Walden....cc	City	.12.2	.10	..9	.p.	..45	..35	..60	..1.45	.3.55	..5.00	..4

NAME of PLACE.	Population in 1890.	Miles from Chicago.	Tier.	Township.	R.R.	Time in Hrs. and Minutes.	Cost One Way.	Cost of Round Trip.	Cost of 10 Rides.	Cost of 25 Rides.	Cost of Monthly Ticket.	What Depot.
Walker............		.50.0	..11	..4	ʈʈ	....	$1.51	$....	$....	$....	$....	....
Warrenhurst........		.37.4	..8	..4	ʈʈ	....	.1.12					
Warrenton..........	..25	.37.0	..2	..6	.l.	.1.19	.1.10	.1.85	.7.50	.8.50	.9.50	..3
Wasco..............	..25	.41.5	..7	..2	.u.	.1.28	.1.25	.2.25	.8.75	11.50	.....	..5
Washington Heights.	.2,283	.12.0	..10	..9	.p.	..45	..36	...60	.1.45	.3.55	.5.00	..3
Waukegan..........	.4,915	.35.6	..2	..7	.f.	.1.15	.1.07	.1.90	.7.15	.8.90	.9.70	..2
Wayne.............	..225	.35.3	..7	..4	.e.	....	.1.00	.1.85	.7.10	.8.70	.9.70	..2
Wentworth.........		.13.3	..9	..7	.w.	..45	..38	...50	.2.00	.4.75	......	..6
West Hinsdale.....cc		.17.8	..9	..6	.j.	..38	..53	...80	.3.40	.4.50	.6.50	..3
Western Springs....	..451	.15.3	..9	..7	.j.	..28	..46	...69	.3.00	.4.15	.6.00	..3
Wheaton............	.1,022	.24.9	..8	..5	.e.	..52	..75	.1.25	.5.00	.6.25	.7.50	..2
Wheeler............	..75	.37.1	Ind	Ind	.o.	.1.40	.1.10	.1.85	.9.00	......	13.00	..3
Wheeling...........	..811	.20.9	..5	..6	.v.	.1.21	..71	.1.20	.4.75	.7.10	.10.85	..5
Whitings...........	..750	.16.8	Ind	Ind	.q.	..50	..50	...60	.2.50	.5.70	.9.50	..4
Wildwood.........cc	..City	.16.2	..10	..9	.c.	.1.00	..46	...60	.1.90	.4.15	.6.95	..1
Willard's.........cc	..City	.13.7	..10	..9	.o.	..40	..41	...50	.1.85	.4.30	.7.00	..3
Willow Springs......	..250	.17.5	..9	..7	.i.	..57	..53	.1.00	.2.50	.5.50	......	..3
Wilmette ...	.1,458	.14.0	..5	..8	.f.	..37	..42	...70	.2.80	.4.20	.6.25	..2
Wilmington.........	.1,576	.52.5	..14	..4	.i.	.2.05	.1.58	.2.90	......	......	......	..3
Windsor Park.....cc	..City	.10.7	..9	..9	.c.	..41	..31	...35	.1.50	.3.20	.5.65	..1
Winfield...........	..76	.27.5	..8	..4	.e.	.1.06	..83	.1.40	.5.50	.6.90	.8.00	..2
Winnetka.....r...	.1,079	.16.5	..5	..8	.f.	..42	..50	...85	.3.30	.4.65	.6.35	..2
Wireton cc		.18.0	..10	..8	.z.	.1.03	..47	...80	.2.00	.4.25	......	..6
Wolfs...............		.44.4	..10	..4	ʈʈ	....	.1.33					
Woodlawn Park ...cc	..City	..7.8	..9	..9	.c.	..32	..23	...25	.1.20	.2.50	.4.40	..1
Woodstock..........	.1,683	.51.3	..3	..3	.h.	.1.48	.1.54	.2.85	.10.30	15.00	......	..2
Worth..............	..186	.17.5	..10	..8	.t.	..57	..47	...85	.2.00	.4.25	......	..6
Yorkville	..375	.50.0	..10	..2	.j.	.1.54	.1.50	......	......	......	......	..3
Youngsdale........cc		.40.0	..7	..3	.c.	....	.1.14	.1.90	......	......	......	..1
Zarleys............		.43.0	.12	..5	.i.	....	.1.30					..3

Examination of the Map on Page 208 shows it to be divided, by straight lines, into squares, each representing a township six miles square. This Diagram corresponds, in its number of spaces, with the number of squares on that Map, and gives the names of all the towns and counties over the area covered by the Map.

To know the name of any town, in which a village or railroad station is located, we count down the left hand column of figures to the tier of towns wanted and then to the right, until we find the number of the town desired, when examination of this Diagram will give the name of the town. Thus we find, by our suburban table, on the preceding pages, that Wheaton is in tier 8, town 5, on the Map. The corresponding space on this diagram shows Wheaton to be in the town of Milton. Hinsdale is in tier 9, town 6, which this Diagram shows to be in Downers Grove.

The names of townships are omitted from the Map, from lack of space, but the name of the town, in which every station on the Map is located, may be found by consulting this Diagram. A study of this Diagram with the Map will well repay the reader.

The location of the county seat is indicated by a black figure, and the name of the county seat is shown by small capitals.

TIER.	TOWN.	TOWN.	TOWN.	TOWN.	TOWN.	TOWN.	TOWN.		
	McHENRY COUNTY.			LAKE COUNTY.					
1	1 Alden.	2 Hebron.	3 Richmond	4 Antioch.	5	6 Newport.	7 Benton.		
2	1 Hartland.	2 Greenwood.	3 McHenry.	4 Grant.	5 Avon.	6 Warren.	7 Waukegan. WAUKEGAN.	Lake........... ....Michigan.	
3	1 Seneca.	2 Dorr. WOODSTOCK.	3 Nunda.	4 Wauconda.	5 Fremont.	6 Libertyville.	7 Shields.		
4	1 Coral.	2 Grafton.	3 Algonquin.	4 Cuba.	5 Ela.	6 Vernon.	7 Deerfield.	TOWN.	
	KANE COUNTY.			COOK COUNTY.					
5	1 Hampshire.	2 Rutland.	3 Dundee.	4 Barrington.	5 Palatine.	6 Wheeling.	7 Northfield.	8 New Trier.	TOWN.
6	1 Burlington.	2 Plato.	3 Elgin.	4 Hanover.	5 Shaumburg.	6 Elk Grove.	7 Maine.	8 Niles.	9 Evanston.
				DU PAGE COUNTY.			Norwood Park.		
7	1 Virgil.	2 Campton.	3 St. Charles.	4 Wayne.	5 Blomingdale.	6 Addison.	7 Leyden.	8 Chicago.	9 Chicago.
8	1 Kaneville.	2 Blackberry.	3 GENEVA. Batavia.	4 Winfield.	5 Milton. WHEATON.	6 York.	7 Proviso. Riverside.	8 Cicero. Chicago.	9 Chicago. CHICAGO
9	1 Big Rock.	2 Sugar Grove.	3 Aurora.	4 Naperville.	5 Lisle.	6 Downers Grove.	7 Lyons.	8 Chicago.	9 Chicago.
	KENDALL COUNTY.			WILL COUNTY.					
10	1 Little Rock.	2 Bristol.	3 Oswego.	4 Wheatland.	5 Du Page	6 Lemont.	7 Palos.	8 Worth.	9 Calumet.
11	1 Fox.	2 Kendall. YORKVILLE.	3 Neausay.	4 Plainfield.	5 Lockport.	6 Homer.	7 Orland.	8 Bremen.	9 Thornton.
12	1 Big Grove.	2 Lisbon.	3 Seward.	4 Troy.	5 Joliet. JOLIET.	6 New Lenox.	7 Frankfort.	8 Rich.	9 Bloom.
	GRUNDY COUNTY.								
13	1 Nettle Creek.	2 Saratoga.	3 Ausable.	4 Channahon.	5 Jackson.	6 Manhattan.	7 Green Garden.	8 Monee.	9 Creto.
14	1 Erienna.	2 Wauponsee. MORRIS.	3 Felix.	4 Wilmington.	5 Florence.	6 Wilton.	7 Peotone.	8 Will.	9 Washington.

Diagram Showing Counties and Townships in Chicago Suburbs.

This Diagram corresponds, in its number of spaces, with the Map on page 208. That Map gives railroad stations. This Diagram gives the names of all townships in which all suburban stations are located. Six towns in the southern part of Grundy County and three towns in the southern part of Will County, are not shown in the Map.

Condensed Summary of the Great Exhibitions.

The wonderfully rapid advance made in every department of human endeavor, during the last forty years, is largely due to the great international fairs which have been held in various parts of the civilized world within the last half century.

These expositions have wrought great good in the following several ways:

They have stimulated the exhibitors to achieve great results and attain high excellence.

By the comparison of one product with another, the people, and the exhibitors themselves, have learned how improvements could be made superior to all that had been produced before.

ADMINISTRATION BUILDING—COLUMBIAN EXPOSITION.

Great multitudes of people have been induced to travel, and in doing so have met new faces, made new acquaintances, and come in contact with new thought.

At the various expositions, those who have attended have studied and learned the best methods, the most approved forms, the highest and best, much of which they have applied to the affairs of their everyday life.

In the study and adoption of the improvements which visitors have seen at the various fairs, their desires and ambitions have been so greatly educated as to create increased demands in every department of manufacture. This has so stimulated all descriptions of human industry as to give employment to millions of people, and cause a general circulation of money among all classes of artisans, mechanics and laborers in every part of the world.

The first of the great international fairs was held in the year 1851, in the Crystal Palace, London, England, the building being constructed in four months, at a cost of $965,000. At this exposition there were 17,900 exhibitors, about one-third of whom were from Great Britain and the British Colonies, the remainder coming from various parts of the world, including Persia, China, Greece, Denmark and countries far distant from England.

At that exhibition most liberal arrangements were made for the admission of 35,000 pupils from schools, the inmates of charitable institutions, and members of the various military organizations. Scientific lectures pertaining to the fair were delivered during its continuance, all of which had wide circulation and important influence in improving the public mind and cultivating the taste of the people.

This exposition resulted in not only giving instruction to over six millions of people who attended the exhibition, but it yielded a profit to the stockholders of $750,000.

The series of international fairs thus auspiciously begun has since been followed by several expositions, largely international in character, by many that have been national, and very many that have been local, though so highly meritorious as to deserve patronage from all parts of the country in which they have been held.

The table herewith gives the main statistics of the eight greatest and most successful international expositions which have been held since, and including, the London Exhibition of 1851.

FACTS CONCERNING EIGHT INTERNATIONAL EXPOSITIONS.

WHERE HELD.	Year When Held.	Acres Occupied by Buildings.	Number of Exhibitors.	Number of Admissions.	Number of Days Open.	Average Attendance Per Day.
London	1851	21	17,000	6,039,195	144	41,938
Paris	1855	24½	22,000	5,162,330	200	25,811
London	1862	23½	29,000	6,211,103	171	36,322
Paris	1867	37	52,000	10,200,000	217	47,470
Vienna	1873	40	42,000	7,254,687	186	39,003
Philadelphia	1876	60	60,000	9,910,996	159	62,333
Paris	1878	60	52,000	13,000,000	194	67,010
Paris	1889	75½	60,000	32,354,111	183	181,170

Held at Chicago, Ill., Beginning May 1, and Closing October 30, 1893.

Director-General of the Columbian Exposition—George R. Davis, of Illinois.

GENERAL OFFICERS OF
The World's Columbian Commission.

President....Thomas W. Palmer, of Michigan.
1st Vice-Pres..Thos. M. Waller, of Connecticut.
2nd Vice-Pres...M. H. de Young, of California.
3rd Vice-Pres..Davidson B. Penn, of Louisiana.
4th Vice-Pres..Gorton W. Allen, of New York.
5th Vice-Pres...A. B. Andrews, of N. Carolina.
Secretary... .....John T. Dickinson, of Texas.
   Vice-Chairman   (Jas. A. McKenzie, of
Executive Committee, { ....Kentucky.

BOARD OF LADY MANAGERS.

President......Mrs. Potter Palmer, of Chicago.
1st Vice-Pres..Mrs. R. Trautmann,of New York.
2nd Vice-Pres...Mrs. E. C. Burleigh, of Maine.
3rd Vice-Pres..Mrs. C. Price, of North Carolina.
4th Vice-Pres...Miss K. L. Minor, of Louisiana.
5th Vice-Pres..Mrs. B. Wilkins, of Dist. of Col.
6th Vice-Pres..Mrs. S. R. Ashley, of Colorado.
7th Vice-Pres...Mrs. F. B. Ginty, of Wisconsin.
8th Vice-Pres...Mrs. M. B. Salisbury, of Utah.
Vice-Pres.-at-Large { Mrs. Russell B. Harrison,
            ....of Montana.
  Vice Chairman   (Mrs. Virginia C. Mere-
Executive Committee, { ....dith, of Indiana.
Secretary...Mrs. Susan G. Cooke, of Tennessee.

**RESIDENTS OF CHICAGO APPOINTED BY PRESIDENT
OF THE WORLD'S COLUMBIAN COMMISSION.**

Mrs. B. M. H. Palmer...........Lake Shore Drive.
Mrs. S. Thatcher, Jr..............River Forest.
Mrs. Jas. A. Mulligan....... ....190 Pine St.
Frances Dickinson, M. D......... 70 State St.
Miss Sara T. Hallowell.........Palmer House.
Mrs. George L. Dunlap......328 Dearborn Av.
Mrs. L. Brace Shattuck....5300 Woodlawn Av.
Mrs. Annie C. Meyers....Great Northern Hotel.
Mrs. M. R. M. Wallace......3817 Michigan Av.
Mrs. Myra Bradwell........1428 Michigan Av.
Mrs. Jas. R. Doolittle, Jr...24 Groveland Park.
Mrs. Matilda B. Carse. .....145 Ashland Boul.
Martha H. Ten Eyck........5704 Madison Av.
Mrs. M. I. Sandes............Ravenswood, Ill.
Mrs. Leander Stone.........3352 Indiana Av.
Mrs. Gen. A. L. Chetlain....543 North State St.
Frances E. Willard..............Evanston, Ill.

GENERAL OFFICERS OF
The World's Columbian Exposition.

President...........Harlow N. Higinbotham.
Vice-President............Ferdinand W. Peck.
2nd Vice-President..........Robert A. Waller.
Secretary..............Howard O. Edmonds.
Treasurer...... ....Anthony F. Seeberger.
Auditor...............William K. Ackerman.
Attorney.............:.....William K. Carlisle.
Traffic Manager..................E. E. Jaycox.

BOARD OF REFERENCE AND CONTROL.

Wm. T. Baker.	Edwin Walker.
H. N. Higinbotham.	H. B. Stone.
R. A. Waller.	E. P. Ripley.
L. J. Gage.	John J. P. Odell.

EXECUTIVE COMMITTEE,

Consisting of the President, Vice-President,
Ex-Presidents who are members of the Board,
the Director-General and the Chairmen of
the Standing Committees.

Harlow N. Higinbotham...........President.	
Ferdinand W. Peck............Vice President.	
Ferdinand W. Peck.	Chas. L. Hutchinson.
Henry B. Stone.	James W. Ellsworth.
Edwin Walker.	Robert C. Clowry.
Wm. D. Kerfoot.	John J. P. Odell.
Charles H. Schwab.	H. N. Higinbotham.
Alexander H. Revell.	Thies J. Lefens.
Edward P. Ripley.	Lyman J. Gage.
George R. Davis.	William T. Baker.

STANDING COMMITTEE ON FINANCE.

Ferd. W. Peck, Chairman.

Elbridge G. Keith.	John J. P. Odell.
Lyman J. Gage.	H. N. Higinbotham.

SPECIAL COMMITTEE ON CEREMONIES.

Edward F. Lawrence, Chairman.

James W. Ellsworth.	Charles H. Wacker.
Charles T. Yerkes.	William D. Kerfoot.
Charles H. Schwab.	Charles Henrotin.
Alexander H. Revell.	E. C. Culp, Secretary.

COUNCIL OF ADMINISTRATION

From the World's Columbian Commission.
George V. Massey, of Delaware.
James W. St. Clair, of West Virginia.

From the World's Columbian Exposition.
Harlow N. Higinbotham, of Chicago.
Charles H. Schwab, of Chicago.

WORLD'S CONGRESS AUXILIARY.

President................Charles C. Bonney.	Treasurer................ ......Lyman J. Gage
Vice-President.... ....Thomas B. Bryan.	Secretary.............Benjamin Butterworth

BOARD OF MANAGEMENT OF UNITED STATES GOVERNMENT EXHIBIT.

HON. EDWIN WILLITS, Chairman.
SEVELLON A. BROWN, Chief Clerk of the
Department of State, to represent that de-
partment.
ALLURED B. NETTLETON, Assistant Secretary
of the Treasury, to represent the Treasury
Department.
MAJOR CLIFTON COMLY, U. S. A., to repre-
sent the War Department.
CAPTAIN R. W. MEADE, U. S. N., to represent
the Navy Department.
A. D. HAZEN, Third Assistant Postmaster
General, to represent the Post Office Depart-
ment.
HORACE A. TAYLOR, Commissioner of Rail-
roads, to represent the Department of the
Interior.
ELIJAH C. FOSTER, General Agent of the
Department of Justice, to represent that
department.
EDWIN WILLITS, Assistant Secretary of
Agriculture, to represent the Department of
Agriculture.
DR. G. BROWN GOODE, Assistant Secretary
Smithsonian Institution, to represent that
institution and the National Museum.
J. W. COLLINS, Assistant-in-Charge Division
of Fisheries, to represent the United States
Fish Commission.
F. T. BICKFORD, Secretary.

View of the Southern Portion of the Exposition Grounds.

To learn the location of the various prominent buildings and features of special interest, the reader is recommended to begin the examination near the Administration Building (No. 1), which is quickly reached, upon arrival at the grounds, from steamboat pier or railroad station. Afterwards, follow these numbers as they come in order, and the general location of the principal objects on the grounds is soon understood. See explanations more in detail on the following pages.

Places of General Interest.

1. Administration Building.	19. Harbor for All Vessels.	37. Occupied by Norway.
2. Electric Fountain.	20. Entrance to Basin.	38. Occupied by Ecuador.
3. Machinery Building.	21. Statue of the Republic.	39. Occupied by Guatemala.
4. Saw-Mill in Operation.	22. Music Hall.	40. Occupied by Costa Rica.
5. Stock Pavilion.	23. Liberal Arts Building.	41. Occupied by Turkey.
6. Agricultural Implements.	24. U. S. Govt. Building.	42. Occupied by Sweden.
7. Dairy Exhibit, Butter, etc.	25. Fisheries Building.	43. Occupied by Colombia.
8. Grounds for Use of Stock.	26. Battle Ship—Man-of-War.	44. Nicaragua Location.
9. Forestry Building.	27. Occupied by Gt. Britain.	45. Occupied by Brazil.
10. Leather Exhibit.	28. Canada Headquarters.	46. Northern Part of Lagoon.
11. Krupp Guns, for Warfare.	29. Occupied by Russia.	47. Fine Arts Building.
12. Ethnological Exhibit.	30. Occupied by Germany.	48. Illinois Building.
13. Convent of La Rabida.	31. Occupied by Austria.	49. Northwest Lagoon.
14. Agricultural Building.	32. Occupied by Ceylon.	50. Occupied by Japan House.
15. Casino, with Restaurant.	33. Occupied by France.	51. Eastern Lagoon.
16. Pier. Movable Sidewalk.	34. Space Occupied by Iowa.	52. Wooded Island.
17. Lake, South of Pier.	35. Fifty-seventh Street.	53. Bridge and Lagoon.
18. Lake, North of Pier.	36. Annex to Art Exhibit.	54. Location of Rose Garden.

Numbers Correspond with Numbers in Illustration Above.

Northern Portion of the World's Fair Grounds, at Jackson Park.

In viewing the general exterior of the grounds, the visitor may make use of numerous small boats, which will carry passengers through the canals and the lagoons. The Circular Elevated Railway, having its southern terminus at No. 12, and its northern ending at No. 24, will also greatly assist in easily going from one portion of the grounds to another, enabling the visitor to study the general features of interest without the weariness resulting from continuous walking.

Buildings and Notable Localities.

55. View of Hunter's Camp.
56. Woman's Building.
57. Fifty-ninth St. Entrance.
58. Fifty-seventh St. Entrance.
59. Libby Glass Works.
60. Japanese Bazaar.
61. View of Dutch Settlement.
62. View of German Village.
63. View of Street in Cairo.
64. Algeria and Tunis.
65. Panorama of Volcano.
66. Morocco Exhibits.
67. Chinese Village & Theater.
68. Captive Balloon.
69. Ingleside Street.
70. Indian Village.
71. Nursery Exhibit.

72. Depot — Cottage Grove Cable Cars.
73. Venice Murano Company.
74. R. R. Station on Illinois Central.
75. Hagenbeck Animal Show.
76. Dutch Settlement.
77. Location of Natatorium.
78. Panorama of Bernese Alps.
79. View of Turkish Village.
80. View of Moorish Palace.
81. In this vicinity are a Cider Press, a model of St. Peter's at Rome, a Chinese Tea House, Fire and Guard Station, etc.
82. View of Austrian Village.
83. View of Dahomey Village.

84. View of Roman House.
85. Shows Nursery Exhibit.
86. Cottage Grove Avenue Entrance to Midway Plaisance.
87. Sliding Railway, just south of Midway Plaisance.
88. Sixtieth Street Entrance to Exposition Grounds.
89. "Puck" and "Judge" Buildings.
90. Horticultural Building.
91. Sixty-third St. Entrance.
92. Transportation Building.
93. Mines & Mining Building.
94. Electricity Building.
95. North Canal.
96. R. R. Station, on Grounds.

For Location of State Buildings, See Page 228.

Bird's-eye View of the Exposition on Pages 218 and 219.

On the preceding pages you will observe a bird's-eye view of the buildings and grounds of the Columbian Exposition. Please understand that this sketch does not do justice to the affair. The purpose of that view, pre-

MACHINERY HALL.

sented on pages 218 and 219, is to give the reader an idea of the relative location of the different buildings and the various leading objects of interest which present themselves to the eyes in a journey about the grounds.

You are desirous of seeing the Fair to the best advantage. Such being the case, we advise you to take first a cursory examination of the grounds and buildings, that you may understand the outlines of the plan. When you know the location of all the principal features of interest, you can afterward study the Fair in detail.

VIEW LOOKING SOUTH ACROSS LAGOON.

With that purpose in mind, we will take a general view of the Exposition Buildings and their surroundings from an imaginary two-hundred foot elevation, about one quarter of a mile to the southeast of the grounds. Consequently, as we cast our eyes over the grounds we look toward the northwest.

The space occupied by the Exposition includes 633 acres, 553 acres belonging to Jackson Park, and 80 acres to Midway Plaisance (*Play-zance*), the location of which is designated by the double row of figures that extend away in the distance at the upper edge of our picture.

The buildings cover about 149 acres. The galleries in the buildings give 50 acres of additional space for the exhibits. The stock sheds extend over 40 acres. The waterways and lagoons cover 61 acres, and the wooded island contains 16 acres.

Excepting the Art Building, the framework of all these buildings is made of wood, to furnish which a thickly covered forest of 5,000 acres would be required. Upon the frame has been nailed, in solid slabs and blocks, a material called "staff," which is fireproof, and made of plaster, cement and hemp. Being mixed in water, it is, in the beginning, a soft mortar, set in molds of every conceivable ornamental design. When hard, it is in readiness to be used as a covering for the wooden frame, and. when nailed in place and painted, has all the appearance of solid masonry, and will last for several years in any climate, and for generations in a warm and dry climate.

The permission to use these grounds was obtained on condition that the buildings should all be taken down at the close of the Exposition, and the grounds restored to their original condition for park and pleasure purposes. To erect these buildings, advertise the Fair. conduct the Exposition through to the end, remove the buildings and restore the park, will cost about $22,000.000. To raise this large sum of money, an organization was effected, composed of leading citizens of Chicago, through whose efforts the people subscribed $5.000.000 as stock to the enterprise. The city of Chicago subscribed $5,000,000. and Congress appropriated $2,500,000. Beyond that amount. the managers borrowed what money was necessary to carry the enterprise to a successful conclusion. What the returns will be no one can know, as the great and widespread educational influence of such an éxposition cannot be measured—in money. The supposition is that the money realized from the sale of the buildings at the close of the Fair, together with the receipts from admission and sale of privileges, will fairly reimburse the projectors and subscribers to the enterprise.

It should be remembered by the visitor that the Fair is in honor of the 400th anniversary of the discovery of the Western World, and the landing of Columbus upon the newly discovered hemisphere on October 12, 1492, as described on page 36. Hence the name Columbian Exposition, and the many reminders of Columbus which you will see as you attend the Fair.

With these preliminary remarks we will begin our journey of inspection throughout the grounds, starting near the point where we leave the railroad train, upon arrival at the Exposition grounds, and following the numbers as they grow larger. The first conspicuous object that arrests our attention is:

1. Administration Building.— This is a highly ornamented edifice, being exceedingly rich in relief work and sculpture. Here are the headquarters of the Managers of the Exposition, the Fire and Police Departments, the press, and the authorities having charge of foreign affairs. Here also are a bank, the post office and the department where general information is obtained concerning the Fair. The Administration Building was designed by Richard M. Hunt, architect, of New York, and cost $550,-000. It is 262 feet square. Height of outer dome, 277½ feet. Height of inner dome, 188 feet. Diameter of dome, 120 feet. The four pavilions, one being at each corner, are 82½ feet square and 74 feet high. The entrances are 50 feet wide and 37 feet high. The floor area of this building covers a little over four acres.

2. Electric Fountain.—Diameter, 150 feet; cost, $50,000. Stands at the head of the basin, directly east of the Administration Building. Was designed and made in Paris. Through the aid of electricity, its waters present many colors, which are, of course, only seen to advantage in the night time.

3. Machinery Hall.—Size, 840 feet long and 492 feet wide. Roof trusses, 100 feet high. Width of span, 130 feet. Area of floor, 17½ acres. Designed by Peabody & Stearns, architects, Boston. Cost, $1,200,000. The placing of machinery in position, and removing it, are aided by an elevated traveling crane. There is an annex to this building in the rear, at the westward, which is 550

MANUFACTURES AND LIBERAL ARTS BUILDING.

feet long by 490 feet wide. Floor area of the annex, a little over 6 acres. This building, architecturally, would serve as a railroad train house, and at the close of the Fair will probably be sold for that purpose. Directly adjoining this building, on the south, are the pump works, power house and machine shops.

4. Saw-Mill.—Immediately south of the Machinery Building is the edifice devoted to the exhibition of machinery for sawing timber. Is 300 feet long, 125 feet wide. Cost $35,000. This is an especially important exhibit to all persons engaged in the lumber industry.

5. Stock Pavilion, 440 feet long and 280 feet wide. Designed to accommo-

UNITED STATES GOVERNMENT BUILDING.

date the people while they witness a display of the various domestic animals which will be placed on exhibition.

6. Agricultural Implements. — Directly south of the Agricultural Building, and on the vacant ground west of the pond, is a display of windmills and agricultural implements.

AGRICULTURAL BUILDING.

7. Dairy Exhibit.—Size of building, 200 by 100 feet. Cost $30,000. Arranged for the display of dairy machinery, and the processes for converting milk into butter, cheese, etc.

8. Stock Barns, with pavilion, cover 40 acres, and cost $335,000. Southeastward from the stock grounds is the crematory for the burning of garbage, and here also are the latest and most improved methods for the disposal of sewage. This, of itself, is a very important exhibit.

9. Forestry Building.— Size, 528 by 208 feet. Floor area, 2½ acres. Cost, $100,000. Composed wholly of woods and timbers, many of the woods having the bark on. No iron used in the construction of this building, wooden bolts and pegs taking the place of nails. Each State exhibits several specimens of its native trees.

10. Leather Exhibit.—North of the Forestry Building is an edifice devoted to an exhibition of all the different leathers, from the finest kid and morocco to the strongest sole leather, together with an exemplification of the processes for converting skins into leather. Size of building: 600 feet long, 150 feet wide.

11. Krupp's Gun Works. — North of the leather exhibit are stationed several of the monster Krupp guns.

12. Ethnological Exhibit.—In this location are exhibited primitive modes of life, as shown at different periods, among various tribes and classes of people in certain portions of the world. In this vicinity an Indian school is conducted, and in the immediate neighborhood the circular overhead railway has its southern terminus, its northern ending being in front of the United States Government Building.

13. Convent of La Rabida.—Cost of building, $50,-000. Is a reproduction of the convent in Spain in which, it is supposed, Columbus developed his idea of an undiscovered country to the westward. It was at this convent, in 1492, that Columbus, when traveling on foot, in a destitute condition, applied for food and shelter, and, by the good Father De Marchena, the prior of the institution, was kindly received. To him Columbus unfolded his plans for exploration, and, becoming interested, he secured for Columbus an introduction to the court of Ferdinand and Isabella. It is believed that the assistance thus rendered to Columbus, at a critical time of need, proved the means by which the navigator was enabled to discover the American Continent.

14. Agriculture.—Size of building: 800 feet long, 500 feet wide. Height of cornice, 65 feet; height of dome, 130 feet; floor area, 15 acres. Size of annex

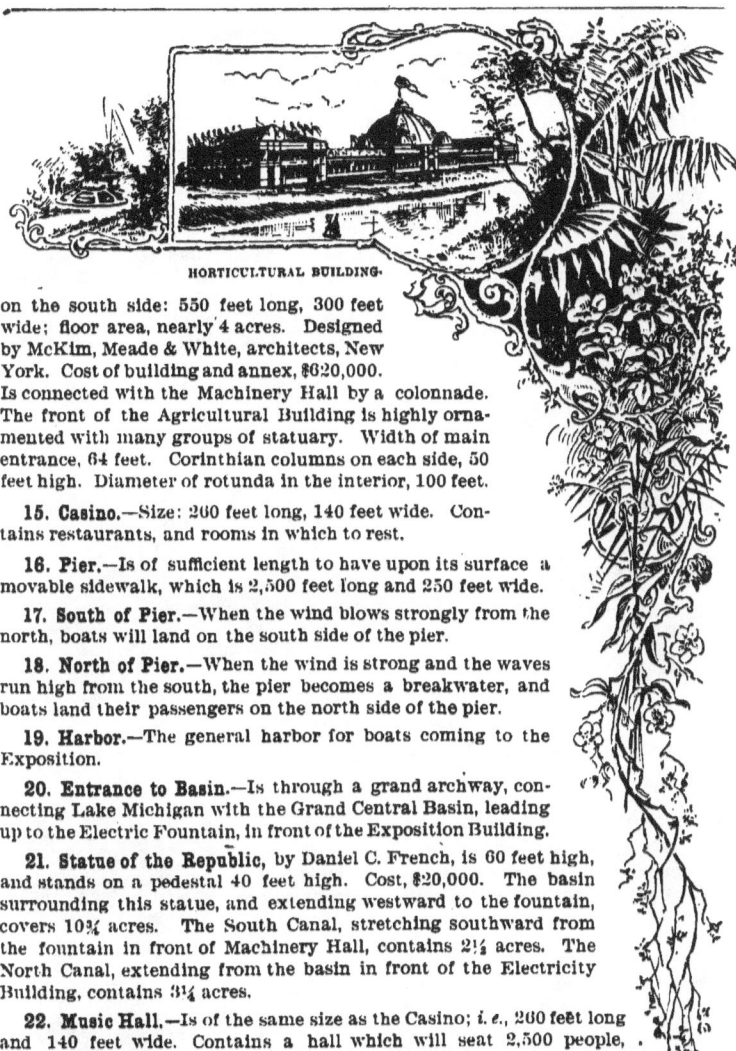

HORTICULTURAL BUILDING.

on the south side: 550 feet long, 300 feet wide; floor area, nearly 4 acres. Designed by McKim, Meade & White, architects, New York. Cost of building and annex, $620,000. Is connected with the Machinery Hall by a colonnade. The front of the Agricultural Building is highly ornamented with many groups of statuary. Width of main entrance, 64 feet. Corinthian columns on each side, 50 feet high. Diameter of rotunda in the interior, 100 feet.

15. **Casino.**—Size: 260 feet long, 140 feet wide. Contains restaurants, and rooms in which to rest.

16. **Pier.**—Is of sufficient length to have upon its surface a movable sidewalk, which is 2,500 feet long and 250 feet wide.

17. **South of Pier.**—When the wind blows strongly from the north, boats will land on the south side of the pier.

18. **North of Pier.**—When the wind is strong and the waves run high from the south, the pier becomes a breakwater, and boats land their passengers on the north side of the pier.

19. **Harbor.**—The general harbor for boats coming to the Exposition.

20. **Entrance to Basin.**—Is through a grand archway, connecting Lake Michigan with the Grand Central Basin, leading up to the Electric Fountain, in front of the Exposition Building.

21. **Statue of the Republic,** by Daniel C. French, is 60 feet high, and stands on a pedestal 40 feet high. Cost, $20,000. The basin surrounding this statue, and extending westward to the fountain, covers 10¾ acres. The South Canal, stretching southward from the fountain in front of Machinery Hall, contains 2½ acres. The North Canal, extending from the basin in front of the Electricity Building, contains 3¼ acres.

22. **Music Hall.**—Is of the same size as the Casino; i. e., 260 feet long and 140 feet wide. Contains a hall which will seat 2,500 people, besides an orchestra and chorus of 500 singers and musicians, presenting the best music known to the world down to the present time. Music Hall is connected with the Casino by a structure known as the Peristyle, which is 600 feet long, 60 feet wide and 60 feet high. The Peristyle contains 48 columns, representing the States and Territories. The whole structure is exceedingly grand in its ornamentation, and cost, including the Casino and Music Hall, $300,000.

23. **Manufactures and Liberal Arts.**—Size of the building: 1,687 feet long and 787 feet wide. Height of the four corner pavilions, 97 feet; height of walls, 66 feet; height of four center pavilions, 122 feet; height of roof over central hall, 245½ feet; height of roof truss over central hall, 211 feet; height, from the floor up, 201 feet. Span of truss, 382 feet; span in the clear, 352 feet. Weight of truss, 300,000 pounds. Ground covered by building, 30½ acres; floor area, including galleries, 44 acres. Designed by Geo. B. Post, architect, of New York, and cost $1,700,000.

The central hall in this edifice is 1,280 by 380 feet, the whole surrounded by a nave 107 feet wide, both hall and nave being enclosed by a 50-foot gallery. It is the largest building in the world, will seat 75,000 persons in the central hall, and the entire building will accommodate 300,000 people. There are 7,000,000 feet of lumber in the floor, of which there were 215 carloads of flooring, requiring 5 carloads of nails to fasten this flooring in position. The floor area is equal to the space occupied by 20 buildings the size of the Chicago Auditorium, the iron and steel in the roof being sufficient in quantity to build two Brooklyn Bridges. The lumber in the building requires all the timber that could be grown on 1,100 acres of densely timbered pine forest. The building, with its interior laid off in streets and lighted by 20,000 electric lights, is, of itself, one of the greatest wonders ever seen upon earth.

24. United States Government.—Size of building, 415 by 345 feet; area of floor, 6 acres; height of dome, 236 feet; diameter of dome, 120 feet. Designed by Government Architect Windrim, and cost $400,000.

TRANSPORTATION BUILDING.

Includes an exhibit by each of the Departments at Washington, showing the various coins and paper money coined and engraved by Government. The life-saving department will also give exhibitions.

25. Fisheries.—Size of building, 365 by 165 feet. The annexes are connected with the main building by circular arcades, each annex being 135 feet in diameter. Floor area, 3 acres. Designed by Henry Ives Cobb, architect, of Chicago, and cost $225,000. General fisheries exhibit in the main building, angling in the west annex, and aquaria in the east annex. Salt-water fish shown in tanks holding 40,000 gallons of salt water, brought from the Atlantic Ocean, condensed for shipment to one-fifth its usual bulk, and restored to its normal saline density by fresh water at the tanks. A whale, sharks, jelly fish, devil fish, and a thousand other specimens, alive, are all shown here.

26. Battle Ship.—At this point is a ship—the Illinois—modeled after the most approved ideas in battle-ship architecture. Length of ship, 348 feet; width, 69 feet; height from water line to top of military mast, 76 feet. Designed by Frank W. Grogan, and cost $100,000. Its purpose is to exhibit the equipment necessary in a modern man-of-war.

Across the breakwater, at the westward, on the edge of the lagoon, is a building 84 by 45 feet in size, three stories in height, designed as a model of the Government Life-Saving Station, exhibitions being made from time to time of the methods pursued in rescuing persons that are shipwrecked near shore. Close to this building are the edifices devoted to a Lighthouse and a Weather Bureau.

To the northward, across the lagoon, is a Fire and Guard Station, and to the eastward of this is a building in which we can get a clam bake when we desire.

27. Great Britain.—As we return from our visit to the Battle Ship and go northward, across the inlet, to the lagoon, we see, at the right, the imposing edifice known as the headquarters for the officers having in charge the exhibits from Great Britain.

The following, excepting numbers 34, 35 and 36, are the locations assigned for buildings which belong to various foreign countries:

28. Canada. **29.** Russia. **30.** Germany. **31.** Austria. **32.** Ceylon. **33.** France. **34.** Iowa. **35.** Fifty-seventh Street. **36.** Annex to Art Exhibit. **37.** Norway. **38.** Ecuador. **39.** Guatemala. **40.** Costa Rica. **41.** Turkey. **42.** Sweden. **43.** Colombia. **44.** Nicaragua. **45.** Brazil.

46. Lake.—South of the Fine Arts Exhibit. Contains 7½ acres.

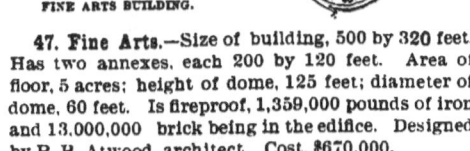

FINE ARTS BUILDING.

47. Fine Arts.—Size of building, 500 by 320 feet. Has two annexes, each 200 by 120 feet. Area of floor, 5 acres; height of dome, 125 feet; diameter of dome, 60 feet. Is fireproof, 1,359,000 pounds of iron and 13,000,000 brick being in the edifice. Designed by P. B. Atwood, architect. Cost, $670,000.

48. Illinois Building.—Southward from the Fine Arts Gallery, across the lake, is the imposing building which represents the State of Illinois. Size, 450 by 160 feet; floor area, three and one-fifth acres; height of dome, 236 feet. Contains trophies owned by the State, a portion of the building being occupied by the Illinois State Women's Exhibit. Designed by Boyington & Co., architects, of Chicago, and cost $250,000.

49. Lagoon.—This part of the lagoon extends eastward to Lake Michigan, and contains 3¾ acres.

50. Japan House.—Japan was one of the earliest of the foreign nations to make arrangements for this Exposition, her appropriation of $630,765 being so munificent as to call forth the warmest commendation.

As a just compliment to Japan for her liberality and enterprise, the north part of the wooded island has been set apart for the Japanese Building, the edifice here erected, surrounded with its gardens and flowers, to forever remain as a part of the permanent attractions of Jackson Park.

51. Lagoon.—Lying to the eastward of the Wooded Island.

52. Wooded Island.—Contains 16 acres, largely devoted to floriculture and horticulture.

53. Lagoon.—This body of water near here, connecting the interior waterways with Lake Michigan, contains 3¾ acres,

FISHERIES BUILDING.

54. Rose Garden.—Devoted to an exhibition of every variety of rose that is grown, with the methods of propagation, culture, etc.

55. Hunter's Camp.—Illustrating methods of tenting and necessary equipments when hunting.

56. Woman's Building. — Size, 388 by 199 feet; area of floors, 3½ acres. Contains model of hospital, kindergarten, kitchen, refreshment rooms, library, bureau of information, ladies' parlors, resting rooms, dressing rooms, etc. Prepared for and devoted to, the exclusive occupancy and use of women. Designed by Miss Sophia G. Hayden, architect, of Boston. Cost, $138,000.

57. Fifty-ninth Street Entrance from Midway Plaisance.

58. Fifty - seventh Street Entrance.—This is a popular and much-traveled entrance, at the northern part of the grounds. The State and Foreign Buildings are in the vicinity of this entrance.

59. Libby Glass Works. — This designates the location of the first of a series of special exhibits which are found along the Midway Plaisance, the entrance to which is in this vicinity.

The numbers that follow indicate locations. and the names after the numbers explain the character of the exhibits, thus:

60. Japanese Bazaar. **61.** Dutch Settlement. **62.** German Village. **63.** Street in Cairo. **64.** Algeria and Tunis. **65.** Panorama of Volcano. **66.** Morocco Exhibits. **67.** Chinese Village and Theater. **68.** Captive Balloon. **69.** Ingleside Street. **70.** Indian Village. **71.** Nursery Exhibit. **72.** Depot. **73.** Venice Murano Company. **74.** Railroad Station. **75.** Hagenbeck Animal Show. **76.** Dutch Settlement. **77.** Natatorium. **78.** Panorama of Bernese Alps. **79.** Turkish Village. **80.** Moorish Palace. **81.** In this vicinity are a Cider Press, a model of St. Peter's at Rome. a Chinese Tea House, Fire and Guard Station, etc. **82.** Austrian Village.

MINES AND MINING BUILDING.

83. Dahomey Village.   **84.** Roman House. **85.** Nursery Exhibit. **86.** Cottage Grove Avenue Entrance to Midway Plaisance. **87.** Sliding Railway, just south of Midway Plaisance. **88.** Sixtieth Street Entrance to Exposition Grounds. **89.** "Puck" and "Judge" Buildings.

90. Horticultural Building. — Size, 998 by 250 feet; floor area, 6½ acres; height of dome, 132 feet; diameter of dome, 180 feet. Designed by W. L. B. Jenney, architect, of Chicago. Cost, $300,000. This building has a central pavilion and two end pavilions, making three courts in the interior. In the center court, under the dome, there are very tall palms, bamboos and tree ferns. Surrounding the Horticultural Building, flowers are planted in great profusion. Upon the wooded island, across the lagoon from the Horticultural Building, there are also a great variety of flowers and aquatic plants.

At the opening of the Exposition, hundreds of thousands of tulips will illuminate the grounds, the later months seeing all the flowers, in great profusion, in their season, a great chrysanthemum exhibit forming a prominent part of the horticultural display during the closing days of the Fair.

91. Sixty-third Street Entrance. — The various places where entrance may be had to the grounds are a matter of interest. This has long been a favorite point of entrance with passengers on the Illinois Central Railroad.

92. Transportation Building. — Size, 960 by 256 feet; floor area, 9¼ acres. Adler & Sullivan, architects, of Chicago. Cost, $370,000. The cupola in the center of the building is 166 feet high, and is reached by eight elevators, which are, of themselves, a part of the exhibit.

The great main entrance is superb in ornamentation, is overlaid with gold, and presents a wonderfully beautiful appearance.

The Transportation Building contains every imaginable contrivance for carrying purposes, from the most primitive of olden times, to the electric road vehicle, the Hercules locomotive and the balloon. See the illustrations on page 224, showing various modes of transportation.

93. Mines and Mining Building.—

Architect, S. S. Beman, of Chicago. Cost, $265,000. Size, 700 by 350 feet; floor area, 8½ acres; height to cornice on main fronts, 65 feet. The main central entrances are 90 feet to the center of the arch. The gallery is 25 feet above the main floor, is 60 feet wide, and extends entirely around the building. The central hall is 630 feet long, the clear space in the center being 115 feet high.

The exhibit in this building includes an immense display of specimens of every description of ore in the rough, processes

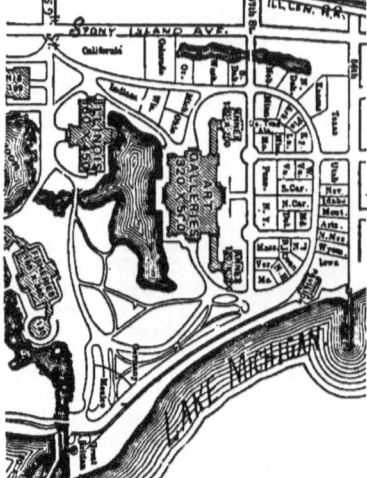

LOCATION OF STATE BUILDINGS—LOOKING WEST.

of reduction of ore to metals, and a great variety of marbles and precious stones. The geological cabinets of the world have freely yielded of their stores for this Exposition, no other such collection ever having been gathered before.

94. Electricity Building.—Size, 690

by 345 feet. The nave, or main body of the building, extending northward from the Grand Entrance, is 115 feet wide and 112 feet high; height of the roof of the balance of the building, 62 feet. There are 4

ELECTRICITY BUILDING.

domes and 10 towers, the two highest being each 195 feet high. Floor area, 9½ acres. Van Brunt & Howe, architects, of Kansas City. Cost, $410,000.

This is one of the most interesting and important exhibits of the Exposition. We, as a civilized people, have just entered the outer edge of the great

domain of electricity. In this field lie warmth and intensity of heat, mechanical and healing power, common light and brilliant illumination. What the future has before us, we may reasonably imagine from an examination of the wonderful results already achieved by the electricians, whose experiments are constantly developing the new and useful, down to the present time. The reader should not fail to behold the power and perfection attained in electric lighting, which is revealed by the grand illumination of this building at night.

95. North Canal.—This is a

charming waterway for small craft, and contains 3¼ acres. From the bridge at the north end of this canal, the view is taken which is shown on page 220, entitled "View Looking South Across Lagoon."

96. Railroad Station.—Into this

building enter the terminal tracks of numerous railways.

The reader must understand that this description of the grounds is written some months in advance of the actual placing of the goods upon exhibition. Our main purpose in this description is to tell you where the buildings stand, and what it is intended they shall contain. When the formal opening takes place, May 1, 1893, the visitor will realize that this description of the Great Fair of 1893 is but a mild word-painting of the Exposition, which will then deserve another chapter, descriptive in detail of the advancement of civilization as made manifest in the Great International Fair of 1893.

Amount of Appropriations for Use by the Several States.

STATE BUILDING, NORTH DAKOTA.

STATE BUILDING, TEXAS.

STATE BUILDINGS.

Several of the State Buildings, to be used as headquarters by people from each State, are shown herewith.

All of the States and Territories will participate in the Exposition. The 31 States and 2 Territories mentioned below, have each m a d e appropriations through their legislatures.

Up to July 1st, 1892, forty States and Territories had determined to erect buildings on the ground. These buildings will, for the most part, be two stories high, will average 50 by 100 feet in size, and will cost from $10,000 to $100,000 each, with the exception of the Illinois Building, which cost $250,000.

ILLINOIS STATE BUILDING. WORLD'S COLUMBIAN EXPOSITION CHICAGO 1893

TOTAL AMOUNTS.

M a n y of the States which have m a d e appropriations, are raising additional amounts to expend u p o n their representation at the Fair. These additional amounts aggregate more than $750,000. The total expenditure by the States and Territories will be nearly $5,000,000.

The following nine States are raising funds by stock subscriptions:

Alabama	$20,000	Kansas	$100,000
Arkansas	40,000	Oregon	50,000
Florida	50,000	South Dakota	25,000
Georgia	100,000	Total	$385,000

STATE BUILDING, DELAWARE.

STATE BUILDING, WISCONSIN.

Amount Appropriated by Each State for Columbian Exhibit.

Arizona	$30,000	Louisiana	$36,000
California	300,000	Maine	40,000
Colorado	100,000	Maryland	60,000
Delaware	10,000	Massachusetts	150,000
Idaho	20,000	Michigan	100,000
Illinois	800,000	Minnesota	50,000
Indiana	75,000	Missouri	150,000
Iowa	130,000	Montana	50,000
Kentucky	100,000	Nebraska	50,000
N. Hampshire	$25,000	Vermont	$15,000
New Jersey	70,000	Virginia	25,000
New Mexico	25,000	Washington	100,000
New York	300,000	West Virginia	40,000
North Carolina	25,000	Wisconsin	65,000
North Dakota	25,000	Wyoming	30,000
Ohio	125,000		
Pennsylvania	300,000	Total	$3,471,000
Rhode Island	50,000		

STATE BUILDING, WEST VIRGINIA.

STATE BUILDING, MASSACHUSETTS.

AT THE COLUMBIAN EXPOSITION.

Amounts of Money Appropriated by Each of the Foreign Governments.

ARGENTINE REPUBLIC.—Senor Don Julio Victorica, Buenos Ayres, Argentine Republic —$100,000.

AUSTRIA. — Marquis Olivier Bacquehem, Vienna, Austria—$102,300.

BELGIUM.—Monsieur A. Vercruysse, 3 Rue de l'Orangerie, Brussels, Belgium—$57,900.

BRAZIL. — Senhor Marechal Jose Simeao de Olveira, Rio de Janeiro, Brazil—$600,000.

BRITISH GUIANA. — Hon. B. Howell Jones, Georgetown, British Guiana—$25,000.

BRITISH HONDURAS. — Hon. John H. Phillips, Belize, British Honduras—$7,500.

CANADA. — Prof. William Saunders, Ottawa, Canada—$100,000.

CAPE COLONY. — L. Wiener, Esq., M. L. A., Cape Town, Africa —$50,-000.

CEYLON.— J. J. Grinlinton, M. L. C., Colombo, Ceylon — $65,600.

COLOMBIA.—Senor Don Carlos Martinez Silva, Bogota, Colombia— $100,000.

COSTA RICA.— Senor Don David J. Guzman, San Jose, Costa Rica — $150,000.

CUBA. — Exmo. Senor Don Antonio C. Telleria, Havana, Cuba — $25,-000.

DENMARK.—Dr. Emil Meyer, Copenhagen, Denmark— $67,000.

DUTCH GUIANA.— Baron Schimmelphennick, Paramaribo, Dutch Guiana—$10,000.

DUTCH WEST INDIES.—Hon. J. H. R. Beaujon, Curacoa, West Indies—$5,000.

ECUADOR.—Dr. Eduardo Arosemena,Guayaquil, Ecuador—$125,000.

FRANCE.—Monsieur C. Krantz, Avenue de la Bourdonnais, No. 22, Paris, France— $733,400.

GERMANY.— Hon. Ad. Wermuth, Wilhelmstrasse, No. 74, Berlin, Germany—$690,-200.

GREAT BRITAIN.—Sir Henry Trueman Wood, John Street, Adelphi, London, England— $291,990.

GUATEMALA.—Senor Don Manuel Lemus, Guatemala City, Guatemala—$200,000.

HAWAIIAN ISLANDS.—His Excellency, Samuel Parker, Honolulu, Hawaiian Islands.

HAYTI. — Charles A. Preston, Esq., 72 West Nineteenth St., New York City—$25,000.

HONDURAS.—Dr. R. Fritzgartner, Tegucigalpa, Honduras—$20,000.

JAMAICA.—Lieut.-Col. C. J. Ward, C. M. G., Kingston, Jamaica—$24,333.

JAPAN. — His Excellency, Togama Kawano, Tokio, Japan—$630,765.

KOREA.—Mr. Ye Wan Yong, Seoul, Korea.

LIBERIA.—Hon. A. B. King, Monrovia, Liberia.

MAURITIUS.—Mr. W. Arthur Edwards, Island of Mauritius.

MEXICO.—Senor Lic. Miguel Serrano, Apartado No. 533, Mexico City, Mexico—$50,000.

NETHERLANDS. — Jhr. S. Van Citters, The Hague, Holland.

NEW CALEDONIA. —Monsieur L. Gauharou, Noumea, New Caledonia.

NEW SOUTH WALES.—Hon. Arthur Renwick, 73 Phillip Street, Sydney, New South Wales— $243,325.

NICARAGUA.— Don Antonio Salaverri, Managua, Nicaragua—$30,000.

NORWAY.—His Excellency, H. R. Astrup, Christiania, Norway—$50,280.

PARAGUAY.— Senor Don Benjamin Aceval, Asuncion, Paraguay— $100,-000.

PERSIA. — Hon. E. Spencer Pratt, Teheran, Persia.

LOTTO PORTRAIT OF COLUMBUS,

Recommended by the Columbian Exposition Authorities for Use on the Souvenir Coins.

PERU.—Don Eduardo Habich, Lima, Peru.— $140,000.

PORTO RICO.—Senor Don Jose G. del Valle, San Juan, Porto Rico.

RUSSIA. — Hon. Privy Councillor Behr, St. Petersburg, Russia—$46,320.

SALVADOR.—Dr. Esteban Castro, San Salvador, Salvador—$12,500.

SPAIN.—His Excellency, Count of Casa Miranda, Madrid, Spain—$14,000.

SWEDEN. —Herr Generaldirektor Rich. Akerman, Stockholm, Sweden—$53,600.

TRANSVAAL.—His Excellency, General Joubert, Transvaal, Africa.

TRINIDAD. — His Excellency, Sir Frederick Broome, K. C. M. G., Port of Spain, Trinidad, West Indies—$15,000.

TURKEY.—Hakky Bey, Constantinople, Turkey.

URUGUAY.—Senor Don Frederico R. Vidiella, Montevideo, Uruguay—$24,000.

Men to whom the public are indebted for much labor performed in behalf of the Exposition.

William T. Baker....443 Rand-McNally Bldg.
C. K. G. Billings......... ....2 Madison St.
Thomas B. Bryan....401 Rand-McNally Bldg.
Edward B. Butler...............199 Adams St.
Benj. Butterworth.........Union League Club.
Isaac N. Camp.........State and Jackson Sts.
Wm. J. Chalmers........Fulton and Union Sts.
Robert C. Clowry ....150 Washington St.
Charles H. Chappell.....Chicago & Alton R. R.
George R. Davis..........Rand-McNally Bldg.
Arthur Dixon....................299 Fifth Av.
James W. Ellsworth..........Phenix Building.
Geo. P. Engelhard...........358 Dearborn St.
Lyman J. Gage............First National Bank.
Charles Henrotin.............169 Dearborn St.
H. N. Higinbotham........Marshall Field & Co.
Chas. L. Hutchinson.....Corn Exchange Bank.
Elbridge G. Keith........Metropolitan Nat. Bank.
Wm. D. Kerfoot............85 Washington St.
Wm. P. Ketcham.....Hoyne & Blue Island Avs.
Milton W. Kirk........Care Jas. S. Kirk & Co.
Edward F. Lawrence........First National Bank.
Thies J. Lefens.........Room 1, 80 La Salle St.

Andrew McNally.........Rand-McNally Bldg.
Adolph Nathan........Franklin & Jackson Sts.
Robert Nelson..................2801 Fifth Av.
John J. P. Odell..........Union National Bank.
Ferd. W. Peck...........110 Auditorium Bldg.
Eugene S. Pike..............164 Dearborn St.
Washington Porter...........108 Dearborn St.
Alexander H. Revell..Wabash Av. & Adams St.
Edward P. Ripley...207 Rand-McNally Bldg.
A. M. Rothschild...............203 Monroe St.
George Schneider...........115 Dearborn St.
Charles H. Schwab......128 Washington St.
Paul O. Stensland..........409 Milwaukee Av.
Henry B. Stone..........208 Washington St.
Charles H. Wacker.......171 N. Desplaines St.
Edwin Walker.............616 Rookery Bldg.
Robert A. Waller...............164 La Salle St.
H. Washburne........... ....City Hall.
John C. Welling........... ...78 Michigan Av.
Fred. S. Winston.............Monadnock Bldg.
G. H. Wheeler................2020 State St.
Charles T. Yerkes.........444 North Clark St.

The regular meetings of the Directory occur on the second Friday of each month.

Chiefs of Different Departments.

A—Agriculture, Food and Food Products, Farming Machinery and Appliances. W. I. Buchanan, of Iowa, Chief.

B—Horticulture, Viticulture and Floriculture. J. M. Samuels, of Kentucky, Chief. Bureau of Floriculture (sub-division of same). John Thorp, of New York, Chief.

C—Live Stock, Domestic and Wild Animals. Eber W. Cottrell, of Michigan, Chief.

D—Fish, Fisheries, Fish Products and Apparatus of Fishing. J. W. Collins, United States Fish Commission, Chief.

E—Mines, Mining and Metallurgy. F. J. V. Skiff, of Colorado, Chief.

F—Machinery. L. W. Robinson, United States Navy, Chief.

G—Transportation Exhibits—Railways, Vessels, Vehicles. Willard A. Smith, of Illinois, Chief.

H—Manufactures. James Allison, of Ohio Chief.

J—Electricity and Electrical Appliances. J. P. Barrett, of Illinois, Chief.

K—Fine Arts—Pictorial, Plastic and Decorative. Halsey C. Ives, of Missouri, Chief.

L—Liberal Arts, Education, Engineering, Public Works, Architecture, Music and the Drama. S. H. Peabody, of Illinois, Chief. Musical Bureau, Prof. William L. Tomlins, Director.

M—Ethnology, Archæology, Progress of Labor and Invention—Isolated and Collective Exhibits. F. W. Putnam, of Harvard University, Chief.

N—Forestry and Forest Products. W. I. Buchanan, of Iowa, Acting Chief.

O—Publicity and Promotion. Moses P. Handy, of Pennsylvania, Chief.

P—Foreign Affairs. Walker Fearn, of Louisiana, Chief.

Calendar for Use when Making Appointments at the Exposition.

CALENDAR FOR 1893.																																										

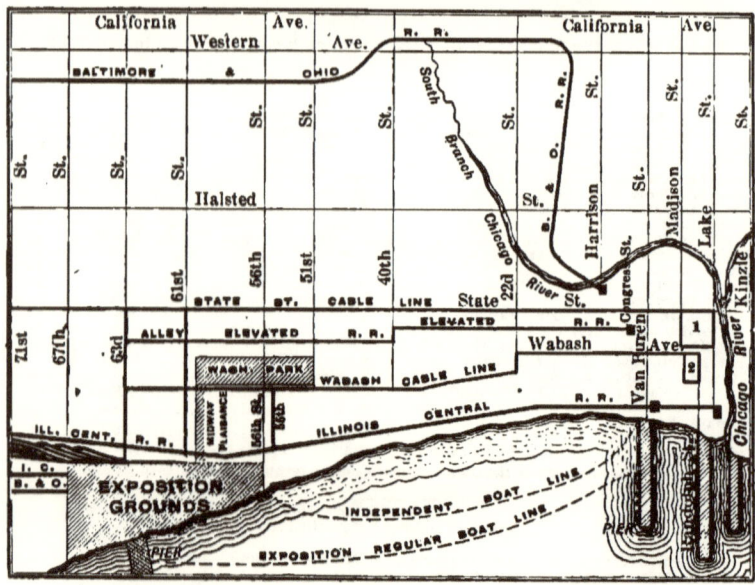

Map Looking Westward, Showing Various Car and Boat Lines.

Names of the six regular lines, their charges, and time required to go to the Exposition. Distance, 7 miles from Madison Street to 63rd Street.

NAME OF LINE.	Where to Take Boats or Cars.	How Often in Minutes Boats and Cars Start.	Charge One Way in Cents.	Charge Round Trip in Cents.	Time Required to Go in Minutes.	Hours in Which Boats and Cars Run.
Regular Boat Line...	Van Buren St. Pier	..45 *..	..15..	..25..	..45..	...9 A. M. to 5 : 30 P. M.
Indep'nt Boat Line.,	Van Buren St. Pier	.. .60....	..15..	..25..	..35‖‖	......10 A. M. to 5 P. M.
Illinois Central R. R.	At Any Station....	10 to 30‖	..23..	..25..	..32..	5 : 25 A. M. to12, night.
Wabash Cable Line..	At Any Street. ...	..1 to 2½	...5..	..10..	..53..	5 : 23 A. M. to 11 :34 P.M.†
Elevated Railroad...	At Any Station....	...4....	...5..	..10..	..34..	....5 A. M. to 8 P. M.‡
State St. Cable Line.	At Any Street......	..1 to 2½	...5..	..10..	..56..	...5 A. M. to 12 : 10 A. M.†

* During the World's Fair period, the number of boats will be so greatly increased that one will leave the pier every 5 minutes.

† Horse cars occasionally all night.

‡ Trains every 18 minutes all night.

‖ From 5 P. M. till 6 : 20 P. M., trains every 5 minutes.

‖‖ Passengers landed north of Exposition.

Explanation Concerning Various Lines Going to the Exposition.

The Boat Lines make no stop, after leaving the northern pier, until they reach their destination at the Exposition.

The Illinois Central Trains leave at foot of " Lake St." and stop at " Van Buren St.," " 16th St.," " 22nd St.," " 27th St.," "31st St.," " 35th St." (Douglas Station), "39th St." (Oakland), " 43rd St.," " 47th St." (Kenwood), " 50th St." (Madison Park), "53rd St." (Hyde Park), " 57th St." (South Park), " 60th St.," " 63rd St." (Woodlawn Park), " 67th St." (Oakwoods).

The Wabash Avenue Cable Line starts at Randolph St., and stops for passengers at any street crossing.

The Elevated Railroad Cars start at Congress St. and stop, for the letting off and taking on of passengers, at the following stations: " Hubbard Court," " 12th St.," " 18th St.," " 22nd St.," " 26th St.," " 29th St.," " 31st St.," " 33rd St.," " 35th St.," "39th St.," " Indiana Av. and 40th St.," "43rd St.," " 47th St.," " 51st St.," " 55th St.," " 58th St.," " 61st St.," " 63rd St. and

South Park Av.," " Cottage Grove Av.," " Lexington Av.," " Madison Av.," " Stony Island Av.," " Jackson Park."

The State Street Cable Line starts at Lake St. and stops at all street corners when required by passengers to do so.

The Baltimore & Ohio Trains start from Harrison St. Station, and make a circuit of about 20 miles, reaching the Exposition grounds from their south side, as shown by the line above which are the letters B. & O. The Illinois Central and other lines, as shown by black marks, have access to the Exposition in the southern part of the grounds. The Baltimore & Ohio does not compete with the other direct lines in carrying passengers from the business center of the city, but will carry the passengers of the Northern Pacific Railway to the grounds, and may serve as a connecting line with some other roads. It is expected, at this writing, that most passengers from the west and north of the city will leave their trains, on arrival at depots, and take the direct lines to the Exposition.